PHILIP'S

C000254061

STREE

East Yorkshire Northern Lincolnshire

First published in 2002 by

Philip's, a division of
Octopus Publishing Group Ltd
2-4 Heron Quays, London E14 4JP

Second edition 2005
First impression 2005
EYLBA

ISBN-10 0-540-08763-7 (pocket)
ISBN-13 978-0-540-08763-1 (pocket)

© Philip's 2005

Ordnance Survey®

This product includes mapping data licensed from Ordnance Survey® with the permission of the Controller of Her Majesty's Stationery Office. © Crown copyright 2005. All rights reserved. Licence number 100011710.

No part of this publication may be reproduced, stored in a retrieval system or transmitted in any form or by any means, electronic, mechanical, photocopying, recording or otherwise, without the permission of the Publishers and the copyright owner.

To the best of the Publishers' knowledge, the information in this atlas was correct at the time of going to press. No responsibility can be accepted for any errors or their consequences.

The representation in this atlas of a road, track or path is no evidence of the existence of a right of way.

Ordnance Survey and the OS Symbol are registered trademarks of Ordnance Survey, the national mapping agency of Great Britain.

Post Office is a trade mark of Post Office Ltd in the UK and other countries.

Printed by Toppan, China

Contents

III **Key to map symbols**

IV **Key to map pages**

VI **Route planning**

X **Administrative and Postcode boundaries**

1 **Street maps** at 1⅓ inches to 1 mile

122 **Street maps** at 2⅔ inches to 1 mile

154 **Street maps of centres of Beverley, Kingston-upon-Hull and York** at 5⅓ inches to 1 mile

157 **Index** of towns and villages

159 **Index** of streets, hospitals, industrial estates, railway stations, schools, shopping centres, universities and places of interest

Digital Data

The exceptionally high-quality mapping found in this atlas is available as digital data in TIFF format, which is easily convertible to other bitmapped (raster) image formats.

The index is also available in digital form as a standard database table. It contains all the details found in the printed index together with the National Grid reference for the map square in which each entry is named.

For further information and to discuss your requirements, please contact Philip's on 020 7644 6932 or james.mann@philips-maps.co.uk

Key to map symbols

22a	**Motorway** with junction number
	Primary route – dual/single carriageway
	A road – dual/single carriageway
	B road – dual/single carriageway
	Minor road – dual/single carriageway
	Other minor road – dual/single carriageway
	Road under construction
	Tunnel, covered road
	Rural track, private road or narrow road in urban area
	Gate or obstruction to traffic (restrictions may not apply at all times or to all vehicles)
	Path, bridleway, byway open to all traffic, road used as a public path
	Pedestrianised area
DY7	**Postcode boundaries**
	County and unitary authority boundaries
	Railway, tunnel, railway under construction
	Tramway, tramway under construction
	Miniature railway
Walsall	**Railway station**
	Private railway station
South Shields	**Metro station**
	Tram stop, tram stop under construction
	Bus, coach station

	Ambulance station
	Coastguard station
	Fire station
	Police station
	Accident and Emergency entrance to hospital
H	**Hospital**
	Place of worship
i	**Information Centre** (open all year)
	Shopping Centre
P P&R	**Parking, Park and Ride**
PO	**Post Office**
	Camping site, caravan site
	Golf course
	Picnic site
Prim Sch	**Important buildings, schools, colleges, universities and hospitals**
	Built up area
	Woods
River Ouse	**Tidal water, water name**
	Non-tidal water – lake, river, canal or stream
	Lock, weir, tunnel
Church	**Non-Roman antiquity**
ROMAN FORT	**Roman antiquity**
87 / 246	**Adjoining page indicators and overlap bands** The colour of the arrow and the band indicates the scale of the adjoining or overlapping page (see scales below)

Enlarged mapping only

	Railway or bus station building
	Place of interest
	Parkland

Acad	**Academy**	Inst	**Institute**	Recn Gd	**Recreation Ground**
Allot Gdns	**Allotments**	Ct	**Law Court**	Resr	**Reservoir**
Cemy	**Cemetery**	L Ctr	**Leisure Centre**	Ret Pk	**Retail Park**
C Ctr	**Civic Centre**	LC	**Level Crossing**	Sch	**School**
CH	**Club House**	Liby	**Library**	Sh Ctr	**Shopping Centre**
Coll	**College**	Mkt	**Market**	TH	**Town Hall/House**
Crem	**Crematorium**	Meml	**Memorial**	Trad Est	**Trading Estate**
Ent	**Enterprise**	Mon	**Monument**	Univ	**University**
Ex H	**Exhibition Hall**	Mus	**Museum**	W Twr	**Water Tower**
Ind Est	**Industrial Estate**	Obsy	**Observatory**	Wks	**Works**
IRB Sta	**Inshore Rescue Boat Station**	Pal	**Royal Palace**	YH	**Youth Hostel**
		PH	**Public House**		

■ The small numbers around the edges of the maps identify the 1 kilometre National Grid lines

■ The dark grey border on the inside edge of some pages indicates that the mapping does not continue onto the adjacent page

The scale of the maps on the pages numbered in blue is 4.2 cm to 1 km • 2⅔ inches to 1 mile • 1: 23810

0 ¼ ½ ¾ 1 mile

0 250 m 500 m 750 m 1 kilometre

The scale of the maps on pages numbered in green is 2.1 cm to 1 km • 1⅓ inches to 1 mile • 1: 47620

0 ¼ ½ ¾ 1 mile

0 250m 500m 750m 1 kilometre

The scale of the maps on pages numbered in red is 8.4 cm to 1 km • 5⅓ inches to 1 mile • 1: 11900

0 220 yards 440 yards 660 yards ½ mile

0 125 m 250 m 375 m ½ kilometre

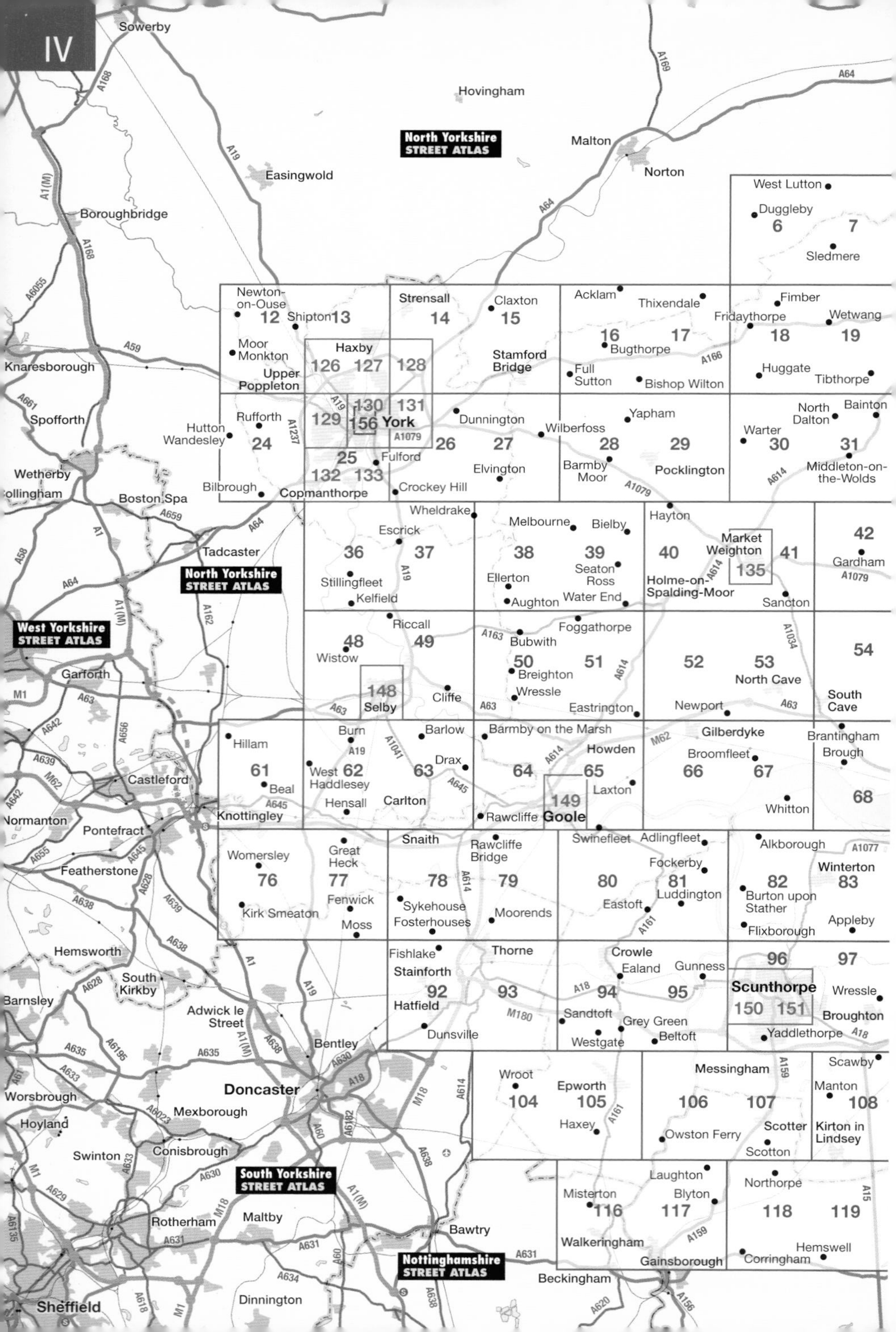
Sowerby
Hovingham
North Yorkshire STREET ATLAS
Malton
Norton
Easingwold
Boroughbridge
West Lutton
Duggleby 6
7
Sledmere
Newton-on-Ouse 12
Shipton 13
Strensall 14
Claxton 15
Acklam
Thixendale
16
17
Bugthorpe
Full Sutton
Bishop Wilton
Fimber
Fridaythorpe 18
Wetwang 19
Huggate
Tibthorpe
Moor Monkton
Haxby
126 127 128
Upper Poppleton
Stamford Bridge
Knaresborough
Spofforth
Rufforth
Hutton Wandesley
24
129 130 131
156 York
Dunnington
26 27
Wilberfoss
Yapham
28 29
Barmby Moor
Pocklington
North Dalton
Bainton
Warter 30
31
Middleton-on-the-Wolds
25
132 133
Fulford
Elvington
Crockey Hill
Bilbrough
Copmanthorpe
Wetherby
Collingham
Boston Spa
Tadcaster
North Yorkshire STREET ATLAS
Wheldrake
Escrick
36 37
Stillingfleet
Kelfield
Melbourne
Bielby
38 39
Ellerton
Seaton Ross
Aughton
Water End
Hayton
40
Market Weighton
135
41
Holme-on-Spalding-Moor
Sancton
42
Gardham
West Yorkshire STREET ATLAS
Garforth
Riccall
48 49
Wistow
148 Selby
Cliffe
Bubwith
Foggathorpe
50 51
Breighton
Wressle
Eastrington
52 53
North Cave
Newport
54
South Cave
Castleford
Hillam
61
Beal
Burn
West Haddlesey 62
Barlow
63
Drax
Hensall
Carlton
Barmby on the Marsh
64
Howden 65
149 Goole
Laxton
Rawcliffe
Gilberdyke
Broomfleet
66 67
Whitton
Brantingham
Brough
68
Knottingley
Normanton
Pontefract
Featherstone
Womersley
76
Great Heck
77
Kirk Smeaton
Fenwick
Moss
Snaith
78
Sykehouse
Fosterhouses
Rawcliffe Bridge
79
Moorends
Swinefleet
Adlingfleet
80
Fockerby
81
Luddington
Eastoft
Alkborough
82
Burton upon Stather
Flixborough
Winterton 83
Appleby
Hemsworth
South Kirkby
Barnsley
Adwick le Street
Fishlake
Thorne
Stainforth
92
Hatfield
93
Dunsville
Crowle
Ealand
94
Sandtoft
Westgate
Gunness
95
Grey Green
Beltoft
96 97
Scunthorpe
150 151
Wressle
Broughton
Yaddlethorpe
Bentley
Doncaster
Worsbrough
Hoyland
Mexborough
Swinton
Conisbrough
Wroot
104
Epworth
105
Haxey
Messingham
106 107
Owston Ferry
Scotter
Scotton
Scawby
Manton
108
Kirton in Lindsey
South Yorkshire STREET ATLAS
Rotherham
Maltby
Bawtry
Laughton
Misterton
116
Blyton
117
Walkeringham
Gainsborough
Northorpe
118 119
Hemswell
Corringham
Nottinghamshire STREET ATLAS
Beckingham
Sheffield
Dinnington

Key to map pages

156 Map pages at 5⅓ inches to 1 mile

141 Map pages at 2⅔ inches to 1 mile

113 Map pages at 1⅓ inches to 1 mile

Scale

0 5 10 15 20 km

0 5 10 miles

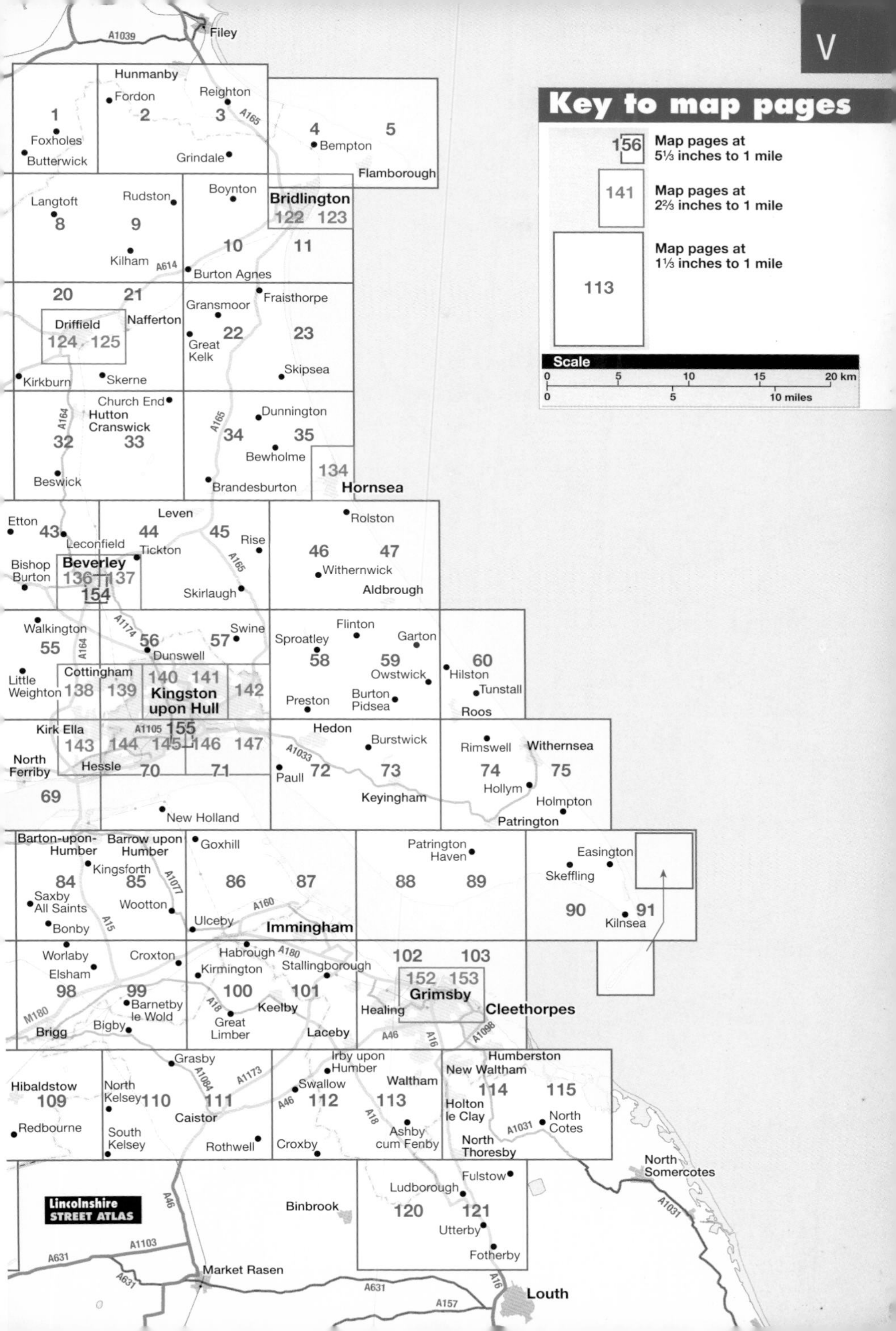
Filey
A1039
Hunmanby
Fordon
Reighton
1
2
3
A165
4
5
Foxholes
Butterwick
Grindale
Bempton
Flamborough
Langtoft
Rudston
Boynton
Bridlington
122 123
8
9
10
11
Kilham
A614
Burton Agnes
20
21
Gransmoor
Fraisthorpe
Driffield
124 125
Nafferton
22
23
Great Kelk
Kirkburn
Skerne
Skipsea
Church End
Hutton Cranswick
A164
32
33
A165
34
35
Dunnington
Bewholme
134
Beswick
Brandesburton
Hornsea
Etton
43
Leven
44
45
Rise
Rolston
Leconfield
Tickton
46
47
Bishop Burton
Beverley
136 137
154
A165
Withernwick
Aldbrough
Skirlaugh
Walkington
A1174
Swine
Flinton
55
A164
56
57
Sproatley
Garton
Dunswell
58
59
60
Little Weighton
Cottingham
138
139
140 141
142
Kingston upon Hull
Owstwick
Hilston
Tunstall
Preston
Burton Pidsea
Roos
Kirk Ella
A1105
155
Hedon
143
144
145
146
147
Burstwick
Rimswell
Withernsea
North Ferriby
Hessle
70
71
A1033
72
73
74
75
Paull
Hollym
69
Keyingham
Holmpton
New Holland
Patrington
Barton-upon-Humber
Barrow upon Humber
Goxhill
Patrington Haven
Easington
Kingsforth
A1077
84
85
86
87
88
89
Skeffling
Saxby All Saints
Wootton
A160
90
91
Bonby
A15
Ulceby
Immingham
Kilnsea
Worlaby
Croxton
Habrough
A180
102
103
Elsham
Kirmington
Stallingborough
152 153
98
99
100
101
Grimsby
Barnetby le Wold
Keelby
Healing
Cleethorpes
M180
A18
Great Limber
Brigg
Bigby
Laceby
A46
A16
A1098
Grasby
Irby upon Humber
Humberston
A1084
A1173
Waltham
New Waltham
Hibaldstow
North Kelsey
Swallow
114
115
109
110
111
A46
112
113
Holton le Clay
Caistor
A18
North Cotes
Redbourne
Ashby cum Fenby
A1031
South Kelsey
Rothwell
Croxby
North Thoresby
North Somercotes
Fulstow
Ludborough
Lincolnshire STREET ATLAS
A46
Binbrook
120
121
A1031
Utterby
A1103
A631
Fotherby
Market Rasen
A631
A631
A16
Louth
A157

Route planning

Scale
0 5 10 15 km
0 5 10 miles
Easingwold
Malton
Norton
Strensall
Haxby
City of York
York
Upper Poppleton
Stamford Bridge
Pocklington
Market Weighton
Holme-on-Spalding-Moor
Tadcaster
Bishopthorpe
Copmanthorpe
Sherburn in Elmet
Barlby
Selby
Howden
Gilberdyke
North Cave
Goole
Snaith
Carlton
Knottingley
Ferrybridge
Hovingham

Filey
Filey Bay
Primrose Valley
Hunmanby
Hunmanby Moor
Reighton Gap
Reighton
Speeton
Buckton
Bempton
Flamborough
Sewerby
Bridlington
West Hill
Hilderthorpe
BRIDLINGTON BAY
Lebberston
Gristhorpe
Flixton
Folkton
Muston
Willerby
Staxton
Yedingham
Ganton
East Heslerton
Sherburn
Potter Brompton
West Heslerton
Brompton
Fordon
Wold Newton
Foxholes
Burton Fleming
Grindale
Butterwick
Helperthorpe
Weaverthorpe
Octon
Thwing
East Lutton
West Lutton
Octon Cross Roads
Boynton
Rudston
Kirby Grindalythe
Langtoft
Bessingby
Carnaby
Haisthorpe
Thornholme
Sledmere
Cottam
Kilham
Burton Agnes
Ruston Parva
Harpham
Fraisthorpe
Fimber
Garton-on-the-Wolds
Lowthorpe
Nafferton
Gransmoor
Barmston
Wetwang
Elmswell
Little Driffield
Driffield
Driffield Canal
Great Kelk
Lissett
Gembling
Ulrome
Kelleythorpe
Foston on the Wolds
Wansford
Tibthorpe
Kirkburn
Southburn
Skerne
Brigham
Church End
Beeford
Skipsea
Skipsea Brough
North Dalton
Bainton
Hutton
Hutton Cranswick
Rotsea
North Frodingham
Dunnington
East Riding of Yorkshire
Hempholme
Bewholme
Atwick
Middleton-on-the-Wolds
Watton
Watton Beck
Kilnwick
North Cliff
Hornsea
Lund
Beswick
Burshill
Brandesburton
Holme on the Wolds
Lockington
Baswick Steer
Seaton
Thorpe
Hornsea Mere
Hornsea Bridge
South Dalton
Scorborough
Aike
Leven
Leven Canal
Sigglesthorne
Rolston
Catwick
Goxhill
Arram
Etton
Leconfield
Eske
Little Hatfield
Mappleton
Goodmanham
Gardham
Cherry Burton
Routh
Long Riston
Rise
Great Hatfield
Great Cowden
Tickton
Arnold
Withernwick
Molescroft
Beverley
Weel
Meaux
Skirlaugh
New Ellerby
Bishop Burton
Marton
West Newton
Aldbrough
East Newton
Walkington
Woodmansey
North Newbald
Old Ellerby
South Newbald
Bentley
Wawne
Thearne
Flinton
Garton
Swine
Coniston
Dunswell
Grimston
High Hunsley
Skidby
Bransholme
Sutton on Hull
Thirtleby
Sproatley
Humbleton
Fitling
Hilston
Ganstead
Kingston-upon-Hull
Cottingham
Little Weighton
Rowley
Bilton
Lelley
Owstwick
Tunstall
Everthorpe
Epplewort
Riplingham
Sutton Ings
Stoneferry
Elstronwick
North End
Preston
Burton Pidsea
Roos
Waxholme
West End
South Cave
Newland
Sculcoates
Summergangs
West End
Kirk Ella
Willerby
East Ella
Marfleet
Salt End
Hedon
Brantingham
West Ella
Anlaby
Haven Side
Rimswell
Ellerker
Swanland
Elloughton
Welton
Northfield
Hessle
KINGSTON UPON HULL
Burstwick
Halsham
East End
Paull
Camerton
Brough
North Ferriby
Thorngumbald
Ryehill
Keyingham
Humber Bridge
HUMBER
Ottringham
Whitton
Goxhill Haven
Little Humber
Winestead
Redcliff Channel
Barton Waterside
New Holland
Thorney Crofts
Read's Island
Winteringham
Barton-upon-Humber
Barrow Haven
Patrington
West Halton
South Ferriby
Goxhill
Barrow upon Humber
South End
East Halton
Sunk Island
Winterton
Kingsforth
Horkstow
New River Ancholme
Thealby
Saxby All Saints
Burnham
Thornton Curtis
North Killingholme
Roxby
Wootton
North
Bonby
Ulceby Skitter
South Killingholme
Ulceby
Immingham
Appleby
ROTTERDAM 12:30
ZEEBRUGGE 12:45
A1039
A165
A64
A614
A166
A1035
A1079
A164
A1033
A63
A1174
A15
A160
A1077
A1034
B1229
B1255
B1259
B1253
B1249
B1252
B1251
B1248
B1242
B1244
B1243
B1230
B1233
B1237
B1238
B1239
B1240
B1231
B1362
B1218
B1206
B1204
B1211

Ellerton
Laytham
Water End
Holme-on-Spalding-Moor
Sancton
Bishop Burton
Molescroft
Beverley
Aughton
North Duffield
Harthorpe
A163
Moor End
Sand Hole
Foggathorpe
North Cliffe
North Newbald
Walkington
Bubwith
Highfield
Rascal Moor
South Cliffe
South Newbald
A1035
Bentley
A163
Gunby
Gribthorpe
Willitoft
Hotham
High Hunsley
B1230
A164
Skidby
Barlby
Osgodby
Menthorpe
Breighton
Spaldington
A614
Bursea
Little Weighton
Cottingham
Lund
South Duffield
Cliffe
Foulness
North Cave
Rowley
Everthorpe
Eppleworth
East Common
Hemingbrough
Wressle
Brind
B1228
North Howden
Portington
Hive
West End
South Cave
Riplingham
Newsholme
Cavil
Sandholme
Scalby
Newport
A63
Kirk Ella
Willerby
Barlow
A63
Barmby on the Marsh
Eastrington
B1230
Gilberdyke
Brantingham
A1041
Long Drax
Derwent
Howden
M62
Staddlethorpe
Market Weighton Canal
Ellerker
West Ella
Anlaby
Asselby
Knedlington
Kilpin Pike
Balkholme
Elloughton
Welton
Swanland
B1231
Drax
Boothferry
Kilpin
Broomfleet
Brough
Northfield
Hessle
Ouse
North Ferriby
Camblesforth
A645
Newland
Laxton
Hook
Skelton
Airmyn
Hirst Courtney
Blacktoft
Faxfleet
Whitton
Humber Bridge
Carlton
Saltmarshe
Yokefleet
Goole
Ousefleet
Redcliff Channel
Barton Waterside
Snaith
East Cowick
Rawcliffe
Reedness
Whitgift
Winteringham
Read's Island
Barton-upon-Humber
West Cowick
Rawcliffe Bridge
Old Goole
Swinefleet
Little Reedness
Alkborough
A645
Dutch River
West Halton
A1077
Walcot
Pollington
Southfield Reservoir
Adlingfleet
A161
Trent
South Ferriby
B1218
Aire and Calder Navigation
Fockerby
Garthorpe
Coleby
Winterton
Kingsforth
Burton Stather
A1077
B1430
Horkstow
M18
A614
Burton upon Stather
Thealby
Pincheon Green
Luddington
B1204
Saxby All Saints
Burnham
Roxby
Don
Eastoft
Normanby
North
Moorends
B1392
Flixborough
Fosterhouses
A161
Amcotts
Appleby
B1207
Bonby
B1206
Far Bank
Fishlake
Doncaster North Services
Thorne
Crowle
Flixborough Stather
Dragonby
Lincolnshire
Worlaby
Canal Side
Stainforth & Keadby Canal
Windsor
A1077
Kirk Bramwith
Stainforth
Wike Well End
Ealand
Keadby
B1216
Gunness
Crosby
Santon
Elsham
A18
A18
Frodingham
Hatfield
A146
A18
Scunthorpe
Wressle
Barnby Dun
Burringham
Brumby
M180
A18
Wrawby
Dunscroft
Althorpe
M181
A1029
Kirk Sandall
Hatfield Woodhouse
Sandtoft
M180
Woodhouse
Derrythorpe
B1450
Ashby
Broughton
Brigg
Dunsville
West End
Grey Green
Westgate
Yaddlethorpe
B1208
A18
Edenthorpe
Belton
Beltoft
Bottesford
Mill Place
Somerby
A630
Armthorpe
Church Town
West Butterwick
East Butterwick
Scawby
B1434
Nutwell
M18
Thorne
Epworth
Messingham
B1207
Sturton
Howsham
Doncaster
Wroot
A159
B1398
A15
Cantley
Epworth Turbary
B1400
Manton
Cadney
Branton
A161
Low Burnham
Susworth
Hibaldstow
Auckley
Kelfield
Scotterthorpe
Lidget
Blaxton
Owston Ferry
Scotter
North Kelsey
Upperthorpe
Haxey
B1206
Laughton Forest
Finningley
B1396
Westwoodside
East Lound
Scotton
Kirton in Lindsey
Redbourne
Robin Hood Doncaster Sheffield International Airport
Craiselound
East Ferry
South Kelsey
Wildsworth
B1206
B1400
Auckley
A614
Idle
Laughton
Northorpe
A638
B6463
Misson
Misterton
West Stockwith
Blyton
B1205
Grayingham
Waddingham
Brandy Wharf
Thornton le Moor
Austerfield
East Stockwith
Pilham
Eau
Blyborough
Snitterby
Spital Hill
Newington
Walkerith
Aisby
Willoughton
South Owersby
Kingerby
Bawtry
A159
B1398
Atterby
Harworth
Walkeringham
Morton
Bishop Norton
Bircotes
Scaftworth
Everton
Gringley on the Hill
Gainsborough
Corringham
Hemswell
A15
Spital in the Street
Glentham
Bishopbridge
Scrooby
Cuckoo Hill
A631
A631
Caenby
Serlby
A638
Mattersey Thorpe
Wiseton
Beckingham
Springthorpe
Harpswell
Hemswell Cliff
Caenby Corner
Normanby-by-Spital
Toft next Newton
Blyth Services
Ranskill
B6045
Mattersey
B1403
Clayworth
Saundby
Heapham
Glentworth
Blyth
Torworth
A634
North Wheatley
Bole
Upton
Owmby-by-Spital
Lound
Lea
A156
Knaith Park
B1241
Fillingham
Saxby
A620
South Wheatley
Sturton le Steeple
Kexby
Barnby Moor
Sutton
Hayton
Willingham by Stow
Spridlington
Faldingworth
A1
A638
Knaith
B1398
Clarborough
Gate Burton
Normanby by Stow
Ingham
Cold Hanworth
North Leverton with Habblesthorpe
Littleborough
Hackthorn
Welham
Stow
Cammeringham
West Retford
Marton
Thorpe in the Fallows
Snarford
Scofton
Ranby
Babworth
RETFORD
Coates
A1500
Brattleby
Welton Hill
A620
Ordsall
South Leverton
Sturton by Stow
Aisthorpe
Welton
A46
B6079
Grove
Cottam
Brampton
Scampton
Dunholme
Worksop
B6420
Eaton
Treswell
Rampton
Torksey
B1241
Bransby
A57
A638
Woodbeck
Church Laneham
Broxholme
North Carlton
Scothern
A1
Headon
Stokeham
Fenton
Ingleby
Till
Langworth
Gamston
Upton
Laneham
South Carlton
A15
Sudbrooke
Elkesley
Askham
Laughterton
A156
Kettlethorpe
Saxilby
Odder
B1398
Riseholme
Nettleham
Hardwick
Poulter
West Drayton
Markham Moor
Darlton
East Drayton
Dunham
Newton on Trent
A57
Burton
A158
Bothamsall
Markham Moor Services
A57
Ragnall
Broadholme
Reepham
Carburton
A614
Haughton
Milton
East Markham
Fledborough
Thorney
Skellingthorpe
Lincoln
Ermine
North Greetwell
Cherry Willingham
Bevercotes
West Markham
North Clifton
St Giles

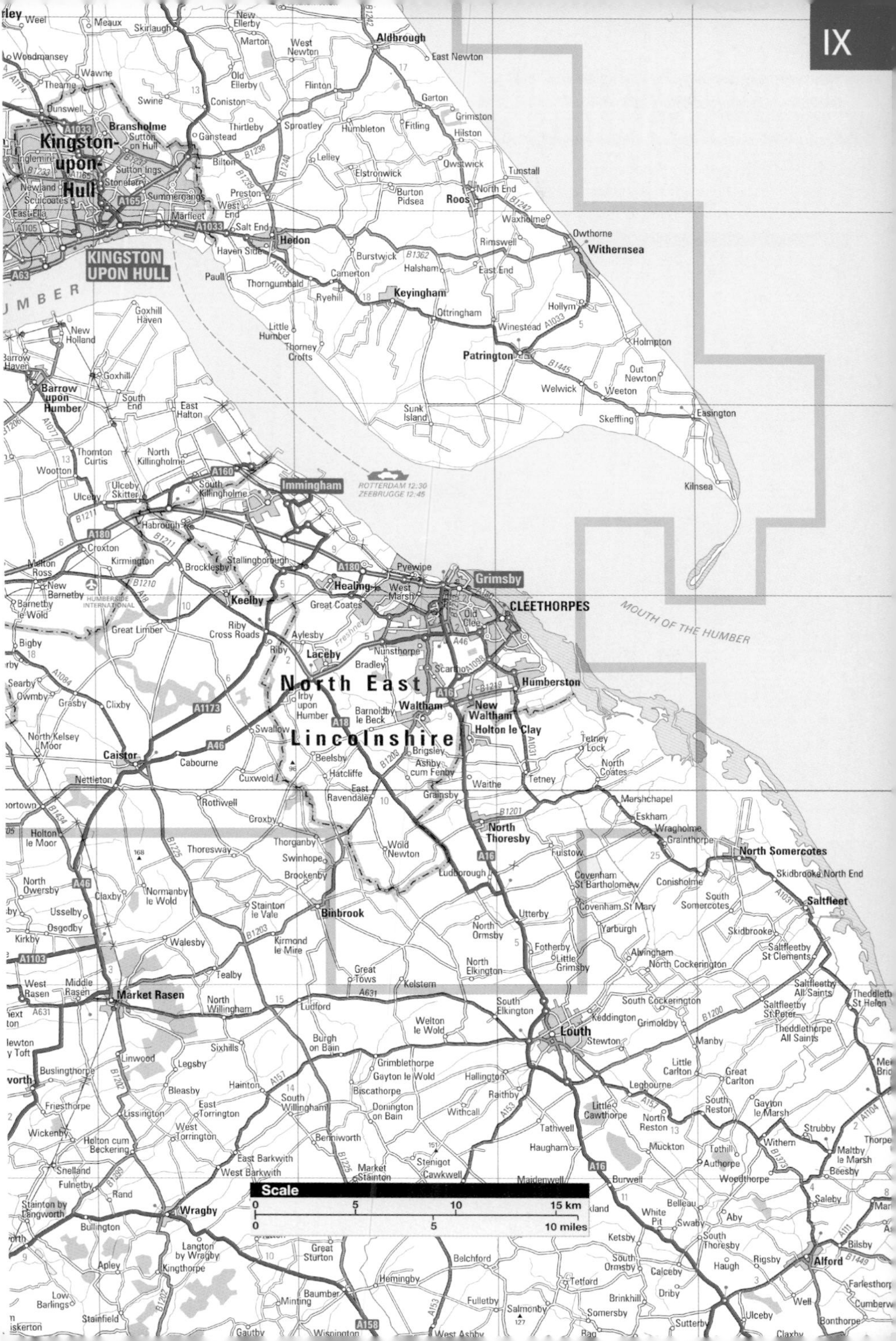
Weel
Meaux
Skirlaugh
New Ellerby
Marton
West Newton
Aldbrough
East Newton
Woodmansey
Wawne
Old Ellerby
Flinton
Thearne
Swine
Coniston
Garton
Dunswell
Grimston
Bransholme
Sutton on Hull
Thirtleby
Sproatley
Humbleton
Fitling
Hilston
Kingston-upon-Hull
Ganstead
Inglemire
Bilton
Lelley
Owstwick
Tunstall
Sutton Ings
Elstronwick
Newland
Stoneferry
Burton Pidsea
North End
Sculcoates
Summergangs
Preston
Roos
East Ella
West End
Waxholme
Marfleet
Salt End
Owthorne
Hedon
Rimswell
Withernsea
KINGSTON UPON HULL
Haven Side
Burstwick
Halsham
East End
Paull
Camerton
Thorngumbald
Ryehill
Keyingham
Hollym
HUMBER
Goxhill Haven
Ottringham
Little Humber
Winestead
New Holland
Thorney Crofts
Holmpton
Patrington
Barrow Haven
Goxhill
Barrow upon Humber
South End
Out Newton
East Halton
Welwick
Weeton
Sunk Island
Easington
Skeffling
Thornton Curtis
North Killingholme
Wootton
Immingham
ROTTERDAM 12:30
ZEEBRUGGE 12:45
South Killingholme
Ulceby
Ulceby Skitter
Kilnsea
Habrough
Croxton
Kirmington
Stallingborough
Melton Ross
Brocklesby
Pyewipe
Grimsby
New Barnetby
Healing
West Marsh
Barnetby le Wold
HUMBERSIDE INTERNATIONAL
Keelby
Great Coates
CLEETHORPES
MOUTH OF THE HUMBER
Old Clee
Great Limber
Riby Cross Roads
Aylesby
Freshney
Bigby
Riby
Laceby
Nunsthorpe
Bradley
Scartho
Searby
North East Lincolnshire
Humberston
Owmby
Grasby
Clixby
Irby upon Humber
Barnoldby le Beck
Waltham
New Waltham
Holton le Clay
North Kelsey Moor
Swallow
Tetney Lock
Caistor
Cabourne
Beelsby
Brigsley
Ashby cum Fenby
North Coates
Hatcliffe
Nettleton
Cuxwold
Waithe
Tetney
East Ravendale
Rothwell
Grainsby
Marshchapel
Croxby
Eskham
Wragholme
Grainthorpe
Holton le Moor
North Thoresby
Thoresway
Thorganby
Wold Newton
Fulstow
North Somercotes
Swinhope
Skidbrooke North End
North Owersby
Brookenby
Ludborough
Covenham St Bartholomew
Conisholme
Claxby
Normanby le Wold
South Somercotes
Saltfleet
Usselby
Stainton le Vale
Binbrook
Covenham St Mary
Utterby
Osgodby
Yarburgh
Kirkby
Walesby
Kirmond le Mire
North Ormsby
Skidbrooke
Saltfleetby St Clements
Fotherby
Alvingham
Little Grimsby
North Cockerington
Tealby
North Elkington
Great Tows
West Rasen
Middle Rasen
Kelstern
Saltfleetby All Saints
Theddlethorpe St Helen
Market Rasen
North Willingham
Ludford
South Elkington
South Cockerington
Saltfleetby St Peter
Keddington
Grimoldby
Welton le Wold
Theddlethorpe All Saints
Louth
Stewton
Manby
Burgh on Bain
Sixhills
Linwood
Legsby
Grimblethorpe
Little Carlton
Buslingthorpe
Gayton le Wold
Hallington
Great Carlton
Hainton
South Willingham
Biscathorpe
Raithby
Legbourne
Bleasby
Friesthorpe
East Torrington
Donington on Bain
Withcall
Little Cawthorpe
South Reston
Gayton le Marsh
Lissington
North Reston
Tathwell
West Torrington
Wickenby
Holton cum Beckering
Benniworth
Strubby
Muckton
Withern
Tothill
Haugham
Maltby le Marsh
Stenigot
Authorpe
East Barkwith
West Barkwith
Cawkwell
Snelland
Market Stainton
Maidenwell
Beesby
Fulnetby
Rand
Burwell
Woodthorpe
Scale
0 5 10 15 km
0 5 10 miles
Stainton by Langworth
Wragby
Saleby
Belleau
White Pit
Aby
Swaby
Bullington
Ketsby
South Thoresby
Langton by Wragby
Great Sturton
Belchford
South Ormsby
Bilsby
Calceby
Rigsby
Apley
Kingthorpe
Haugh
Alford
Tetford
Hemingby
Driby
Farlesthorpe
Baumber
Brinkhill
Low Barlings
Minting
Fulletby
Well
Salmonby
Cumberworth
Somersby
Stainfield
Ulceby
Bonthorpe
Sutterby
Gautby
Wispington
West Ashby
Bag Enderby
Claxby
A1033
A1165
A165
A1105
A63
A160
A180
A18
A1077
A46
A1173
A1084
A1031
A16
A1098
B1219
A631
A1103
A157
A153
A1104
A111
A158
B1242
B1240
B1238
B1362
B1445
B1211
B1210
B1203
B1201
B1225
B1202
B1200
B1373
B1449
B1399
B1434

Administrative and Postcode boundaries

County and unitary authority boundaries

Postcode boundaries

Area covered by this atlas

Scale

0 5 10 15 20 25 30 35 40 km

0 5 10 15 20 25 miles

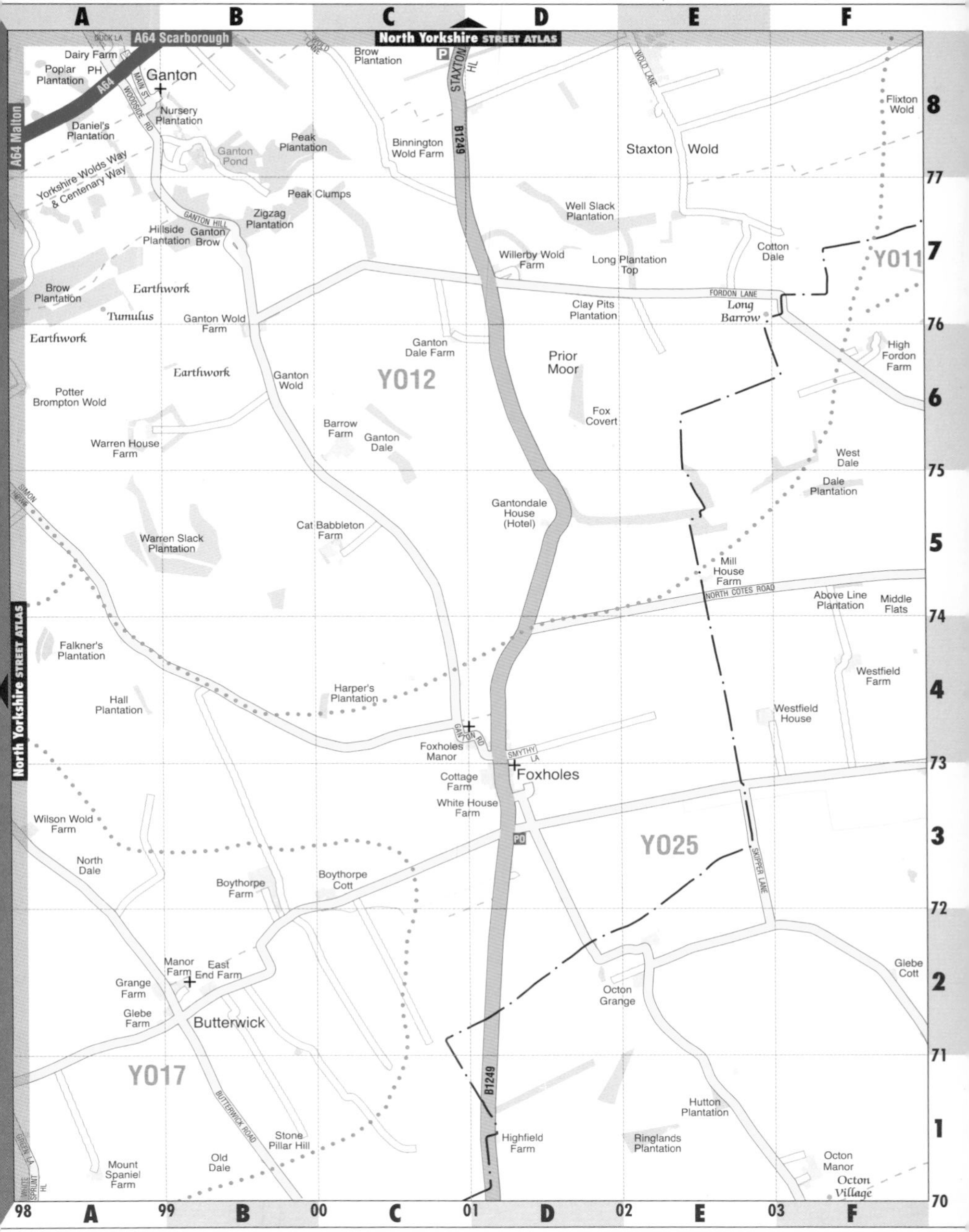
A
B
C
D
E
F
A64 Scarborough
North Yorkshire STREET ATLAS
A64 Malton
Dairy Farm
Poplar Plantation
PH
Ganton
Nursery Plantation
Daniel's Plantation
Ganton Pond
Peak Plantation
Brow Plantation
Binnington Wold Farm
STAXTON HL
B1249
Staxton Wold
Flixton Wold
Yorkshire Wolds Way & Centenary Way
Peak Clumps
Zigzag Plantation
Hillside Plantation
Ganton Brow
GANTON HILL
Well Slack Plantation
Willerby Wold Farm
Long Plantation Top
Cotton Dale
YO11
Brow Plantation
Earthwork
Tumulus
Ganton Wold Farm
Clay Pits Plantation
FORDON LANE
Long Barrow
Earthwork
Ganton Dale Farm
Prior Moor
High Fordon Farm
Earthwork
Ganton Wold
YO12
Potter Brompton Wold
Fox Covert
Barrow Farm
Ganton Dale
Warren House Farm
West Dale
Dale Plantation
Gantondale House (Hotel)
Cat Babbleton Farm
Warren Slack Plantation
Mill House Farm
NORTH COTES ROAD
Above Line Plantation
Middle Flats
Falkner's Plantation
Westfield Farm
Harper's Plantation
Hall Plantation
Westfield House
Foxholes Manor
GANTON RD
SMYTHY LA
Foxholes
Cottage Farm
White House Farm
Wilson Wold Farm
PO
YO25
North Dale
Boythorpe Farm
Boythorpe Cott
SKIPPER LANE
Manor Farm
East End Farm
Grange Farm
Glebe Cott
Octon Grange
Glebe Farm
Butterwick
YO17
B1249
Hutton Plantation
BUTTERWICK ROAD
Stone Pillar Hill
Highfield Farm
Ringlands Plantation
Mount Spaniel Farm
Old Dale
Octon Manor
Octon Village
WOLD LANE
WOODSIDE RD
MAIN ST
SIMON HOWE
GREEN LA
WHITE SPRUNT HL
98
99
00
01
02
03
77
76
75
74
73
72
71
70
8
7
6
5
4
3
2
1

1

F8
1 OWSTON RD
2 MITFORD RD
3 MITFORD CL
4 OUTGAITS CL
5 WENTWORTH WY
6 SIMPSON AVE
7 HIGH CFT
8 CASTLE HL
9 BOWLING GN LA
10 CHURCH HL
11 HUNGATE CT
12 VICARAGE CL
13 FONTAYNE RD
14 BARDNEY RD
15 ROWEDALE CL
16 AMBREY CL
17 PARK RISE
18 OLIVER'S CL
19 ROSEMOOR CL
20 HARBOROUGH CL

Scale: 1⅓ inches to 1 mile
0 ¼ ½ mile
0 250m 500m 750m 1 km

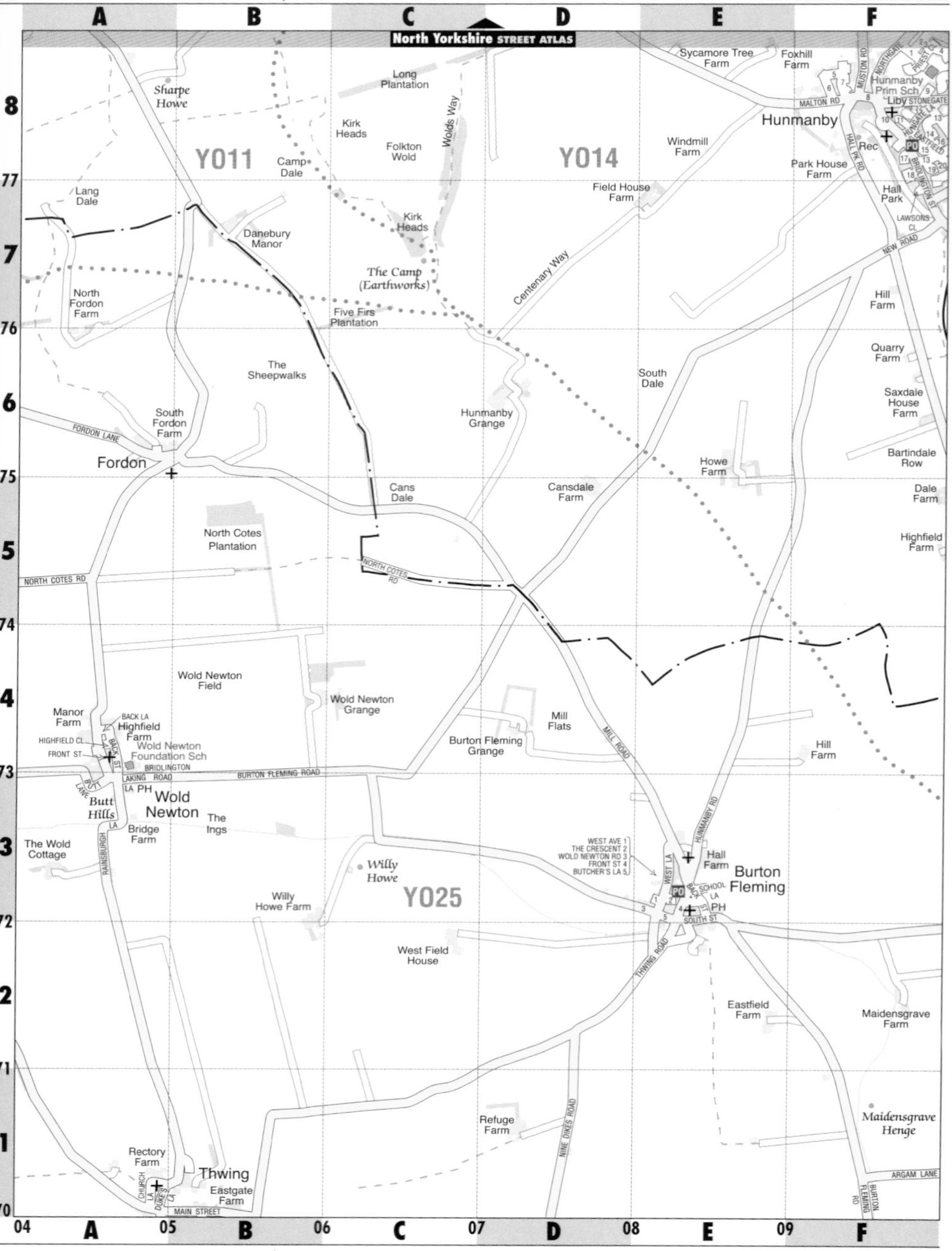

1

9

Scale: 1⅓ inches to 1 mile

0 ¼ ½ mile

0 250m 500m 750m 1 km

A8
1 WRANGHAM DR
2 LENNOX CL
3 BURLYN RD
4 CHERRY RD
5 HAWKE GARTH
6 MANOR GDNS
7 CECIL RD
8 HOWES RD
9 WATSON CL
10 HAMERTON RD
11 HAMERTON CL
12 GRIMSTON RD
13 STRICKLAND RD
14 PERCY RD
15 HAVERCROFT RD
16 COWLINGS CL

4

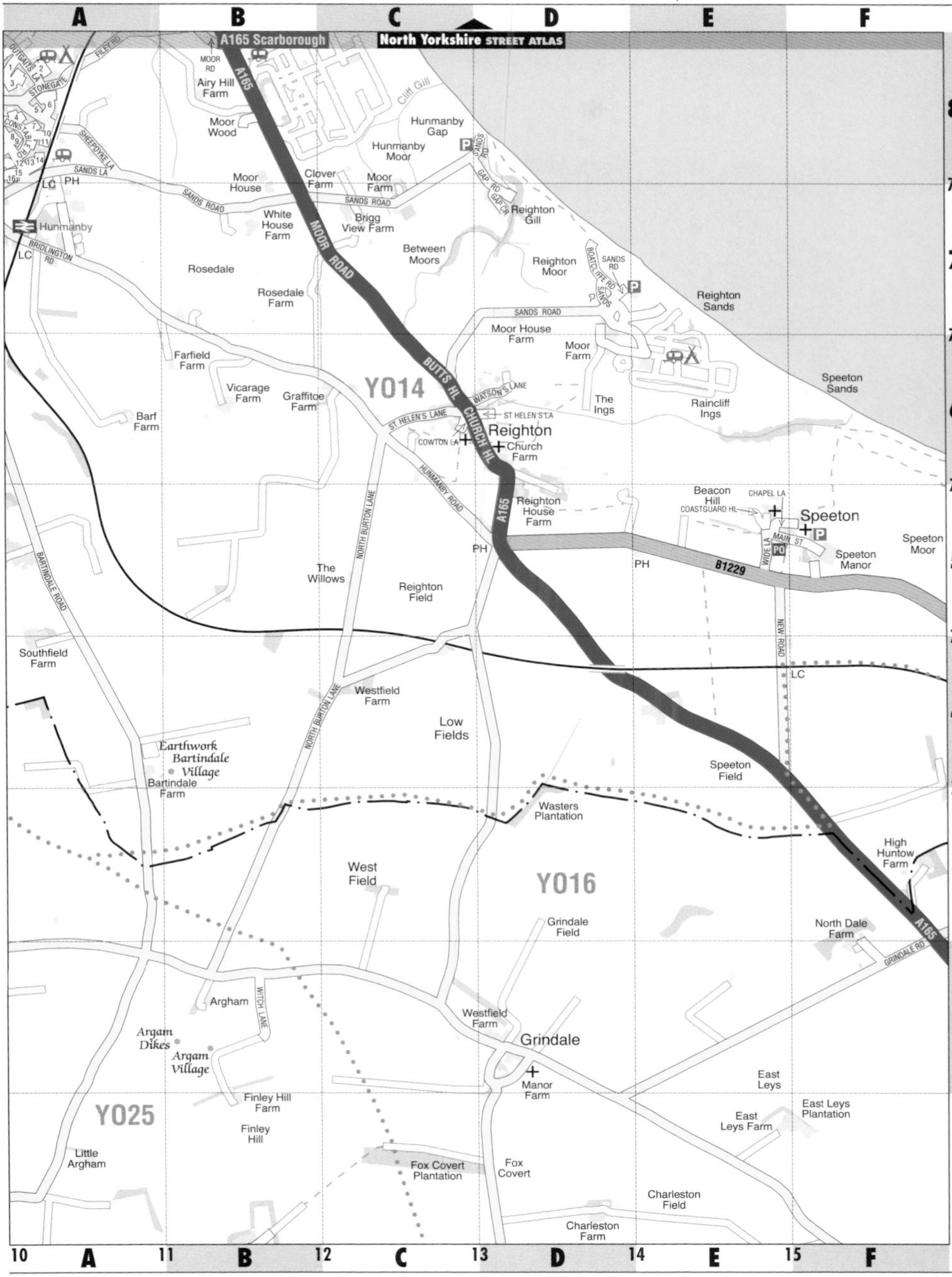

10

4

3

Scale: 1⅓ inches to 1 mile
0 ¼ ½ mile
0 250m 500m 750m 1 km

C4
1 WALMSLEY CL
2 GRANGE CL
3 COLLINGWOOD RD
4 THE MEADOWS
5 RINGLEY MDWS

D4
1 THE PADDOCK
2 SPRING LA
3 ST MICHAEL'S WK
4 BYEDALES
5 GILLUS LA
6 CHURCH LA
7 ACREDYKES
8 VICARAGE LA
9 CLARK CR

122 3 123

For full street detail of the highlighted area see pages 122 and 123.

Scale: 1⅓ inches to 1 mile
0 ¼ ½ mile
0 250m 500m 750m 1 km
A B C D E F
8 76 7 75 6 74 5 73 4 72 3 71 2 70 1 69
22 23 24 25 26 27
Scab Scar
Thornwick Bay
Holmes Scar
North Cliff
West Scar
Flamborough Cliffs Nature Reserve
Sixpenny Hill Plantation
Holiday Centre
Thornwick Farm
THORNWICK RD
PH
NORTH MARINE ROAD
ST DAVID LANE
1 NORTH MARINE RD
2 MARINE VALLEY
3 NORTH MOOR RD
Breil Nook
Breil Head
Cradle Head
North Moor
Northcliff Farm
Stottle Bank Nook
The Grange
Hotel
B1255
YO15
Flamborough Head Golf Club
Selwicks Bay
BEMPTON LA
B1229
CRAIKEWELLS
Flatmere Plantation
Kindle Scar
Flamborough Outer Headland Nature Reserve
GULL NOOK
EAST SCAR
MERESIDE VW
CH
Tower
Flamborough Head
Seaways Farm
B1259
SELWICK DR
Lighthouse
Flamborough CE VC Prim Sch
CARTER LA
Castle
FLAEN RD
FLAEN CL
TOWER ST
SEA ROAD
CONSTABLE ROAD
LIGHTHOUSE ROAD
Head Farm
Mast
Ocean View Farm
Liby
High Stacks
B1255
LA
SOUTH SEA ROAD
Flamborough
Old Fall Plantation
Cattlemere Scar
Beacon Farm
Visitor Centre
South Landing Nature Reserve
The Timoneer
South Landing
South Cliff
Hartendale Crag
Beacon Hill
SOUTH SEA RD
Great Scars

A2
1 WOODCOCK RD
2 BEECH GR
3 BEECH AVE
4 GARENDS RD
5 NORTH END
6 CHAPEL ST
7 HIGH ST
8 GREENSIDE
9 MERESIDE
10 SCHOOL LA
11 OGLE RD
12 POST OFFICE ST
13 DOG AND DUCK SQ
14 ALLISON LA
15 STYLEFIELD RD
16 CASTLE CR
17 STOTTLEBINK
18 CONSTABLE CL
19 CHURCH ST
20 WATER LA
21 WEST ST
22 HARTENDALE CL
23 BUTLERS LA
24 CHURCH LA
25 CHURCH CL
26 SOUTH SEA AVE

Scale: 1⅓ inches to 1 mile
0 ¼ ½ mile
0 250m 500m 750m 1 km

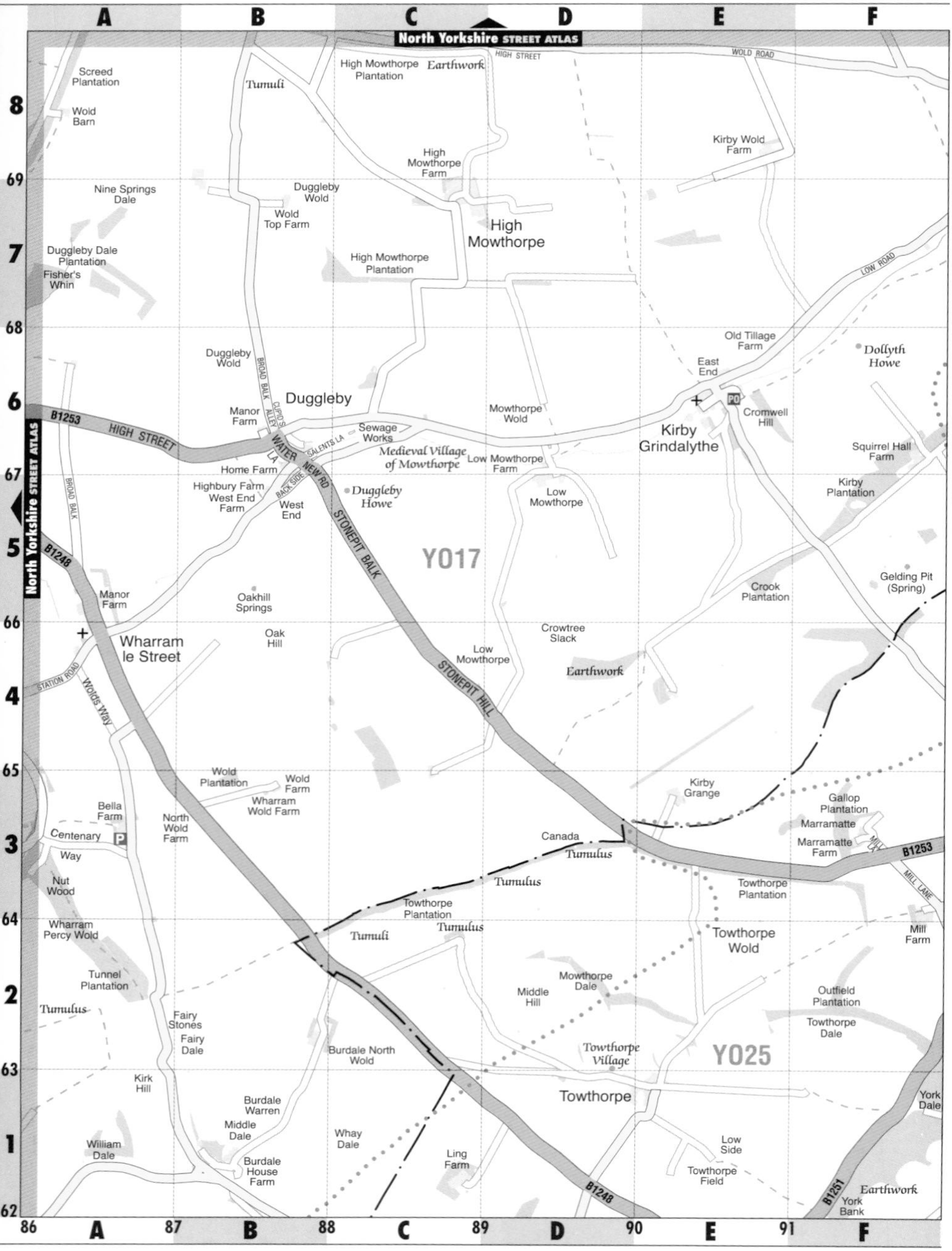
A B C D E F
North Yorkshire STREET ATLAS
HIGH STREET
WOLD ROAD
Screed Plantation
Wold Barn
Tumuli
High Mowthorpe Plantation
Earthwork
Kirby Wold Farm
High Mowthorpe Farm
Nine Springs Dale
Duggleby Wold
Wold Top Farm
High Mowthorpe
Duggleby Dale Plantation
Fisher's Whin
High Mowthorpe Plantation
LOW ROAD
Old Tillage Farm
Dollyth Howe
Duggleby Wold
BROAD BALK
CUPID'S ALLEY
Duggleby
East End
PO
Manor Farm
Mowthorpe Wold
Cromwell Hill
B1253
HIGH STREET
Sewage Works
SALENTS LA
WATER LA
Kirby Grindalythe
Squirrel Hall Farm
Medieval Village of Mowthorpe
Low Mowthorpe Farm
Home Farm
NEW RD
Highbury Farm
West End Farm
BACK SIDE
West End
Duggleby Howe
Low Mowthorpe
Kirby Plantation
STONEPIT BALK
YO17
B1248
Crook Plantation
Gelding Pit (Spring)
Manor Farm
Oakhill Springs
Oak Hill
Crowtree Slack
Wharram le Street
Low Mowthorpe
STATION ROAD
Wolds Way
STONEPIT HILL
Earthwork
Wold Plantation
Wold Farm
Kirby Grange
Gallop Plantation
Bella Farm
Wharram Wold Farm
North Wold Farm
Marramatte
Canada
Centenary Way
P
Tumulus
Marramatte Farm
MILL LA
B1253
Nut Wood
Tumulus
Towthorpe Plantation
MILL LANE
Towthorpe Plantation
Wharram Percy Wold
Tumuli
Tumulus
Towthorpe Wold
Mill Farm
Tunnel Plantation
Mowthorpe Dale
Middle Hill
Outfield Plantation
Tumulus
Fairy Stones
Fairy Dale
Towthorpe Dale
Burdale North Wold
Towthorpe Village
YO25
Kirk Hill
Towthorpe
York Dale
Burdale Warren
Middle Dale
Whay Dale
Low Side
William Dale
Ling Farm
Burdale House Farm
Towthorpe Field
B1248
B1251
Earthwork
York Bank
8 69 7 68 6 67 5 66 4 65 3 64 2 63 1 62
86 87 88 89 90 91

18

Scale: 1⅓ inches to 1 mile
0 ¼ ½ mile
0 250m 500m 750m 1 km

8

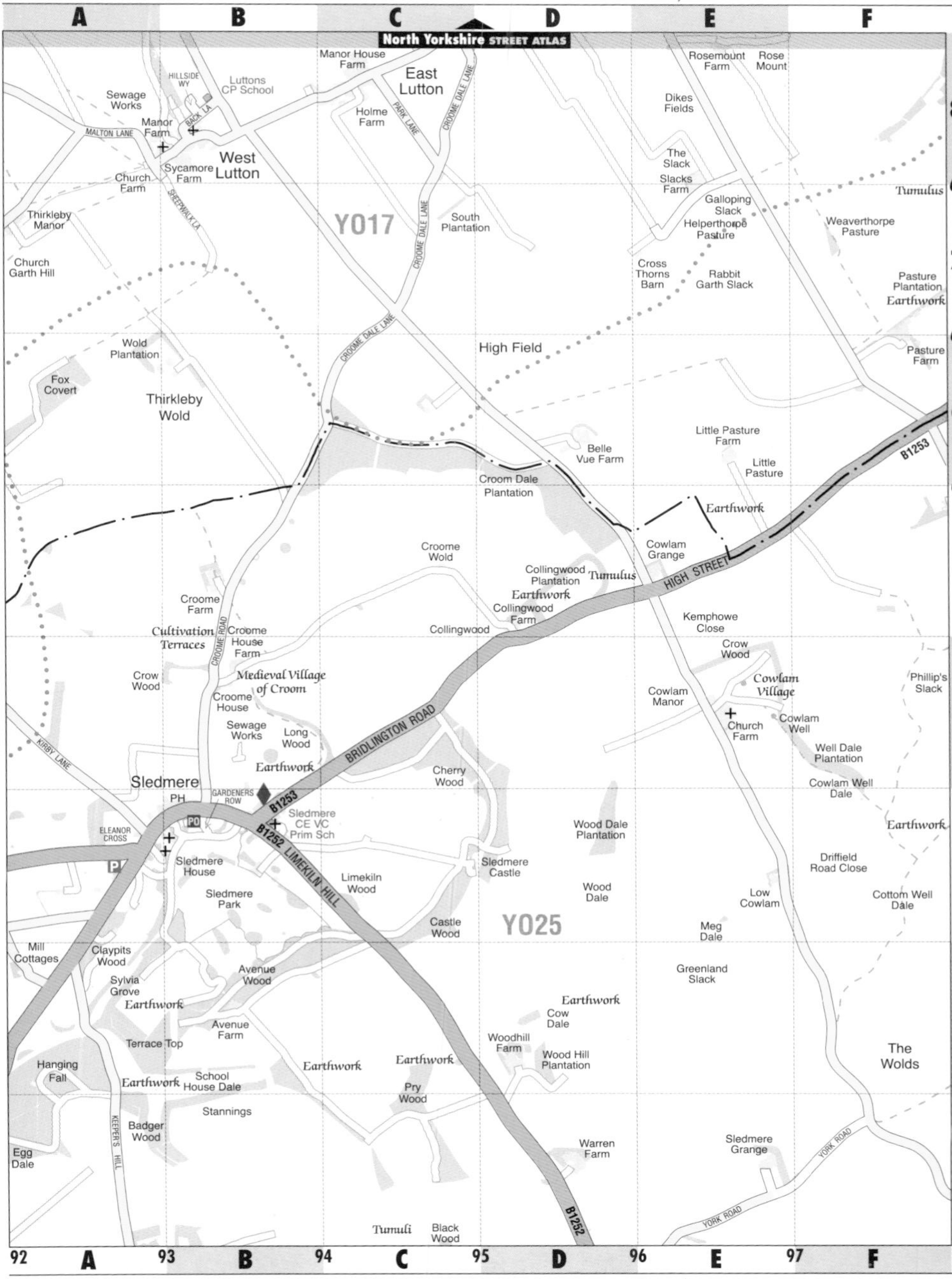
A
B
C
D
E
F
North Yorkshire STREET ATLAS
Manor House Farm
East Lutton
Rosemount Farm
Rose Mount
HILLSIDE WY
Luttons CP School
Sewage Works
BACK LA
CROOME DALE LANE
PARK LANE
Holme Farm
Dikes Fields
MALTON LANE
Manor Farm
West Lutton
Sycamore Farm
Church Farm
The Slack
Slacks Farm
Galloping Slack
Helperthorpe Pasture
Tumulus
Thirkleby Manor
SHEEPWALK LA
YO17
South Plantation
Weaverthorpe Pasture
Church Garth Hill
Cross Thorns Barn
Rabbit Garth Slack
Pasture Plantation
Earthwork
Wold Plantation
High Field
Pasture Farm
Fox Covert
Thirkleby Wold
Little Pasture Farm
Belle Vue Farm
Little Pasture
B1253
Croom Dale Plantation
Earthwork
Croome Wold
Cowlam Grange
Collingwood Plantation
Tumulus
HIGH STREET
Earthwork
Croome Farm
Collingwood Farm
Kemphowe Close
Cultivation Terraces
Croome House Farm
CROOME ROAD
Collingwood
Crow Wood
Crow Wood
Medieval Village of Croom
Cowlam Manor
Cowlam Village
Phillip's Slack
Croome House
BRIDLINGTON ROAD
Church Farm
Cowlam Well
Sewage Works
Long Wood
Well Dale Plantation
KIRBY LANE
Earthwork
Cherry Wood
Sledmere
GARDENERS ROW
Cowlam Well Dale
PH
B1253
Sledmere CE VC Prim Sch
PO
ELEANOR CROSS
Wood Dale Plantation
Earthwork
B1252 LIMEKILN HILL
P
Sledmere House
Sledmere Castle
Driffield Road Close
Limekiln Wood
Sledmere Park
Wood Dale
Low Cowlam
Cottom Well Dale
Castle Wood
YO25
Meg Dale
Mill Cottages
Claypits Wood
Avenue Wood
Greenland Slack
Sylvia Grove
Earthwork
Earthwork
Cow Dale
Avenue Farm
Terrace Top
Woodhill Farm
Hanging Fall
Earthwork
Earthwork
Wood Hill Plantation
The Wolds
Earthwork
School House Dale
Pry Wood
Stannings
Badger Wood
KEEPER'S HILL
Warren Farm
Sledmere Grange
YORK ROAD
Egg Dale
B1252
YORK ROAD
Tumuli
Black Wood
8
69
7
68
6
67
5
66
4
65
3
64
2
63
1
62
92
93
94
95
96
97

19
8

7
1

Scale: 1⅓ inches to 1 mile
0 ¼ ½ mile
0 250m 500m 750m 1 km

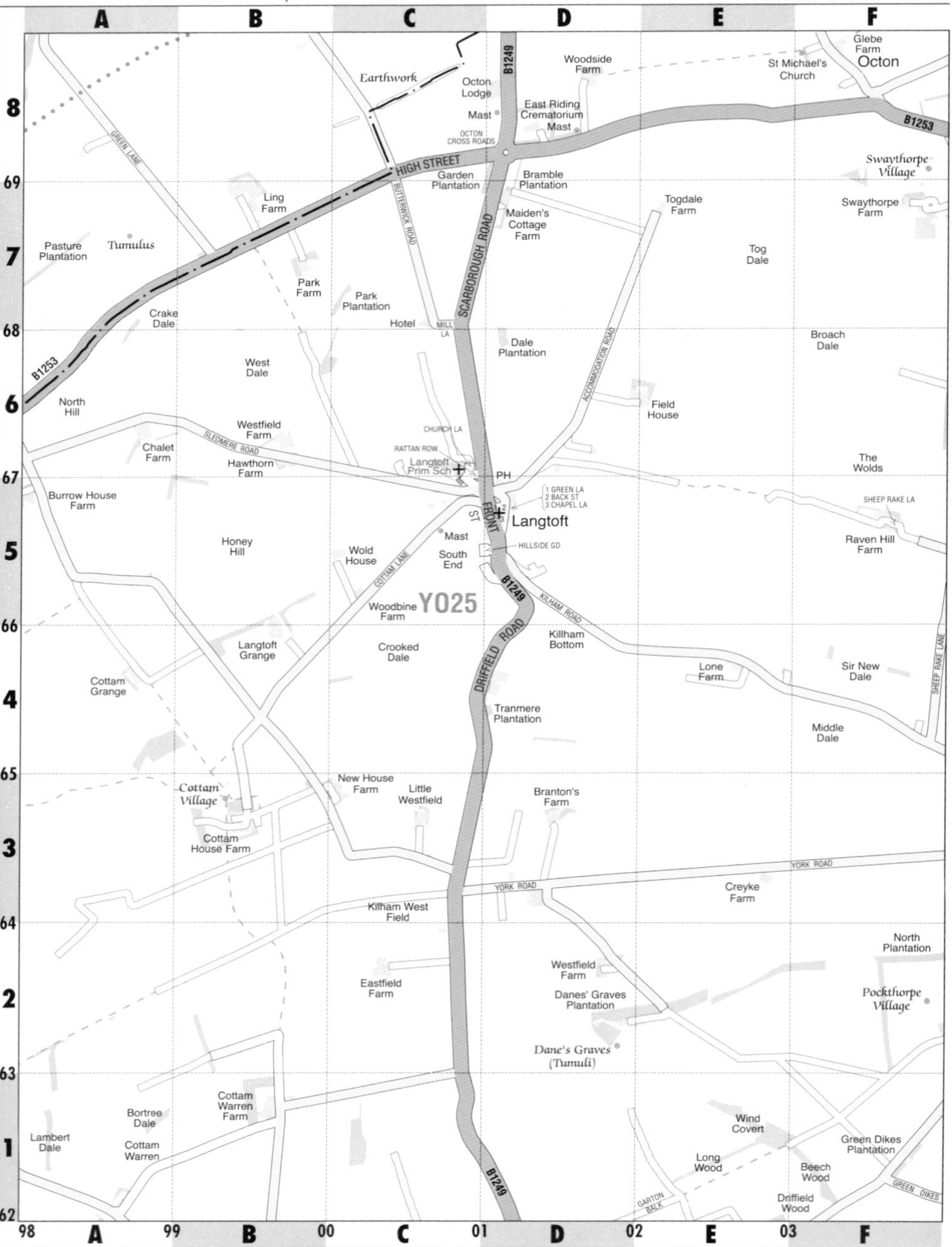

7
20

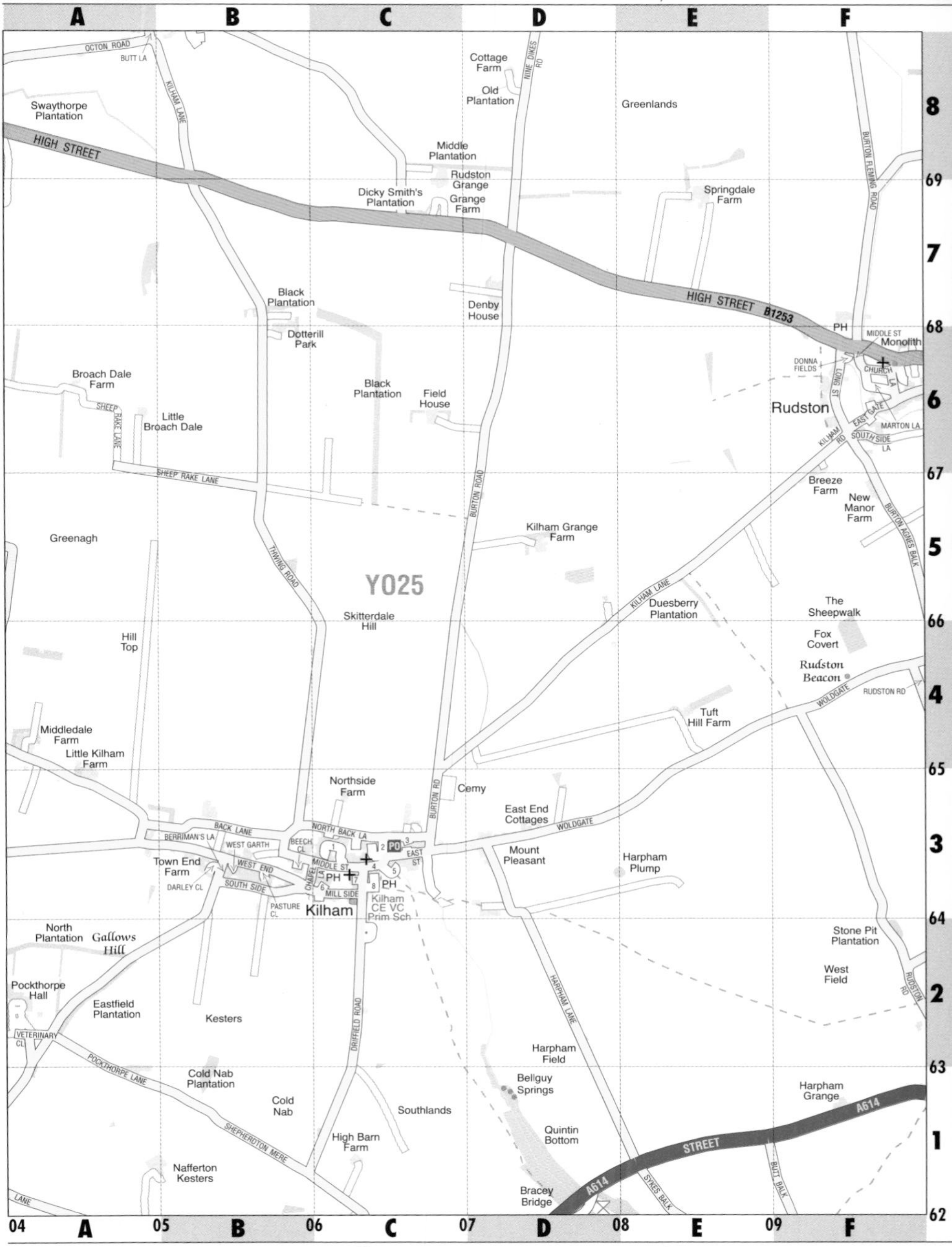

C3
1 CHANTRY MDWS
2 CHURCH LA
3 ROPERY CL
4 CHURCH ST
5 BAKEHOUSE LA
6 MILL SIDE CL
7 SOUTH CL
8 SOUTH GR

9
3

Scale: 1⅓ inches to 1 mile
0 ¼ ½ mile
0 250m 500m 750m 1 km

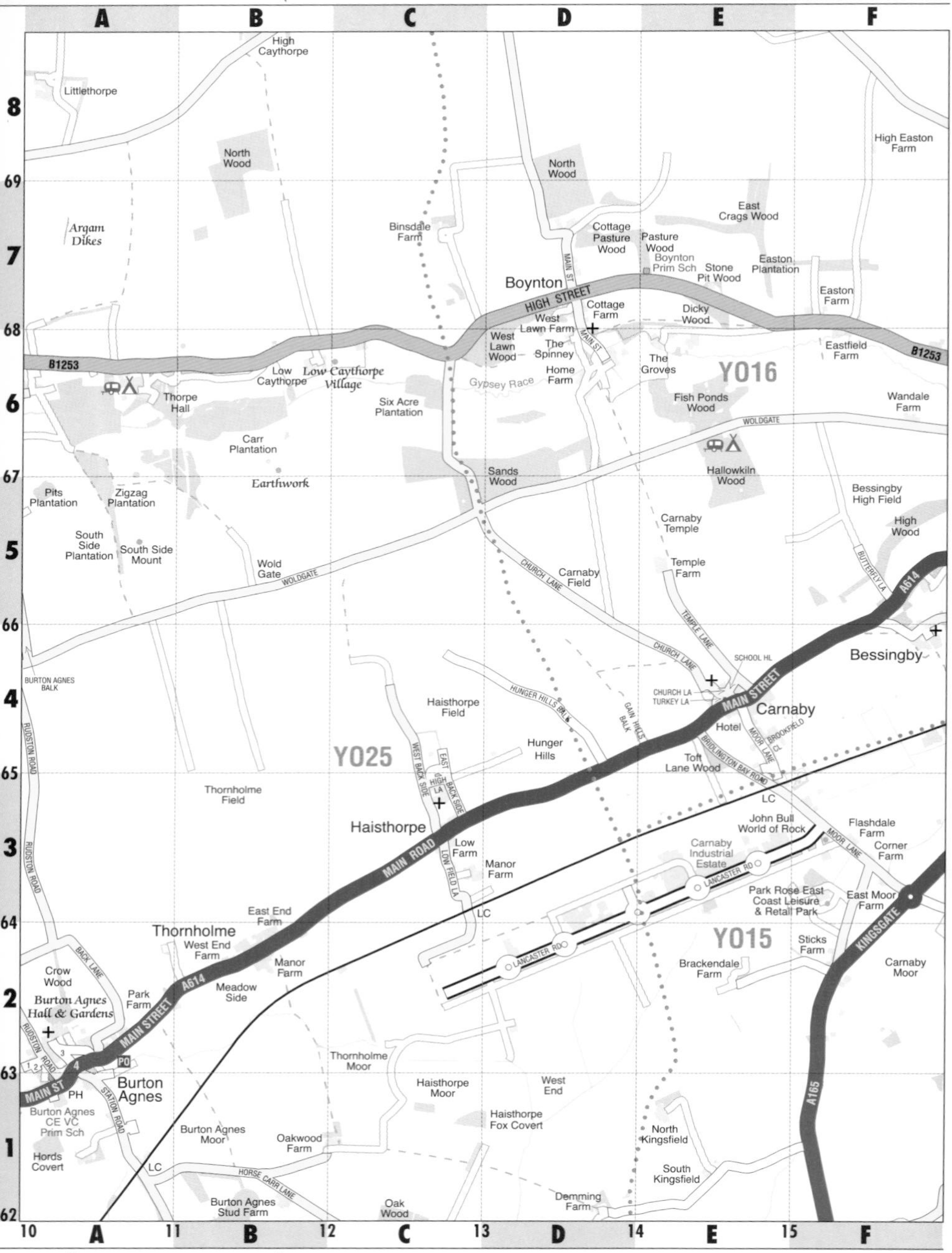

A2
1 ST MARTIN'S DR
2 ST MARTIN'S CL
3 SHADY LA
4 HOSPITAL HL

9
22

Scale: 1⅓ inches to 1 mile
0 ¼ ½ mile
0 250m 500m 750m 1 km

4

A
B
C
D
E
F
122
123
8
69
7
68
6
67
5
66
4
65
3
64
2
63
1
62
16
17
18
19
20
21
The Grange
Hill Field
YO16
Stackyard Plantation
Marton
Leys Plantation
Long Wood
YO15
Gell-spring Plantation
Home Farm
Dyke Wood
Nature Reserve
Needles Plantation
Dykes End
GRINDALE LANE
SCARBOROUGH ROAD
A165
BEMPTON LANE
PINFOLD LANE
FLAMBOROUGH RD
MARTON GATE
B1255
Charity Farm
CHURCH LA
HIGH SEWERBY RD
MOOR RD
CH
Sewerby Hall
Sewerby Rocks
County Farm
HADDON RD
TRENTHAM DR
THORESBY AV
THORESBY CL
JOHNSON AV
DARWIN RD
MOUNT CR
BEMPTON OVAL
AIREDALE DR
THORNTONDALE DR
WHARFEDALE DR
W CRAYKE
KEPPEL DR
MORDACKS RD
THE GRAYKE
MAPLE RD
SANDSACRE AVE
WHEATLEY DR
BEECH DR
VIKING ROAD
MAIN ST
CLIFF WK
PH
PO
Model Village
LC
Sewerby Fields
Rock Ends
Sewerby
Sch
Prim Sch
BURSTALL HL
MILL LANE
DANES CFT
B1255 MARTON ROAD
SEWERBY RD
HARLAND RD
OMEGA RD
LIMEKILN LANE
Old Town
FORTYFOOT
ST COLUMBA RD
LAMBERT RD
QUEENSGATE
EIGHTH AVE
SECOND AV
FIRST AV
NORTH MARINE DRIVE
EASTON RD
WESTGATE
HIGH ST
SOUTH BACK LA
LEYS RD
GYPSEY RD
CHANTRY CT
BROOKLAND RD
ST JOHN'S ST
APPLEGARTH
JUBILEE AV
Cemy
BUTTS CL
Coll
ST ALBAN RD
ST AIDAN RD
MILNER RD
BRETT ST
Bridlington RUFC
Bridlington Town FC
B1254
BRIDLINGTON
Bridlington & District
H
BESSINGBY HL
CARLTON ST
TRINITY RD
TENNYSON AVE
PROMENADE
MIDWAY AV
Bridlington
A1038
QUAY RD
Liby
Mus
BESSINGBY RD
HILDERTHORPE RD
A614
WRIGHT CR
CORNFIELD CR
THORNTON ROAD
HARRINGTON
MATSON RD
KENT SQ
West Hill
Ind Est
BESSINGBY WY
GEORGIAN WY
ST JAMES RD
CARDIGAN RD
EAST RD
RICHMOND ST
HORSFORTH AV
WINDSOR CR
S MARINE DR
Spa Theatre
BRICK KILN BALK
MAIN ST
Middle Wood
Hilderthorpe
KINGSGATE
KINGSTON RD
Church Plantation
Hilderthorpe Village
BELVEDERE RD
BELVEDERE GR
BELVEDERE PARADE
1 KINGSTON CR
2 TRAFALGAR CR
3 AVOCET WAY
4 TEAL GARTH
5 HERON MEWS
6 CURLEW GREEN
7 KINGFISHER DR
8 PARTRIDGE CL
9 KINGSTON CL
10 BELVEDERE CL
Bridlington Bay
Southcliff Caravan Park
Wilsthorpe Covert
Bridge Farm
Hill Farm
Wilsthorpe Village
Cliff Farm
Sewage
Wilsthorpe
YO15
Auburn Farm
Auburn Village
P

For full street detail of the highlighted area see pages 122 and 123.

23

Scale: 1⅓ inches to 1 mile
0 ¼ ½ mile
0 250m 500m 750m 1 km

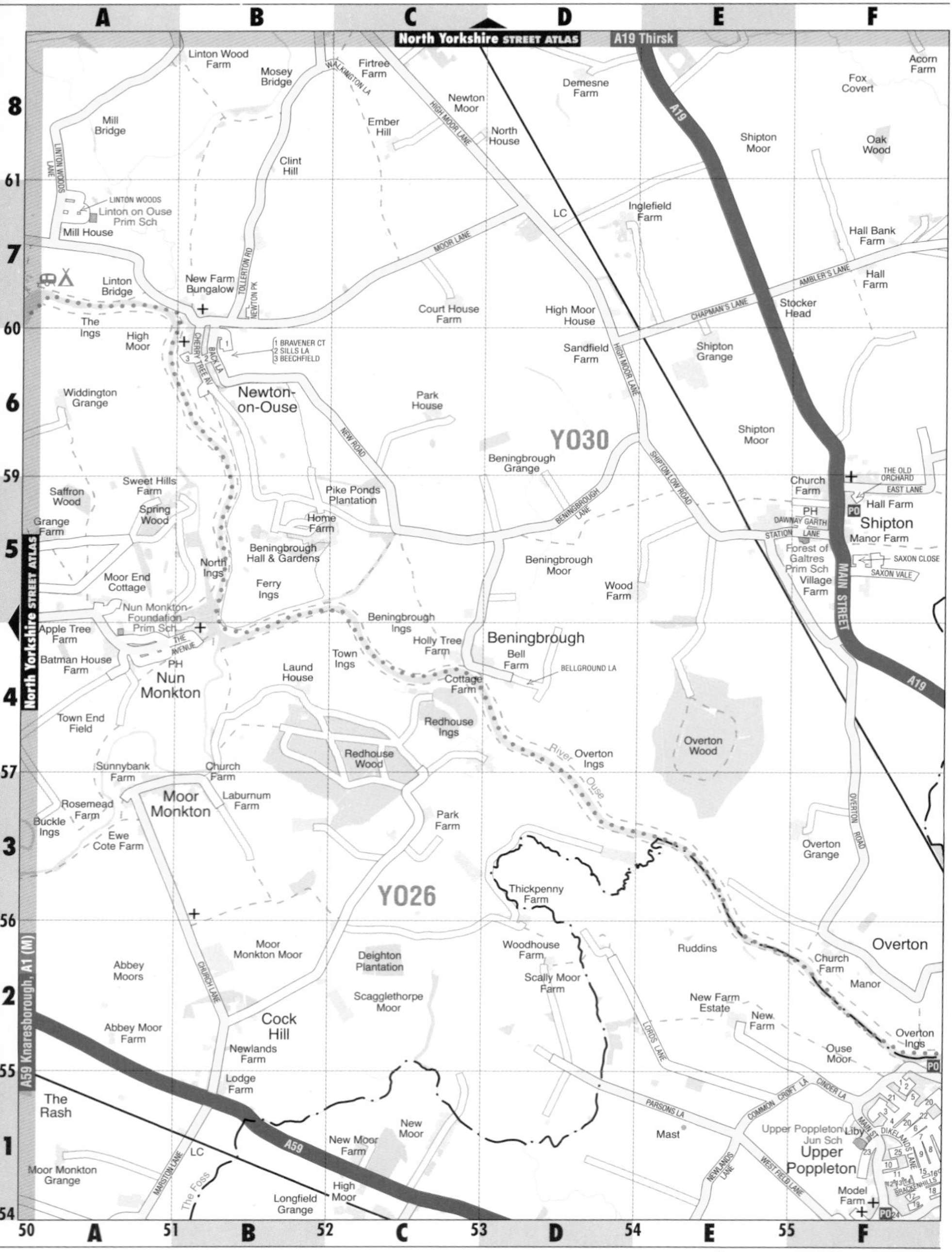

24

F1
1 RIVERSIDE WALK
2 RIVERSIDE GDNS
3 BANKSIDE CL
4 SPRINGFIELD RD
5 LITTLEFIELD CL
6 MONTAGUE WALK
7 EBOR WAY
8 PEAR TREE AVE
9 ELM TREE AVE
10 LIMEGARTH
11 CHANTRY GAP
12 GROVE GD
13 CHANTRY GR
14 CHANTRY AVE
15 APPLE GARTH
16 CHERRY GROVE
17 SYCAMORE VIEW
18 FAIRWAY DR
19 DIKELANDS CL
20 NETHER WY
21 RIVERSVALE DR
22 ALLERTON DR
23 SCHOOL LA
24 STATION RD
25 BEECH WY

Scale: 1⅓ inches to 1 mile
0 ¼ ½ mile
0 250m 500m 750m 1 km

14

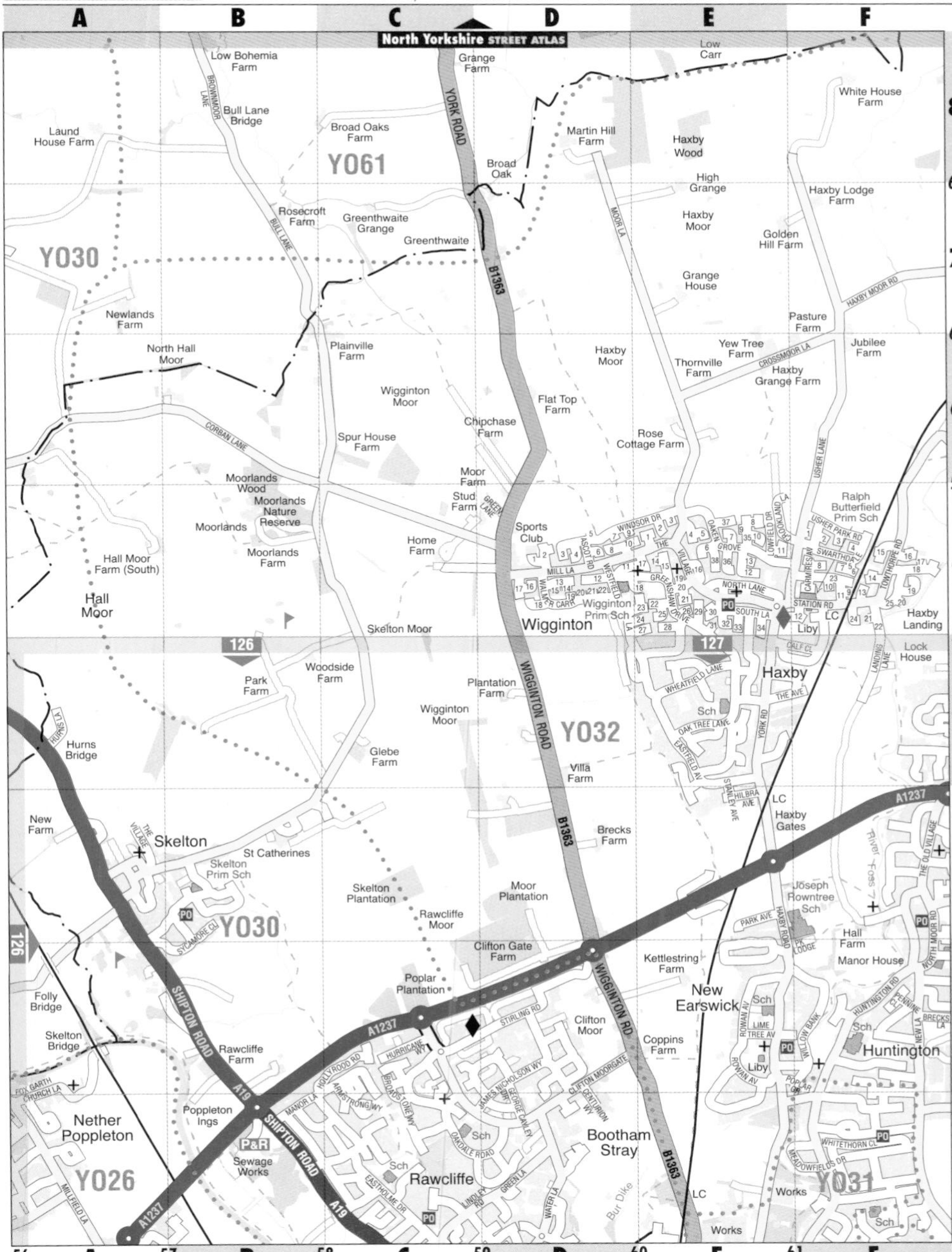

For full street detail of the highlighted area see pages 126 and 127.

129
128

130

A7
1 LEYFIELD CL
2 MOORLAND GARTH
3 WILKINSON WY
4 FOSSLAND VW
5 RIVERSIDE WK
6 LOW CFT
7 WOOD CL
8 ADLINGTON CL
9 FIRBANK CL
10 OSMINGTON GDNS
11 MELCOMBE AVE
12 PORTISHAM PL
13 LADYSMITH MS
14 SUSSEX WY
15 PELHAM PL

B7
1 ORCHARD WY
2 MIDDLECROFT GR
3 GLEBE CL
4 STATION SQ
5 HIGHLANDS AVE
6 OAKLANDS
7 HALLARD WY
8 THE WILLOWS
9 WEST END CL
10 OAK TREE WY

13

B8
1 LAKESIDE GR
2 THOMPSON DR
3 THE SWALLOWS
4 BLACKLEE CL
5 NORTHFIELDS
6 NETHERWOODS
7 LITTLETHORPE CL

C8
1 CHAPMAN CL
2 BRUNSWICK CL
3 PULLEYN CL
4 STUART CL
5 COULSON CL
6 CUNDALL CL

Scale: 1⅓ inches to 1 mile
0 ¼ ½ mile
0 250m 500m 750m 1 km

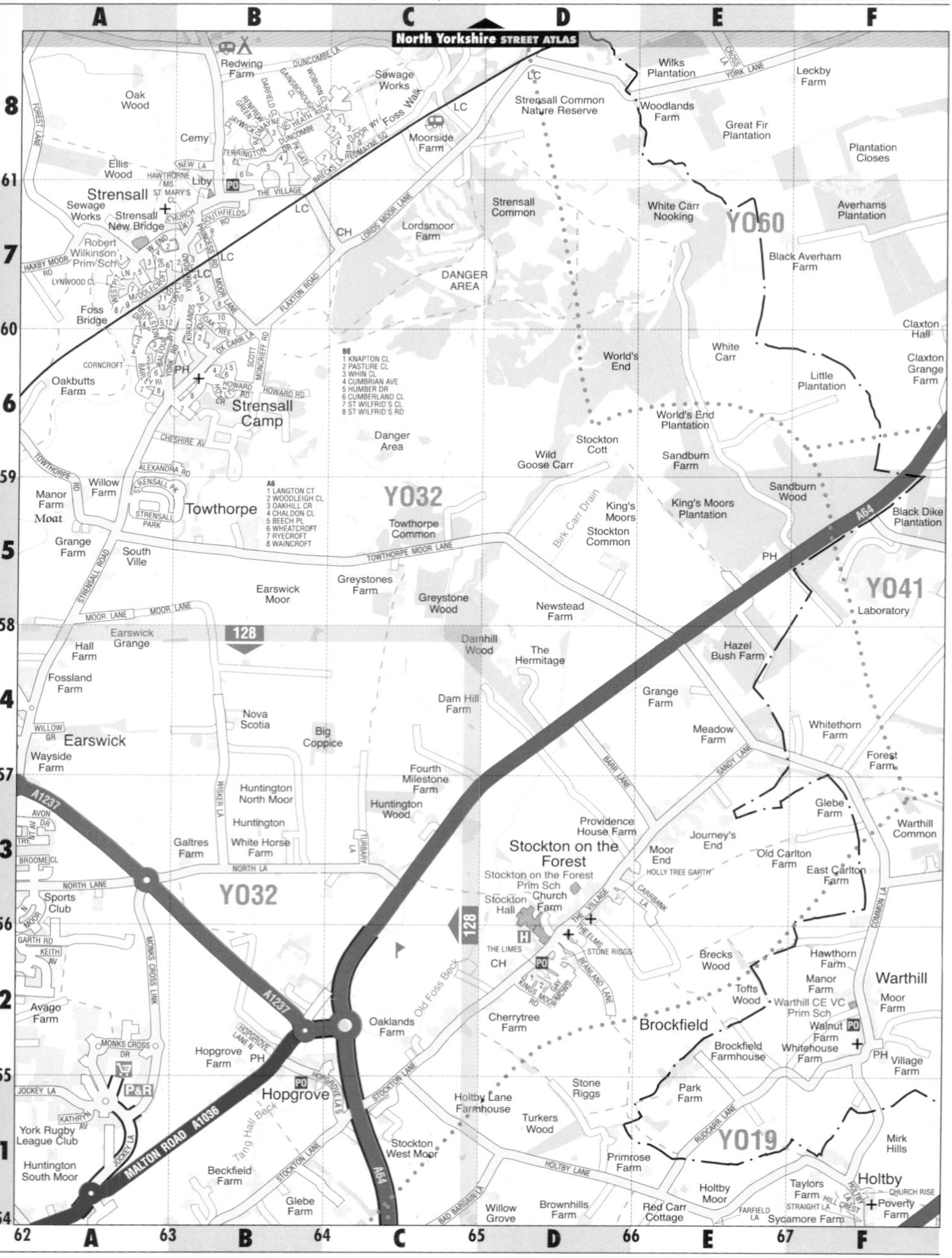

D2
1 CHAUMONT WY
2 MARMIAM DR

For full street detail of the highlighted area see page 128.
13
131
26

Scale: 1⅓ inches to 1 mile
0 ¼ ½ mile
0 250m 500m 750m 1 km

16

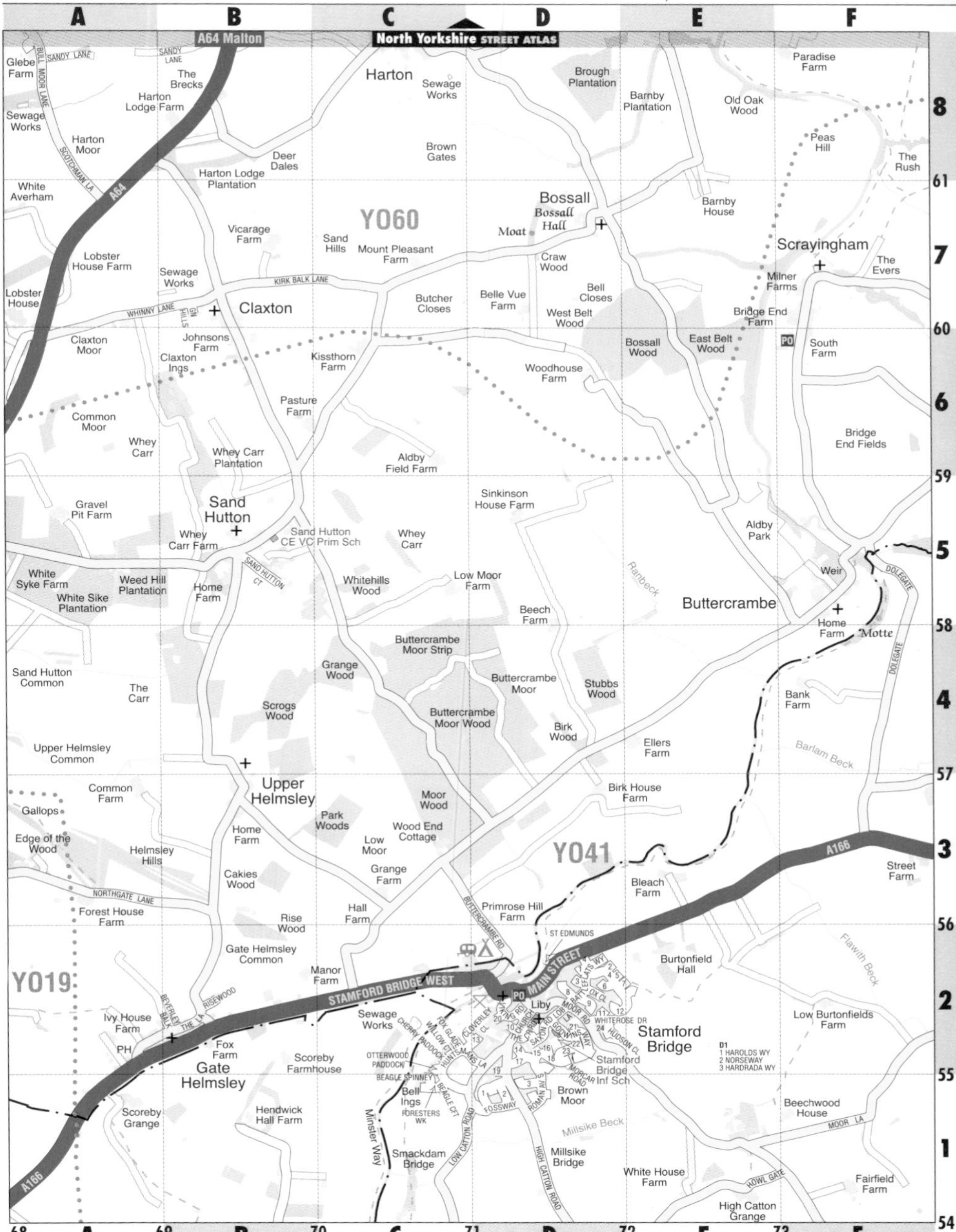
A B C D E F
A64 Malton
North Yorkshire STREET ATLAS
Glebe Farm
SANDY LANE
BULL MOOR LANE
SCOTCHMAN LA
The Brecks
Harton Lodge Farm
Sewage Works
Harton Moor
Harton
Sewage Works
Brown Gates
Deer Dales
Harton Lodge Plantation
Brough Plantation
Barnby Plantation
Paradise Farm
Old Oak Wood
Peas Hill
The Rush
White Averham
A64
Bossall
Bossall Hall
Moat
Barnby House
YO60
Vicarage Farm
Sand Hills
Mount Pleasant Farm
Craw Wood
Scrayingham
The Evers
Lobster House Farm
Sewage Works
KIRK BALK LANE
Butcher Closes
Belle Vue Farm
Bell Closes
Milner Farms
Lobster House
WHINNY LANE
GIN HILLS
Claxton
West Belt Wood
Bridge End Farm
Claxton Moor
Johnsons Farm
Claxton Ings
Kissthorn Farm
Woodhouse Farm
Bossall Wood
East Belt Wood
PO
South Farm
Common Moor
Pasture Farm
Whey Carr
Whey Carr Plantation
Aldby Field Farm
Bridge End Fields
Gravel Pit Farm
Sand Hutton
Sinkinson House Farm
Whey Carr Farm
Sand Hutton CE VC Prim Sch
Whey Carr
Aldby Park
SAND HUTTON CT
Ranbeck
Weir
DOLEGATE
White Syke Farm
White Sike Plantation
Weed Hill Plantation
Home Farm
Whitehills Wood
Low Moor Farm
Beech Farm
Buttercrambe
Home Farm
Motte
Buttercrambe Moor Strip
Sand Hutton Common
The Carr
Grange Wood
Buttercrambe Moor
Stubbs Wood
Bank Farm
Scrogs Wood
Buttercrambe Moor Wood
Birk Wood
Ellers Farm
Barlam Beck
Upper Helmsley Common
Common Farm
Upper Helmsley
Birk House Farm
Gallops
Moor Wood
Park Woods
Edge of the Wood
Home Farm
Wood End Cottage
Low Moor
YO41
A166
Helmsley Hills
Cakies Wood
Grange Farm
Bleach Farm
Street Farm
NORTHGATE LANE
Forest House Farm
Primrose Hill Farm
BUTTERCRAMBE RD
Hall Farm
Rise Wood
ST EDMUNDS
Flawith Beck
Gate Helmsley Common
MAIN STREET
Burtonfield Hall
YO19
Manor Farm
STAMFORD BRIDGE WEST
PO
Liby
FLATS WY
OX CL
BATTLE
MOOR RD
LOB LA
WHITEROSE DR
RISEWOOD
BEVERLEY BALK
THE LA
Ivy House Farm
Sewage Works
CHERRY PADDOCK
WILLOW CT
FOX GLADE
HUNTS
MANS LA
CLOVERLEY CL
THE CHURCH
SAXON RD
GODWINSWAY
HUDSON CL
Stamford Bridge
Low Burtonfields Farm
PH
Fox Farm
Gate Helmsley
Scoreby Farmhouse
OTTERWOOD PADDOCK
BEAGLE SPINNEY
Stamford Bridge Inf Sch
MORCAR ROAD
D1
1 HAROLDS WY
2 NORSEWAY
3 HARDRADA WY
Bell Ings
BEAGLE CFT
FORESTERS WK
FOSSWAY
ROMAN AV S
Brown Moor
Scoreby Grange
Hendwick Hall Farm
Minster Way
Beechwood House
MOOR LA
Millsike Beck
LOW CATTON ROAD
HIGH CATTON ROAD
Smackdam Bridge
Millsike Bridge
White House Farm
HOWL GATE
Fairfield Farm
A166
High Catton Grange
8 61 7 60 6 59 5 58 4 57 3 56 2 55 1 54
68 A 69 B 70 C 71 D 72 E 73 F

27

D2
1 BRIDLINGTON RD
2 DERWENT CL
3 DANESWELL CL
4 BURTON FIELDS RD
5 GARROWBY VW
6 KINGSWAY
7 DARLEY CL
8 WHARTON RD
9 ST JOHN'S RD
10 CHURCH LA
11 EGREMONT CL
12 BURTON FIELDS CL
13 HEATHER BANK
14 TOSTIG CL
15 FAIRFAX
16 SCHOOL CL
17 ROMAN AVE N
18 GODWINSWAY
19 BUTTS CL
20 VIKING CL
21 MIDGLEY CL
22 BROWN MOOR
23 FURLONG RD
24 ETTY CL

16

15

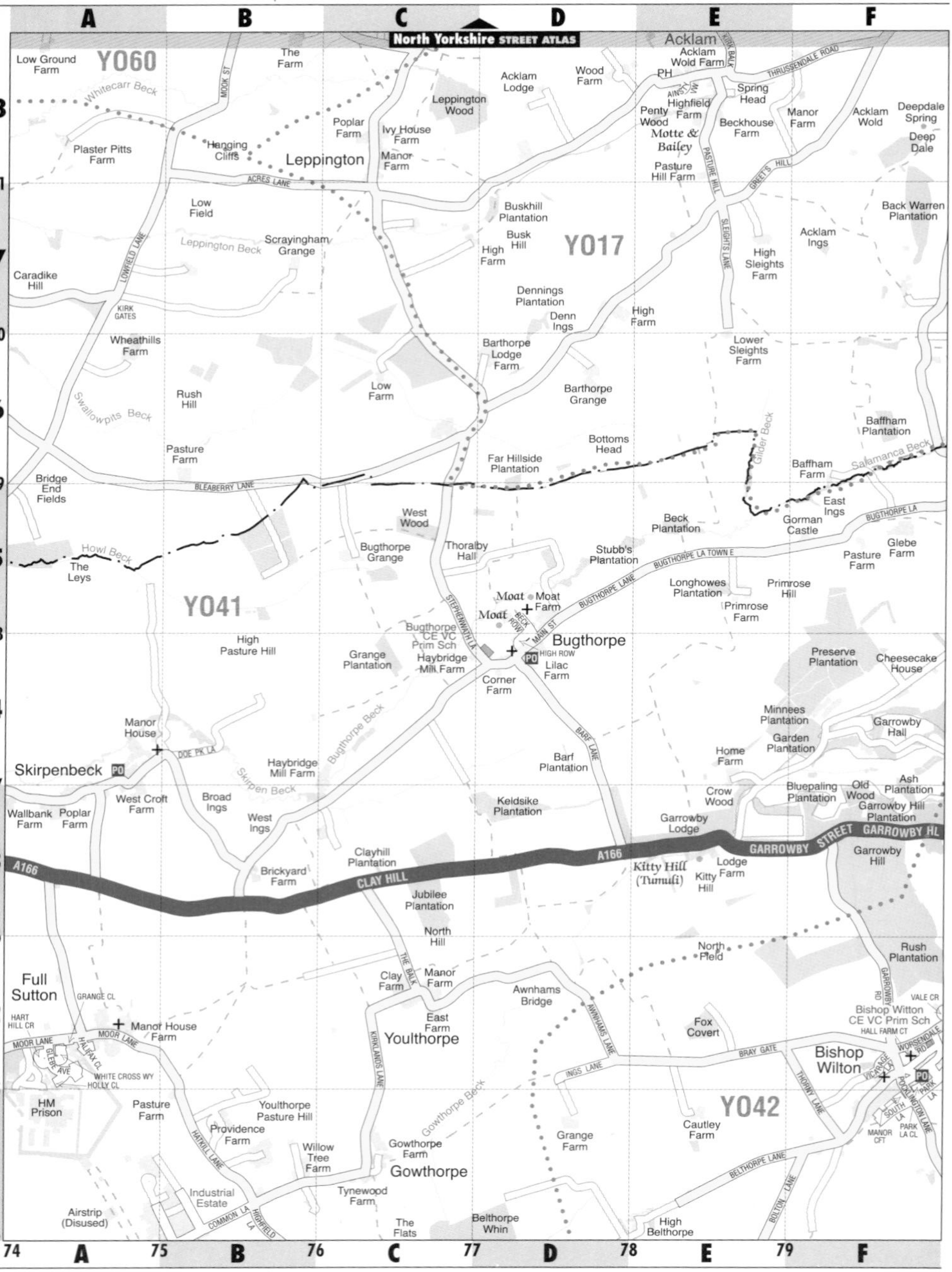
Scale: 1⅓ inches to 1 mile
North Yorkshire STREET ATLAS
YO60
YO17
YO41
YO42
Acklam
Leppington
Bugthorpe
Skirpenbeck
Full Sutton
Youlthorpe
Gowthorpe
Bishop Wilton
Low Ground Farm
The Farm
Acklam Wold Farm
Acklam Lodge
Wood Farm
Leppington Wood
Poplar Farm
Ivy House Farm
Manor Farm
Hanging Cliffs
Plaster Pitts Farm
Spring Head
Highfield Farm
Penty Wood
Motte & Bailey
Beckhouse Farm
Acklam Wold
Deepdale Spring
Deep Dale
Pasture Hill Farm
Low Field
Buskhill Plantation
Busk Hill
High Farm
Scrayingham Grange
Back Warren Plantation
Acklam Ings
High Sleights Farm
Caradike Hill
Dennings Plantation
Denn Ings
Wheathills Farm
Lower Sleights Farm
Barthorpe Lodge Farm
Low Farm
Barthorpe Grange
Rush Hill
Baffham Plantation
Bottoms Head
Pasture Farm
Far Hillside Plantation
Baffham Farm
Bridge End Fields
East Ings
Gorman Castle
West Wood
Beck Plantation
Thoralby Hall
Stubb's Plantation
Bugthorpe Grange
Glebe Farm
The Leys
Longhowes Plantation
Primrose Hill
Moat
Moat Farm
Primrose Farm
Bugthorpe CE VC Prim Sch
High Pasture Hill
Grange Plantation
Haybridge Mill Farm
Lilac Farm
Corner Farm
Preserve Plantation
Cheesecake House
Minnees Plantation
Garden Plantation
Garrowby Hall
Manor House
Home Farm
Barf Plantation
Haybridge Mill Farm
Crow Wood
Bluepaling Plantation
Old Wood
Ash Plantation
Garrowby Hill Plantation
West Croft Farm
Broad Ings
Wallbank Farm
Poplar Farm
West Ings
Keldsike Plantation
Garrowby Lodge
Clayhill Plantation
Brickyard Farm
Kitty Hill (Tumuli)
Kitty Hill
Lodge Farm
Garrowby Hill
Jubilee Plantation
North Hill
North Field
Rush Plantation
Clay Farm
Manor Farm
Awnhams Bridge
East Farm
Manor House Farm
Fox Covert
Bishop Wilton CE VC Prim Sch
HM Prison
Pasture Farm
Youlthorpe Pasture Hill
Providence Farm
Willow Tree Farm
Gowthorpe Farm
Grange Farm
Cautley Farm
Industrial Estate
Tynewood Farm
Airstrip (Disused)
The Flats
Belthorpe Whin
High Belthorpe
Whitecarr Beck
Leppington Beck
Swallowpits Beck
Howl Beck
Bugthorpe Beck
Skirpen Beck
Gilder Beck
Salamanca Beck
Gowthorpe Beck
MOOK ST
ACRES LANE
LOWFIELD LANE
KIRK GATES
BLEABERRY LANE
KIRK BALK
THRUSSENDALE ROAD
AINSTY
PASTURE HILL
GREETS HILL
SLEIGHTS LANE
BUGTHORPE LA
BUGTHORPE LA TOWN E
BUGTHORPE LANE
STEPHENWATH LA
BECK ROW
MAIN ST
HIGH ROW
BARF LANE
DOE PK LA
A166
CLAY HILL
GARROWBY STREET
GARROWBY HL
THE BALK
KIRKLANDS LANE
AWNHAMS LANE
INGS LANE
BRAY GATE
THORNY LANE
GARROWBY RD
VALE CR
HALL FARM CT
WORSENDALE RD
VICARAGE LA
POCKLINGTON LANE
PARK LA
SOUTH LA
PARK LA CL
MANOR CFT
BELTHORPE LANE
BOLTON LANE
HATKILL LANE
COMMON LA
HIGHFIELD LA
GRANGE CL
HART HILL CR
MOOR LANE
HALIFAX CL
GLEBE AVE
WHITE CROSS WY
HOLLY CL
PH
PO

Scale: 1⅓ inches to 1 mile
0 ¼ ½ mile
0 250m 500m 750m 1 km

18

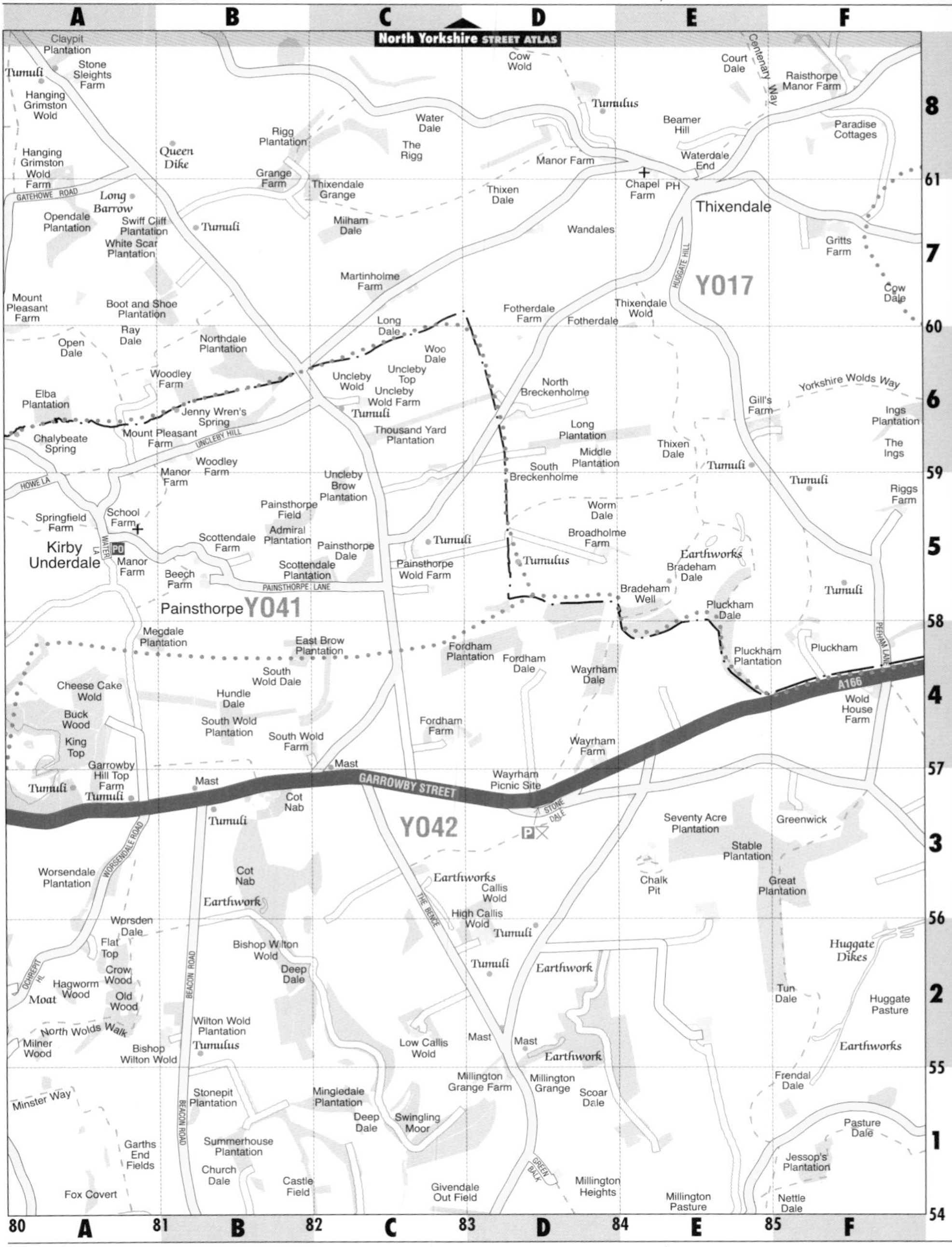

29
18

17
6

Scale: 1⅓ inches to 1 mile
0 ¼ ½ mile
0 250m 500m 750m 1 km

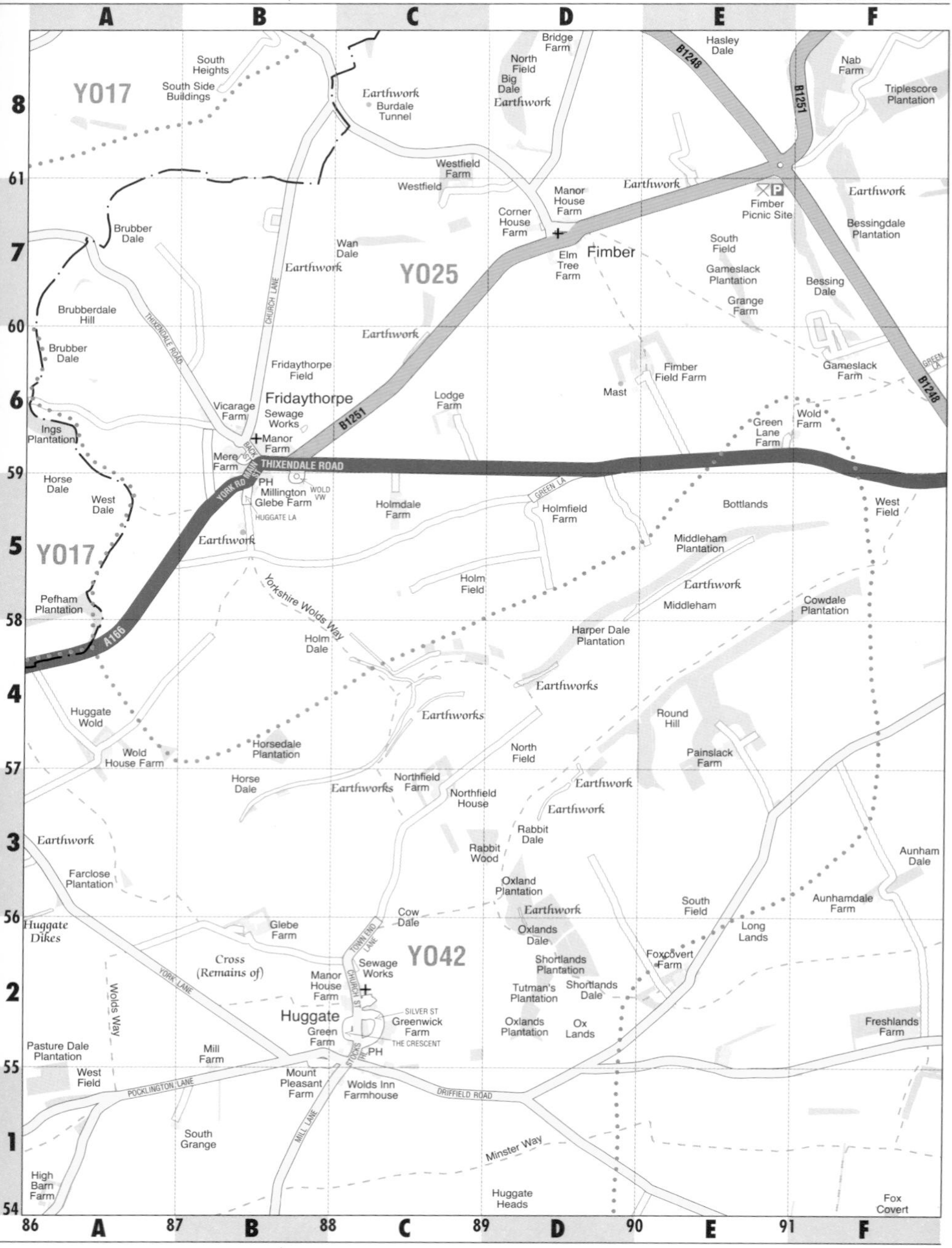

17
30

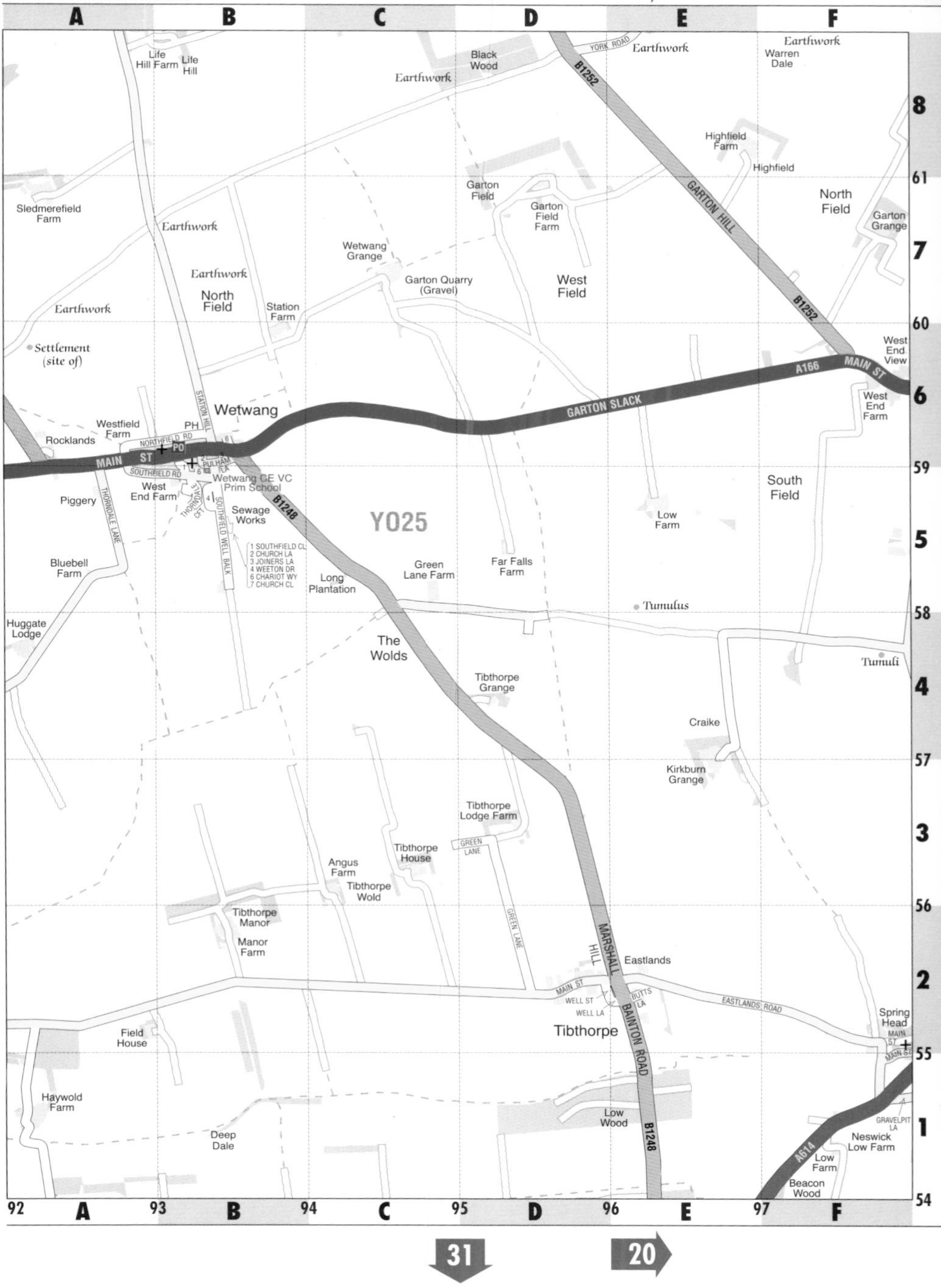

Scale: 1⅓ inches to 1 mile
0 ¼ ½ mile
0 250m 500m 750m 1 km
7
20
A B C D E F
Life Hill Farm
Life Hill
Black Wood
YORK ROAD
Earthwork
Earthwork
Warren Dale
Earthwork
B1252
Highfield Farm
Highfield
Sledmerefield Farm
Earthwork
Garton Field
Garton Field Farm
GARTON HILL
North Field
Garton Grange
Wetwang Grange
Earthwork
Garton Quarry (Gravel)
West Field
North Field
Station Farm
Earthwork
B1252
Settlement (site of)
West End View
A166
MAIN ST
STATION HILL
Wetwang
GARTON SLACK
West End Farm
Westfield Farm
PH
Rocklands
NORTHFIELD RD
PO
MAIN ST
PULHAM LA
SOUTHFIELD RD
Wetwang CE VC Prim School
South Field
West End Farm
Piggery
THORNDALE LANE
THORNDALE CFT
SOUTHFIELD WELL BALK
Sewage Works
B1248
YO25
Low Farm
1 SOUTHFIELD CL
2 CHURCH LA
3 JOINERS LA
4 WEETON DR
6 CHARIOT WY
7 CHURCH CL
Bluebell Farm
Green Lane Farm
Far Falls Farm
Long Plantation
Tumulus
Huggate Lodge
The Wolds
Tumuli
Tibthorpe Grange
Craike
Kirkburn Grange
Tibthorpe Lodge Farm
GREEN LANE
Tibthorpe House
Angus Farm
Tibthorpe Wold
Tibthorpe Manor
GREEN LANE
Manor Farm
MARSHALL HILL
Eastlands
MAIN ST
WELL ST
WELL LA
BUTTS LA
EASTLANDS ROAD
Spring Head
Field House
Tibthorpe
BAINTON ROAD
MAIN ST
Haywold Farm
Low Wood
GRAVELPIT LA
Neswick Low Farm
Deep Dale
B1248
A614
Low Farm
Beacon Wood
8
61
7
60
6
59
5
58
4
57
3
56
2
55
1
54
92 A 93 B 94 C 95 D 96 E 97 F
31
20

Scale: 1⅓ inches to 1 mile

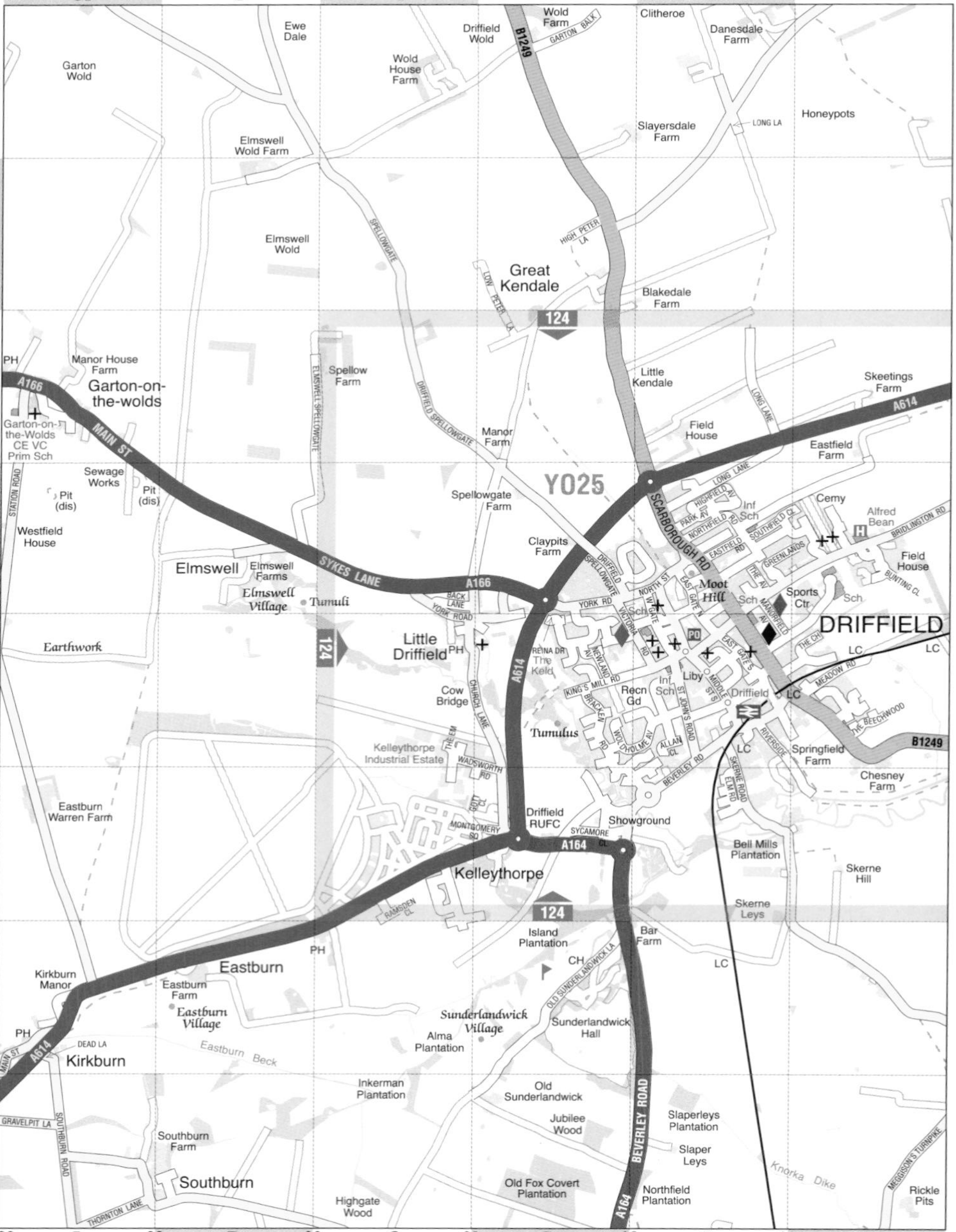

A B C D E F
98 99 00 01 02 03
8 7 6 5 4 3 2 1
61 60 59 58 57 56 55 54

For full street detail of the highlighted area see pages 124 and 125.

Scale: 1⅓ inches to 1 mile
0 ¼ ½ mile
0 250m 500m 750m 1 km

9
22

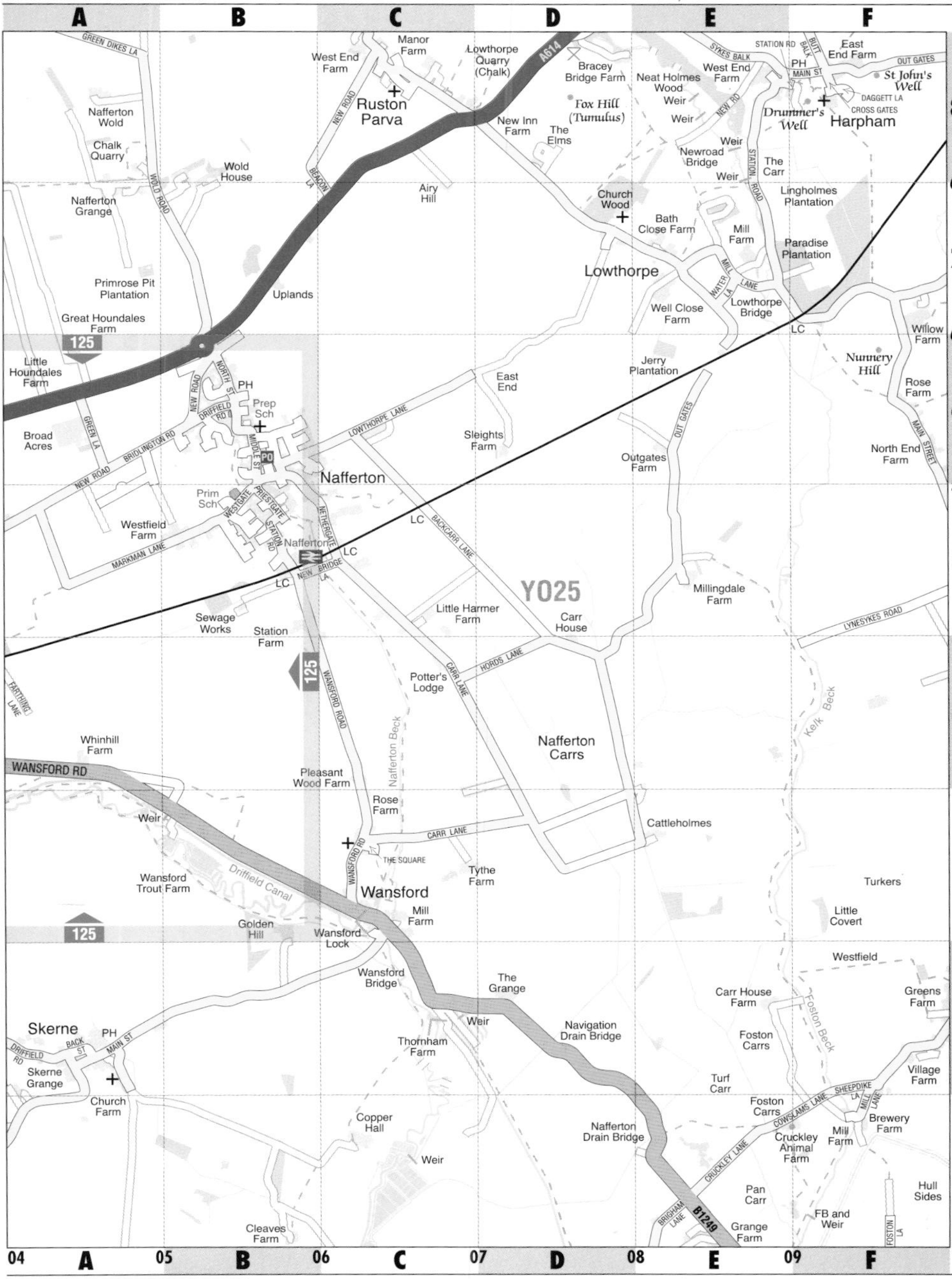
A
B
C
D
E
F
8
61
7
60
6
59
5
58
4
57
3
56
2
55
1
54
04
05
06
07
08
09
GREEN DIKES LA
Manor Farm
West End Farm
Lowthorpe Quarry (Chalk)
A614
Bracey Bridge Farm
Neat Holmes Wood
West End Farm
SYKES BALK
STATION RD
BUTT BALK
East End Farm
OUT GATES
PH
MAIN ST
St John's Well
DAGGETT LA
CROSS GATES
Drummer's Well
Harpham
Fox Hill (Tumulus)
Weir
Ruston Parva
NEW ROAD
Nafferton Wold
Chalk Quarry
New Inn Farm
The Elms
NEW RD
Newroad Bridge
STATION ROAD
The Carr
Wold House
WOLD ROAD
BEACON LA
Airy Hill
Church Wood
Lingholmes Plantation
Nafferton Grange
Bath Close Farm
Mill Farm
Paradise Plantation
Lowthorpe
WATER LA
MILL LANE
Primrose Pit Plantation
Uplands
Well Close Farm
Lowthorpe Bridge
Great Houndales Farm
LC
Willow Farm
125
Little Houndales Farm
NORTH ST
NEW ROAD
PH
East End
Jerry Plantation
Nunnery Hill
Rose Farm
Prep Sch
DRIFFIELD RD
GREEN LA
BRIDLINGTON RD
LOWTHORPE LANE
Broad Acres
MIDDLE ST
PO
Sleights Farm
OUT GATES
MAIN STREET
North End Farm
Outgates Farm
NEW ROAD
Nafferton
Prim Sch
WESTGATE
PRIESTGATE
NETHERGATE
Westfield Farm
STATION RD
BACKCARR LANE
Nafferton
MARKMAN LANE
NEW BRIDGE LA
YO25
Millingdale Farm
Sewage Works
Station Farm
Little Harmer Farm
Carr House
LYNESYKES ROAD
125
HORDS LANE
Potter's Lodge
CARR LANE
FARTHING LANE
WANSFORD ROAD
Kelk Beck
Whinhill Farm
Nafferton Carrs
Nafferton Beck
WANSFORD RD
Pleasant Wood Farm
Rose Farm
Weir
Cattleholmes
CARR LANE
WANSFORD RD
THE SQUARE
Tythe Farm
Wansford Trout Farm
Driffield Canal
Wansford
Turkers
Mill Farm
Little Covert
Golden Hill
125
Wansford Lock
Westfield
Wansford Bridge
The Grange
Carr House Farm
Greens Farm
Foston Beck
Skerne
PH
Weir
Navigation Drain Bridge
Foston Carrs
BACK ST
MAIN ST
DRIFFIELD RD
Thornham Farm
Village Farm
Skerne Grange
Turf Carr
SHEEPDIKE LA
MILL LANE
Church Farm
Foston Carrs
COWSLAMS LANE
Copper Hall
Nafferton Drain Bridge
Cruckley Animal Farm
Mill Farm
Brewery Farm
CRUCKLEY LANE
Weir
Pan Carr
Hull Sides
FB and Weir
BRIGHAM LANE
B1249
Cleaves Farm
Grange Farm
FOSTON LA

For full street detail of the highlighted area see page 125.

33
22

21
10

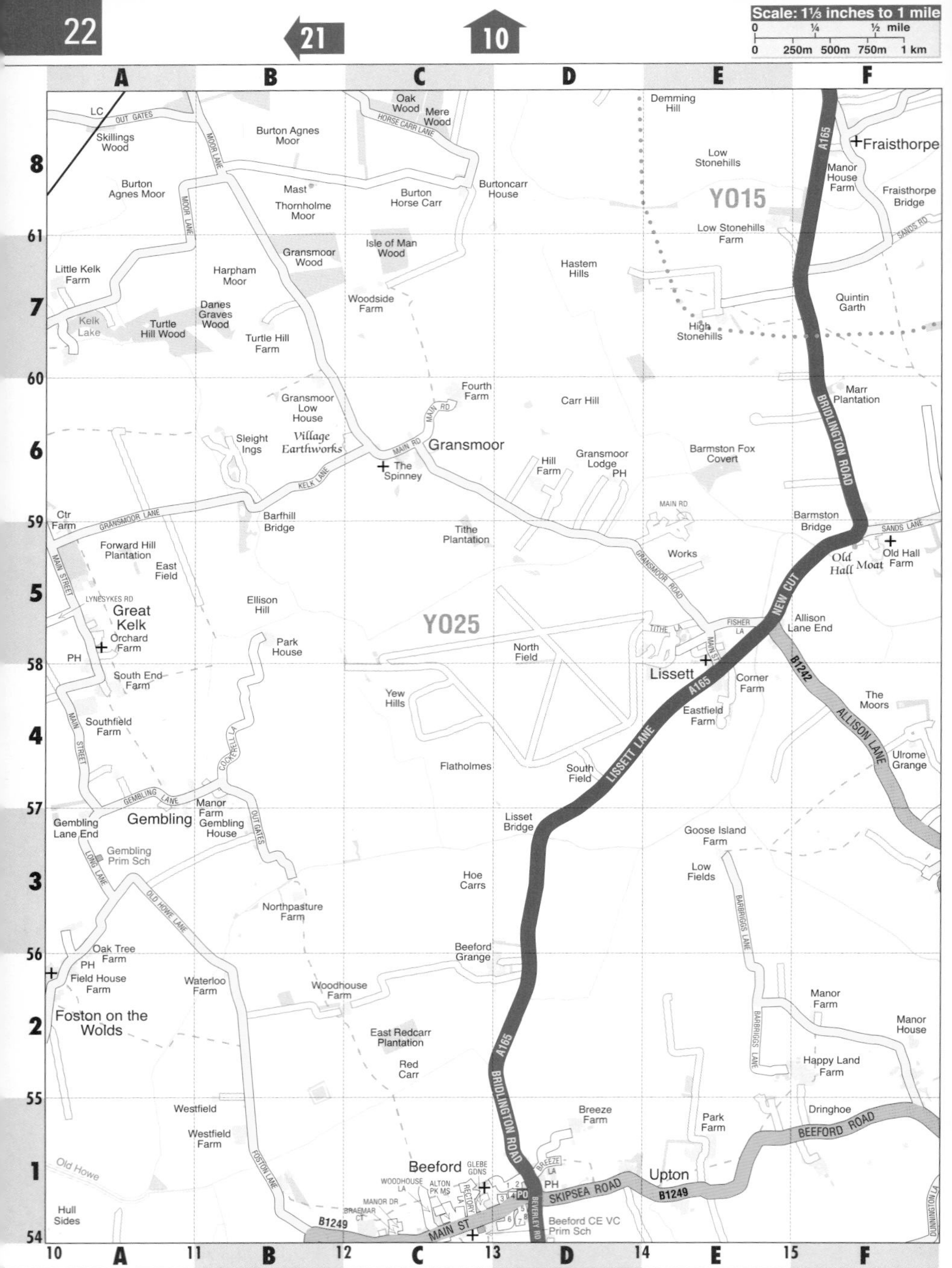

21
34

D1
1 CHURCH LA
2 ST LEONARD'S CL
3 WHARRAM FIELD
4 NEWSAM CL
5 MEADOW CL
6 ASHLEIGH DR
7 BARONWOOD CR
8 WELBURN CT

Scale: 1⅓ inches to 1 mile

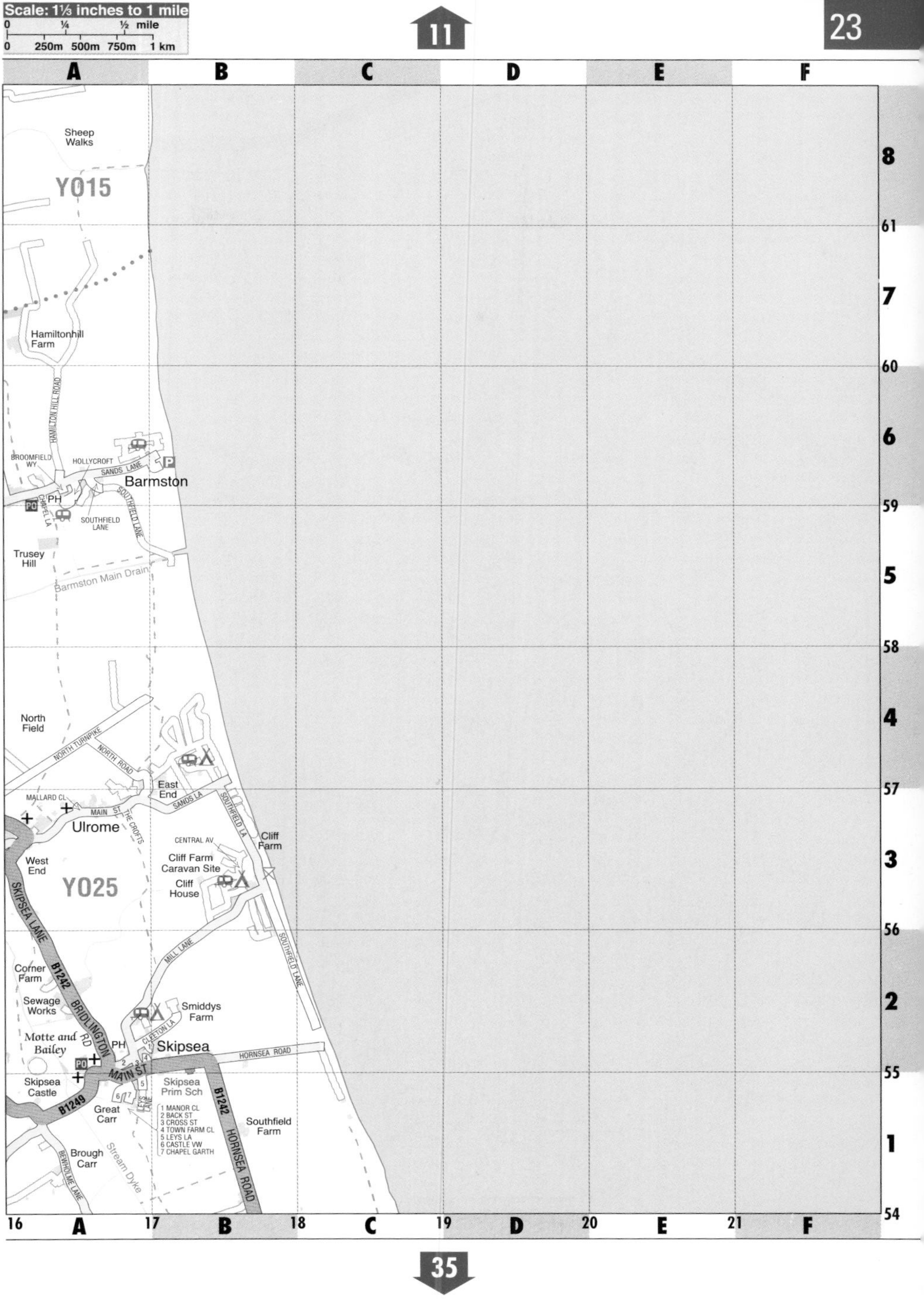

B
D
F
Sheep Walks
YO15
Hamiltonhill Farm
HAMILTON HILL ROAD
BROOMFIELD WY
HOLLYCROFT
SANDS LANE
Barmston
PH
CHAPEL LA
SOUTHFIELD LANE
SOUTHFIELD LANE
Trusey Hill
Barmston Main Drain
North Field
NORTH TURNPIKE
NORTH ROAD
East End
SANDS LA
MALLARD CL
MAIN ST
THE CROFTS
Ulrome
SOUTHFIELD LA
Cliff Farm
CENTRAL AV
Cliff Farm Caravan Site
Cliff House
West End
YO25
SKIPSEA LANE
MILL LANE
SOUTHFIELD LANE
Corner Farm
B1242
BRIDLINGTON RD
Sewage Works
Smiddys Farm
Motte and Bailey
PH
CLEETON LA
Skipsea
HORNSEA ROAD
MAIN ST
Skipsea Castle
B1249
Skipsea Prim Sch
B1242
HORNSEA ROAD
Great Carr
1 MANOR CL
2 BACK ST
3 CROSS ST
4 TOWN FARM CL
5 LEYS LA
6 CASTLE VW
7 CHAPEL GARTH
Southfield Farm
Brough Carr
BEWHOLME LANE
Stream Dyke
8
61
7
60
6
59
5
58
4
57
3
56
2
55
54
16
17
18
19
20
21

12

Scale: 1⅓ inches to 1 mile
0 ¼ ½ mile
0 250m 500m 750m 1 km

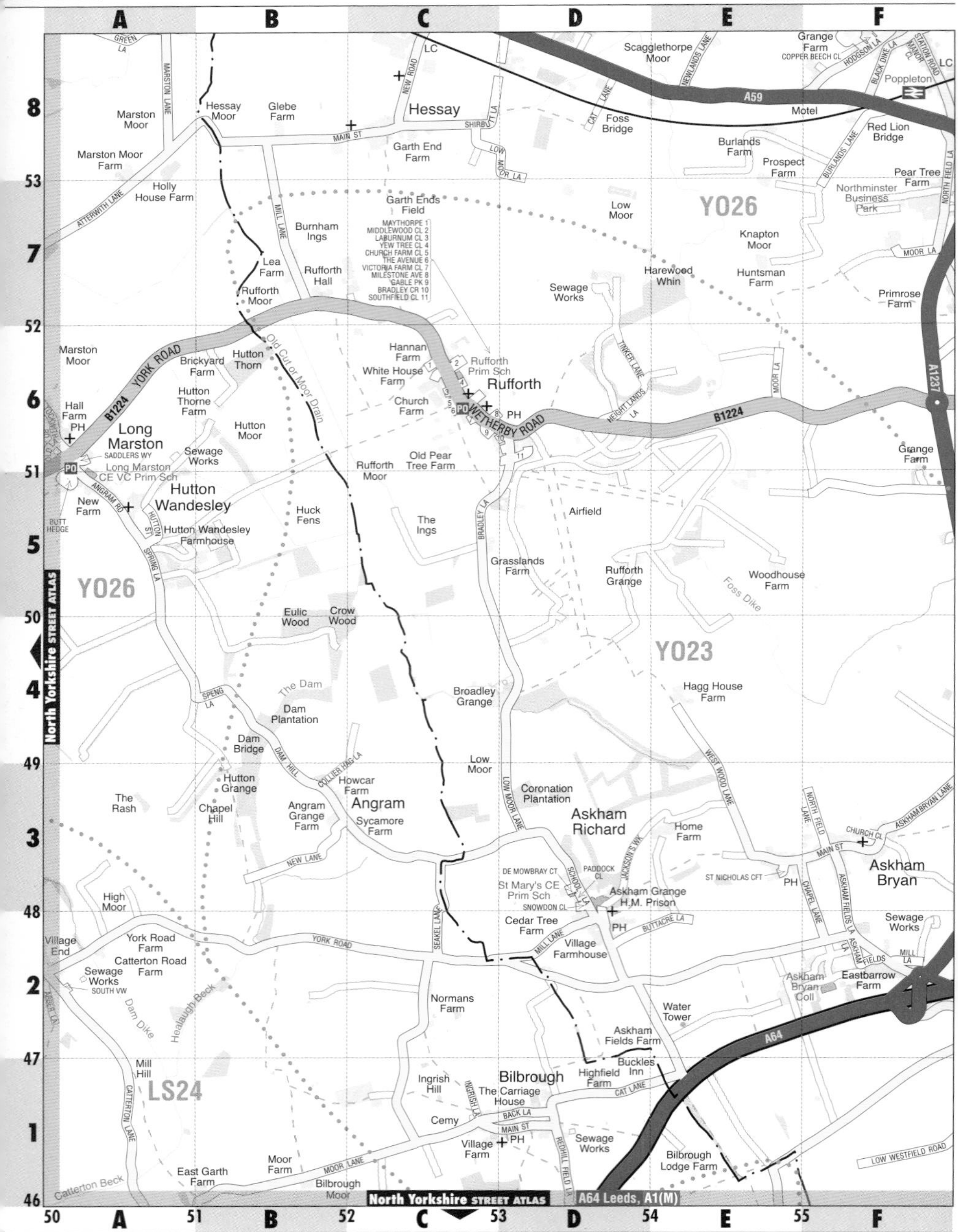
A
B
C
D
E
F
8
53
7
52
6
51
5
50
4
49
3
48
2
47
1
46
50
51
52
53
54
55
GREEN LA
MARSTON LANE
Hessay Moor
Glebe Farm
Marston Moor
Marston Moor Farm
Holly House Farm
ATTERWITH LANE
LC
NEW ROAD
Hessay
MAIN ST
SHIRBUTT LA
LOW MOOR LA
Garth End Farm
Scagglethorpe Moor
NEWLANDS LANE
CAT LANE
Foss Bridge
A59
Grange Farm
COPPER BEECH CL
HODGSON LA
BLACK DIKE LA
MANOR CL
STATION ROAD
LC
Poppleton
Motel
Red Lion Bridge
Burlands Farm
BURLANDS LANE
Prospect Farm
Pear Tree Farm
NORTH FIELD LA
Northminster Business Park
YO26
Garth Ends Field
MAYTHORPE 1
MIDDLEWOOD CL 2
LABURNUM CL 3
YEW TREE CL 4
CHURCH FARM CL 5
THE AVENUE 6
VICTORIA FARM CL 7
MILESTONE AVE 8
GABLE PK 9
BRADLEY CR 10
SOUTHFIELD CL 11
MILL LANE
Burnham Ings
Low Moor
Knapton Moor
MOOR LA
Lea Farm
Rufforth Hall
Rufforth Moor
Sewage Works
Harewood Whin
Huntsman Farm
Primrose Farm
Marston Moor
YORK ROAD
B1224
Brickyard Farm
Hutton Thorn
Old Cut or Moor Drain
Hannah Farm
White House Farm
Rufforth Prim Sch
Rufforth
Church Farm
PO
WETHERBY ROAD
PH
TINKER LANE
HEIGHT LANDS LA
MOOR LA
B1224
A1237
Hall Farm
PH
Long Marston
Hutton Thorne Farm
Hutton Moor
Sewage Works
SADDLERS WY
Long Marston CE VC Prim Sch
Hutton Wandesley
Old Pear Tree Farm
Rufforth Moor
Grange Farm
New Farm
ANGRAM RD
HUTTON ST
BUTT HEDGE
Hutton Wandesley Farmhouse
Huck Fens
The Ings
BRADLEY LA
Airfield
SPRING LA
YO26
Grasslands Farm
Rufforth Grange
Woodhouse Farm
Foss Dike
Eulic Wood
Crow Wood
YO23
The Dam
Broadley Grange
Hagg House Farm
SPENG LA
Dam Plantation
Dam Bridge
DAM HILL
COLLIER HAG LA
Low Moor
WEST WOOD LANE
Hutton Grange
Howcar Farm
Coronation Plantation
LOW MOOR LANE
The Rash
Chapel Hill
Angram Grange Farm
Angram
Askham Richard
Home Farm
NORTH FIELD LANE
ASKHAM BRYAN LANE
CHURCH CL
MAIN ST
Sycamore Farm
JACKSON'S WK
NEW LANE
DE MOWBRAY CT
SCHOOL LA
PADDOCK CL
ST NICHOLAS CFT
Askham Bryan
PH
St Mary's CE Prim Sch
Askham Grange H.M. Prison
High Moor
SNOWDON CL
CHAPEL LANE
ASKHAM FIELDS LA
Sewage Works
Cedar Tree Farm
PH
BUTTACRE LA
York Road Farm
YORK ROAD
SEAKEL LANE
MILL LANE
Village Farmhouse
ASKHAM LA
FIELDS LA
MILL LA
Village End
Catterton Road Farm
Sewage Works
SOUTH VW
Eastbarrow Farm
Askham Bryan Coll
Normans Farm
Water Tower
Dam Dike
Healaugh Beck
ABBER LA
A64
Askham Fields Farm
Mill Hill
Buckles Inn
Ingrish Hill
Bilbrough
Highfield Farm
LS24
CATTERTON LANE
INGRISH LA
The Carriage House
CAT LANE
BACK LA
Cemy
MAIN ST
Village Farm
PH
Sewage Works
REDHILL FIELD LA
LOW WESTFIELD ROAD
Bilbrough Lodge Farm
Moor Farm
East Garth Farm
MOOR LANE
Catterton Beck
Bilbrough Moor
North Yorkshire STREET ATLAS
A64 Leeds, A1(M)

Scale: 1⅓ inches to 1 mile
0 ¼ ½ mile
0 250m 500m 750m 1 km

126 127 131

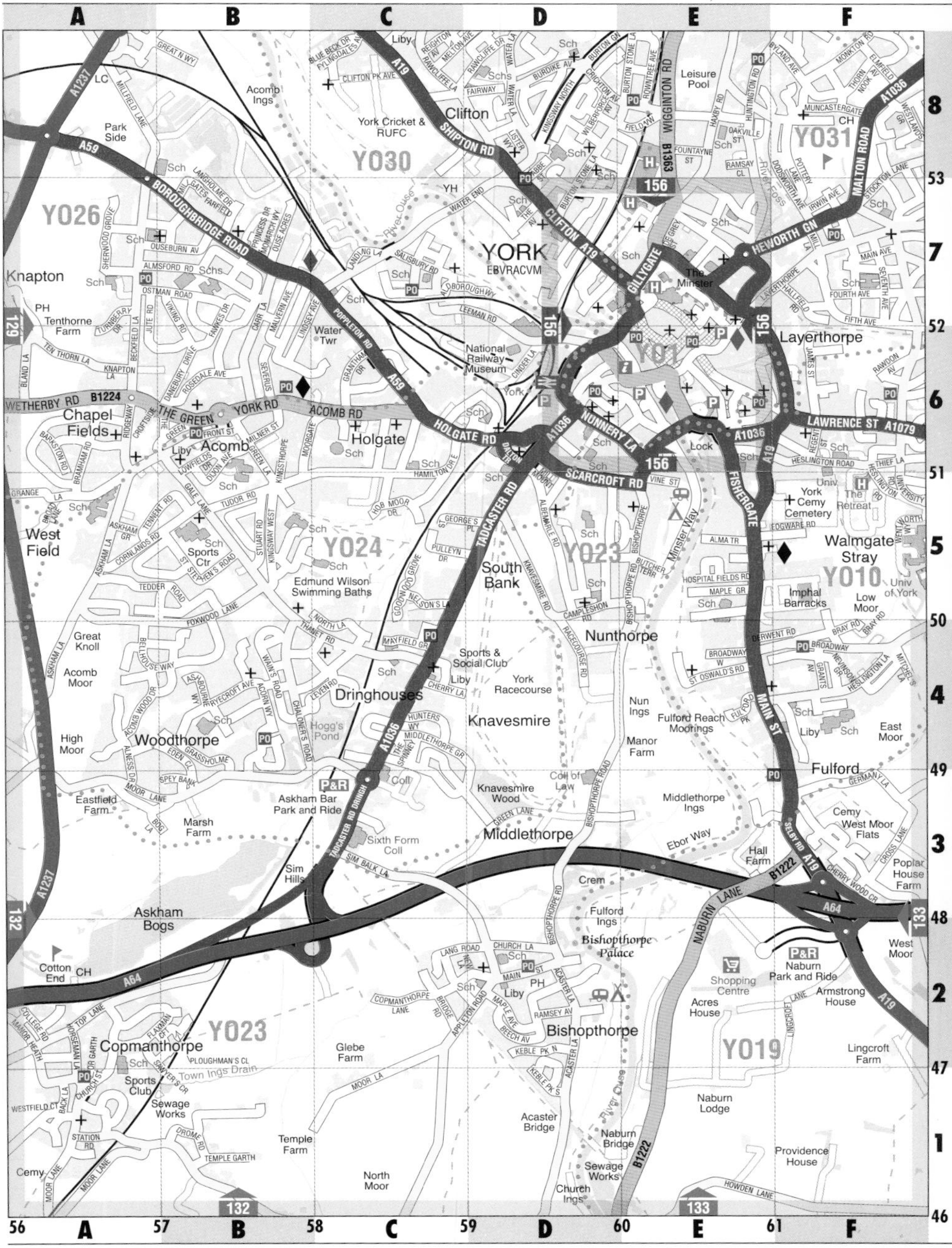

36 26

For full street detail of the highlighted area see pages 129, 130, 132 and 133.

For full street detail of the highlighted area see page 156.

F7
1 GORSE HL
2 HOLLY TREE CFT
3 ASPEN CL
4 ORCHARD CTS
5 PETERCROFT CL
6 KENDAL CL
7 UNDERCROFT
8 THORNCROFT
9 SAWYERS WK
10 CONEYCROFT
11 KEEPERS WY
12 WESTWOOD MEWS
13 SCAUDERCROFT
14 GREENCROFT CT
15 LIME TREE MEWS
16 OX CALDER CL
17 GREENCROFT LA
18 GREENSIDE
19 ASHDALE RD
20 THE GREEN
21 HUNTERS WOOD WY
22 DEERSTONE WY
23 GREENSIDE WLK
24 GREENSIDE CL

Scale: 1⅓ inches to 1 mile
0 ¼ ½ mile
0 250m 500m 750m 1 km

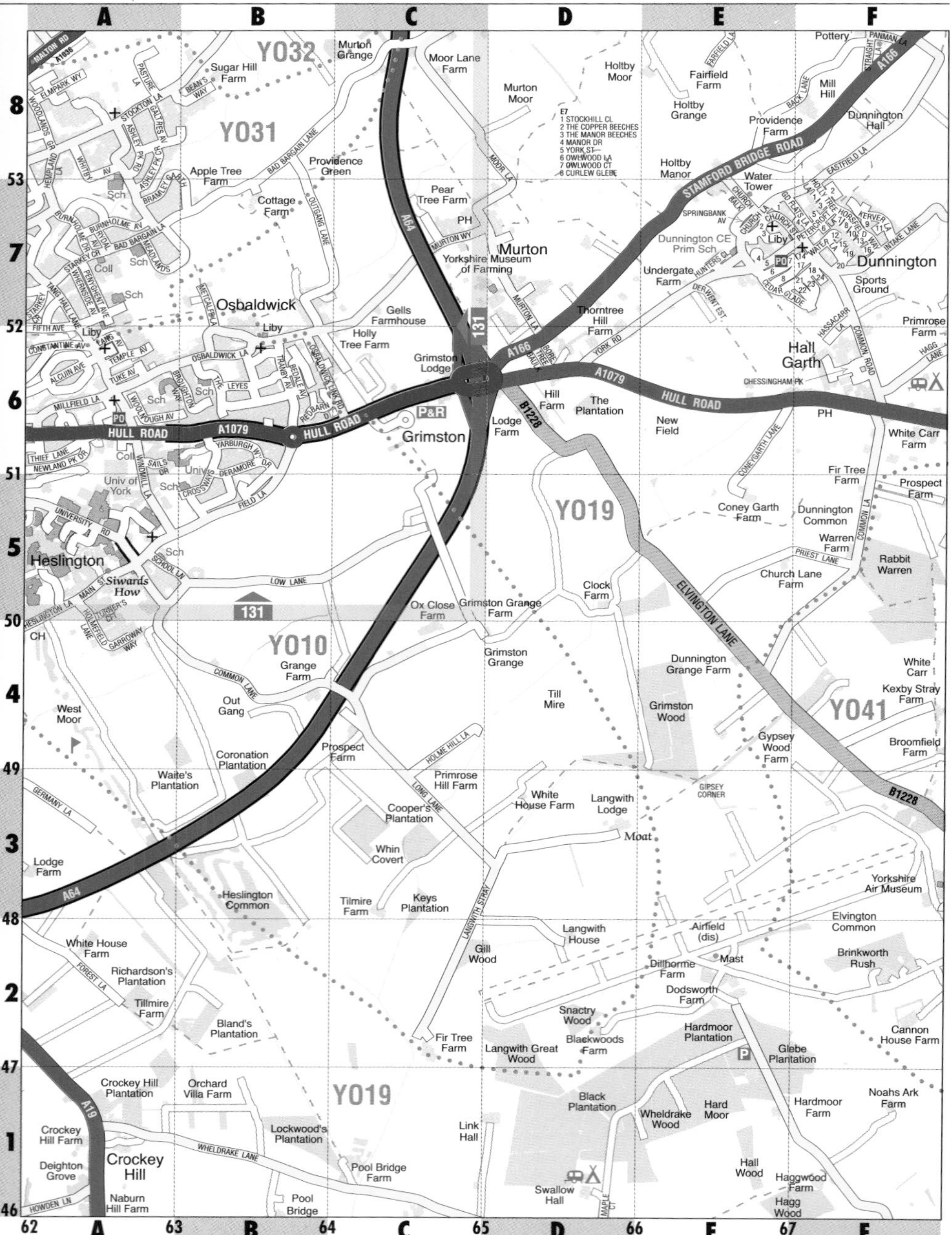

For full street detail of the highlighted area see page 131.

Scale: 1⅓ inches to 1 mile
0 ¼ ½ mile
0 250m 500m 750m 1 km

15

28

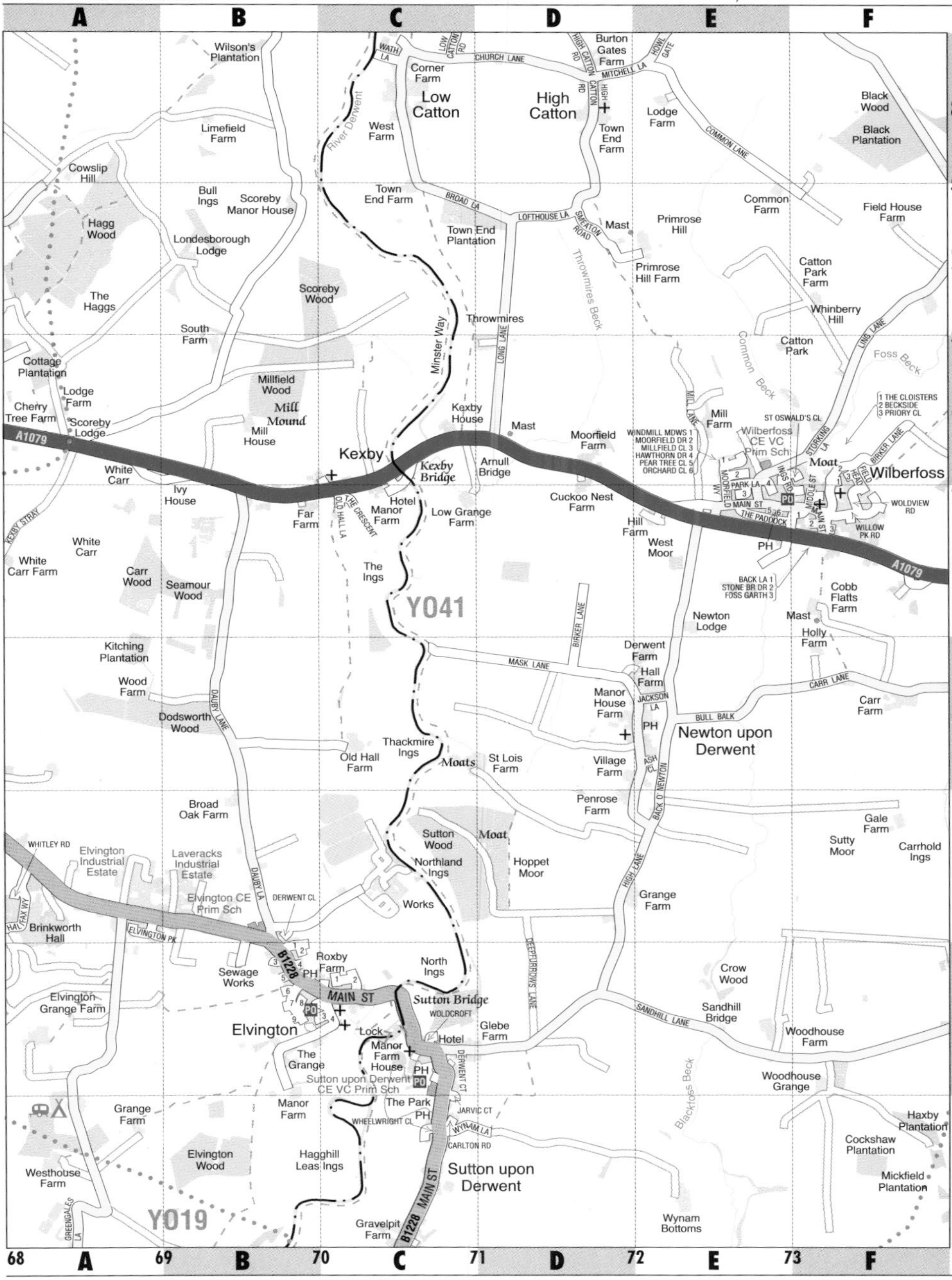

B2
1 WHITE HOUSE GR
2 BEECH CL
3 LORRAINE AVE
4 HILLGARTH CT
5 DOVECOTE GARTH
6 BECK CL
7 BECKSIDE
8 BELVOIR AVE
9 ALVIN WK

C2
1 RIVERSIDE CL
2 RIVERSIDE GDNS
3 CHURCH GN
4 CHURCH LA

38

28

27
16

Scale: 1⅓ inches to 1 mile
0 ¼ ½ mile
0 250m 500m 750m 1 km

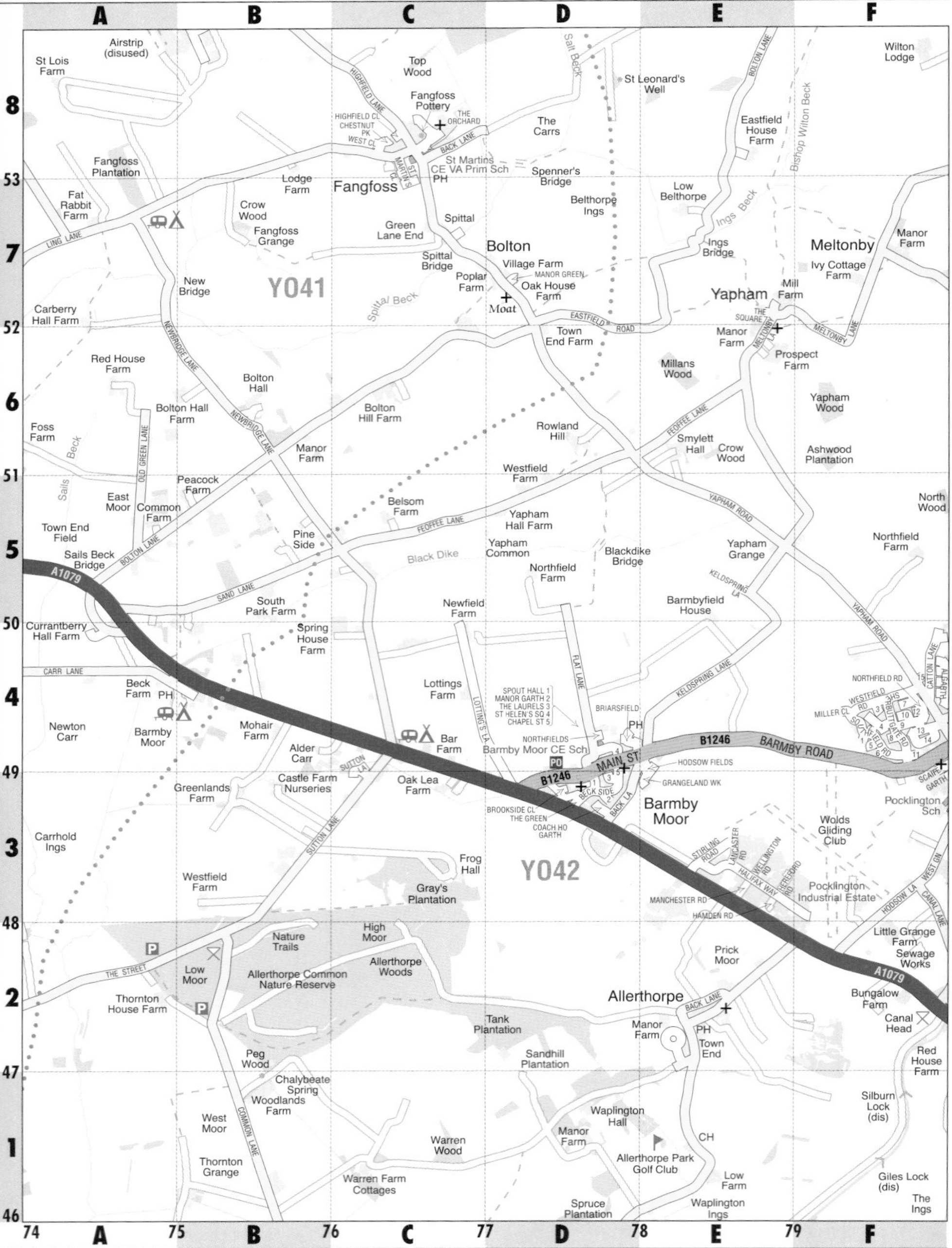
A
B
C
D
E
F
8
53
7
52
6
51
5
50
4
49
3
48
2
47
1
46
74
75
76
77
78
79
St Lois Farm
Airstrip (disused)
Top Wood
Fangfoss Pottery
HIGHFIELD LANE
HIGHFIELD CL
CHESTNUT PK
WEST CL
THE ORCHARD
BACK LANE
ST MARTINS CL
St Martins CE VA Prim Sch
PH
Fangfoss
Salt Beck
St Leonard's Well
The Carrs
Spenner's Bridge
BOLTON LANE
Eastfield House Farm
Bishop Wilton Beck
Wilton Lodge
Fangfoss Plantation
Lodge Farm
Fat Rabbit Farm
Crow Wood
Fangfoss Grange
LING LANE
Green Lane End
Spittal
Belthorpe Ings
Low Belthorpe
Ings Beck
Ings Bridge
Bolton
Village Farm
MANOR GREEN
Oak House Farm
Spittal Bridge
Poplar Farm
Moat
Meltonby
Manor Farm
Ivy Cottage Farm
Mill Farm
Yapham
THE SQUARE
MELTONBY LA
MELTONBY LANE
New Bridge
YO41
Spittal Beck
Carberry Hall Farm
EASTFIELD ROAD
Town End Farm
Manor Farm
Prospect Farm
Millans Wood
Red House Farm
NEWBRIDGE LANE
Bolton Hall
Bolton Hill Farm
Yapham Wood
Bolton Hall Farm
Foss Farm
Beck
OLD GREEN LANE
Rowland Hill
FEOFFEE LANE
Smylett Hall
Crow Wood
Ashwood Plantation
Manor Farm
Westfield Farm
Sails
East Moor
Peacock Farm
Common Farm
Belsom Farm
Yapham Hall Farm
YAPHAM ROAD
North Wood
Town End Field
Pine Side
FEOFFEE LANE
Yapham Common
Blackdike Bridge
Yapham Grange
Northfield Farm
Sails Beck Bridge
BOLTON LANE
Black Dike
Northfield Farm
A1079
SAND LANE
KELDSPRING LA
South Park Farm
Newfield Farm
Barmbyfield House
YAPHAM ROAD
Currantberry Hall Farm
Spring House Farm
CARR LANE
FLAT LANE
Beck Farm
PH
Lottings Farm
SPOUT HALL 1
MANOR GARTH 2
THE LAURELS 3
ST HELEN'S SQ 4
CHAPEL ST 5
BRIARSFIELD
KELDSPRING LANE
NORTHFIELD RD
CATTON LANE
ALGARTH
WESTFIELD RD
MILLER CL
Newton Carr
Barmby Moor
Mohair Farm
LOTTING'S LA
Bar Farm
NORTHFIELDS
PH
B1246
BARMBY ROAD
Alder Carr
Barmby Moor CE Sch
PO
MAIN ST
HODSOW FIELDS
SUTTON LA
Castle Farm Nurseries
Oak Lea Farm
B1246
GRANGELAND WK
SCAIFE GARTH
Greenlands Farm
BECK SIDE
BACK LA
Barmby Moor
Pocklington Sch
BROOKSIDE CL
THE GREEN
COACH HO GARTH
Wolds Gliding Club
Carrhold Ings
SUTTON LANE
Frog Hall
STIRLING ROAD
LANCASTER RD
WELLINGTON RD
HALIFAX WAY
HEREFORD RD
YO42
Westfield Farm
Gray's Plantation
MANCHESTER RD
Pocklington Industrial Estate
HODSOW LA
WEST GN
CANAL LANE
HAMDEN RD
High Moor
Nature Trails
Little Grange Farm
Sewage Works
Prick Moor
P
THE STREET
Low Moor
Allerthorpe Woods
Allerthorpe Common Nature Reserve
A1079
Thornton House Farm
P
Allerthorpe
BACK LANE
Bungalow Farm
Canal Head
Tank Plantation
Manor Farm
PH
Town End
Red House Farm
Peg Wood
Sandhill Plantation
Chalybeate Spring
Woodlands Farm
Silburn Lock (dis)
West Moor
COMMON LANE
Waplington Hall
Manor Farm
Warren Wood
CH
Allerthorpe Park Golf Club
Thornton Grange
Warren Farm Cottages
Low Farm
Giles Lock (dis)
Spruce Plantation
Waplington Ings
The Ings

27
39

F4
1 DALMAIS CL
2 BURNS CL
3 WESTFIELD CL
4 ORCHARD GD
5 WELLINGTON CL
6 MEADOWFIELD CL
7 NORTHFIELD RISE
8 HALIFAX CL
9 ORCHARD WY
10 ORCHARD CL
11 ST JOHN'S CL
12 NORTHFIELD CL
13 SHERBUTTGATE DR
14 SHERBUTTGATE RD
15 ANDREW'S CT

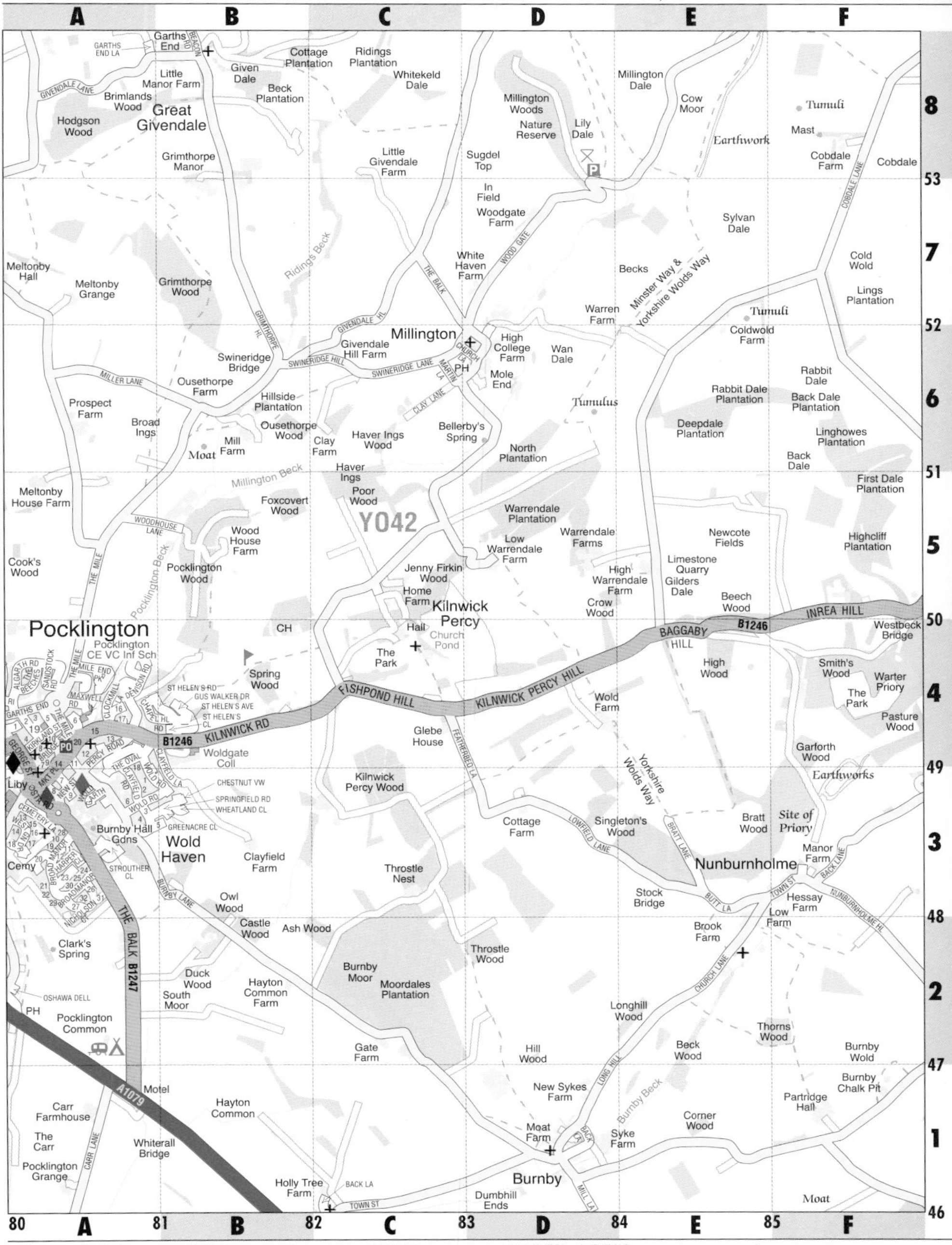
A
B
C
D
E
F
Garths End
GARTHS END LA
BEACON RD
Cottage Plantation
Ridings Plantation
Given Dale
Little Manor Farm
Whitekeld Dale
Millington Dale
GIVENDALE LANE
Brimlands Wood
Beck Plantation
Hodgson Wood
Great Givendale
Millington Woods
Nature Reserve
Lily Dale
Cow Moor
Tumuli
Mast
Earthwork
Grimthorpe Manor
Little Givendale Farm
Sugdel Top
Cobdale Farm
Cobdale
COBDALE LANE
In Field
Woodgate Farm
Sylvan Dale
WOOD GATE
Ridings Beck
White Haven Farm
THE BALK
Meltonby Hall
Meltonby Grange
Grimthorpe Wood
Becks
Minster Way & Yorkshire Wolds Way
Cold Wold
Lings Plantation
Warren Farm
Tumuli
Coldwold Farm
GRIMTHORPE HL
GIVENDALE HL
Millington
Givendale Hill Farm
CHURCH LA
High College Farm
Wan Dale
Swineridge Bridge
SWINERIDGE HILL
SWINERIDGE LANE
MARTIN LA
PH
Mole End
Rabbit Dale
MILLER LANE
Ousethorpe Farm
Hillside Plantation
CLAY LANE
Rabbit Dale Plantation
Back Dale Plantation
Prospect Farm
Tumulus
Broad Ings
Ousethorpe Wood
Bellerby's Spring
Deepdale Plantation
Linghowes Plantation
Mill Farm
Moat
Clay Farm
Haver Ings Wood
North Plantation
Back Dale
Millington Beck
Haver Ings
Poor Wood
Meltonby House Farm
Foxcovert Wood
First Dale Plantation
YO42
Warrendale Plantation
WOODHOUSE LANE
Wood House Farm
Warrendale Farms
Newcote Fields
Highcliff Plantation
Low Warrendale Farm
Cook's Wood
Pocklington Wood
Jenny Firkin Wood
Limestone Quarry
Pocklington Beck
THE MILE
High Warrendale Farm
Gilders Dale
Home Farm
Kilnwick Percy
Beech Wood
Crow Wood
INREA HILL
Pocklington
CH
Hall
Church Pond
BAGGABY HILL
B1246
Westbeck Bridge
Pocklington CE VC Inf Sch
The Park
High Wood
Smith's Wood
Spring Wood
Warter Priory
FISHPOND HILL
KILNWICK PERCY HILL
The Park
ALGARTH RD
THE BEECHES
SANDSTOCK RD
MILE END PK
MAXWELL RD
CLOCKMILL
DENISON RD
ST HELEN'S RD
GUS WALKER DR
ST HELEN'S AVE
ST HELEN'S CL
CHAPEL HL
Wold Farm
Pasture Wood
GARTHS END
THE MILL
KIRKLAND ST
BRIDGE ST
GEORGE ST
MKT PL
PO
PERCY ROAD
B1246
KILNWICK RD
Glebe House
Garforth Wood
Woldgate Coll
THE OVAL
CLAYFIELD RD
WOLD RD
CLAYFIELD LA
Yorkshire Wolds Way
Earthworks
Liby
NEW ST
WOLD GARTH
CHESTNUT VW
SPRINGFIELD RD
WHEATLAND CL
Kilnwick Percy Wood
FEATHERBED LA
CEMETERY LA
WEST GN
Burnby Hall Gdns
GREENACRE CL
Wold Haven
Cottage Farm
LOWFIELD LANE
Singleton's Wood
BRATT LANE
Bratt Wood
Site of Priory
Cemy
Clayfield Farm
Throstle Nest
Manor Farm
BACK LANE
BROAD MANOR
STROUTHER CL
Nunburnholme
BROADMANOR
NICHOLSON CT
BURNBY LANE
Owl Wood
Stock Bridge
BUTT LA
TOWN ST
Hessay Farm
NUNBURNHOLME HL
THE BALK B1247
Castle Wood
Ash Wood
Brook Farm
Low Farm
Clark's Spring
Throstle Wood
CHURCH LANE
Burnby Moor
Moordales Plantation
Duck Wood
OSHAWA DELL
South Moor
Hayton Common Farm
Longhill Wood
PH
Pocklington Common
Thorns Wood
Gate Farm
Beck Wood
Burnby Wold
Hill Wood
Motel
A1079
New Sykes Farm
Burnby Chalk Pit
Burnby Beck
Carr Farmhouse
Hayton Common
LONG HILL
Partridge Hall
Corner Wood
The Carr
Whiterall Bridge
Moat Farm
BACK LA
Syke Farm
CARR LANE
Pocklington Grange
Burnby
Holly Tree Farm
BACK LA
TOWN ST
Dumbhill Ends
MILL LA
Moat
8
53
7
52
6
51
5
50
4
49
3
48
2
47
1
46
80
A
81
B
82
C
83
D
84
E
85
F

A4
1 EDWARD ST
2 VICTORIA RD
3 MURRAY CL
4 BRINDLEGATE
5 SCHOOL LA
6 BEECH CT
7 PEM LANE
8 KIRKGATE
9 MARKET ST
10 HALLGATE
11 THE AVENUE
12 CHERRY ORCH MEWS
13 VOLAGE CT
14 ST PETER'S SQ
15 LONDON ST
16 TARGET LA
17 PAYTON CL
18 CLAYFIELD CL
19 POCKLINGTON COM JUN SCH
20 UNION ST

A3
1 WOLDGATE VW
2 KILNWICK GARTH
3 PINEWOOD RD
4 PINEWOOD CT
5 PINEWOOD CL
6 VALENTINE CL
7 DEAN'S LA
8 REGENT ST PAVEMENT
9 WILLOW CT
10 THE LILACS
11 MCSHANE CT
12 MACDONALD CT
13 SYMONS WY
14 BECK VW
15 GARRICK CL
16 COMRIE DR
17 WAITE CL
18 TURNBULL DR
19 FETHERSTON CL
20 BROWNING RD
21 SAUNDERS CRES
22 THURLOW AVE
23 DORRINGTON CL
24 KINGS CL
25 MCGRATH CL
26 HART DR
27 LORD DR
28 MAY CT
29 RUNDLE CT
30 JENKINGS CL
31 ALBRIGHT CL
32 MORGAN CL

29
18

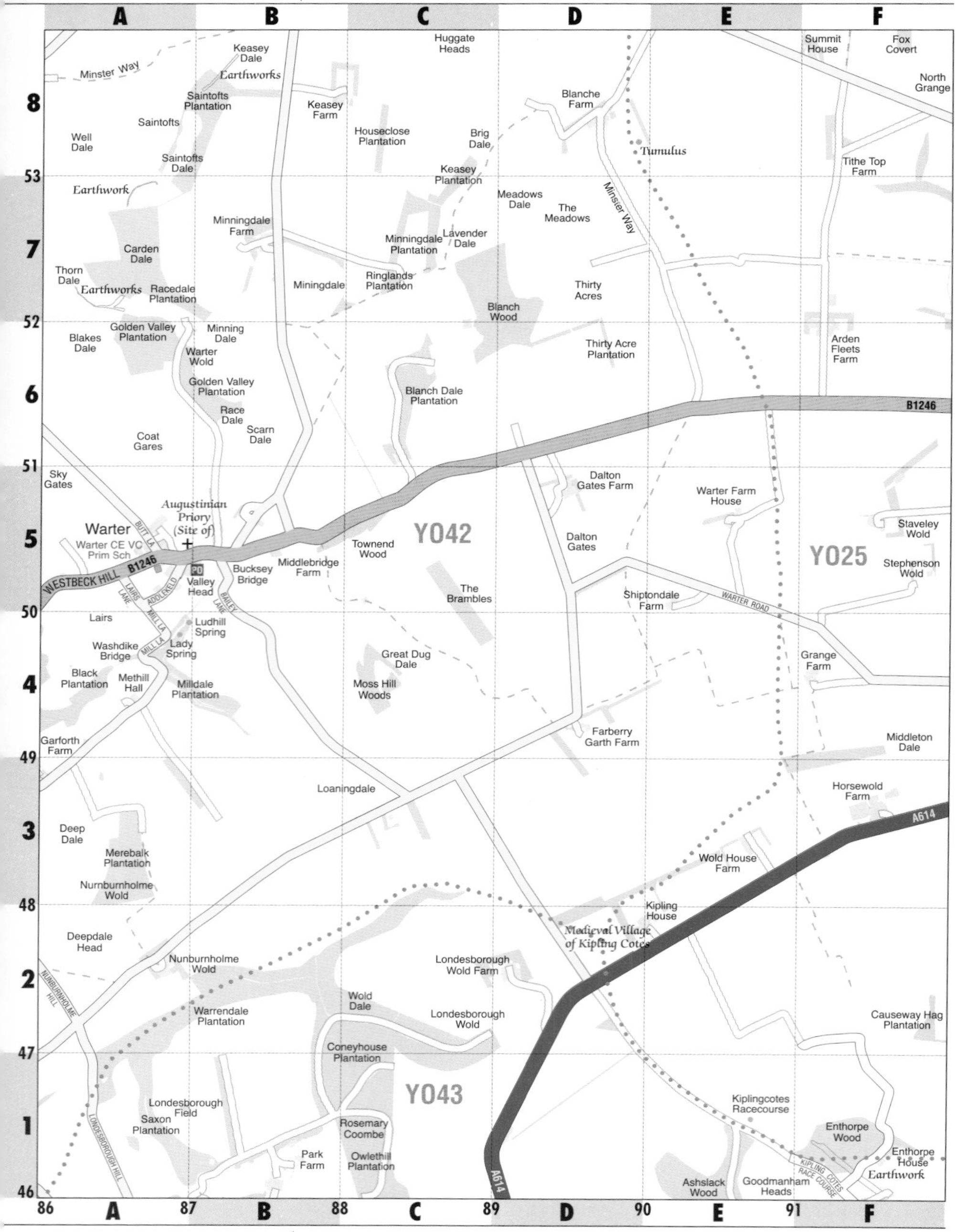
Scale: 1⅓ inches to 1 mile
0 ¼ ½ mile
0 250m 500m 750m 1 km
A B C D E F
8 53 7 52 6 51 5 50 4 49 3 48 2 47 1 46
86 87 88 89 90 91
Minster Way
Keasey Dale
Earthworks
Huggate Heads
Summit House
Fox Covert
North Grange
Saintofts Plantation
Keasey Farm
Blanche Farm
Saintofts
Well Dale
Houseclose Plantation
Brig Dale
Tumulus
Saintofts Dale
Keasey Plantation
Tithe Top Farm
Earthwork
Meadows Dale
The Meadows
Minster Way
Minningdale Farm
Minningdale Plantation
Lavender Dale
Carden Dale
Thorn Dale
Earthworks
Racedale Plantation
Miningdale
Ringlands Plantation
Thirty Acres
Blanch Wood
Golden Valley Plantation
Minning Dale
Blakes Dale
Warter Wold
Arden Fleets Farm
Thirty Acre Plantation
Golden Valley Plantation
Blanch Dale Plantation
Race Dale
B1246
Scarn Dale
Coat Gares
Sky Gates
Dalton Gates Farm
Augustinian Priory (Site of)
Warter Farm House
Warter
Warter CE VC Prim Sch
BUTT LA
YO42
Staveley Wold
Townend Wood
Dalton Gates
YO25
Stephenson Wold
Middlebridge Farm
B1246
WESTBECK HILL
PO
Bucksey Bridge
Valley Head
LAIRS LANE
ADDLEKELD
BAILEY LANE
The Brambles
Shiptondale Farm
WARTER ROAD
Lairs
Ludhill Spring
MILL LA
Washdike Bridge
Lady Spring
Great Dug Dale
Grange Farm
Black Plantation
Methill Hall
Milldale Plantation
Moss Hill Woods
Farberry Garth Farm
Garforth Farm
Middleton Dale
Loaningdale
Horsewold Farm
A614
Deep Dale
Merebalk Plantation
Wold House Farm
Nunburnholme Wold
Kipling House
Deepdale Head
Medieval Village of Kipling Cotes
Nunburnholme Wold
Londesborough Wold Farm
NUNBURNHOLME HILL
Wold Dale
Warrendale Plantation
Londesborough Wold
Causeway Hag Plantation
Coneyhouse Plantation
YO43
Londesborough Field
Kiplingcotes Racecourse
Saxon Plantation
LONDESBOROUGH HILL
Rosemary Coombe
Enthorpe Wood
Park Farm
Owlethill Plantation
Enthorpe House
KIPLING COTES RACE COURSE
Earthwork
A614
Ashslack Wood
Goodmanham Heads

29
41

Scale: 1⅓ inches to 1 mile
0 ¼ ½ mile
0 250m 500m 750m 1 km

19
32

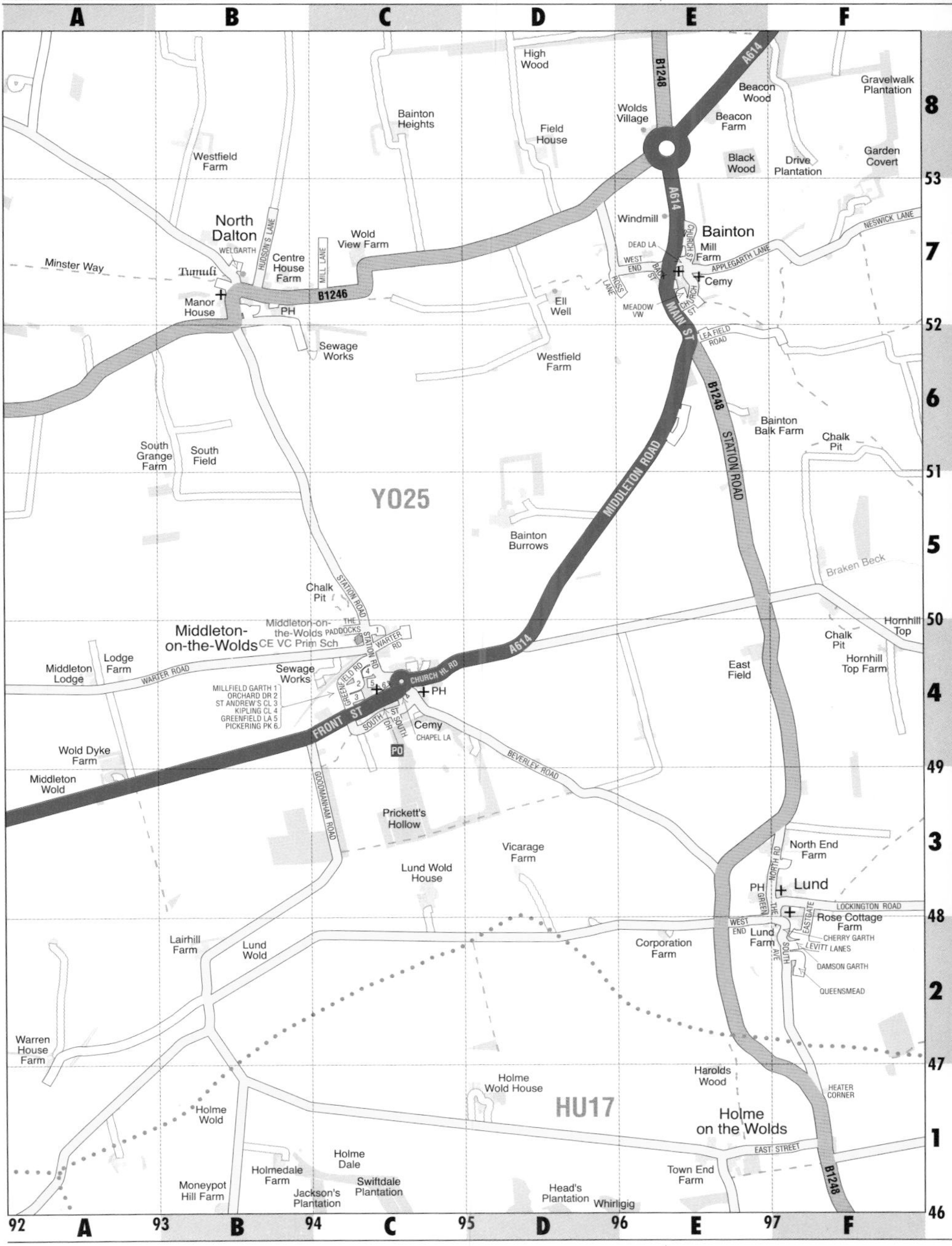

42
32

31
20
Scale: 1⅓ inches to 1 mile

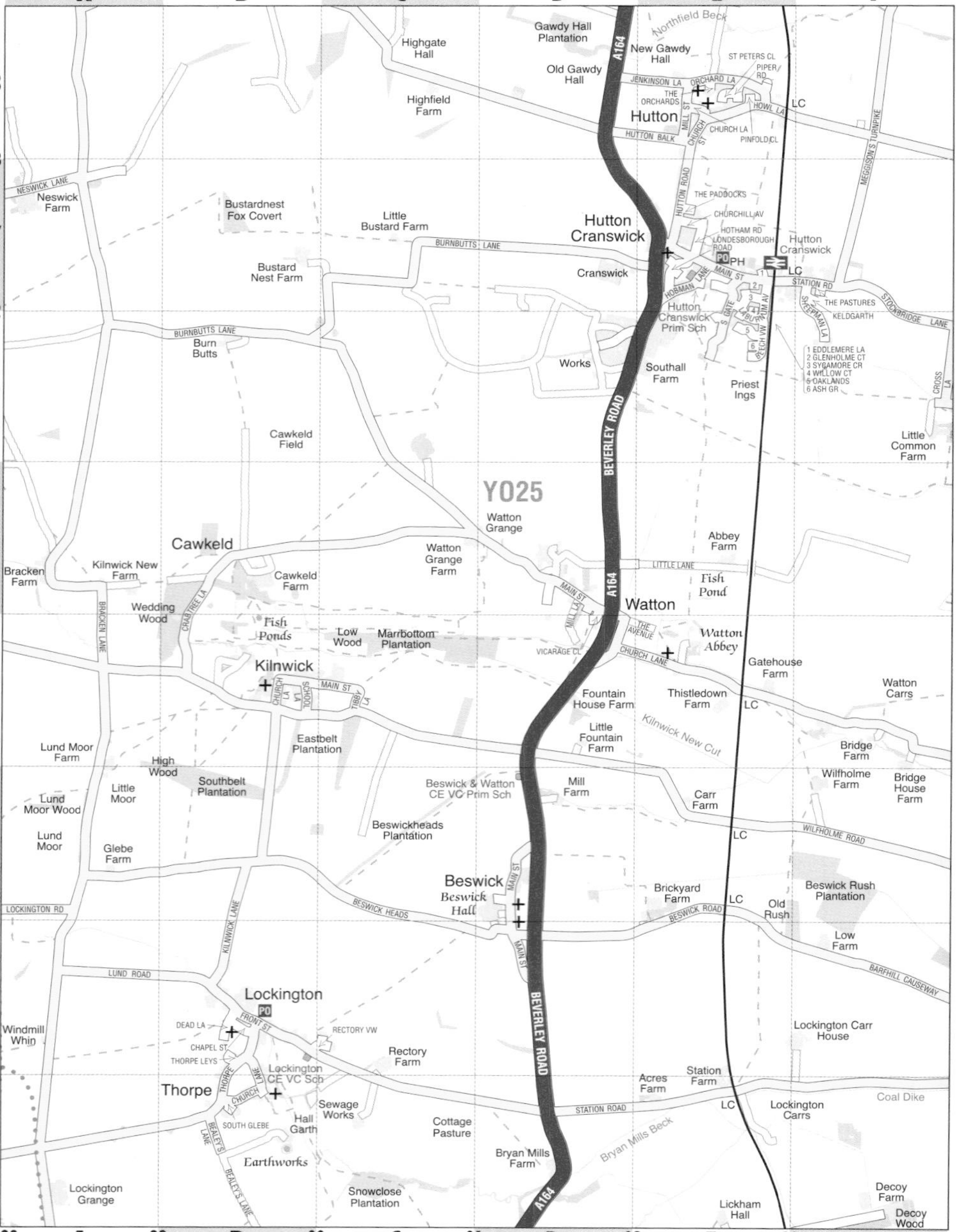

31
43

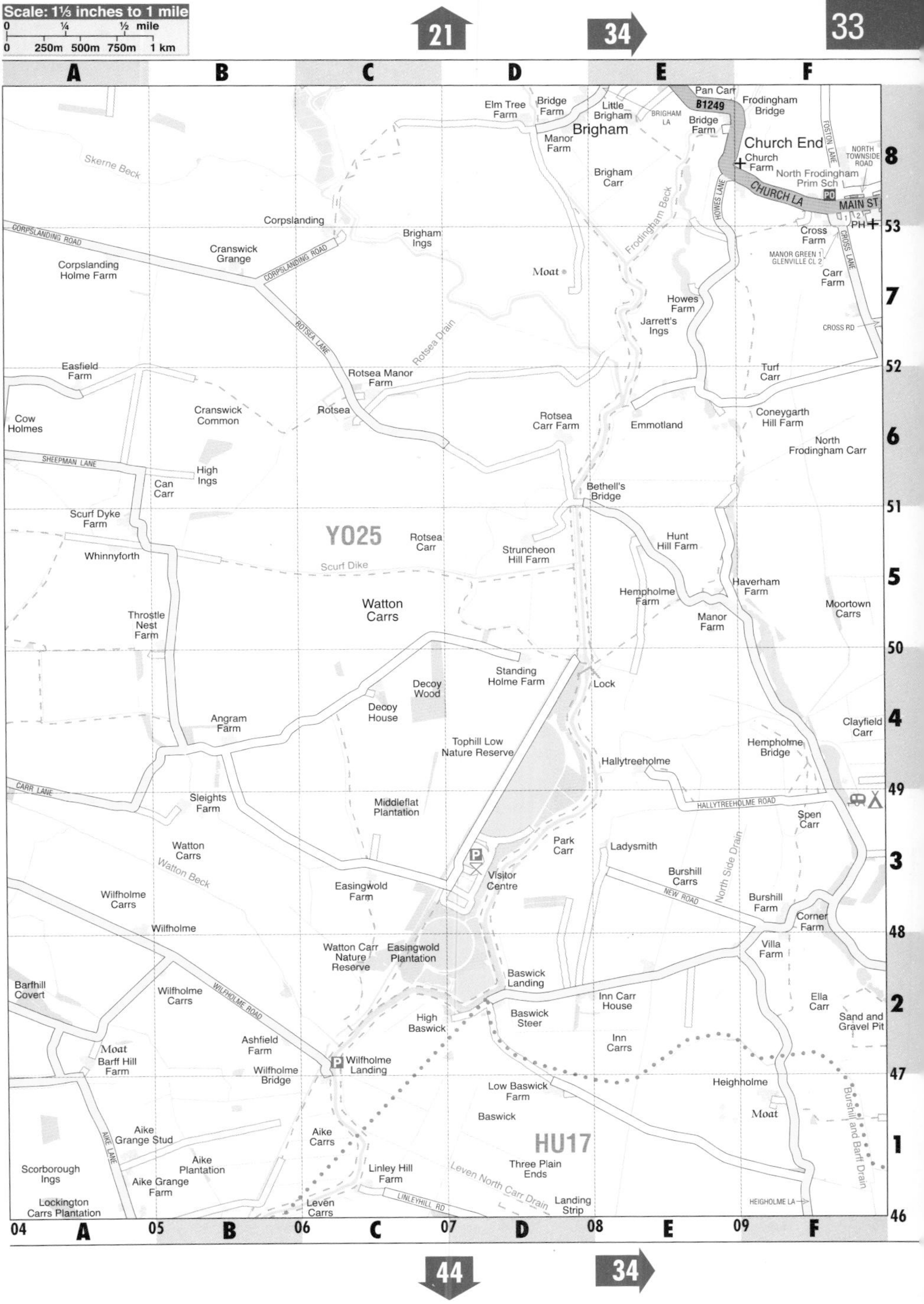
Scale: 1⅓ inches to 1 mile
0 ¼ ½ mile
0 250m 500m 750m 1 km
21
34
A B C D E F
Pan Carr
B1249
Elm Tree Farm
Bridge Farm
Little Brigham
BRIGHAM LA
Bridge Farm
Frodingham Bridge
Manor Farm
Brigham
Church End
FOSTON LANE
NORTH TOWNSIDE ROAD
Skerne Beck
Church Farm
North Frodingham Prim Sch
Brigham Carr
HOWES LANE
CHURCH LA
PO
MAIN ST
PH
Corpslanding
CORPSLANDING ROAD
Brigham Ings
Frodingham Beck
Cross Farm
CROSS LANE
MANOR GREEN 1
GLENVILLE CL 2
Cranswick Grange
CORPSLANDING ROAD
Corpslanding Holme Farm
Moat
Carr Farm
Howes Farm
Jarrett's Ings
ROTSEA LANE
Rotsea Drain
CROSS RD
Easfield Farm
Rotsea Manor Farm
Turf Carr
Cow Holmes
Cranswick Common
Rotsea
Rotsea Carr Farm
Emmotland
Coneygarth Hill Farm
North Frodingham Carr
SHEEPMAN LANE
High Ings
Can Carr
Bethell's Bridge
Scurf Dyke Farm
YO25
Rotsea Carr
Hunt Hill Farm
Whinnyforth
Struncheon Hill Farm
Scurf Dike
Haverham Farm
Hempholme Farm
Watton Carrs
Moortown Carrs
Throstle Nest Farm
Manor Farm
Standing Holme Farm
Decoy Wood
Lock
Decoy House
Clayfield Carr
Angram Farm
Tophill Low Nature Reserve
Hempholme Bridge
Hallytreeholme
CARR LANE
Sleights Farm
Middleflat Plantation
HALLYTREEHOLME ROAD
Spen Carr
Watton Carrs
Park Carr
Ladysmith
Watton Beck
P
Visitor Centre
Burshill Carrs
NEW ROAD
North Side Drain
Wilfholme Carrs
Easingwold Farm
Burshill Farm
Corner Farm
Wilfholme
Watton Carr Nature Reserve
Easingwold Plantation
Villa Farm
Barfhill Covert
Wilfholme Carrs
WILFHOLME ROAD
Baswick Landing
Inn Carr House
Ella Carr
Baswick Steer
Sand and Gravel Pit
High Baswick
Moat
Barff Hill Farm
Ashfield Farm
Inn Carrs
P
Wilfholme Landing
Wilfholme Bridge
Heigholme
Low Baswick Farm
Burshill and Barff Drain
Moat
Baswick
Aike Grange Stud
AIKE LANE
Aike Carrs
HU17
Scorborough Ings
Aike Plantation
Linley Hill Farm
Three Plain Ends
Leven North Carr Drain
Aike Grange Farm
Lockington Carrs Plantation
Leven Carrs
LINLEYHILL RD
Landing Strip
HEIGHOLME LA
8
53
7
52
6
51
5
50
4
49
3
48
2
47
1
46
04 A 05 B 06 C 07 D 08 E 09 F
44
34

33
22

Scale: 1⅓ inches to 1 mile
0 ¼ ½ mile
0 250m 500m 750m 1 km

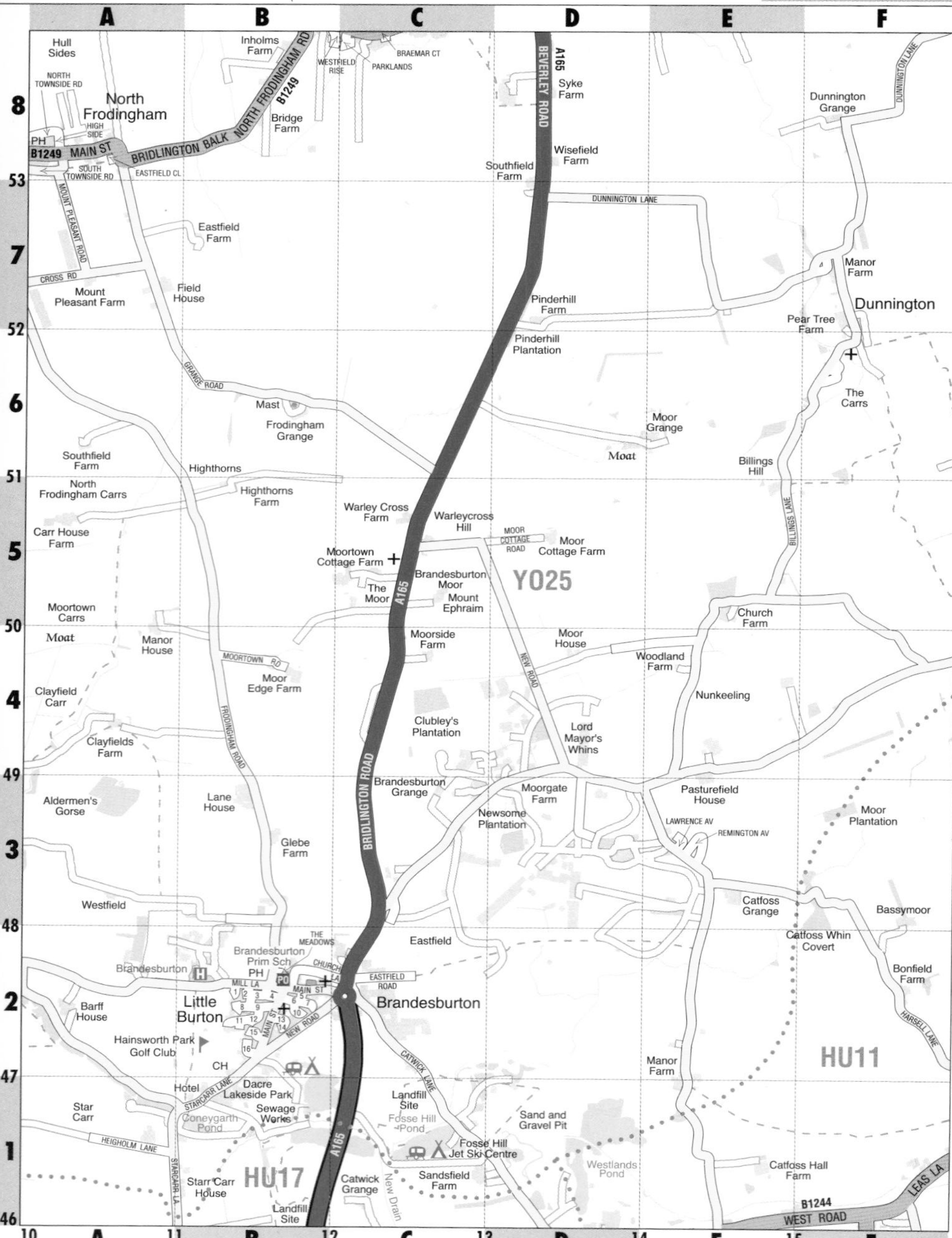

B2
1 PARK AVE
2 ALTOFT CL
3 LITTLE BURTON
4 CHARTER'S LA
5 CROSS HL
6 BOARDMAN LA
7 BOARDMAN PK
8 MAPLE WK
9 ST QUINTIN PK
10 ALDERMANS WY
11 HYMERS CL
12 REEDSWAY
13 STOCKWELL LA
14 BARLEY GARTH
15 THE POPLARS
16 ELMFIELD DR

33
45

Scale: 1⅓ inches to 1 mile
0 ¼ ½ mile
0 250m 500m 750m 1 km

23

A
B
C
D
E
F
Skipsea Grange
B1242 HORNSEA ROAD
BEWHOLME LANE
Low Bonwick
CH
Skirlington Leisure Park
Far Grange Country Park
Visitor Centre
Rec
Low Skirlington Farm
High Skirlington
High Bonwick
High Grounds
YO25
SKIPSEA ROAD
LONG LANE
North Field
Works
GARDHAM LANE
North End Farm
Cliff Farm
North End
NORTH RD
CALAM VILLAS
CHURCH LA
CLIFF RD
STOW RD
Hill Top Farm
CANHAM LA
PH
Field House Farm
BEWHOLME ROAD
Atwick
HORNSEA ROAD
Hall
NORTH RD
Laburnum Farm
Bewholme
FAR LA
WATER LA
SKIPSEA RD
Bewholme Prim Sch
ATWICK RD
CATFOSS RD
Model Farm
SEATON RD
Double Gates
134
B1242
Little Atwick
Eastfield Farm
CLIFF RD
BEWHOLME LANE
Little Arram
WESTHOLME AV
NUTANA AV
Northfield House
Arram Hall
North Cliff
CLIFF ROAD
ATWICK ROAD
BELVEDERE PK
Birk Crag
Northfield Farm
Springfield Farm
NORTHGATE
CARLTON AV
ASHCROFT DR
DRAYCOTT AVE
NICHOLAS ST
CLIFTON ST
ESPL
HU18
Honeysuckle Farm
Hotel
Seaton Hold
HU11
Westfield Farm
EASTGATE
MARINE DR
Sch
WESTWOOD AV
Sports Ground
Liby
CLIFF RD
NEW ROAD
Leisure Centre
Coll
NEWBEGIN
SANDS LA
SOUTH PROM
HORNSEA
PASTURE RD
BURTON RD
Poplar Farm
B1244
PH
Council Offices
MARVELGARTH LANE
BEWHOLME LANE
MILL LANE
SEATON RD
Swan I
Seaton Grange
Brockholme
SOUTHGATE
Cemy
HORNSEA BURTON RD
Common Farm
BREAMER LANE
Lady I
Hornsea Mere Nature Reserve
BURTON RD
THE CR
Buttercup Farm
TRINITY RD
Beverley Farm
Seaton
HORNSEA ROAD
EBOR AV
South Cliff
RANBY DR
MAIN ST
B1244
HULL ROAD
MARLBOROUGH AV
Low Wood
PICKERING AV
Southorpe Village
EDENFIELD AV
Hornsea Burton
ROLSTON RD
TANSLEY LA
MANOR PARK
BUTCHERS ROW
WASSAND ROAD
Hornsea Rail Trail
B1242
Decoy Plantation
Southorpe Farm
POTTERS WAY
GRUNDILL LA
Wassand Hall & Gardens
SOUTHORPE RD
8
53
7
52
6
51
5
50
4
49
3
48
2
47
1
46
16
17
18
19
20
21

For full street detail of the highlighted area see page 134.

A1
1 COMMON LA
2 NICHOLSON LA
3 BACK LA
4 WITTYS PADDOCK
5 MIDDLE LA

46

132

D8
1 MAIN ST
2 FERRY FARM CL
3 MAYPOLE GR
4 ST MATTHEW'S CL

133

Scale: 1⅓ inches to 1 mile
0 ¼ ½ mile
0 250m 500m 750m 1 km

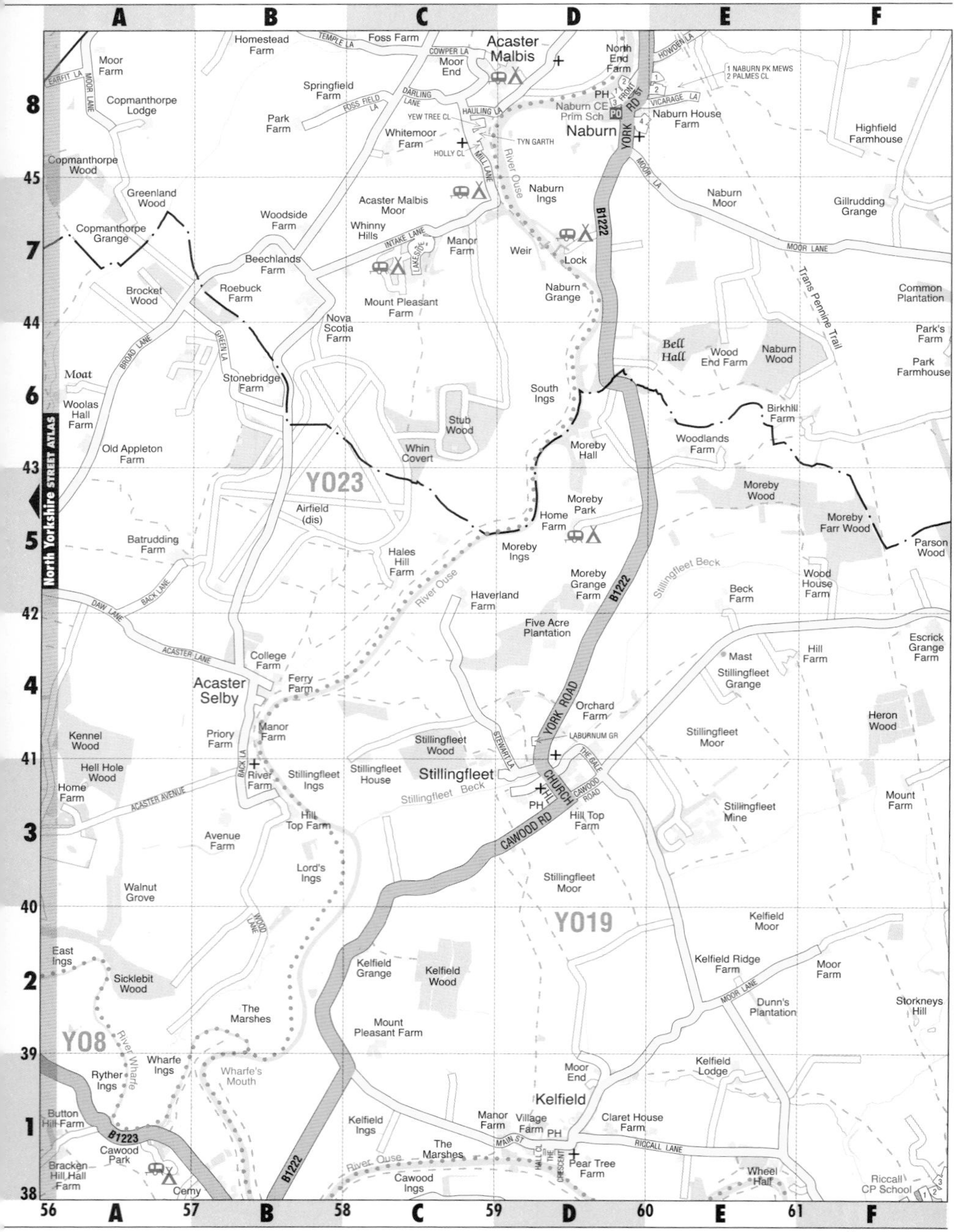

48

F1
1 COPPERGATE
2 ELMS CL
3 NORTHFIELD LA

Scale: 1⅓ inches to 1 mile
0 ¼ ½ mile
0 250m 500m 750m 1 km

26
38

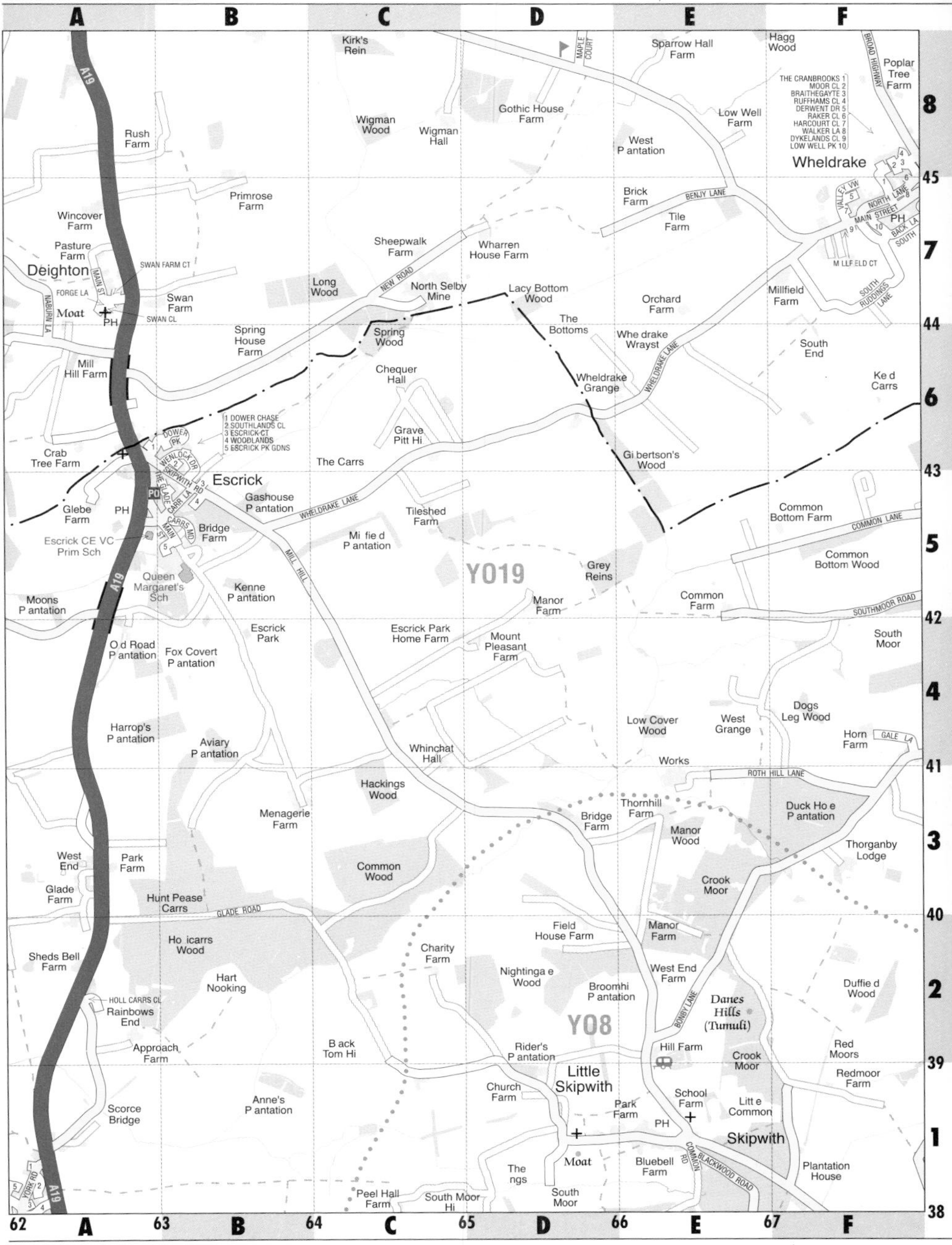

37
27

Scale: 1⅓ inches to 1 mile
0 ¼ ½ mile
0 250m 500m 750m 1 km

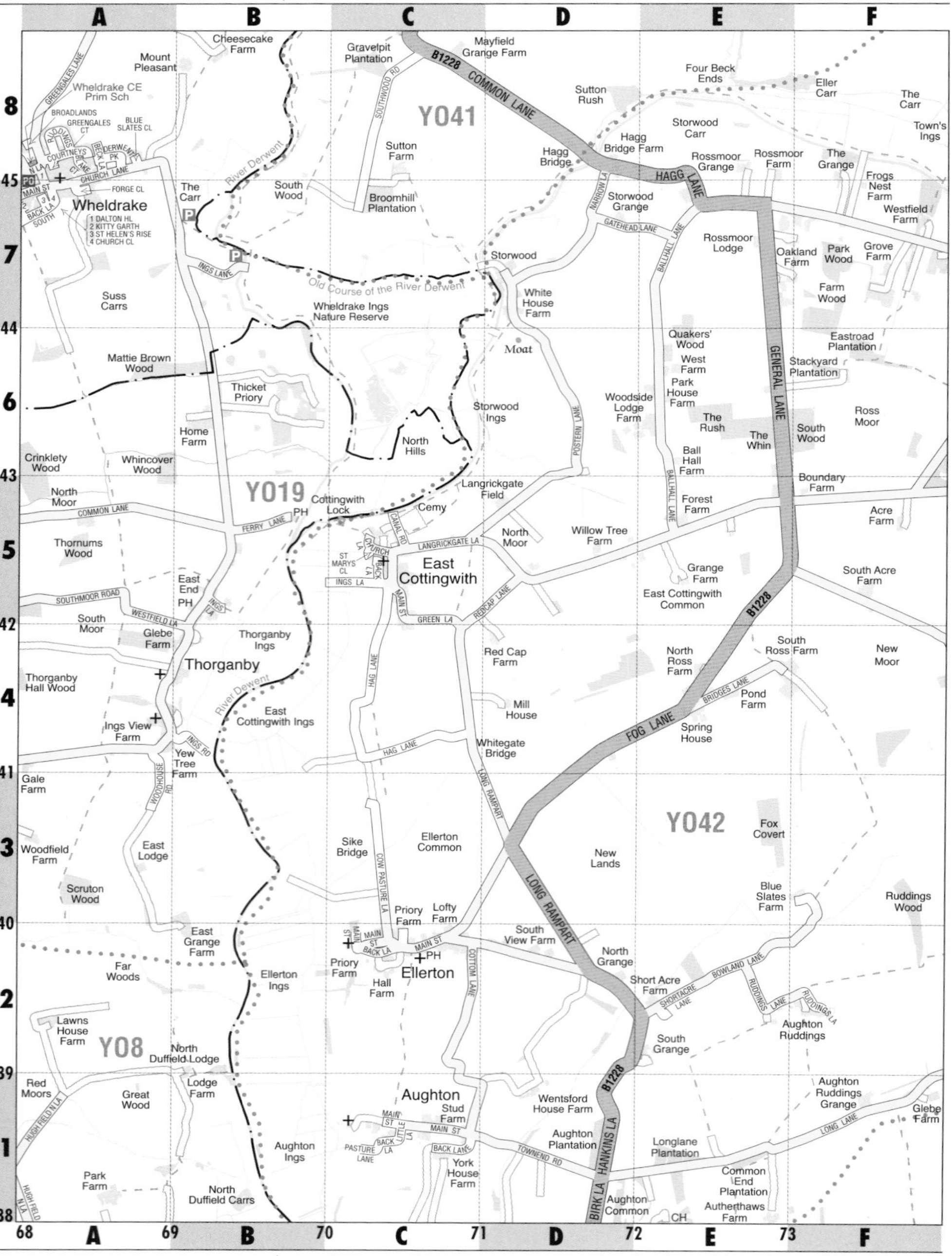

37
50

Scale: 1⅓ inches to 1 mile
0 ¼ ½ mile
0 250m 500m 750m 1 km

28
40

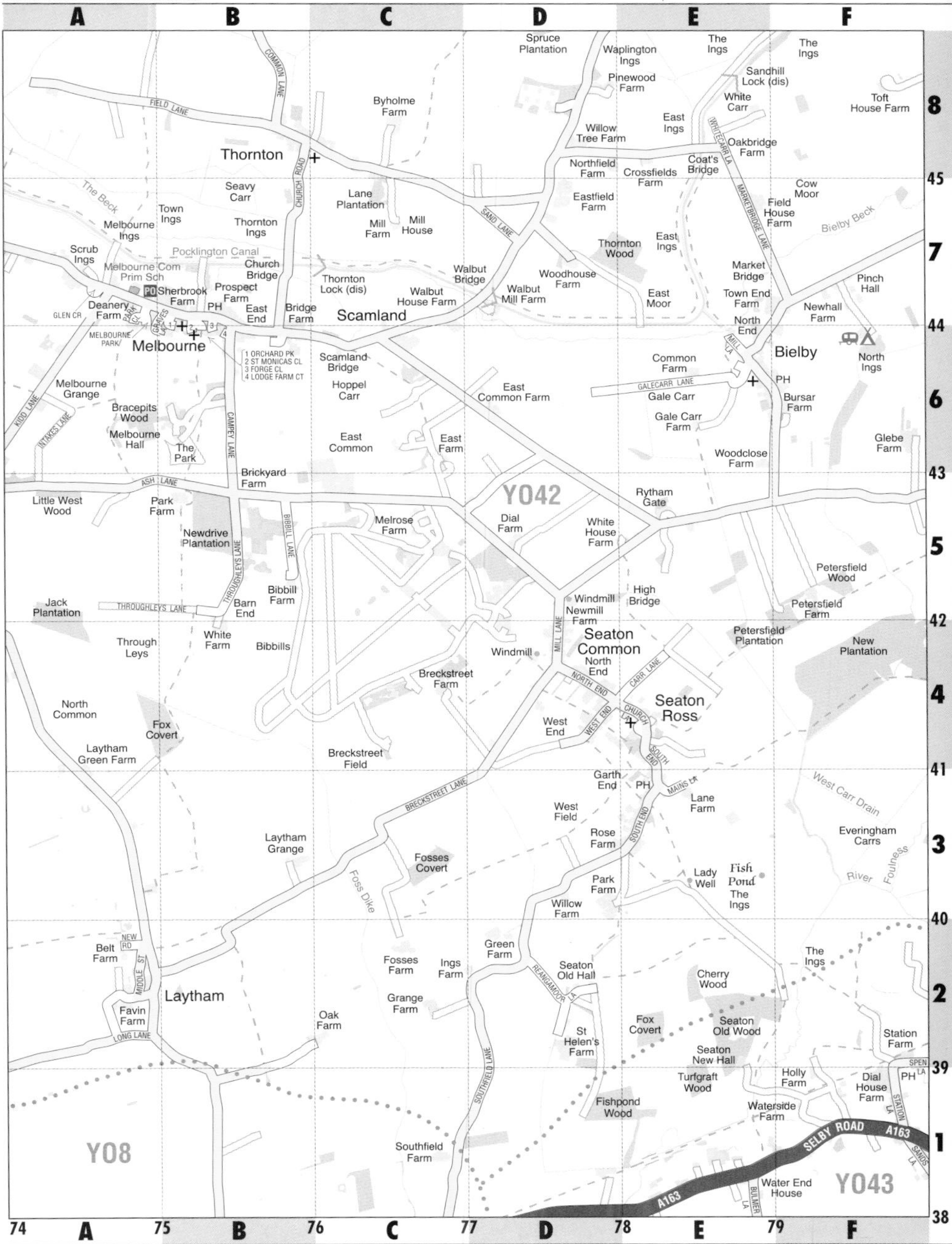

51
40

39
29

Scale: 1⅓ inches to 1 mile
0 ¼ ½ mile
0 250m 500m 750m 1 km

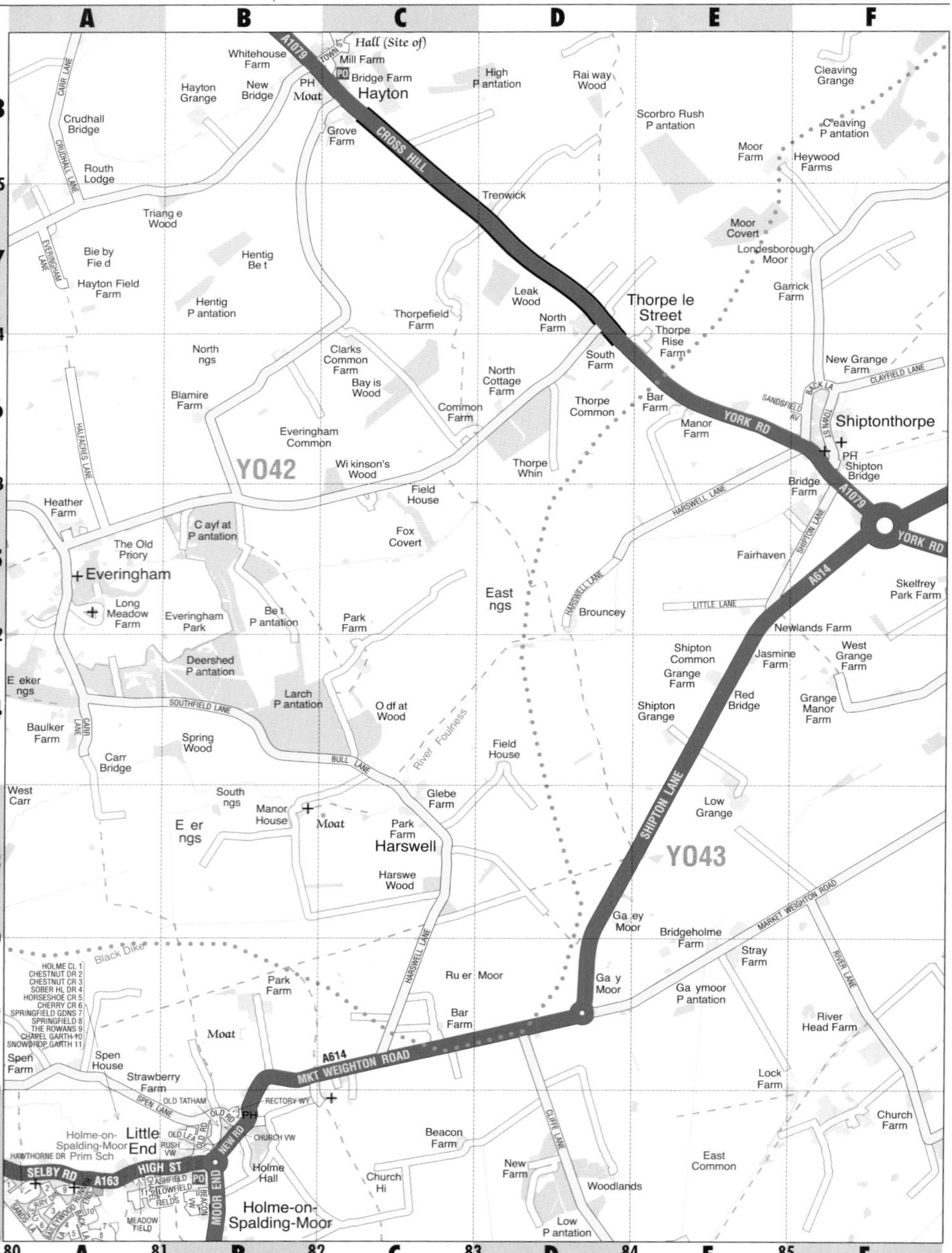

39
52

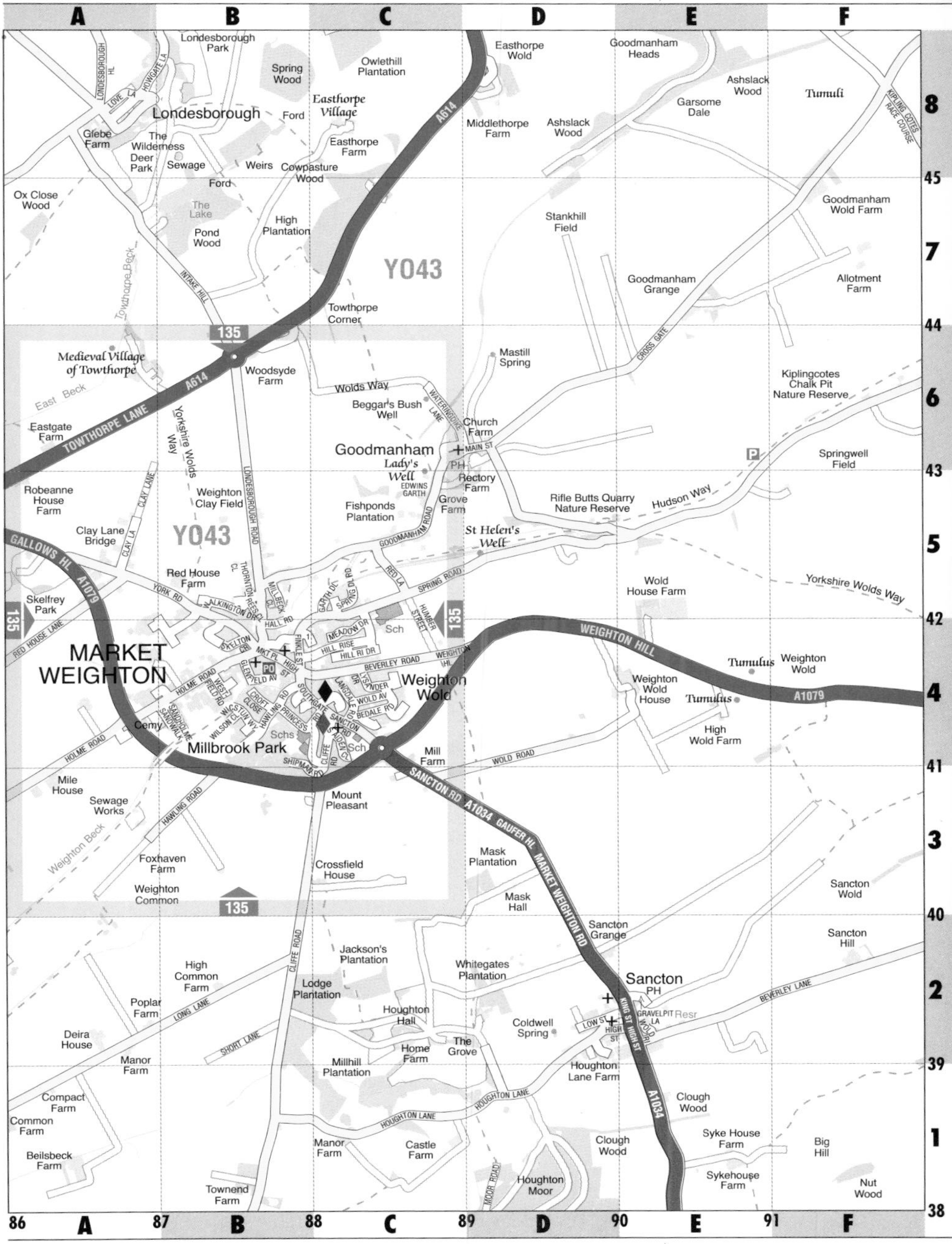

For full street detail of the highlighted area see page 135.

41
31

Scale: 1⅓ inches to 1 mile
0 ¼ ½ mile
0 250m 500m 750m 1 km

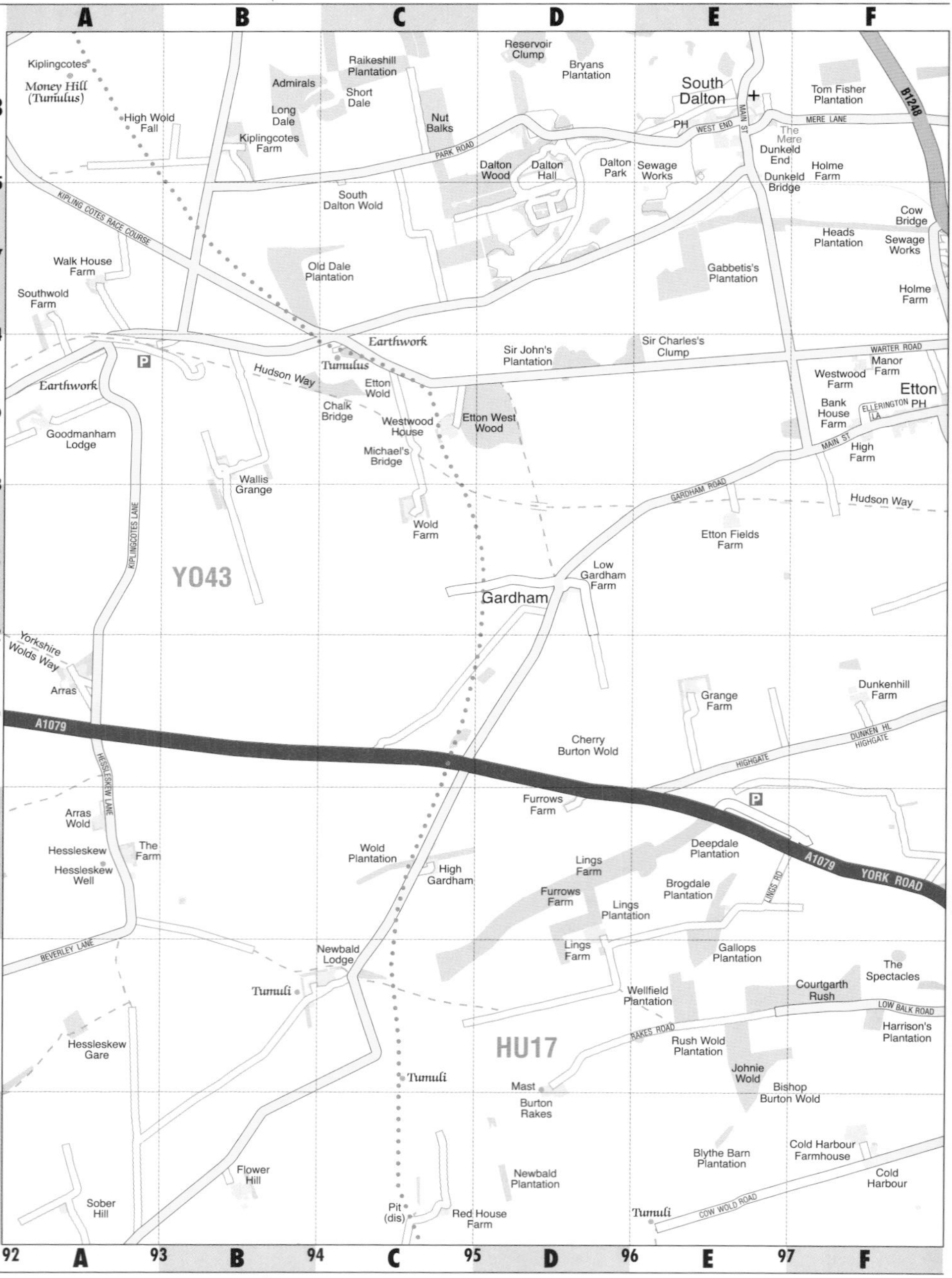

41
54

Scale: 1⅓ inches to 1 mile
0 ¼ ½ mile
0 250m 500m 750m 1 km

32
44
For full street detail of the highlighted area see page 136.

D6
1 BYGOT CL
2 PASTURE CL
3 CASTLE CL
4 WYNDHAM CL
5 THE POPLARS
6 SHIPTON CR
7 GRANGE RD
8 CRANSWICK CL

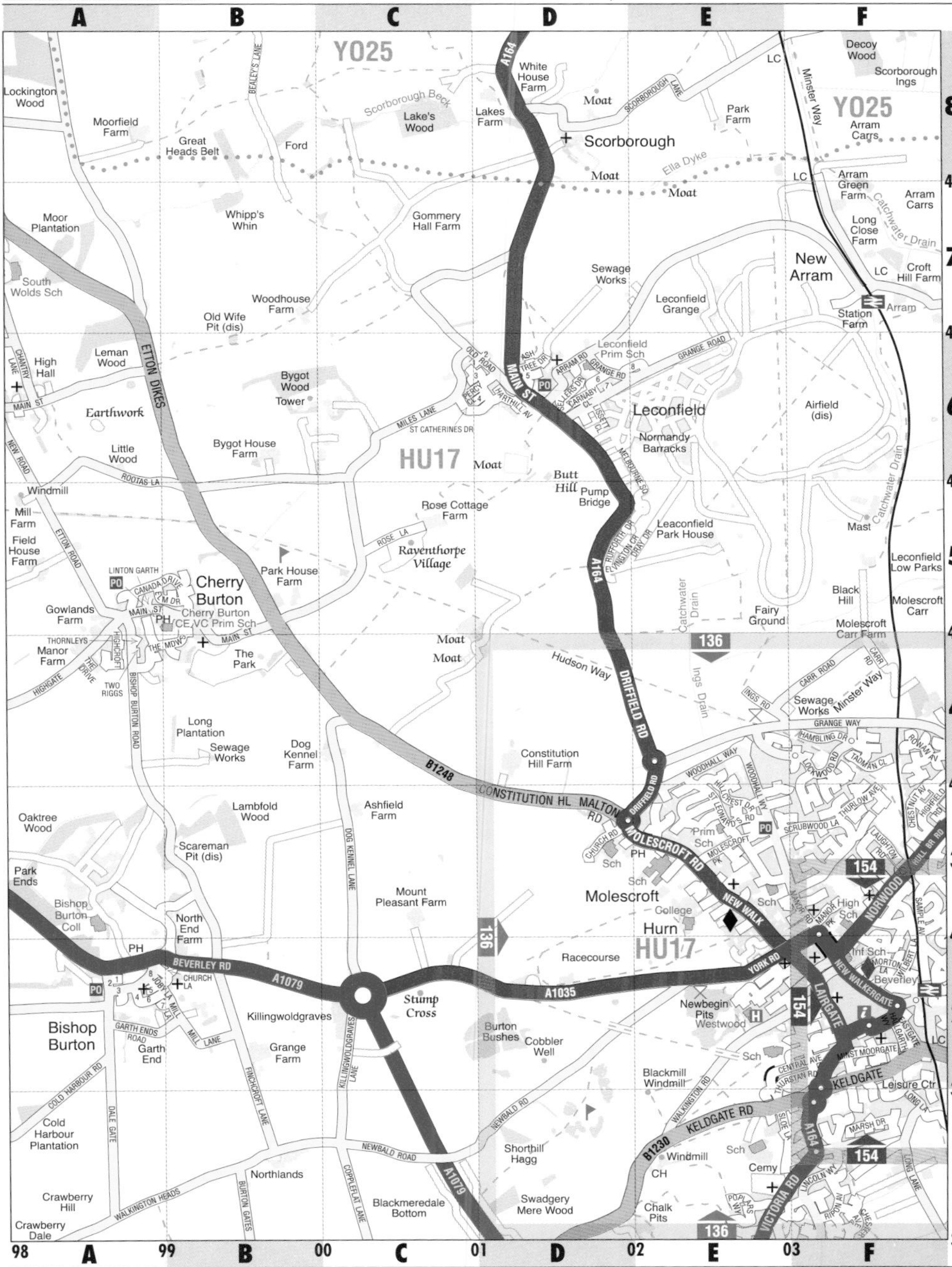

A2
1 COTTAGE FIELD
2 FINKLE ST
3 BRYAN MERE
4 RATTEN ROW
5 COLD HARBOUR VW
6 CALLAS
7 CALAIS CFT
8 PUDDING GATE

55
44
For full street detail of the highlighted area see page 154.

43
33

Scale: 1⅓ inches to 1 mile
0 ¼ ½ mile
0 250m 500m 750m 1 km

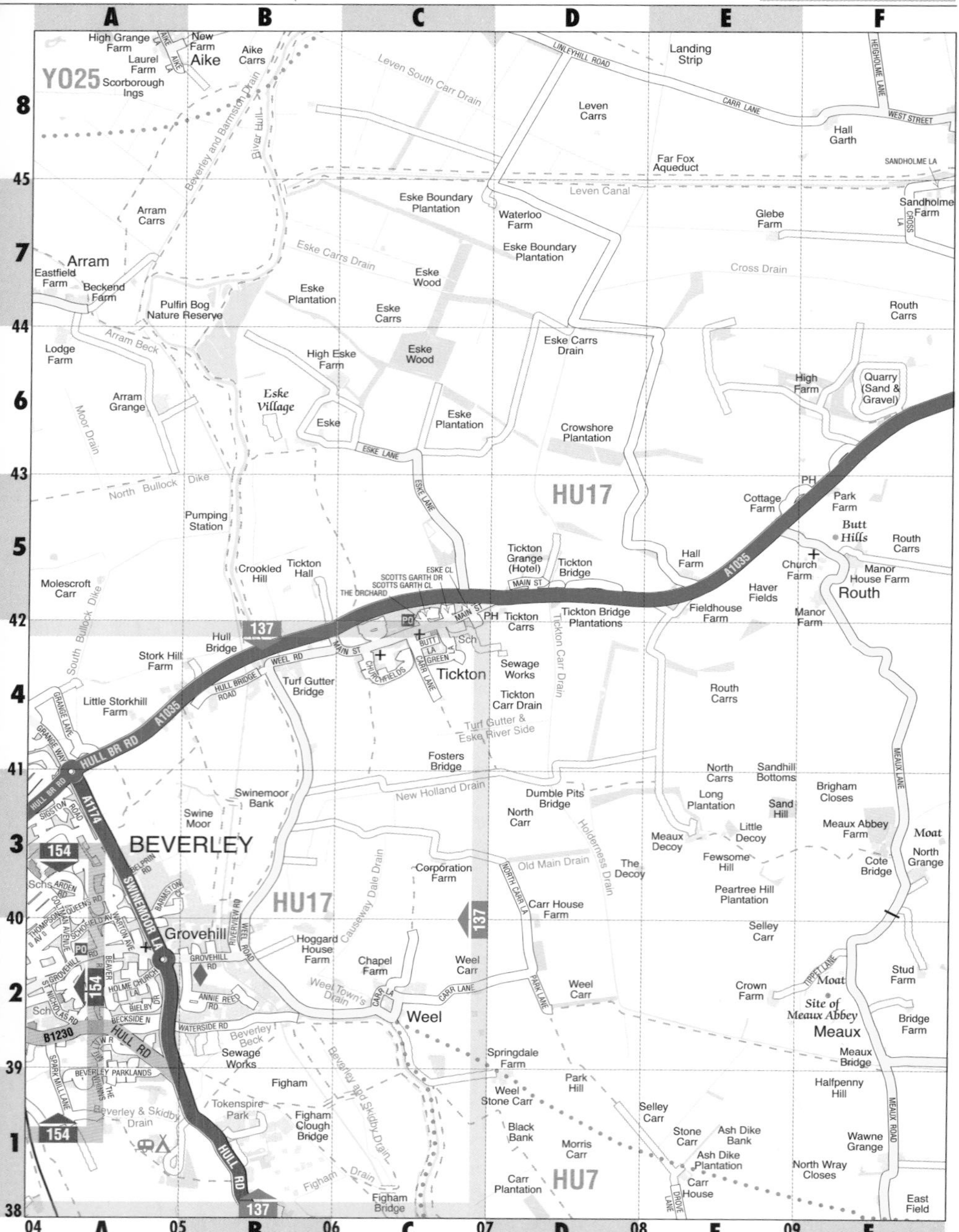

136
56
For full street detail of the highlighted area see page 154.
For full street detail of the highlighted area see page 137.

Scale: 1⅓ inches to 1 mile
0 ¼ ½ mile
0 250m 500m 750m 1 km

34
46

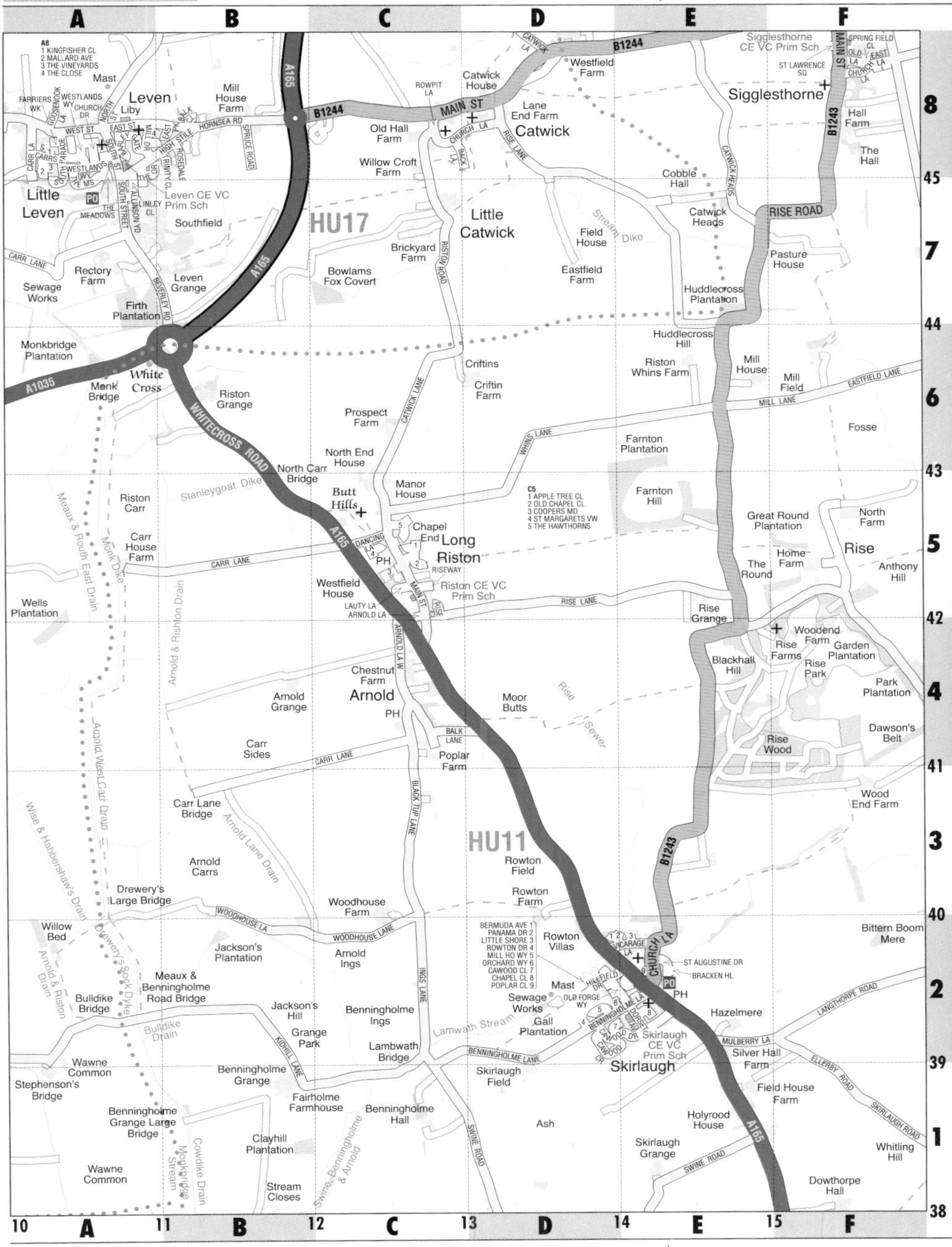

57
46

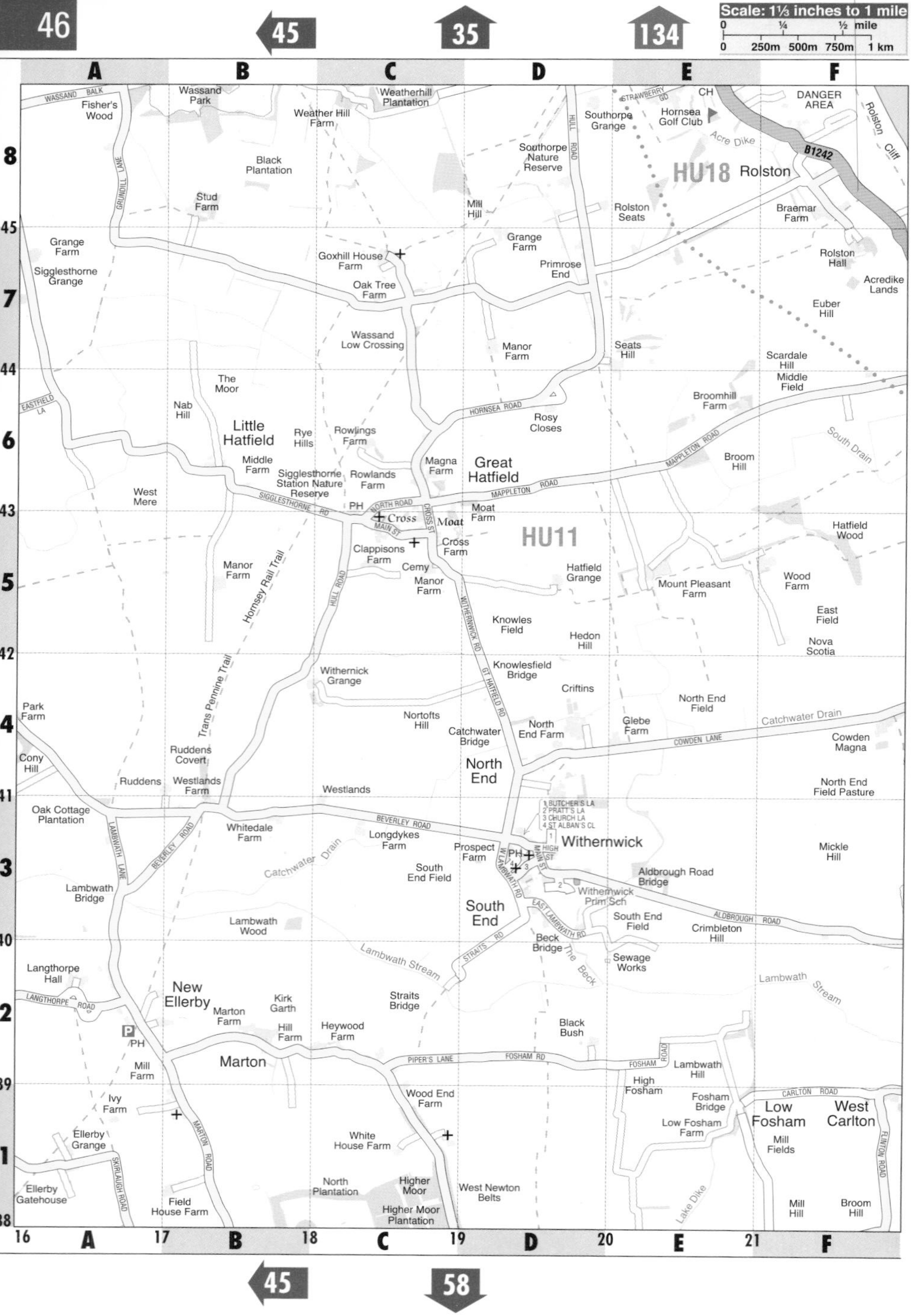
45
35
134
Scale: 1⅓ inches to 1 mile
0 ¼ ½ mile
0 250m 500m 750m 1 km
Wassand Park
Fisher's Wood
Weatherhill Plantation
Weather Hill Farm
Southorpe Grange
Hornsea Golf Club
DANGER AREA
Rolston Cliff
B1242
Black Plantation
Southorpe Nature Reserve
HU18
Rolston
Stud Farm
Mill Hill
Rolston Seats
Braemar Farm
Grange Farm
Sigglesthorne Grange
Goxhill House Farm
Primrose End
Rolston Hall
Acredike Lands
Oak Tree Farm
Euber Hill
Wassand Low Crossing
Manor Farm
Seats Hill
Scardale Hill
Middle Field
The Moor
Broomhill Farm
Nab Hill
Rosy Closes
Little Hatfield
Rye Hills
Rowlings Farm
Magna Farm
Great Hatfield
Broom Hill
Middle Farm
Sigglesthorne Station Nature Reserve
Rowlands Farm
West Mere
Moat Farm
Cross
Moat
HU11
Hatfield Wood
Clappisons Farm
Cross Farm
Cemy
Manor Farm
Hatfield Grange
Mount Pleasant Farm
Wood Farm
East Field
Knowles Field
Hedon Hill
Nova Scotia
Hornsey Rail Trail
Withernick Grange
Knowlesfield Bridge
Criftins
North End Field
Trans Pennine Trail
Park Farm
Nortofts Hill
Catchwater Bridge
North End Farm
Glebe Farm
Catchwater Drain
Cowden Magna
Cony Hill
Ruddens Covert
North End
Ruddens
Westlands Farm
Westlands
North End Field Pasture
Oak Cottage Plantation
Whitedale Farm
Longdykes Farm
Prospect Farm
Withernwick
Mickle Hill
South End Field
Aldbrough Road Bridge
Lambwath Bridge
Withernwick Prim Sch
South End
South End Field
Crimbleton Hill
Lambwath Wood
Beck Bridge
Sewage Works
Lambwath Stream
The Beck
Langthorpe Hall
New Ellerby
Kirk Garth
Straits Bridge
Marton Farm
Hill Farm
Heywood Farm
Black Bush
Mill Farm
Marton
Lambwath Hill
High Fosham
Ivy Farm
Wood End Farm
Fosham Bridge
Low Fosham
West Carlton
Low Fosham Farm
Ellerby Grange
White House Farm
Mill Fields
Ellerby Gatehouse
North Plantation
Higher Moor
West Newton Belts
Field House Farm
Higher Moor Plantation
Mill Hill
Broom Hill
Lake Dike
Acre Dike
South Drain
WASSAND BALK
GRUNDILL LANE
HULL ROAD
STRAWBERRY GD
EASTFIELD LA
HORNSEA ROAD
MAPPLETON ROAD
SIGGLESTHORNE RD
NORTH ROAD
MAIN ST
CROSS ST
WITHERNWICK RD
GT HATFIELD RD
COWDEN LANE
BEVERLEY ROAD
LAMBWATH LANE
1 BUTCHER'S LA
2 PRATT'S LA
3 CHURCH LA
4 ST ALBAN'S CL
HIGH ST
W LAMBWATH RD
E LAMBWATH RD
STRAITS RD
ALDBROUGH ROAD
LANGTHORPE ROAD
PIPER'S LANE
FOSHAM RD
FOSHAM ROAD
CARLTON ROAD
FLINTON ROAD
MARTON ROAD
SKIRLAUGH ROAD
PH
CH
A B C D E F
8 7 6 5 4 3 2 1
45 44 43 42 41 40 39 38
16 17 18 19 20 21
45
58

Scale: 1⅓ inches to 1 mile

0 ¼ ½ mile

0 250m 500m 750m 1 km

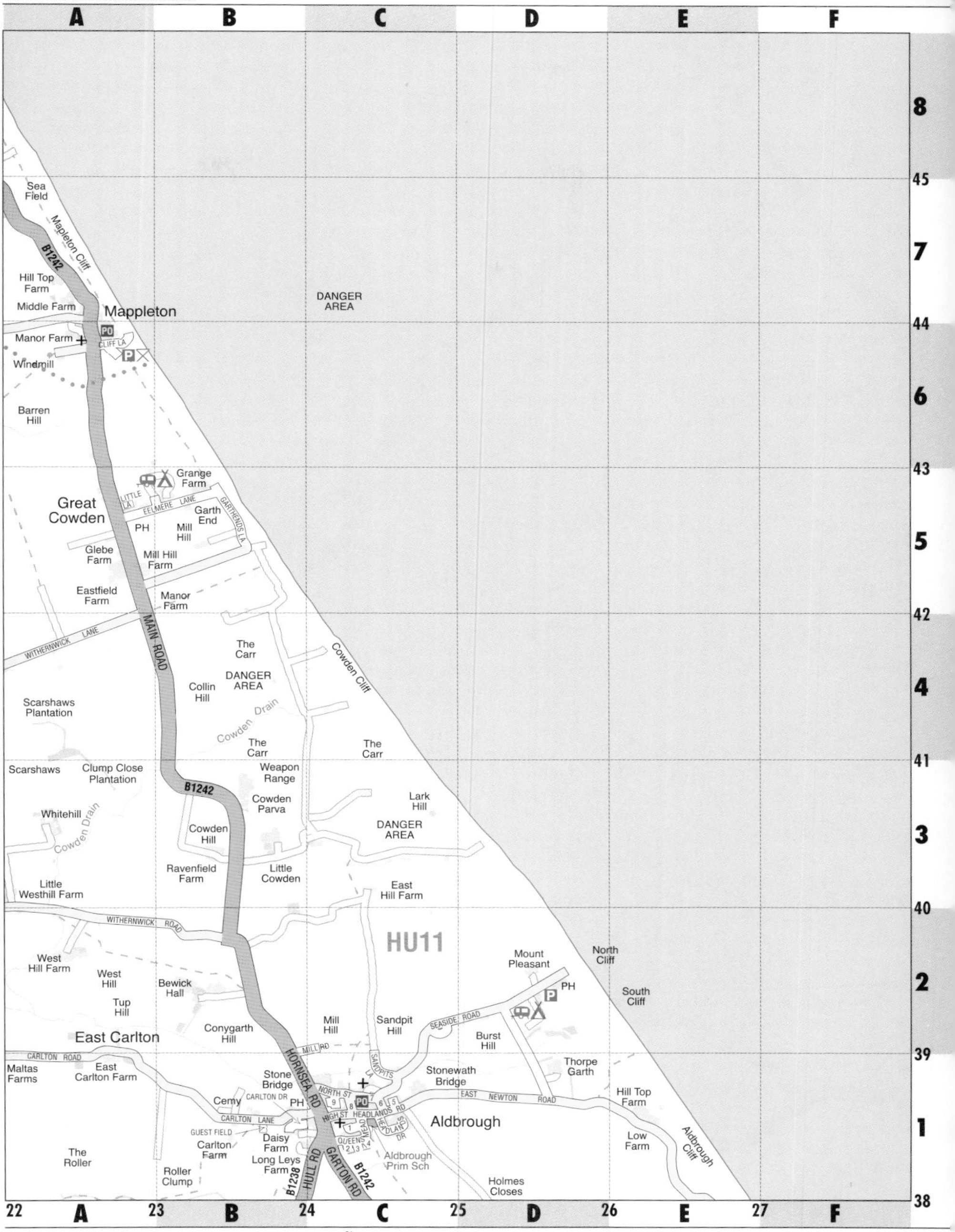
A
B
C
D
E
F
8
45
7
44
6
43
5
42
4
41
3
40
2
39
1
38
22
23
24
25
26
27
Sea Field
Mapleton Cliff
B1242
Hill Top Farm
Middle Farm
Mappleton
DANGER AREA
PO
Manor Farm
CLIFF LA
P
Windmill
Barren Hill
Grange Farm
LITTLE LA
EELMERE LANE
GARTHENDS LA
Great Cowden
Garth End
PH
Mill Hill
Glebe Farm
Mill Hill Farm
Eastfield Farm
Manor Farm
WITHERNWICK LANE
MAIN ROAD
The Carr
Cowden Cliff
DANGER AREA
Collin Hill
Scarshaws Plantation
Cowden Drain
The Carr
The Carr
Scarshaws
Clump Close Plantation
Weapon Range
B1242
Cowden Parva
Lark Hill
Whitehill
Cowden Drain
Cowden Hill
DANGER AREA
Ravenfield Farm
Little Cowden
Little Westhill Farm
East Hill Farm
WITHERNWICK ROAD
HU11
Mount Pleasant
North Cliff
West Hill Farm
West Hill
Bewick Hall
PH
P
South Cliff
Tup Hill
Mill Hill
Sandpit Hill
SEASIDE ROAD
Burst Hill
East Carlton
Conygarth Hill
MILL RD
HORNSEA RD
CARLTON ROAD
Thorpe Garth
Maltas Farms
East Carlton Farm
Stone Bridge
SANDPITS LA
Stonewath Bridge
Hill Top Farm
NORTH ST
EAST NEWTON ROAD
Cemy
CARLTON DR
PH
PO
CARLTON LANE
HIGH ST
HEADLANDS RD
Aldbrough
GUEST FIELD
Daisy Farm
QUEENSMEAD
HEADLANDS DR
Low Farm
Aldbrough Cliff
Carlton Farm
The Roller
Long Leys Farm
Aldbrough Prim Sch
Roller Clump
B1238
HULL RD
GARTON RD
B1242
Holmes Closes

C1
1 ELM GROVE
2 CEDAR GROVE
3 WILLOW GROVE
4 ASH GROVE
5 WENTWORTH GROVE
6 NOTTINGHAM RD
7 CHURCH ST
8 CROSS ST
9 CASTLE PARK

59

B8
1 SHERBURN ST
2 MARKET PL
3 CARDINALS CL
4 OLD BOYS SCHOOL LA
5 GOLD THREAD LA
6 KING ST

D6
1 GREENWAYS DR
2 GREEN WAYS
3 MOORFIELDS
4 HILL TOP RD
5 CHURCH WK
6 GARTH CL
7 GEORGE ST
8 CHURCH HL
9 WOODALL CT

36

F8
1 ASH GR
2 HAWTHORNS
3 CHURCH ST
4 HALL FARM CL
5 VIKING DR
6 THE CRESCENT
7 NORSEMAN CL
8 WEST CT
9 KELFIELD RD

Scale: 1⅓ inches to 1 mile
0 ¼ ½ mile
0 250m 500m 750m 1 km

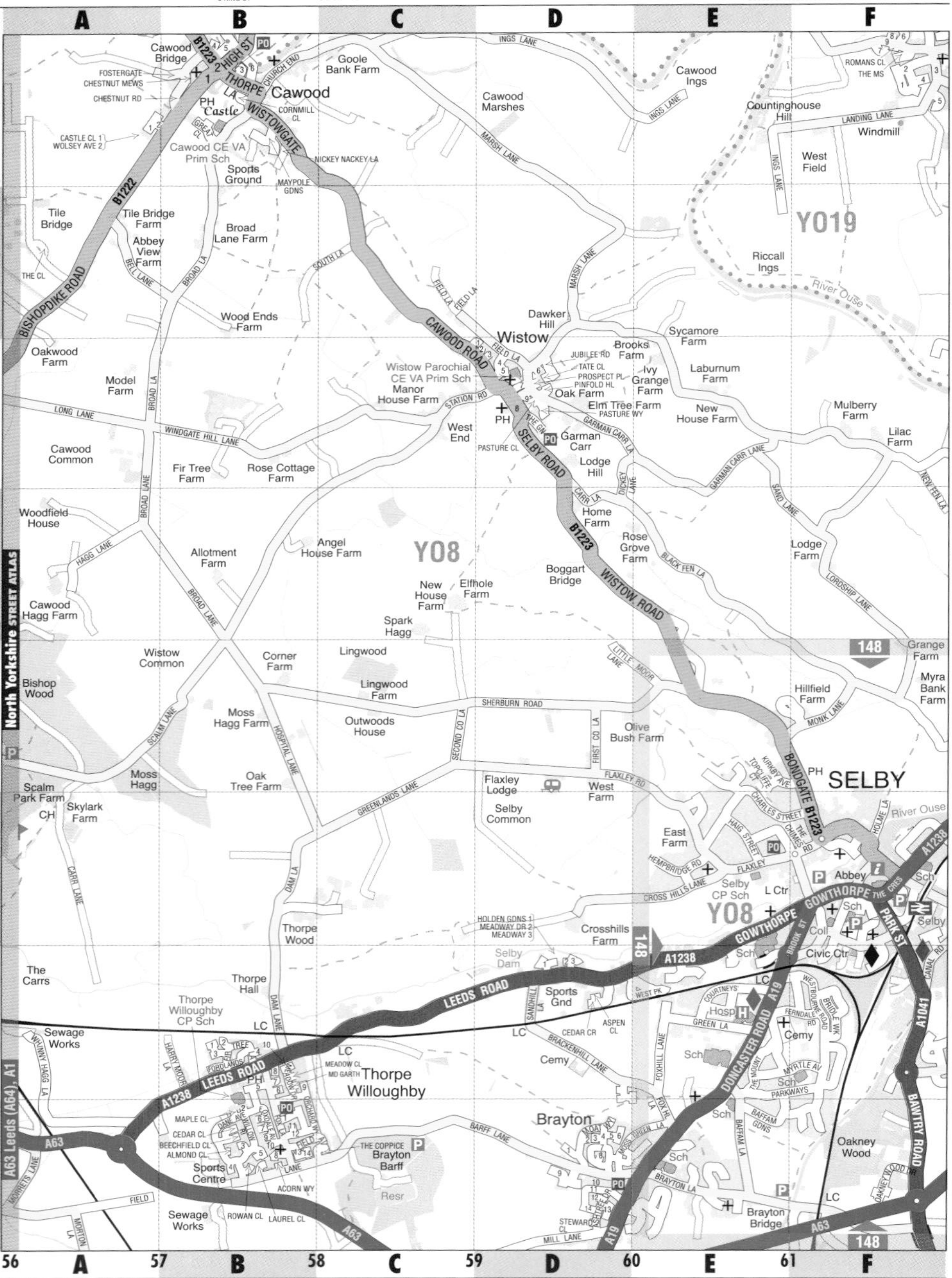

56 A 57 B 58 C 59 D 60 E 61 F

B1
1 SANDWAY DR
2 LIMETREE CL
3 LABURNUM CL
4 BIRCH CL
5 OAK DR
6 SAXON CL
7 NORMAN CL
8 BRAMBLES
9 STUART GR
10 TUDOR CL
11 SANDWAY CL
12 SANDWAY AVE
13 WOOD LA
14 WOOD CL

B2
1 FIR TREE WY
2 PINE TREE CL
3 THE FIR TREES
4 FIR TREE CL
5 LONDESBOROUGH GR
6 BARFF GR
7 FRANCIS CT
8 HOLLY GR
9 LINDEN WY
10 HAWTHORNE CL

62

D1
1 EVERGREEN WY
2 CONIFERS CL
3 GREENACRES GR
4 GREENACRES DR
5 SANDIACRES
6 GREENFIELD DR
7 GREENACRES CR
8 GREENACRES CL
9 ST WILFRID'S CR
10 BARFF CL
11 THE POPLARS
12 MAPLE GR
13 CHERRY TREE CL
14 WILLOW BANK

Scale: 1⅓ inches to 1 mile

0 ¼ ½ mile

0 250m 500m 750m 1 km

A8
1 MANOR GARTH
2 BACK LA
3 SILVER ST
4 NOVA SCOTIA WY
5 DANES CT
6 KING RUDDING CL

37
50

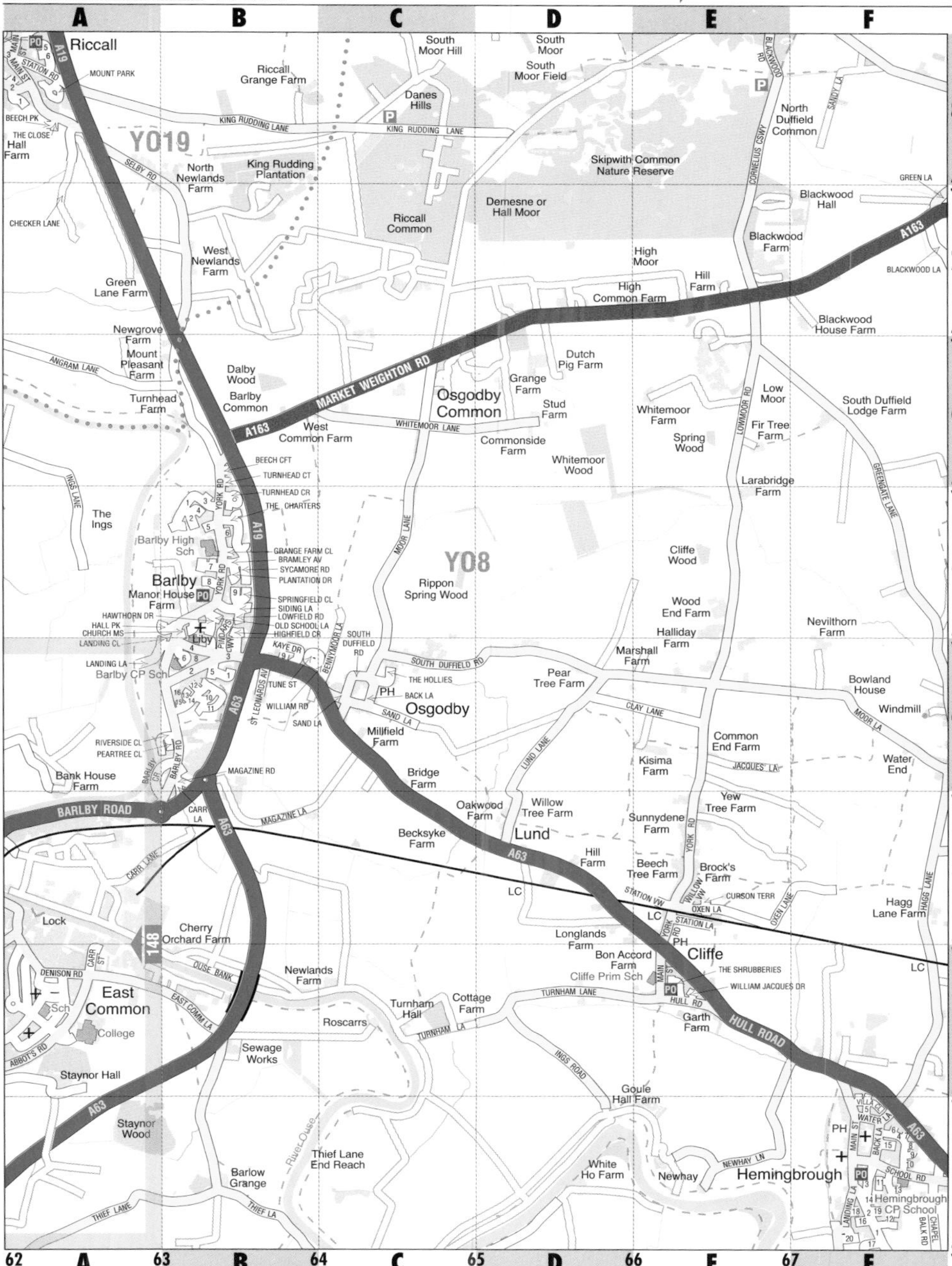

B4
1 GEORGE TERR
2 BARLBY BY-PASS
3 HIGHFIELD VW
4 HOWDEN RD
5 WILFREDS RD
6 ACORN CL
7 CHERRY TREE WK
8 WILFREDS GR
9 THOMPSON CL
10 MAPLE TREE AVE
11 WOODLANDS VIEW
12 CHERRY TREE CT
13 WOODLANDS CT
14 WOODLANDS DR
15 WOODLANDS CL
16 LORDSHIP LA

B5
1 RIVER VW
2 RIVER CL
3 NORTHFIELD
4 DERWENT DR
5 KINGS CL
6 MOOR LA
7 GROVE PK
8 GLEBE GARTH
9 SPRINGFIELD DR

63
50

F1
1 BARMBY FERRY RD
2 MILL LA
3 GARTHENDS LA
4 CHESTNUT GARTH
5 MANOR CL
6 CHESTNUT RISE
7 CHESTNUT CFT
8 CHESTNUT DR
9 CHESTNUT CT
10 CHESTNUT AVE
11 FERRY CL
12 ST MARY'S AVE
13 CARR CL
14 MILL GARTH
15 THE CLOISTERS
16 SOUTHLANDS
17 MILLFIELD RD
18 DURHAM CL
19 NURSERY CL
20 ORCHARD END

A7
1 WILLOW DR
2 OAK RD
3 WESTFIELD RD
4 GARTH AVE
5 MANOR DR
6 MANOR CL

49

38

D7
1 MEADOWFIELD
2 VICARAGE CL
3 STAITHE ST
4 CHURCH CL
5 HONEY POT
6 MANOR CT

Scale: 1⅓ inches to 1 mile
0 ¼ ½ mile
0 250m 500m 750m 1 km

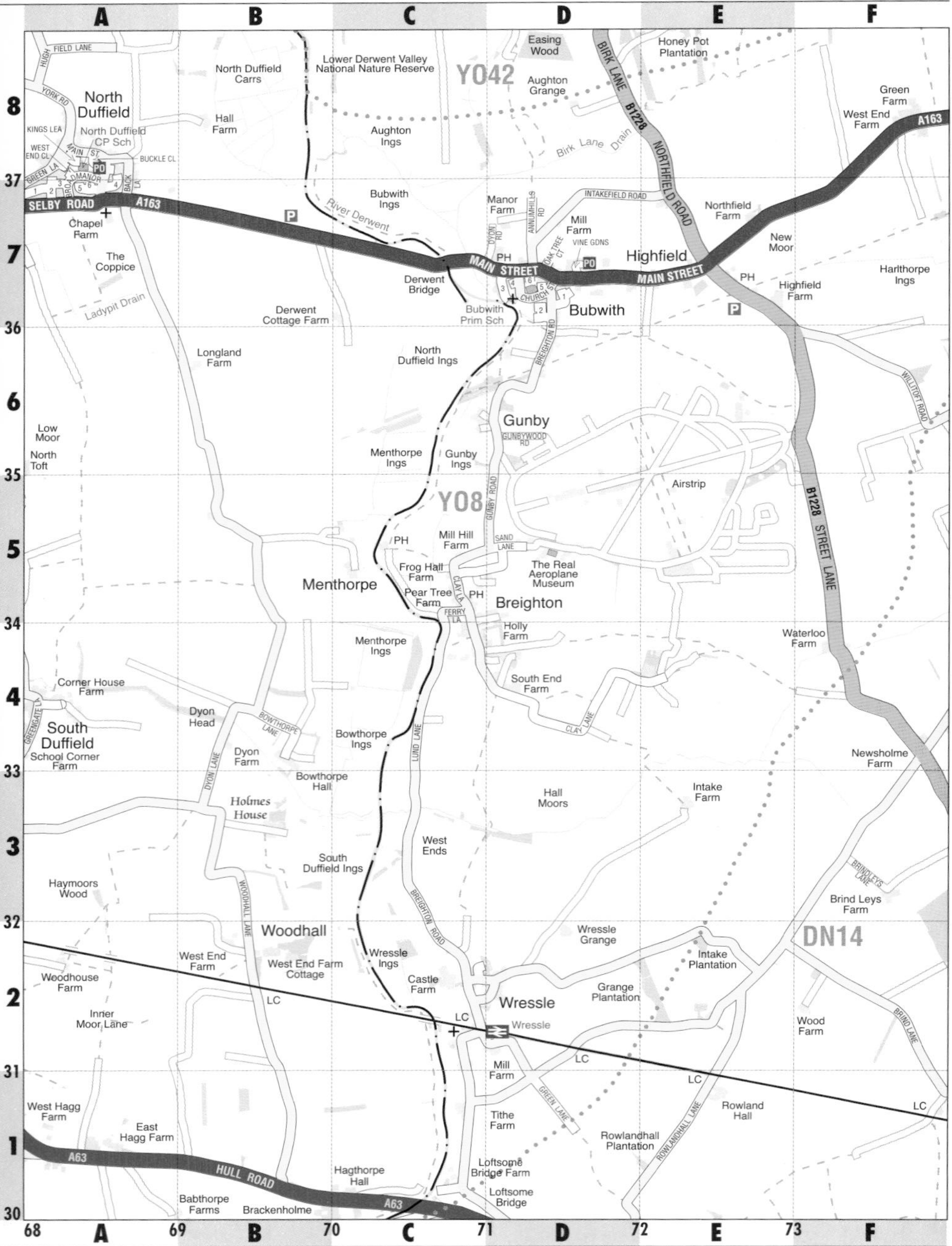

49

64

Scale: 1⅓ inches to 1 mile
0 ¼ ½ mile
0 250m 500m 750m 1 km

39
52

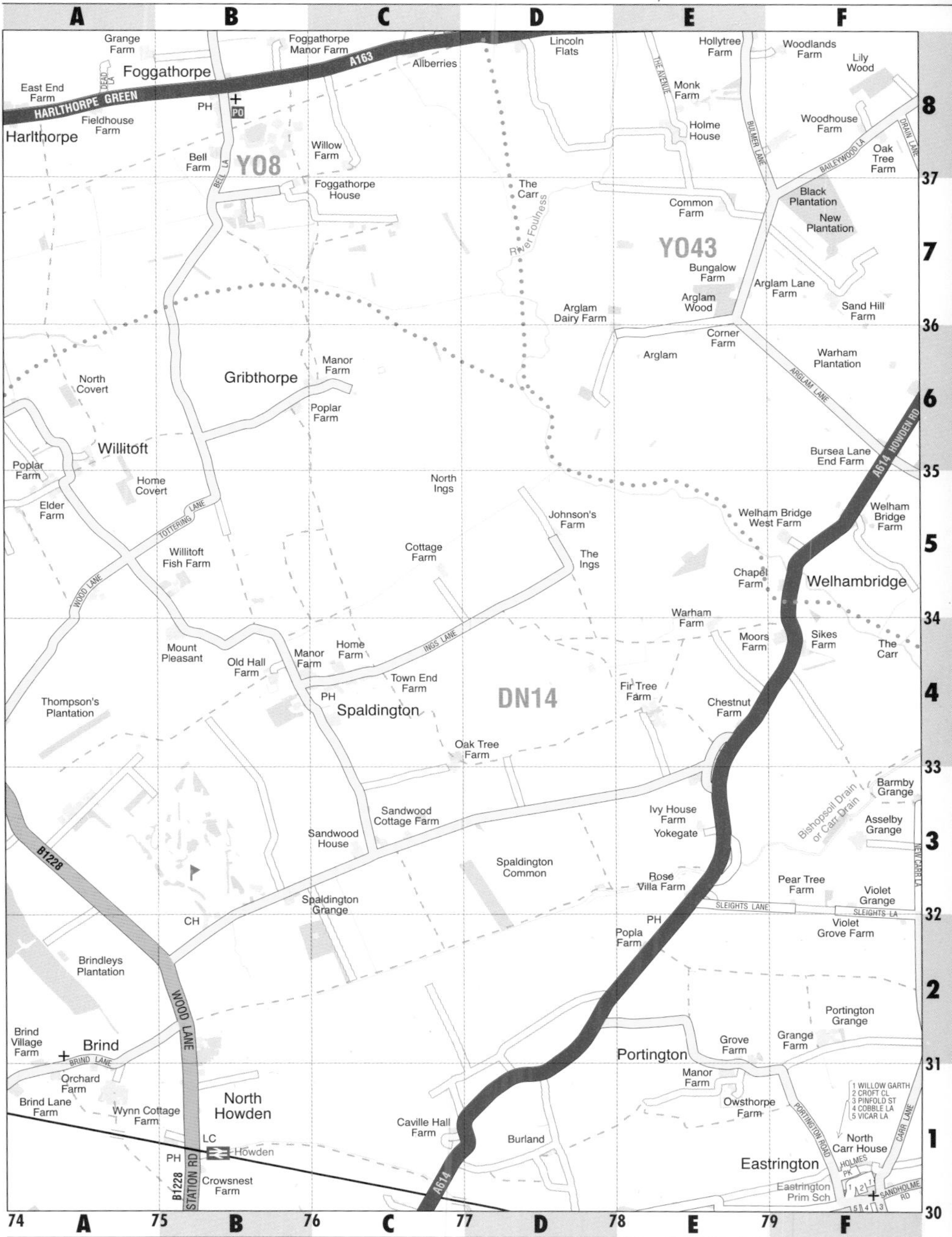

65
52

51
40

Scale: 1⅓ inches to 1 mile
0 ¼ ½ mile
0 250m 500m 750m 1 km

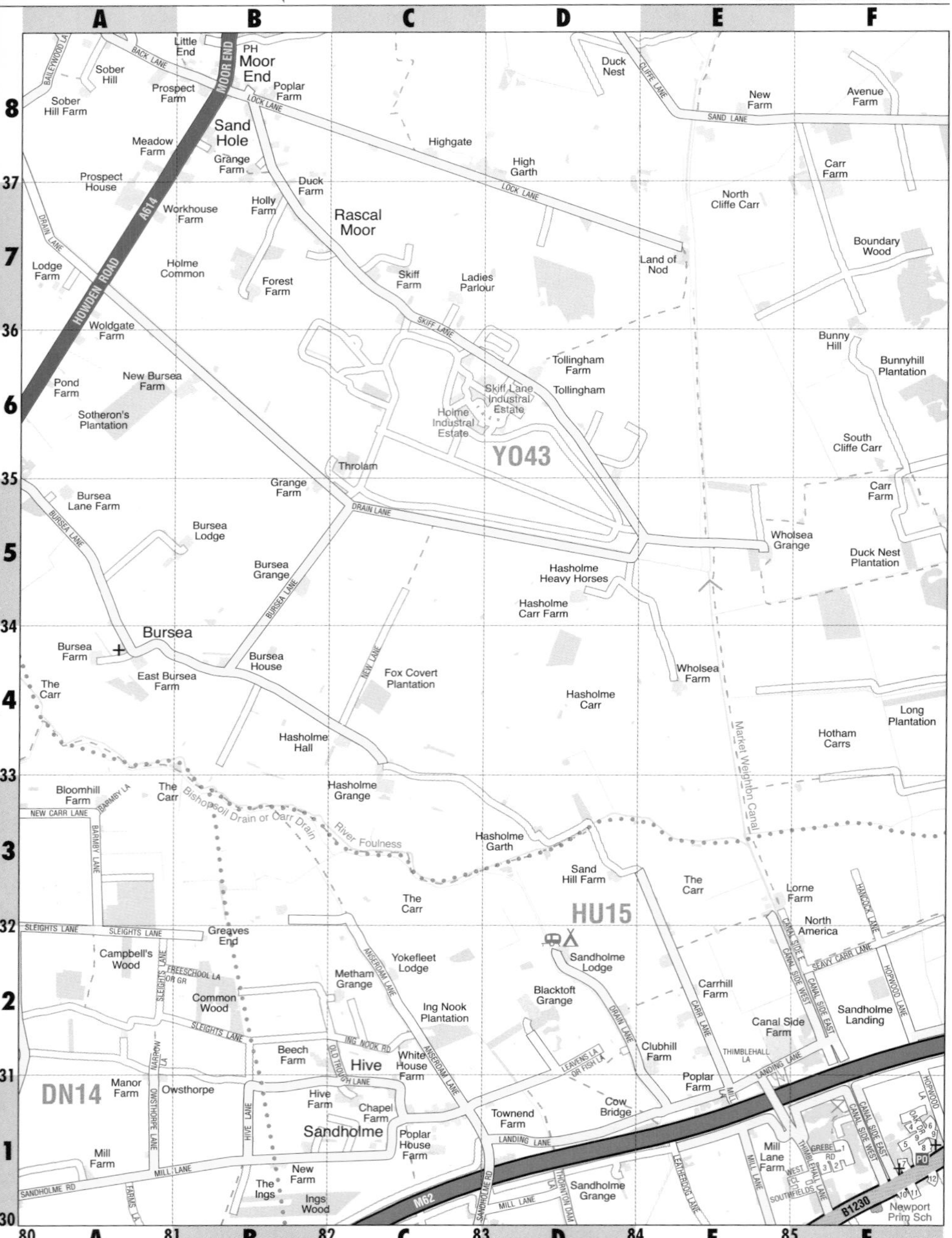

51
66

F1
1 TEAL RD
2 GADWALL CL
3 POCHARD CL
4 BRIAR CL
5 HAWTHORN CL
6 THE SPINNEY
7 OCEAN DR
8 BLACKTHORN CL
9 MEADOW LA
10 TURKS HEAD GDNS
11 VILLAGE FARM CL
12 NETTLE HILL

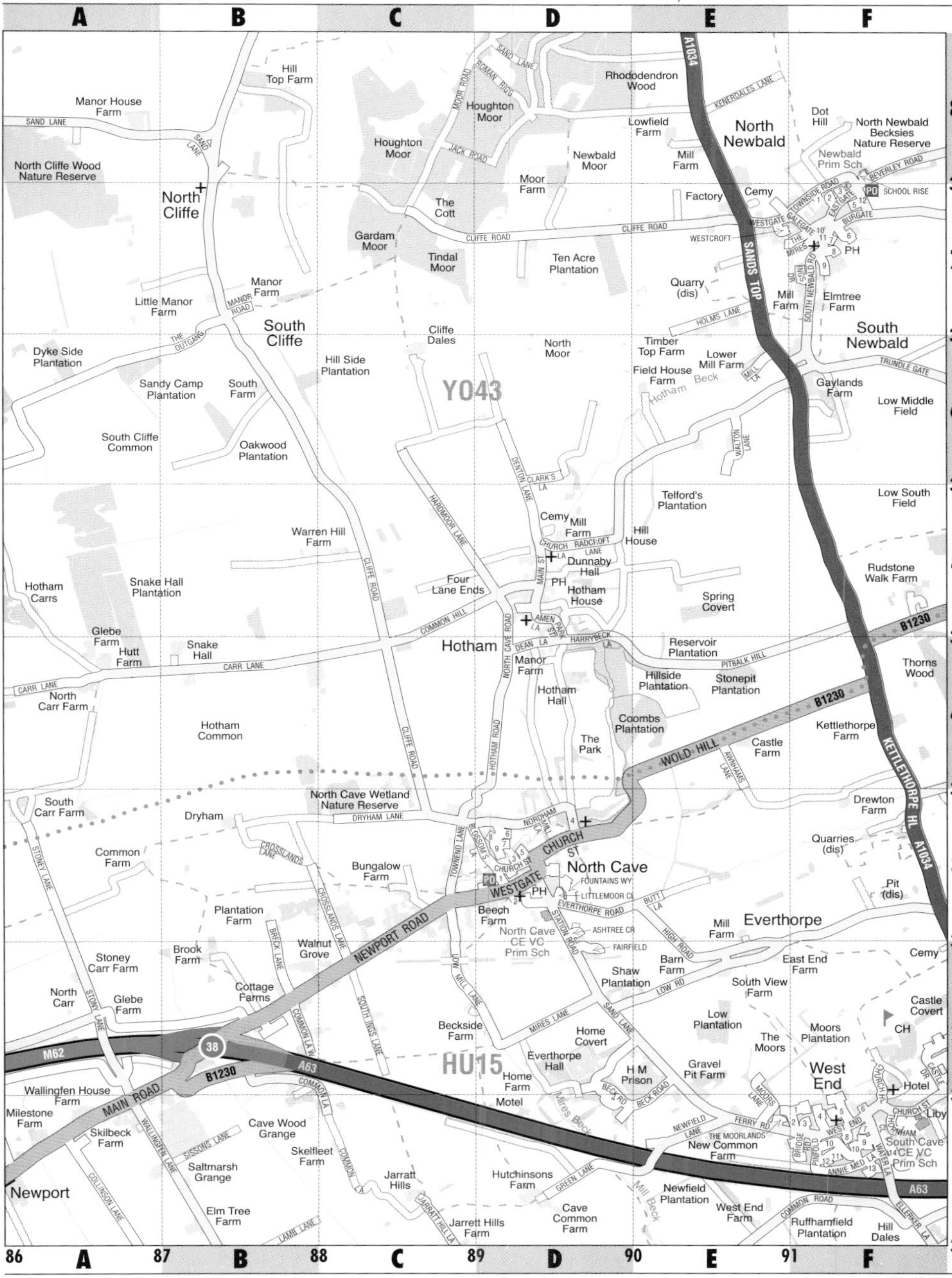
A
B
C
D
E
F
8
37
7
36
6
35
5
34
4
33
3
32
2
31
1
30
86
87
88
89
90
91
Hill Top Farm
Manor House Farm
SAND LANE
SAND LANE
North Cliffe Wood Nature Reserve
North Cliffe
SAND LANE
MOOR ROAD
ROMAN RIGG
Houghton Moor
Houghton Moor
JACK ROAD
Rhododendron Wood
A1034
KENERDALES LANE
Lowfield Farm
North Newbald
Dot Hill
North Newbald Becksies Nature Reserve
Newbald Prim Sch
BEVERLEY ROAD
SCHOOL RISE
Newbald Moor
Mill Farm
Moor Farm
The Cott
Factory
Cemy
TOWNSIDE ROAD
EASTGATE
GALEGATE
BURGATE
WESTGATE
WESTCROFT
THE MIRES
Gardam Moor
CLIFFE ROAD
CLIFFE ROAD
Tindal Moor
Ten Acre Plantation
SANDS TOP
PH
Quarry (dis)
Manor Farm
Little Manor Farm
MANOR ROAD
Mill Farm
SOUTH NEWBALD RD
Elmtree Farm
HOLMS LANE
THE OUTGANG
South Cliffe
Cliffe Dales
North Moor
Timber Top Farm
Lower Mill Farm
South Newbald
Dyke Side Plantation
Hill Side Plantation
Field House Farm
Hotham Beck
MILL LA
TRUNDLE GATE
Gaylands Farm
Sandy Camp Plantation
South Farm
YO43
Low Middle Field
South Cliffe Common
Oakwood Plantation
WALTON LANE
DENTON LANE
CLARK'S LA
HARDMOOR LANE
Telford's Plantation
Low South Field
Cemy
Mill Farm
Hill House
Warren Hill Farm
CHURCH LA
RADCROFT LANE
CLIFFE ROAD
Dunnaby Hall
MAIN ST
Snake Hall Plantation
Four Lane Ends
PH
Hotham House
Spring Covert
Rudstone Walk Farm
Hotham Carrs
COMMON HILL
AMEN LA
PARK ST
NORTH CAVE ROAD
DEAN LA
HARRYBECK LA
B1230
Glebe Farm
Hutt Farm
Snake Hall
Hotham
Reservoir Plantation
Thorns Wood
CARR LANE
CARR LANE
Manor Farm
PITBALK HILL
North Carr Farm
Hotham Hall
Hillside Plantation
Stonepit Plantation
B1230
Hotham Common
HOTHAM ROAD
CLIFFE ROAD
Coombs Plantation
Kettlethorpe Farm
The Park
WOLD HILL
ANNHAMS LANE
Castle Farm
KETTLETHORPE HL
South Carr Farm
North Cave Wetland Nature Reserve
Drewton Farm
Dryham
DRYHAM LANE
NORDHAM
MILL LA
STONEY LANE
CROSSLANDS LANE
TOWNEND LANE
BLOSSOM'S LA
CHURCH ST
CHURCH ST
Quarries (dis)
A1034
Common Farm
Bungalow Farm
North Cave
WESTGATE
PH
FOUNTAINS WY
LITTLEMOOR CL
Pit (dis)
Plantation Farm
Beech Farm
EVERTHORPE ROAD
BUTT LA
North Cave CE VC Prim Sch
ASHTREE CR
STATION ROAD
Mill Farm
Everthorpe
BRECK LANE
CROSSLANDS LANE
HIGH ROAD
Stoney Carr Farm
Brook Farm
Walnut Grove
NEWPORT ROAD
FAIRFIELD
Barn Farm
Shaw Plantation
East End Farm
Cemy
LOW MILL LANE
LOW RD
South View Farm
North Carr
Glebe Farm
Cottage Farms
STONY LANE
COMMON LA
SOUTH INGS LANE
Low Plantation
Castle Covert
Beckside Farm
MIRES LANE
SAND LANE
Home Covert
Moors Plantation
CH
M62
38
The Moors
Everthorpe Hall
HU15
H M Prison
Gravel Pit Farm
West End
CHURCH HL
CASTLE ST
Hotel
B1230
A63
Home Farm
MOORS LANE
Wallingfen House Farm
COMMON LA
BECK RD
BECK ROAD
Motel
Milestone Farm
MAIN ROAD
Mires Beck
NEWFIELD LANE
FERRY RD
WEST END
CHURCH ST
Liby
Skilbeck Farm
WALLINGFEN LANE
Cave Wood Grange
THE MOORLANDS
New Common Farm
BRIDGE RD
PINFOLD
THORNHAM
South Cave CE VC Prim Sch
SISSONS LANE
Saltmarsh Grange
Skelfleet Farm
COMMON LANE
ANNIE MED LA
WATER LA
COLLINSON LANE
Jarratt Hills
Hutchinsons Farm
GREEN LANE
Newfield Plantation
A63
Newport
JARRATT HILL LA
Mill Beck
COMMON ROAD
Elm Tree Farm
LAMB LANE
Jarrett Hills Farm
Cave Common Farm
West End Farm
Ruffhamfield Plantation
ELLERKER LA
Hill Dales
A
B
C
D
E
F

Scale: 1⅓ inches to 1 mile
0 ¼ ½ mile
0 250m 500m 750m 1 km

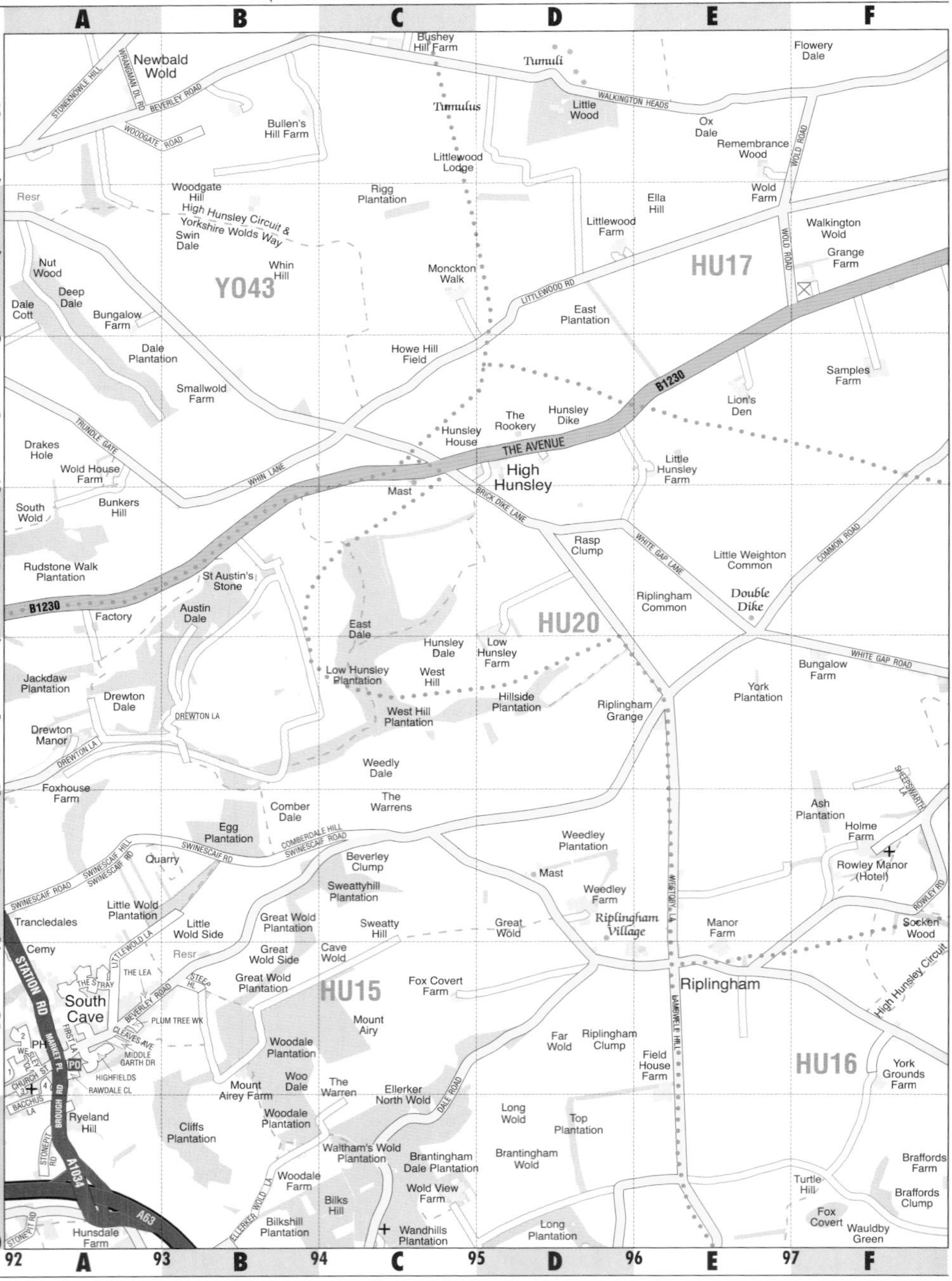

A2
1 CASTLE RISE
2 THE PARKLANDS
3 WOLD VW
4 SOUTHCOTE CL

Scale: 1⅓ inches to 1 mile

0 ¼ ½ mile

0 250m 500m 750m 1 km

B7
1 LAWSON CL
2 FERGUSON RD
3 ALL HALLOWS RD
4 WEST MILL RISE
5 TAYLORS CL

B8
1 WESTFIELD GARTH
2 MIDDLEHOWE GN
3 BIRCH LEA
4 SAUNDERS CFT

C8
1 AUTHERD GARTH
2 WAUDBY CL
3 MEADOW WY
4 SHERWOOD CL

D8
1 SPEEDWELL LA
2 THE HAVEN
3 HAYWARD CL
4 NIGHTINGALE CL
5 HUZZARD CL
6 ORIEL CL
7 ASH DENE

43 136 56

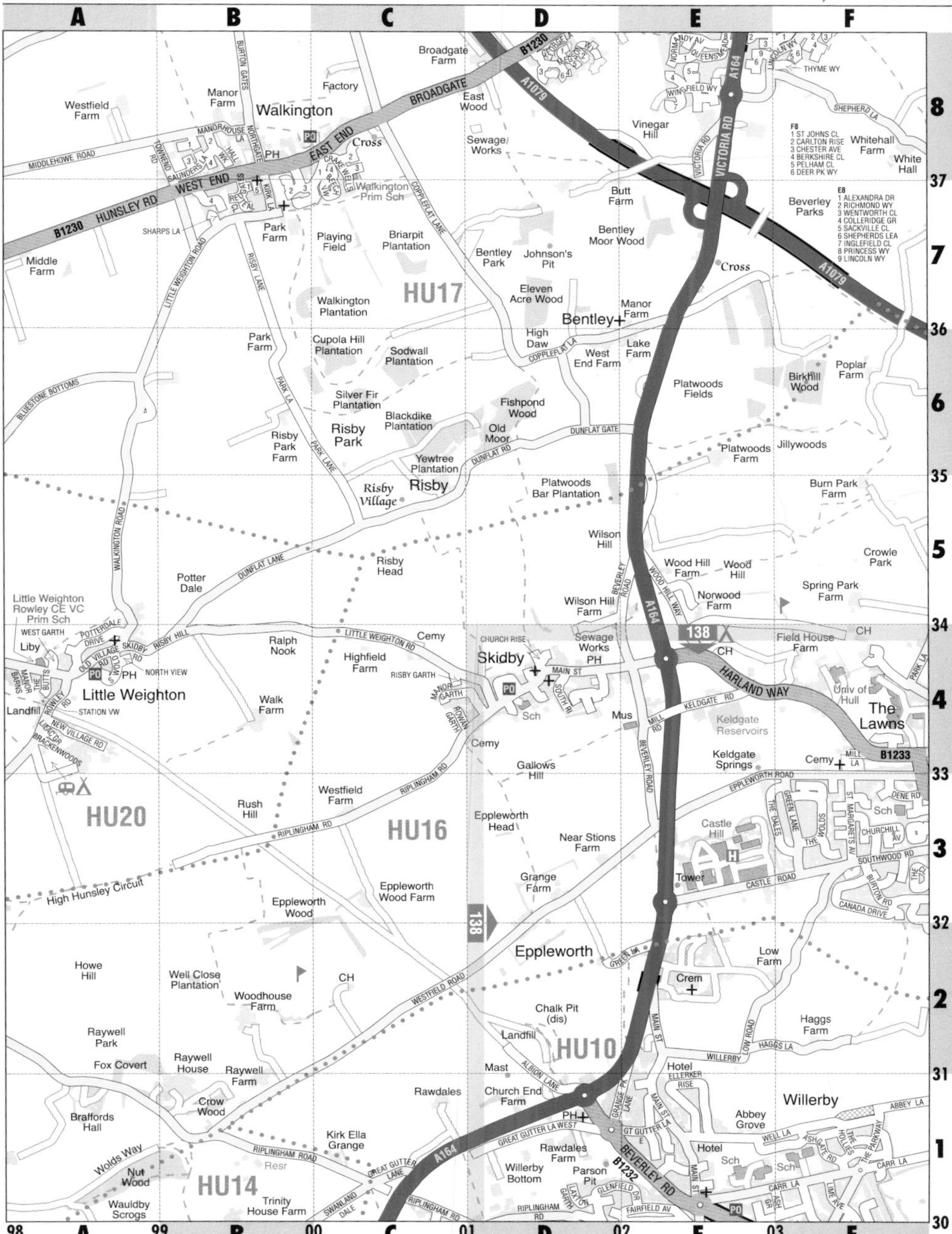

69 139 143

For full street detail of the highlighted area see page 138.

F6
1 ARNCLIFFE CL
2 KETTLEWELL CL
3 WYTHERSTONE CL
4 KILKOY DR
5 SEDBURY CL
6 TRENT PK
7 KINGSBURY WY
8 RAINSWOOD CL
9 FRENSHAM CL
10 RAUCEBY CL
11 GRANTHAM AVE
12 EMBERTON PK
13 THURLSTONE CL
14 GREYGARTH CL
15 KINDERSCOUT CL
16 SAPPERTON CL
17 'YKEHAM CL
18 ƷEDGEBROOK GR
19 QUARRINGTON GR
20 WOOLSTHORPE GR
21 SLEIGHTHOLME CL
22 BRECON DR
23 SALCEY CL
24 BRANDON WY
25 LANGLEY PK
26 EMBERTON PK
27 BLACKWATER WY
28 FINDON CL
29 SALTWELL PK
30 KELBERDALE CL
31 NOSELEY WY
32 HIGHGROVE WY
33 CHURCH RD
34 PENNYHOLME CL

55 137 44

Scale: 1⅓ inches to 1 mile
0 ¼ ½ mile
0 250m 500m 750m 1 km

144 138 145

For full street detail of the highlighted area see pages 139 and 140.

F5
1 BROOKFIELD CL
2 GRIMSCOTT CL
3 CAMBEAK CL
4 DULVERTON CL
5 ASHWORTHY CL
6 COOKBURY CL
7 PADSTOW CL
8 MALPAS CL
9 PENROSE CL
10 KINGSCOTT CL
11 TOWAN CL
12 CAMELFORD CL
13 BLISLAND CL
14 CHERITON CL
15 HARLEQUIN DR
16 FOXGLOVE CL
17 JASMINE GR
18 BEAMSLEY WY
19 MASPIN CL
20 BOSTON CT
21 EVERSFIELD CL
22 KEYNES PK
23 LAVENDER CL
24 FERRY MDW PK
25 KNOLE PK
26 SHILLING CL
27 HARTSHOLME PK
28 TOLLYMORE PK
29 MARBURY PK
30 BRADGATE PK
31 TEMPLEWATERS
32 PARCEVALL DR

Scale: 1⅓ inches to 1 mile
0 ¼ ½ mile
0 250m 500m 750m 1 km

A6
1 HARLECH CL
2 LEITHOLM CL
3 BORTHWICK CL
4 SNOWHILL CL
5 RISHWORTH CL
6 RANNOCH CL
7 APPIN CL
8 MOORFOOT CL
9 RANGELEY CL
10 HELVELLYN CL
11 GRASSINGTON CL
12 WHERNSIDE CL
13 WHITEHOPE CL
14 BLACKHOPE CL
15 PYKESTONE CL
16 DALKEITH CL
17 LADYSIDE CL
18 PENDLE CL
19 SADDLEWORTH CL

45
58

A5
1 ABINGDON GARTH
2 BINBROOK GARTH
3 SELWORTHY CL
4 RINGSTEAD GARTH
5 COSFORD GARTH
6 HAYDOCK GARTH
7 SKILGATE CL
8 ALLERFORD DR
9 LYNMOUTH CL
10 BOSSINGTON CL
11 PITSFOLD CL
12 CLEEVE DR
13 MYLOR CL
14 FINNINGLEY GARTH
15 GATWICK GARTH
16 HUCKNALL GARTH
17 INNSWORTH GARTH
18 YATESBURY GARTH
19 SWINDERBY GARTH
20 ENSTONE GARTH

B5
1 JASON GARTH
2 KINLOSS GARTH
3 LEEMING GARTH
4 MANSTON GARTH
5 DRUMMOND CT
6 LEADHILLS WY
7 DOWNHILL DR
8 MAIDEN CT
9 NEATSHEAD GARTH

146
58
147
For full street detail of the highlighted area see pages 141 and 142.

57

46

Scale: 1⅓ inches to 1 mile

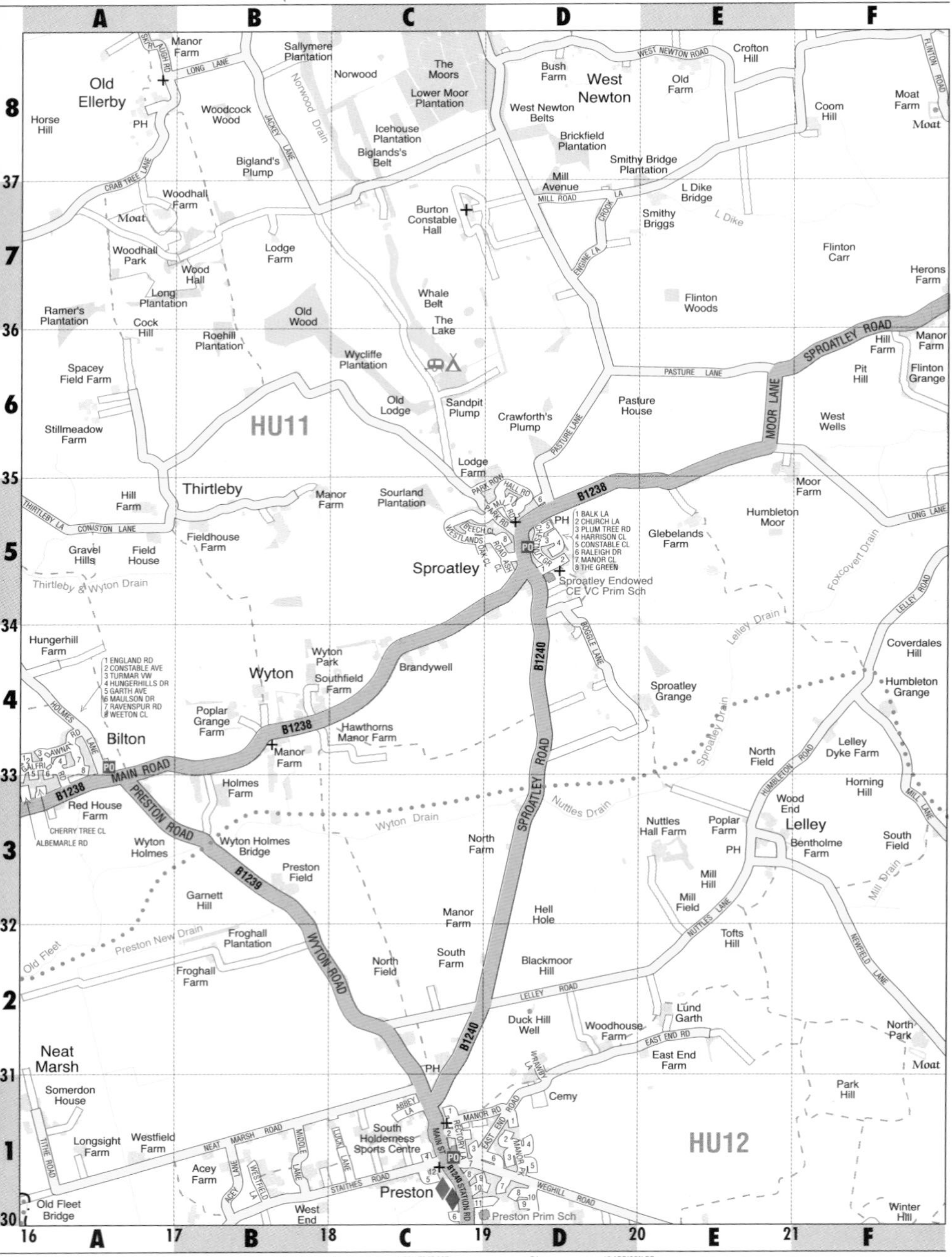

C1
1 NESS LA
2 KIRK RD
3 THORNTON GR
4 PINFOLD CT
5 VILLAGE FARM RD
6 HELMS AV
7 SCHOOL RD
8 SYCAMORE CL
9 BROCKLE BANK CT
10 OAK TREE EST
11 ELDON DR
12 CHAPEL CL

D1
1 HIGHFIELD RISE
2 GARBUTT CL
3 GRASSAM CL
4 ELLIS CL
5 HUNTER CL
6 PEACE WK
7 RANDS EST
8 WATKINSON CL
9 BARTLETT CL
10 ADDISON RD

142

72

Scale: 1⅓ inches to 1 mile
0 ¼ ½ mile
0 250m 500m 750m 1 km

47 60

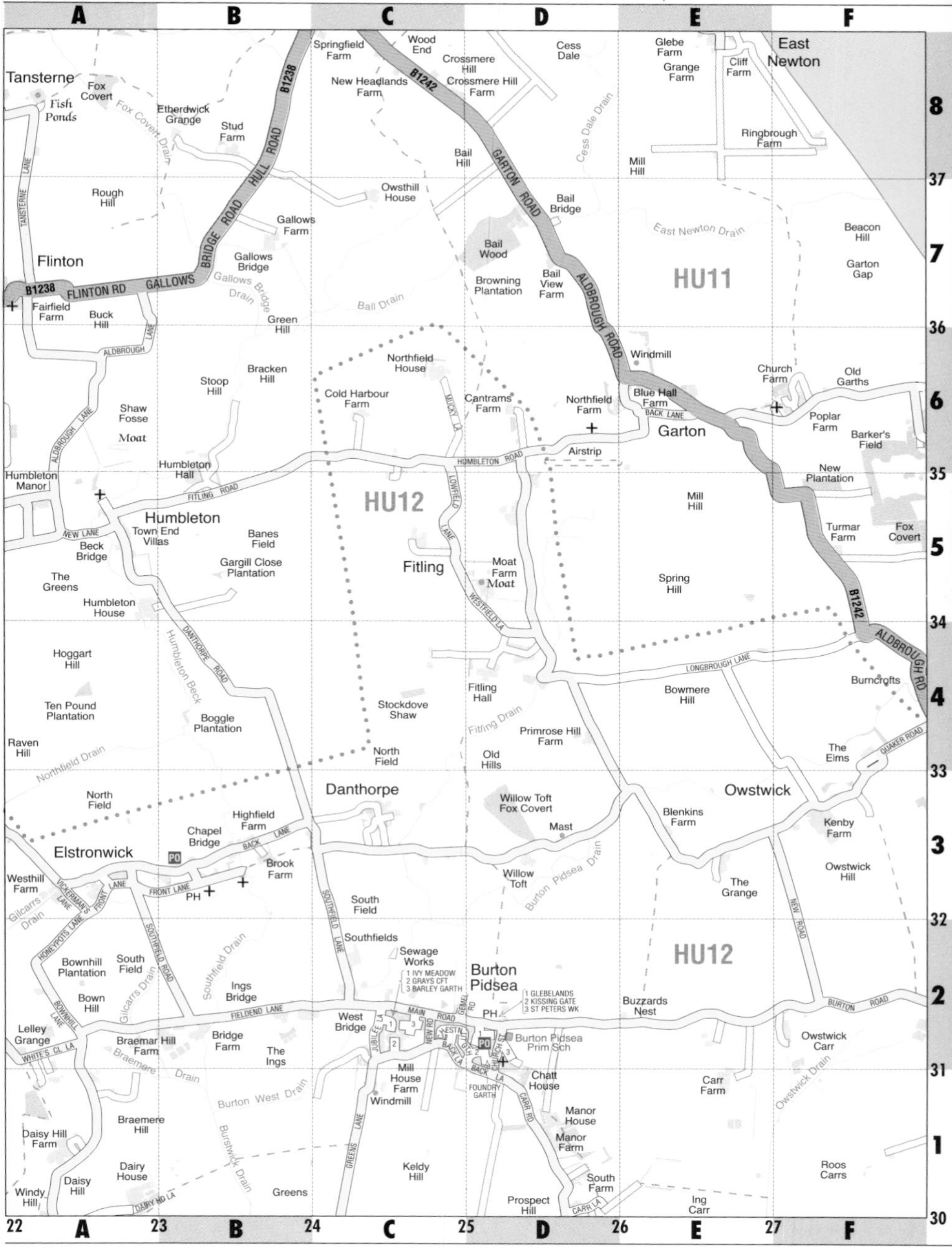

73 60

59

Scale: 1⅓ inches to 1 mile
0 ¼ ½ mile
0 250m 500m 750m 1 km

A
B
C
D
E
F
8
37
7
36
6
35
5
34
4
33
3
32
2
31
1
30
28
29
30
31
32
33
Great Parks
The Mount
Moat Farm
Moat
Sewage Works
Grimston Garth
Grimston Park
Bracken Hill
Norwood Plantation
HU11
Admiral Storr's Tower
Glebe Farm
Tunstall Pastures
TOWER ROAD
Mayfield Farm
Mount Farm
Hilston
Pit (dis)
PASTURES LANE
HOGSEA LANE
QUAKER RD
Gills Mere
Monkwith
B1242
The Furze
Roos Furze
East Furze
North End Farm
Mill Hill
ALDBROUGH ROAD
West Furze
Glebe Farm
PASTURES LANE
RECTORY LA
HU12
Church Farm
FURZE ROAD
Westhill Farm
Furze Farm
Town Farm
MAIN ST
Manor Farm
SEASIDE LANE
SEASIDE LANE
Tunstall
Kiln House
Elmtree Farm
Carr Farm
PH
Kiln Well
KILNHOUSE LA
Cliff Farm
BURTON ROAD
ROSTUN ROAD
Poplar Farm
NORTH END RD
North End Villas
North End
East Field
Tunstall Hall
Sewage Works
PINFOLD LA
Hill Top Farm
Cote Farm
Roos CE VC Prim Sch
1 HINCH GARTH
2 BEECHWOOD VWS
3 PILMAR LA
Round Close Plantation
MAIN ST
PILMAR LANE
B1242
SOUTHFIELD LANE
Tunstall Drain
RECTORY RD
PO
INGLEPOOL CORNER
Roos
PH
Tedder Hill
Cherry Hill
HU19
Redhouse Farm
EASTFIELD EST
WITHERNSEA RD
HODGSON LA
Broom Hill
SOUTH PK
Thirtle Bridge
CHESTNUT GARTH
THIRTLE BR LA
Renish
AMB LA
SOUTH END RD
ELM GARTH
Burnham Carrs
Butcher Bridge

59

74

Scale: 1⅓ inches to 1 mile
0 ¼ ½ mile
0 250m 500m 750m 1 km

A8
1 DEER PK CT
2 PRIORY PARK GR
3 PRIORY PARK CL
4 CHURCH LA
5 OLD VICARAGE LA
6 ORCHARD CL
7 THE MEADOWS
8 HILLCREST
9 HILLSIDE CL
10 CHESTNUT GREEN

A7
1 PINE TREE LA
2 ROSE LEA CL
3 HILLAM HALL VW
4 HILLAM HALL LA
5 HILLAM HALL CL
6 BEDFORDS FOLD

62

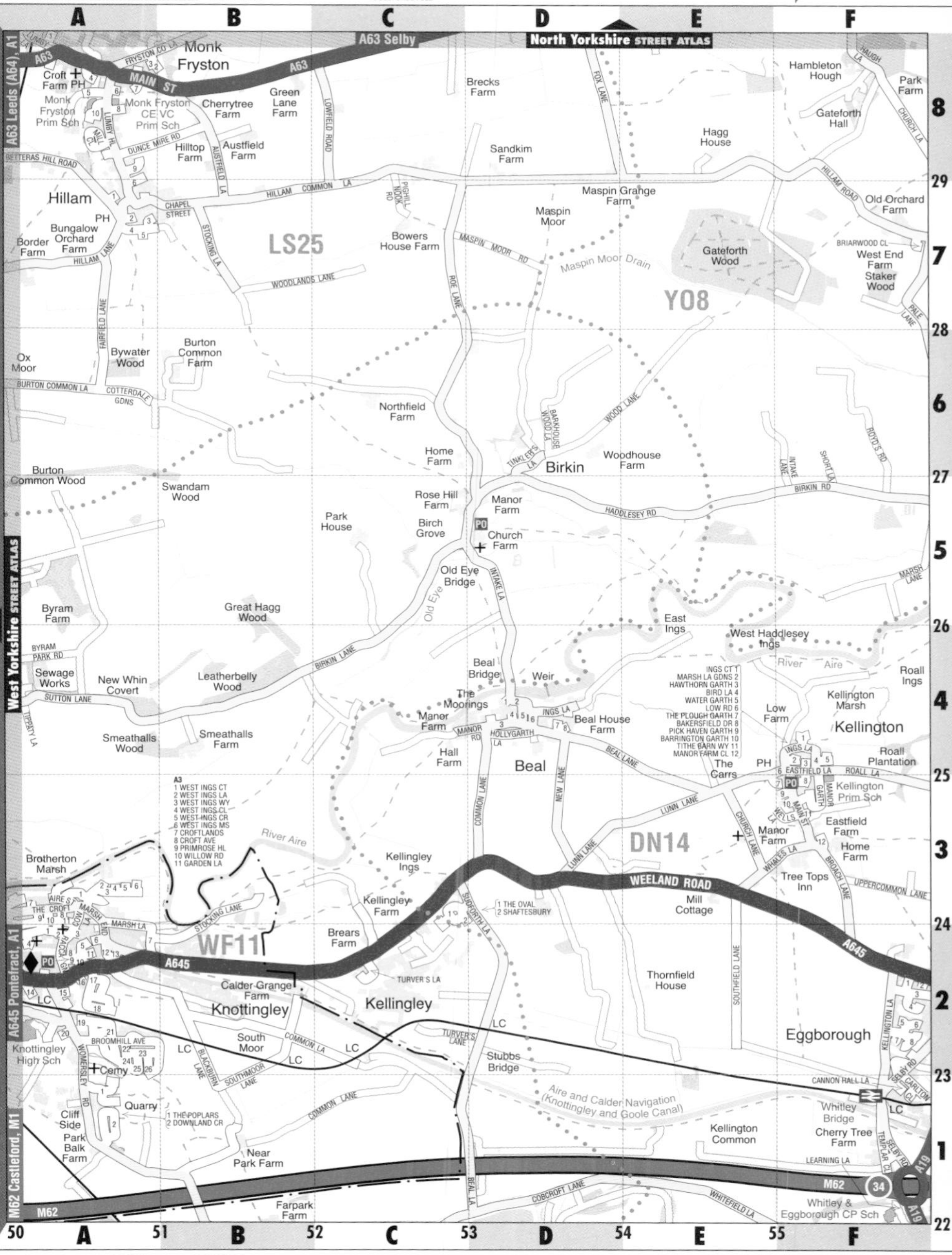

A2
1 PRIMROSE VALE
2 TITHE BARN RD
3 SUNNY BANK
4 ST BOLTOPHS CL
5 FOUNDRY LA
6 FERNLEY GREEN CL
7 TRUNDLES LA
8 GRENLEY ST
9 LAMB INN RD
10 EAST VW
11 RACCA AVE
12 HARKER ST
13 LOW GN
14 MIDDLE LA
15 GILLANN ST
16 WEELAND CT
17 SPRINGFIELDS AVE
18 SPRINGFIELDS
19 BROOMHILL GR
20 QUARRY AVE
21 BROOMHILL WK
22 BROOMHILL PL
23 BROOMHILL CL
24 BROOMHILL SQ
25 BROOMHILL CR
26 BROOMHILL DR

76

D4
1 GARTH MILL
2 MARSH LA
3 MAIN ST
4 RIVERDALE
5 CRAVEN GARTH
6 BROAD LA
7 VILLAGE FARM CT
8 GABLES CL

62

F2
1 WESTFIELD RD
2 WESTFIELD CL
3 WESTFIELD AVE
4 WESTFIELD GR
5 TABARD HAMLET
6 TABARD RD
7 THE TABARDS
8 THE HAMLET

61
48
148

Scale: 1⅓ inches to 1 mile
0 ¼ ½ mile
0 250m 500m 750m 1 km

61
77

Scale: 1⅓ inches to 1 mile
0 ¼ ½ mile
0 250m 500m 750m 1 km

49
64

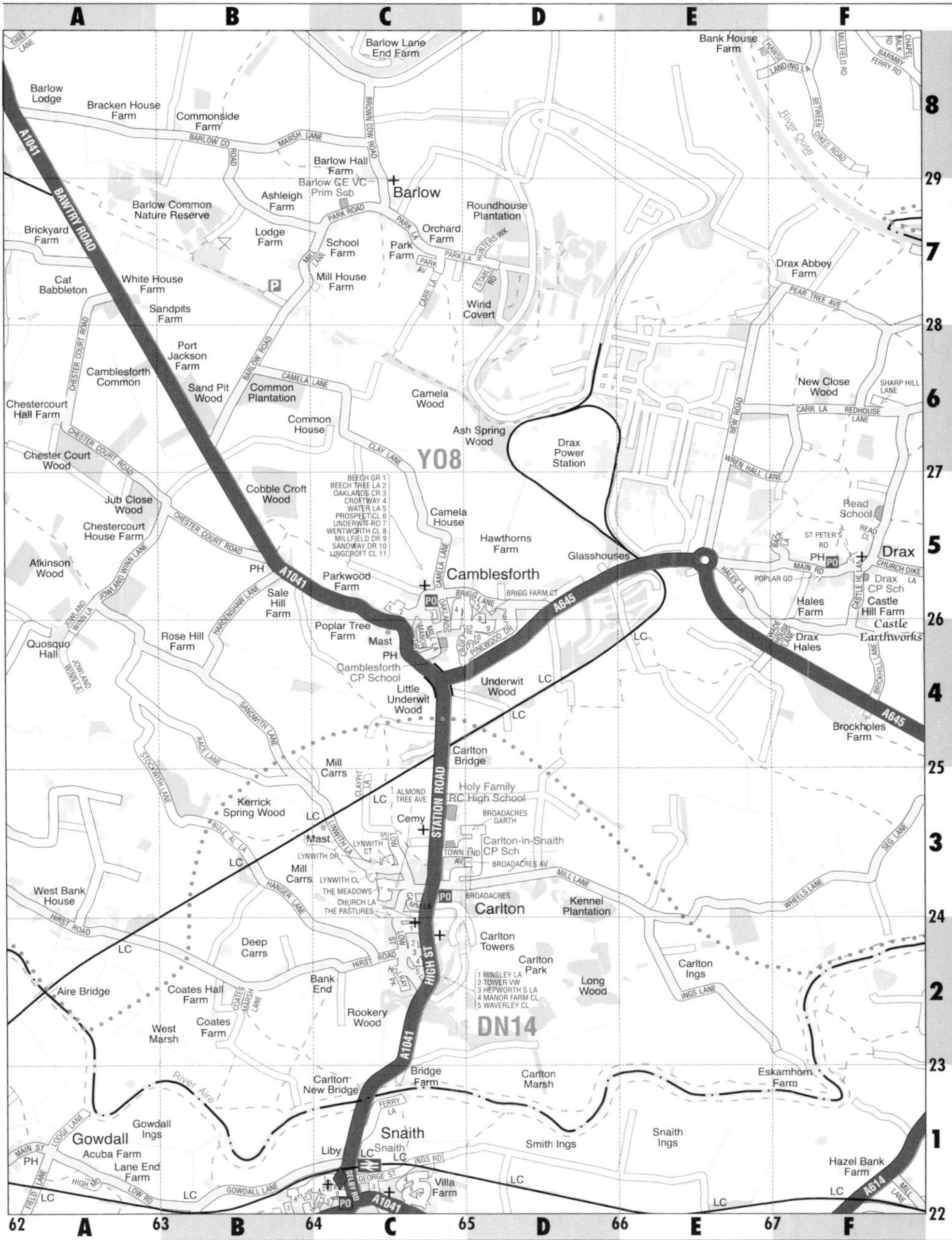

B1
1 PRIORY WAY
2 DAWNAY GARTH
3 MARINA AVE
4 YARBURGH CL

C1
1 PRIORY LA
2 CHURCH LA
3 BUTTLE LA
4 VILLA FIELDS
5 LODGE GDNS
6 SAFFRON DR
7 LABURNUM CL
8 BUTTER MKT
9 MARKET PL
10 JASMINE CL

78
64

63
50

Scale: 1⅓ inches to 1 mile
0 ¼ ½ mile
0 250m 500m 750m 1 km

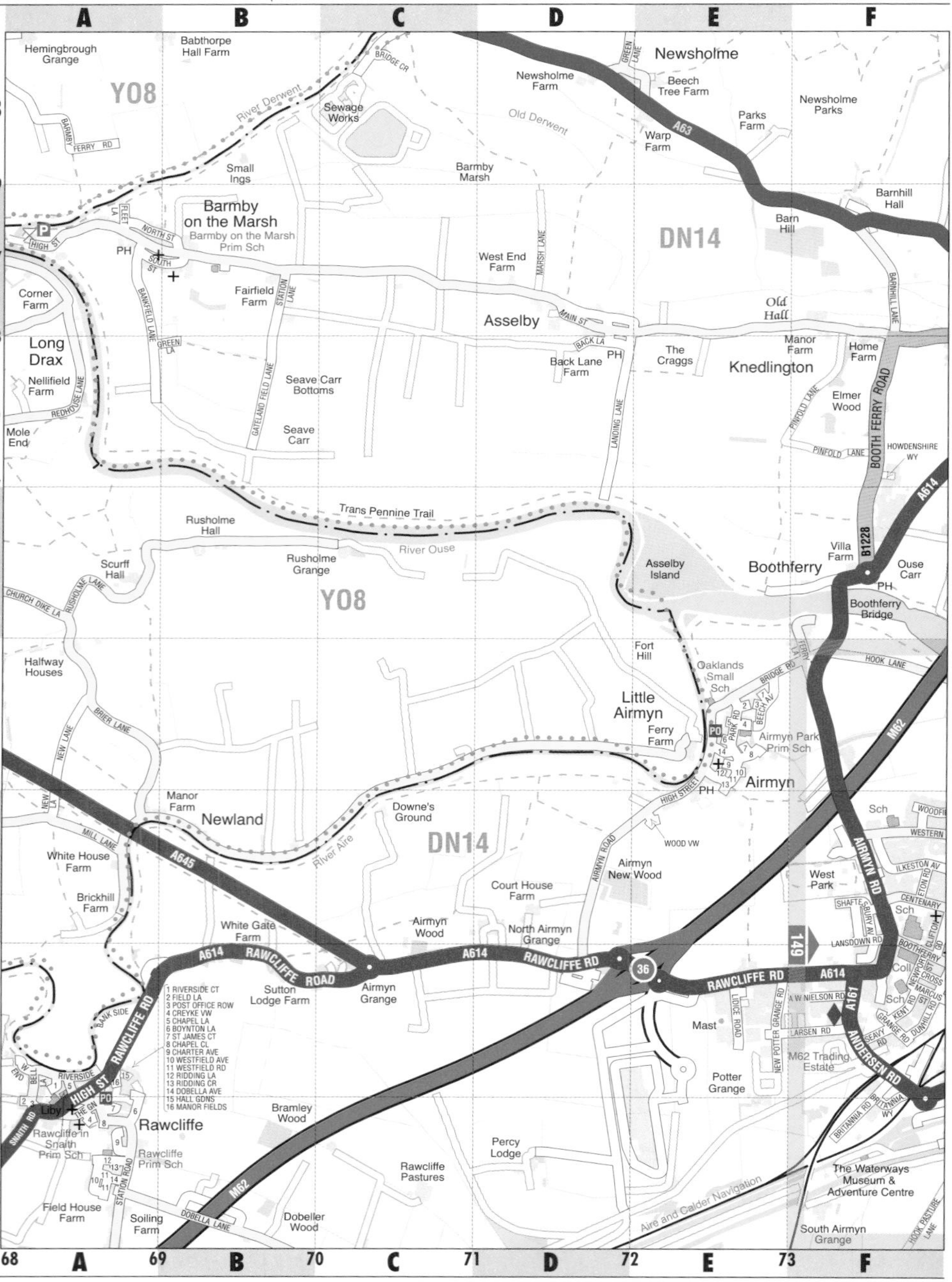

63
79

E4
1 BEECH GR
2 CHESTNUT AVE
3 BEECH AVE
4 PERCY DR
5 HALL CL
6 PARK CL
7 COURTS CL
8 WOODLAND WY
9 ST DAVID'S VW
10 PARSONS CL
11 PARSON'S WK
12 CHURCH VW
13 THE CROSSINGS
14 THE PADDOCK

Scale: 1⅓ inches to 1 mile
0 ¼ ½ mile
0 250m 500m 750m 1 km

A7
1 GOWDALL WY
2 WILLERBY DR
3 WRANGBROOK CL
4 SANDHOLME WY
5 WOODINGS CT
6 SPRINGHEAD CL
7 BATTY LA
8 DREWTON CT
9 WEIGHTON CT
10 BRIERLEY CL
11 MINSTER CT
12 MILTON CL
13 THE VINERY
14 KENSINGTON GDNS
15 ST JOHN'S ST
16 ST PETER'S CL
17 MARSH END
18 SKIRLAW CL
19 PEARTREE PK
20 NORTHOLMBY ST

51
66

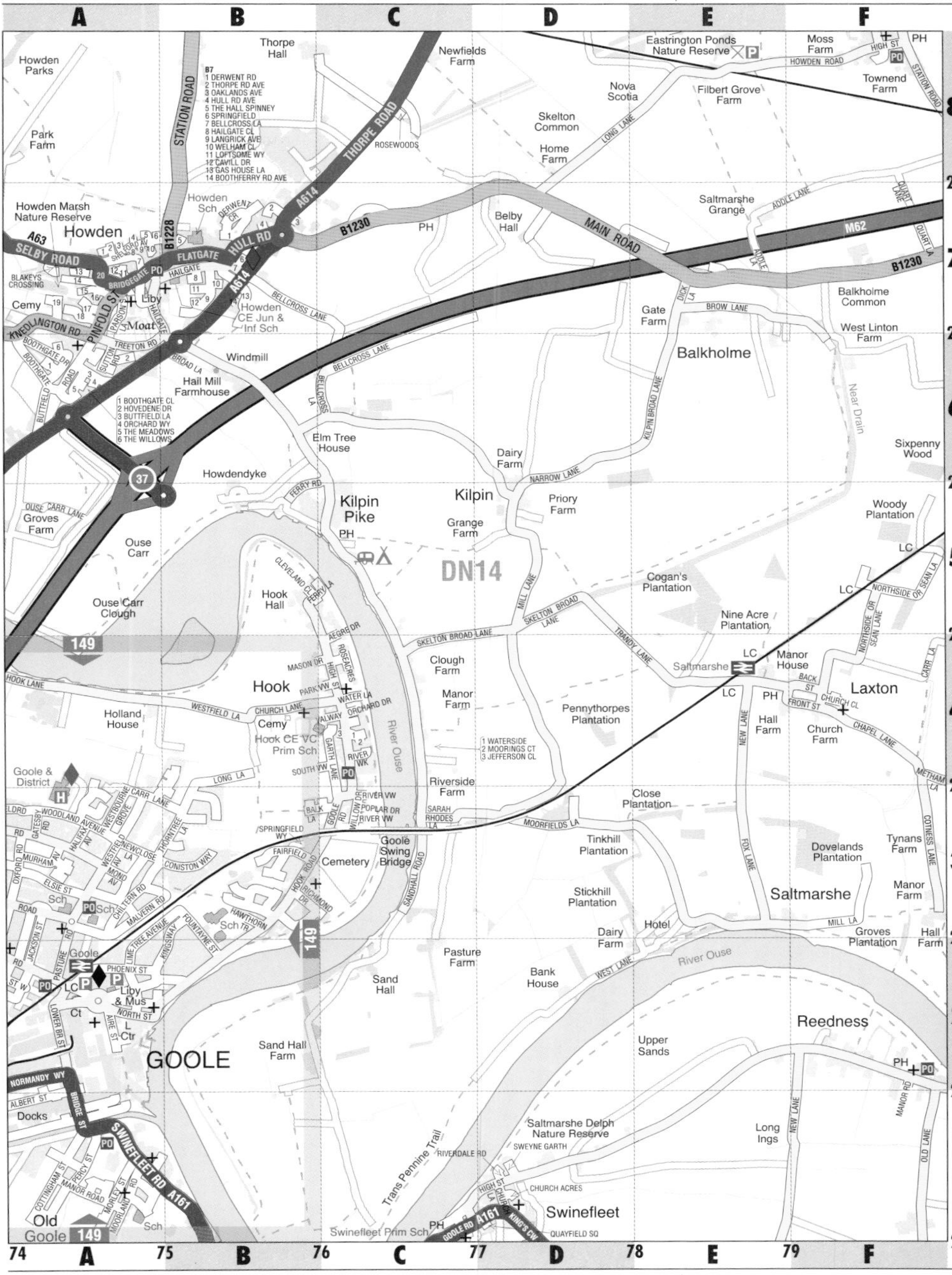

80
66

For full street detail of the highlighted area see page 149.

65
52

D8
1 SANDHOLME CL
2 THE PEPPERCORNS
3 VICTORIA DR
4 ST STEPHEN'S CR
5 HANSARD CR
6 HANSARD DR
7 WILLOW GN
8 CHAPEL MEADOWS
9 BISHOP CT
10 MANOR DR
11 CHAPEL GARTH
12 WESTBROOK RD
13 THE PADDOCK
14 SYCAMORE CL
15 CHESTNUT DR
16 CHERRY CT
17 LABURNUM WK

Scale: 1⅓ inches to 1 mile
0 ¼ ½ mile
0 250m 500m 750m 1 km

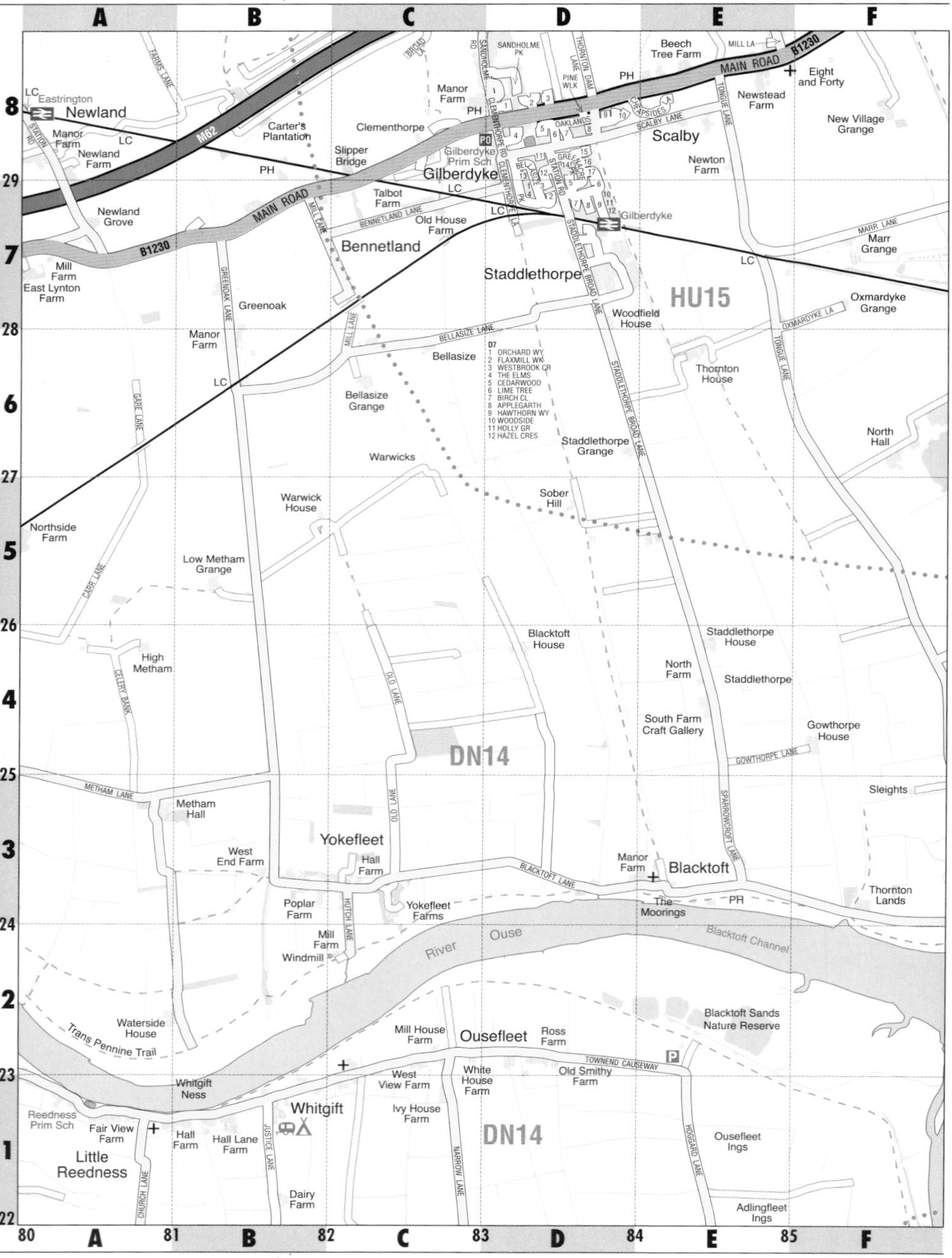
A B C D E F
8 29 7 28 6 27 5 26 4 25 3 24 2 23 1 22
80 81 82 83 84 85
Eastrington
Newland
Manor Farm
Newland Farm
Newland Grove
Mill Farm
East Lynton Farm
M62
Carter's Plantation
Slipper Bridge
MAIN ROAD
B1230
Clementhorpe
Manor Farm
Gilberdyke Prim Sch
Gilberdyke
Talbot Farm
Old House Farm
Bennetland
BENNETLAND LANE
MILL LANE
GREENOAK LANE
Greenoak
Manor Farm
BELLASIZE LANE
Bellasize
Bellasize Grange
Staddlethorpe
SANDHOLME PK
THORNTON DAM LANE
PINE WLK
OAKLANDS
Beech Tree Farm
MILL LA
Eight and Forty
Newstead Farm
SCALBY LANE
Scalby
New Village Grange
Newton Farm
MARR LANE
Marr Grange
Oxmardyke Grange
OXMARDYKE LA
TONGUE LANE
HU15
Woodfield House
Thornton House
STADDLETHORPE BROAD LANE
D7
1 ORCHARD WY
2 FLAXMILL WK
3 WESTBROOK CR
4 THE ELMS
5 CEDARWOOD
6 LIME TREE
7 BIRCH CL
8 APPLEGARTH
9 HAWTHORN WY
10 WOODSIDE
11 HOLLY GR
12 HAZEL CRES
Staddlethorpe Grange
North Hall
Warwicks
Sober Hill
Warwick House
Northside Farm
GARE LANE
CARR LANE
Low Metham Grange
High Metham
CELERY BANK
Blacktoft House
Staddlethorpe House
North Farm
Staddlethorpe
OLD LANE
South Farm Craft Gallery
Gowthorpe House
GOWTHORPE LANE
DN14
METHAM LANE
Metham Hall
Sleights
SPARROWCROFT LANE
Yokefleet
West End Farm
Hall Farm
BLACKTOFT LANE
Manor Farm
Blacktoft
Thornton Lands
Poplar Farm
HUTCH LANE
Yokefleet Farms
The Moorings
Mill Farm
Windmill
River Ouse
Blacktoft Channel
Blacktoft Sands Nature Reserve
Waterside House
Trans Pennine Trail
Mill House Farm
Ousefleet
Ross Farm
TOWNEND CAUSEWAY
Whitgift Ness
West View Farm
White House Farm
Old Smithy Farm
Whitgift
Ivy House Farm
DN14
Reedness Prim Sch
Fair View Farm
Hall Farm
Hall Lane Farm
JUSTICE LANE
NARROW LANE
HOGGARD LANE
Ousefleet Ings
Little Reedness
CHURCH LANE
Dairy Farm
Adlingfleet Ings

65
81

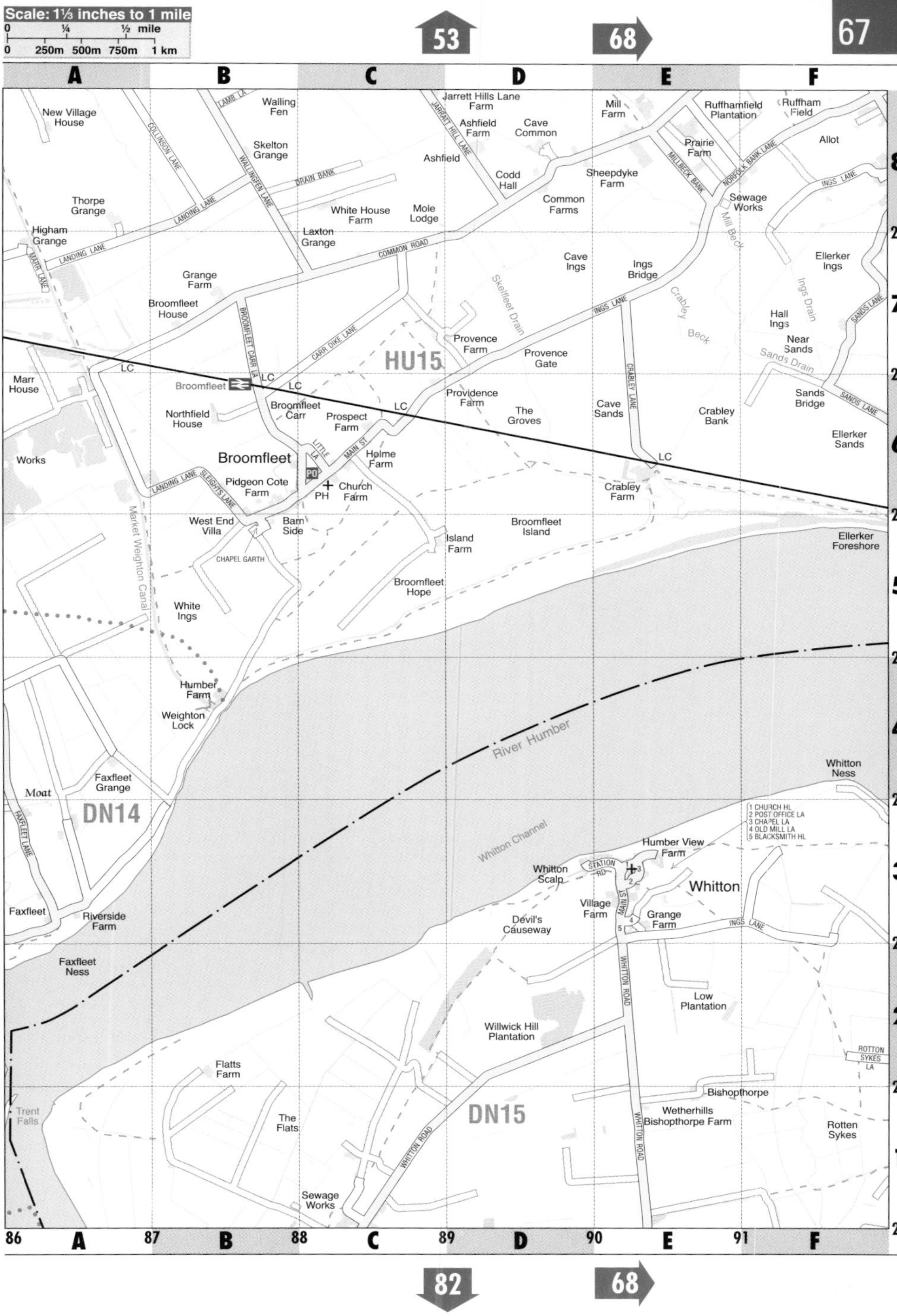
Scale: 1⅓ inches to 1 mile
0 ¼ ½ mile
0 250m 500m 750m 1 km
53
68
A B C D E F
New Village House
Walling Fen
Jarrett Hills Lane Farm
Ashfield Farm
Cave Common
Mill Farm
Ruffhamfield Plantation
Ruffham Field
Skelton Grange
Ashfield
Prairie Farm
Allot
Codd Hall
Sheepdyke Farm
Sewage Works
Thorpe Grange
White House Farm
Mole Lodge
Common Farms
Higham Grange
Laxton Grange
Cave Ings
Ings Bridge
Ellerker Ings
Grange Farm
Broomfleet House
Hall Ings
Provence Farm
Provence Gate
Near Sands
HU15
Marr House
Broomfleet
Northfield House
Broomfleet Carr
Prospect Farm
Providence Farm
The Groves
Cave Sands
Crabley Bank
Sands Bridge
Ellerker Sands
Works
Broomfleet
Holme Farm
Pidgeon Cote Farm
Church Farm
PH
PO
Crabley Farm
West End Villa
Barn Side
Island Farm
Broomfleet Island
Ellerker Foreshore
CHAPEL GARTH
Broomfleet Hope
White Ings
Humber Farm
Weighton Lock
River Humber
Whitton Ness
Moat
Faxfleet Grange
DN14
1 CHURCH HL
2 POST OFFICE LA
3 CHAPEL LA
4 OLD MILL LA
5 BLACKSMITH HL
Whitton Channel
Humber View Farm
Whitton Scalp
Whitton
Village Farm
Grange Farm
Faxfleet
Riverside Farm
Devil's Causeway
Faxfleet Ness
Low Plantation
Willwick Hill Plantation
Flatts Farm
Bishopthorpe
Trent Falls
The Flats
DN15
Wetherhills Bishopthorpe Farm
Rotten Sykes
Sewage Works
LAMB LA
COLLINSON LANE
WALLINGFEN LANE
DRAIN BANK
LANDING LANE
MARR LANE
COMMON ROAD
JARRATT HILL LANE
MILLBECK BANK
NORFOLK BANK LANE
INGS LANE
Mill Beck
Ings Drain
SANDS LANE
Crabley Beck
Sands Drain
Skelfleet Drain
BROOMFLEET CARR LA
CARR DIKE LANE
CRABLEY LANE
LITTLE LA
MAIN ST
SLEIGHTS LANE
Market Weighton Canal
FAXFLEET LANE
STATION RD
MAIN ST
WHITTON ROAD
ROTTON SYKES LA
LC
8 29 7 28 6 27 5 26 4 25 3 24 2 23 1 22
86 87 88 89 90 91
82
68

C7
1 SPINDLEWOOD
2 STOCKBRIDGE PK
3 CHURCH LA
4 CHURCH VIEW
5 DORSEY WY
6 THORNHAM'S WY

D5
1 BROADACRE PK
2 MEDLAR DR
3 BROADLEY CROFT
4 ASPEN WLK
5 FAIRFIELD VIEW
6 WISKE AVE
7 LOXLEY WY
8 MEDEN AVE
9 DEARNE CT
10 AIRE CL
11 FIR CL
12 WILLOW DR
13 ELLOUGHTONTHORPE WY
14 MYRTLE WY
15 HONEYSUCKLE CL
16 ALDER CL

67

54

E6
1 CHAPEL HILL
2 TEMPLE WK
3 LADYWELL GATE

Scale: 1⅓ inches to 1 mile
0 ¼ ½ mile
0 250m 500m 750m 1 km

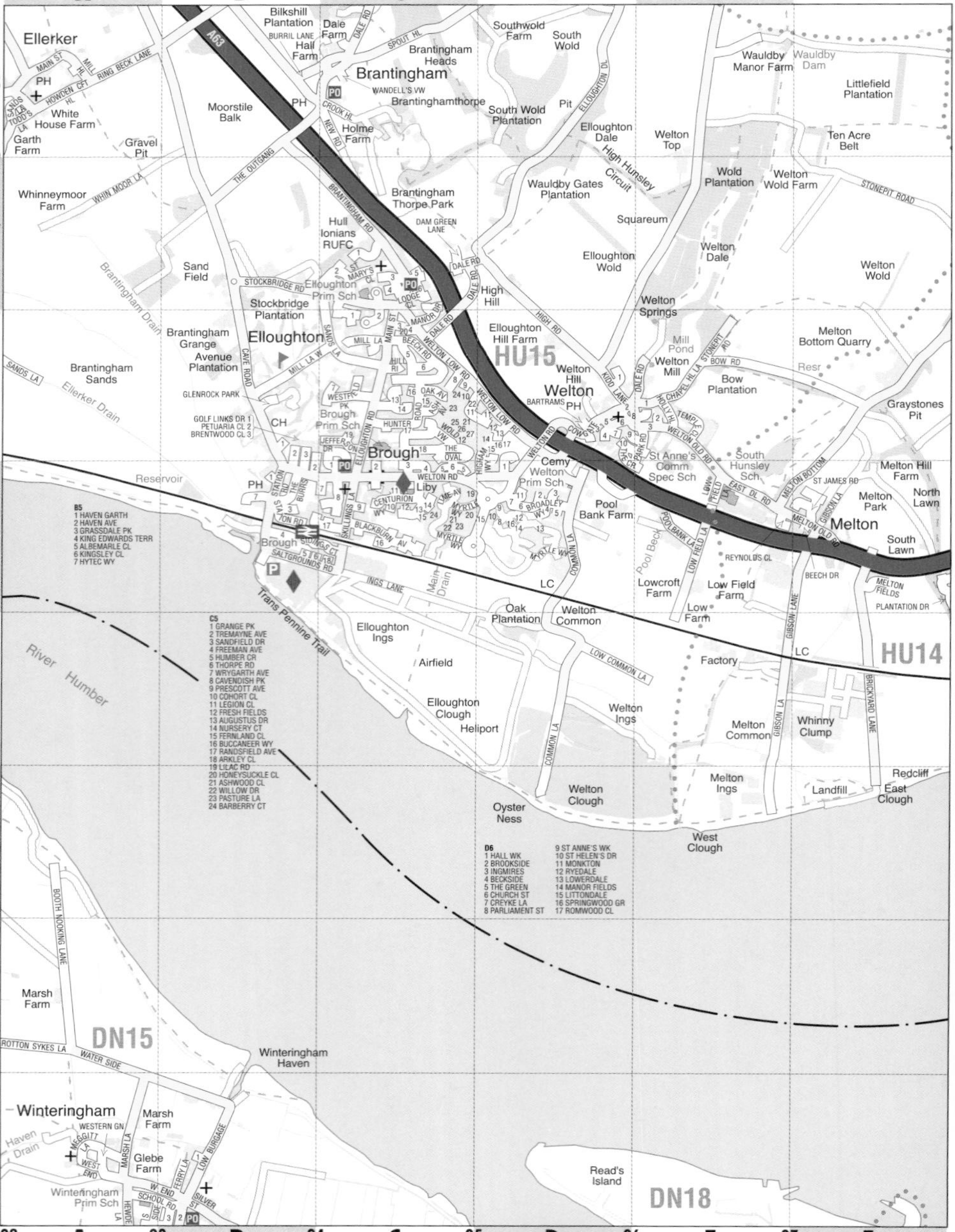

B1
1 ORCHARD DR
2 HIGH BURGAGE
3 BACK LA

67

83

C6
1 DROVERS RISE
2 VICARAGE GD
3 CHAPEL MEWS
4 PINE WK
5 HOBSON RD
6 HARLAND RD
7 LARCHMONT CL
8 WOODLANDS LA
9 PLOVER DR
10 THORNTON
11 FRYSTON
12 LASTINGHAM
13 CHANTRYS DR
14 RANSOME WAY
15 ELM AVE
16 LAMBERT AVE
17 WOODLAND AVE
18 SPRINGFIELD AVE
19 ATKINSON DR
20 ST PAULINUS CRES
21 COVINGTON
22 LOWERDALE
23 LINTON
24 CARLTON
25 WINTRINGHAM
26 ROMBALDS CFT
27 PINEFIELD PL

B6
1 WEST FIELD LA
2 QUEENSBURY WAY
3 STRATTON PK
4 HUMBERDALE CL
5 HUMBER VIEW
6 COPPER BEECH CL

C7
1 BEECH GR
2 THE PADDOCK
3 EASENBY CL
4 GREENACRES

A5
1 THE PADDOCK
2 GREENWAYS
3 WOODGATES MOUNT
4 SWANLAND GARTH
5 WOODLANDS RI
6 WOODGATES CL
7 THE RISE
8 WEST PARKLANDS DR
9 PARKLANDS DR
10 PARKLANDS CR
11 ASHTON HALL DR
12 SPINNEY CFT CL
13 ROXTON HALL DR
14 ASHDALE PK
15 TURNER'S LA

E1
1 ROPERY LA
2 TRINITY WK
3 VICTORIA DR
4 STABLE LA
5 SHADWELL RI
6 PONDS WY
7 WESTERN DR
8 REGENCY CT
9 COUNCIL TERR
10 CASTLEDYKE W
11 FLEETGATE
12 MALTBY LA
13 HUNGATE
14 CHAPEL LA

F1
1 VICTORY WAY
2 HARRIER RD
3 NURSERY CL
4 SEDGE CL
5 QUEEN'S AVE
6 OVERTON CT
7 TYSONS CL
8 GREENWAY
9 WHISTON WAY
10 TREECE GN
11 WILLOW DR
12 SOUTERGATE
13 CATHERINE ST

139
143
140
For full street detail of the highlighted area see page 155.

Scale: 1⅓ inches to 1 mile
0 ¼ ½ mile
0 250m 500m 750m 1 km

69
85

E2
1 WENTWORTH CRES
2 WESTBURN AVE
3 FULFORD CRES
4 GLENEAGLES CRES
5 ALBERT ST
6 PEPLOE CRES

For full street detail of the highlighted area see pages 144 and 145.

For full street detail of the highlighted area see pages 146 and 147.

147

C7
1 PRINCES AVE
2 SHIELDS RD
3 ANDREW LA
4 HARDYS RD
5 BURNSALLS RD
6 ROBSON WY
7 BEECH AVE
8 CEDAR CT
9 OAK GR
10 POPLAR GR
11 FOTHERBIE GARTH
12 HALES CR
13 WESTLANDS CL
14 CLOEBERRY WY
15 GREEN RD
16 HERON CL
17 DRAPER'S LA
18 WARN AVE
19 KETWELL LA
20 WAYFBAIN LA
21 CHURCH GARTH
22 SPENCER CL
23 LAMBERT PK RD
24 HAVEN STAITHES
25 WESTWICK
26 WOODMARKETGATE
27 IVESON CL
28 GEORGE ST
29 KING'S PL
30 ST AUGUSTINE'S GARTH
31 MARKET PL
32 DRAPER'S LA
33 DISTAFF LA
34 ST MEWS

58

Scale: 1⅓ inches to 1 mile
0 ¼ ½ mile
0 250m 500m 750m 1 km

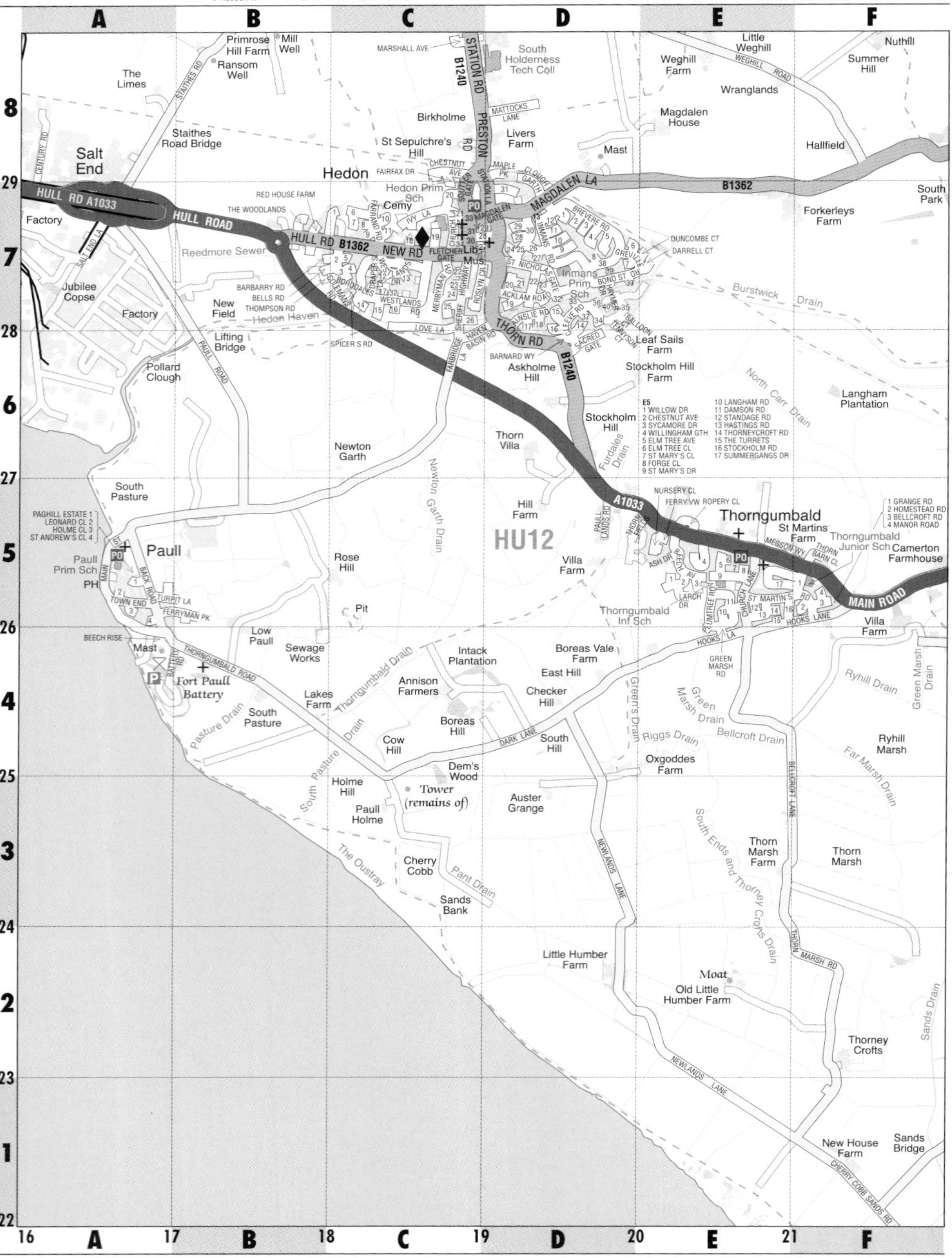

71

87

D7
1 ALBINA GARTH
2 HAVEN GARTH
3 GUY GARTH
4 POULTNEY GARTH
5 CONSTABLE GARTH
6 BETHELL CT
7 VILLIERS CT
8 MAGDALEN CT
9 ALURED GARTH
10 HOLCROFT GARTH
11 FLEET GARTH
12 BECK GARTH
13 THIRTY ACRE LA
14 WYNTRYNGHAM CL
15 WATERLAND CL
16 CHAYTOR CL
17 ANDERSONS CL
18 MANDERVILLE CL
19 HILDYARD CL
20 ADELIZA GARTH
21 APPLE GARTH
22 CHARLES ST
23 STOCKHOLM PK
24 ST ANTHONY'S DR
25 ST ANTHONY'S PK
26 FEWSON GARTH
27 NEVILLE GARTH
28 CHAPELRY GARTH
29 ALISON GARTH
30 WATSON DR
31 CHERRY TREE LA
32 BERKELEY DR
33 HARRINGTON CT
34 GARVEY WY
35 CROMWELL RD
36 GIBSON LA
37 STEPHENSON CL
38 ST MARY'S DR
39 ST MICHAEL'S DR
40 ELWYN WY

Scale: 1⅓ inches to 1 mile
0 ¼ ½ mile
0 250m 500m 750m 1 km

A6
1 ELM TREE FARM RD
2 NORTH RISE
3 NETTLETON GARTH
4 BURNHAM AVE
5 RAINES CLOSE
6 CHESTNUT CL
7 STATION RD

59
74

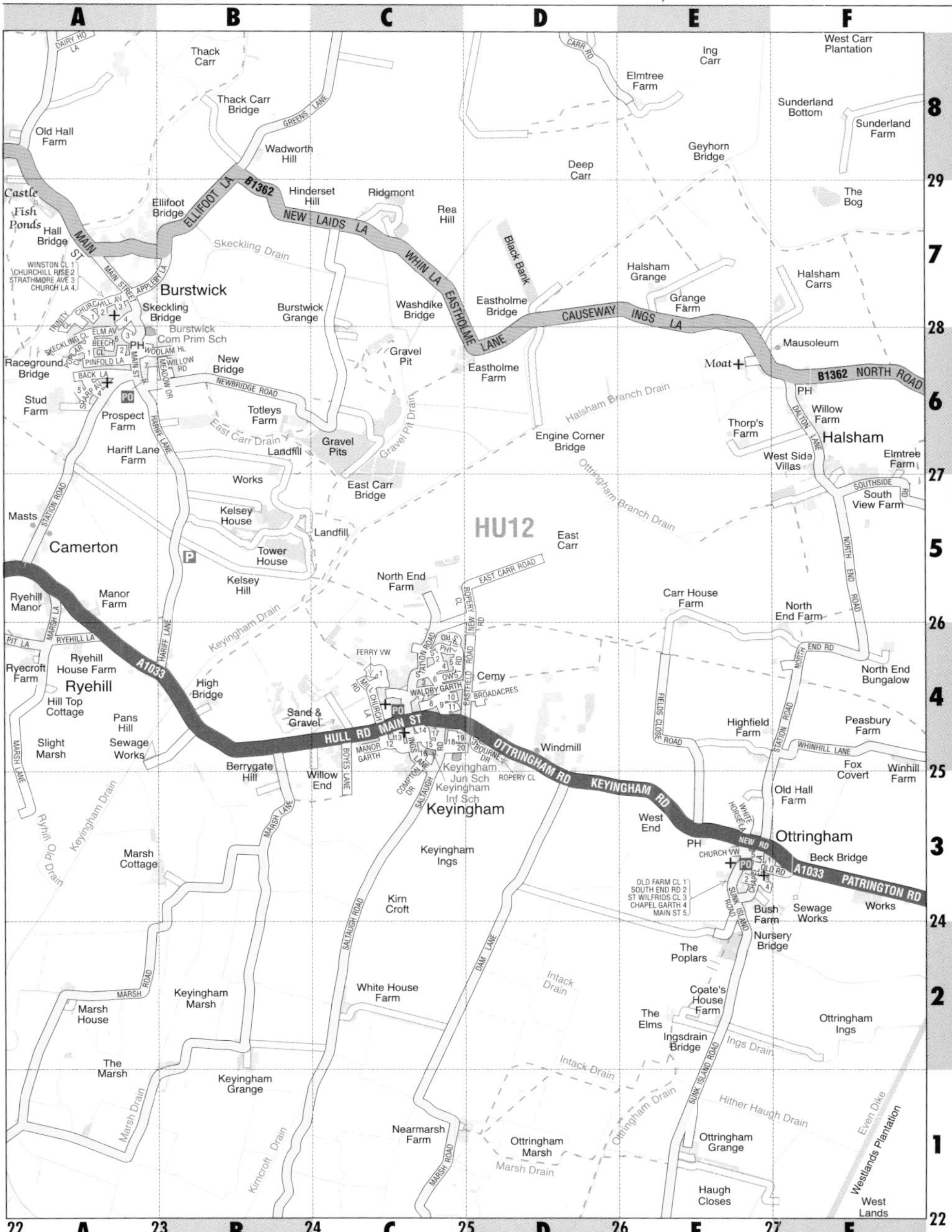

C4
1 EBOR MANOR
2 ALBEMARLE RD
3 KELSEY DR
4 LANGDALE DR
5 ETHERINGTON CL
6 SEYMOUR RD
7 ELM TREE CL
8 WESTERDALE CL
9 MARRITT WY
10 MAUDE CL
11 OMBLER CL
12 MAISTER RD
13 CHAPEL LA
14 BECK LA
15 SCHOOL LA
16 KIRNCROFT CL
17 JELLISON WK
18 GRIFFITHS WY
19 MELVILLE CL
20 RUSSELL DR

88
74

73
60

F7
1 HUBERT ST
2 CAMMIDGE ST
3 GEORGE ST
4 ALMA ST
5 WALTER ST
6 EDWARD ST

Scale: 1⅓ inches to 1 mile
0 ¼ ½ mile
0 250m 500m 750m 1 km

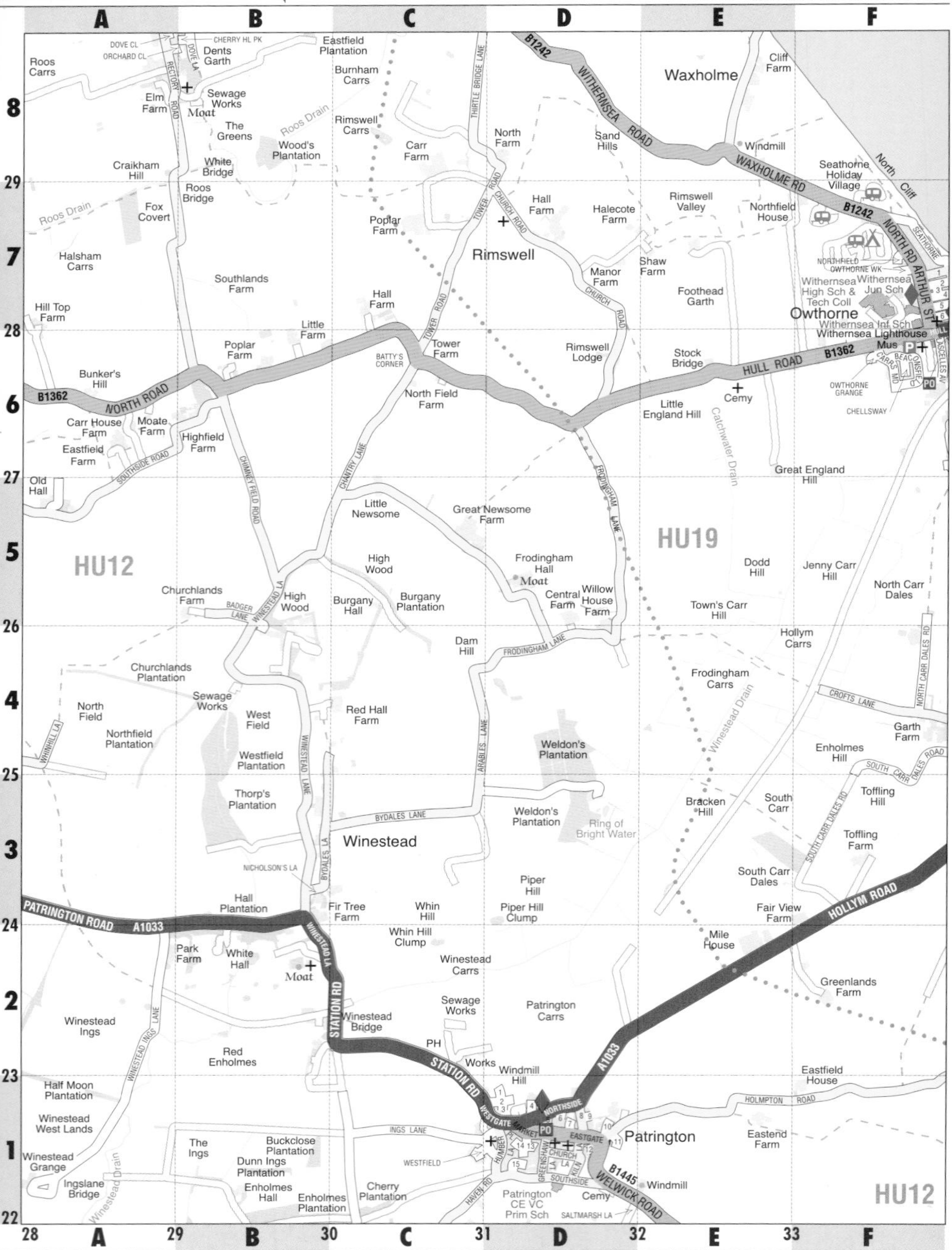

73
89

D1
1 HUNTER CL
2 GUARDIANS RD
3 FRANCIS WY
4 WESTGATE MANOR
5 PUMP ROW
6 NORTHSIDE CT
7 CHURCH VW
8 TITHE BARN LA
9 TITHE BARN CL
10 CLARKS LA
11 BEECH DR
12 THE CLOSE
13 THE CRESCENT
14 ST PATRICK'S GN
15 SAFFRON GARTH

Scale: 1⅓ inches to 1 mile

0 ¼ ½ mile

0 250m 500m 750m 1 km

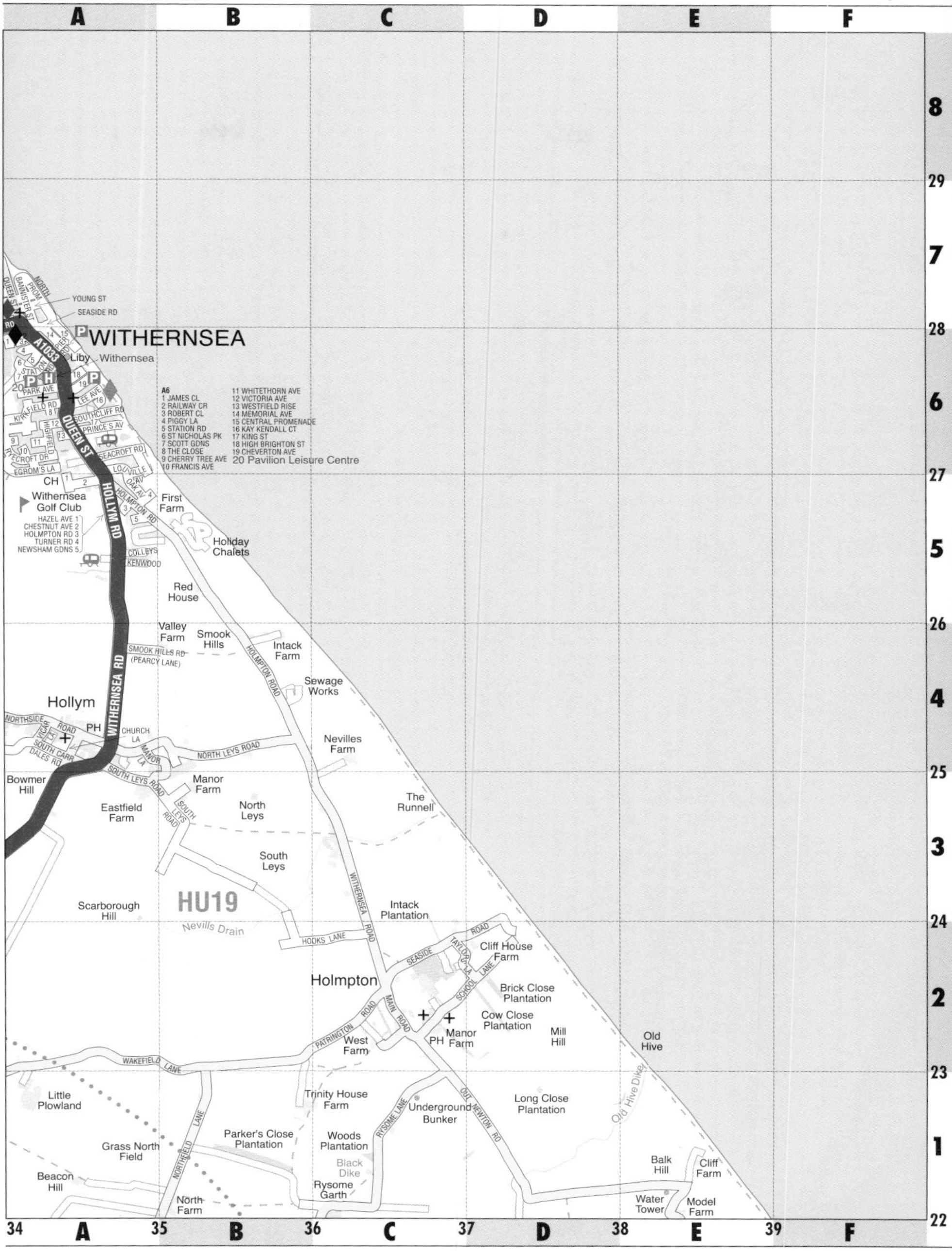

90

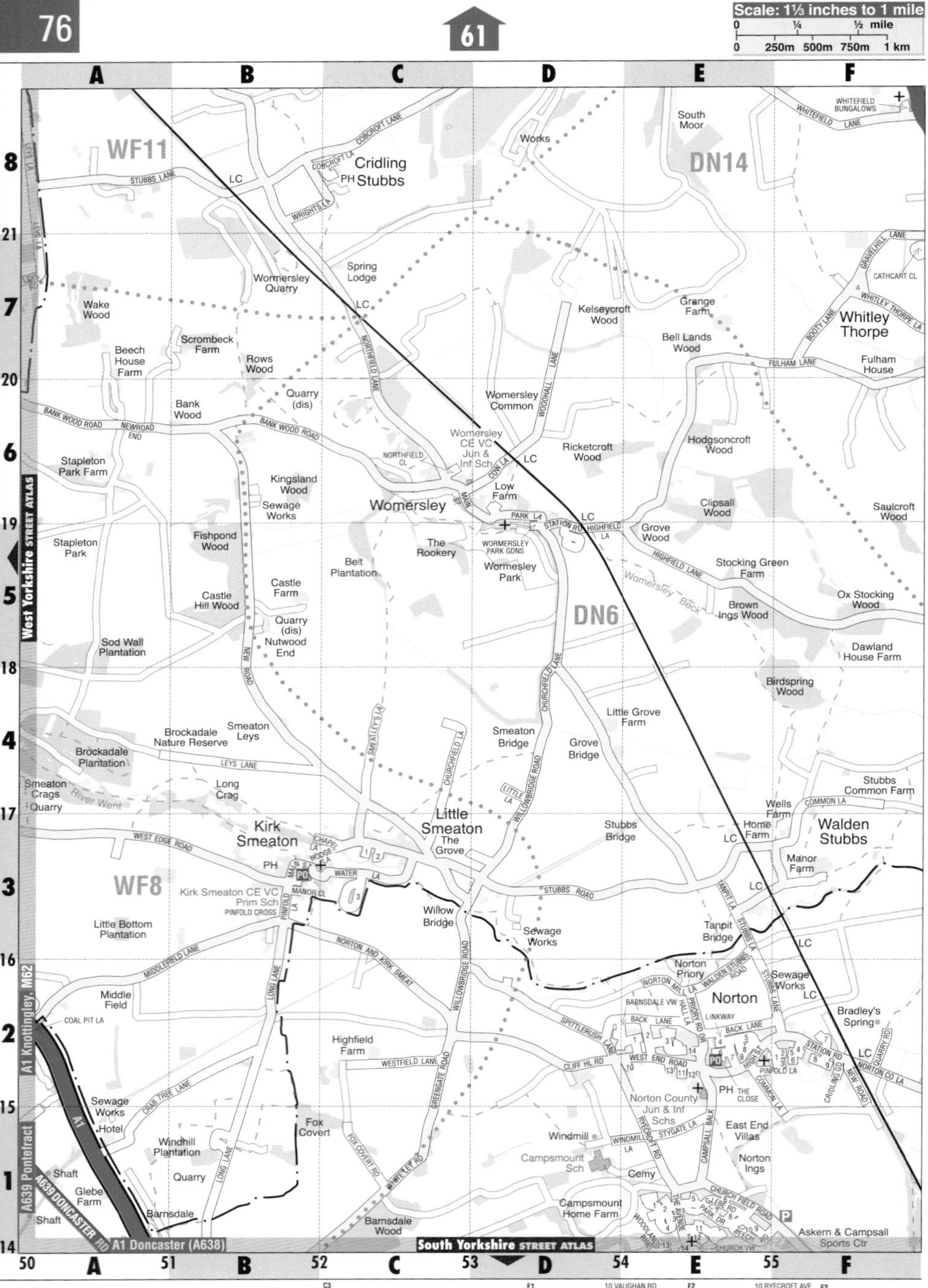

C3
1 WENTDALE
2 STAN VALLEY
3 SPRINGFIELD CR

E1
1 TENNYSON AVE
2 SHAKESPEARE AVE
3 BYRON AVE
4 WORDSWORTH AVE
5 WELLINGTONIA DR
6 LANGLEYS RD
7 EAST VW
8 GRANGE RD
9 WILLOW RD
10 VAUGHAN RD
11 CAMPSALL PK RD
12 CAMPSALL HALL RD
13 SHERWOOD CL
14 HIGH ST

E2
1 BROC-O-BANK
2 NEWTHORPE RD
3 FORRESTER'S CL
4 TRAFFORD RD
5 ARUNDEL RD
6 ADELAIDE RD
7 HEADINGLEY RD
8 ORCHARD DR
9 ORCHARD CL
10 RYECROFT AVE
11 FIR TREE DR
12 MANOR CL
13 WINDMILL MD
14 KIPLIN DR

F2
1 LYNDHURST DR
2 LYNDHURST CL
3 LYNDHURST RISE
4 ASHBURNHAM CL
5 ASHBURNHAM WK
6 DENVER RD
7 MANOR GARTH
8 SWAN SYKE DR
9 DRYHURST CL

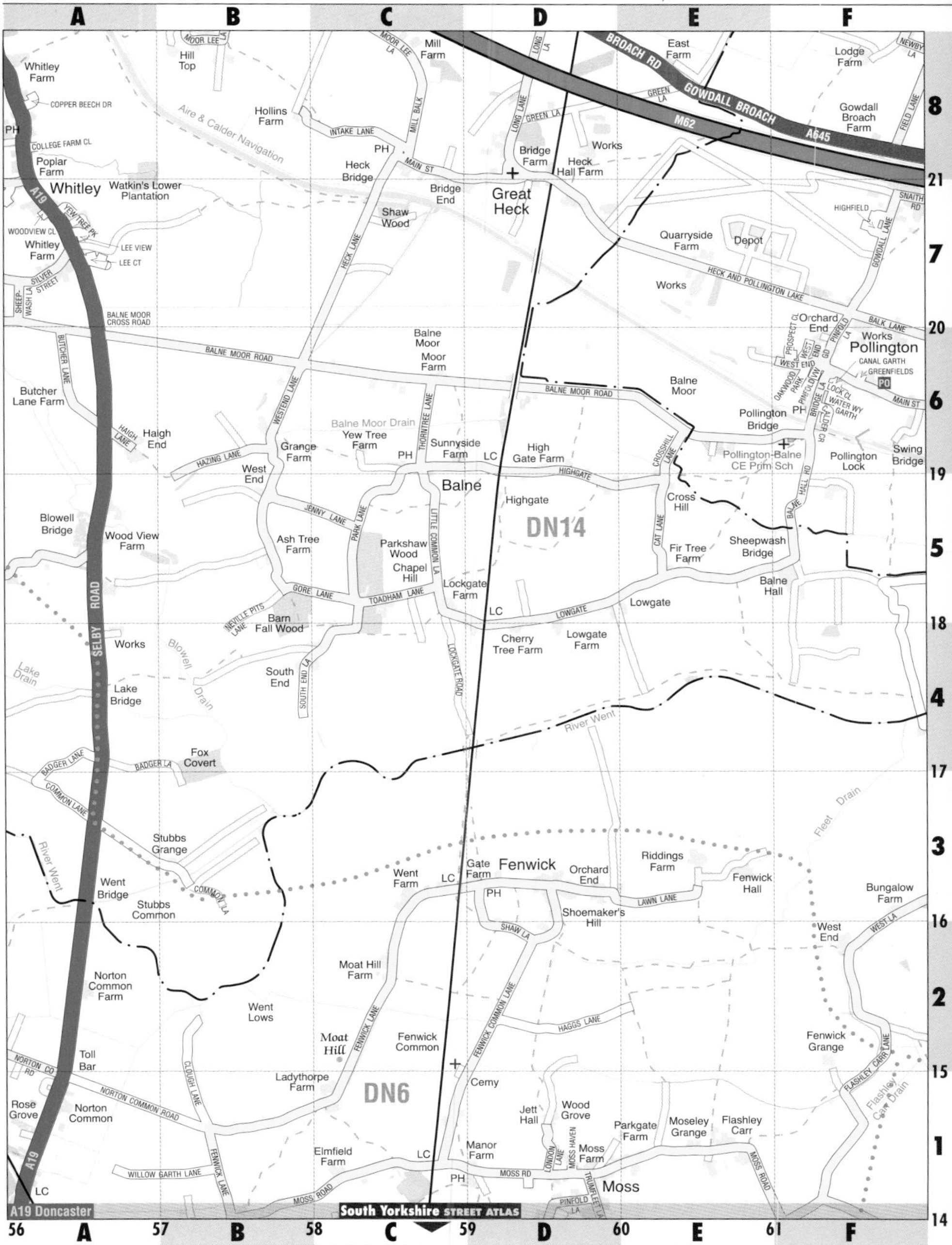
A
B
C
D
E
F
8
21
7
20
6
19
5
18
4
17
3
16
2
15
1
14
56
57
58
59
60
61
Whitley Farm
COPPER BEECH DR
PH
COLLEGE FARM CL
Poplar Farm
Whitley
Watkin's Lower Plantation
A19
YEW TREE PK
WOODVIEW CL
Whitley Farm
LEE VIEW
LEE CT
SILVER STREET
SHEEPWASH LA
BALNE MOOR CROSS ROAD
Hill Top
MOOR LEE LA
Hollins Farm
Aire & Calder Navigation
MOOR LEE LA
Mill Farm
MILL BALK
INTAKE LANE
PH
Heck Bridge
MAIN ST
Bridge End
Shaw Wood
HECK LANE
LONG LA
LONG LANE
GREEN LA
Bridge Farm
Great Heck
Heck Hall Farm
Works
BROACH RD
East Farm
GREEN LA
GOWDALL BROACH
M62
A645
Lodge Farm
NEWBY LA
Gowdall Broach Farm
FIELD LANE
SNAITH RD
HIGHFIELD
GOWDALL LANE
Quarryside Farm
Depot
Works
HECK AND POLLINGTON LANE
Orchard End
BALK LANE
Works
Pollington
PROSPECT CL
WEST END
WEST END
PINFOLD GD
CANAL GARTH
GREENFIELDS
PO
OAKWOOD PARK
PINFOLD VW
LOCK CL
WATER WY GARTH
MAIN ST
BUTCHER LANE
BALNE MOOR ROAD
Balne Moor
Moor Farm
Butcher Lane Farm
HAIGH LANE
Haigh End
WESTEND LANE
Balne Moor Drain
THORNTREE LANE
BALNE MOOR ROAD
Balne Moor
Pollington Bridge
PH
BRIDGE LA
CALDER CR
HAZING LANE
Grange Farm
Yew Tree Farm
PH
Sunnyside Farm
LC
High Gate Farm
CROSSHILL LANE
Pollington-Balne CE Prim Sch
Pollington Lock
Swing Bridge
West End
HIGHGATE
Balne
Highgate
Cross Hill
BALNE HALL RD
JENNY LANE
PARK LANE
LITTLE COMMON LA
DN14
CAT LANE
Blowell Bridge
Wood View Farm
Ash Tree Farm
Parkshaw Wood
Fir Tree Farm
Sheepwash Bridge
Chapel Hill
Lockgate Farm
Balne Hall
GORE LANE
TOADHAM LANE
NEVILLE PITS LANE
Barn Fall Wood
LC
LOWGATE
Lowgate
SELBY ROAD
Works
Blowell Drain
LOCKGATE ROAD
Cherry Tree Farm
Lowgate Farm
Lake Drain
Lake Bridge
South End
SOUTH END LA
River Went
BADGER LANE
BADGER LA
Fox Covert
COMMON LANE
Fleet Drain
River Went
Stubbs Grange
Went Bridge
Stubbs Common
COMMON LA
Went Farm
LC
Gate Farm
Fenwick
PH
Orchard End
Riddings Farm
LAWN LANE
Fenwick Hall
Bungalow Farm
SHAW LA
Shoemaker's Hill
West End
WEST LA
Norton Common Farm
Moat Hill Farm
Went Lows
FENWICK COMMON LANE
HAGGS LANE
Moat Hill
FENWICK LANE
Fenwick Common
Fenwick Grange
FLASHLEY CARR LANE
Flashley Carr Drain
NORTON CO RD
Toll Bar
Ladythorpe Farm
Cemy
DN6
NORTON COMMON ROAD
CLOUGH LANE
Rose Grove
Norton Common
Jett Hall
Wood Grove
Parkgate Farm
Moseley Grange
Flashley Carr
A19
Elmfield Farm
LC
Manor Farm
LONDON LANE
MOSS HAVEN
Moss Farm
MOSS ROAD
WILLOW GARTH LANE
FENWICK LANE
PH
MOSS RD
TRUMFLEET LA
Moss
LC
MOSS ROAD
PINFOLD LA

77
63

C8
1 ROLAND SIMPSON CL
2 THE CHASE
3 BEAN GDNS
4 SOUTH PARKWAY
5 PARK GDNS
6 OAKDALE CL
7 HALL CL
8 COURT GDNS
9 THE PARKWAY
10 MITTEN AVE
11 WALNUT CRES
12 SYCAMORE CL

Scale: 1⅓ inches to 1 mile
0 ¼ ½ mile
0 250m 500m 750m 1 km

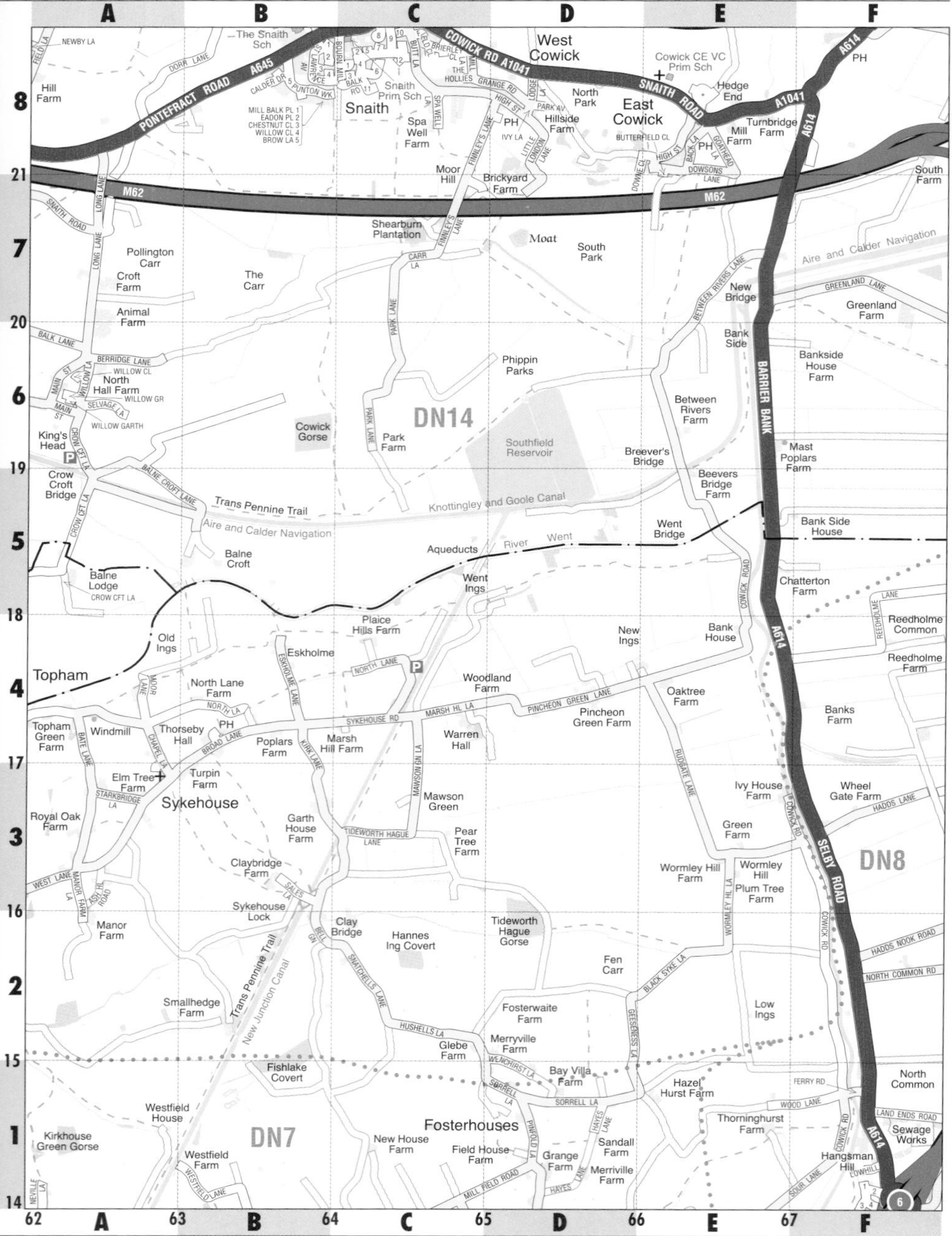

77
92

F1
1 QUAYSIDE 1
2 WATERSIDE RD
3 WATERSIDE
4 QUAY RD

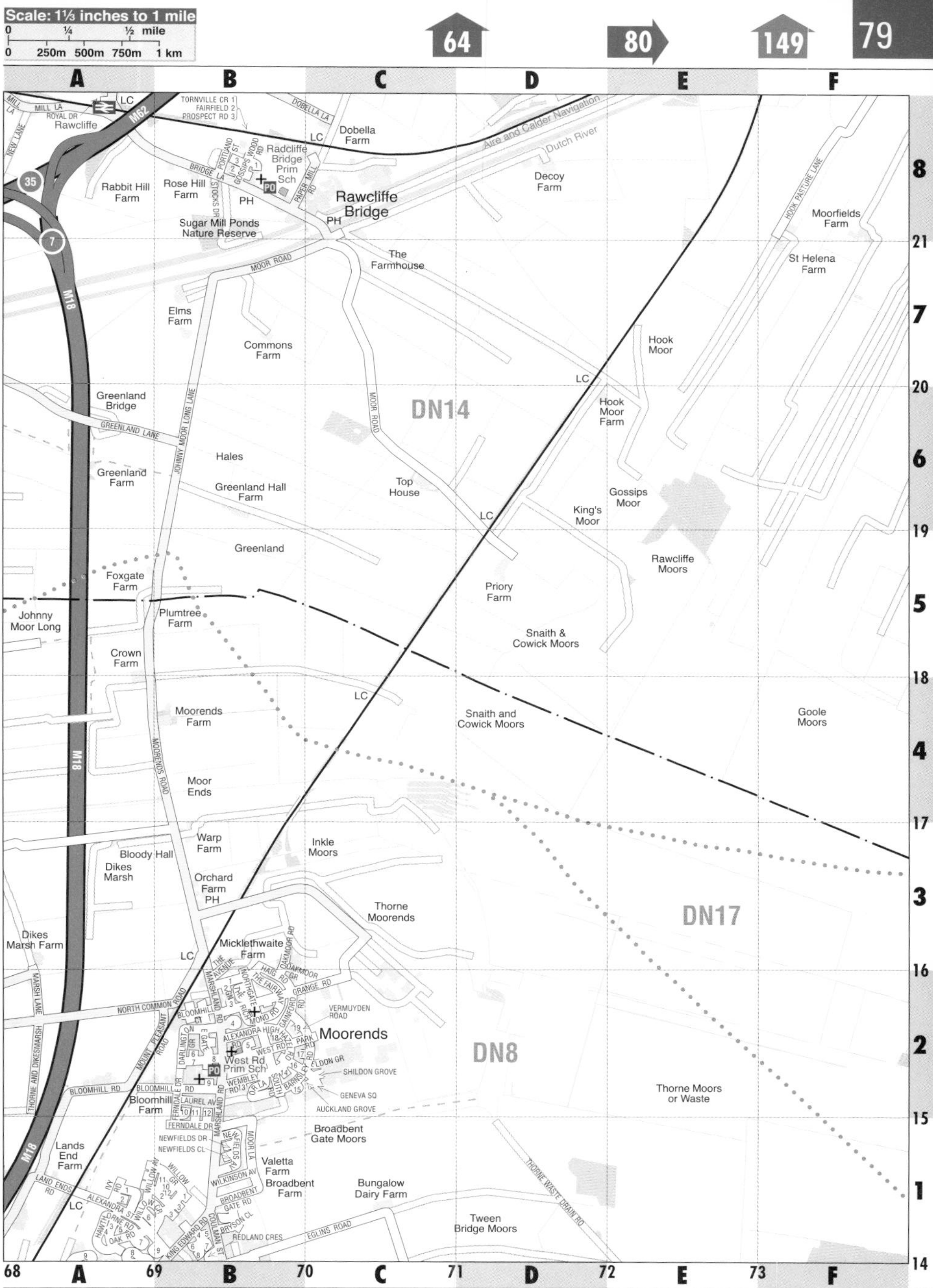

A1
1 WALNUT RD
2 BIRCHWOOD CL
3 CHERRY TREE DR
4 HAWTHORNE AVE
5 HAWTHORNE GR
6 WILLOW RD
7 OAK CR
8 CORONA DR
9 HIGHFIELD CR

B1
1 MAPLE RD
2 CEDAR RD
3 WILLOW GR
4 KINGS CT RD
5 JAMES CT
6 EDWARD CT
7 CHARLES CT
8 HENRY CT
9 KING EDWARD CR
10 HOLLY WK
11 HOLLY RD
12 MAPLE RD

B2
1 MICKLETHWAITE RD
2 MICKLETHWAITE GR
3 GRANGE GR
4 BLOOMHILL CL
5 THE HERMITAGE
6 ALDER GR
7 BELVEDERE DR
8 NEWHOLME DR
9 BLOOM HL GR
10 ROWAN CL
11 LABURNUM AVE
12 MULBERRY AVE
13 DUNELM CR
14 KENTS GDNS
15 SILKSTONE OVAL
16 LOCARNO RD
17 WINDLESTONE SQ
18 GAINFORD SQ
19 THRISLINGTON SQ

149
79
65

Scale: 1⅓ inches to 1 mile
0 ¼ ½ mile
0 250m 500m 750m 1 km

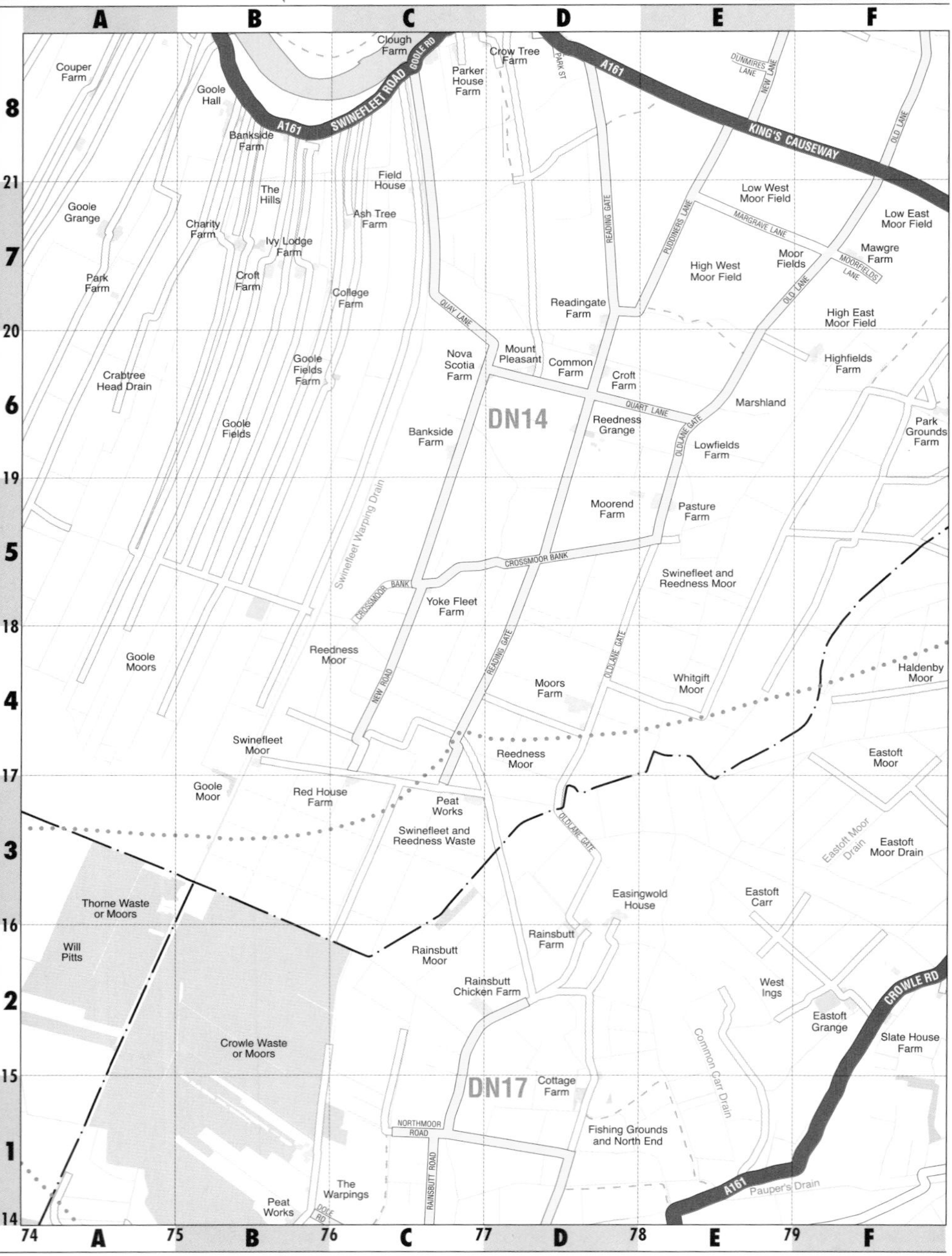

79
94

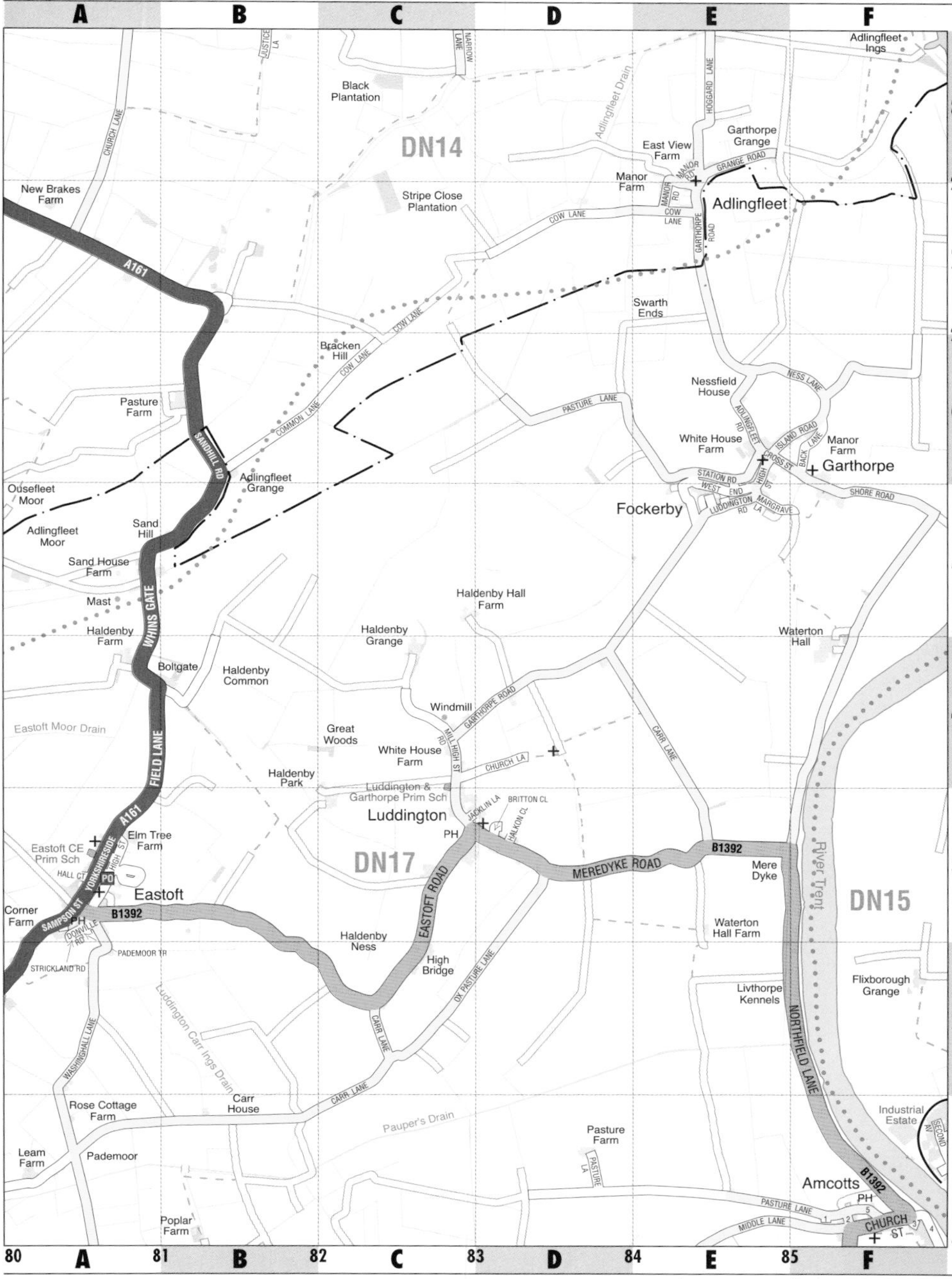

F1
1 BELTHORN RD
2 CHAPEL ST
3 CROSS LA
4 TRENT SIDE
5 DARK LA

81
67

Scale: 1⅓ inches to 1 mile
0 ¼ ½ mile
0 250m 500m 750m 1 km

81
96

A5
1 FARNDALE WY
2 NORTHLANDS AVE
3 FOWLER CT
4 BOYNTON CR
5 HILLSMERE GR
6 BOSTON CL
7 WATERLOW DR
8 PLYMOUTH CL
9 LEEK HILL
10 WESTWINDS RD
11 MALKINSON CL
12 HAWTHORNE CL
13 BLANKNEY CT
14 MARKET ST
15 QUEEN ST
16 CHURCH SIDE

A7
1 BEAULAH VILLAS
2 BEAULAHLAND
3 SKINNERS LA
4 QUEEN ELIZABETH AVE
5 OLD POST OFFICE LA

83

E8
1 SUNNYBANK
2 TOFTS RD
3 BRADWELL CL
4 MILSON CL
5 PELHAM CL
6 MASONS CT
7 NICHOLAS CT
8 GEORGINA CT
9 GODDARD CL
10 HARROWDYKE
11 BERETUN GN
12 GRANGE AVE
13 MOUNT AVE
14 BEACON AVE
15 PARKDALE
16 ELMDALE
17 WELTON CL
18 STEVENSON'S WY
19 HARVEST AVE
20 SHARPE CL
21 MALKIN RD
22 HESSLE VW
23 TEAL DR
24 RIVERBANK RISE
25 FURNISS CT

69

Scale: 1⅓ inches to 1 mile
0 ¼ ½ mile
0 250m 500m 750m 1 km

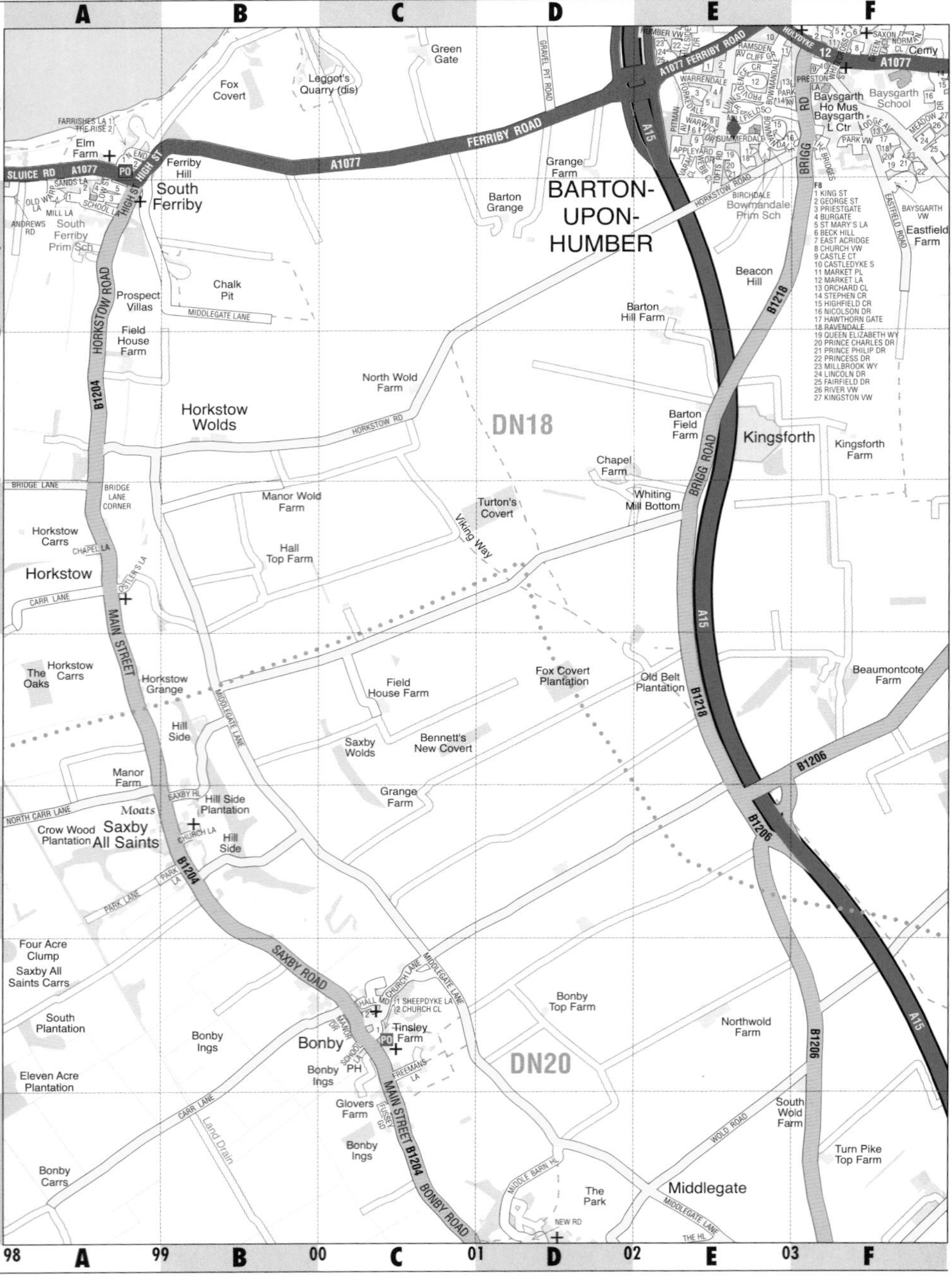

83

98

Scale: 1⅓ inches to 1 mile
0 ¼ ½ mile
0 250m 500m 750m 1 km

C8
1 HARVEST RISE
2 THE BRAMBLES
3 ROWAN CL
4 HEDGEROW CL
5 SCHOFIELD CL
6 HAWTHORN RISE
7 MILLFIELDS WY
8 PADDOCK RISE
9 MIDDLEGATE CL
10 HIGHFIELDS
11 GLEN HALL RISE

70

86

D8
1 JOHN HARRISON'S CL
2 WILLOW GDNS
3 CROSS ST
4 CHURCHSIDE
5 BECK LA
6 GLANFORD GR
7 BARRICK CL
8 THE SPINNEY

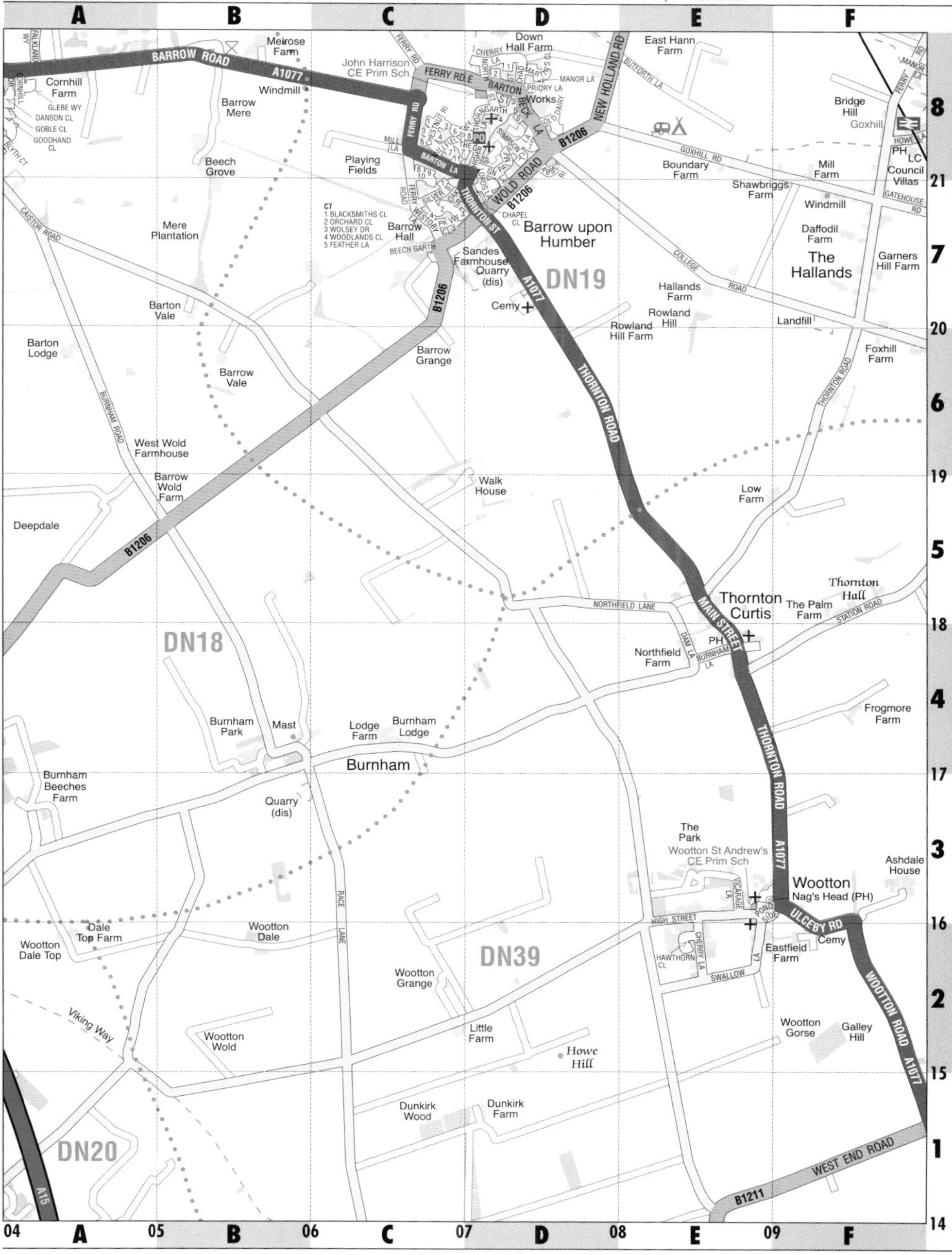

99

86

A8
1 STOTHARDS LA
2 GREENGATE LA
3 PIDGEON COTE LA
4 WESTFIELD RD
5 CHURCH ST
6 CHESTNUT WY
7 ROWEN CT
8 JASMINE CT
9 THE BRIDLES

85
71

Scale: 1⅓ inches to 1 mile
0 ¼ ½ mile
0 250m 500m 750m 1 km

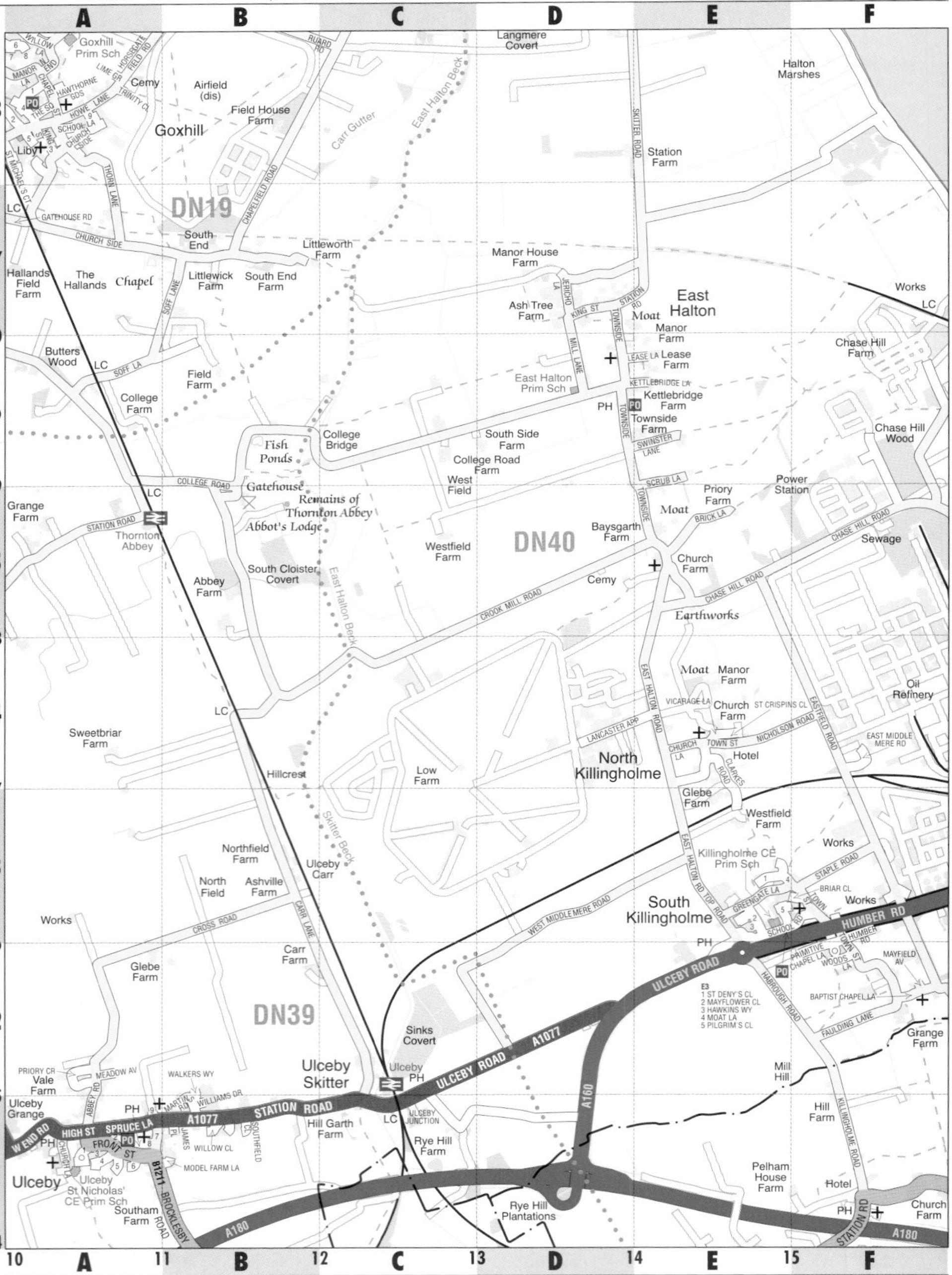

A1
1 HALLCROFT
2 STEPHEN CL
3 FORGE CR
4 MOUNT ROYALE CL
5 PITMOOR LA
6 NELTHORPE CL
7 CORONATION RD
8 PARKS CL
9 ADVENT CT

85
100

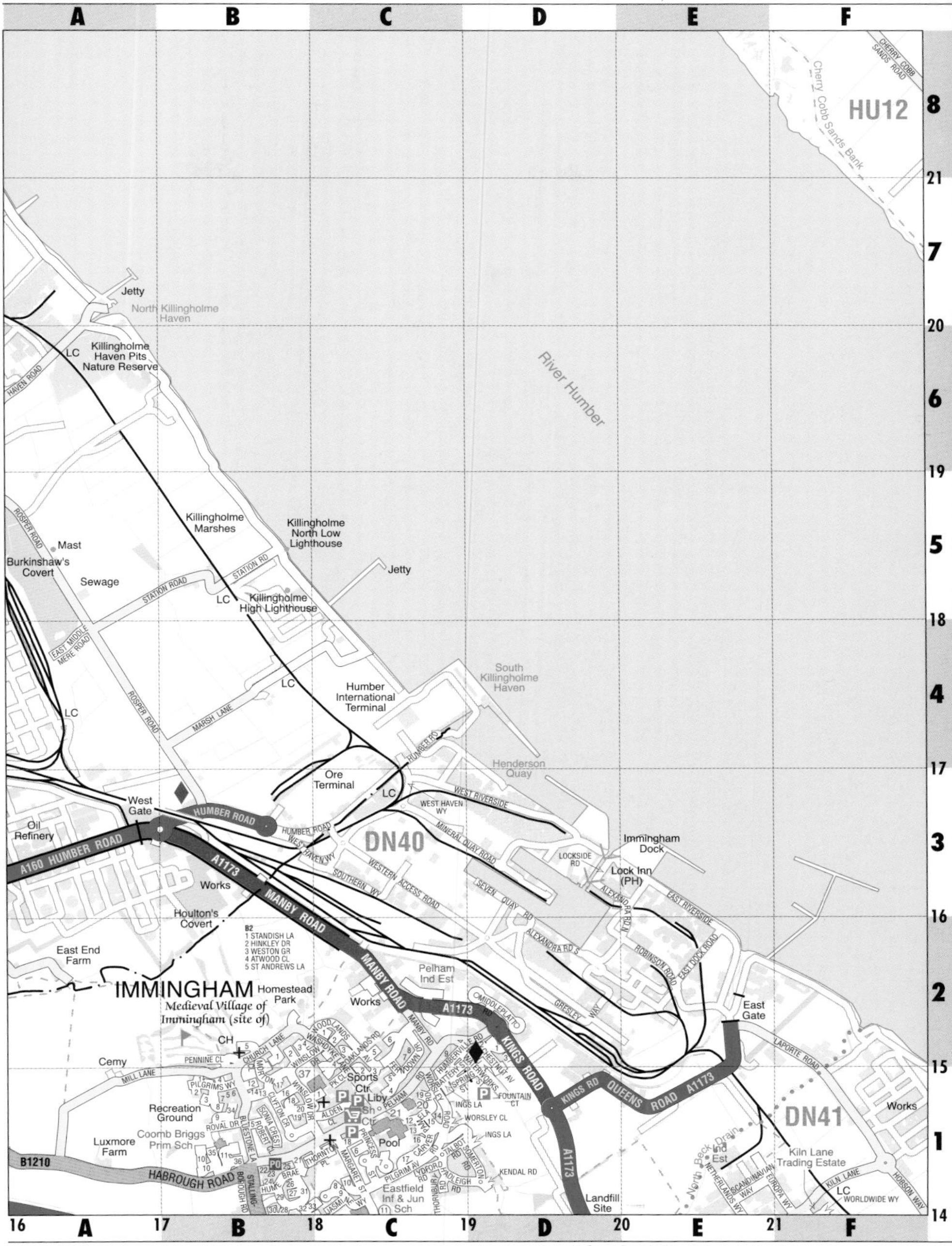
A
B
C
D
E
F
8
21
7
20
6
19
5
18
4
17
3
16
2
15
1
14
16
17
18
19
20
21
HU12
Cherry Cobb Sands Bank
CHERRY COBB SANDS ROAD
River Humber
Jetty
North Killingholme Haven
Killingholme Haven Pits Nature Reserve
HAVEN ROAD
LC
Killingholme Marshes
Killingholme North Low Lighthouse
Killingholme High Lighthouse
Jetty
ROSPER ROAD
Mast
Burkinshaw's Covert
Sewage
STATION ROAD
STATION RD
EAST MIDDLE MERE ROAD
MARSH LANE
South Killingholme Haven
Humber International Terminal
HUMBER RD
Henderson Quay
Ore Terminal
West Gate
HUMBER ROAD
Oil Refinery
A160 HUMBER ROAD
A1173
MANBY ROAD
WEST RIVERSIDE
WEST HAVEN WY
MINERAL QUAY ROAD
DN40
WESTERN ACCESS ROAD
SOUTHERN WY
SEVEN QUAY RD
Immingham Dock
LOCKSIDE RD
Lock Inn (PH)
ALEXANDRA RD N
ALEXANDRA RD S
EAST RIVERSIDE
ROBINSON ROAD
EAST DOCK ROAD
GRESLEY WAY
Works
Houlton's Covert
B2
1 STANDISH LA
2 HINKLEY DR
3 WESTON GR
4 ATWOOD CL
5 ST ANDREWS LA
East End Farm
IMMINGHAM
Homestead Park
Medieval Village of Immingham (site of)
Pelham Ind Est
Works
MIDDLEPLATT RD
KINGS ROAD
KINGS RD
QUEENS ROAD
East Gate
LAPORTE ROAD
CH
Cemy
PENNINE CL
MILL LANE
CHURCH LANE
PILGRIMS WY
Sports Ctr
Liby
Sh Ctr
Pool
Recreation Ground
Coomb Briggs Prim Sch
Luxmore Farm
B1210
HABROUGH ROAD
ROYAL DR
PRINCESS
PELHAM RD
PILGRIM AV
INGS LA
WORSLEY CL
FOUNTAIN CT
KENDAL RD
Eastfield Inf & Jun Sch
Landfill Site
DN41
Works
North Beck Drain
Ind Est
Kiln Lane Trading Estate
KILN LANE
WORLDWIDE WY
HOBSON WAY
EUROPA WY
SCANDINAVIAN WAY
NETHERLANDS WY

B1
1 MAIDEN CL
2 VIKING CL
3 MILLHOUSE RISE
4 CLEVELAND CL
5 HAZEL CFT
6 LYDIA CT
7 JACKSON MEWS
8 ST ANDREWS WY
9 HELEN CR
10 ANCHOLME AVE
11 STEEPING DR
12 HOLLINGSWORTH AVE
13 LANSDOWN RD
14 BALFOUR PL
15 STAINTON DR
16 AINSWORTH RD
17 HOLBECK PL
18 LEYDEN CL
19 CHILTON CL
20 BRADFORD RD
21 BLOSSOM WY
22 HIGHFIELD AVE
23 LINDUM AVE
24 MACKENZIE PL
25 CLARENCE CL
26 BOWMAN WY
27 HAMISH WK
28 KINLOCH WY
29 JAMES WY
30 KISHORN CT
31 HIGHLAND TARN
32 OBAN CT
33 PADDOCK CT
34 VALDA VALE
35 CALDER CL
36 AIRE CL
37 Allerton Prim Sch

C1
1 ALLERTON DR
2 SPINNEY CL
3 BEECHWOOD AVE
4 MUIRFIELD CFT
5 BERWICK CT
6 MAYFLOWER AVE
7 ROUNDWAY
8 JAPONICA HILL
9 MAGNOLIA RISE

101

10 CUSHMAN CR
11 ORKNEY PL
12 DEANE RD
13 EATON RD
14 SACKVILLE CL
15 SACKVILLE RD
16 COLLIER RD
17 BREWSTER AVE
18 CRAIK HILL AVE
19 PAM CL
20 Canon Peter Hall CE Prim Sch
21 The Immingham Sch

C2
1 COPSE CL
2 CEDAR DR
3 MAPLE GR
4 ROSE GDNS
5 ASH TREE CL
6 HOYLAKE DR
7 SUNNINGDALE DR
8 BIRKDALE DR
9 WILLOW TREE CL

88

D2
1 HAWTHORN AVE
2 LARCH CL
3 TRENCHARD CL

87
73

Scale: 1⅓ inches to 1 mile

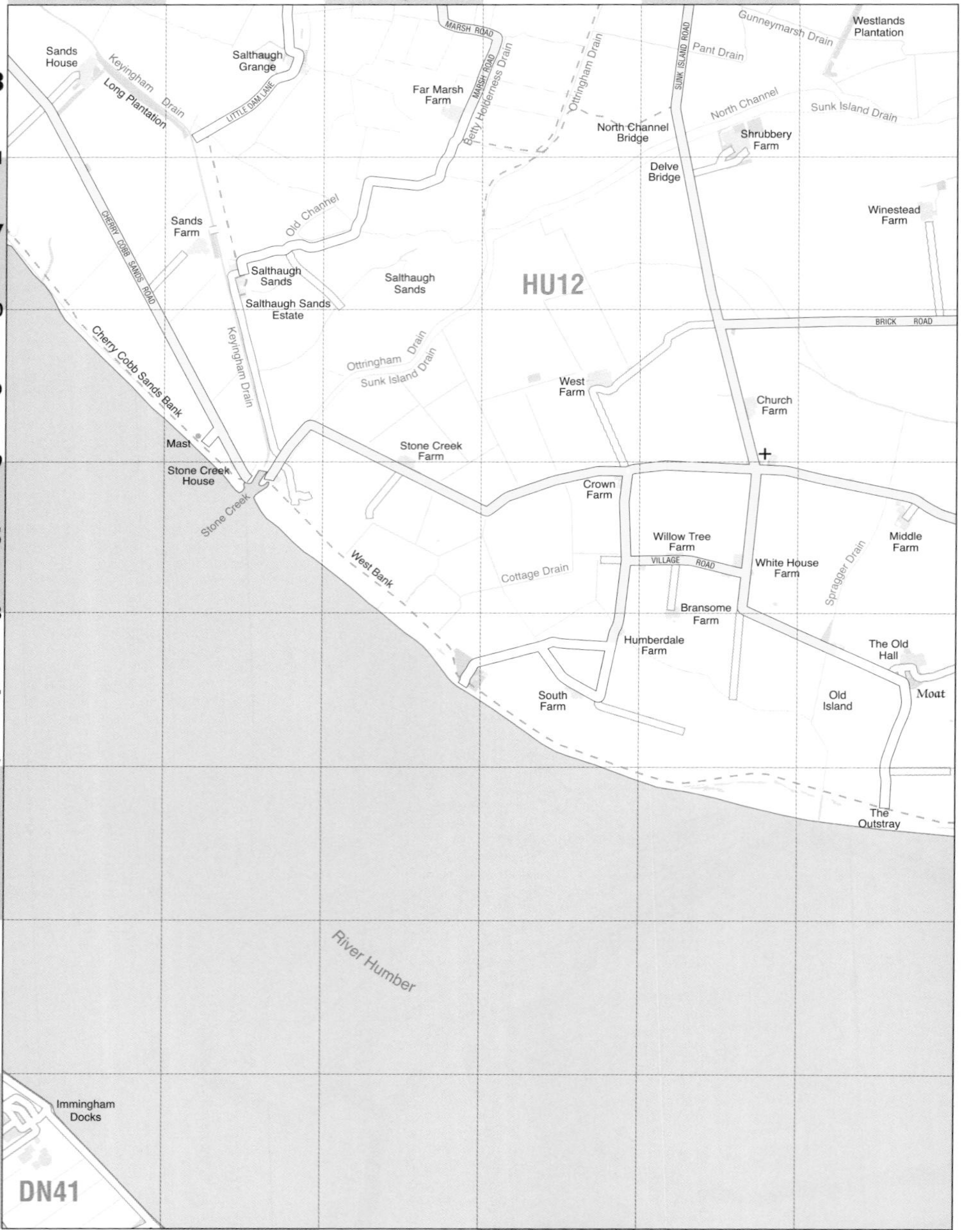
A
B
C
D
E
F
Sands House
Keyingham Drain
Long Plantation
Salthaugh Grange
LITTLE DAM LANE
MARSH ROAD
Far Marsh Farm
Betty Holderness Drain
Ottringham Drain
SUNK ISLAND ROAD
Gunneymarsh Drain
Pant Drain
Westlands Plantation
North Channel
Sunk Island Drain
North Channel Bridge
Shrubbery Farm
Delve Bridge
Winestead Farm
CHERRY COBB SANDS ROAD
Sands Farm
Old Channel
Salthaugh Sands
Salthaugh Sands
Salthaugh Sands Estate
HU12
BRICK ROAD
Cherry Cobb Sands Bank
Keyingham Drain
Ottringham Drain
Sunk Island Drain
West Farm
Church Farm
Mast
Stone Creek Farm
Stone Creek House
Stone Creek
Crown Farm
Willow Tree Farm
Middle Farm
Spragger Drain
West Bank
VILLAGE ROAD
White House Farm
Cottage Drain
Bransome Farm
Humberdale Farm
The Old Hall
Moat
South Farm
Old Island
The Outstray
River Humber
Immingham Docks
DN41
8
21
7
20
6
19
5
18
4
17
3
16
2
15
1
14
22
23
24
25
26
27

87
102

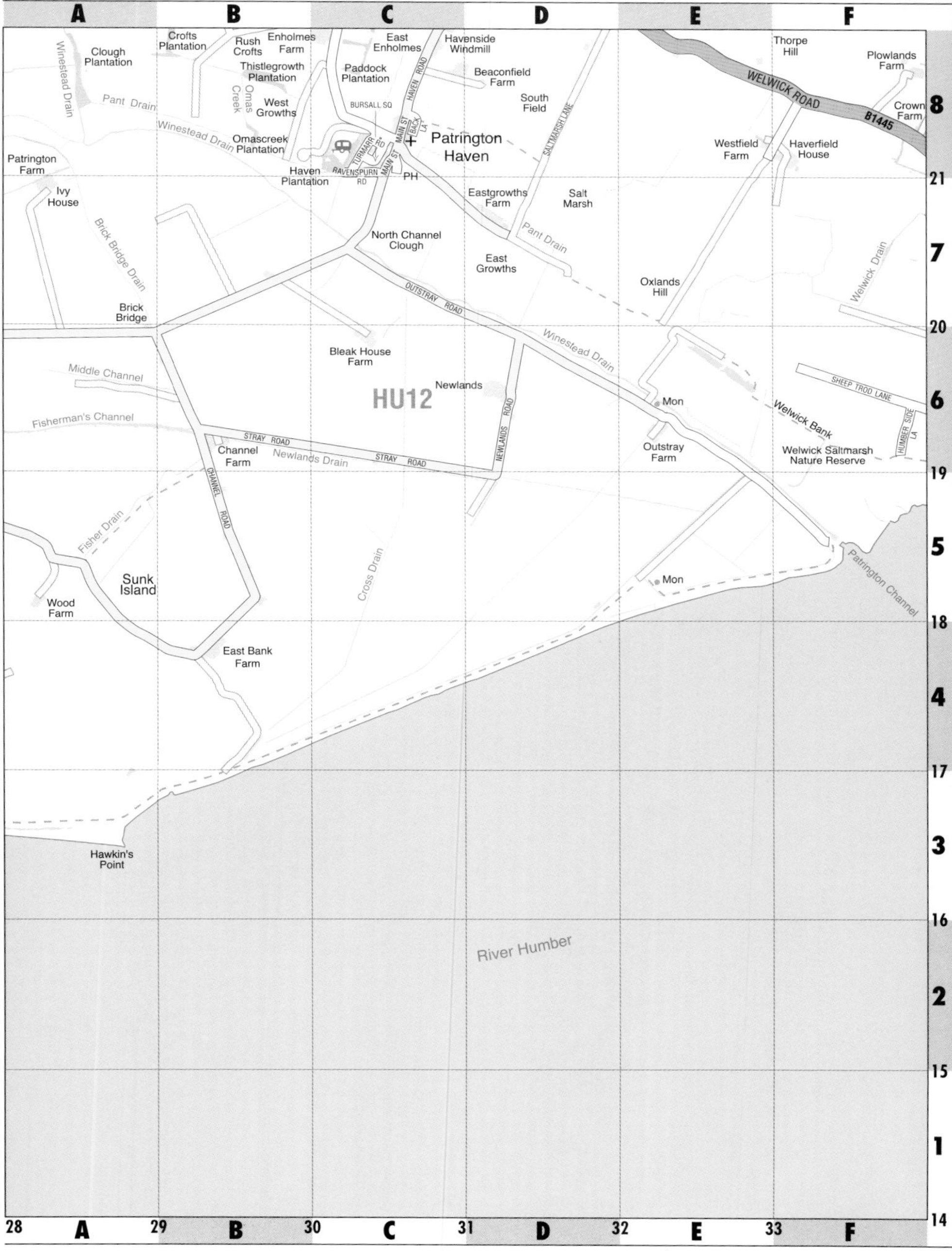
A
B
C
D
E
F
Clough Plantation
Crofts Plantation
Rush Crofts
Enholmes Farm
East Enholmes
Havenside Windmill
Thorpe Hill
Plowlands Farm
Winestead Drain
Thistlegrowth Plantation
Paddock Plantation
Beaconfield Farm
WELWICK ROAD
Pant Drain
Omas Creek
West Growths
BURSALL SQ
HAVEN ROAD
South Field
Crown Farm
B1445
Winestead Drain
Omascreek Plantation
TURMARR RD
MAIN ST
BACK LA
Patrington Haven
SALTMARSH LANE
Westfield Farm
Haverfield House
Patrington Farm
Haven Plantation
RAVENSPURN RD
PH
Ivy House
Eastgrowths Farm
Salt Marsh
Brick Bridge Drain
North Channel Clough
Pant Drain
East Growths
Welwick Drain
Oxlands Hill
OUTSTRAY ROAD
Brick Bridge
Winestead Drain
Bleak House Farm
Middle Channel
Newlands
HU12
SHEEP TROD LANE
Mon
Welwick Bank
Fisherman's Channel
NEWLANDS ROAD
HUMBER SIDE LA
STRAY ROAD
Channel Farm
Newlands Drain
Outstray Farm
Welwick Saltmarsh Nature Reserve
CHANNEL ROAD
Fisher Drain
Cross Drain
Mon
Patrington Channel
Sunk Island
Wood Farm
East Bank Farm
Hawkin's Point
River Humber
8
21
7
20
6
19
5
18
4
17
3
16
2
15
1
14
28
29
30
31
32
33

89

75

Scale: 1⅓ inches to 1 mile
0 ¼ ½ mile
0 250m 500m 750m 1 km

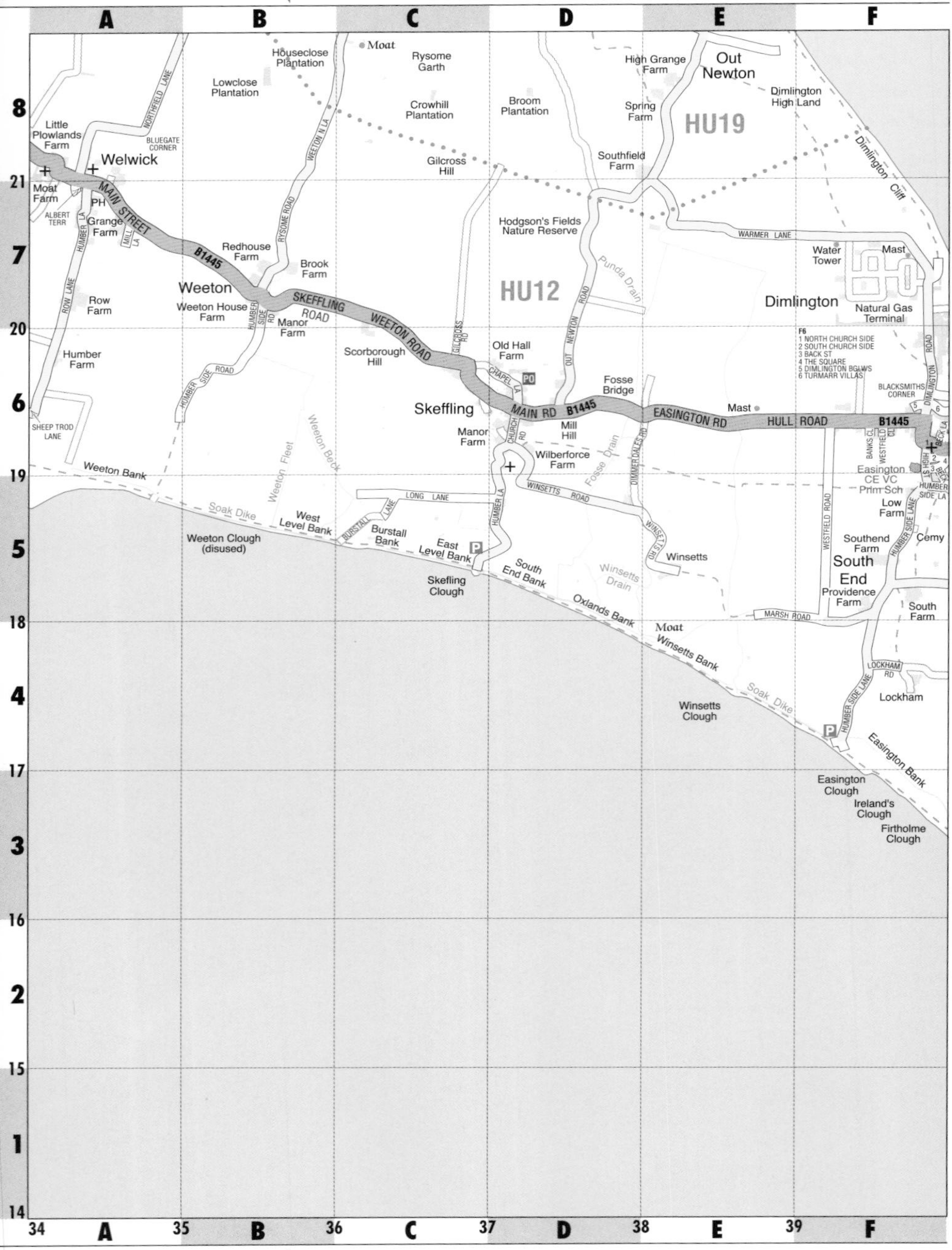

A
B
C
D
E
F
8
21
7
20
6
19
5
18
4
17
3
16
2
15
1
14
34
35
36
37
38
39
Moat
Houseclose Plantation
Rysome Garth
High Grange Farm
Out Newton
Lowclose Plantation
Crowhill Plantation
Broom Plantation
Spring Farm
Dimlington High Land
HU19
Little Plowlands Farm
NORTHFIELD LANE
BLUEGATE CORNER
Welwick
WEETON N LA
Gilcross Hill
Southfield Farm
Dimlington Cliff
Moat Farm
PH
ALBERT TERR
MAIN STREET
Grange Farm
HUMBER LA
MILL LA
RYSOME ROAD
Hodgson's Fields Nature Reserve
WARMER LANE
Redhouse Farm
B1445
Brook Farm
Punda Drain
Water Tower
Mast
Weeton
SKEFFLING ROAD
HU12
Dimlington
Row Farm
ROW LANE
Weeton House Farm
HUMBER SIDE RD
Manor Farm
WEETON ROAD
OUT NEWTON ROAD
Natural Gas Terminal
Humber Farm
Scorborough Hill
GILCROSS RD
Old Hall Farm
F6
1 NORTH CHURCH SIDE
2 SOUTH CHURCH SIDE
3 BACK ST
4 THE SQUARE
5 DIMLINGTON BGLWS
6 TURMARR VILLAS
HUMBER SIDE ROAD
CHAPEL LA
PO
Fosse Bridge
DIMLINGTON ROAD
BLACKSMITHS CORNER
Skeffling
MAIN RD
EASINGTON RD
Mast
HULL ROAD
SHEEP TROD LANE
Weeton Beck
Manor Farm
CHURCH RD
Mill Hill
BECK LA
Weeton Bank
Weeton Fleet
Wilberforce Farm
Fosse Drain
DIMMER DALES RD
BANKS CL
WESTFIELD CL
HIGH ST
Easington CE VC Prim Sch
Soak Dike
LONG LANE
WINSETTS ROAD
HUMBER SIDE LA
West Level Bank
BURSTALL LANE
Burstall Bank
HUMBER LA
Low Farm
Weeton Clough (disused)
WINSETTS RD
WESTFIELD ROAD
Southend Farm
Cemy
East Level Bank
P
South End Bank
Winsetts
HUMBER SIDE LANE
Skeffling Clough
Winsetts Drain
South End
Providence Farm
Oxlands Bank
MARSH ROAD
South Farm
Moat
Winsetts Bank
LOCKHAM RD
Lockham
Soak Dike
Winsetts Clough
Easington Bank
Easington Clough
Ireland's Clough
Firtholme Clough

89

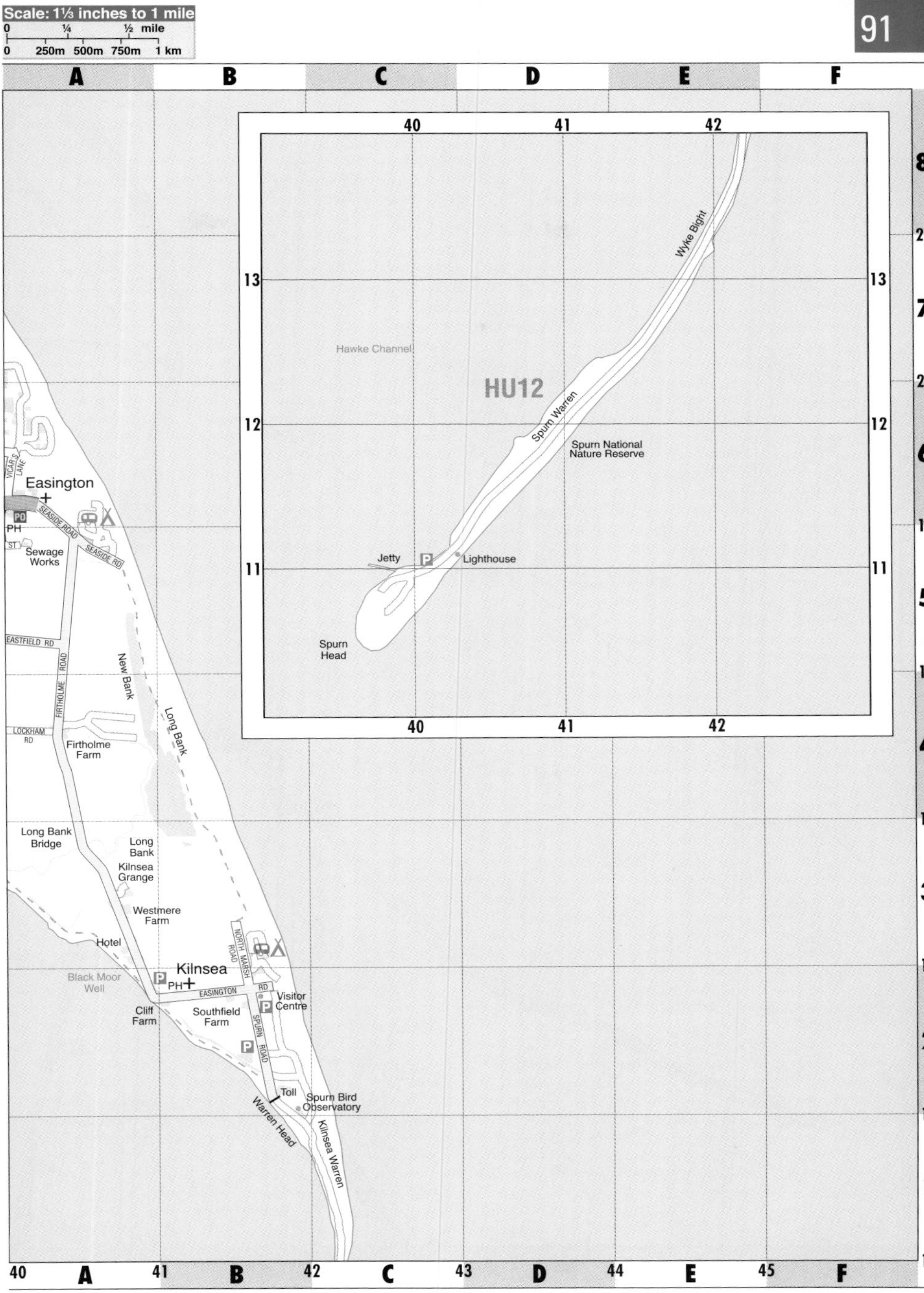
Scale: 1⅓ inches to 1 mile
0 ¼ ½ mile
0 250m 500m 750m 1 km
A
B
C
D
E
F
8
7
6
5
4
3
2
1
21
20
19
18
17
16
15
14
40
41
42
43
44
45
13
12
11
Wyke Bight
Hawke Channel
HU12
Spurn Warren
Spurn National
Nature Reserve
Jetty
Lighthouse
Spurn
Head
VICAR'S LANE
Easington
PO
PH
ST
SEASIDE ROAD
SEASIDE RD
Sewage
Works
EASTFIELD RD
FIRTHOLME ROAD
New Bank
Long Bank
LOCKHAM RD
Firtholme
Farm
Long Bank
Bridge
Long
Bank
Kilnsea
Grange
Westmere
Farm
Hotel
NORTH MARSH ROAD
Black Moor
Well
Kilnsea
PH
EASINGTON RD
Visitor
Centre
Cliff
Farm
Southfield
Farm
SPURN ROAD
Toll
Spurn Bird
Observatory
Warren Head
Kilnsea Warren

C6
1 SILVER ST
2 NEW GREEN
3 THORNE RD
4 BREEZEMOUNT CT
5 KENNETH AVE
6 ASHFIELD GR
7 BEECH CR
8 NUTFIELDS GR
9 DR ANDERSON AVE
10 CROSSWAYS
11 HOLME GDNS
12 BOOTHAM RD
13 DUKE ST
14 KINGSWAY
15 STANLEY GDNS
16 STANLEY RD
17 THOMAS RD

78

E4
1 AMBROSE AVE
2 BRABBS AVE
3 WESTFIELD VILLAS
4 WESTFIELD RD
5 SPRINGFIELD AVE
6 LEYLAND AVE
7 BROCKENHURST RD
8 MANOR GD
9 EPWORTH RD (WEST)

Scale: 1⅓ inches to 1 mile
0 ¼ ½ mile
0 250m 500m 750m 1 km

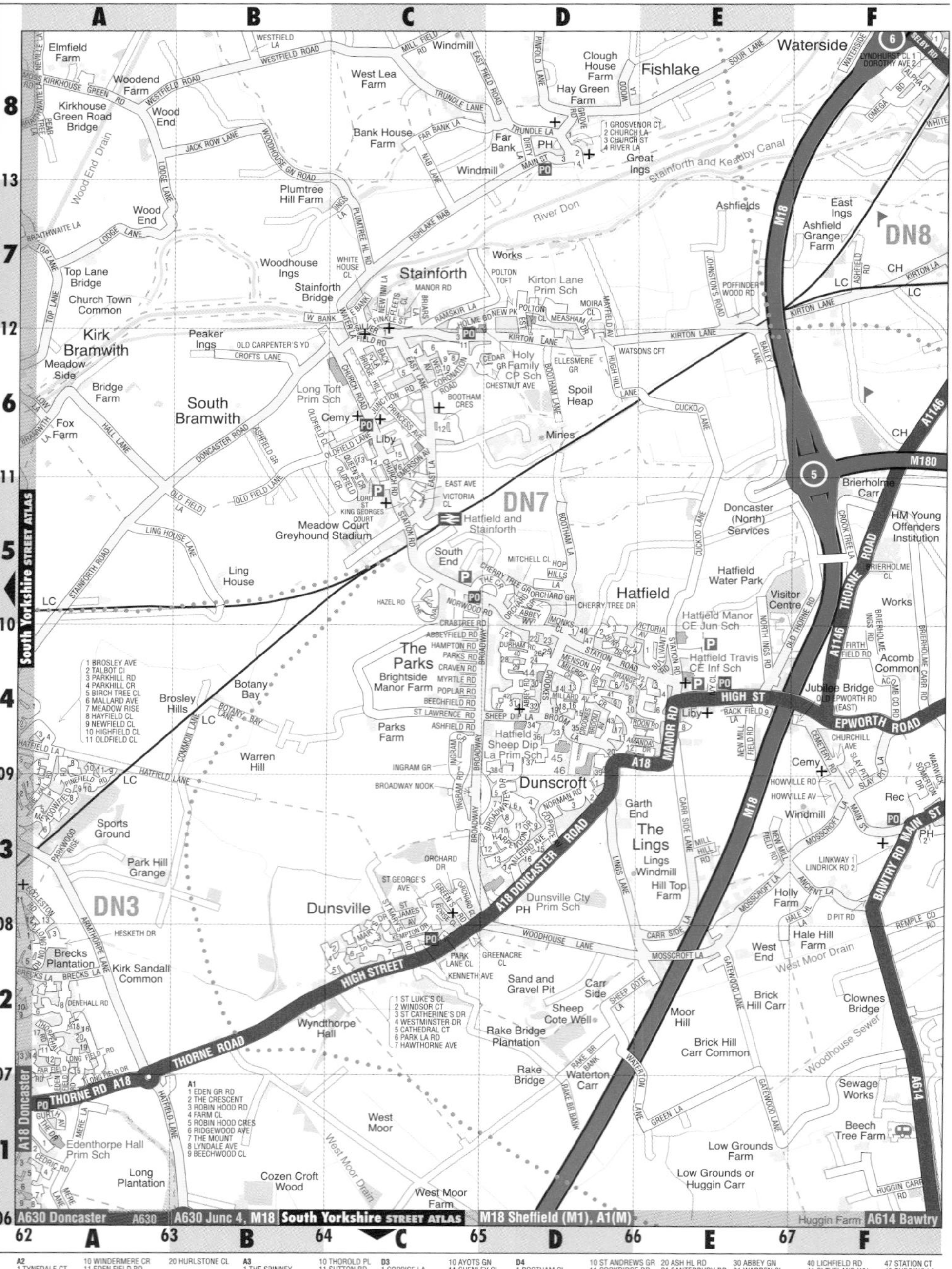

A2
1 TYNEDALE CT
2 GRANGE PK
3 TARLETON CL
4 HAREWOOD AVE
5 CURZEN CR
6 ELIZABETH AVE
7 REDHALL CL
8 NEWHALL RD
9 DERWENT DR
10 WINDERMERE CR
11 EDEN FIELD RD
12 HARVEST CL
13 EDENCROFT DR
14 FAR FIELD CL
15 MEADOW CFT
16 FOTHERGILL DR
17 FERNHALL CL
18 HOLMSHAW CL
19 HAMPSON GARDENS
20 HURLSTONE CL

A3
1 THE SPINNEY
2 ST ANDREW'S WY
3 LIMEDALE VW
4 PINEFIELD AVE
5 MILL FIELD CT
6 GREENFIELD CL
7 HEATHFIELD CL
8 WHEATFIELD CL
9 LOWFIELD CL
10 THOROLD PL
11 SUTTON RD
12 LONGTON RD

D3
1 COPPICE LA
2 DANUM RD
3 NORMAN DR
4 ASTON GN
5 BRETTON CL
6 HARPENDON DR
7 WIDFORD GN
8 AMWELL GN
9 BARNET GN
10 AYOTS GN
11 SHENLEY CL
12 HARPENDEN CL
13 HODDESDON CR
14 NASEBY CL
15 BLENHEIM CL
16 BOSWORTH CL

D4
1 BOOTHAM CL
2 NETTLEHOLME
3 HOMESTEAD GARTH
4 BRACKEN HEEN CL
5 GRANGE CL
6 LINDEN CL
7 KING'S CL
8 PARKSTONE GR
9 TOLLESBY LA
10 ST ANDREWS GR
11 COOKRIDGE DR
12 PARKWAYS
13 MILCROFT CR
14 THOMPSON NOOK
15 ROSEBERRY AVE
16 THOMPSON DR
17 NUNTHORPE CL
18 MILLARD NOOK
19 WHITE HO CL
20 ASH HL RD
21 CANTERBURY RD
22 GLENCOE CL
23 PRESCOTT GR
24 INVERNESS RD
25 BALMORAL RD
26 BRAMAR RD
27 ST EDWINS CL
28 YORK RD
29 WINCHESTER RD
30 ABBEY GN
31 WARREN CL
32 ABBEY GDNS
33 OAKLAND AVE
34 BROADWATER DR
35 LODGE CT
36 LEVERSTOCK GN
37 KINSBOURNE GN
38 BROADLANDS CL
39 COPPICE GR
40 LICHFIELD RD
41 CLEVELAND WY
42 WARRENNE RD
43 MARTON GR
44 HATFIELD CROOKESBROOM PRIM SCH
45 HATFIELD VISUAL ARTS COLL
46 CHASE SPECIAL SCH
47 STATION CT
48 PUDDING LA

Scale: 1⅓ inches to 1 mile
0 ¼ ½ mile
0 250m 500m 750m 1 km

A8
1 CASSON'S RD
2 HIGHFIELD CR
3 MARSDEN GR
4 LIME TREE GR
5 UPR KENYON ST
6 LWR KENYON ST
7 BELLWOOD CR
8 BROOKFIELD CL
9 FOSTER RD
10 DURHAM AVE
11 GODFREY RD
12 BOATING DYKE WY
13 CAPSTAN WY
14 ASHBURNHAM RD
15 BROWNS LA
16 QUEEN ST
17 QUEEN'S CT
18 CHAPEL LA
19 BELLE VUE TERR
20 THE GREEN
21 HORSE FAIR GN
22 FAIRTREE WK
23 MIDDLEBROOK LA
24 SILVER ST
25 PINFOLD LA
26 DUNSTAN DR
27 CLIFTON CT
28 KENYON CL
29 WINDLASS CL
30 DUNSTAN DR
31 ANCHOR CL

79

B8
1 INGLENOOK DR
2 REDLAND CR
3 ALBERT ST
4 COULMAN RD
5 COULMAN ST
6 LOCKWOOD CL
7 TENNYSON AVE
8 CHURCH CL
9 HAYNES GN
10 HOUPS RD
11 LITTLEWOOD RD
12 COVENTRY RD
13 TITHE BARN LA
14 DANUM CL
15 HAYNES GDNS
16 TRAVIS CL
17 TRAVIS GR
18 TRAVIS AVE
19 ALWYN RD

94

A7
1 ASHFIELD AVE
2 CANAL VW
3 CHEVIOT CL
4 MALVERN CL
5 QUANTOCK CL
6 MARINA VW
7 WENDAN RD
8 WEST CT
9 PICKERING GR
10 PARK VIEW
11 PARK CRES
12 SOUTH WOOD DR
13 ASH TREE RD
14 GREEN TOP FST SCH

B7
1 HAYNES GR
2 HAYNES CL
3 CHESTNUT AVE
4 ELM TREE GR
5 PEEL HL RD
6 WIKE GATE GR
7 WIKE GATE CL
8 PEEL CASTLE RD
9 MARLBOROUGH RD
10 MILLER CL
11 OLDFIELD RD
12 FENLAND RD
13 ST MICHAEL'S CL
14 SOUTHFIELD CL
15 AXHOLME GN
16 ST GEORGES RD
17 SWANLAND CL
18 MOWBRAY RD
19 ST GEORGES CL
20 PASHLEY RD
21 BEECH TREE AVE
22 THE CROFT
23 SWANLAND CT

104
94

93
80

D8
1 COX LA
2 CRANIDGE CL
3 JUSTICE HALL LA
4 BOWLING GN LA
5 CHAPEL ST
6 PRINTING OFFICE LA
7 LOW CROSS ST
8 CROSS SLACK
9 KESTEVEN GR

D7
1 VICAR'S WK
2 CHANCERY LA
3 WEST TERRACE ST
4 HIGH ST
5 MARKET CT
6 THE PADDOCKS
7 QUEENS DR
8 SOUTHFIELD RD
9 CROWLAND RD
10 LABURNUM GR
11 MULBERRY DR
12 ST JAMES CL
13 LINCOLN CL
14 WOLDS CL
15 REGENT DR

Scale: 1⅓ inches to 1 mile
0 ¼ ½ mile
0 250m 500m 750m 1 km

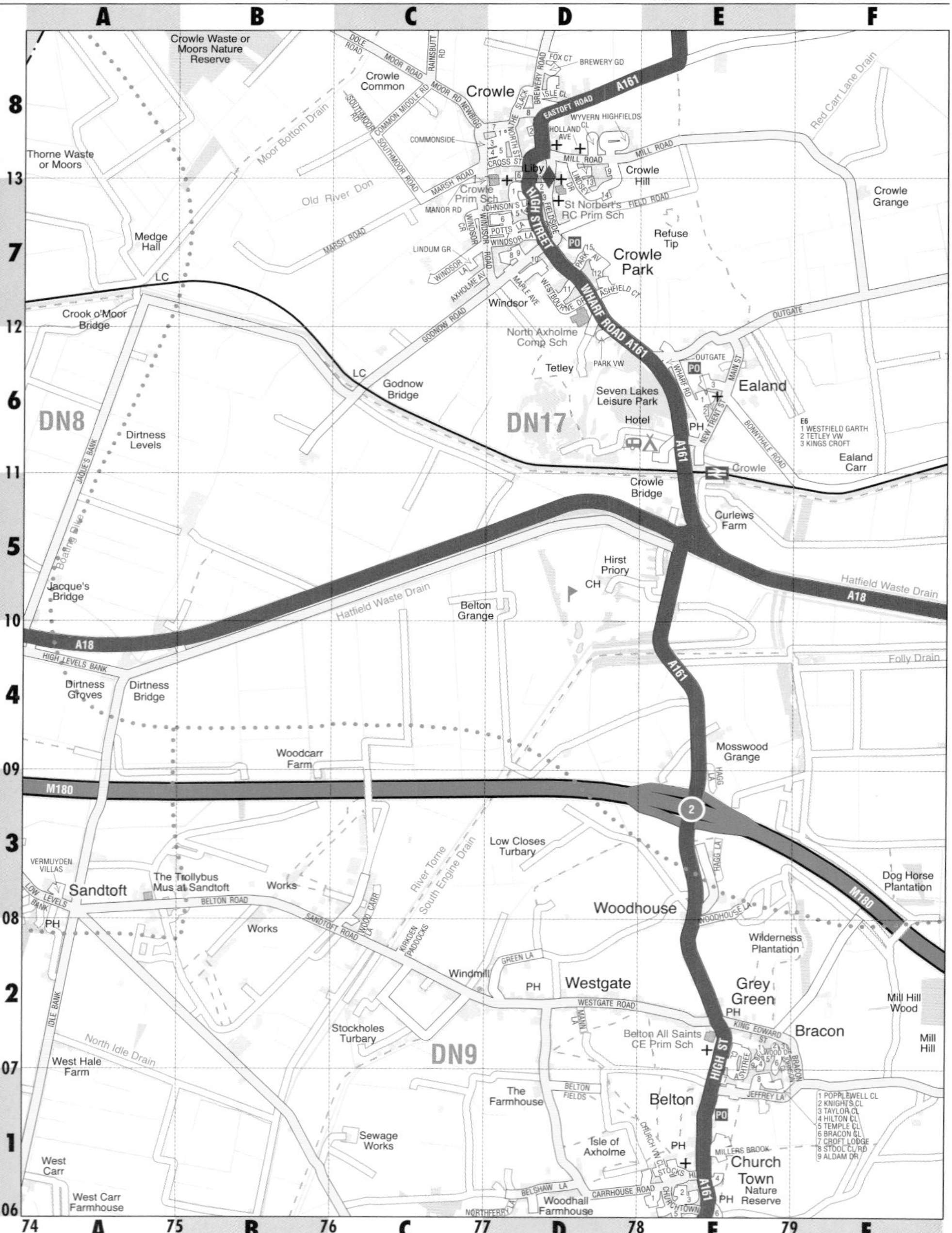

93
105

E1
1 SOUTHFIELD
2 KEEPER'S WY
3 POACHER'S CFT
4 MEADOWBANK
5 CHERRY GR
6 BELGRAVE CL

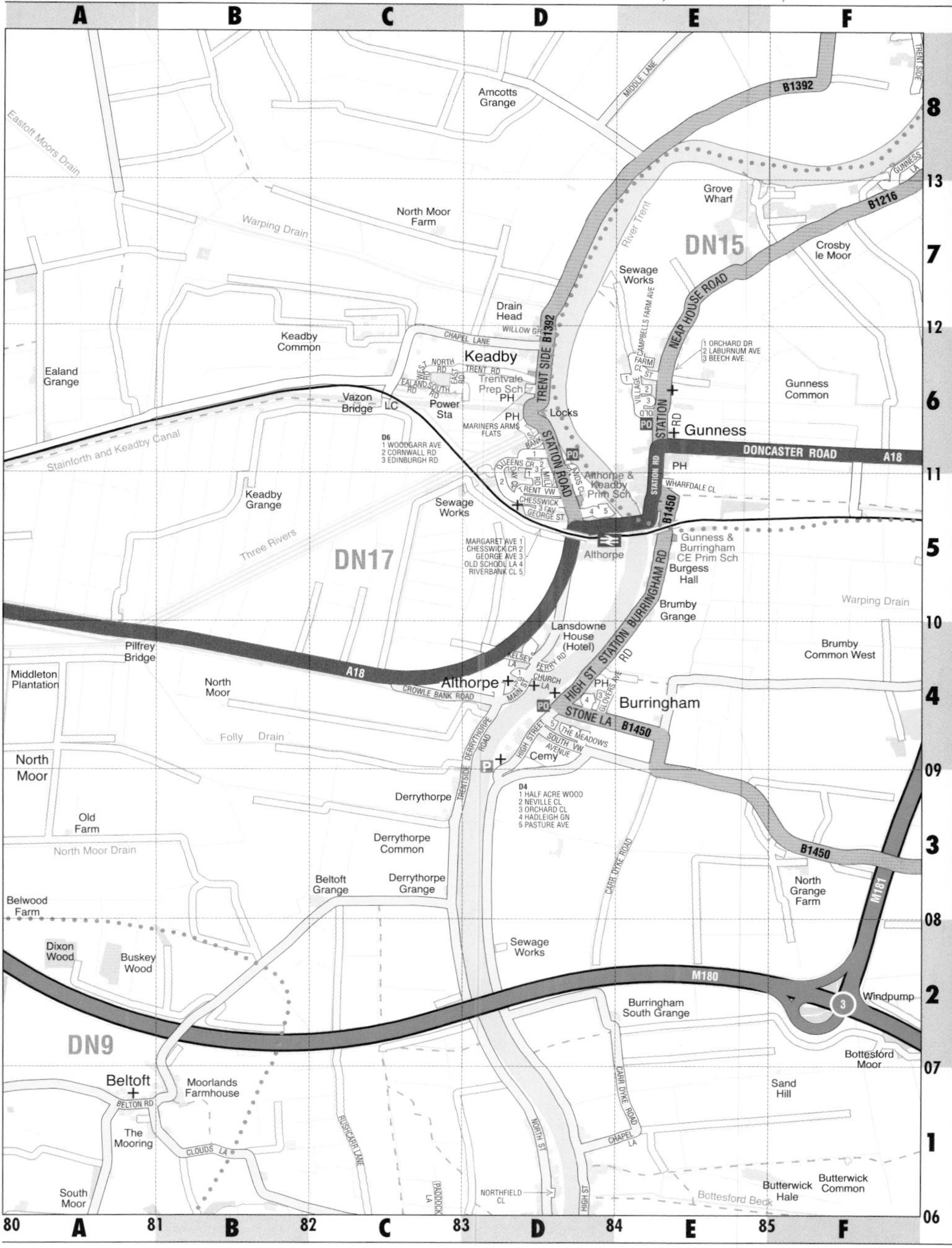
Scale: 1⅓ inches to 1 mile
0 ¼ ½ mile
0 250m 500m 750m 1 km
81
96
150
A B C D E F
8
13
7
12
6
11
5
10
4
09
3
08
2
07
1
06
80 81 82 83 84 85
Eastoft Moors Drain
Amcotts Grange
MIDDLE LANE
B1392
TRENT SIDE
GUNNESS LA
Grove Wharf
B1216
North Moor Farm
Warping Drain
River Trent
DN15
Crosby le Moor
Sewage Works
NEAP HOUSE ROAD
CAMPBELLS FARM AVE
Drain Head
WILLOW GR
CHAPEL LANE
Keadby Common
Keadby
TRENT SIDE B1392
1 ORCHARD DR
2 LABURNUM AVE
3 BEECH AVE
Ealand Grange
NORTH RD
WEST RD
TRENT RD
EAST RD
EALAND RD
SOUTH RD
Trentvale Prep Sch
FARM CL
VILLAGE ST
Gunness Common
Vazon Bridge
LC
Power Sta
PH
Locks
OLD STATION RD
Gunness
Stainforth and Keadby Canal
D6
1 WOODGARR AVE
2 CORNWALL RD
3 EDINBURGH RD
MARINERS ARMS FLATS
BANK
STATION ROAD
DONCASTER ROAD
A18
QUEENS CR
OAK CL
MILL RD
STATION RD
Althorpe & Keadby Prim Sch
RENT VW
WHARFDALE CL
Keadby Grange
Sewage Works
CHESSWICK
FAV
GEORGE ST
B1450
Three Rivers
DN17
MARGARET AVE 1
CHESSWICK CR 2
GEORGE AVE 3
OLD SCHOOL LA 4
RIVERBANK CL 5
Althorpe
Gunness & Burringham CE Prim Sch
Burgess Hall
BURRINGHAM RD
Brumby Grange
Warping Drain
Lansdowne House (Hotel)
STATION RD
Pilfrey Bridge
Brumby Common West
Middleton Plantation
North Moor
A18
KELSEY LA
FERRY RD
CHURCH LA
Althorpe
CROWLE BANK ROAD
MAIN ST
HIGH ST
PH
GLOVERS AVE
Burringham
STONE LA
B1450
Folly Drain
THE MEADOWS
SOUTH VW
AVENUE
HIGH STREET
TRENTSIDE DERRYTHORPE ROAD
North Moor
Cemy
P
Derrythorpe
D4
1 HALF ACRE WOOD
2 NEVILLE CL
3 ORCHARD CL
4 HADLEIGH GN
5 PASTURE AVE
Old Farm
North Moor Drain
Derrythorpe Common
CARR DYKE ROAD
B1450
Beltoft Grange
Derrythorpe Grange
North Grange Farm
Belwood Farm
M181
Dixon Wood
Buskey Wood
Sewage Works
M180
Windpump
Burringham South Grange
3
DN9
Bottesford Moor
Beltoft
Moorlands Farmhouse
BELTON RD
Sand Hill
CARR DYKE ROAD
The Mooring
RUSHCARR LANE
NORTH ST
CHAPEL LA
CLOUDS LA
Butterwick Hale
Butterwick Common
South Moor
PADDOCK LA
NORTHFIELD CL
HIGH ST
Bottesford Beck
106
96
150

B7
1 PRIMROSE WY
2 POPPY CL
3 WOODALE CL
4 BETONY CL
5 COLTSFOOT CL
6 FLETCHER CL
7 BLACKTHORN CL
8 AVENSWOOD LA
9 ST MARY'S CT
10 HERON CL
11 PIPPIN CT
12 RUSSET CL
13 SEDGEWOOD WY
14 LUNEBURG PL
15 AVE ROUEN
16 AVE LOURDES
17 AVE FONTENAY

95

E2
1 CHERRY MOUNT
2 ROWAN CR
3 CHARTERHOUSE DR
4 ROSSALL CL
5 OUNDLE CL
6 MILL HL DR

82

7 QUEENSWOOD RD
8 CHELTENHAM CL
9 OAKLEIGH
10 RICHMOND DR
11 MILL CFT
12 BURNET DR
13 HOLLY CL
14 PLANTAIN CL
15 PIMPERNEL WY
16 JONQUIL AVE
17 CHAMOMILE CL
18 TAMARISK WY
19 LAUREL WY
20 WILKINSON WY
21 JOHNSON DR
22 NUTWOOD VW
23 PEACH TREE CL
24 HONEYSUCKLE CT

Scale: 1⅓ inches to 1 mile
0 ¼ ½ mile
0 250m 500m 750m 1 km

A B C D E F

A B C D E F

For full street detail of the highlighted area see pages 150 and 151.

95

D1
1 TYDEMAN CL
2 HOLSTEIN DR
3 HALES CL
4 HALLBROOK CT
5 LAXTON GR
6 TALISMAN DR
7 LAMBOURNE RI
8 BRAMLEY CR
9 RIBSTON CL

107

10 CONFERENCE CT
11 WORCESTER CL
12 RILESTON PL
13 MALLING WK
14 MERRYWEATHER CT
15 STURMER CT
16 PIPPIN DR
17 WREN CL
18 MARTIN CL
19 FIELDFARE CL
20 HAZEL GR
21 GARDENIA DR
22 AUBRETIA DR
23 ARMERIA DR
24 ACORN WY
25 MONTBRETIA DR
26 DUNNOCK CL

D2
1 OAKWOOD RI
2 CROSSBECK RD
3 MAGDALEN CL
4 BRUNEL CL
5 GIRTON CL
6 NUFFIELD CL
7 MOUNTBATTEN CL
8 ST CATHERINES CR
9 CAVENDISH RD
10 TRINITY RD
11 DOWNING CR
12 NEWNHAM CR
13 PEMBROKE AVE
14 THORNHOLME DR
15 WAYSIDE CL
16 KNIGHT'S CT
17 TEMPLAR CT
18 EMMANUEL DR
19 CHURCH LA
20 OLD SCHOOL LA
21 REPTON DR
22 SILVER BIRCH RI
23 BEECHES AVE
24 COPPER BEECH WK
25 ROSEWOOD WY
26 CAMPBELL AVE
27 HORNBEAM AVE
28 FIR CL

Scale: 1⅓ inches to 1 mile
0 ¼ ½ mile
0 250m 500m 750m 1 km

83
98

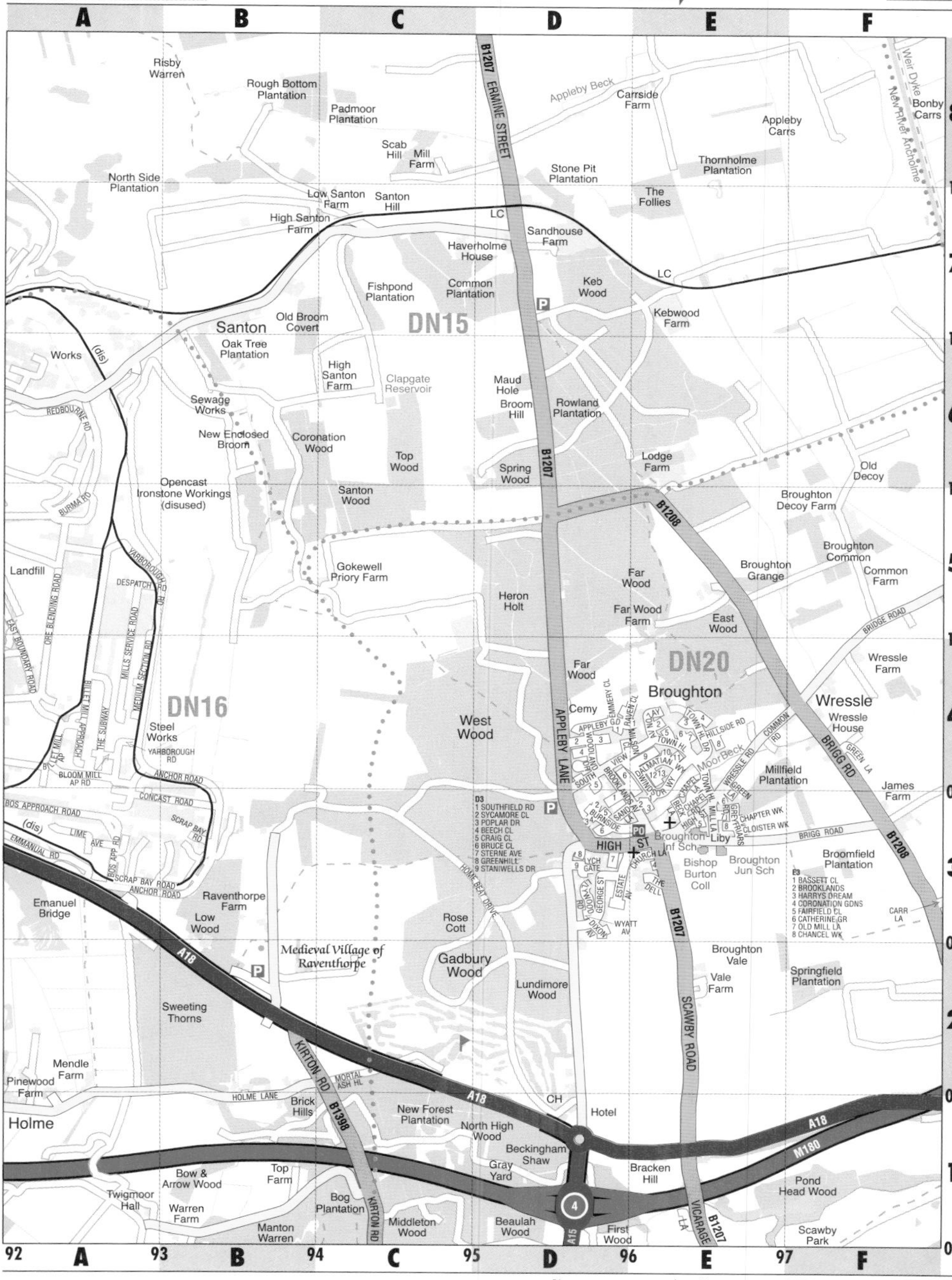

108
98

D4
1 HERON HOLT
2 WESTMINSTER RD
3 THE BLACKTHORNS
4 WESTWOOD
5 TRINITY CT
6 YARBOROUGH CR

E4
1 BADGER WY
2 RUE DE NOZAY
3 BEECHWOOD CR
4 PINETREE CL
5 CHESTNUT GR
6 SCHOOL HOUSES
7 HUNTS CL
8 EASTWOOD DR
9 ST BERNARD'S CL
10 AIREDALE CL
11 LABRADOR DR
12 BEAGLE CL
13 DANE CL

97
84

F7
1 WOODLAND DR
2 DOLL LA
3 DUNNS PADDOCK
4 MALTKILN LA

Scale: 1⅓ inches to 1 mile
0 ¼ ½ mile
0 250m 500m 750m 1 km

A
B
C
D
E
F
8
13
7
12
6
11
5
10
4
09
3
08
2
07
1
06
98
99
00
01
02
03
Bonby Carrs
Bonby Carr Drain
Soak Drain
Worlaby New Ings
Clarkson's Carr Farm
CARR LANE
Worlaby Catchwater
Worlaby Causeway Drain
Worlaby Carrs
LC
Worlaby Carrs Farm
Clough Plantation
Elsham May Bank Drain
Elsham Carr Drain
Land Drain
Rennison's Carr Farm
Old River Ancholme
Decoy Covert
Elsham Carrs
Carr Side Plantation
Tweedmoor Plantation
Moor Plantation
New Plantation
LOW ROAD
NEW RD
MAIN ST
TOP RD
GRANGE FIELD
THE HILL
Almshouse
Worlaby Prim Sch
PH
Worlaby
Hillside Plantation
Elsham Hill
B1206
B1204
ELSHAM ROAD
WASHDYKE LANE
Mast
Water Treatment Works
Quarry (dis)
MIDDLEGATE LANE
Deepdale Plantation
VICARAGE LA
CHURCH ST
HALL LA
NEW ST
CHAPEL LA
FRONT ST
FIRTREE DR
BARNETBY LA
Elsham
Barton Belt
Elsham Hall Country & Wildlife Park
Moat Wood
Old Lane Holt
Snowdale
Southside Plantation
Tumuli
CH
Botany Bay
Timaru Farm
Wrawby Plantation
Low Moor Drain
Great Moor
M180
Little Moor
Wrawby Moor
DN20
Planker Dike
BRIDGE ROAD
Broughton Bridge
Broughton Carrs
Sewage Works
Low Moor Drain (West)
Little Carr Drain
West Drain
White Hills
Melton Road Farm
MELTON ROAD
Carr Drain
Chicken Farm
STAR CARR LA
STAR CARR LANE
Three Tree Farm
Castlethorpe Carr Farm
Carr Farm
Wrawby Carrs
Wits End
Top Farm
A18
1 MARKHAM WY
2 ECCLES CT
3 CHAPEL LA
4 FRANKLAND CL
5 VICARAGE RD
GILLATTS CL
OLD MILL LA
VICARAGE AV
MILLVIEW GD
Wrawby
Grey Farm
MILL LA
Castlethorpe Bridge
Low Farm
C3
1 SUNNINGDALE AVE
2 DAVY CR
3 NORTHERN AVE
4 HIGHFIELD GR
BARTON RD
DOVECOTE MW
Wrawby Postmill
Wrawby St Mary's CE Prim Sch
Bridge Farm
PH
BRIGG ROAD
THE OLD STACK YARD
HIGH FIELD RD
KETTLEBY LANE
Skegger Beck
GRAMMAR SCHOOL LA
BRICKYARD LANE
Catchwater
St Mary's RC Prim Sch
Vale of Ancholme Tech Coll
Springfield
St Helens
Castlethorpe Covert
The Mount
Mount Farm
Coal Dyke End
Brigg Prim Sch
WRAWBY ROAD
Kettleby House
Moat
LC
KETTLEBY VW
WINSTON WY
SPRINGFIELD RI
Kettleby Carrs Farm
Sewage Works
B1208
Works
Sir John Nelthorpe Sch
Cemy
BRIGG
Carr Farm
A1084
Woodlands Farm
THE MOORINGS
Works
Liby
PO
1 OAKFIELD CL
2 WILLOWBROOK DR
Priory Farm
PH
A18 BRIDGE ST
BIGBY RD
BIGBY HIGH ROAD
ASHDOWN CL
MAPLE CL
Castlethorpe
SCAWBY RD
East Side
Brigg Prep Sch
Brigg
LC
THE COPSE
Pingley Farm
Howsham Farm
Scawby Brook
Ancholme Leisure Centre
Island Carr
TENNYSON CL
PINGLEY MD
Howsham Barff Wood
B1434
PH
BROOK LA
CHURCH LA
Westrum
New River Ancholme
Old River Ancholme
CADNEY RD
WESTRUM LA
Kettleby Beck
LN7
Mill Place
Bentley Farm
Froghall Carrs

B2
1 CHERRY TREE AVE
2 KINGSWAY
3 COLTON ST
4 CARY LA
5 MARKET LA
6 EXCHANGE PL
7 ANCHORAGE ST
8 MARKET PL
9 PARADISE PL
10 BRIDGE ST
11 RIVERSIDE
12 TEAL CL
13 THE NARROW BOATS
14 MILLERS QUAY
15 MILL CL
16 ANCHORS WY
17 KILN LA
18 WEST TERR
19 ENGINE ST
20 FORRESTER ST
21 JAMES ST
22 FOXGLOVE CL
23 POPPYFIELD WY
24 BRAMBLE WY

97
109

C2
1 PRESTON DR
2 HAWTHORN AVE
3 MAGRATH CT
4 DIXON CL
5 WESLEY RD
6 OLD COURTS RD
7 GRAMMAR SCHOOL RD S
8 WRAWBY ST
9 ELWES ST
10 THE BOTTLINGS
11 ANCHOLME GDNS
12 ST CLARES WK
13 CROSS ST
14 GARDEN ST
15 QUEEN ST
16 BIGBY RD
17 PRINCES ST
18 NEW ST
19 HOLME CL
20WELLBECK CL
21 CHAPEL WY
22 ST JAMES RD
23 GLANFORD RD
24 HEDGEROW LA
25 YARBOROUGH RD
26 SPRINGFIELD RD
27 NICOLGATE LA
28 DUDLEY RD

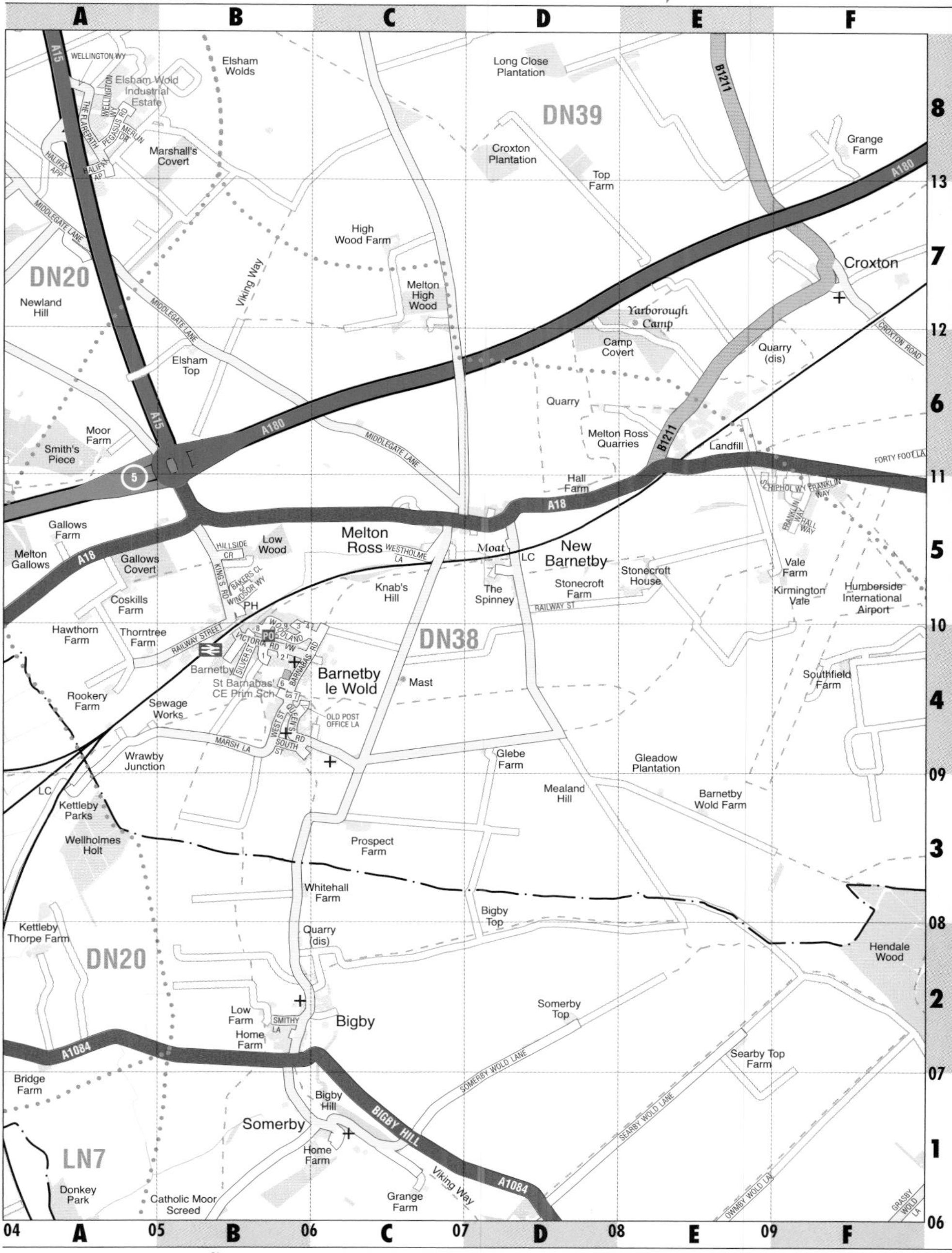

B4
1 ST MARY'S AVE
2 WALKER'S CL
3 SYCAMORE CL
4 BIRCH WY
5 WILLOW CL
6 CUTHBERT AVE
7 SMITHY LA
8 CHESTNUT GR
9 OAK GR

99
86

Scale: 1⅓ inches to 1 mile
0 ¼ ½ mile
0 250m 500m 750m 1 km

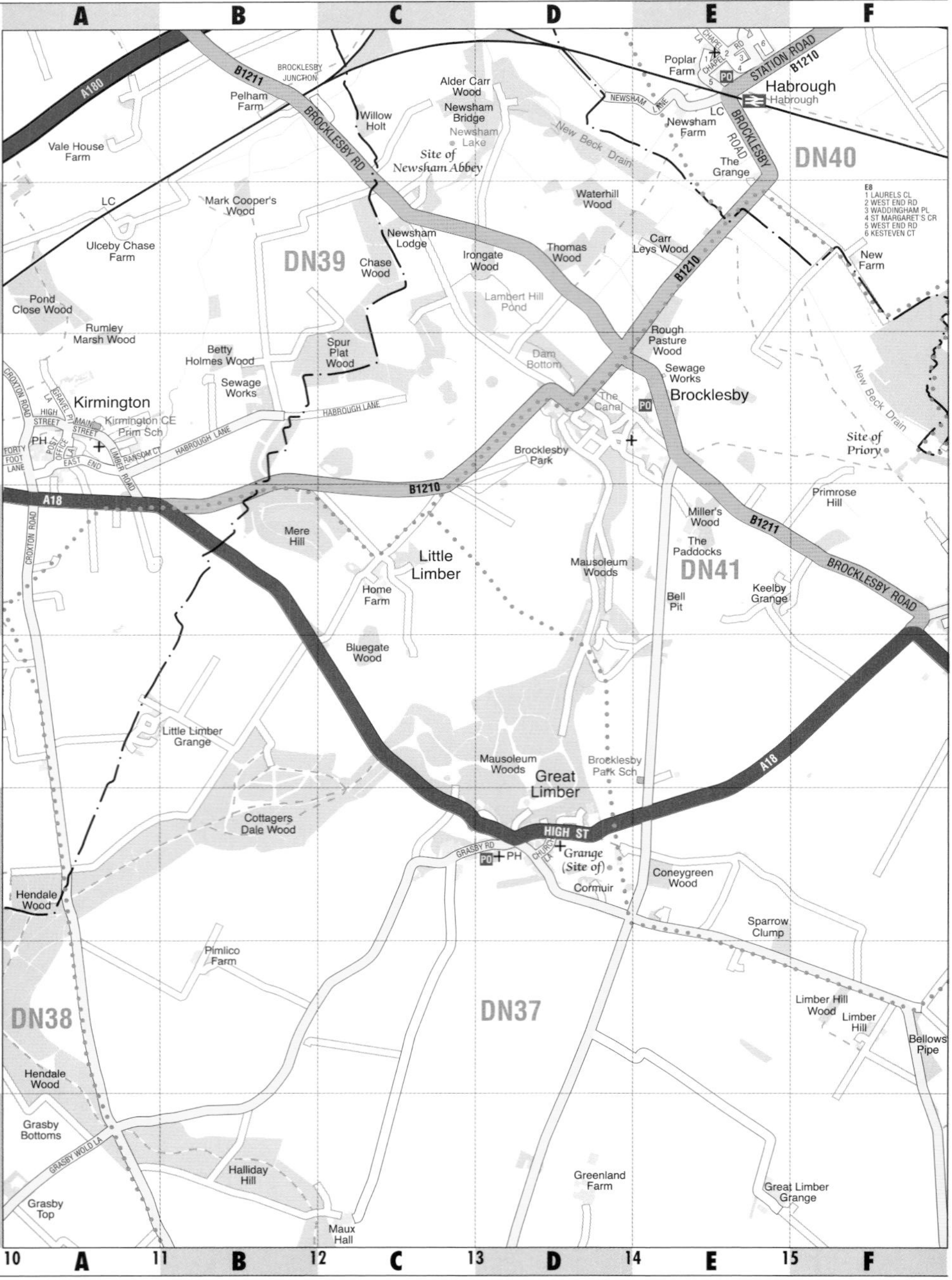

99
111

Scale: 1⅓ inches to 1 mile
0 ¼ ½ mile
0 250m 500m 750m 1 km

87
102

B8
1 KISHORN CT
2 KINLOCH WY
3 PERTH WY
4 TUMMEL CT
5 OBAN CT

C8
1 GUERNSEY GR
2 ALDERNEY WY
3 ORKNEY PL
4 SHETLAND WY
5 FAIRISLE RISE

F5
1 APPLE TREE CT
2 MALLARD CL
3 SWALLOW DR
4 WREN CL
5 CARLTON RD
6 IVY FARM CT
7 PINNEY'S CT
8 MAPLE GR
9 FORD'S AVE
10 MCVEIGH CT
11 BEVERLEY CT
12 WESTWOOD RD
13 ASHLEIGH CT
14 FORSYTHIA AVE
15 BLUEBELL CT
16 SALADINE CT
17 CORNFLOWER CL
18 ROOKERY RD
19 PRIMROSE CL

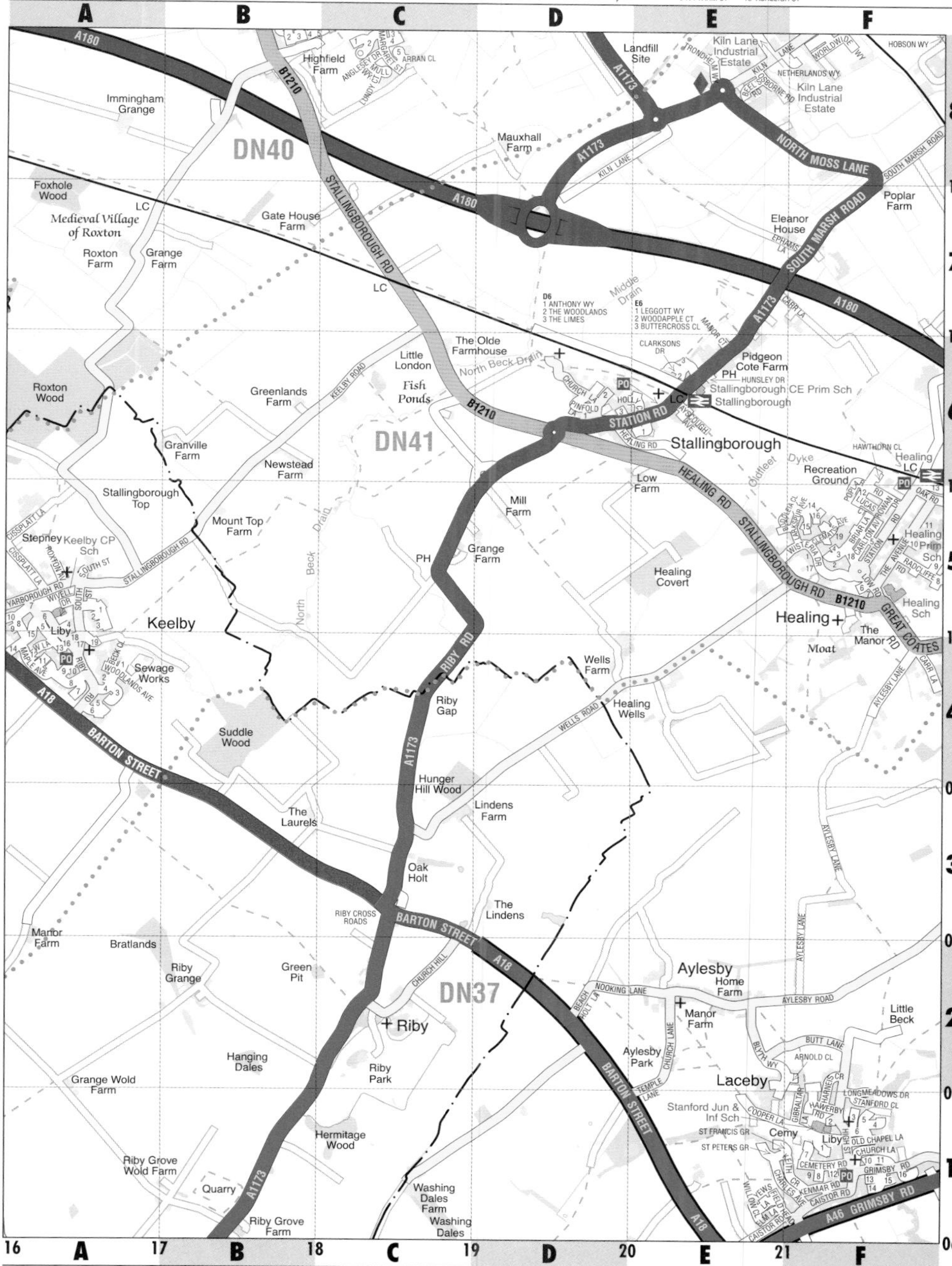

A4
1 MIDFIELD WY
2 ROWAN CL
3 RAITHBY AVE
4 SUDDLE WY
5 THORNTON GDN
6 COTHAM GDN
7 LONGMEADOW RI
8 MILSON RD
9 CADDLE RD
10 KAREN AVE
11 HULBERRY CL
12 MAPLE CL
13 HALLS LA
14 MILL LA
15 PELHAM CR
16 ST MARTIN'S PL
17 ST BARTHOLOMEW'S CL
18 KING ST
19 CHURCH LA

A5
1 EASTFIELD RD
2 TOMLINE RD
3 WINDSOR CL
4 MANOR CL
5 VICTORIA RD
6 MANOR ST
7 BROADWAY
8 ST ANNE'S RD
9 WEST VIEW CL
10 CHURCHILL AVE

112
102

F1
1 THE MEAD
2 BUTTERFIELD CL
3 SEED CL LA
4 PHILLIPS LA
5 AUSTIN GARTH
6 NEW CHAPEL LA
7 CEMETERY CR
8 KNIGHTS CL
9 ST MARGARET'S CL
10 FIELD CL
11 SPRING LA
12 ALTOFT CL
13 WHITGIFT CL
14 GRANGE AVE
15 TREVOR CL
16 GEORGE BUTLER CL

C4
1 SERVICE RD 22
2 SERVICE RD 23
3 SERVICE RD 4
4 SERVICE RD 5
5 SERVICE RD 25
6 HEMSWELL DR
7 SCOTT CL
8 SERVICE RD 6
9 SERVICE RD 7
10 SERVICE RD 17
11 SERVICE RD 18
12 SERVICE RD 1
13 SERVICE RD 19
14 SERVICE RD 20
15 SERVICE RD 2
16 BINBROOK WY
17 SERVICE RD 3
18 SERVICE RD 16
19 SERVICE RD 15
20 BARMOUTH DR

101

88

Scale: 1⅓ inches to 1 mile
0 ¼ ½ mile
0 250m 500m 750m 1 km

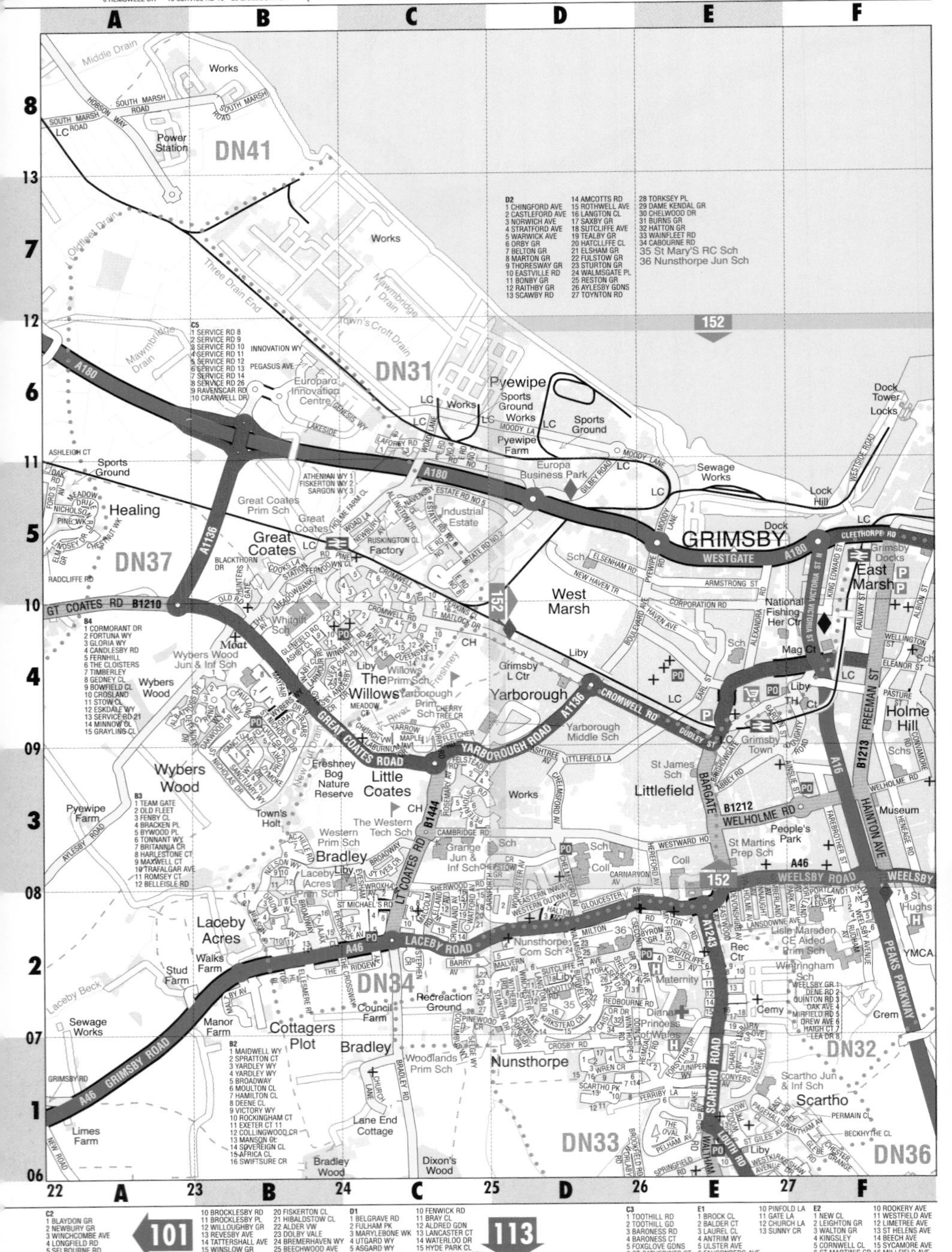

C2
1 BLAYDON GR
2 NEWBURY GR
3 WINCHCOMBE AVE
4 LONGFIELD RD
5 SELBOURNE RD
6 CLARENDON RD
7 THORNTON GR
8 WELLBECK RD
9 WELBECK PL
10 BROCKLESBY RD
11 BROCKLESBY PL
12 WILLOUGHBY GR
13 REVESBY AVE
14 TATTERSHALL AVE
15 WINSLOW GR
16 BARDNEY GDNS
17 GOXHILL GDNS
18 WICKENBY CL
19 WIRRAL AVE
20 FISKERTON CL
21 HIBALDSTOW CL
22 ALDER VW
23 DOLBY VALE
24 BREMERHAVEN WY
25 BEECHWOOD AVE
26 WYMARK VW
27 DALE VW
28 TALLERT WY

101

D1
1 BELGRAVE RD
2 FULHAM PK
3 MARYLEBONE WK
4 UTGARD WY
5 ASGARD WY
6 HAMPSTEAD PK
7 FINSBURY DR
8 EASON RD
9 WALLIS CT
10 FENWICK RD
11 BRAY CL
12 ALDRED GDN
13 LANCASTER CT
14 WATERLOO DR
15 HYDE PARK CL
16 BUCKINGHAM GDN
17 BUCKINGHAM GR

113

C3
1 TOOTHILL RD
2 TOOTHILL GD
3 BARONESS RD
4 BARONESS CT
5 FOXGLOVE GDNS
6 ST CATHERINES CT
7 DOWNING CL
8 MAGDALENE RD

E1
1 BROCK CL
2 BALDER CT
3 LAUREL CL
4 ANTRIM WY
5 ULSTER AVE
6 FAUCONBERG AVE
7 SOPHIA AVE
8 PELHAM AVE
9 PELHAM PL
10 PINFOLD LA
11 GATE LA
12 CHURCH LA
13 SUNNY CR

E2
1 NEW CL
2 LEIGHTON GR
3 WALTON GR
4 KINGSLEY
5 CORNWELL CL
6 ST MARTIN'S CR
7 FRUSHER AVE
8 HOMEFIELD AVE
9 RUPERT RD
10 ROOKERY AVE
11 WESTFIELD AVE
12 LIMETREE AVE
13 ST HELENS AVE
14 BEECH AVE
15 SYCAMORE AVE
16 MILLFIELD AVE
17 LYNDHURST AVE
18 MELBOURNE AVE
19 CRAGSTON AVE

For full street detail of the highlighted area see pages 152 and 153.

114

B2
1 CHATSWORTH PL
2 BALMORAL RD
3 CURZON CT
4 TERRINGTON PL
5 CRIDLING PL
6 KENILWORTH RD
7 HAVERSTOE PL
8 IRBY CT
9 ORMSBY CL
10 GREEN HL
11 CHERRY DALE
12 MILL GARTH
13 BELMONT CL
14 RAVENHILL CL
15 BRAMPTON WY

C1
1 PYTCHLEY WK
2 FITZWILLIAM MEWS
3 WELLS CR
4 BECKSIDE CL
5 BULLFINCH LA
6 WOODLAND WK
7 BECK WK
8 GREENFINCH DR
9 WINDERMERE CR
10 CONISTON CR
11 GRASMERE GR
12 DERWENT DR
13 ENNERDALE CL
14 CHAFFINCH DR
15 BRAMBLE WY
16 VIOLET CL
17 HAREWOOD GR
18 HAMPTON CL
19 CONISTON CR
20 LALRGATE PL
21 ARDEN VILLAGE
22 MARIGOLD WK
23 CRANBOURNE CL
24 DELAMERE CT
25 LAMBOURN CT
26 BURNHAM REACH
27 WESTPORT RD
28 MEADOW VW
29 HAYLING MERE

C2
1 PENSHURST RD
2 THORESBY PL
3 RUFFORD RD
4 BLENHEIM PL
5 WOODSLEY AVE
6 WENDOVER RI
7 LINDSEY RD
8 PARKER ST
9 GUNBY PL
10 LYNTON RI
11 CRAITHIE RD
12 MINSHULL RD
13 WEEKES RD
14 CAENBY RD
15 WESLEY CR
16 BILLINGHAY CT
17 LANSDOWN LINK
18 BURLEY AVE
19 ESKHAM CL
20 MARSHCHAPEL CL
21 LUDBOROUGH WY
22 BEESBY DR
23 BUTTERWICK CL
24 WALTHAM GR
25 ALVINGHAM AVE
26 QUORN MEWS
27 CATTISTOCK RD

D1
1 CHELSEA WK
2 ROCHESTER CT
3 MAYFAIR CT
4 FAIRFIELD CT
5 WHITEHALL RD
6 SOUTH VW
7 FIELDHOUSE RD
8 KINGSTON CL
9 WEYFORD RD
10 WESTBURY PK
11 GROVENOR CT
12 CUMBERLAND RD
13 RUSSELL CT
14 CAVENDISH CL
15 BERNERS RD
16 CLEE NESS DR
17 ASHWOOD DR
18 SINDERSON RD
19 HURSTLEA DR
20 CARRINGTON DR
21 POPLAR DR
22 CARLTON CL
23 NEWLANDS PK
24 FOREST WY
25 ROYAL CT

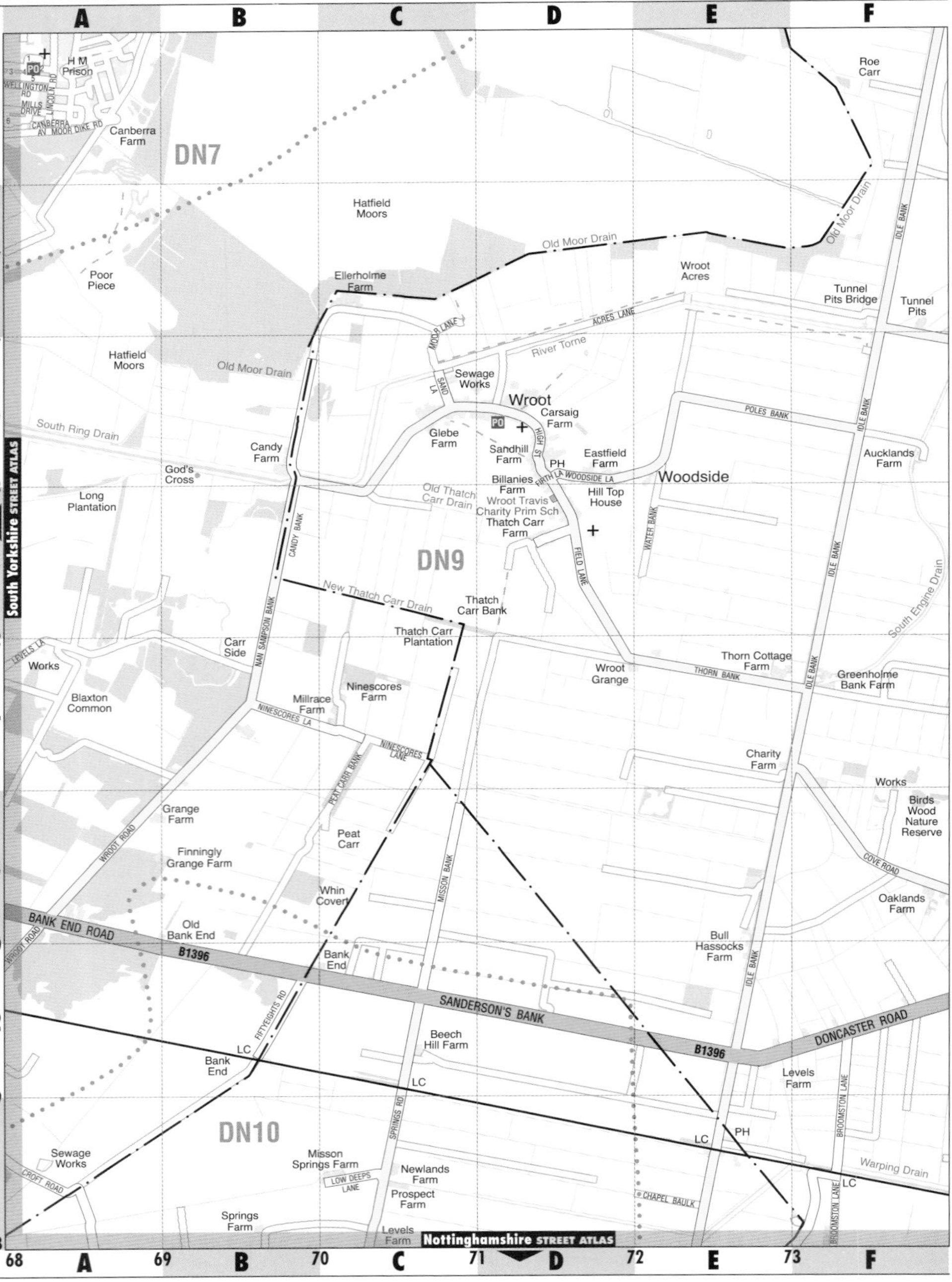
H M Prison
Canberra Farm
DN7
Hatfield Moors
Old Moor Drain
Poor Piece
Ellerholme Farm
Wroot Acres
Tunnel Pits Bridge
Tunnel Pits
Roe Carr
Sewage Works
Wroot
Carsaig Farm
Glebe Farm
Sandhill Farm
Eastfield Farm
Woodside
Candy Farm
God's Cross
Long Plantation
Billanies Farm
Hill Top House
Wroot Travis Charity Prim Sch
Thatch Carr Farm
DN9
Aucklands Farm
New Thatch Carr Drain
Thatch Carr Bank
Thatch Carr Plantation
Carr Side
Works
Blaxton Common
Millrace Farm
Ninescores Farm
Wroot Grange
Thorn Cottage Farm
Greenholme Bank Farm
Charity Farm
Birds Wood Nature Reserve
Grange Farm
Finningly Grange Farm
Peat Carr
Whin Covert
Oaklands Farm
Old Bank End
Bank End
Bull Hassocks Farm
BANK END ROAD
B1396
SANDERSON'S BANK
DONCASTER ROAD
Beech Hill Farm
Levels Farm
DN10
Sewage Works
Misson Springs Farm
Newlands Farm
Prospect Farm
Springs Farm
Levels Farm
Warping Drain
South Yorkshire STREET ATLAS
Nottinghamshire STREET ATLAS

Scale: 1⅓ inches to 1 mile
0 ¼ ½ mile
0 250m 500m 750m 1 km

D6
1 MANLEY CT
2 STANFIELD RD
3 MORFIELD GR
4 SOUTHFIELD DR
5 GUISEFIELD RD
6 BIRCHFIELD RD
7 THE LIDGETT
8 MASSEY CL
9 TREE CL
10 CORONATION CR
11 AXHOLME DR

D7
1 FERNBANK
2 FIELDS CL
3 ORCHARD CFT
4 SWALLOW CT
5 CARRSIDE
6 NICHOLSON WY

94

E6
1 CASTLE DR
2 VINEGARTH
3 WESLEY CL
4 CHURCH ST
5 MARKET PL
6 CHAPEL ST
7 MANOR CT RD
8 FAIRFIELD CFT
9 ROOKERY CFT
10 PINFOLD
11 NEWLAND VW
12 MOORLAND WY
13 QUEEN ST
14 POPPLEWELL TERR
15 REAPER'S RISE
16 CHERRY ORCHARD
17 SOUTH FURLONG CFT
18 FERN CFT
19 WOODLAND WY
20 MOWBRAY CT
21 LINDSEY CT
22 HOLLINGSWORTH LA

106

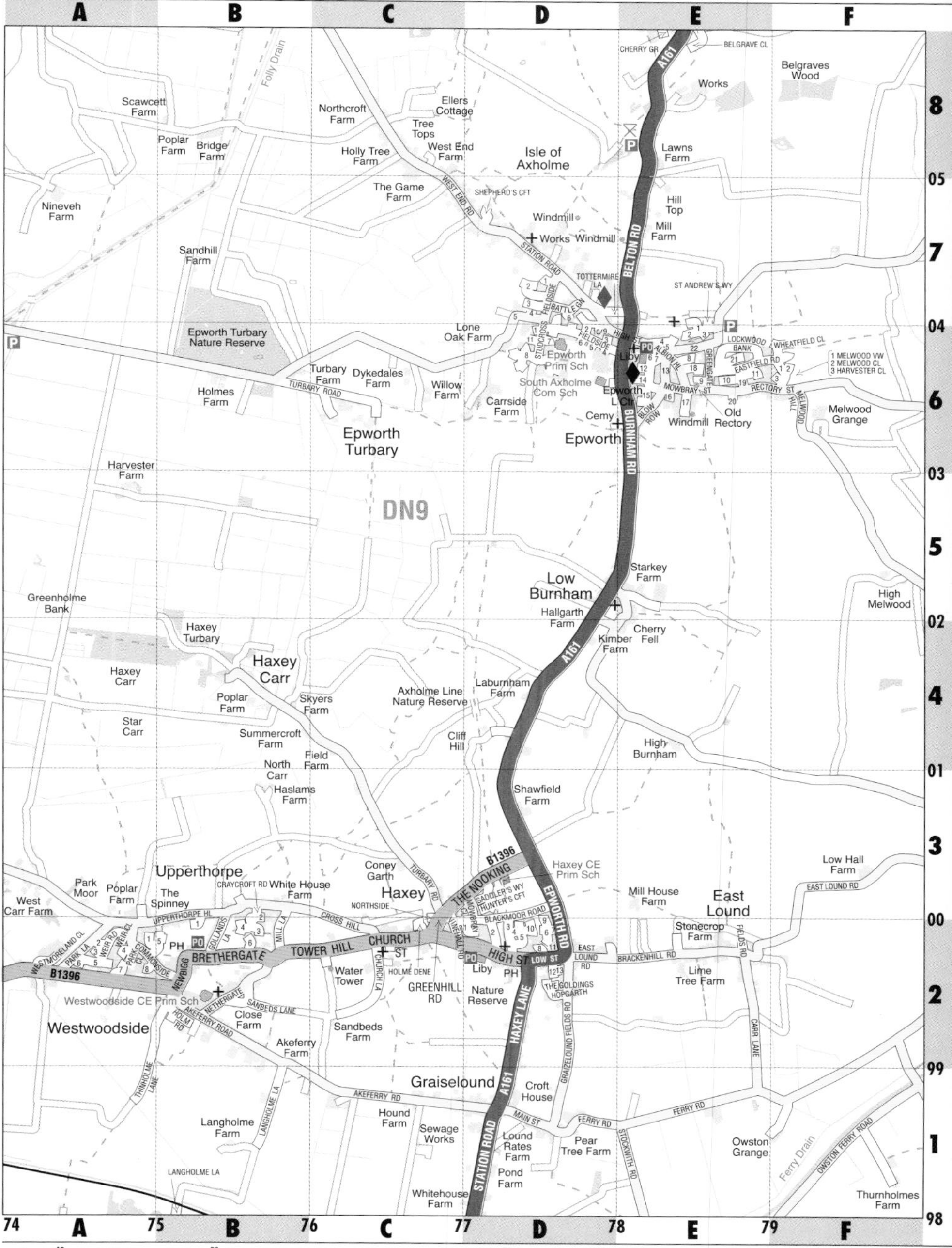

A2
1 THE ROWANS
2 AXHOLME RD
3 COLLEYWELL CL
4 PARK DR
5 THE MEADOWS
6 MOORLANDS
7 DREWRY LA
8 WEAVERS CFT

B2
1 TAVELLA CT
2 HIGHFIELD CR
3 WESTLAND RD
4 CHAPEL CL
5 THE BIRCHES
6 CRACKLE HILL

116

D2
1 HALLCROFT RD
2 MARLBOROUGH AVE
3 LOWCROFT AVE
4 LOWCROFT CL
5 ASH TREE DR
6 REAPER'S WY
7 GRANARY CFT
8 HAXEY GRANGE
9 HAYFIELD CL
10 LOWCROFT MD
11 BURRELLS CL
12 CHATSWOTH WY
13 FARRRIERS FOLD

106

105
95
D8
1 THE CROFT
2 FARM LA
3 PARKLANDS

Scale: 1⅓ inches to 1 mile
0 ¼ ½ mile
0 250m 500m 750m 1 km

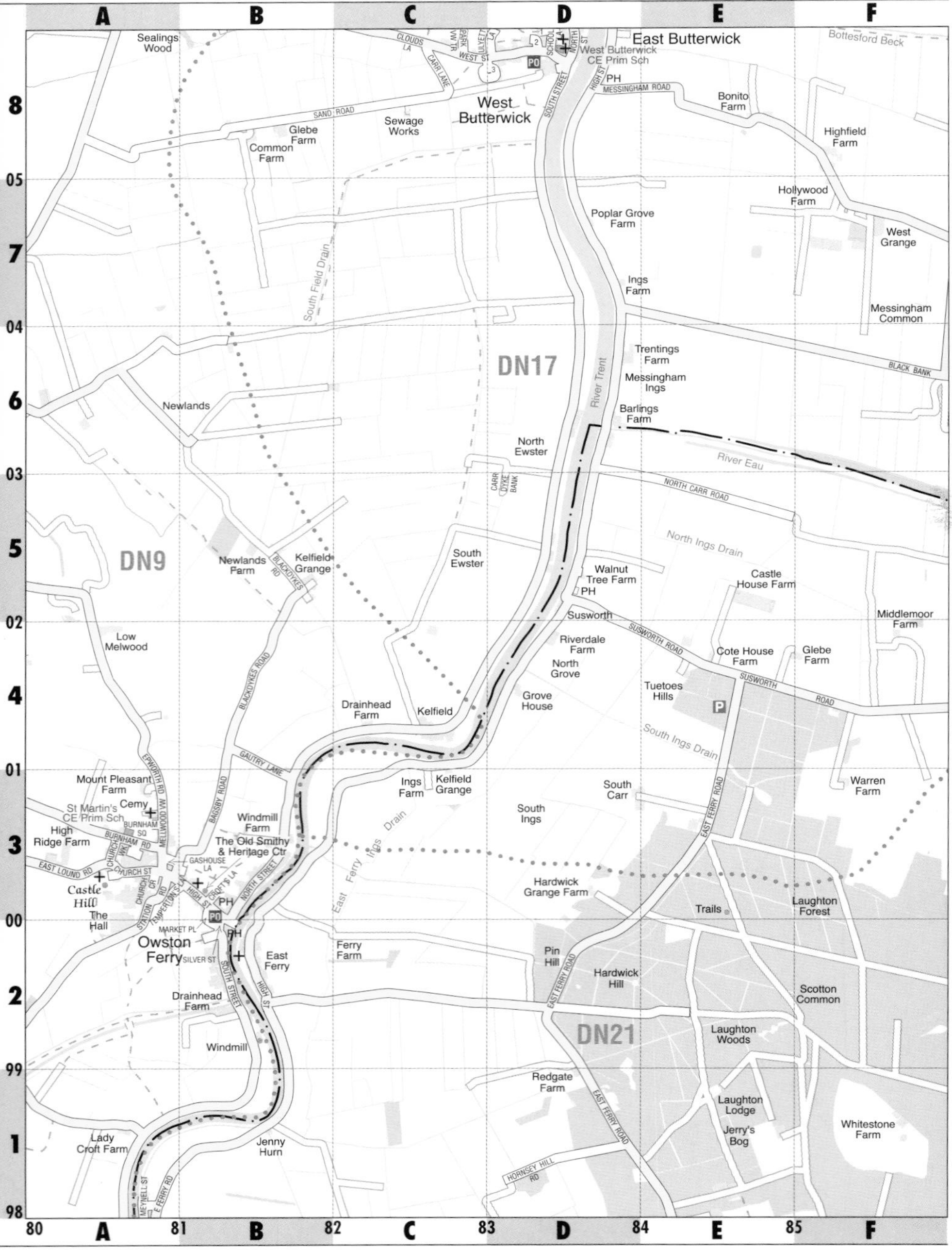

105
117

Scale: 1⅓ inches to 1 mile
0 ¼ ½ mile
0 250m 500m 750m 1 km

96
108

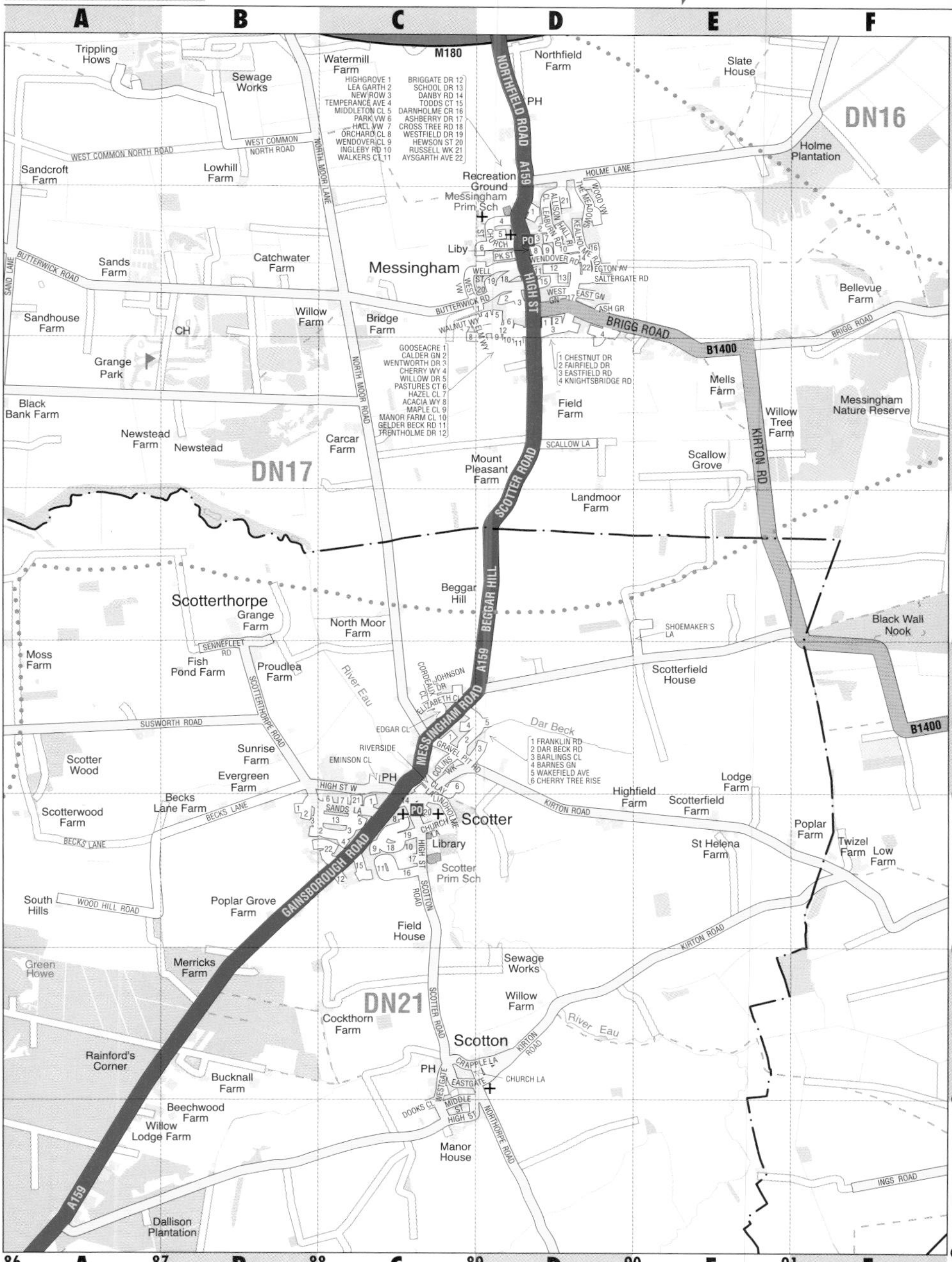

B3
1 BELLBUTTS VW
2 LARK RISE
3 ASH GR

C3
1 POPLAR GR
2 ROOKLANDS
3 BEECHWOOD DR
4 CHESTNUT CL
5 PINETREE AVE
6 BRAMLEY GR
7 CEDAR CL
8 ORCHARD AVE
9 ST PETER'S GR
10 CECIL CL
11 MILL CR
12 SOUTHCLIFFE RD
13 WAKERLEY RD
14 HOBB LA
15 CHARLES AVE
16 WESTCLIFFE RD
17 REVILL CL
18 ASTLEY CR
19 ST PETER'S RD
20 THE GREEN
21 CROWN GDNS
22 THE ROOKERY

118
108

107
97

F5
1 DICKINSON CL
2 COCKETTS LA
3 BARNSIDE
4 OLD SCHOOL DR
5 MEADOW CT
6 ST ALBANS CL
7 CHAPEL CT
8 SARGENT'S WY

Scale: 1⅓ inches to 1 mile
0 ¼ ½ mile
0 250m 500m 750m 1 km

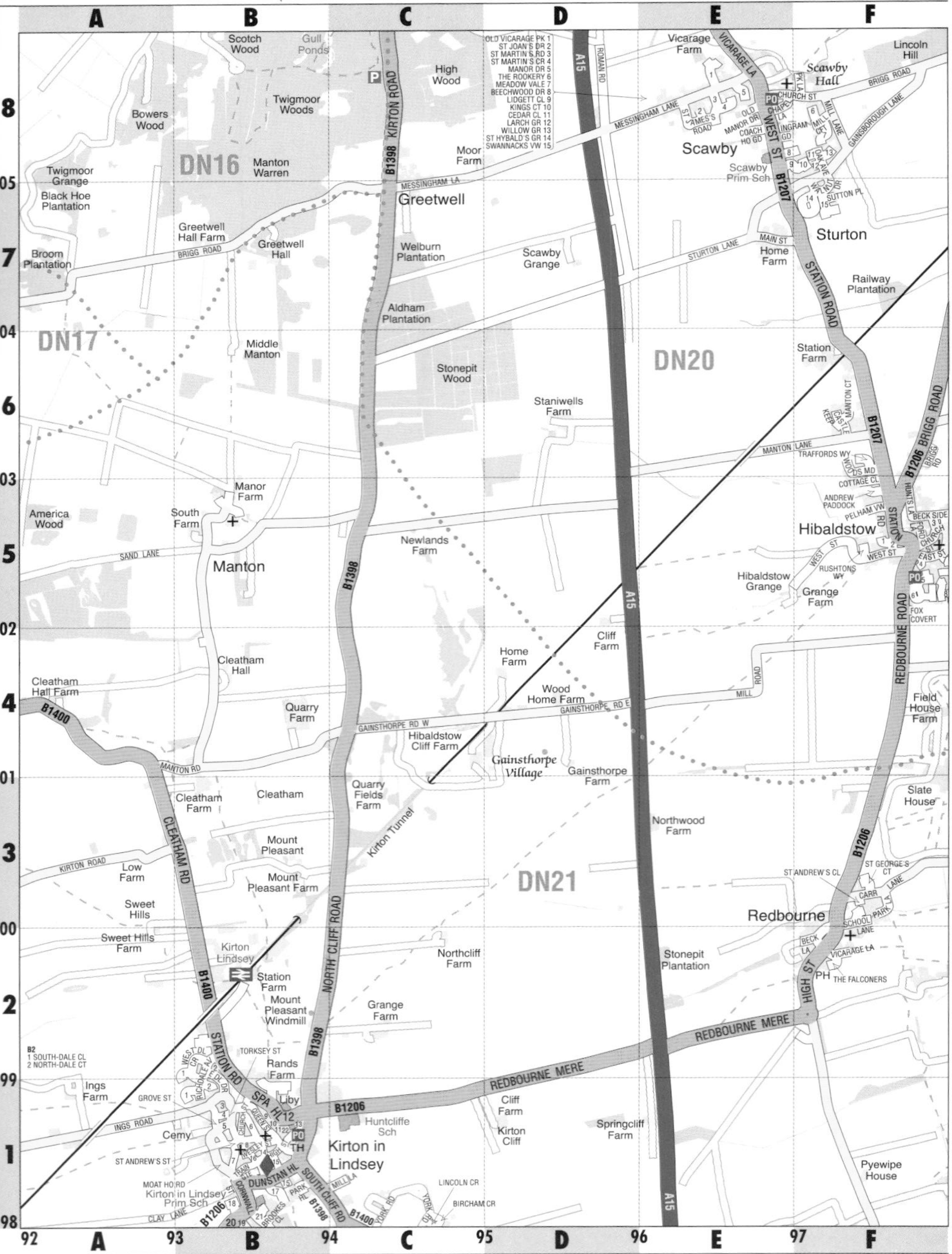

B1
1 HIGHFIELD DR
2 ORCHARD CL
3 WHITEWELL CL
4 DARWIN ST
5 TURNER ST
6 MARCH ST
7 CORNWALL ST
8 OLD SCHOOL YD
9 SUNNY HILL
10 UNICORN ROW
11 GEORGE ST
12 KING EDWARD ST
13 SYLVESTER ST
14 WRAY ST
15 EAST CROSS ST
16 WEST CROSS ST
17 DUNSTAN VILLAS
18 LOWFIELD CL
19 GRAYINGHAM RD
20 GAINSBOROUGH RD
21 FAIRFIELDS
22 MARKET PL

107
119

Scale: 1⅓ inches to 1 mile
0 ¼ ½ mile
0 250m 500m 750m 1 km

98
110

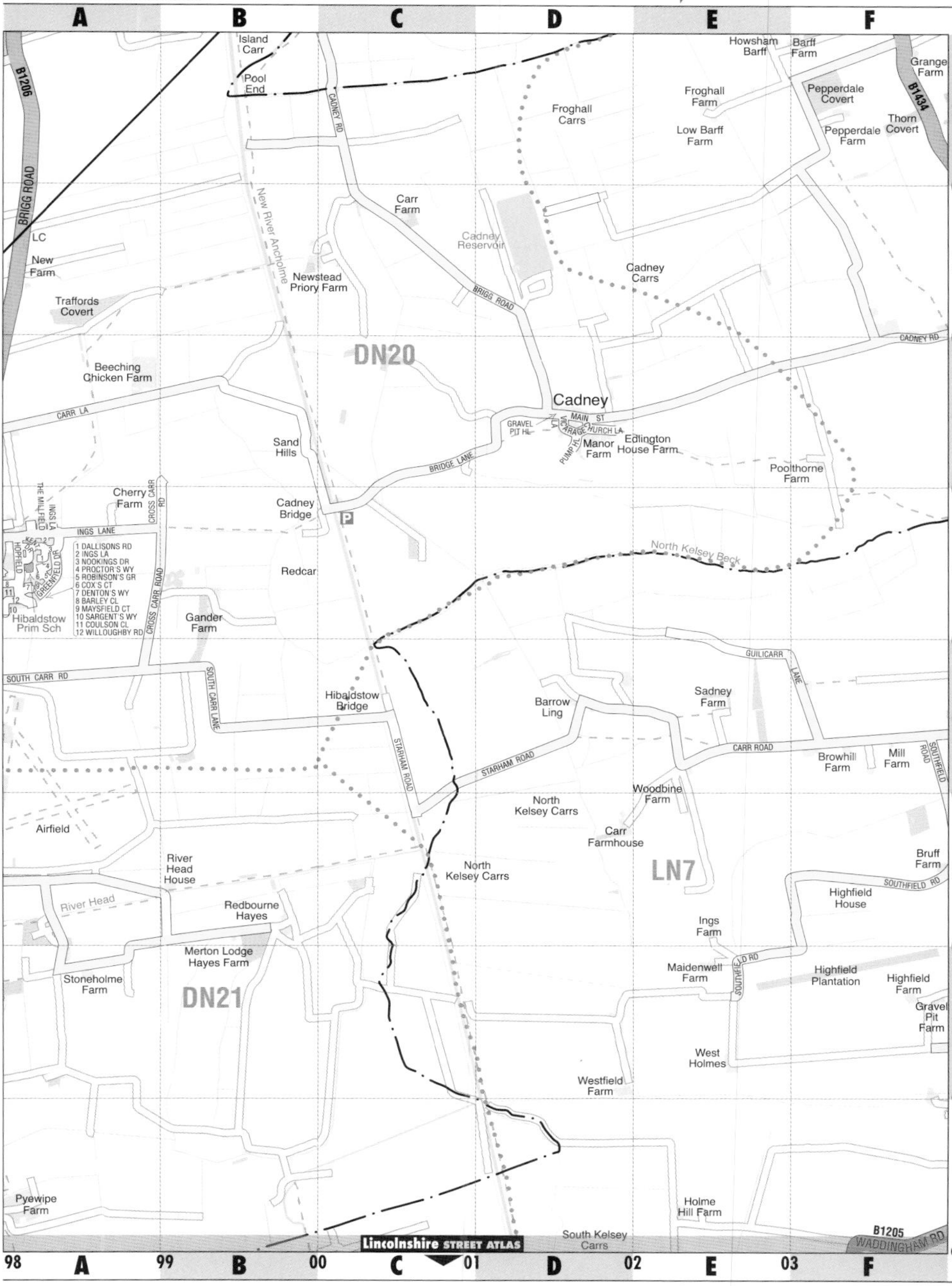

110

109
99
Scale: 1⅓ inches to 1 mile
0 ¼ ½ mile
0 250m 500m 750m 1 km

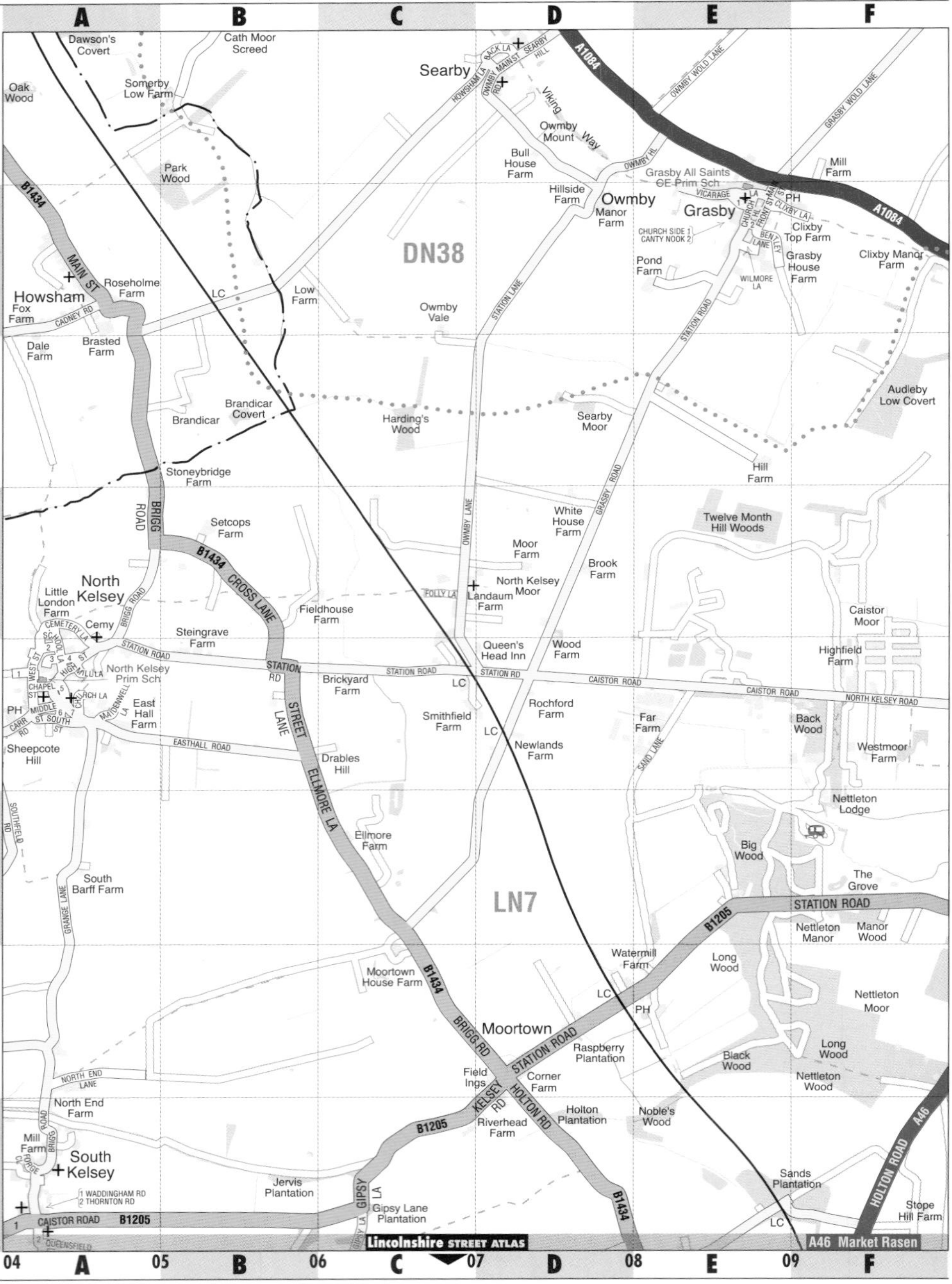

109

A4
1 OCCUPATION LA
2 LINDUM WK
3 PATRICKS CL
4 OLD SCHOOL LA
5 HALLS LA
6 GREEN LA
7 CHURCH ST

Scale: 1⅓ inches to 1 mile
0 ¼ ½ mile
0 250m 500m 750m 1 km

100
112

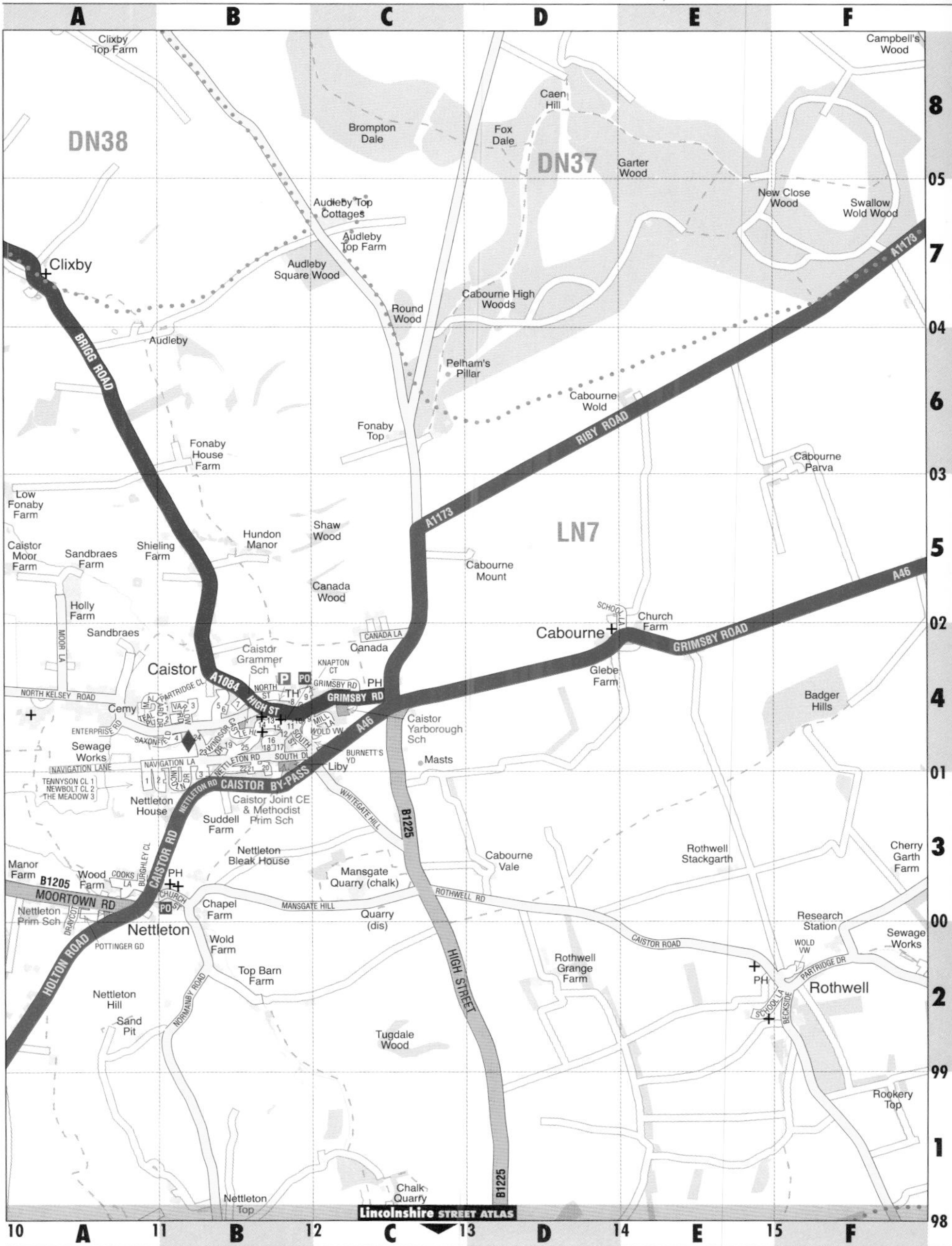

B4
1 PHEASANT CT
2 PLOVER SQ
3 AYSCOUGH GR
4 SAXON WY
5 KEYWORTH DR
6 HANSARD CR
7 CHERRY HOLT
8 GEORGE MEWS
9 THE ROPEWALK
10 BUTTER MKT
11 MARKET PL
12 PLOUGH HL
13 CHAPEL ST
14 CHURCH ST
15 BANK LA
16 FOUNTAIN ST
17 HORSE MKT
18 WESTBROOKE GR
19 CHICHESTER DR
20 WESTWOLD RD
21 RISEDALE
22 RAWLINSON AVE
23 MILLFIELDS
24 HERSEY RD
25 CROMWELL VW

112

111
101

Scale: 1⅓ inches to 1 mile

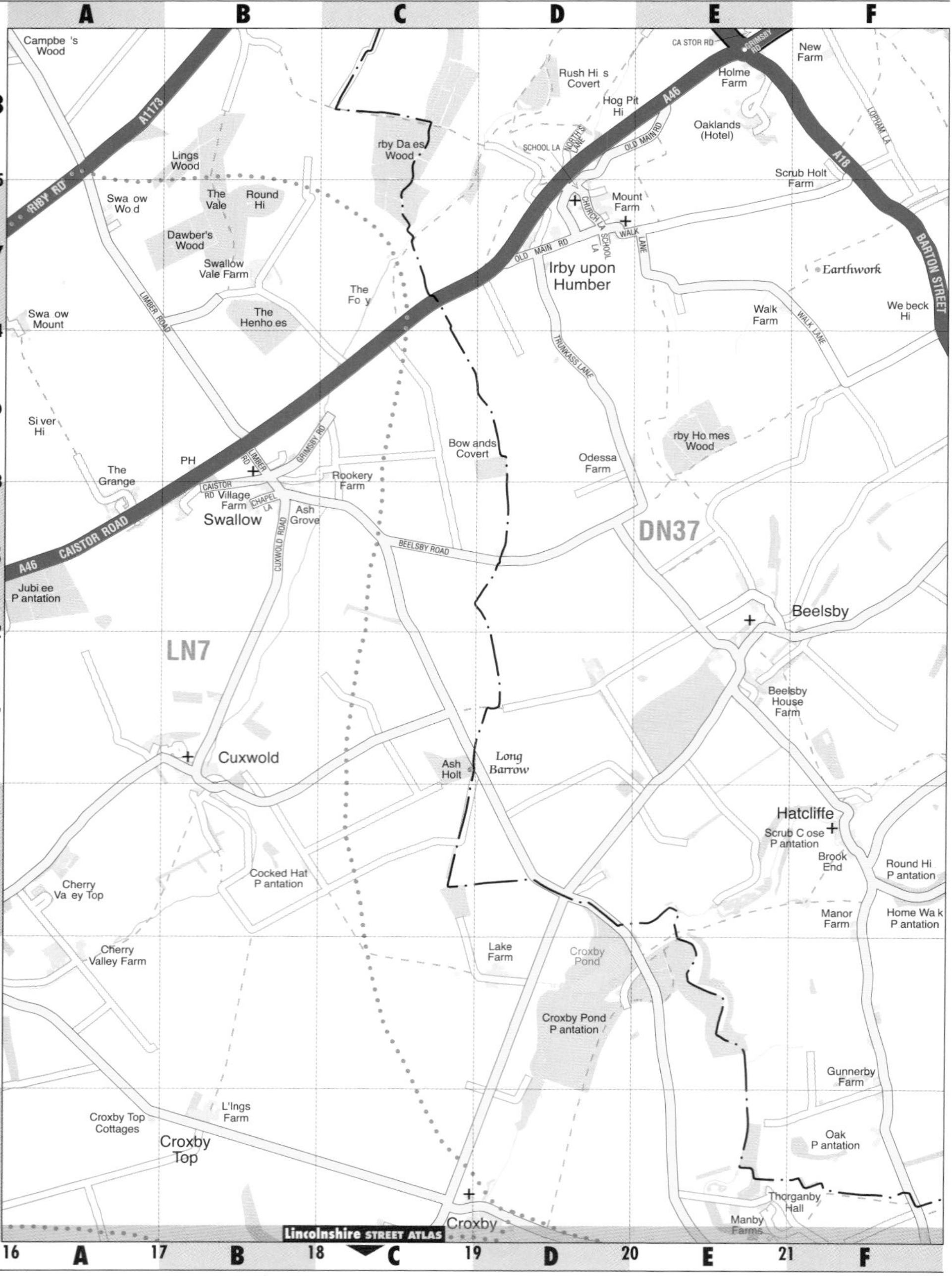
A B C D E F
8 7 6 5 4 3 2 1
05 04 03 02 01 00 99 98
16 17 18 19 20 21
Campbe 's Wood
RIBY RD
A1173
Lings Wood
Swa ow Wo d
The Vale
Round Hi
Dawber's Wood
Swallow Vale Farm
LIMBER ROAD
Swa ow Mount
The Henho es
rby Da es Wood
The Fo y
Rush Hi s Covert
Hog Pit Hi
SCHOOL LA
NORTH'S LANE
OLD MAIN RD
Mount Farm
CHURCH LA
SCHOOL LA
WALK LANE
Irby upon Humber
A46
CA STOR RD
GRIMSBY RD
Holme Farm
New Farm
Oaklands (Hotel)
Scrub Holt Farm
A18
LOPHAM LA
BARTON STREET
Earthwork
Walk Farm
WALK LANE
We beck Hi
TRUNKASS LANE
Si ver Hi
The Grange
PH
LIMBER RD
GRIMSBY RD
CAISTOR RD
Village Farm
CHAPEL LA
Swallow
Ash Grove
Rookery Farm
Bow ands Covert
Odessa Farm
rby Ho mes Wood
DN37
A46 CAISTOR ROAD
CUXWOLD ROAD
BEELSBY ROAD
Jubi ee P antation
Beelsby
LN7
Beelsby House Farm
Cuxwold
Ash Holt
Long Barrow
Hatcliffe
Scrub C ose P antation
Brook End
Round Hi P antation
Cherry Va ey Top
Cocked Hat P antation
Manor Farm
Home Wa k P antation
Cherry Valley Farm
Lake Farm
Croxby Pond
Croxby Pond P antation
Gunnerby Farm
Croxby Top Cottages
L'Ings Farm
Croxby Top
Oak P antation
Thorganby Hall
Croxby
Manby Farms

111

Scale: 1⅓ inches to 1 mile
0 ¼ ½ mile
0 250m 500m 750m 1 km

102
114

D8
1 WORLABY RD
2 BAYSWATER PL
3 WELL VALE
4 BRIAR LA
5 CORNFIELD CL
6 SAGEFIELD CL
7 SPRINGWOOD CR
8 WALESBY CL
9 AMOS CL
10 WINDLESHAM AVE
11 RYDAL AVE
12 KIDDIER AVE
13 BAYONS AVE
14 ELIZABETH CL

E8
1 LARDEN AVE
2 ALLESTREE DR
3 BARBARA CL
4 FLEETWOOD CL
5 RIVAN AVE
6 RIVAN GR
7 ADELPHI DR
8 WOOD CL
9 HEATHERDALE CL
10 ORCHARD CFT
11 HILARY RD
12 EASTBOURNE WY
13 BEATTY AVE
14 CROXBY GR
15 WESTBOURNE GR
16 SPURN AVE
17 LINWOOD AVE
18 DOVEDALE DR
19 TAUNTON WY
20 BRACKEN PK
21 TONBRIDGE
22 WICKLOW AVE
23 GRAMPIAN WY
24 LANCING WY
25 SOUTHWOLD CR
26 CHILTERN WY
27 DERRY WY
28 THE COPSE
29 HAWTHORNE AVE
30 LINDSEY RISE
31 COLLEGE AVE
32 COLLEGE GDNS

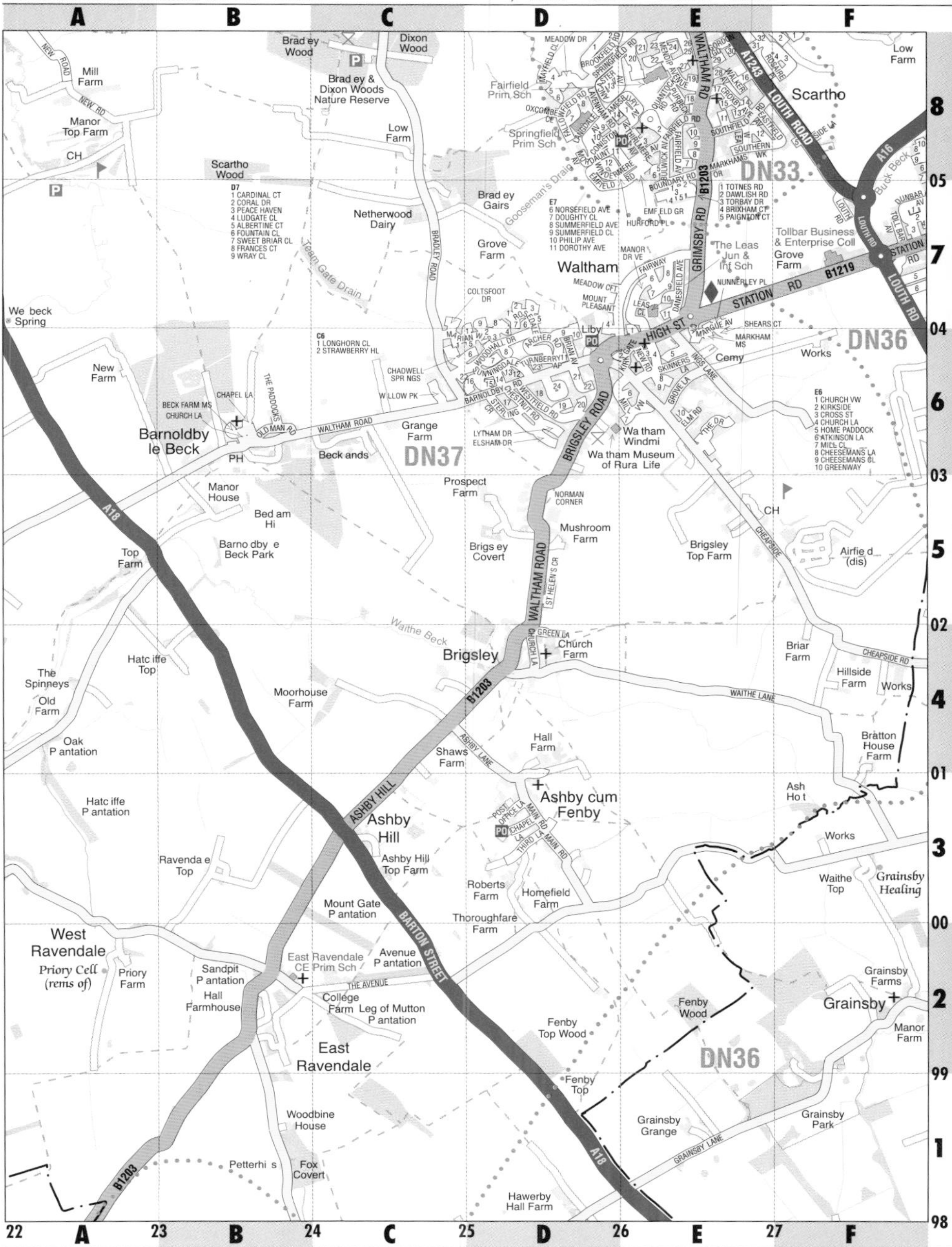

D6
1 DRURY CL
2 WHEATFIELD DR
3 BARKWORTH CT
4 HARVEST CR
5 OLD FARM CT
6 ALDERLEY EDGE
7 ASHBOURNE
8 LINDRICK WK
9 NEVILLE TURNER WY
10 ORCHARD CT
11 PEAR TREE CL
12 SUNNINGDALE
13 CARNOUSTIE
14 BIRKDALE
15 GLENEAGLES
16 MUIRFIELD
17 CHESTNUT CL
18 MAYFAIR CR
19 CHILTERN DR
20 COTSWOLD DR
21 LABURNHAM AVE
22 LABURNHAM CL
23 ASCOT RD
24 SALISBURY AVE

120
114

F7
1 DURSLEY AVE
2 CONISBOROUGH AVE
3 PEMBERTON DR
4 LINDISFARNE AVE
6 HAWTHORNE AVE
7 MAPLE GR

F8
1 SHAW DR
2 WESTKIRKE AVE
3 KENSINGTON PL
4 CHRISTINE PL
5 BRAETON LA
6 JOSEPH OGLE CL
7 MARTIN WY
8 HUNTSMANS CH
9 ELLEN WY
10 LAVENDER GR

A7
1 SHAFTESBURY MEWS
2 CHANDLERS CL
3 DRURY LA
4 ADELPHI CT
5 DUNBAR AVE
6 ALDWYCH CFT
7 BARBICAN WY
8 PICCADILLY
9 DOMINION CL
10 WYNDHAM RD
11 FARMHOUSE MEWS
12 SAVOY CT
13 GREENLANDS AVE
14 THE ORCHARD
15 KAYMILE CL
16 RUTLAND DR
17 CHARLES AVE
18 MARGARET PL
19 WADDINGHAM PL
20 GRANGE FARM LA

113

103

D8
1 STANILAND WY
2 CHIPPENDALE CL
3 SHERATON DR
4 WOODFIELD CL
5 EASTFIELD
6 ROWAN DR
7 BURCOM AVE
8 COULAM PL
9 CHAPMAN CR
10 ASHWOOD DR
11 ANDREW RD
12 VISCOUNT WY
13 HUMBERSTON AVE

Scale: 1⅓ inches to 1 mile
0 ¼ ½ mile
0 250m 500m 750m 1 km

A B C D E F

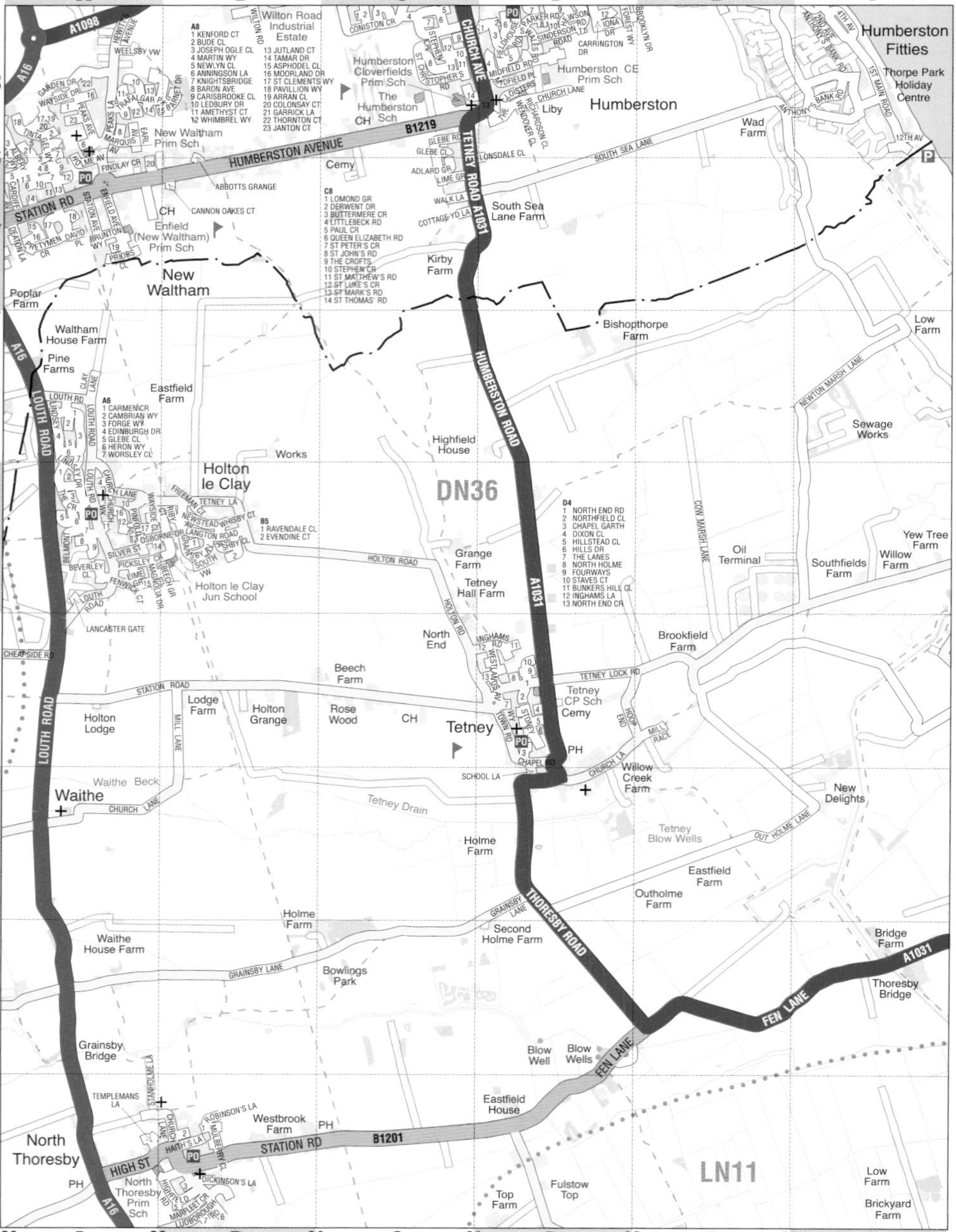

28 A 29 B 30 C 31 D 32 E 33 F

A5
1 PELHAM RD
2 YARBOROUGH CL
3 HAYS CL
4 EASTFIELD RISE
5 BEAUMONDE
6 WOLD VW
7 HOLTON MT
8 HOLTON CT
9 MOUNT PLEASANT
10 ST PETER'S CL
11 PEPPERCORN WK
12 CAMPIONS CL
13 GARTHWAY
14 PINFOLD GDNS
15 SOUTHFIELD RD
16 SARGE CL
17 NURSERY GDNS

B1
1 PLUMTREE LA
2 OLD PLUMTREE LA
3 BORMAN'S LA
4 SMITH FIELD
5 HIGHFIELD CL
6 CAMPIONS' LA
7 MUMBY CL

113

121

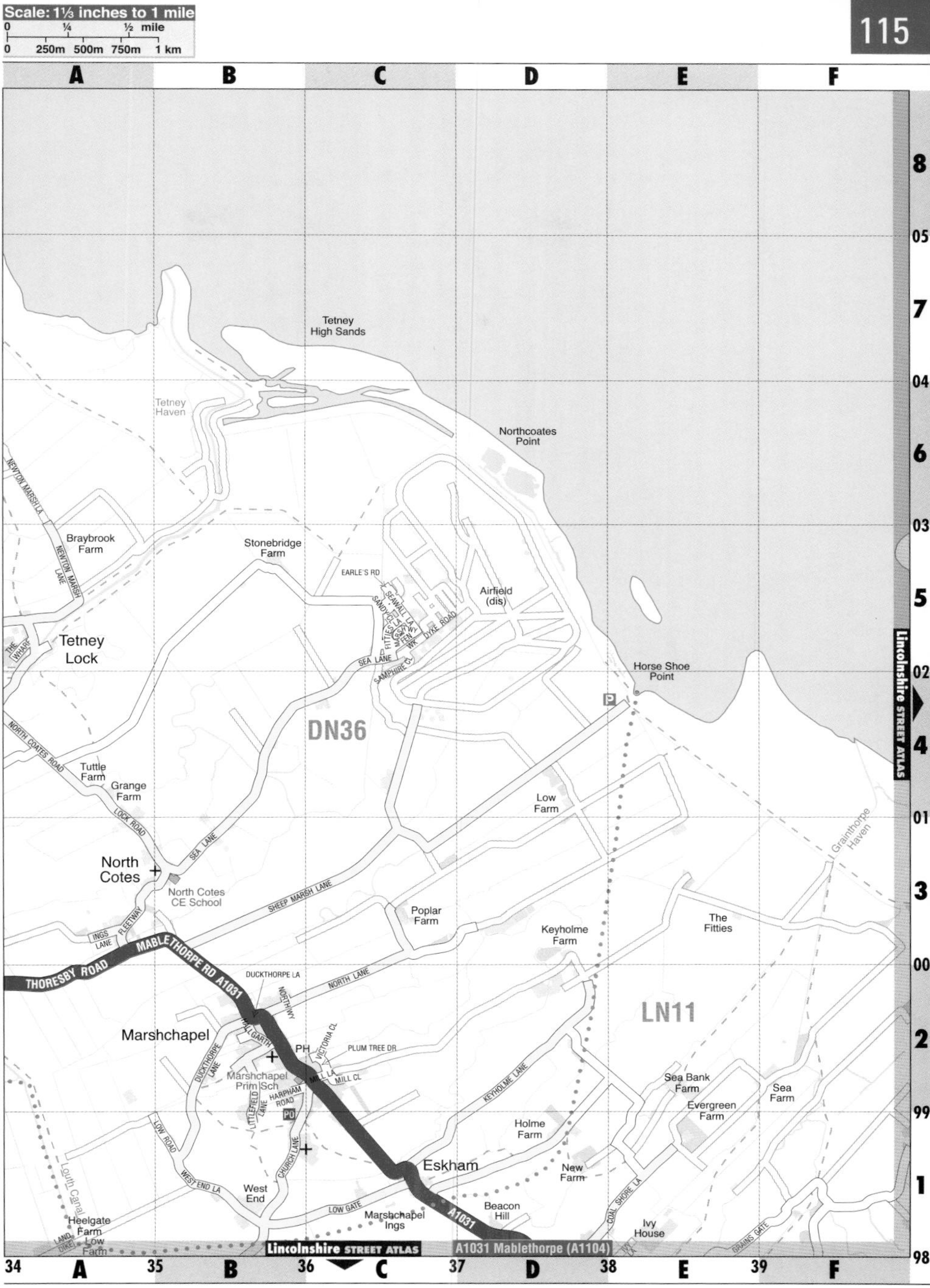
Scale: 1⅓ inches to 1 mile
Tetney High Sands
Tetney Haven
Northcoates Point
NEWTON MARSH LA
Braybrook Farm
NEWTON MARSH LANE
Stonebridge Farm
EARLE'S RD
SEAWALL LA
SANDY CL
FITTIES LA
MARSH WY
FEN WK
DYKE ROAD
Airfield (dis)
Tetney Lock
THE WHARF
SEA LANE
SAMPHIRE CL
Horse Shoe Point
DN36
NORTH COATES ROAD
Tuttle Farm
Grange Farm
LOCK ROAD
Low Farm
Grainthorpe Haven
North Cotes
SEA LANE
North Cotes CE School
SHEEP MARSH LANE
Poplar Farm
Keyholme Farm
The Fitties
INGS LANE
FLEETWAY
MABLETHORPE RD A1031
THORESBY ROAD
DUCKTHORPE LA
NORTH WY
NORTH LANE
LN11
Marshchapel
HALLGARTH
PH
VICTORIA CL
PLUM TREE DR
DUCKTHORPE LANE
Marshchapel Prim Sch
MILL LA
MILL CL
HARPHAM ROAD
LITTLEFIELD LANE
PO
KEYHOLME LANE
Sea Bank Farm
Evergreen Farm
Sea Farm
LOW ROAD
Holme Farm
CHURCH LANE
Eskham
New Farm
Louth Canal
WEST END LA
West End
Beacon Hill
COAL SHORE LA
LOW GATE
Marshchapel Ings
A1031
Ivy House
GRAINS GATE
Heelgate Farm
LAND DIKE
Low Farm
Lincolnshire STREET ATLAS
A1031 Mablethorpe (A1104)

Scale: 1⅓ inches to 1 mile
0 ¼ ½ mile
0 250m 500m 750m 1 km

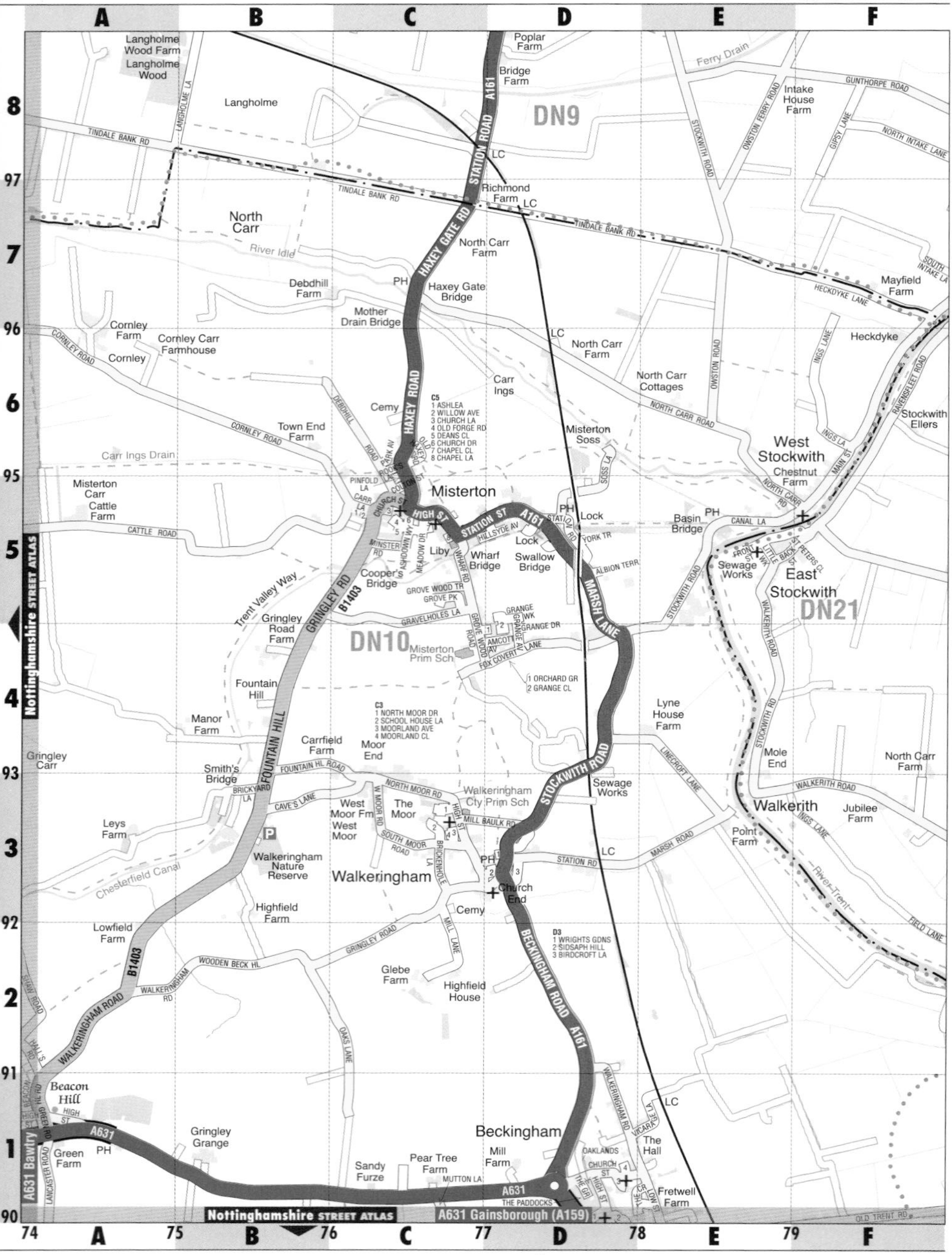

D1
1 RAVENCROFT LA
2 THE LIMES
3 RECTORY GDNS
4 CHURCH VW

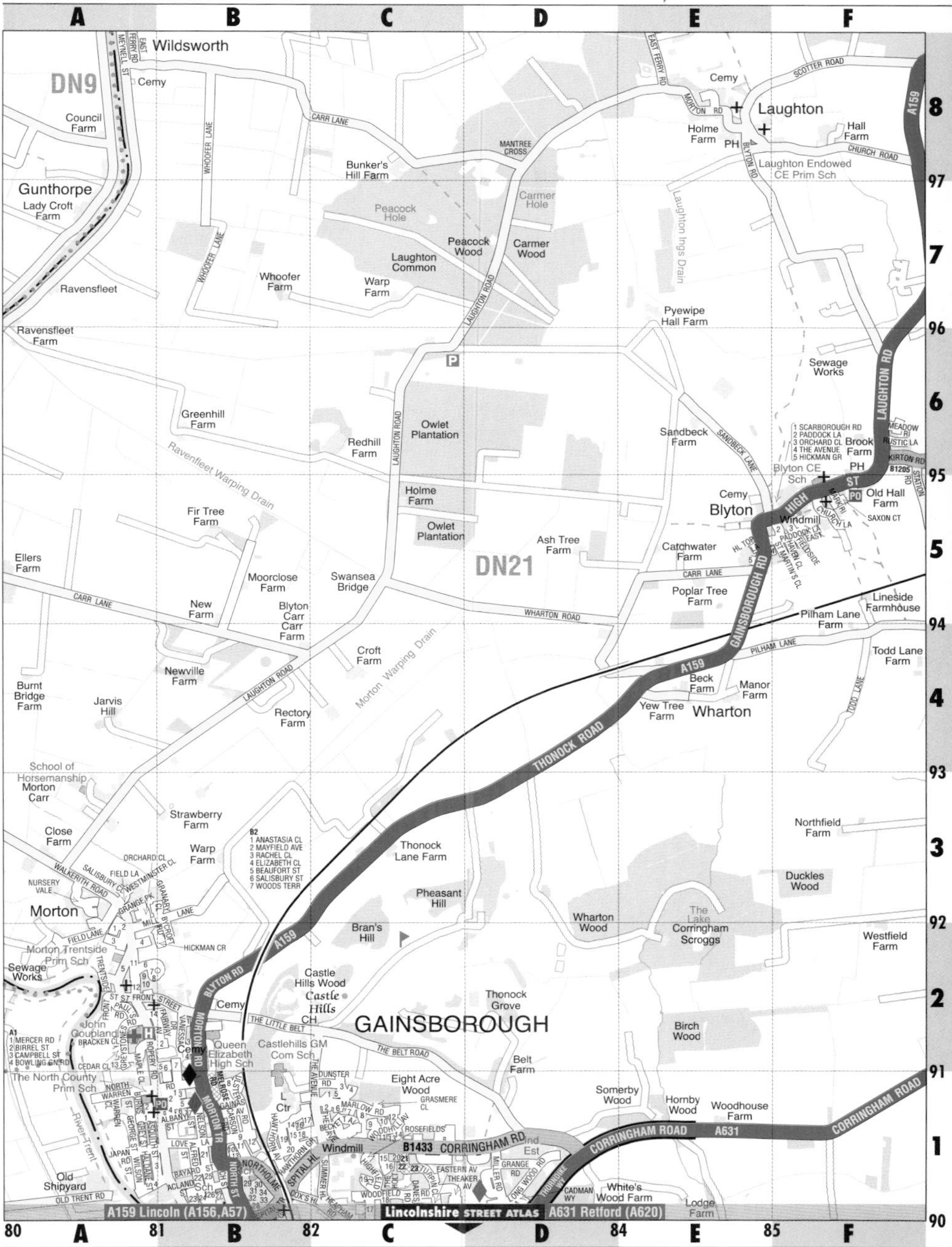

118

A1
1 MERCER RD
2 BIRREL ST
3 CAMPBELL ST
4 BOWLING GN RD

B2
1 ANASTASIA CL
2 MAYFIELD AVE
3 RACHEL CL
4 ELIZABETH CL
5 BEAUFORT ST
6 SALISBURY ST
7 WOODS TERR

A2
1 SOUTHLANDS AVE
2 SOUTHLANDS GD
3 SOUTHLANDS DR
4 MORTON CL
5 CROOKED BILLET ST
6 NORTH ST
7 CROSS ST
8 SOUTH ST
9 WEST ST
10 CHAPEL LA
11 WALKERITH RD
12 DOG AND DUCK LA
13 WILLOW CL
14 WOODLAND AVE

B1
1 HOTSPUR RD
2 NOEL ST
3 MOWBRAY ST
4 CURZON ST
5 MELROSE RD
6 HENLEY CT
7 ROWSTON CL
8 OLD SHOWFIELDS
9 CONNAUGHT RD
10 ARKWRIGHT ST
11 EDWARD RD
12 ARTHUR RD
13 CROMFORD ST
14 BEECH AVE
15 CHESTNUT AVE
16 BIRCH GR
17 ASH GR
18 LABURNUM AVE
19 ACACIA AVE
20 LIME TREE AVE
21 GARFIELD ST
22 LINCOLN ST
23 BALFOUR ST
24 CECIL ST
25 FORSTER ST
26 FAWCETT ST
27 SCOTT ST
28 DRILL HALL LA
29 CARLISLE ST
30 CHARLES ST
31 TOWER ST
32 TENNYSON ST
33 RECTORY AVE
34 JUBILEE CRES
35 CROSS ST

C1
1 HAWTON CL
2 STIRLING CL
3 MILTON RD
4 ARUNDEL CL
5 MILTON CL
6 DUNBAR CL
7 PENDEEN CL
8 IONA CL
9 SYCAMORE DR
10 LAUREL CL
11 LARCH CT
12 HARROW CL
13 ASPEN CT
14 OAK TREE AVE
15 REDMAN CL
16 BRAMLEY CT
17 NEWLANDS
18 CHERRY TREE RD
19 FIELDING WY
20 BLACKTHORN CL
21 BIRCHWOOD VW
22 THE ALDERS
23 THE ROWANS

117
107

Scale: 1⅓ inches to 1 mile
0 ¼ ½ mile
0 250m 500m 750m 1 km

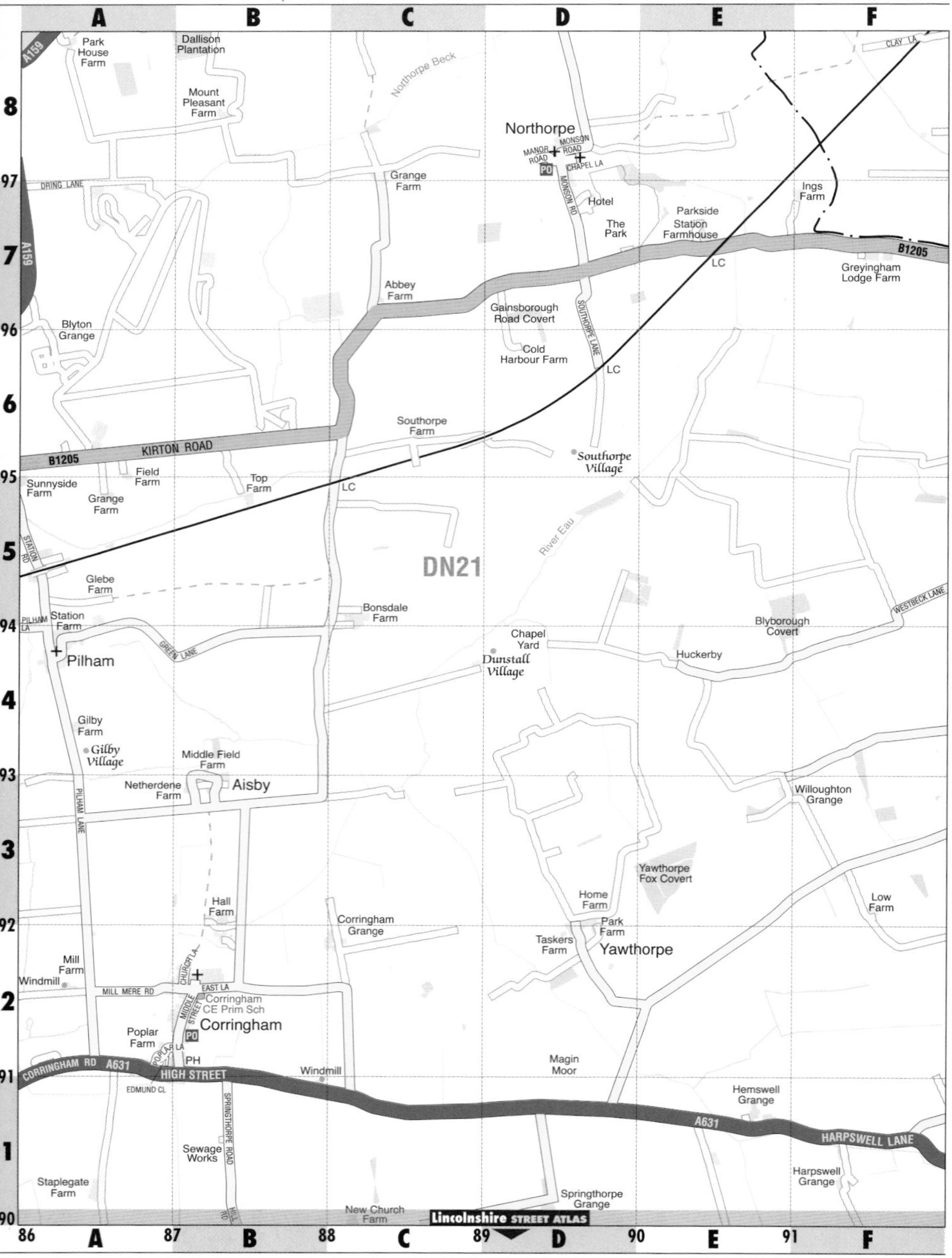
A B C D E F
8
97
7
96
6
95
5
94
4
93
3
92
2
91
1
90
86 87 88 89 90 91
A159
Park House Farm
Dallison Plantation
Mount Pleasant Farm
Northorpe Beck
Northorpe
MANOR ROAD
MONSON ROAD
CHAPEL LA
PO
MONSON RD
Hotel
The Park
Parkside Station Farmhouse
Ings Farm
CLAY LA
B1205
Greyingham Lodge Farm
LC
DRING LANE
Grange Farm
Abbey Farm
Gainsborough Road Covert
Cold Harbour Farm
SOUTHORPE LANE
Blyton Grange
Southorpe Farm
KIRTON ROAD
Southorpe Village
Sunnyside Farm
Field Farm
Grange Farm
Top Farm
River Eau
DN21
STATION RD
Glebe Farm
Bonsdale Farm
PILHAM LA
Station Farm
GREEN LANE
Pilham
Chapel Yard
Dunstall Village
Huckerby
Blyborough Covert
WESTBECK LANE
Gilby Farm
Gilby Village
Middle Field Farm
Netherdene Farm
Aisby
PILHAM LANE
Willoughton Grange
Yawthorpe Fox Covert
Hall Farm
Corringham Grange
Home Farm
Park Farm
Taskers Farm
Yawthorpe
Low Farm
Mill Farm
Windmill
CHURCH LA
MILL MERE RD
EAST LA
Corringham CE Prim Sch
MIDDLE STREET
Corringham
Poplar Farm
POPLAR LA
PH
CORRINGHAM RD
A631
HIGH STREET
EDMUND CL
Windmill
Magin Moor
Hemswell Grange
SPRINGTHORPE ROAD
Sewage Works
HARPSWELL LANE
Harpswell Grange
Staplegate Farm
HILL RD
New Church Farm
Springthorpe Grange

117

Scale: 1⅓ inches to 1 mile
0 ¼ ½ mile
0 250m 500m 750m 1 km

C8
1 YORK RD
2 LINCOLN CR
3 BIRCHAM CR
4 HENLOW CL
5 HALTON CL
6 CRANWELL CL
108

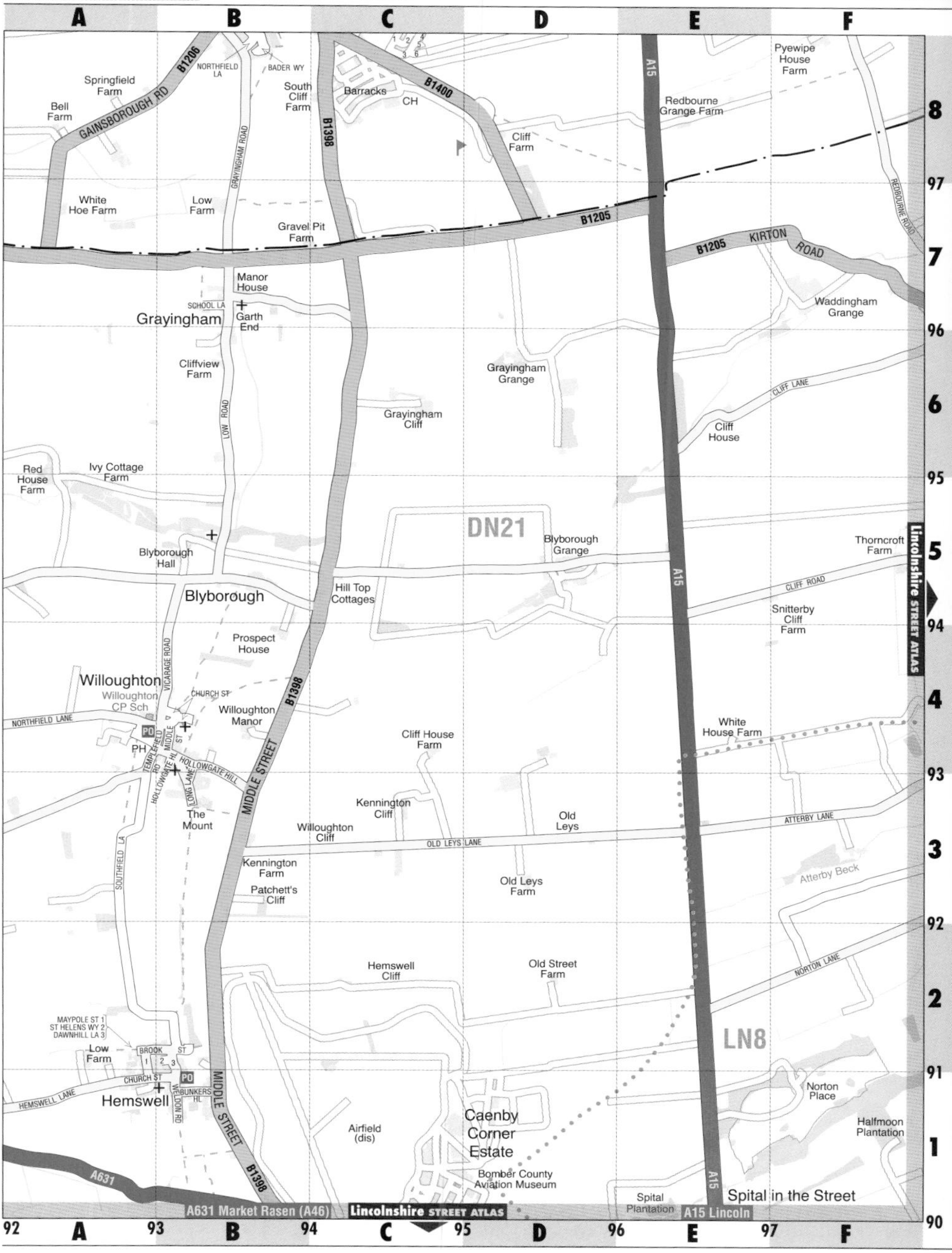

113

Scale: 1⅓ inches to 1 mile
0 ¼ ½ mile
0 250m 500m 750m 1 km

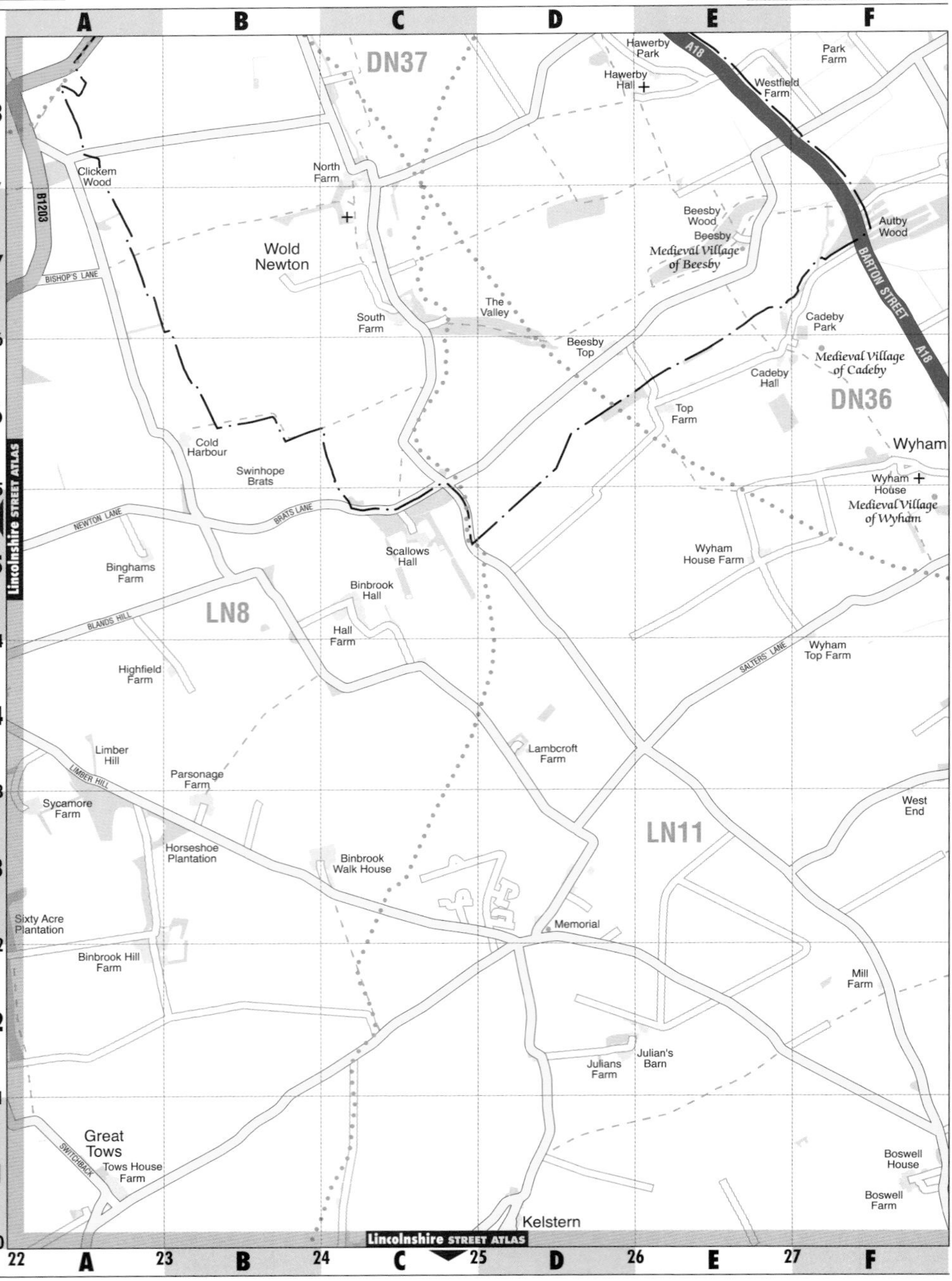

A B C D E F
8 97 7 96 6 95 5 94 4 93 3 92 2 91 1 90
22 23 24 25 26 27
DN37
Hawerby Park
Hawerby Hall
A18
Westfield Farm
Park Farm
Clickem Wood
B1203
North Farm
Beesby Wood
Beesby
Medieval Village of Beesby
Autby Wood
BARTON STREET
Wold Newton
BISHOP'S LANE
The Valley
South Farm
Beesby Top
Cadeby Park
Medieval Village of Cadeby
Cadeby Hall
DN36
Top Farm
Wyham
Cold Harbour
Swinhope Brats
Wyham House
Medieval Village of Wyham
NEWTON LANE
BRATS LANE
Scallows Hall
Wyham House Farm
Binghams Farm
Binbrook Hall
LN8
BLANDS HILL
Hall Farm
Wyham Top Farm
SALTERS' LANE
Highfield Farm
Limber Hill
LIMBER HILL
Lambcroft Farm
Parsonage Farm
Sycamore Farm
West End
LN11
Horseshoe Plantation
Binbrook Walk House
Sixty Acre Plantation
Memorial
Binbrook Hill Farm
Mill Farm
Julians Farm
Julian's Barn
Great Tows
SWITCHBACK
Tows House Farm
Boswell House
Boswell Farm
Kelstern

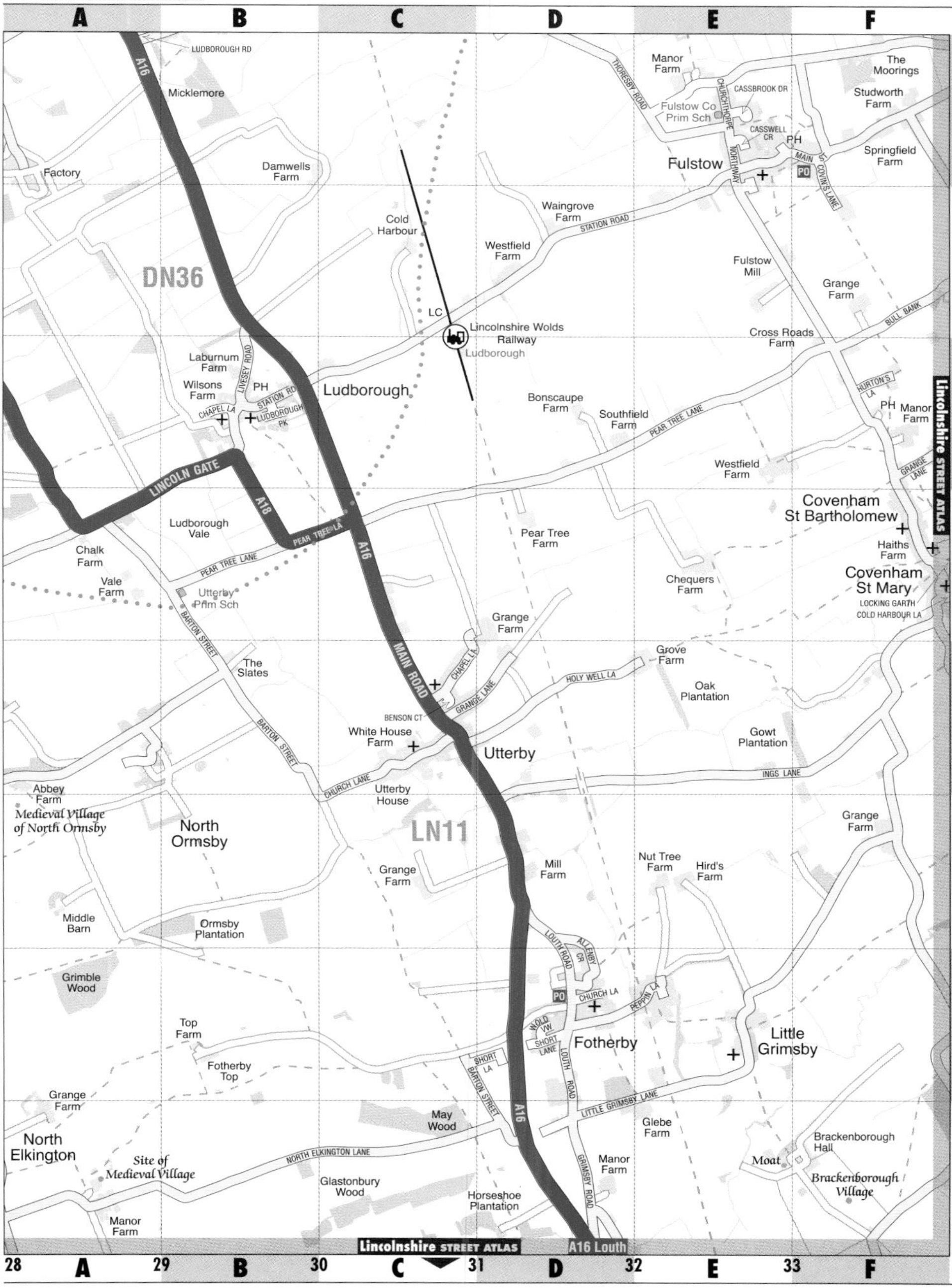
A
B
C
D
E
F
8
97
7
96
6
95
5
94
4
93
3
92
2
91
1
90
28
29
30
31
32
33
LUDBOROUGH RD
A16
Micklemore
Factory
Damwells Farm
Cold Harbour
DN36
LC
Lincolnshire Wolds Railway
Ludborough
Laburnum Farm
LIVESEY ROAD
Wilsons Farm
PH
STATION RD
CHAPEL LA
LUDBOROUGH PK
LINCOLN GATE
A18
Ludborough Vale
PEAR TREE LA
PEAR TREE LANE
Chalk Farm
Vale Farm
Utterby Prim Sch
BARTON STREET
The Slates
MAIN ROAD
CHAPEL LA
GRANGE LANE
BENSON CT
White House Farm
Utterby
CHURCH LANE
Utterby House
Abbey Farm
Medieval Village of North Ormsby
North Ormsby
LN11
Grange Farm
Middle Barn
Ormsby Plantation
Grimble Wood
Top Farm
Fotherby Top
Grange Farm
North Elkington
Site of Medieval Village
Manor Farm
NORTH ELKINGTON LANE
Glastonbury Wood
May Wood
Horseshoe Plantation
SHORT LA
Manor Farm
THORESBY ROAD
CHURCHTHORPE
CASSBROOK DR
Fulstow Co Prim Sch
CASSWELL CR
NORTHWAY
Fulstow
MAIN
COVIN'S LANE
PO
The Moorings
Studworth Farm
Springfield Farm
Waingrove Farm
STATION ROAD
Westfield Farm
Fulstow Mill
Grange Farm
BULL BANK
Cross Roads Farm
HURTON'S LA
Manor Farm
Bonscaupe Farm
Southfield Farm
PEAR TREE LANE
Westfield Farm
GRANGE LANE
Covenham St Bartholomew
Pear Tree Farm
Haiths Farm
Chequers Farm
Covenham St Mary
LOCKING GARTH
COLD HARBOUR LA
Grange Farm
Grove Farm
HOLY WELL LA
Oak Plantation
Gowt Plantation
INGS LANE
Grange Farm
Mill Farm
Nut Tree Farm
Hird's Farm
LOUTH ROAD
ALLENBY CR
CHURCH LA
PEPPIN LA
WOLD VW
SHORT LANE
Fotherby
Little Grimsby
LITTLE GRIMSBY LANE
Glebe Farm
Manor Farm
GRIMSBY ROAD
Brackenborough Hall
Moat
Brackenborough Village
A16 Louth
Lincolnshire STREET ATLAS

10
4

D6
1 TRENTHAM MEWS
2 NORTH PINFOLD WY
3 PINFOLD CT
4 PINFOLD CL
5 CHATSWORTH CL
6 SANDRINGHAM CL
7 THORESBY MEWS
8 BALMORAL CL

A B C D E F

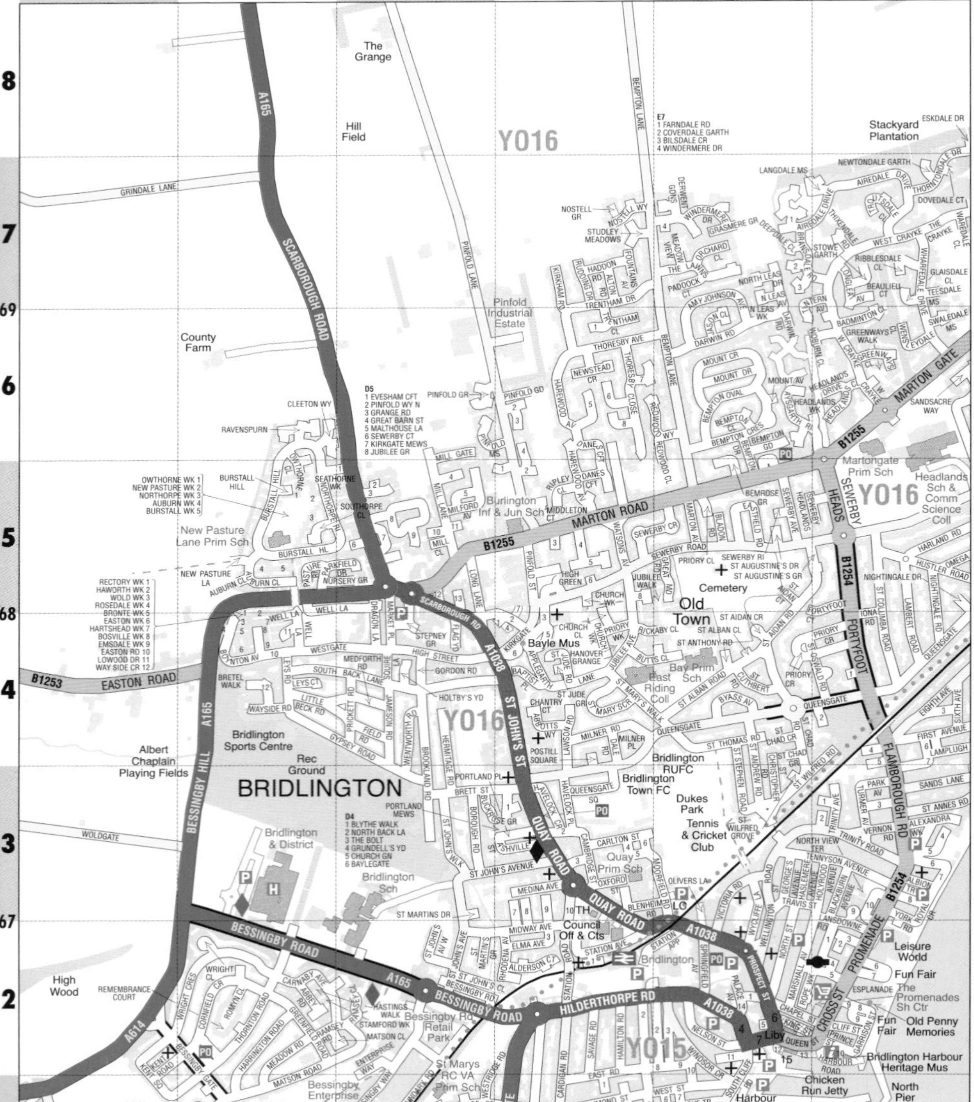

A B C D E F

C5
1 SEATHORNE RD
2 WYKENHAM CL
3 ELLERBURN DR
4 MILLFIELD RD
5 MILFORD CR
6 NEW PASTURE CL
7 SCARBOROUGH RD
8 SCARBOROUGH CR
9 THE HOLLOWS
10 MILL CT
11 MILLBANK
12 SHORT LA
13 STEPNEY AVE

D2
1 ADMIRALS MS
2 NEW BURLINGTON RD
3 ELMA VILLAS

10

D3
1 BURLINGTON GDNS
2 HAVELOCK ST
3 SWINDON ST
4 GILBERT ST
5 THOMPSON ST
6 HILL ST
7 MELBOURNE AVE
8 WESTBOURNE AVE
9 ASHBOURNE AVE
10 STATION AVE

11

F2
1 CLARENCE RD
2 WESTMORLAND GR
3 WESTMORLAND AVE
4 PRINCESS ST
5 PRINCESS TERR
6 FORT TERR
7 REGENT TERR
8 MARLBOROUGH TERR
9 THE CRESCENT
10 BRITANNIA CT

F3
1 TRINITY GR
2 TRINITY MEWS
3 SWANLAND AVE
4 ALEXANDRA CT
5 ALEXANDRA DR
6 GLADSTONE TERR
7 BRIGHT CR
8 CARLISLE RD
9 LANSDOWNE CR
10 PROVIDENCE PL

F4
1 FORTYFOOT GR
2 PARK VW
3 SEVENTH AVE
4 EDGECLIFFE VILLAS
5 CANTON VILLAS
6 LAMPLUGH SQ
7 LAMPLUGH LA

A7
1 NIDDERDALE CL
2 CALDERDALE CL
3 YORDAS CT
4 CARROWAY CL
5 LYTH CL
6 MARTON CT

4

A
B
C
D
E
F
8
7
69
6
5
68
4
3
67
2
1
66
19
20
21
PH
Martonia Caravan Park
JEWISON LANE
SHEEPRAKE LA
FLAMBOROUGH ROAD B1255
Marton
Marton Valley Caravan Park
West Wood
Marton Hall
Leys Plantation
Gell-spring Plantation
Home Farm Plantation
Home Farm
Maidlands Plantation
Bridlington Links & Heritage Park
Dyke Wood
Danes Dyke Nature Reserve
Needles Plantation
Danes Dyke Farm
YO16
YO15
Long Wood
PLANTATION VW
Crow Plantation
CEDAR CT
CADMAN RD
KEPPEL DR
MORDACKS RD
MORDACKS DR
MARTON VW
WILLOWDALE CL
THE CRAYKE
THE GLIMPSE
ANNERLEY DR
MARTONGATE
KESTREL DR
WOODLANDS CL
CHESTNUT CL
FORESTERS WY
VIKING ROAD
POPLAR DR
MAPLE ROAD
ROSEWOOD WALK
VIKING RD
WILLOW DR
Charity Farm Caravan Park
Westfield Plantation
West Wood
CHURCH LANE
Sewerby Park
HIGH SEWERBY ROAD
Crow Wood
CH
MOOR ROAD
Pheasant Plantation
Pigeoncote Plantation
Home Farm
SEWERBY PK CL
Sewerby Hall & Gardens
Dykes End
Liby
SANDGATE RD
BEACON RD
SANDSACRE AVE
WHEATLEY DRIVE
BEECH DRIVE
BARLEY RI
CATLANDS RD
OAKWELL AV
CLOVERLEY RD
SANDSACRE ROAD
PO
SEAGATE
MAIN ST
CLIFF ROAD
PH
SEWERBY ROAD
RIVIERA DR
Sewerby Village
SEAGATE VIEW
HORSESHOE DR
Bondville Model Village
Sewerby Rocks
LC
Sewerby Fields
Rock Ends
SEWERBY ROAD
Sewerby
LIMEKILN LANE
GREAME ROAD
A6
1 SANDSACRE DR
2 MAPEL CL
3 ROSEWOOD CL
4 LABURNUM CT
5 BIRCH CL
6 CLOVERLEY RD
OMEGA CL
Headland Way
LIMEKILN LA
EIGHTH AVENUE
SECOND AVE
THIRD AVE
FOURTH AVE
FIFTH AVE
NORTH MARINE DR
North Sands
ROAD
ALEXANDRA PR
P

11

20 20

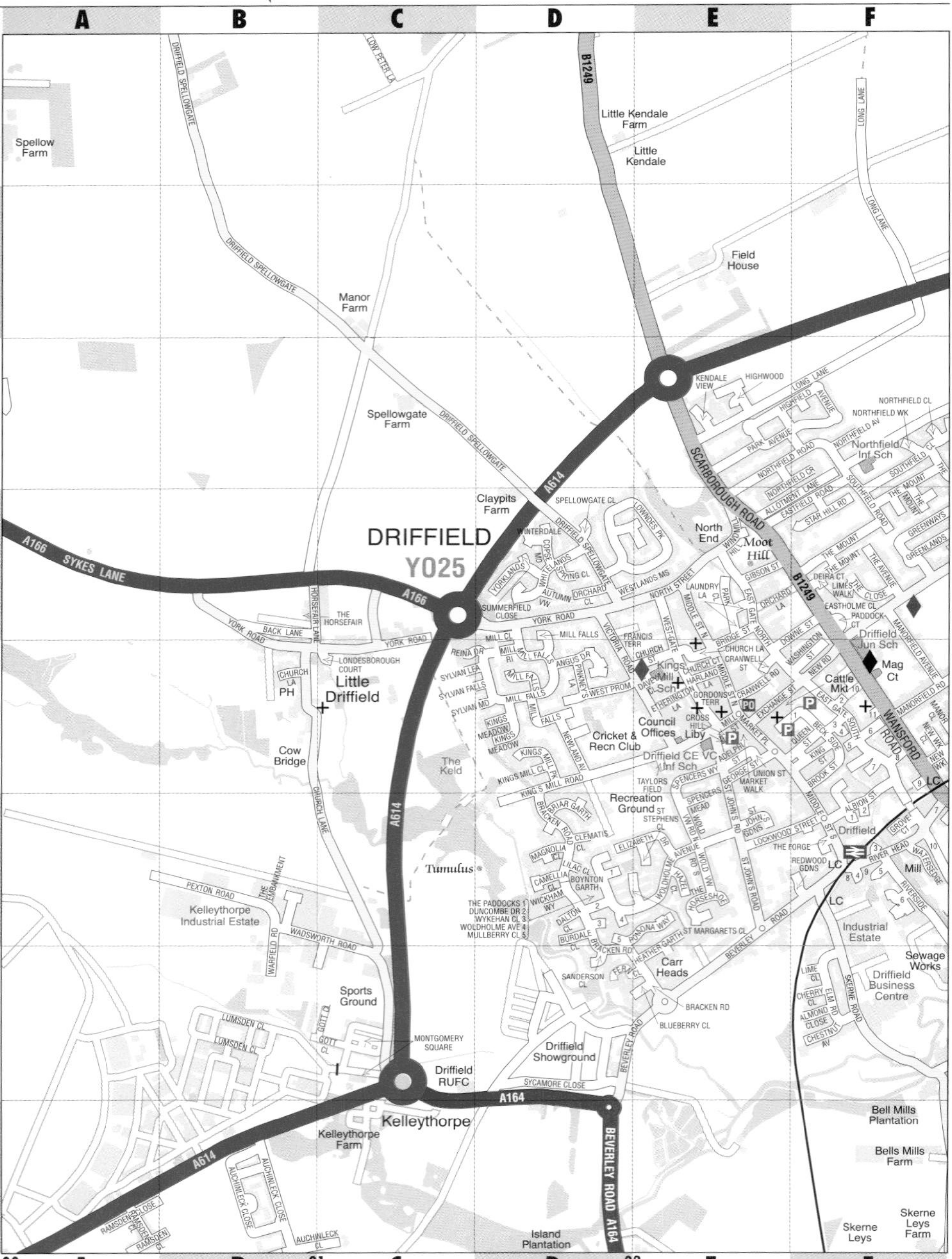

F3
1 ST JOHN'S WK
2 ST JOHN'S PL
3 RIVER HEAD DR
4 GEORGIAN MEWS
5 RIVERSIDE MEWS
6 RIVERSIDE CL
7 ANDERSON ST
8 WOODLANDS
9 BEECHLANDS
10 BEECHWOOD LA

F4
1 PROVIDENCE PL
2 JEVANS CT
3 GALLOWAY LA
4 GALLOWAY CT
5 BRIDGE LA
6 DUNN'S LA
7 NAYFIELD CL
8 HARPER ST
9 FAWCETT GDNS
10 EASTERFIELD CT
11 LANGLEY GARTH

20 20

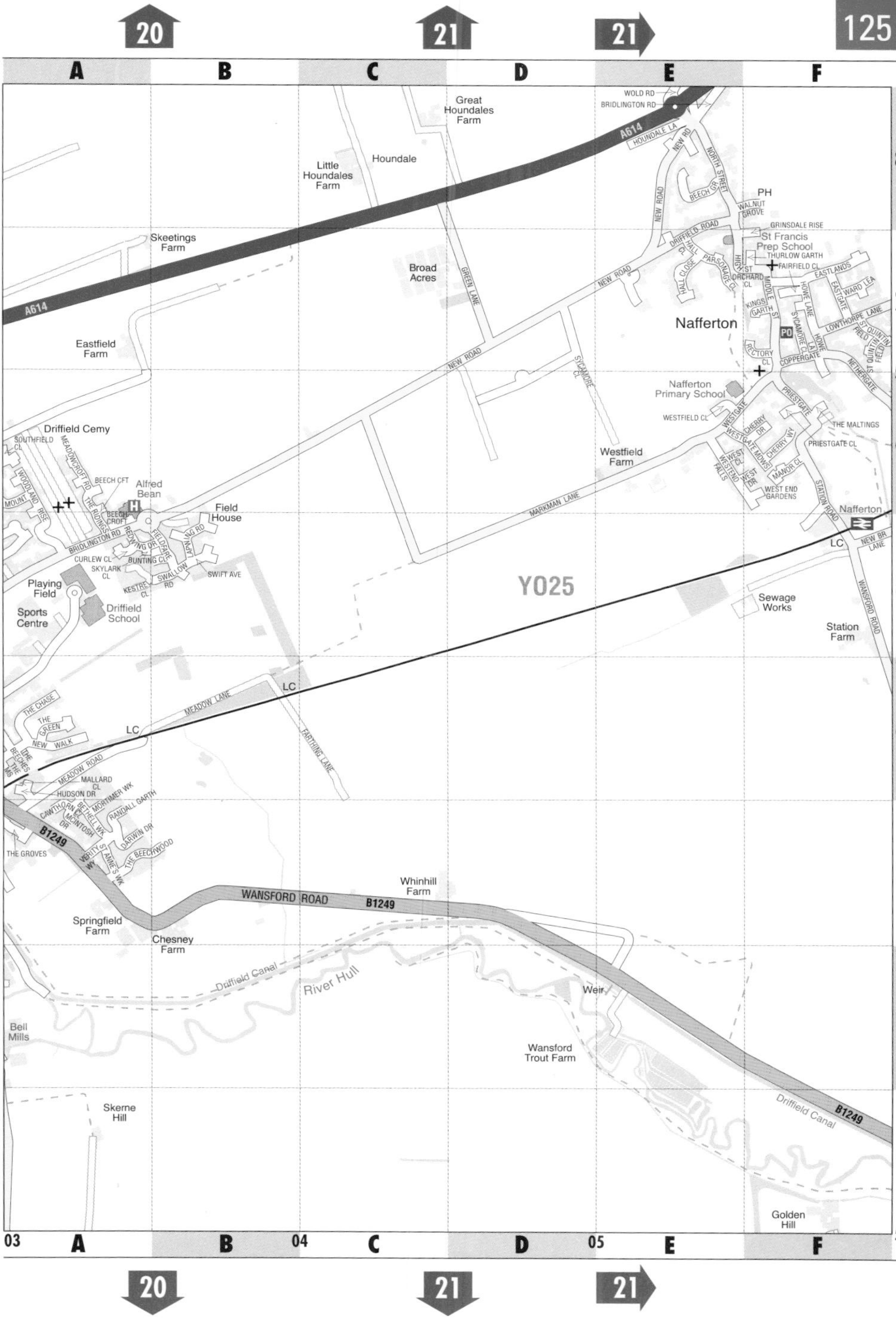
20
21
21
A
B
C
D
E
F
8
7
59
6
5
58
4
3
57
2
1
56
03
04
05
WOLD RD
BRIDLINGTON RD
A614
HOUNDALE LA
Great Houndales Farm
Houndale
Little Houndales Farm
Skeetings Farm
Broad Acres
GREEN LANE
NEW ROAD
NEW RD
NORTH STREET
BEECH GR
PH
WALNUT GROVE
DRIFFIELD ROAD
GRINSDALE RISE
St Francis Prep School
THURLOW GARTH
FAIRFIELD CL
EASTLANDS
WARD LEA
HALL CLOSE
PARSONAGE CL
HIGH ST
ORCHARD CL
MIDDLE ST
KINGS GARTH
HOWE LANE
EASTGATE
LOWTHORPE LANE
Nafferton
PO
SYCAMORE CL
RECTORY CL
COPPERGATE
NETHERGATE
Eastfield Farm
SYCAMORE CL
Nafferton Primary School
WESTFIELD CL
WESTGATE
CHERRY DR
PRIESTGATE
THE MALTINGS
PRIESTGATE CL
CHERRY WY
Westfield Farm
WESTGATE MDWS
WESTEND FALLS
WEST CL
WEST DR
MANOR CL
WEST END GARDENS
STATION ROAD
Nafferton
LC
NEW BR LANE
Driffield Cemy
SOUTHFIELD CL
MEADOWCROFT RD
WOODLAND RISE
MOUNT
BEECH CFT
Alfred Bean
H
THE RUDINGS
BEECH CROFT
Field House
LAPWING RD
BRIDLINGTON RD
REDWING DR
FIELDFARE
BUNTING CL
CURLEW CL
SKYLARK CL
KESTREL CL
SWALLOW RD
SWIFT AVE
MARKMAN LANE
YO25
Playing Field
Sports Centre
Driffield School
Sewage Works
Station Farm
WANSFORD ROAD
LC
MEADOW LANE
THE CHASE
THE GREEN
NEW WALK
LC
FARTHING LANE
THE BEECHES
MEADOW ROAD
MALLARD CL
HUDSON DR
MORTIMER WK
CAWTHORN CL
BETHELL WK
MCINTOSH DR
RANDALL GARTH
B1249
DARWIN DR
THE BEECHWOOD
THE GROVES
VERITY WY
ST ANNE'S WK
Whinhill Farm
WANSFORD ROAD
B1249
Springfield Farm
Chesney Farm
Driffield Canal
River Hull
Weir
Bell Mills
Wansford Trout Farm
Skerne Hill
Driffield Canal
B1249
Golden Hill

12
13

A
B
C
D
E
F
8
7
57
6
5
56
4
3
55
2
1
54
56
57
58
Hall Moor
Wide Open Farm
CH
Woodside Farm
SKELTON LANE
MOOR LANE
Park Farm
YO32
Wigginton Moor
A19
HURNS LA
Hurns Bridge
Glebe Farm
Skelton Moor
Nova Scotia Plantation
MOOR LANE
New Farm
Hall
Skelton
MOORLANDS LANE
St Catherines
Skelton Moor
ST GILES ROAD
THE VILLAGE
CHURCH LANE
Skelton Prim Sch
BRECKSFIELD
YO30
Skelton Plantation
B5
1 THE GREEN
2 THE MEADOWS
3 ORCHARD VIEW
4 THE WHEELHOUSE
5 THE DELL
6 ARTHUR PLACE
ST GILES RD
THE VALE
PASTURE CL
GRANGE CL
FAIRFIELDS DR
SYCAMORE CL
PO
1 RATCLIFFE CT
2 GREGORY CL
3 ST CATHERINES CL
PH
STRIPE LANE
Rawcliffe Moor
CH
BURTREE AV
PARK CL
Folly Bridge
Tees, East & North Yorkshire Ambulance Service HQ
1 THE ROWMANS
2 THE BEECHES
Rawcliffe Moor Farm
Hotel
1 LANGSETT GR
2 RINGSTONE RD
3 BLAKELEY GR
4 ROSEBERRY GR
Poplar Plantation
SHIPTON ROAD
E2
1 CONINGHAM AVE
2 MANOR PK GR
3 ELMA GR
4 BARTON CL
5 RAWCLIFFE CL
6 CHESHIRE CL
7 DEANHEAD GR
A1237
Clifton Moor Sh Ctr
E3
1 CAITHNESS CL
2 CONWAY CL
3 HATFIELD CL
4 OSBOURNE DR
5 GRENWICH CL
6 SOMERSET CL
7 HIGHGROVE CL
8 LONGWOOD LINK
9 WINSCAR GR
STIRLING RD
River Ouse
Clifton Moor Retail Park
Overton Ings
Skelton Bridge
Rawcliffe Farm
RAWCLIFFE LANDING
RAWCLIFFE VILLAGE
HURRICANE WAY
BLENHEIM CT
ST JAMES
Moat
Tom Cobleighs Riverside Farm
MARLBOROUGH CL
HOLLYROOD RD
AMY JOHNSON WY
Manor Farm
CHURCH LANE
POPPLETON HALL GD
CHURCH LANE
FOX GARTH
MITCHELL WY
LINDLEY WOOD GR
LONGWOOD ROAD
DEER HL GR
AVIATOR CT
MANOR LANE
COBHAM WY
VILLAGE STREET
BROADSTONE WY
A1237
GILLINGWOOD RD
A19
ARMSTRONG WAY
RIVELIN WAY
LANGDALE ROAD
SOUTHWAITH CL
HILLCREST AV
ECCLES CL
MANOR LA
EVA AVENUE
BOOTHWOOD RD
HAREWOOD CL 1
KENSINGTON RD 2
MOREHALL CL
WHARNSCLIFFE DR
RYBURN CL
HARDEN
Nether Poppleton
FLORENCE GR
MANOR PARK ROAD
MANOR WAY
BOLTBY RD
ROUND HL LINK
STUBDEN
Lakeside Prim Sch
EBOR WAY
HUTTON CL
SHIPTON ROAD
RAWCLIFFE CFT
ST MARK'S GR
BILSDALE
THORNTON MOOR CL
DOE PK
DAKDALE ROAD
LOXLEY CL
P&R
HOWARD LINK
RAWCLIFFE WY
VERNON RD
TROUTSDALE AV
STAINDALE CL
NURSERY ROAD
MILLFIELD GD
INGS VIEW
HOWARD DRIVE
MANOR PARK CL
DALE DIKE GR
RISHWORTH GR
MILLFIELD LANE
NURSERY CT
Rawcliffe
ELDWICK CL
MIDWAY AVE
Sewage Works
FURNESS DR
Rawcliffe Inf Sch
LANGSHAW CFT
EASTHORPE DR
YO26
BOWNESS DR
HAVERAH COURT
SANDYRIDGE
PATTERDALE DRIVE
BUTTERMERE DR
WESTHOLME DR
CASTHOLME DRIVE
GREYSTOKE RD
SWINSTY CT
LINTON RD
LONG RIDGE LANE
Rawcliffe Ings
KENTMERE DR
BORROWDALE DR
ANGRAM CL
BEAVERDYKE
ALWYNE DRIVE
ALWYNE GR
CHELKER WY
LONG RIDGE DR
Hotel
WHITE ROSE CL
Poppleton Ings
NORTHOLME DRIVE
SHELLEY GR
PO
RAWCLIFFE LA
CAYLEY CL
ORCHARD RD
WESTMINSTER PLACE
INGS LA
WHITE ROSE WAY
A1237
A19

E1
1 CONISTON CL
2 WASDALE CL
3 GARBURN GR
4 SCAFELL CL
5 LOWESWATER RD
6 FYLINGDALES AVE

F1
1 EMBLETON DR
2 COLEDALE CL
3 LEIGHTON CFT
4 BARMBY CL
5 GRASMERE GR
6 BARDEN CT
7 SOUTHOLME DR
8 MILTON CARR
9 FEWSTON DR
10 REIGHTON DR

12
129

C7
1 PLOUGHLANDS
2 THE GREENWAY
3 FOXCROFT
4 OAK TREE CT

C8
1 DEALTRY AVE
2 ARENHALL CL
3 MINSTER CL
4 UPPERCROFT
5 BECKS CL
6 THE CHESTNUTS
7 COPWOOD GR
8 HESLIN CL
9 RUDDINGS CL
10 HUNTERS CL
11 CORNWOOD WY

13

D8
1 MEADOW LN
2 CHERRY ORCHARD
3 ORCHARD PADDOCK
4 CHERRY PADDOCK

128

A1
1 CALDBECK CL
2 STONELANDS CT
3 BELMONT CL
4 HASTINGS CL
5 HARROW GLADE
6 WIMPOLE CL
7 HALIFAX CT
8 WATER LA
9 TAMWORTH RD
10 LUNDY CLOSE
11 PENTIRE CLOSE

B1
1 HERDWICK CL
2 HEADLEY CL
3 MINCHIN CL

130

128

E2
1 SCAWTON AVE
2 GORMIRE AVE
3 ROLSTON AVE
4 HEATHER CFT
5 BADGER PADDOCK
6 PINEWOOD GR
7 THORNFIELD DR

F1
1 DICKENS CL
2 HOMESTEAD CL
3 CARNOCK CT
4 ANDREW DR
5 MONKTON RD
6 THERESA CL

F3
1 CHEVIOT CL
2 CAMBRIAN CL
3 KENDREW CL
4 MERLIN COVERT
5 FIRWOOD WHIN
6 OAK GLADE

127 14 14

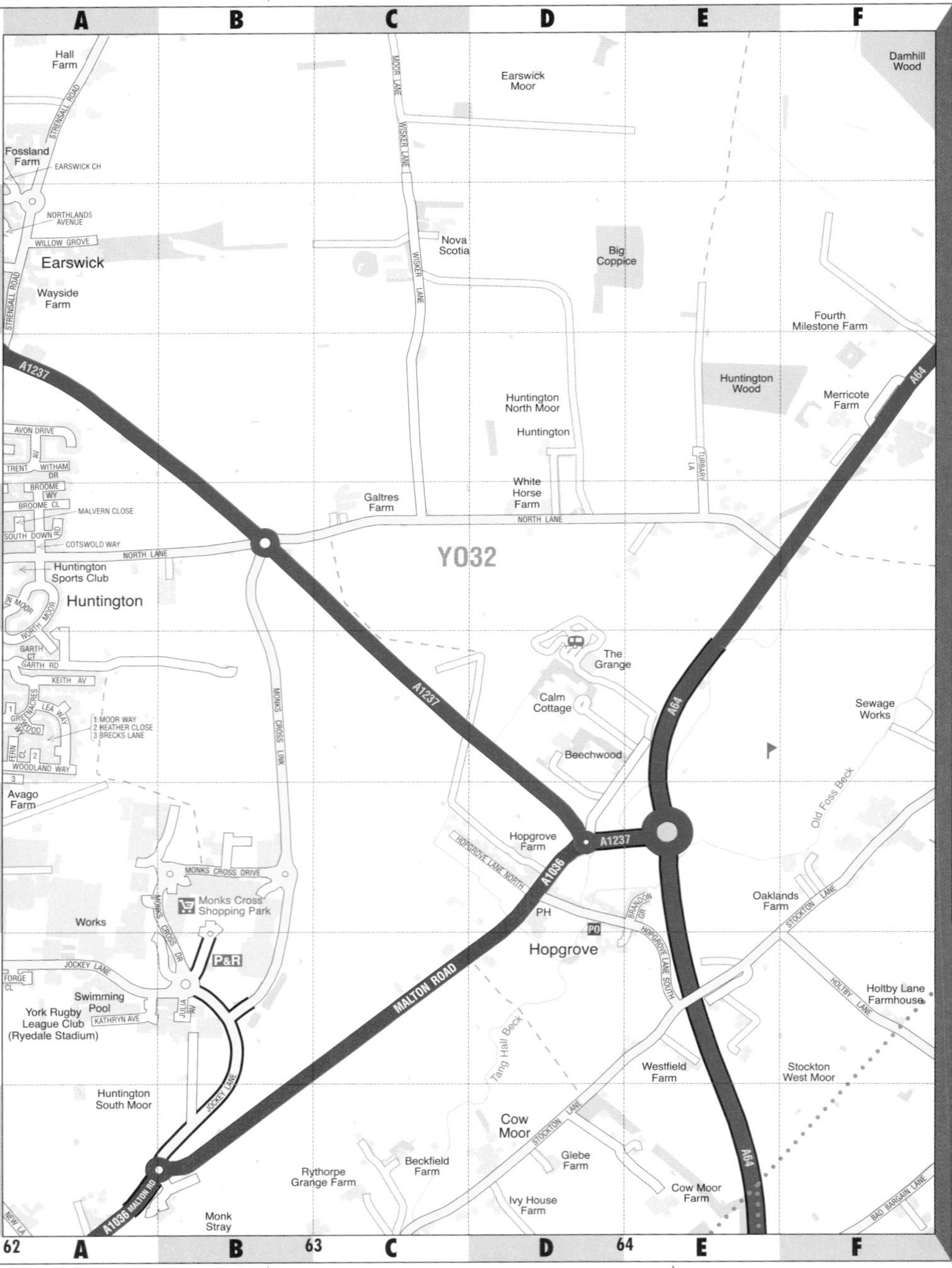
A B C D E F
8 7 57 6 5 56 4 3 55 2 1 54
Hall Farm
STRENSALL ROAD
Fossland Farm
EARSWICK CH
NORTHLANDS AVENUE
WILLOW GROVE
Earswick
Wayside Farm
MOOR LANE
WISKER LANE
Earswick Moor
Nova Scotia
Big Coppice
Damhill Wood
Fourth Milestone Farm
Huntington Wood
Merricote Farm
A64
A1237
Huntington North Moor
Huntington
TURBARY LA
AVON DRIVE
TRENT AV
WITHAM DR
BROOME WY
BROOME CL
MALVERN CLOSE
SOUTH DOWN RD
COTSWOLD WAY
Galtres Farm
White Horse Farm
NORTH LANE
Huntington Sports Club
Huntington
Y032
N MOOR
NORTH MOOR
GARTH CT
GARTH RD
KEITH AV
GREENACRES
LEA WAY
WOOD WY
1 MOOR WAY
2 HEATHER CLOSE
3 BRECKS LANE
FERN CL
WOODLAND WAY
Avago Farm
The Grange
Calm Cottage
Beechwood
Sewage Works
MONKS CROSS LINK
Old Foss Beck
Hopgrove Farm
HOPGROVE LANE NORTH
A1036
MONKS CROSS DRIVE
Monks Cross Shopping Park
Works
PH
PO
BRANDON GR
Oaklands Farm
STOCKTON LANE
Hopgrove
HOPGROVE LANE SOUTH
P&R
JOCKEY LANE
MONKS CROSS DR
FORGE CL
MALTON ROAD
HOLTBY LANE
Holtby Lane Farmhouse
Swimming Pool
York Rugby League Club (Ryedale Stadium)
KATHRYN AVE
JULIA AV
Tang Hall Beck
Westfield Farm
Stockton West Moor
Huntington South Moor
Cow Moor
Glebe Farm
Rythorpe Grange Farm
Beckfield Farm
Cow Moor Farm
Ivy House Farm
BAD BARGAIN LANE
Monk Stray
NEW LA
MALTON RD
62 63 64

127 131 14

F5
1 CHUDLEIGH RD
2 BROMLEY ST
3 ALBANY ST
4 WALWORTH ST N
5 HANOVER ST E
6 UPR HANOVER ST
7 HANOVER ST W
8 STAMFORD ST W
9 WALWORTH ST S
10 STAMFORD ST E
11 KINGSLAND TR
12 BRUNNEL CT
13 ST BARNABAS CT
14 REGENTS CT
15 VICTORIA CT
16 CARLISLE ST
17 CARLETON ST

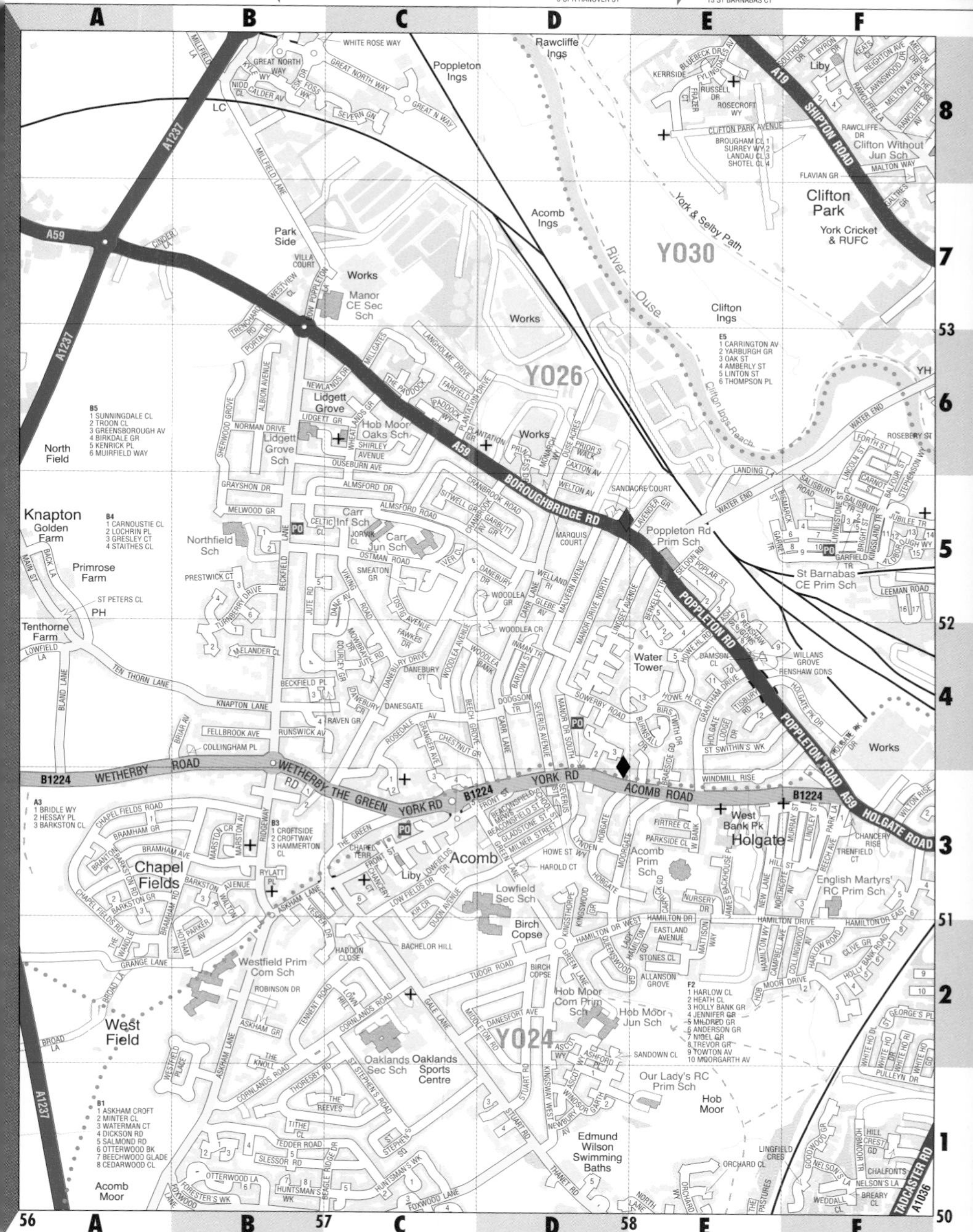

C1
1 THORNWOOD COVERT
2 MAPLEWOOD PADDOCK
3 FOXWOOD LANE
4 HERMAN WALK
5 FIR HEATH CL

C3
1 KIRK VIEW
2 CHURCH MEWS
3 ELMTREE GDNS
4 OAK RISE
5 CROSS ST
6 GALE FARM CT

24

D1
1 WOODFORD PL
2 KEMPTON CL
3 CLAY PL
4 CHESNEY FIELDS
5 ST JAMES PLACE

132

D4
1 PATELY PL
2 HEBDON RISE
3 BAILDON CL

130

E4
1 WINCHESTER GR
2 GARLAND ST
3 WINCHESTER AV
4 CHATSWORTH TERR
5 DILYS GR
6 PEPPERCORN CL
7 BONINGTON CT
8 RENSHAW GDNS
9 HILLARY GARTH
10 SEGRAVE WK
11 MANTHORPE WK
12 CHELWOOD WK
13 BOUTHWAITE DR

F3
1 FALCONER ST
2 ENFIELD CR
3 BARRETT AVE
4 BARBARA GR
5 CAROLINE CL
6 ROBIN GR

A8
1 LINDEN GROVE
2 MARTEN CLOSE
3 RAINSBOROUGH WAY
4 LOCKYER CL

A7
1 BELCOMBE WAY
2 HUDSON CRESCENT
3 CLIFTON PLACE
4 PINFOLD COURT

129

C7
1 UPR NEWBOROUGH ST
2 ALLAN ST
3 MURROUGH WILSON PL
4 FEVERSHAM CR
5 HILLSBOROUGH TERR
6 HUDSON ST

127

E8
1 KIRKHAM AVE
2 THE CROSSWAY
3 LILLING AVE
4 REDGRAVE CL

E5
1 HAWTHORN ST
2 EMMERSON ST
3 FLEMING AVE
4 SCROPE AVE

F8
1 ALBERT CL
2 VICTORIA WY
3 MORRITT CL
4 FOSTON GR
5 THORNFIELD AVE
6 LABURNUM GARTH

For full street detail of the highlighted area see page 156.

59 A B 60 C D 61 E F

A2
1 TOWTON AVE
2 TRENTHOLME DR
3 MOORGARTH AVE
4 WHITE HO GDNS

A3
1 ENFIELD CR
2 WATSON TERR
3 CECILIA PL
4 CAMBRIDGE ST
5 OXFORD ST
6 MOUNT EPHRAIM
7 HOLGATE BR GDNS

129

B1
1 WINDSOR ST
2 HUBERT ST
3 RUBY ST
4 COUNT BE BURGH TERR
5 BALMORAL TERR
6 LICHFIELD CT

133

B2
1 TELFORD TERR
2 PHILADELPHIA TERR
3 ADELAIDE ST

E3
1 BRINKWORTH TERR
2 THOMAS ST
3 HILDA ST
4 GRANVILLE TERR
5 LANSDOWNE TERR
6 HERBERT ST
7 CHAUCER ST
8 DAYSFOOT CT
9 APOLLO ST

F3
1 ST NICHOLAS PL
2 ARNSIDE PL

128
26

A5
1 MELROSE CL
2 APPLEBY PL
3 INGLETON WK
4 WOODHOUSE GR

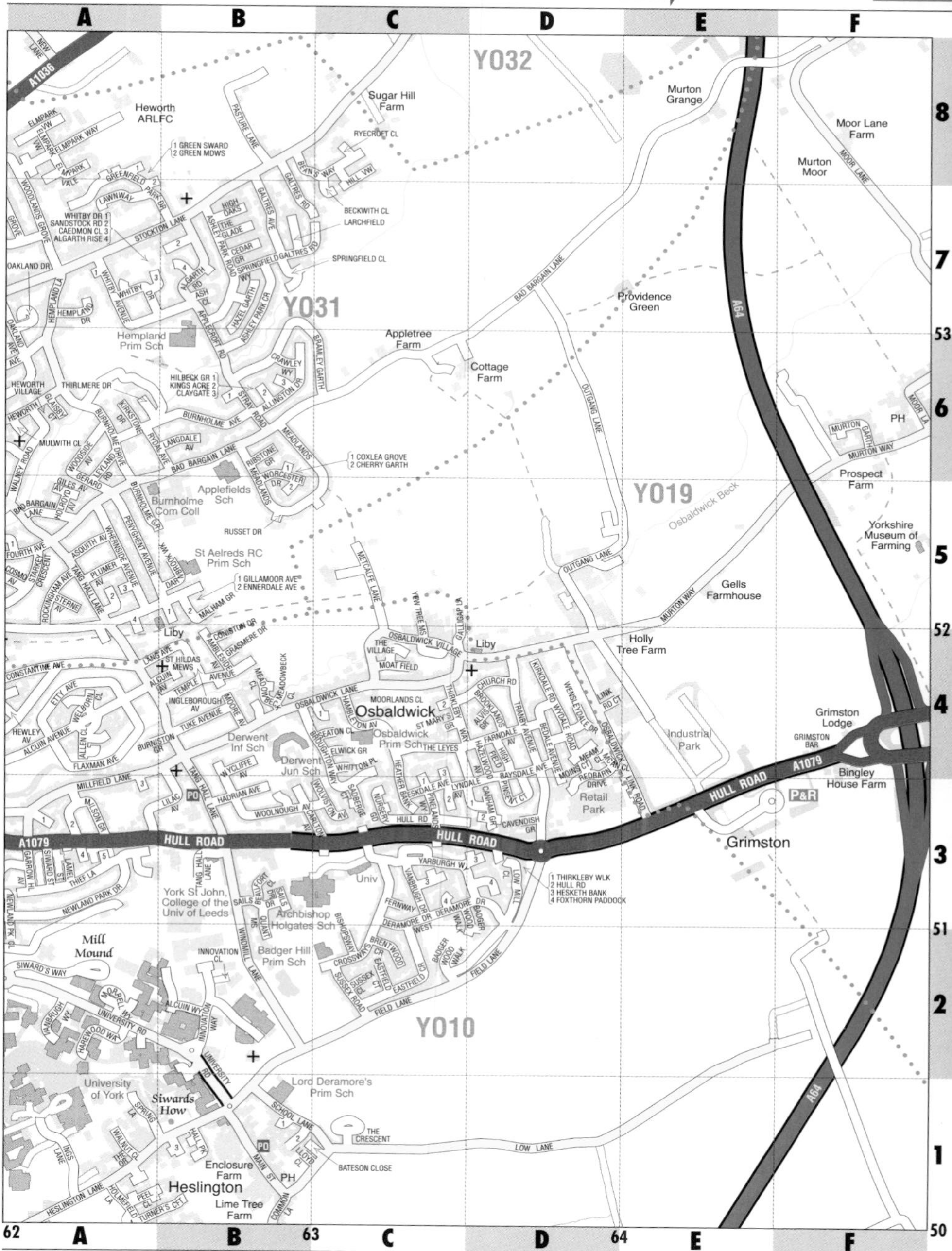

A3
1 HEATHFIELD RD
2 OWSTON AVE
3 WAYNEFLEET GR
4 CYCLE ST
5 NORMAN ST

B1
1 ENCLOSURE GDNS
2 HESLINGTON CT
3 HOLBURNS CFT

C3
1 SHALLOWDALE GR
2 BRACKEN HILL
3 KIMBERLOWS WOOD HILL
4 PINEWOOD HILL

C4
1 VICARAGE GDNS
2 ST THOMAS'S CL
3 GIVENDALE GR

26
26

24

C8
1 HINTON AV
2 LYDHAM CT
3 MARTIN CHEESEMAN CT
4 CRANFIELD PL

129

D8
1 FARMLANDS RD
2 DRINGFIELD CL
3 HERDSMAN RD
4 SANDCROFT CL
5 DEEPDALE

E8
1 TURNMIRE RD
2 SOUTHFIELD CR
3 MEADOW CT
4 THE PASTURES
5 ST HELEN'S RD
6 RAILWAY VW

F8
1 KENSINGTON CT
2 REGENCY MEWS

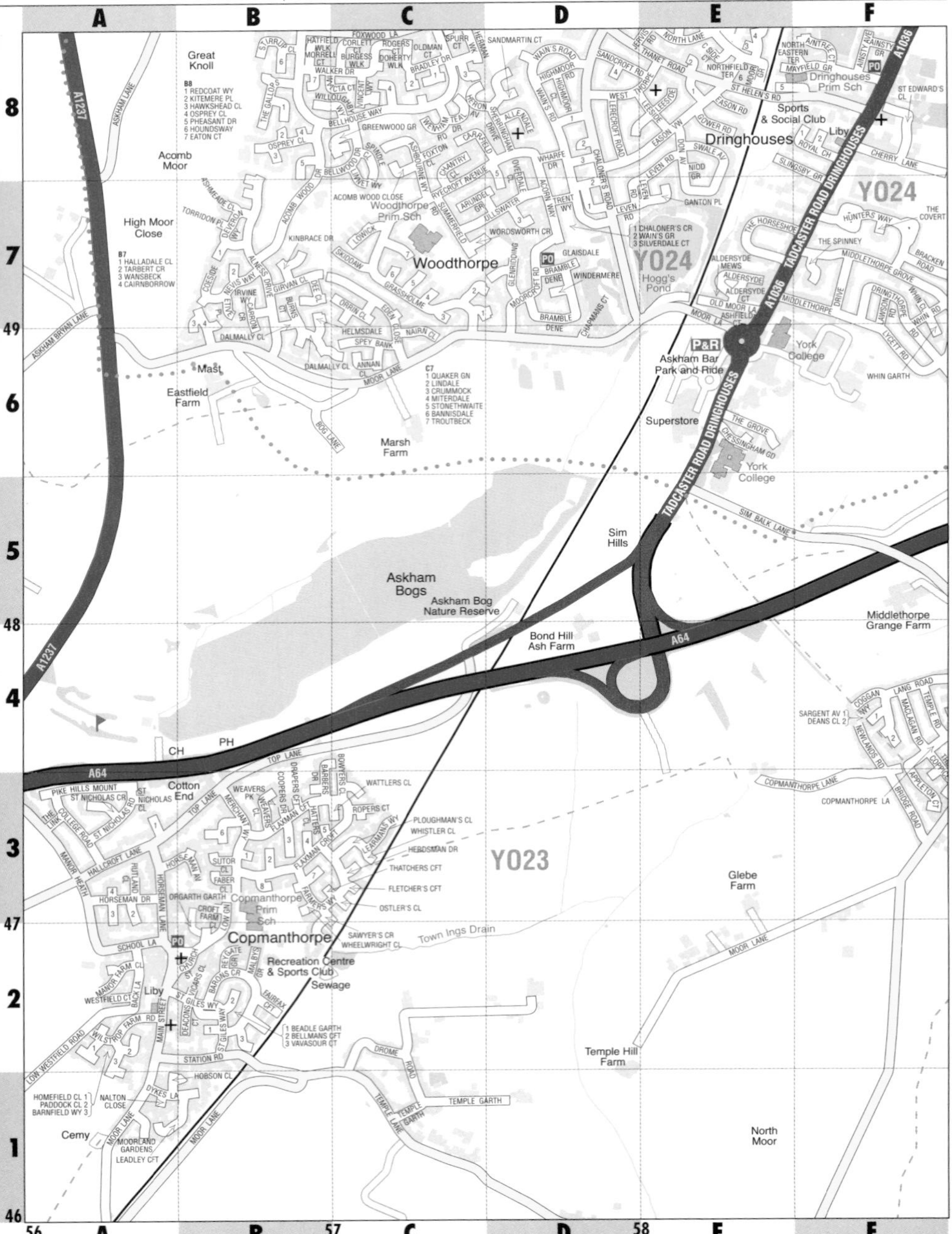

A3
1 LARKFIELD CL
2 HORSEMAN CL
3 LYNWOOD AV
4 LYNWOOD VW

B3
1 SADDLERS CL
2 FARRIERS CFT
3 WAGGONERS DR
4 POTTERS DR
5 WAINERS CL
6 MILLERS CFT
7 LORINERS DR
8 GARDENERS CL

24

36

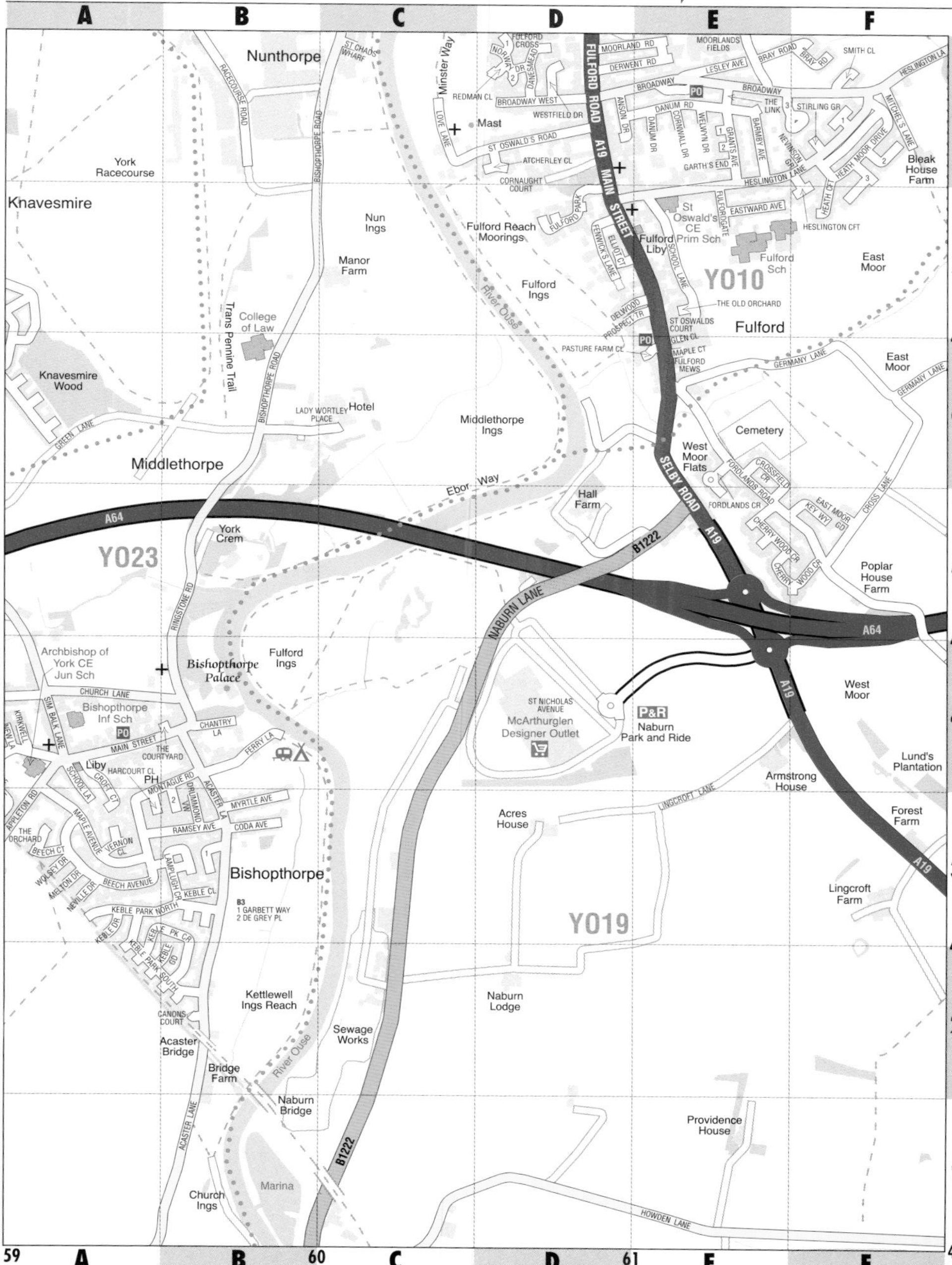
A
B
C
D
E
F
8
7
49
6
5
48
4
3
47
2
1
46
59
60
61
Nunthorpe
York Racecourse
Knavesmire
Knavesmire Wood
Middlethorpe
College of Law
Trans Pennine Trail
BISHOPTHORPE ROAD
RACECOURSE ROAD
ST CHADS WHARF
Nun Ings
Manor Farm
LADY WORTLEY PLACE
Hotel
GREEN LANE
Minster Way
LOVE LANE
Mast
REDMAN CL
ST OSWALD'S ROAD
ATCHERLEY CL
CORNAUGHT COURT
FULFORD CROSS
NORWAY DR
DANESMEAD
BROADWAY WEST
WESTFIELD DR
MOORLAND RD
DERWENT RD
FULFORD ROAD
A19
MAIN STREET
MOORLANDS FIELDS
LESLEY AVE
BROADWAY
PO
ANSON DR
DANUM RD
DANUM DR
CORNWALL DR
WELWYN DR
GRANTS AVE
BARMBY AVE
GARTH'S END
THE LINK
STIRLING GR
NEVINSON GR
HESLINGTON LANE
BRAY ROAD
BRAY RD
SMITH CL
HESLINGTON LA
MITCHEL'S LANE
HEATH MOOR DRIVE
HEATH CFT
Bleak House Farm
HESLINGTON CFT
Fulford Reach Moorings
FULFORD PARK
FENWICK'S LANE
ELLIOT CT
Fulford Liby
SCHOOL LANE
St Oswald's CE Prim Sch
FULFORDGATE
EASTWARD AVE
Fulford Sch
YO10
East Moor
Fulford Ings
River Ouse
DELWOOD
PROSPECT TR
ST OSWALDS COURT
GLEN CL
THE OLD ORCHARD
Fulford
PASTURE FARM CL
MAPLE CT
FULFORD MEWS
GERMANY LANE
East Moor
Middlethorpe Ings
West Moor Flats
Cemetery
SELBY ROAD
Ebor Way
Hall Farm
CROSSFIELD CR
FORDLANDS ROAD
FORDLANDS CR
EAST MOOR GD
KEY WY
CHERRY WOOD CR
CROSS LANE
Poplar House Farm
A64
YO23
York Crem
B1222
NABURN LANE
RINGSTONE RD
Archbishop of York CE Jun Sch
Bishopthorpe Palace
Fulford Ings
CHURCH LANE
Bishopthorpe Inf Sch
SIM BALK LANE
KIRKWELL
NEW LA
MAIN STREET
THE COURTYARD
CHANTRY LA
FERRY LA
Liby
SCHOOL LA
HARCOURT CL
CROFT CT
PH
MONTAGUE RD
DRUMMOND VW
ACASTER LA
MYRTLE AVE
RAMSEY AVE
CODA AVE
APPLETON RD
THE ORCHARD
MAPLE AVENUE
VERNON CL
BEECH CT
WOLSEY DR
MELTON DR
NEVILLE DR
BEECH AVENUE
LAMPLUGH CR
KEBLE CL
Bishopthorpe
B3
1 GARBETT WAY
2 DE GREY PL
KEBLE PARK NORTH
KEBLE DR
KEBLE PK CR
KEBLE GD
KEBLE PARK SOUTH
CANONS COURT
Acaster Bridge
Kettlewell Ings Reach
Sewage Works
Bridge Farm
River Ouse
Naburn Bridge
ACASTER LANE
Church Ings
Marina
ST NICHOLAS AVENUE
McArthurglen Designer Outlet
P&R
Naburn Park and Ride
West Moor
Lund's Plantation
Armstrong House
LINGCROFT LANE
Acres House
Forest Farm
Lingcroft Farm
YO19
Naburn Lodge
Providence House
HOWDEN LANE

35
35

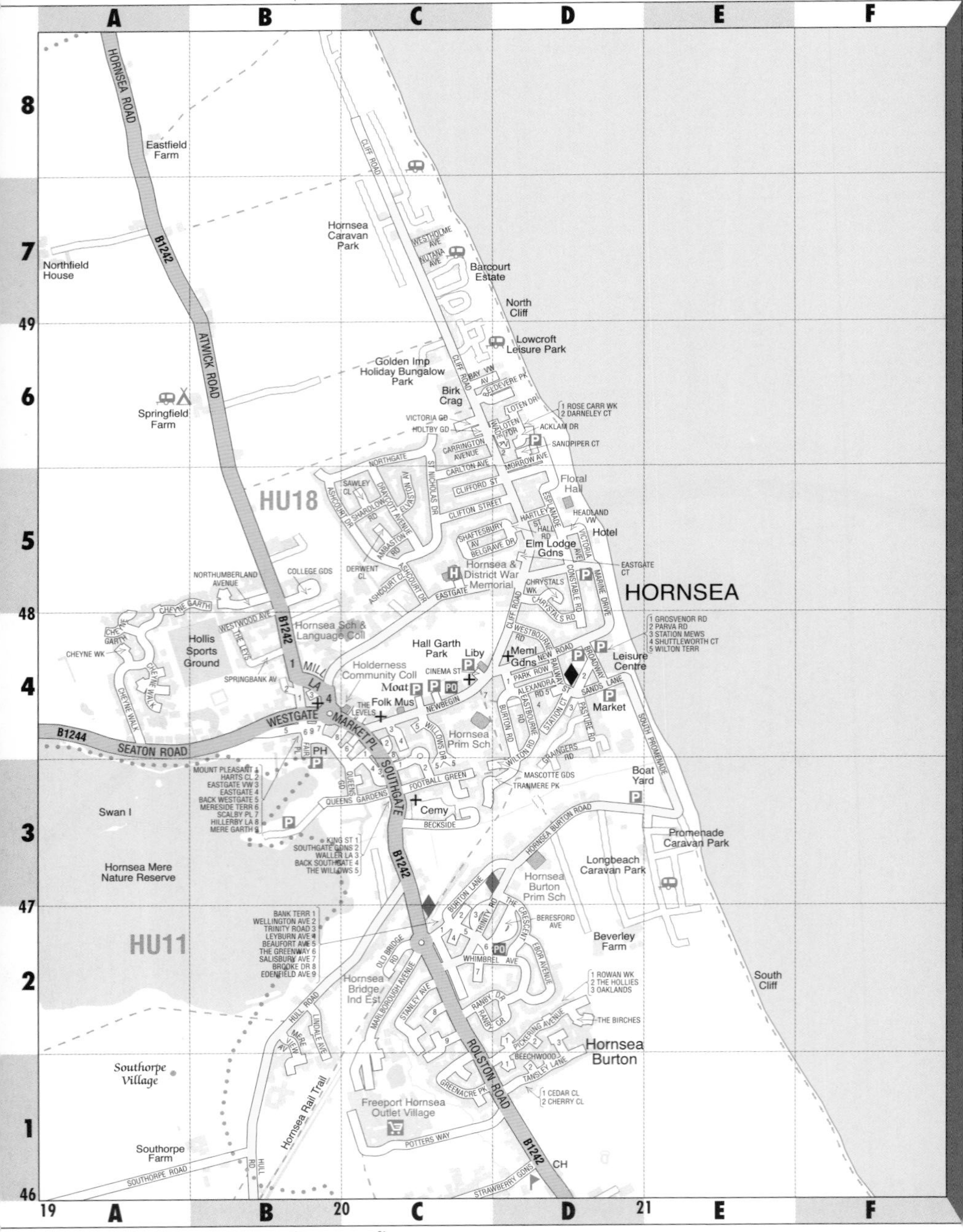
A
B
C
D
E
F
8
7
49
6
5
48
4
3
47
2
1
46
19
20
21
HORNSEA ROAD
Eastfield Farm
B1242
Northfield House
ATWICK ROAD
Springfield Farm
HU18
HU11
Hornsea Caravan Park
CLIFF ROAD
WESTHOLME AVE
NUTANA AVE
Barcourt Estate
North Cliff
Lowcroft Leisure Park
Golden Imp Holiday Bungalow Park
BAY VW
BELVEDERE PK
Birk Crag
VICTORIA GD
HOLTBY GD
1 ROSE CARR WK
2 DARNELEY CT
LOTEN DR
ACKLAM DR
SANDPIPER CT
CARRINGTON AVENUE
CARLTON AVE
MORROW AVE
NORTHGATE
SAWLEY CL
ASHCOURT DR
SHARLOWCOTT RD
DRAYCOTT AVENUE
ELVASTON AV
ST NICHOLAS DR
CLIFFORD ST
CLIFTON STREET
Floral Hall
HARTLEY ST
HALL RD
ESPLANADE
HEADLAND VW
Hotel
SHAFTESBURY AV
BELGRAVE DR
Elm Lodge Gdns
VICTORIA AVE
EASTGATE CT
AMBASTON RD
DERWENT CL
ASHCOURT CL
Hornsea & District War Memorial
CHRYSTALS WK
CHRYSTAL'S RD
CONSTABLE RD
MARINE DRIVE
HORNSEA
NORTHUMBERLAND AVENUE
COLLEGE GDS
CHEYNE GARTH
WESTWOOD AVE
THE LEYS
Hollis Sports Ground
Hornsea Sch & Language Coll
CHEYNE WK
CHEYNE WALK
SPRINGBANK AV
MILL LA
EASTGATE
1 GROSVENOR RD
2 PARVA RD
3 STATION MEWS
4 SHUTTLEWORTH CT
5 WILTON TERR
Hall Garth Park
Liby
Holderness Community Coll
CINEMA ST
Meml Gdns
NEW ROAD
PARK ROW
BROADWAY
RAILWAY ST
Leisure Centre
Moat
PO
ALEXANDRA RD
SANDS LANE
Folk Mus
THE LEVELS
NEWBEGIN
Market
WESTGATE
MARKET PL
B1244
SEATON ROAD
FAIR PL
PH
WILLOWS DR
Hornsea Prim Sch
BURTON RD
EASTBOURNE RD
WILTON RD
STATION CT
PASTURE RD
GRANGERS RD
SOUTH PROMENADE
SOUTHGATE
MOUNT PLEASANT 1
HARTS CL 2
EASTGATE VW 3
EASTGATE 4
BACK WESTGATE 5
MERESIDE TERR 6
SCALBY PL 7
HILLERBY LA 8
MERE GARTH 9
QUEENS GD
QUEENS GARDENS
FOOTBALL GREEN
MASCOTTE GDS
TRANMERE PK
Boat Yard
Swan I
Cemy
BECKSIDE
HORNSEA BURTON ROAD
Promenade Caravan Park
KING ST 1
SOUTHGATE GDNS 2
WALLER LA 3
BACK SOUTHGATE 4
THE WILLOWS 5
Hornsea Mere Nature Reserve
Longbeach Caravan Park
Hornsea Burton Prim Sch
BURTON LANE
TRINITY RD
THE CRESCENT
BERESFORD AVE
BANK TERR 1
WELLINGTON AVE 2
TRINITY ROAD 3
LEYBURN AVE 4
BEAUFORT AVE 5
THE GREENWAY 6
SALISBURY AVE 7
BROOKE DR 8
EDENFIELD AVE 9
Beverley Farm
EBOR AVENUE
WHIMBREL AVE
OLD BRIDGE RD
Hornsea Bridge Ind Est
MARLBOROUGH AVENUE
South Cliff
1 ROWAN WK
2 THE HOLLIES
3 OAKLANDS
HULL ROAD
LINDALE AVE
MERE VIEW AV
STANLEY AVE
RANBY DR
RANBY CR
THE BIRCHES
PICKERING AVENUE
Hornsea Burton
BEECHWOOD
TANSLEY LANE
ROLSTON ROAD
Southorpe Village
GREENACRE PK
1 CEDAR CL
2 CHERRY CL
Hornsea Rail Trail
Freeport Hornsea Outlet Village
POTTERS WAY
Southorpe Farm
HULL RD
SOUTHORPE ROAD
CH
STRAWBERRY GDNS

C4
1 CHAMBERS LA
2 QUALES MEWS
3 BANK ST
4 DESMOND AVE
5 THE WILLOWS
6 MERE WK
7 WITTY'S PASS
8 GRANGER'S YD

35
46

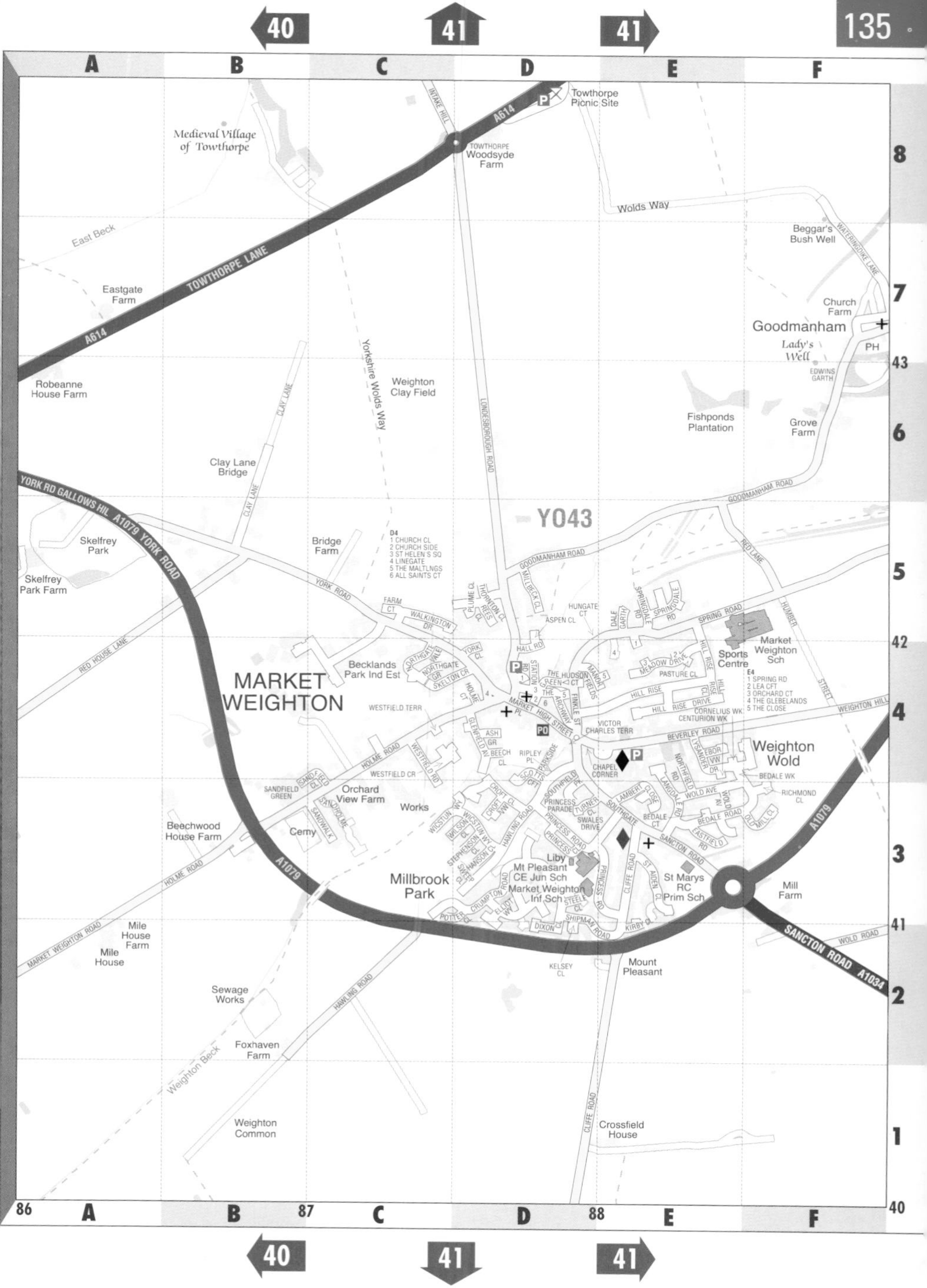
40
41
41
A
B
C
D
E
F
8
7
43
6
5
42
4
3
41
2
1
40
86
87
88
Towthorpe Picnic Site
Medieval Village of Towthorpe
INTAKE HILL
A614
TOWTHORPE
Woodsyde Farm
Wolds Way
Beggar's Bush Well
WATERINGDIKE LANE
East Beck
TOWTHORPE LANE
Eastgate Farm
A614
Church Farm
Goodmanham
Lady's Well
PH
EDWINS GARTH
Robeanne House Farm
Weighton Clay Field
Yorkshire Wolds Way
CLAY LANE
LONDESBOROUGH ROAD
Fishponds Plantation
Grove Farm
Clay Lane Bridge
GOODMANHAM ROAD
YORK RD GALLOWS HIL A1079 YORK ROAD
YO43
CLAY LANE
Skelfrey Park
Bridge Farm
D4
1 CHURCH CL
2 CHURCH SIDE
3 ST HELEN'S SQ
4 LINEGATE
5 THE MALTLNGS
6 ALL SAINTS CT
GOODMANHAM ROAD
RED LANE
Skelfrey Park Farm
YORK ROAD
MILLBECK CL
PLUME CL
THORNTON CL
REES CL
SPRINGDALE RD
SPRINGDALE RD
FARM CT
WALKINGTON DR
HUNGATE CT
ASPEN CL
DALE GARTH
SPRING ROAD
HUMBER
Market Weighton Sch
RED HOUSE LANE
YORK CL
HALL RD
NORTHGATE
VALE
NORTHGATE
GR
SKELTON CR
Becklands Park Ind Est
STATION RD
THE HUDSON
GREEN CT
THE ARCHWAY
MANOR FIELDS
MEADOW DRIVE
PASTURE CL
HILL RISE
Sports Centre
E4
1 SPRING RD
2 LEA CFT
3 ORCHARD CT
4 THE GLEBELANDS
5 THE CLOSE
STREET
MARKET WEIGHTON
HOLME CT
FINKLE ST
HILL RISE
HILL RISE DRIVE
CORNELIUS WK
CENTURION WK
WEIGHTON HILL
WESTFIELD TERR
MARKET HIGH STREET
PL
PO
GLENFIELD AV
VICTOR CHARLES TERR
BEVERLEY ROAD
ASH GR
BEECH CL
RIPLEY PL
PARKSIDE
CHAPEL CORNER
NORTHFIELD
LYSANDER
EBOR VW
DR
Weighton Wold
HOLME ROAD
WESTFIELD RD
SCOTTS CFT
BEDALE WK
WESTFIELD CR
SANDFIELD GREEN
SANDFIELD CL
Orchard View Farm
CROFT CL
SOUTHFIELD
LAMBERT
CLOSE
LANGDALE RD
WOLD AVE
WOLD AV
RICHMOND CL
SANDHOLME
Works
PRINCESS PARADE
TURNER
SOUTHGATE
BEDALE CT
BEDALE ROAD
MILL CL
OLD
Beechwood House Farm
SANDWALK
WICSTUN WY
WILSON
WICSTUN WY
CROFT VW
HAWLING ROAD
SWALES DRIVE
PRINCESS ROAD
SANCTON ROAD
EASTFIELD RD
A1079
Cemy
STEPHENSON CL
HANSON CL
Liby
A1079
HOLME ROAD
SWEEP
Mt Pleasant CE Jun Sch
PRINCESS RD
CLIFFE ROAD
ST AIDEN CL
St Marys RC Prim Sch
Mill Farm
Millbrook Park
CRUMPTON ROAD
Market Weighton Inf Sch
ELLIOT WY
STEELE CL
POTTER CL
DIXON
SHIPMAN ROAD
KIRBY CL
SANCTON ROAD A1034
WOLD ROAD
Mile House Farm
MARKET WEIGHTON ROAD
Mile House
KELSEY CL
Mount Pleasant
HAWLING ROAD
Sewage Works
Foxhaven Farm
Weighton Beck
CLIFFE ROAD
Weighton Common
Crossfield House
40
41
41

43
43

D6
1 WOODHALL DR
2 MOLESCROFT W CL
3 MOLESCROFT AVE
4 MOLESCROFT PK

F7
1 WOODCOATES CL
2 MEADOW BANK
3 BEECH TREE CL
4 BRAMBLE GARTH
5 WILLOW TREE GARTH

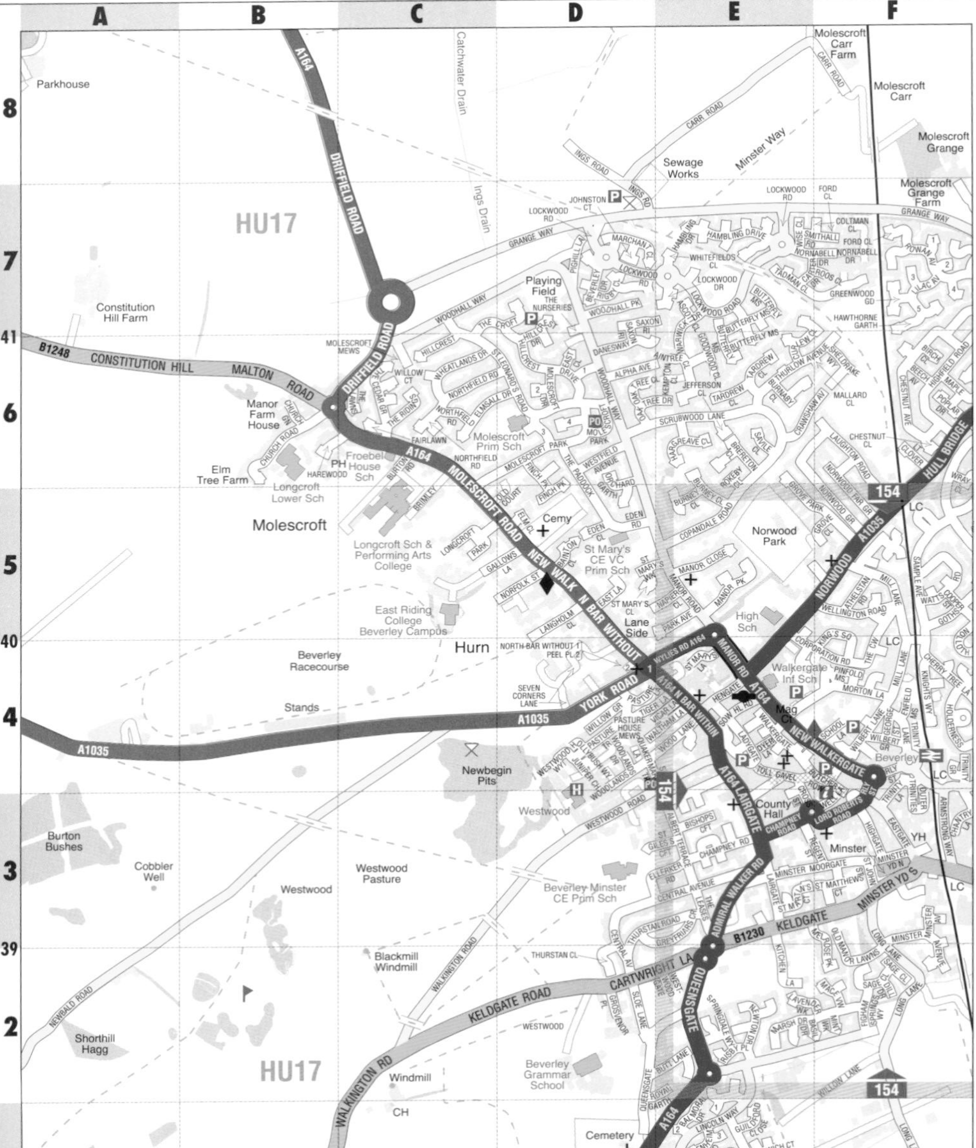

43
55

E1
1 LEATHLEY CL
2 CAVENDISH DR
3 BERKELEY DR
4 HEREFORD CL
5 WINCHESTER AVE
6 OXFORD CL
7 ST ALBANS CL
8 CATHEDRAL CL
9 WELTON CL

For full street detail of the highlighted area see page 154.

A6
1 SOUTHFIELD DR
2 SIGSTON RD
3 EASTFIELD CL
4 SYMMONS CL

44
44

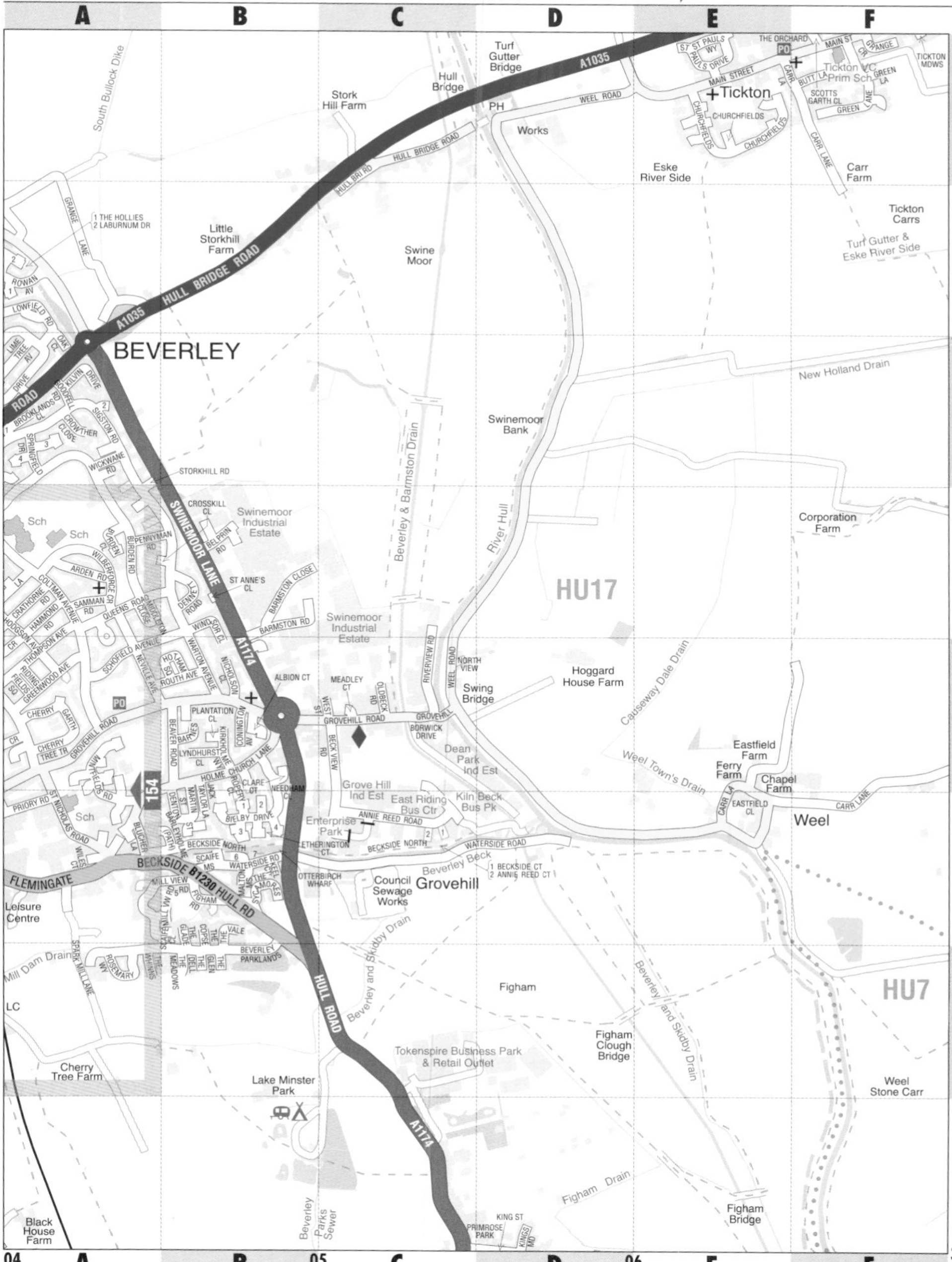

B3
1 TATTERSALL DR
2 HOLGATE CL
3 GILLYON CL
4 AKESTER CL
5 MILL VIEW PL
6 BARKERS MILL
7 MARIN CT

56
44

55
55

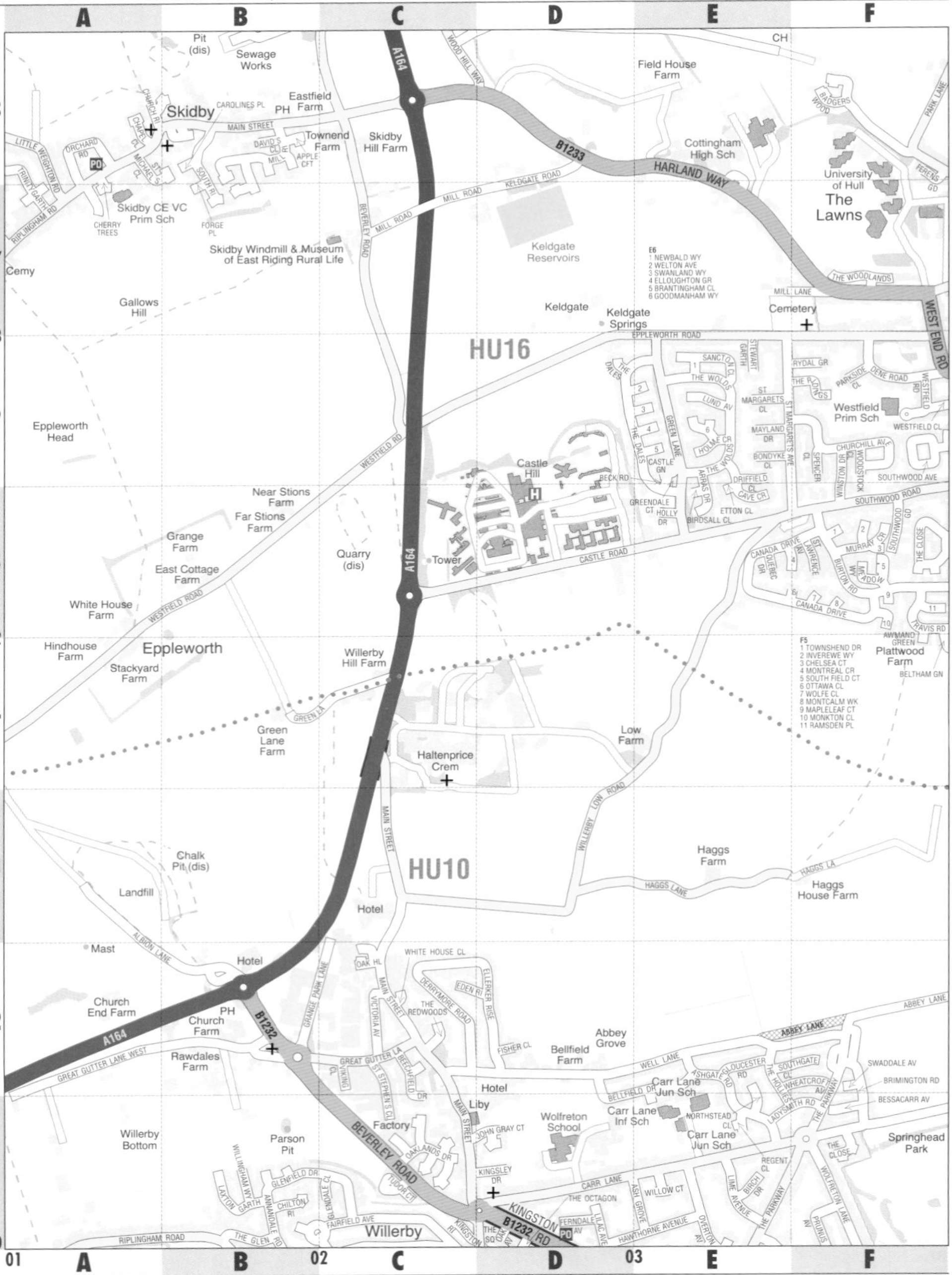
A
B
C
D
E
F
8
7
33
6
5
32
4
3
31
2
1
30
01
02
03
Pit (dis)
Sewage Works
CH
Field House Farm
A164
WOOD HILL WAY
Skidby
CAROLINES PL
PH
Eastfield Farm
MAIN STREET
Townend Farm
Skidby Hill Farm
B1233
HARLAND WAY
Cottingham High Sch
University of Hull
The Lawns
BADGERS WOOD
PARK LANE
FERENS GD
LITTLE WEIGHTON RD
ORCHARD RD
CHURCH RI
CHAPEL
ST MICHAEL'S
DAVID'S CL
MILL RI
APPLE CFT
SOUTH RI
KELDGATE ROAD
MILL ROAD
TRINITY GARTH
RIPLINGHAM RD
Skidby CE VC Prim Sch
CHERRY TREES
FORGE PL
BEVERLEY ROAD
Skidby Windmill & Museum of East Riding Rural Life
Keldgate Reservoirs
E6
1 NEWBALD WY
2 WELTON AVE
3 SWANLAND WY
4 ELLOUGHTON GR
5 BRANTINGHAM CL
6 GOODMANHAM WY
THE WOODLANDS
MILL LANE
Cemy
Gallows Hill
Keldgate
Keldgate Springs
Cemetery
WEST END RD
HU16
EPPLEWORTH ROAD
THE DALES
SANCTON CL
THE WOLDS
STEWART GARTH
RYDAL GR
THE RIDINGS
PARKSIDE CL
DENE ROAD
WESTFIELD RD
LUND AV
ST MARGARETS CL
ST MARGARETS AVE
Westfield Prim Sch
WESTFIELD CL
Eppleworth Head
WESTFIELD RD
GREEN LANE
MAYLAND DR
HOLME CR
CHURCHILL AVE
BONDYKE CL
SPENCER CL
WINSTON DR
WOODSTOCK
Castle Hill
H
BECK RD
CASTLE GN
THE WOLDS
ARRAS DR
DRIFFIELD CL
CAVE CR
SOUTHWOOD AVE
SOUTHWOOD ROAD
Near Stions Farm
Far Stions Farm
GREENDALE CT
HOLLY DR
BIRDSALL CL
ETTON CL
Grange Farm
Quarry (dis)
Tower
CASTLE ROAD
CANADA DRIVE
QUEBEC DR
ST LAWRENCE AV
MURRAY CR
SOUTHWOOD GD
THE CLOSE
BURTON RD
MEADOW
East Cottage Farm
White House Farm
WESTFIELD ROAD
CANADA DRIVE
TRAVIS RD
Hindhouse Farm
Eppleworth
Stackyard Farm
Willerby Hill Farm
F5
1 TOWNSHEND DR
2 INVEREWE WY
3 CHELSEA CT
4 MONTREAL CR
5 SOUTH FIELD CT
6 OTTAWA CL
7 WOLFE CL
8 MONTCALM WK
9 MAPLELEAF CT
10 MONKTON CT
11 RAMSDEN PL
AWMAND GREEN
Plattwood Farm
BELTHAM GN
GREEN LA
Green Lane Farm
Low Farm
Haltenprice Crem
WILLERBY LOW ROAD
MAIN STREET
Chalk Pit (dis)
Haggs Farm
HU10
HAGGS LA
Haggs House Farm
Landfill
HAGGS LANE
Hotel
Mast
ALBION LANE
Hotel
GRANGE PARK LANE
OAK HL
WHITE HOUSE CL
DERRYMORE ROAD
EDEN RI
ELLERKER RISE
THE REDWOODS
VICTORIA AV
Church End Farm
PH
Church Farm
B1232
ABBEY LANE
Abbey Grove
Bellfield Farm
FISHER CL
Rawdales Farm
GREAT GUTTER LANE WEST
GREAT GUTTER LA
VIKING CL
ST STEPHEN'S CL
BEECHFIELD DR
WELL LANE
GLOUCESTER RD
SOUTHGATE CL
ASHGATE RD
THE HOLLIES
WHEATCROFT AV
THE PARKWAY
SWADDALE AV
BRIMINGTON RD
BESSACARR AV
Hotel
BELLFIELD DR
Carr Lane Jun Sch
Liby
Carr Lane Inf Sch
NORTHSTEAD CL
LADYSMITH RD
Factory
Wolfreton School
Carr Lane Jun Sch
Springhead Park
Willerby Bottom
Parson Pit
BEVERLEY ROAD
JOHN GRAY CT
OAKLANDS DR
THE CLOSE
WILLINGHAM WY
GLENFIELD DR
LAYTON GARTH
ANNANDALE RD
CHILTON RI
FAIRFIELD AVE
KINGSLEY DR
TUDOR CT
CARR LANE
REGENT CL
ASH GROVE
WILLOW CT
LIME AVENUE
BIRCH DR
WOLFRETON LANE
THE OCTAGON
KINGSTON RD
B1232
FERNDALE
LILAC AVE
HAWTHORNE AVENUE
OVERTON AV
THE PARKWAY
PRUNUS AV
RIPLINGHAM ROAD
THE GLEN
Willerby
THE SQ
OAK AV
PO

55
143

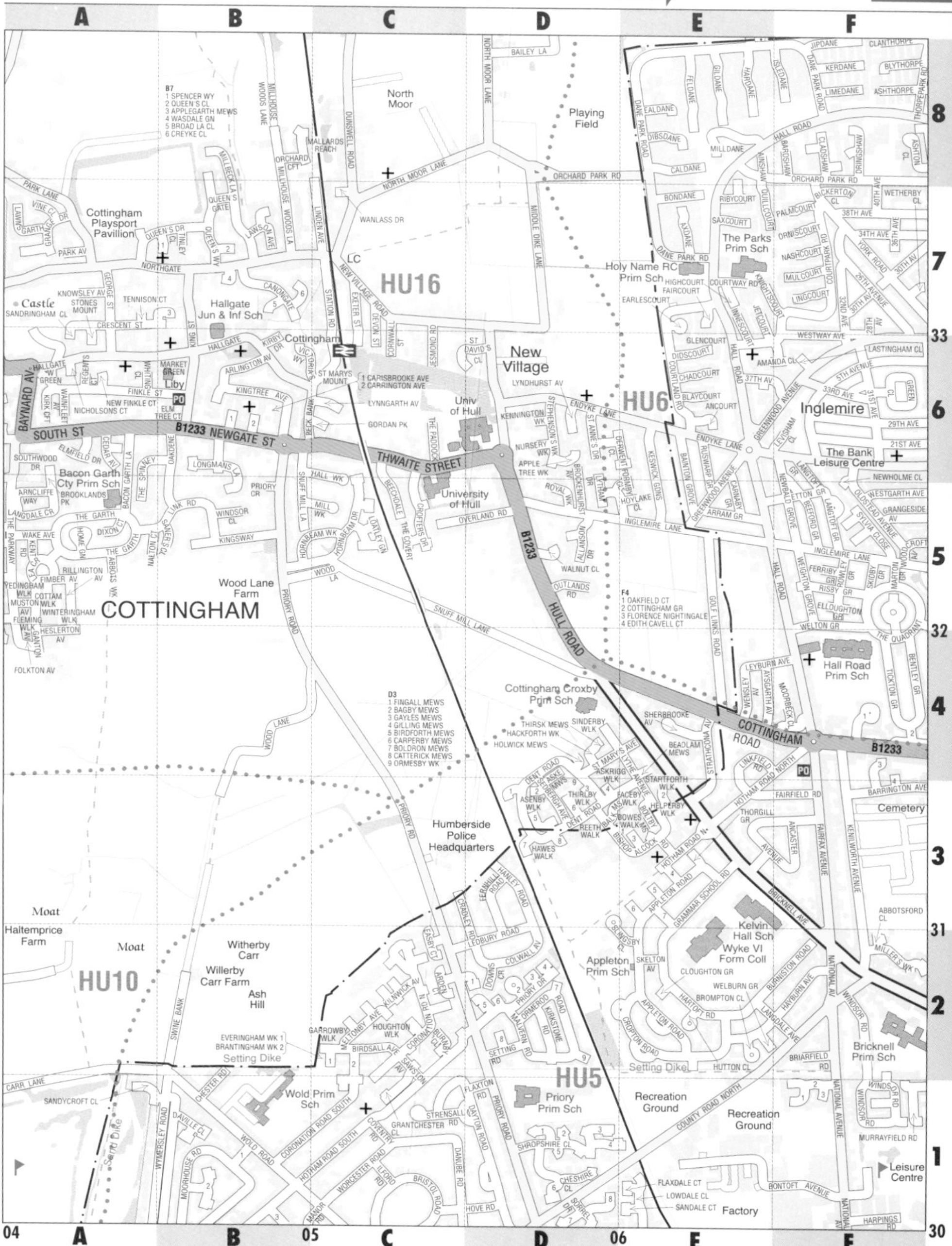

B1
1 MOORHOUSE RD
2 WILLERBY CARR CL
3 HUNSLEY AVE

D1
1 WORCESTERSHIRE CL
2 HERTFORDSHIRE CL
3 YORKSHIRE CL
4 ERNEST KIRKWOOD CL
5 SUSSEX CL
6 WARWICKSHIRE CL
7 HEATHER CL
8 CELANDINE CL

D2
1 ST FRANCIS CT
2 ST THOMAS'S GRANGE
3 ST JUDE'S CT
4 ST EDMUNDS'S CT
5 ST OSWALD CT
6 ST HEDDA'S CT
7 ORMEROD CR
8 SETTING CR
9 MALVERN CR

E3
1 MARSKE WK
2 BURRILL MEWS
3 CALDBERG MEWS
4 SALTON AVE
5 EBBERSTON GR
6 CASTLETON AVE
7 KNAPTON AVE

F1
1 WOOLSHEDS CL
2 WISES FARM RD
3 HAVERFLATS CL

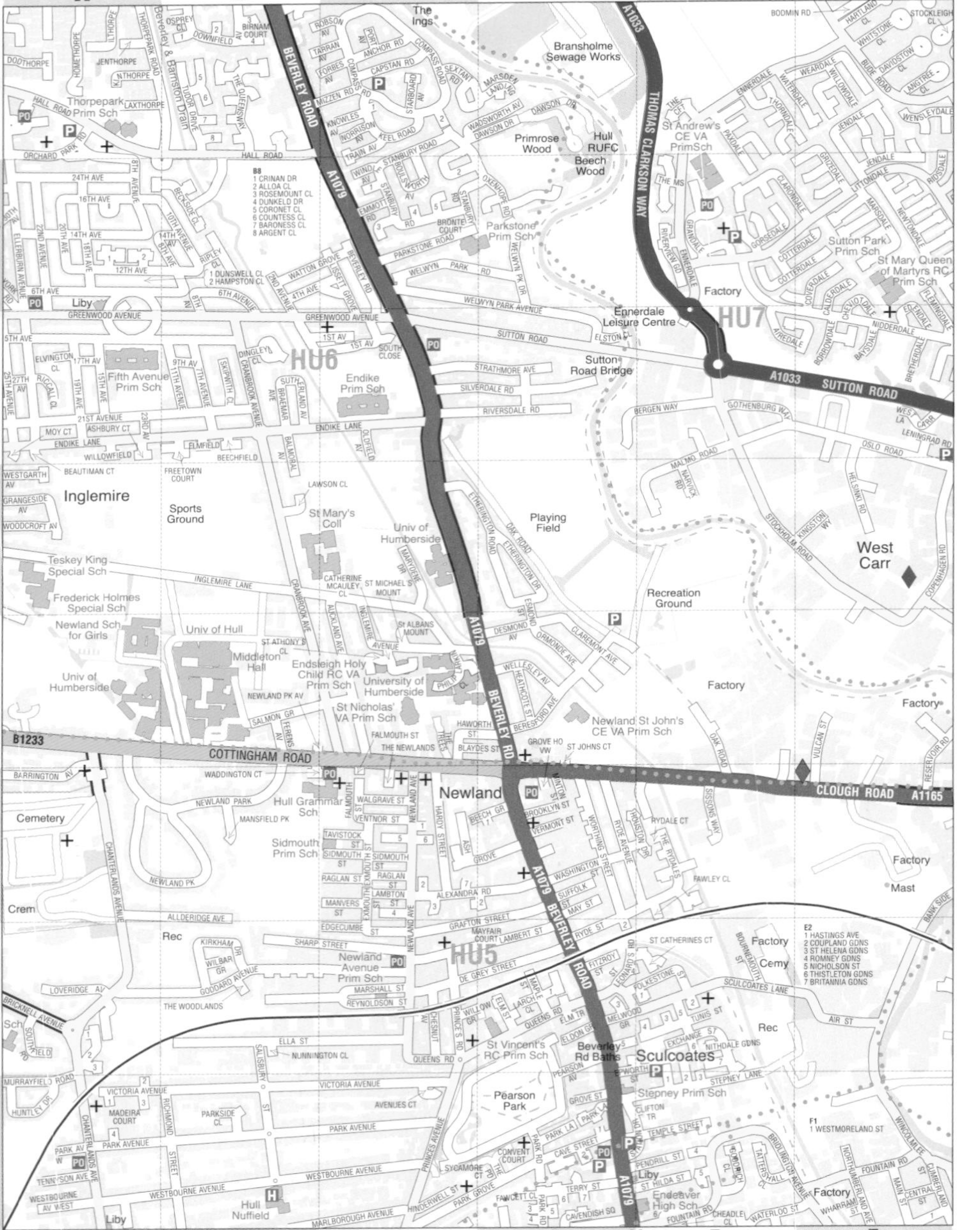
139
C8
1 FLAG WK
2 LARARD AVE
C7
1 BEECHCLIFFE AVE
2 CULLINGWORTH AVE
3 DENHOLME AVE
4 STEETON AVE
5 SILSDEN AVE
56
A
B
C
D
E
F
8
7
33
6
5
32
4
3
31
2
1
30
07
08
09
The Ings
Bransholme Sewage Works
BEVERLEY ROAD
A1079
A1033
THOMAS CLARKSON WAY
Beverley & Barmston Drain
Thorpepark Prim Sch
HALL ROAD
ORCHARD PARK RD
Primrose Wood
Hull RUFC
Beech Wood
St Andrew's CE VA PrimSch
B8
1 CRINAN DR
2 ALLOA CL
3 ROSEMOUNT CL
4 DUNKELD DR
5 CORONET CL
6 COUNTESS CL
7 BARONESS CL
8 ARGENT CL
Parkstone Prim Sch
PARKSTONE ROAD
WELWYN PARK RD
WELWYN PARK AVENUE
Sutton Park Prim Sch
St Mary Queen of Martyrs RC Prim Sch
Factory
Ennerdale Leisure Centre
HU7
HU6
Liby
GREENWOOD AVENUE
SUTTON ROAD
Sutton Road Bridge
A1033 SUTTON ROAD
Fifth Avenue Prim Sch
Endike Prim Sch
ENDIKE LANE
RIVERSDALE RD
SILVERDALE RD
STRATHMORE AVE
Inglemire
Sports Ground
St Mary's Coll
Univ of Humberside
Playing Field
West Carr
Teskey King Special Sch
Frederick Holmes Special Sch
INGLEMIRE LANE
Recreation Ground
Newland Sch for Girls
Univ of Hull
Middleton Hall
Endsleigh Holy Child RC VA Prim Sch
University of Humberside
Univ of Humberside
St Nicholas' VA Prim Sch
Newland St John's CE VA Prim Sch
Factory
B1233
COTTINGHAM ROAD
BEVERLEY RD
CLOUGH ROAD
A1165
Cemetery
Hull Grammar Sch
Newland
Sidmouth Prim Sch
Crem
Rec
HU5
Newland Avenue Prim Sch
Factory
Cemy
Mast
E2
1 HASTINGS AVE
2 COUPLAND GDNS
3 ST HELENA GDNS
4 ROMNEY GDNS
5 NICHOLSON ST
6 THISTLETON GDNS
7 BRITANNIA GDNS
St Vincent's RC Prim Sch
Beverley Rd Baths
Sculcoates
Rec
Stepney Prim Sch
Pearson Park
VICTORIA AVENUE
PARK AVENUE
WESTBOURNE AVENUE
F1
1 WESTMORELAND ST
Hull Nuffield
Liby
Endeavour High Sch
Factory
A1
1 VICTORIA GDNS
2 REGINA CR
3 WHITEHALL GDNS
4 MADISON GDNS
A2
1 ERNEST HL CT
2 RAINHILL RD
3 MARBURY PK
139
C3
1 NEWLAND GR
2 GOULDESBOROUGH CT
3 ST MONICA'S CT
4 MELBOURNE ST
5 TORRINGTON ST
6 WALTER'S TERR
7 THEARNE CL
145
D1
1 CAVE TERR
2 HUDSON GD
3 BARROW CT
4 BROMPTON CT
5 FRIARY CT
6 HAMPSTEAD CT
7 KNIGHTSBRIDGE CT
D2
1 BEACONSFIELD ST
2 SELSEY CL
3 BADEN CL
4 CROMER ST
5 ADDERBURY GR
D3
1 STRATHEARN ST
2 ST AUGUSTINE'S CT
E1
1 FENCHURCH ST
2 FARRINGDON ST
3 CLOVELLY GDNS
4 HADLEIGH CL
5 SCOTNEY CL
6 STAFFORD ST
155

B7
1 PEVENSEY CL
2 PEACEHAVEN CL

57

D8
1 GOLDCREST CL
2 CORMORANT CL
3 LOWLAND CL
4 HOUSEMARTIN DR

142

F5
1 HAMMERSMITH RD
2 SHOREDITCH CL
3 TOTTENHAM CL
4 WILLESDEN CL

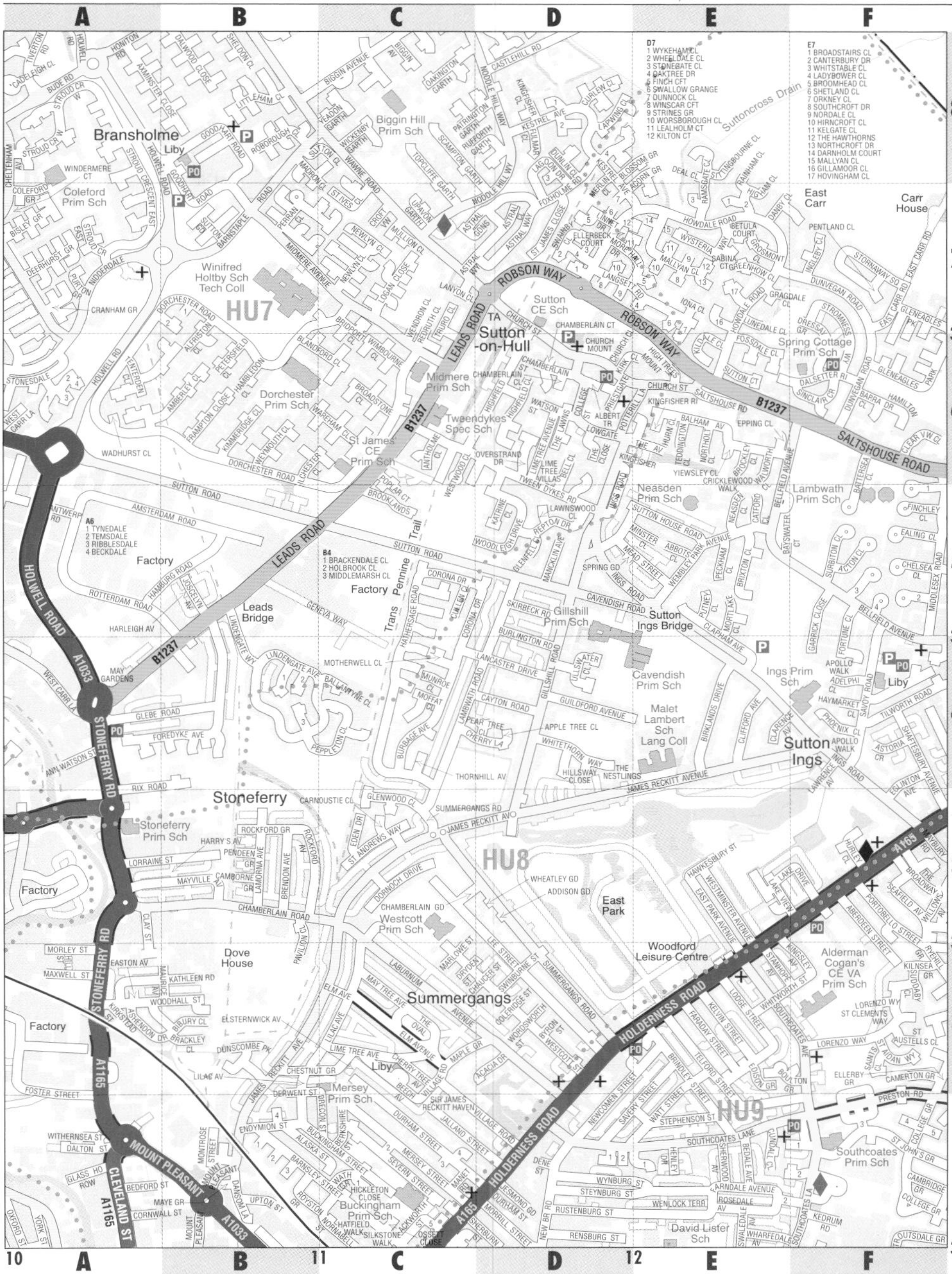

155

B1
1 CUDWORTH GR
2 OAKWELL GR
3 WOMBWELL GR
4 ALSTON AVE

C1
1 DEARNE GR
2 AVON ST
3 DUNELM CL
4 BRANDON CT
5 BUCKINGHAM ST

146

D1
1 JAMES NIVEN CT
2 FERENS CT

142

E1
1 ROTHESAY CL
2 ESKDALE AVE

F1
1 EDGEWARE AVE
2 NORTH COUNTRY CT
3 TRINITY GR
4 WADHAM GR
5 MERTON GR

A5
1 PETERSHAM CL
2 TWICKENHAM CL
3 CHISWICK CL
4 WIMBLEDON CL
5 BELLFIELD AVE
6 HAUXWELL GR
7 PINDERFIELD CL
8 GUY'S CR
9 ALDER HEY DR

B5
1 ALWOODLEY CL
2 ATLANTA CT
3 GANTON CT
4 BELTON CL
5 HARLESTON CL

141

C5
1 DUNMOW CL
2 SHORWELL CL
3 ROOKLEY CL
4 COLDSTREAM CL
5 DRAYTON CL
6 FOYNES GN

57

C6
1 BICKLEIGH GR
2 HARLOW CL
3 ST MARGARETS CT
4 PARKHURST CL

58

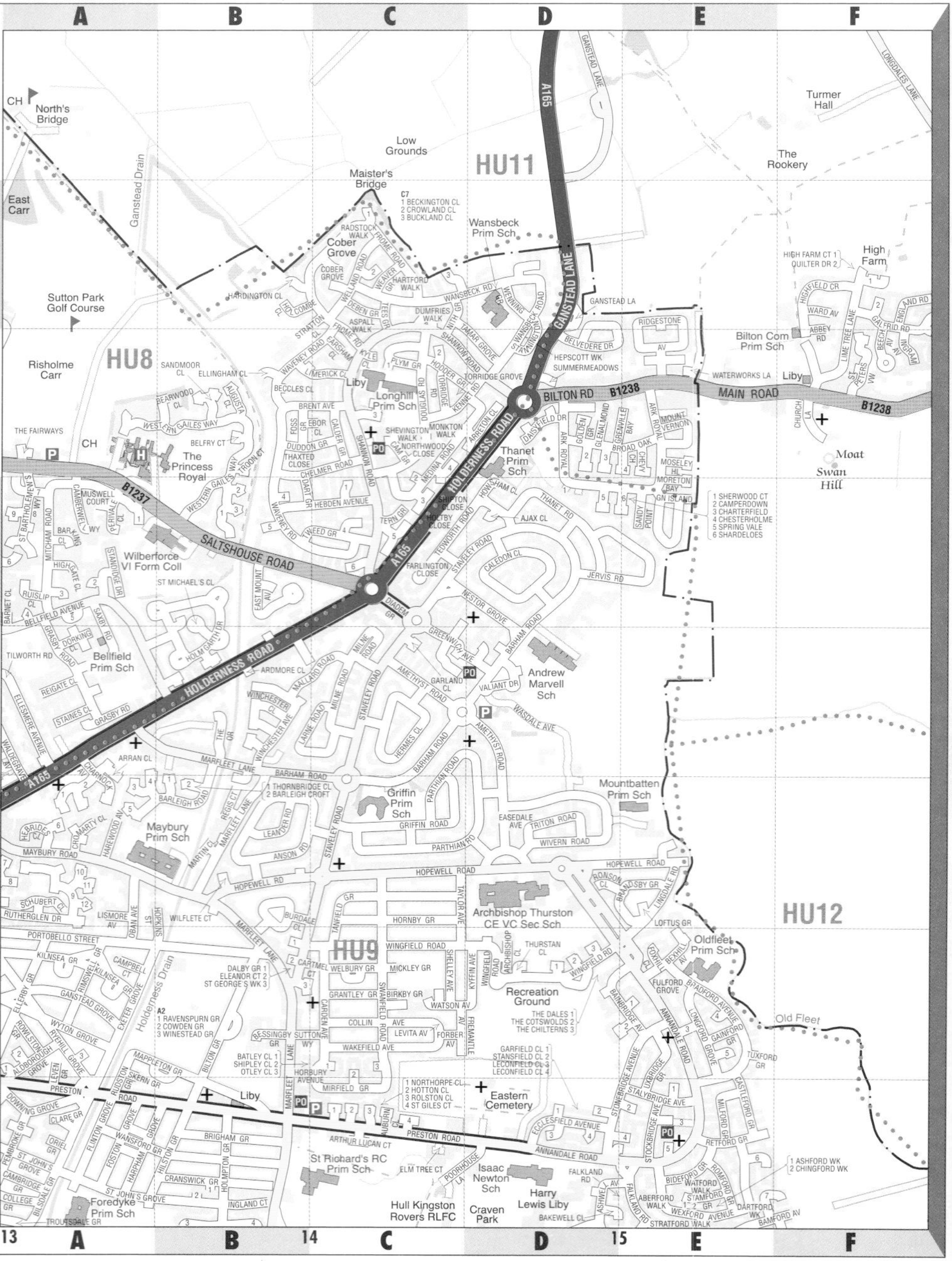

A3
1 FAROES CL
2 SPERRIN CL
3 BROUGHTON CL
4 BROADLAND DR
5 BEAULIEU CT
6 RONALDSWAY CL
7 MAJESTIC CT
8 THE BROADWAY
9 BROADWAY DR
10 GOLDEN CT
11 ZEIGFIELD CT
12 IMPERIAL CT

B1
1 ULROME CT
2 ATWICK CT
3 ENDEAVOUR CR
4 BEWHOLME GR

141

147

58

E1
1 STEMBRIDGE CL
2 CORBRIDGE CL
3 ELMBRIDGE PAR
4 WADEBRIDGE GR
5 IVYBRIDGE WK
6 CHELMSFORD CL
7 CRAYFORD CL

E2
1 FELBRIDGE CL
2 TONBRIDGE GR
3 SLEAFORD AVE
4 STAPLEFORD CL
5 TWYFORD CL

69 138 144

E7
1 CROMWELL CT
2 WOODHILL CL
3 NORWOOD CL
4 WAULDBY CL
5 WEETON WY

E8
1 COLLYNSON CL
2 SETTERWOOD GARTH
3 OAKDALE AV

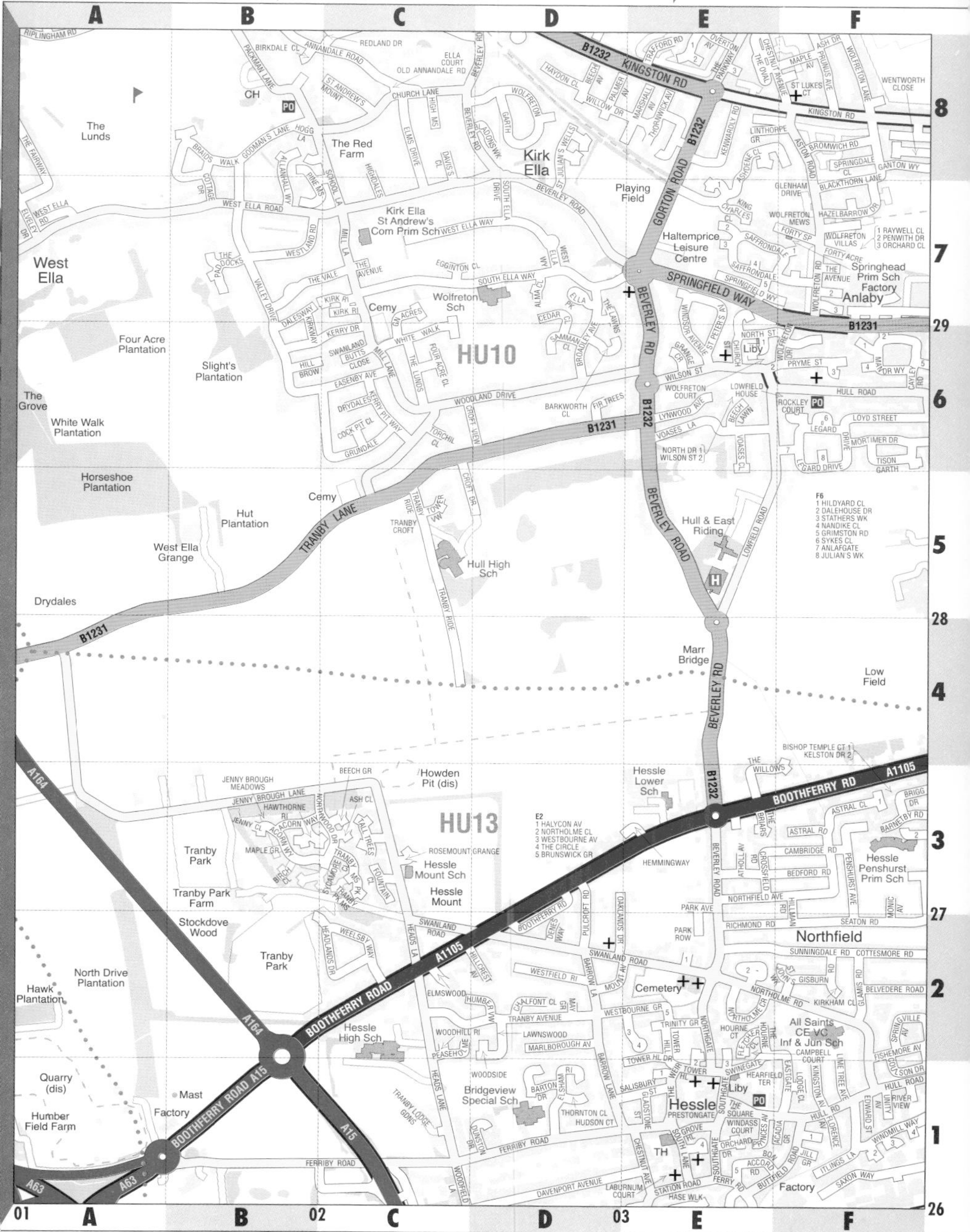

69 69 144

E1
1 SPIRE VW
2 TOWER HILL MEWS
3 VICARAGE LA
4 CLOWES CT
5 FISHWICK AV

F1
1 MARGARET GR
2 BISHOP BLUNT CL
3 BISHOP KEMPTHORNE CL
4 BISHOP GURDON CL

A3
1 BARNETBY RD
2 KELSTON DR
3 YARMOUTH AV
4 WINTHORPE RD
5 BROCKLESBY CL
6 CORRAN GARTH

B7
1 LANGFORD WK
2 HOLLYTREE AV
3 LABURNUM DR
4 ROSEWOOD CL

143

C8
1 PRIMROSE DR
2 COUNTY RD S

139

D8
1 LOCKTON GR
2 HACKNESS GR
3 BARGATE GR
4 SNAINTON GR
5 SORREL DR

E6
1 AIRMYN AVE
2 ST MARTINS AVE

F6
1 HAWTHORN CT

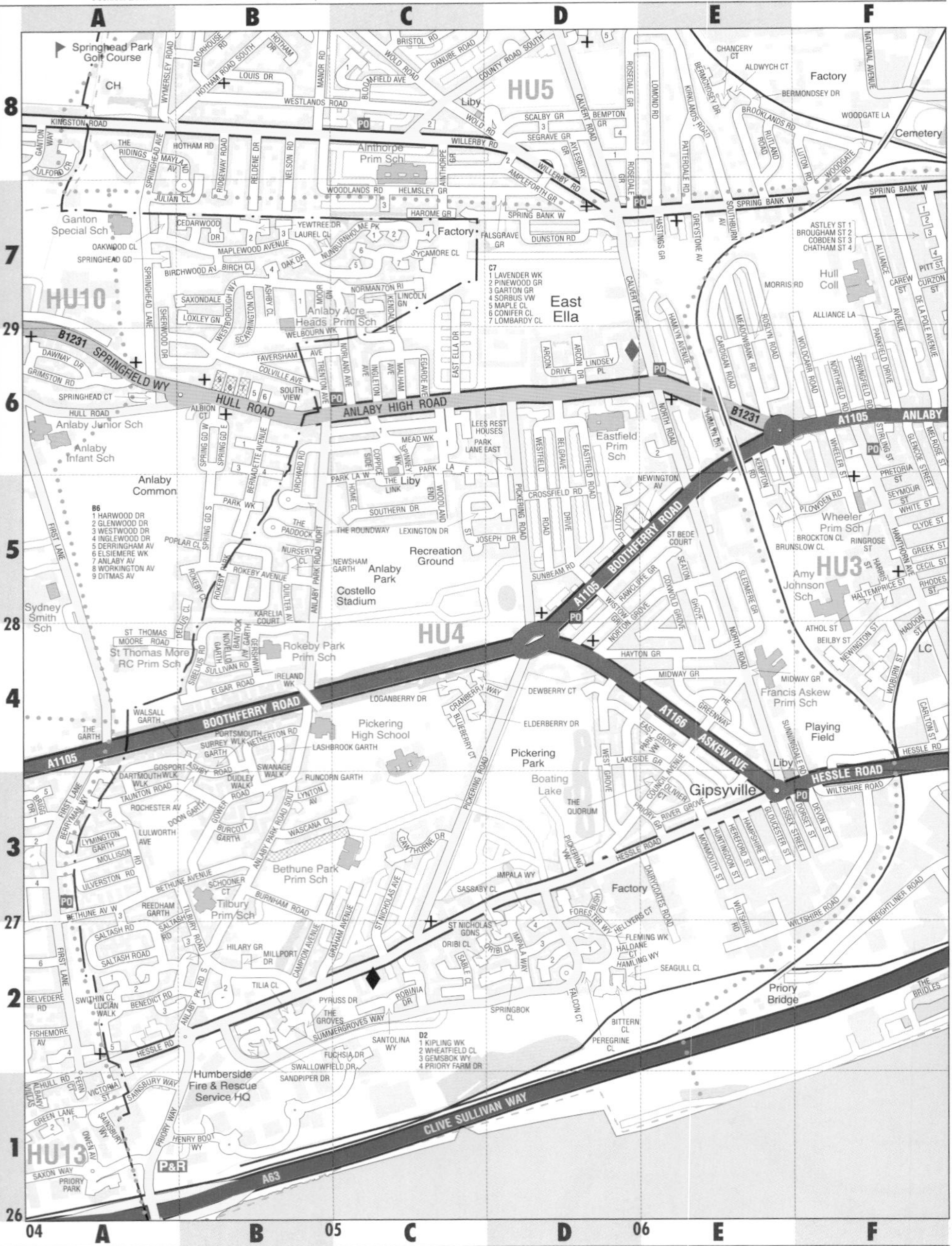

A1
1 BISHOP COCKIN CL
2 CHAPEL CL

143

A2
1 VALENTINE CL
2 BENEDICT CL
3 VINCENT CL
4 NEWLYN CL
5 CRISPIN CL
6 COTTESMORE RD

B2
1 AVONDALE
2 WOOLWICH DR
3 DATCHET GARTH

C6
1 THE GREENWAY

70

For full street detail of the highlighted area see page 155.

A6
1 GRANVILLE ST
2 SANDRINGHAM ST
3 COULTAS CT
4 ACLAND ST
5 LONSDALE ST
6 CARNEGIE ST

B8
1 ROXBURGH ST
2 RICHMOND ST
3 LANARK ST

C6
1 KINGS LEIGH
2 KING'S CROSS CL
3 THORN LEIGH

D8
1 BERKELEY ST
2 CROMWELL CL
3 BROWNING CL
4 LEONARD ST
5 TRAFALGAR ST
6 SHAKESPEARE CL

140
146

A5
1 CORDELLA CL
2 DORADO CL
3 SANDLEMERE CL
4 DARRISMERE VILLAS
5 BRIXHAM CT
6 OTTERBURN ST

B4
1 DIVISION RD
2 SEFTON ST
3 NEWTON ST
4 RIBBLE ST
5 RUGBY ST
6 DEE ST
7 ROSAMOND ST

70

C5
1 LYRIC CL
2 THORNWICK CL
3 BARBERRY CT
4 WINSHIP CL
5 EVER THORPE CL
6 TICHBOURNE CL
7 WESLEY CT
8 BEECH CL
9 CAROL DICKSON CT

D5
1 GOODWIN PAR
2 HAZEL GR
3 FIRETHORN CL
4 NEWPORT CL
5 PEACH TREE CT
6 ELDERWOOD CT
7 QUANTOCK CL
8 BATHURST ST
9 MECHANIC LA

D6
1 BLOOMSBURY CT
2 ARLINGTON ST
3 ALMOND GR
4 BLACKTHORN CT
5 SORBUS CT

146

B7
1 PEMBERTON ST
2 BLYTH ST
3 NAYLOR'S ROW
4 WILSON ST
5 EAST ST
6 ALMA ST

155

C7
1 PELHAM DR
2 EDWARD COLLINS SQ
3 HODGE CT
4 ROSEY ROW
5 ALDERSON MEWS
6 BROADLEY CL
7 DENMARK CT
8 EMILY ST

141

C8
1 NORNABELL ST
2 VICTOR ST
3 BALFOUR ST
4 ARUNDEL ST
5 HORNSEA PAR
6 ST QUINTINS CL

D7
1 BUTTERCUP CL
2 PENISTONE CT
3 BEAUMONT CT
4 BRUMBY'S TERR
5 EMPRINGHAM ST

E8
1 DOVEDALE GR
2 DEEPDALE GR
3 MIDDLEHAM CL
4 BYLAND CT

142
72

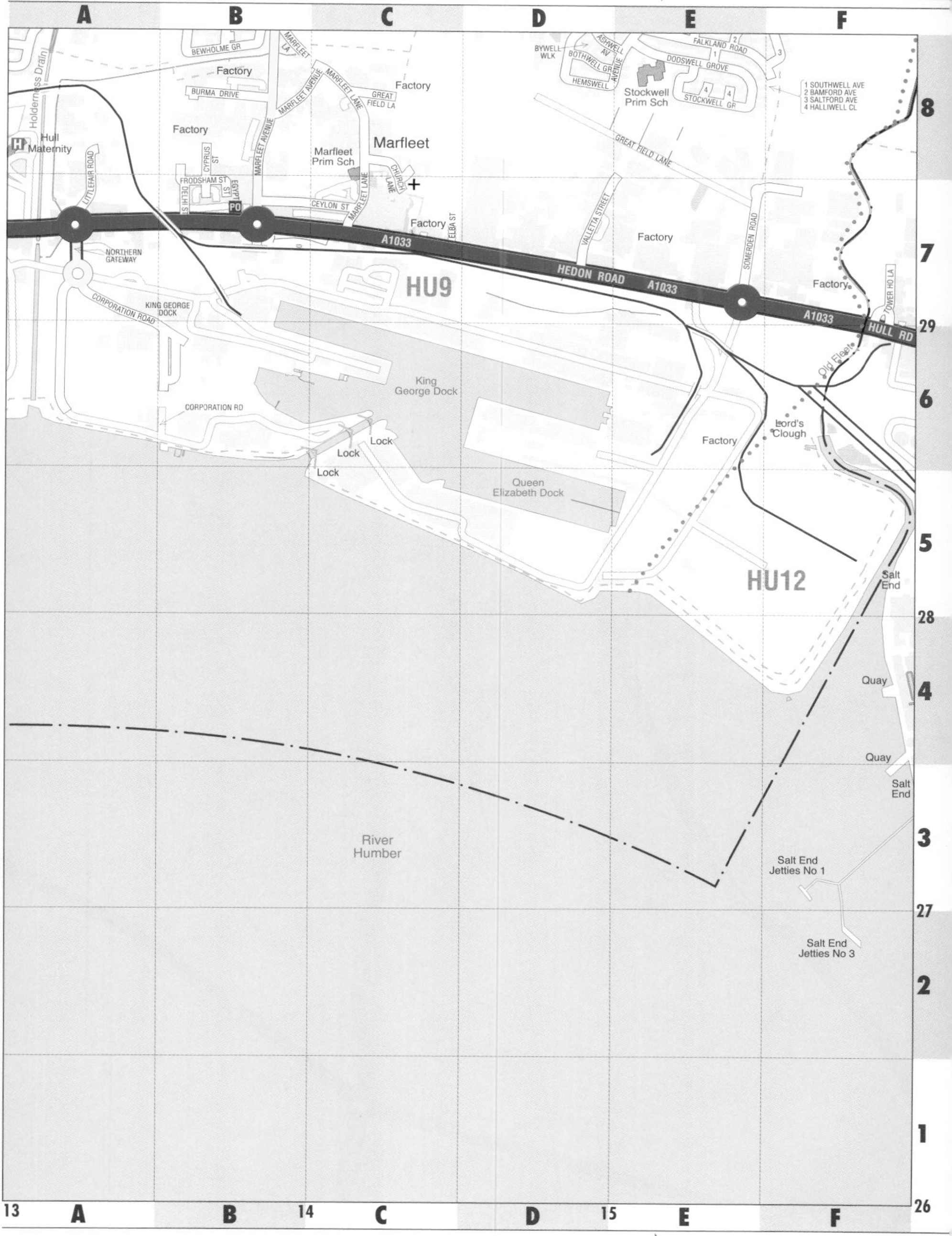
A
B
C
D
E
F
8
7
29
6
5
28
4
3
27
2
1
26
13
14
15
BEWHOLME GR
Factory
BURMA DRIVE
MARFLEET LA
MARFLEET AVENUE
MARFLEET LANE
GREAT FIELD LA
Factory
Marfleet
Marfleet Prim Sch
CHURCH LANE
Holderness Drain
Hull Maternity
LITTLEFAIR ROAD
CYPRUS ST
FRODSHAM ST
DELHI ST
EGYPT ST
PO
CEYLON ST
Factory
ELBA ST
A1033
NORTHERN GATEWAY
CORPORATION ROAD
KING GEORGE DOCK
HU9
HEDON ROAD
A1033
BYWELL WLK
ASHWELL AV
BOTHWELL GR
AVENUE
HEMSWELL
FALKLAND ROAD
DODSWELL GROVE
Stockwell Prim Sch
STOCKWELL GR
1 SOUTHWELL AVE
2 BAMFORD AVE
3 SALTFORD AVE
4 HALLIWELL CL
GREAT FIELD LANE
VALLETTA STREET
Factory
SOMERDEN ROAD
Factory
TOWER HO LA
A1033
HULL RD
Old Fleet
King George Dock
CORPORATION RD
Lock
Lock
Lock
Queen Elizabeth Dock
Lord's Clough
Factory
HU12
Salt End
Quay
Quay
Salt End
River Humber
Salt End Jetties No 1
Salt End Jetties No 3

71
72

C5
1 YORK ST
2 HARPER ST
3 DOUGLAS ST
4 RAINCLIFFE ST
5 LONDESBOROUGH ST
6 HILDA ST
7 PORTHOLME CR
8 SOUTH PAR
9 TURNERS SQ
10 AUDUS ST
11 MARKET PL
12 NEW CHURCH TERR
13 MARKET CROSS SHOP CTR
14 MARKET LA

48

D5
1 MICKLEGATE
2 WREN LA
3 CHURCH HL
4 CHURCH LA
5 CORUNNA CT
6 CHURCH AVE
7 GANT WK
8 ABBEY PL

49 49

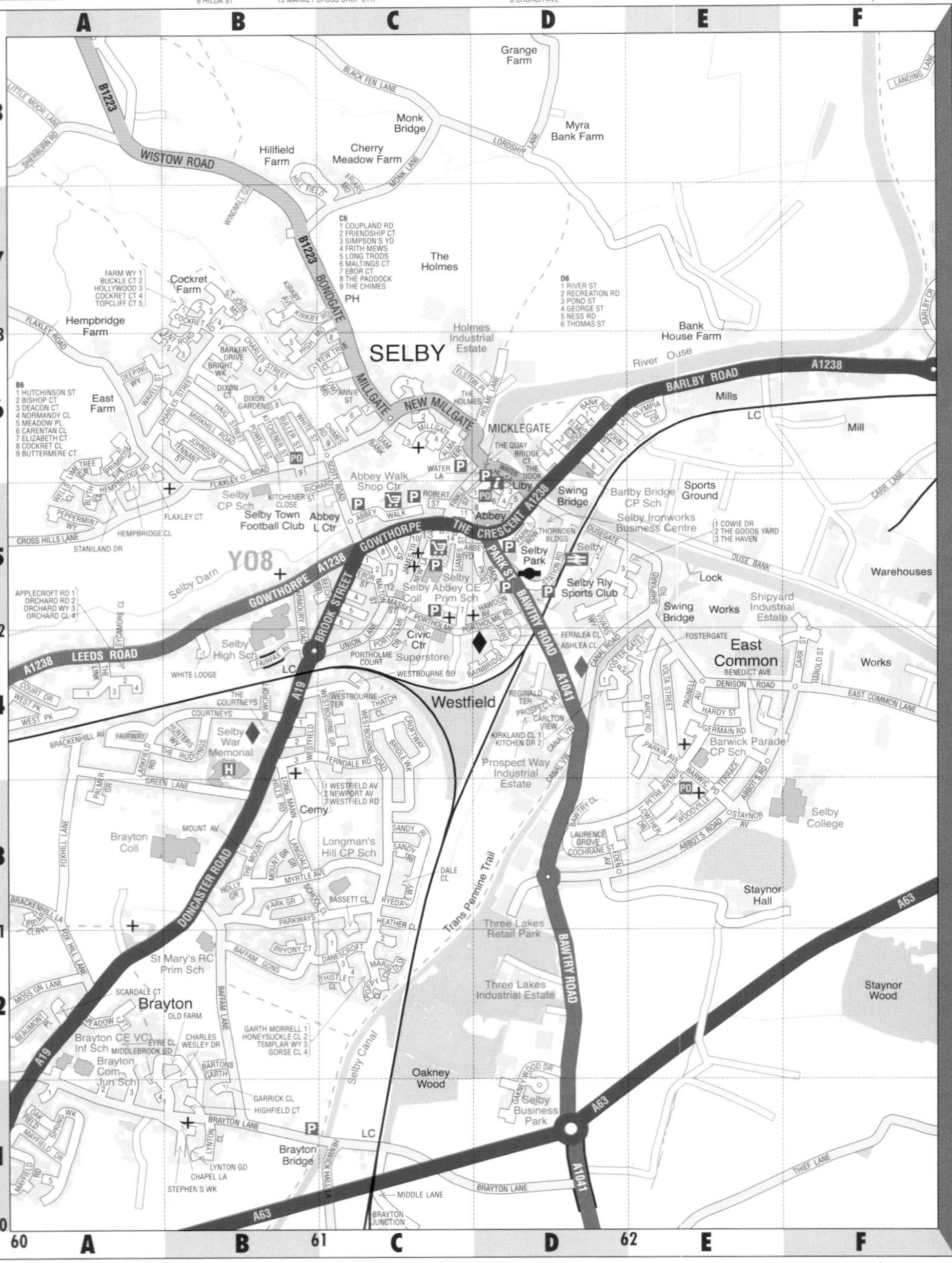

A1
1 MANOR FARM CL
2 HOLMEFIELD CT
3 HOLMEFIELD CL
4 CHILVERS CT
5 MAYFIELD DR

62 63 49

64 65 65

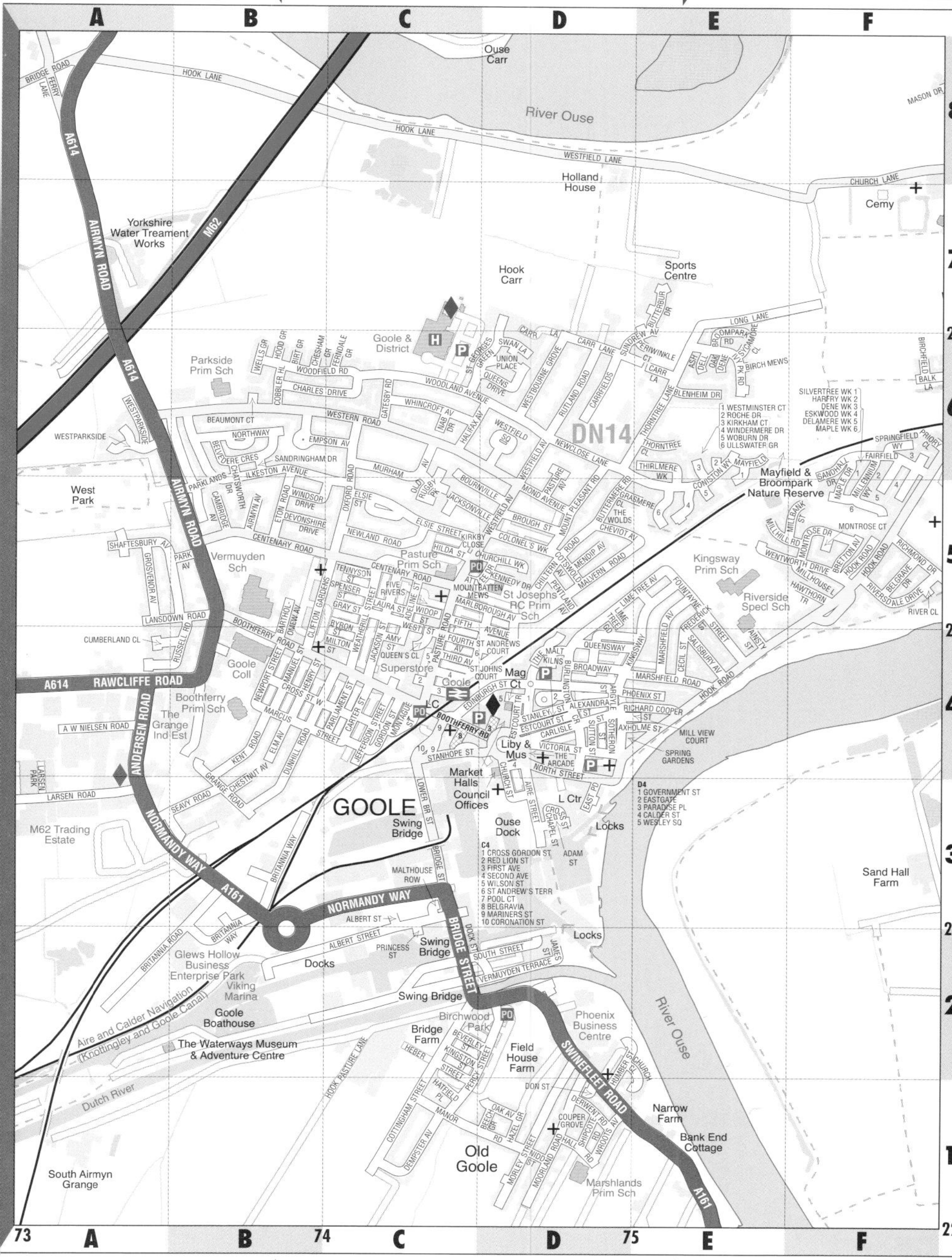
A
B
C
D
E
F
8
7
25
6
5
24
4
3
23
2
1
22
73
74
75
Ouse Carr
River Ouse
HOOK LANE
WESTFIELD LANE
BRIDGE ROAD
FERRY LANE
MASON DR
CHURCH LANE
Cemy
Holland House
Yorkshire Water Treament Works
M62
A614
AIRMYN ROAD
Hook Carr
Sports Centre
Goole & District
H
P
Parkside Prim Sch
LONG LANE
CARR LA
CARR LANE
DN14
WESTPARKSIDE
West Park
Vermuyden Sch
Pasture Prim Sch
St Josephs RC Prim Sch
Mayfield & Broompark Nature Reserve
Kingsway Prim Sch
Riverside Specl Sch
SILVERTREE WK 1
HARFRY WK 2
DENE WK 3
ESKWOOD WK 4
DELAMERE WK 5
MAPLE WK 6
1 WESTMINSTER CT
2 ROCHE DR
3 KIRKHAM CT
4 WINDERMERE DR
5 WOBURN DR
6 ULLSWATER GR
A614 RAWCLIFFE ROAD
ANDERSEN ROAD
Goole Coll
Boothferry Prim Sch
The Grange Ind Est
A W NIELSEN ROAD
LARSEN ROAD
M62 Trading Estate
GOOLE
Swing Bridge
Market Halls
Council Offices
Mag Ct
Liby & Mus
Ouse Dock
L Ctr
Locks
MILL VIEW COURT
SPRING GARDENS
D4
1 GOVERNMENT ST
2 EASTGATE
3 PARADISE PL
4 CALDER ST
5 WESLEY SQ
C4
1 CROSS GORDON ST
2 RED LION ST
3 FIRST AVE
4 SECOND AVE
5 WILSON ST
6 ST ANDREW'S TERR
7 POOL CT
8 BELGRAVIA
9 MARINERS ST
10 CORONATION ST
NORMANDY WAY
A161
BRIDGE STREET
Sand Hall Farm
Glews Hollow Business Enterprise Park
Docks
Viking Marina
Goole Boathouse
Aire and Calder Navigation (Knottingley and Goole Canal)
The Waterways Museum & Adventure Centre
Dutch River
Swing Bridge
Birchwood Park
Bridge Farm
Field House Farm
Phoenix Business Centre
River Ouse
SWINEFLEET ROAD
Narrow Farm
Bank End Cottage
Old Goole
Marshlands Prim Sch
South Airmyn Grange

64 80 65

95
96

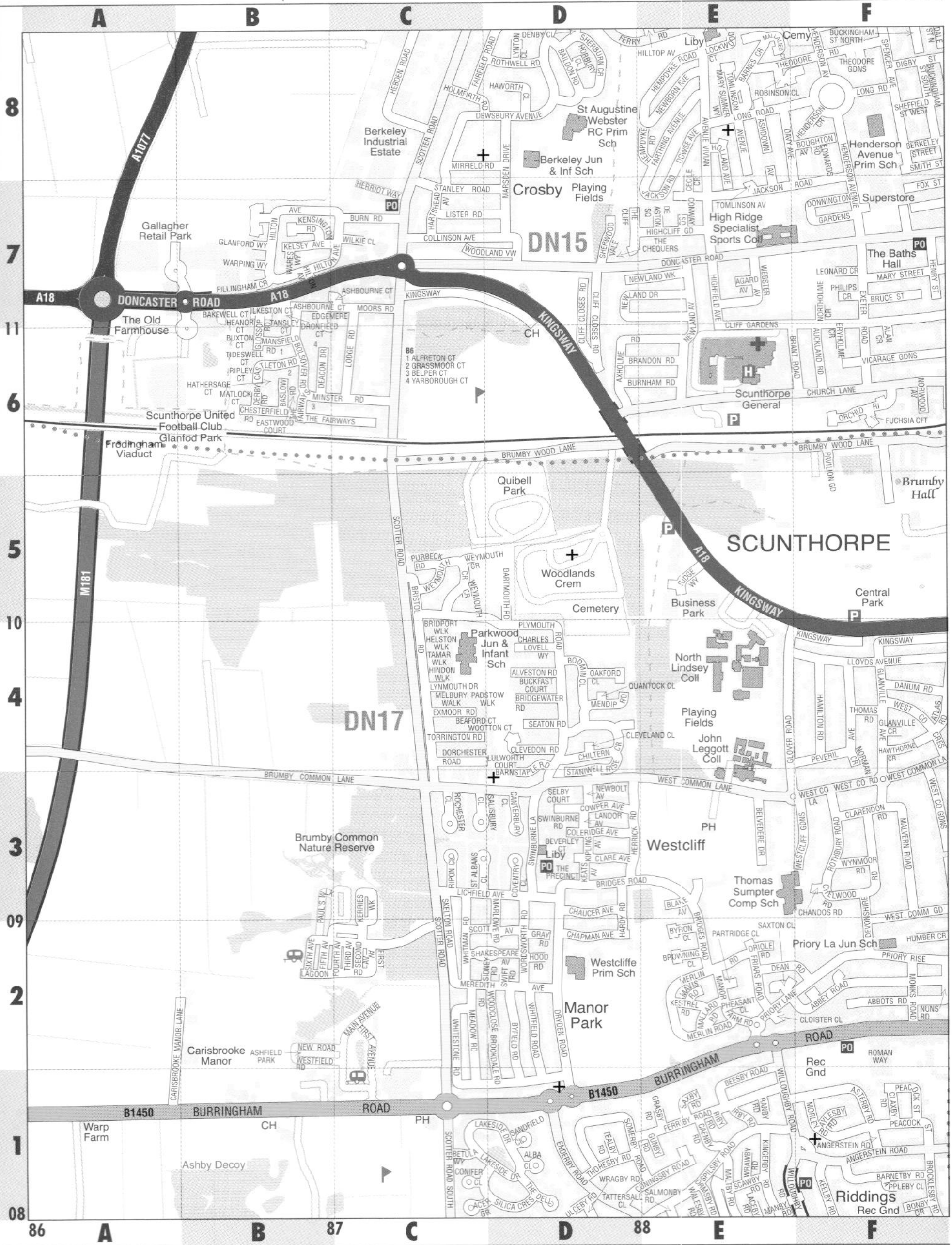
SCUNTHORPE
DN15
DN17
Crosby
Westcliff
Manor Park
Berkeley Industrial Estate
Gallagher Retail Park
The Old Farmhouse
Scunthorpe United Football Club Glanfod Park
Frodingham Viaduct
St Augustine Webster RC Prim Sch
Berkeley Jun & Inf Sch
Playing Fields
High Ridge Specialist Sports Coll
Henderson Avenue Prim Sch
Superstore
The Baths Hall
Scunthorpe General
Brumby Hall
Quibell Park
Woodlands Crem
Cemetery
Business Park
Central Park
Parkwood Jun & Infant Sch
North Lindsey Coll
John Leggott Coll
Brumby Common Nature Reserve
Thomas Sumpter Comp Sch
Priory La Jun Sch
Westcliffe Prim Sch
Carisbrooke Manor
Warp Farm
Ashby Decoy
Riddings Rec Gnd
Rec Gnd
A18
A1077
M181
B1450
DONCASTER ROAD
KINGSWAY
BURRINGHAM ROAD
SCOTTER ROAD
BRUMBY WOOD LANE
BRUMBY COMMON LANE
WEST COMMON LANE
DONCASTER ROAD
CHURCH LANE
CLIFF GARDENS
WILLOUGHBY ROAD
ENDERBY ROAD
CARISBROOKE MANOR LANE
A B C D E F
8 7 6 5 4 3 2 1
86 87 88
11 10 09 08

95
96

B7
1 BELGRAVE SQ
2 FRODINGHAM FOOTPATH
3 CHURCH SQ
4 SOUTHGATE
5 ETHEL CT
6 LESLIE CT
7 KINSLEY WK
8 JUBILEE WY
9 WILSONS CL
10 WALKERS CL
11 GREENS CL
12 MANLEY ST
13 CARLTON ST

B8
1 NORTH ST
2 CROSS ST

C7
1 DAWES LA

96
97

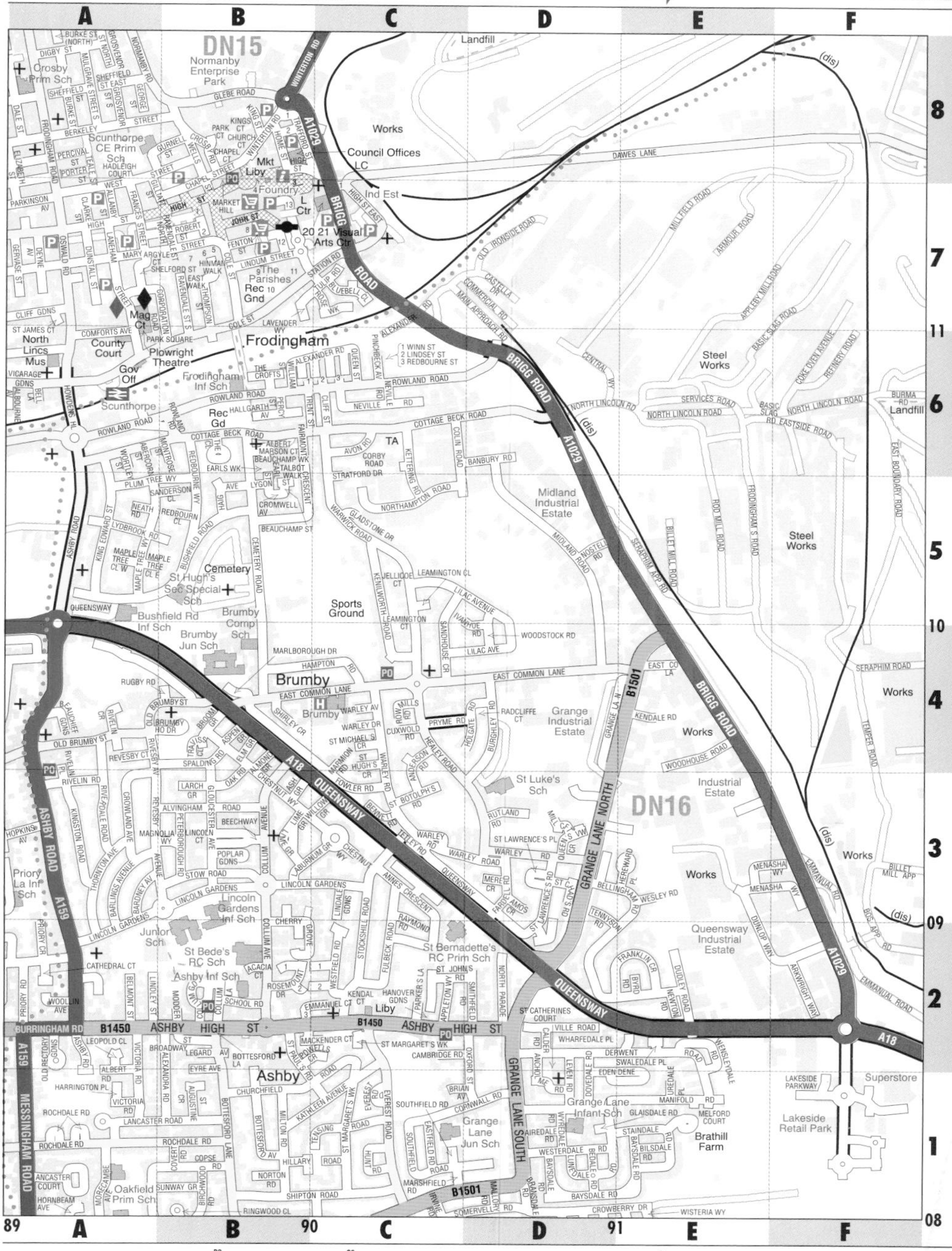

B2
1 ASHBERRY DR
2 ORCHARD CL
3 MACKENDER CT

C2
1 NORTHFIELD CL
2 SPRINGFIELD CL

96
97

102
102

F5
1 FREEMAN WAY
2 THESIGER WK
3 ALBERT PL
4 ALBERT CL
5 COMBER PL

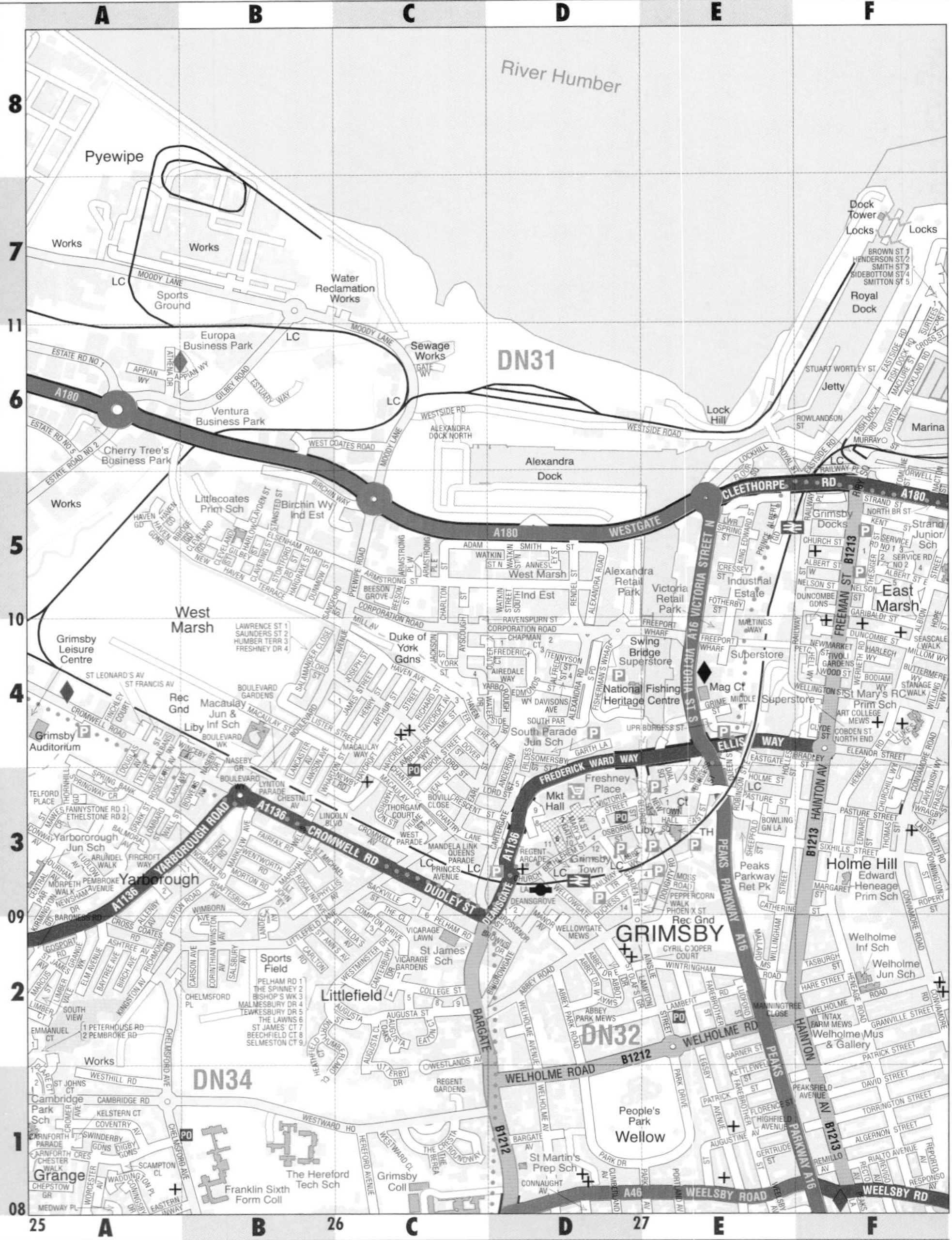

D3
1 GROSVENOR CR
2 GROSVENOR CR
3 E ST MARY'S GATE
4 S ST MARY'S GATE
5 NEW CARTERGATE
6 OLD MARKET PL
7 VICTORIA ST W
8 FLOTTERGATE MALL
9 FRESHNEY PL
10 OLD MARKET PL
11 BULL RING LA
12 ABBEYGATE
13 KEIR HARDIE WK
14 PHYLLIS TAYLOR GDNS

D4
1 RAVENSPURN WY
2 FARNDALE WY
3 WHARFEDALE WY
4 TENNYSON MEWS

E3
1 TOWN HALL ST
2 VICTORIA ST W
3 VICTORIA ST S
4 KEIRHARDIE WK

102
102

A5
1 SALACON WY
2 CALVI CT
3 BRADMAN CT
4 CASSWELL CL
5 MUNSTER CT
6 MANSFIELD CT
7 ACTON CT
8 APPLEBY CT
9 ARNOLD CT
10 WESLEY CT
11 NORFOLK CT
12 SURREY CT
13 SUFFOLK CT
14 SUSSEX CT
15 MARLBOROUGH CL
16 BANBURY CT
17 BELPER CT
18 BEXLEY CT
19 MILFORD CT
20 GUILDFORD ST
21 WORDSWORTH CT
22 WINDSOR CT

103
103

103
103

One-way streets

136 136

House numbers
1 59 HIGH ST

137

Scale: 5⅓ inches to 1 mile
0 110 yards 220 yards
0 125 m 250 m

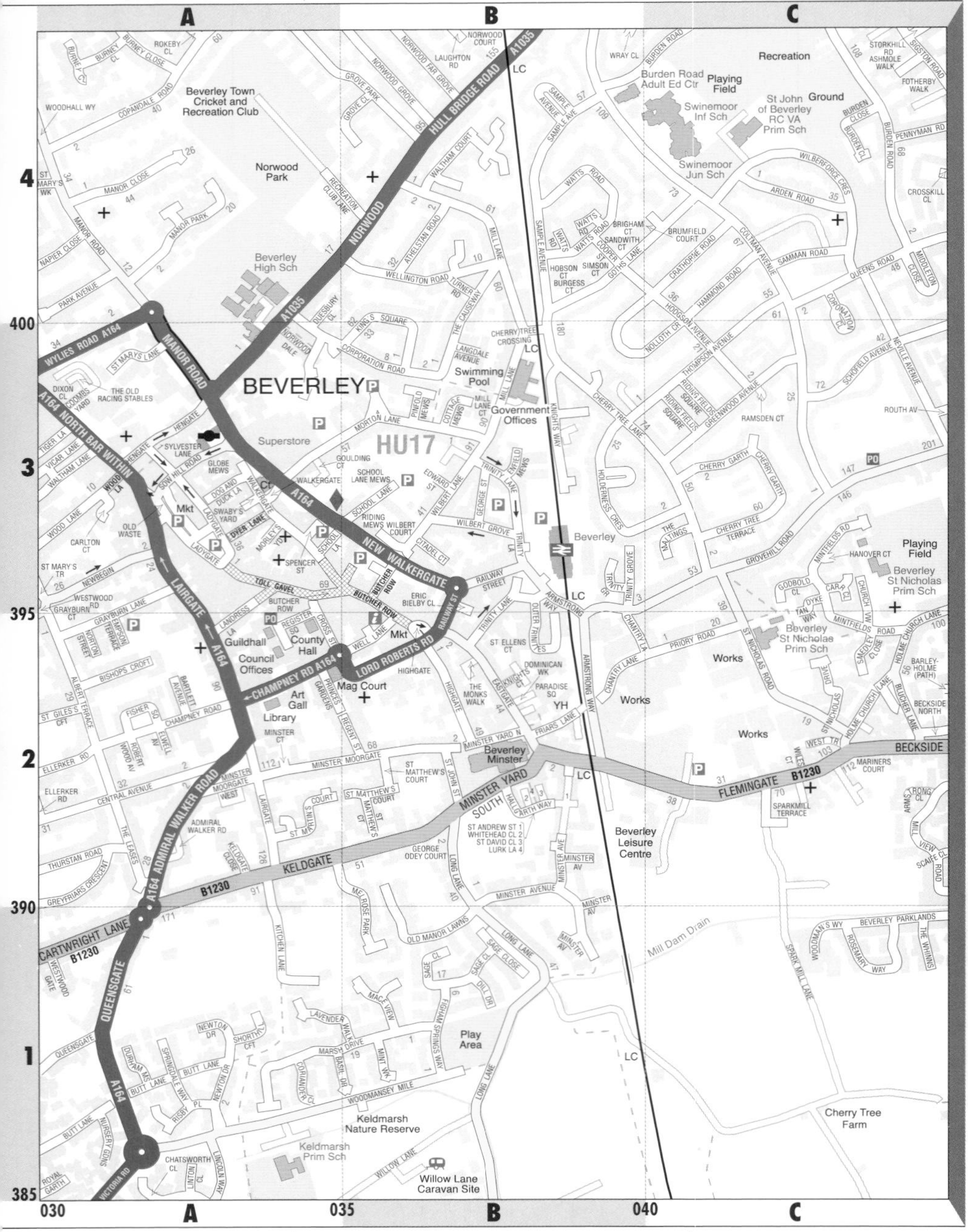

136 136 137

Scale: 5⅓ inches to 1 mile
0 110 yards 220 yards
0 125 m 250 m

One-way streets

House numbers
1 59 HIGH ST

145 140 141 146

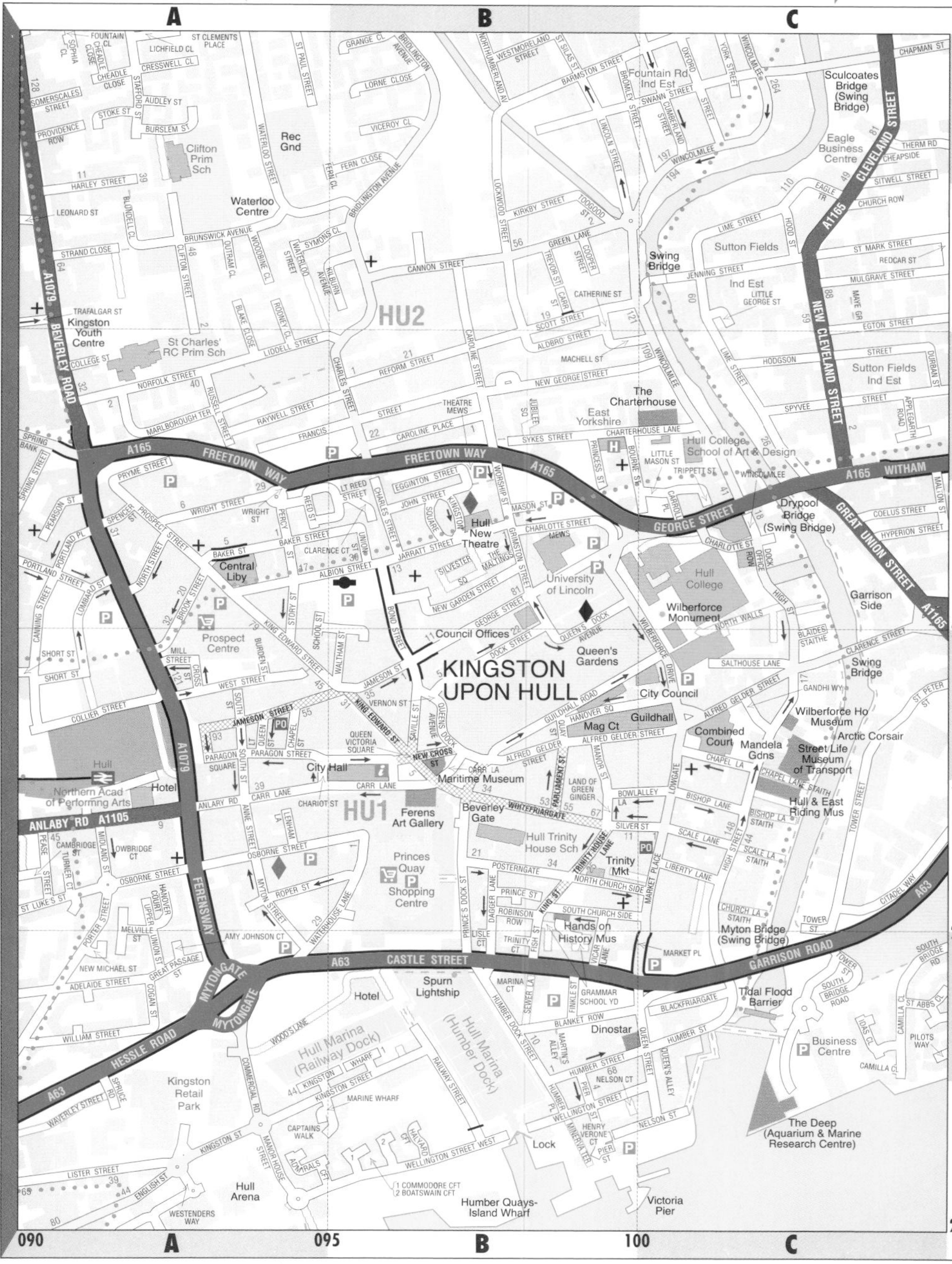

145 145 146 146

One-way streets

130 130

House numbers

1 59 HIGH ST

130

Scale: 5⅓ inches to 1 mile

0 110 yards 220 yards

0 125 m 250 m

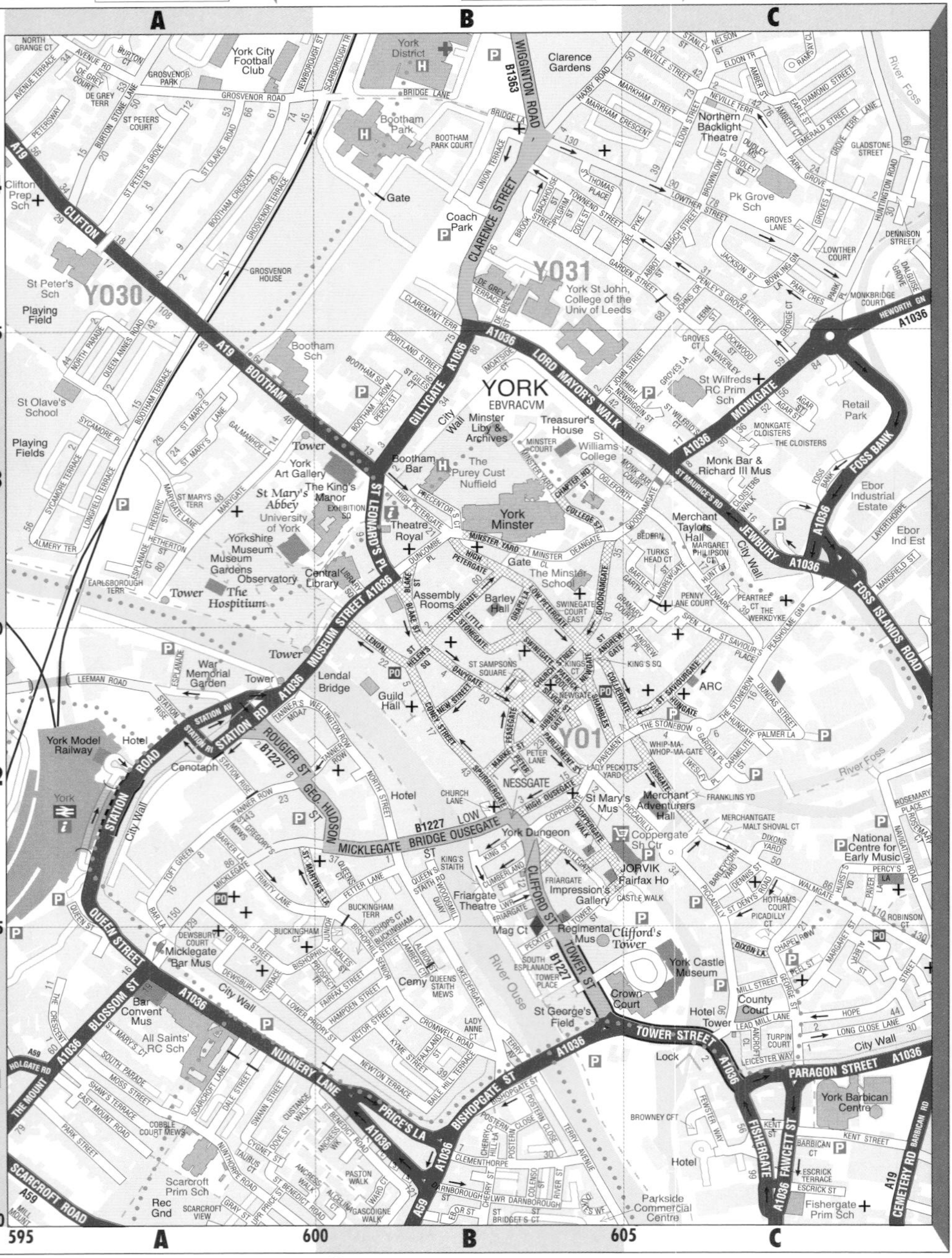

B1
1 VICTORIA ST
2 DRAKE ST
3 SPENCER ST
4 CLEMENT ST

130 130 130

Church Rd **6** Beckenham BR2.......... **53** C6

Place name	Location number	Locality, town or village	Postcode district	Page and grid square
May be abbreviated on the map	Present when a number indicates the place's position in a crowded area of mapping	Shown when more than one place has the same name	District for the indexed place	Page number and grid reference for the standard mapping

Public and commercial buildings are highlighted in magenta **Places of interest** are highlighted in blue with a star★

Abbreviations used in the index

Acad	**Academy**
App	**Approach**
Arc	**Arcade**
Ave	**Avenue**
Bglw	**Bungalow**
Bldg	**Building**
Bsns, Bus	**Business**
Bvd	**Boulevard**
Cath	**Cathedral**
Cir	**Circus**
Cl	**Close**
Cnr	**Corner**
Coll	**College**
Com	**Community**
Comm	**Common**
Cott	**Cottage**
Cres	**Crescent**
Cswy	**Causeway**
Ct	**Court**
Ctr	**Centre**
Ctry	**Country**
Cty	**County**
Dr	**Drive**
Dro	**Drove**
Ed	**Education**
Emb	**Embankment**
Est	**Estate**
Ex	**Exhibition**
Gd	**Ground**
Gdn	**Garden**
Gn	**Green**
Gr	**Grove**
H	**Hall**
Ho	**House**
Hospl	**Hospital**
HQ	**Headquarters**
Hts	**Heights**
Ind	**Industrial**
Inst	**Institute**
Int	**International**
Intc	**Interchange**
Junc	**Junction**
L	**Leisure**
La	**Lane**
Liby	**Library**
Mdw	**Meadow**
Meml	**Memorial**
Mkt	**Market**
Mus	**Museum**
Orch	**Orchard**
Pal	**Palace**
Par	**Parade**
Pas	**Passage**
Pk	**Park**
Pl	**Place**
Prec	**Precinct**
Prom	**Promenade**
Rd	**Road**
Recn	**Recreation**
Ret	**Retail**
Sh	**Shopping**
Sq	**Square**
St	**Street**
Sta	**Station**
Terr	**Terrace**
TH	**Town Hall**
Univ	**University**
Wk, Wlk	**Walk**
Wr	**Water**
Yd	**Yard**

Index of localities, towns and villages

A
Acaster Malbis 36 D8
Acaster Selby 36 B4
Acklam 16 E8
Acomb 129 C3
Adlingfleet 81 E7
Aike 44 A8
Airmyn 64 E4
Aisby 118 B3
Aldbrough 47 C1
Alkborough 82 C8
Allerthorpe 28 E2
Althorpe 95 D4
Amcotts 81 F1
Angram 24 C3
Anlaby 143 F7
Appleby 83 C1
Arnold 45 C4
Arram 44 A7
Ashby 151 B1
Ashby cum Fenby 113 D3
Ashby Hill 113 C3
Askham Bryan 24 F3
Askham Richard 24 D3
Asselby 64 D7
Atwick 35 C5
Aughton 38 C1
Aylesby 101 E2

B
Bainton 31 E7
Balkholme 65 E6
Balne 77 C5
Barlby 49 B5
Barlow 63 C7
Barmby Moor 28 E3
Barmby on the Marsh 64 B7
Barmston 23 A6
Barnetby le Wold 99 C4
Barnoldby le Beck 113 B6
Barrow Hann 70 E1
Barrow Haven 70 C1
Barrow upon Humber 85 D7
Barton-upon-Humber 84 D7
Barton Waterside 69 F2
Beal 61 D4
Beckingham 116 D1
Beeford 22 C1
Beelsby 112 F5
Beltoft 95 A1
Belton 94 E1
Bempton 4 D4
Beningbrough 12 D4
Bennetland 66 C7
Bentley 55 D7
Bessingby 10 F4
Beswick 32 D3
Beverley 154 A3
Bewholme 35 A5
Bielby 39 F6
Bigby 99 C2
Bilbrough 24 D1
Bilton 58 A4
Birkin 61 D6
Bishop Burton 43 A2
Bishopthorpe 133 B3
Bishop Wilton 16 F2
Blacktoft 66 E3
Blyborough 119 B5
Blyton 117 E5
Bolton 28 D7
Bonby 84 C2
Bootham Stray 127 B2
Boothferry 64 E5
Bossall 15 D7
Bottesford 96 D2
Boynton 10 D7
Bracon 94 F2
Bradley 102 B3
Bradley 102 C1
Brandesburton 34 C2
Bransholme 141 A8
Brantingham 68 C8
Brayton 148 A2
Breighton 50 D5
Bridlington 122 B3
Brigg 98 D2
Brigham 33 E8
Brigsley 113 D4
Brind 51 A2
Brockfield 14 E2
Brocklesby 100 E6
Broomfleet 67 B6
Brough 68 C5
Broughton 97 E4
Brumby 151 B4
Bubwith 50 D7
Buckton 4 C4
Bugthorpe 16 D4
Burn 62 D7
Burnby 29 D1
Burnham 85 C3
Burringham 95 E4
Bursea 52 A4
Burstwick 73 B7
Burton Agnes 10 A1
Burton Fleming 2 E3
Burton Pidsea 59 D2
Burton Stather 82 A5
Burton upon Stather 82 B4
Buttercrambe 15 E5
Butterwick 1 B2

C
Cabourne 111 D4
Cadney 109 D6
Caenby Corner Estate 119 D1
Caistor 111 B4
Camblesforth 63 D5
Camerton 73 A5
Canal Side 93 A7
Carlton 63 D3
Carnaby 10 E4
Catwick 45 D8
Cawkeld 32 B5
Cawood 48 B8
Chapel Fields 129 B3
Chapel Haddlesey 62 C5
Cherry Burton 43 B5
Church End 33 F8
Church Town 94 E1
Claxton 15 B7
Cleethorpes 153 C2
Cliffe 49 E2
Clifton 130 A7
Clifton Park 129 F7
Clixby 111 A7
Cock Hill 12 B2
Coleby 82 E6
Coniston 57 F6
Copmanthorpe 132 B2
Corringham 118 B2
Cottagers Plot 102 B2
Cottingham 139 A5
Covenham
St Bartholomew 121 F5
Covenham St Mary 121 F5
Cridling Stubbs 76 C8
Crockey Hill 26 A1
Crosby 150 D7
Crowle 94 D8
Crowle Park 94 D7
Croxby 112 C1
Croxby Top 112 B1
Croxton 99 F7
Cuxwold 112 B4

D
Danthorpe 59 C3
Deighton 37 A7
Dimlington 90 F7
Dragonby 82 E1
Drax 63 F5
Driffield 124 C5
Dringhouses 132 E8
Duggleby 6 B6
Dunnington 26 F7
Dunnington 34 F7
Dunscroft 92 D3
Dunsville 92 B3
Dunswell 56 D5

E
Ealand 94 E6
Earswick 128 A7
Easington 91 A6
Eastburn 20 B2
East Butterwick 106 E8
East Carlton 47 A2
East Common 148 E4
East Cottingwith 38 C5
East Cowick 78 D8
East Ella 144 D7
East Halton 86 E7
East Lound 105 E3
East Lutton 7 C8
East Marsh 152 F5
East Newton 59 F8
Eastoft 81 A3
East Ravendale 113 C2
Eastrington 51 F1
East Stockwith 116 F5
Eggborough 61 F2
Ellerker 68 A8
Ellerton 38 C2
Elloughton 68 C7
Elmswell 20 B5
Elsham 98 F7
Elstronwick 59 A3
Elvington 27 B2
Eppleworth 138 A4
Epworth 105 D6
Epworth Turbary 105 C6
Escrick 37 B5
Eskham 115 C1
Etton 42 F6
Everingham 40 A5
Everthorpe 53 E3

F
Fangfoss 28 C7
Fenwick 77 D3
Ferriby Sluice 83 F7
Fimber 18 D7
Fishlake 92 E8
Fitling 59 C5
Flamborough 5 B2
Flinton 59 A7
Flixborough 82 B1
Flixborough Stather 82 A1
Fockerby 81 E5
Foggathorpe 51 B8
Fordon 2 A6
Fosterhouses 78 C1
Foston on the Wolds 22 A2
Fotherby 121 C2
Foxholes 1 D3
Fraisthorpe 22 F8
Fridaythorpe 18 B6
Frodingham 151 B6
Fulford 133 E7
Full Sutton 16 A2
Fulstow 121 E8

G
Gainsborough 117 C2
Ganstead 57 F5
Ganton 1 A8
Gardham 42 D5
Garthorpe 81 F6
Garton 59 E6

Garton-on-the-Wolds 20 A6
Gateforth 62 A7
Gate Helmsley 15 B2
Gembling 22 A3
Gilberdyke 66 C8
Gipsyville 144 E3
Goodmanham 135 F7
Goole 149 C3
Gowdall 63 A1
Gowthorpe 16 C1
Goxhill 86 B8
Grainsby 113 F2
Graiselound 105 C1
Grange 152 A1
Gransmoor 22 C6
Grant Thorold 153 A4
Grasby 110 E7
Grayingham 119 B7
Great Coates 102 B5
Great Cowden 47 A5
Great Givendale 29 B8
Great Hatfield 46 D6
Great Heck 77 D7
Great Kelk 22 A5
Great Kendale 20 D7
Great Limber 100 D3
Great Tows 120 A1
Greetwell 108 C7
Grey Green 94 E2
Gribthorpe 51 B6
Grimsby 152 E2
Grimston 131 E3
Grindale 3 D2
Grovehill 137 C3
Gunby 50 D6
Gunness 95 E6
Gunthorpe 117 A7

H

Habrough 100 E8
Haisthorpe 10 C3
Hall Garth 26 F6
Halsham 73 F6
Harlthorpe 51 A8
Harpham 21 F8
Harswell 40 C3
Harton 15 C8
Hatcliffe 112 F3
Hatfield 92 D5
Hatfield Woodhouse 93 A3
Haxby 127 D7
Haxey 105 C3
Haxey Carr 105 B4
Hayton 40 C8
Healing 102 A5
Hedon 72 C8
Hemingbrough 49 F1
Hemswell 119 A1
Hensall 62 D2
Heslington 131 B1
Hessay 24 C8
Hessle 143 E1
Heworth 130 F6
Hibaldstow 108 F5
High Catton 27 D8
Highfield 50 E7
High Hunsley 54 D6
High Mowthorpe 6 D7
High Risby 82 F1
Hilderthorpe 11 B4
Hillam 61 A7
Hilston 60 B4
Hirst Courtney 62 F3
Hive 52 C2
Holgate 129 F3
Hollym 75 A4
Holme 97 A1
Holme Hill 152 F3
Holme-on-Spalding-Moor 40 B1
Holme on the Wolds 31 E1
Holmpton 75 C2
Holtby 14 F1
Holton le Clay 114 B5
Hopgrove 128 D2
Horkstow 84 A5
Horkstow Wolds 84 B6
Hornsea 134 D5
Hornsea Burton 134 D2
Hotham 53 D4
Howden 65 A7
Howsham 110 A7
Huggate 18 B2
Humberston 114 E8
Humberston Fitties 114 F8
Humbleton 59 B5
Hunmanby 2 F8
Huntington 127 E3
Hurn 136 C4
Hut Green 62 A2
Hutton 32 E8
Hutton Cranswick 32 D7
Hutton Wandesley 24 A5

I

Immingham 87 B2
Inglemire 139 F6
Irby upon Humber 112 D7

K

Keadby 95 D6
Keelby 101 B5
Kelfield 36 D1
Kelleythorpe 124 C1
Kellingley 61 C2
Kellington 61 F4
Kelstern 120 D1
Kexby 27 C6
Keyingham 73 D3
Kilham 9 C3
Kilnsea 91 B2
Kilnwick 32 B4
Kilnwick Percy 29 C5
Kilpin 65 D5
Kilpin Pike 65 C5
Kingsforth 84 E6
Kingston upon Hull 155 B2
Kirby Grindalythe 6 E6
Kirby Underdale 17 A5
Kirk Bramwith 92 A6
Kirkburn 20 A2
Kirk Ella 143 D8
Kirk Smeaton 76 B3
Kirmington 100 A6
Kirton in Lindsey 108 B1
Knapton 129 A5
Knavesmire 133 A7
Knedlington 64 E6
Knottingley 61 B2

L

Laceby 101 E2
Laceby Acres 102 B2
Langtoft 8 D5
Laughton 117 F8
Laxton 65 F4
Layerthorpe 130 E4
Laytham 39 B2
Leconfield 43 D6
Lelley 58 F3
Leppington 16 C8
Leven 45 A8
Lissett 22 E4
Little Airmyn 64 E4
Little Burton 34 B2
Little Catwick 45 D7
Little Coates 102 C3
Little Driffield 124 C4
Little End 40 A1
Littlefield 152 C2
Little Grimsby 121 E2
Little Hatfield 46 B6
Little Heck 62 D1
Little Leven 45 A7
Little Limber 100 C5
Little Reedness 66 A1
Little Skipwith 37 D1
Little Smeaton 76 C3
Little Weighton 55 A4
Lockington 32 B2
Londesborough 41 B8
Long Drax 64 A6
Long Marston 24 A6
Long Riston 45 C5
Low Burnham 105 D5
Low Catton 27 C8
Low Fosham 46 F1
Low Risby 83 B1
Lowthorpe 21 E7
Ludborough 121 C6
Luddington 81 C3
Lund
Beverley 31 F3
Selby 49 D3

M

Manor Park 150 D2
Manton 108 B5
Mappleton 47 A7
Marfleet 147 C8
Market Weighton 135 B4
Marshchapel 115 B2
Marton 123 D8
Marton 46 B2
Meaux 44 F2
Melbourne 39 B6
Melton 68 F5
Meltonby 28 F7
Melton Ross 99 C5
Menthorpe 50 C5
Messingham 107 C7
Middlegate 84 E1
Middlethorpe 133 B6
Middleton-on-the-Wolds 31 B4
Millbrook Park 135 C3
Millington 29 C6
Misterton 116 C5
Molescroft 136 B5
Monk Fryston 61 B8
Moor End 52 B8
Moorends 79 C2
Moor Monkton 12 A3
Moortown 110 D2
Morton 117 A3
Moss 77 D1
Murton 26 D7

N

Naburn 36 D8
Nafferton 125 E7
Neat Marsh 58 A2
Nether Poppleton 126 A2
Nettleton 111 A2
New Arram 43 F7
New Barnetby 99 D5
New Earswick 127 D3
New Ellerby 46 A2
New Holland 70 E2
Newland
Goole 64 B3
Howden 66 A8
Hull 140 C3
Newport 53 A1
Newsholme 64 E8
Newton-on-Ouse 12 B6
Newton upon Derwent 27 E4
New Village 139 D6
New Waltham 114 A7
Normanby 82 B3
North Cave 53 D3
North Cliffe 53 B8
North Cotes 115 A3
North Dalton 31 B7
North Duffield 50 A8
North Elkington 121 A1
North End
Goxhill 71 A1
Withernwick 46 D4
North Ferriby 69 B4
Northfield 143 F2
North Frodingham 34 A8
North Howden 51 B1
North Kelsey 110 A5
North Killingholme 86 D4
North Newbald 53 E8
North Ormsby 121 B3
Northorpe 118 D8
North Thoresby 114 A1
Norton 76 E2
Nunburnholme 29 E3
Nun Monkton 12 A4
Nunsthorpe 102 D1
Nunthorpe 133 C8

O

Octon 8 F8
Old Clee 153 C2
Old Ellerby 58 A8
Old Goole 149 C1
Old Town 122 E5
Osbaldwick 131 C4
Osgodby 49 C4
Osgodby Common 49 C6
Ottringham 73 F3
Ousefleet 66 D2
Out Newton 90 E8
Overton 12 F2
Owmby 110 D7
Owston Ferry 106 A2
Owstwick 59 E3
Owthorne 74 F7

P

Painsthorpe 17 B5
Patrington 74 E1
Patrington Haven 89 C8
Paull 72 A5
Pilham 118 A4
Pocklington 29 A4
Pollington 77 F6
Portington 51 E2
Preston 58 C1
Pyewipe 152 A8

R

Rascal Moor 52 B7
Rawcliffe
Goole 64 A1
York 126 E2
Rawcliffe Bridge 79 C8
Redbourne 108 F3
Reedness 65 F2
Reighton 3 D6
Riby 101 C2
Riccall 49 A8
Riddings 150 F1
Rimswell 74 D7
Riplingham 54 E2
Risby 55 C5
Rise 45 F5
Rolston 46 E8
Roos 60 A1
Rothwell 111 F2
Routh 44 F5
Roxby 83 A3
Rudston 9 F6
Rufforth 24 C6
Ruston Parva 21 C8
Ryehill 73 A4

S

Salt End 72 A8
Saltmarshe 65 F3
Sancton 41 E2
Sand Hole 52 B8
Sandholme 52 C1
Sand Hutton 15 B5
Sandtoft 94 A3
Santon 97 B7
Saxby All Saints 84 A3
Scalby 66 E8
Scamland 39 C7
Scartho 102 F1
Scawby 108 E8
Scorborough 43 D8
Scotter 107 D3
Scotterthorpe 107 B5
Scotton 107 D2
Scrayingham 15 F7
Sculcoates 140 E2
Scunthorpe 150 F5
Searby 110 C8
Seaton 35 A1
Seaton Common 39 D4
Seaton Ross 39 E4
Selby 148 C6
Sewerby 123 A5
Sewerby Village 123 C6
Shipton 12 F5
Shiptonthorpe 40 F6
Sigglesthorne 45 F8
Skeffling 90 C6
Skelton
Goole 65 C4
York 126 C6
Skerne 21 A2
Skidby 138 B8
Skipsea 23 B2
Skipwith 37 E1
Skirlaugh 45 E2
Skirpenbeck 16 A4
Sledmere 7 B4
Snaith 63 C1
Somerby 99 B1
South Bank 130 A1
South Bramwith 92 B6
Southburn 20 B1
South Cave 54 A2
South Cliffe 53 B7
South Dalton 42 E8
South Duffield 50 A4
South End 46 D3
South End 90 F5
South Ferriby 84 B7
South Field 69 E4
South Kelsey 110 A1
South Killingholme 86 E3
South Newbald 53 F6
Spaldington 51 C4
Speeton 3 F5
Spital in the Street 119 E1
Sproatley 58 C5
Staddlethorpe 66 D7
Stainforth 92 C7
Stallingborough 101 E6
Stamford Bridge 15 E2
Stillingfleet 36 C3
Stockton on the Forest 14 D3
Stoneferry 141 B3
Strensall 14 A7
Strensall Camp 14 B6
Sturton 108 F7
Summergangs 141 C2
Sutton Ings 141 F4
Sutton-on-Hull 141 D6
Sutton upon Derwent 27 C1
Swallow 112 B5
Swanland 69 B6
Swine 57 D6
Swinefleet 65 D1
Sykehouse 78 B3

T

Tang Hall 130 F5
Tansterne 59 A8
Temple Hirst 62 E4
Tetney 114 D4
Tetney Lock 115 A5
Thealby 82 D4
Thearne 56 D7
The Hallands 85 F7
The Lawns 138 F7
The Lings 92 D3
The Parks 92 C4
The Willows 102 C4
Thirtleby 58 B5
Thixendale 17 E7
Thorganby 38 B4
Thorne 93 A8
Thorngumbald 72 E5
Thornholme 10 B2
Thornton 39 B8
Thornton Curtis 85 E5
Thorpe 32 B1
Thorpe le Street 40 D7
Thorpe Willoughby 48 C2
Thwing 2 B1
Tibthorpe 19 D2
Tickton 137 E8
Topham 78 A4
Towthorpe 14 B5
Towthorpe 6 D1
Tunstall 60 C2

U

Ulceby 86 A1
Ulceby Skitter 86 C2
Ulrome 23 A3
Upper Helmsley 15 B3
Upper Poppleton 12 F1
Upperthorpe 105 B3
Upton 22 E1
Utterby 121 D4

V

Victoria Dock Village 146 B5

W

Waithe 114 A3
Walcot 82 C7
Walden Stubbs 76 F3
Walkeringham 116 C3
Walkerith 116 E3
Walkington 55 B8
Walmgate Stray 130 F1
Waltham 113 D7
Wansford 21 C3
Warter 30 A5
Warthill 14 F2
Waterside 92 F8
Watton 32 D5
Wawne 56 E8
Waxholme 74 E8
Weel 137 F3
Weelsby 153 A1
Weeton 90 B7
Weighton Wold 135 F4
Welhambridge 51 F5
Wellow 152 D1
Welton 68 D6
Welwick 90 A8
West Butterwick 106 D8
West Carlton 46 F1
West Carr 140 F5
Westcliff 150 E3
West Cowick 78 D8
West Ella 143 A7
West End 53 F2
Westfield 148 C4
West Field 129 A2
Westgate 94 D2
West Haddlesey 62 A5
West Halton 82 E8
West Hill 122 A1
West Lutton 7 B8
West Marsh 152 B5
West Newton 58 D8
West Ravendale 113 A2
Westrum 98 C1
West Stockwith 116 F6
Westwoodside 105 A2
Wetwang 19 B6
Wharram le Street 6 A4
Wharton 117 E4
Wheldrake 38 A7
Whitgift 66 B1
Whitley 77 A7
Whitley Thorpe 76 F7
Whitton 67 E3
Wigginton 13 D5
Wike Well End 93 B7
Wilberfoss 27 F5
Wildsworth 117 A8
Willerby 138 C1
Willitoft 51 A6
Willoughton 119 A4
Wilsthorpe 11 A2
Winestead 74 C3
Winteringham 68 A1
Winterton 83 A5
Wistow 48 D6
Withernsea 75 A6
Withernwick 46 D3
Wold Haven 29 B3
Wold Newton
Binbrook 120 B7
Hunmanby 2 A3
Womersley 76 C6
Woodhall 50 B2
Woodhouse 94 E3
Woodmansey 56 B8
Woodside 104 E6
Woodthorpe 132 C7
Wootton 85 F3
Worlaby 98 D8
Wrawby 98 E4
Wressle
Broughton 97 F4
Howden 50 D2
Wroot 104 D6
Wybers Wood 102 A3
Wyham 120 F6
Wyton 58 B4

Y

Yaddlethorpe 96 C2
Yapham 28 E7
Yarborough 152 A3
Yawthorpe 118 D2
Yokefleet 66 C3
York 156 B3
Youlthorpe 16 C2

1

1st Ave HU6 140 C6
1st Main Rd DN36 114 F8
10th Ave HU6 140 B7
11th Ave HU6 140 B6
12th Ave
Humberston DN36 114 F8
Kingston upon Hull HU6 140 A7
14th Ave HU6 140 A7
15th Ave HU6 140 A6
16th Ave HU6 140 A7
17th Ave HU6 140 A6
18th Ave HU6 140 A7
19th Ave HU6 140 A6

2

2nd Ave
Humberston DN36 114 F8
Kingston upon Hull HU6 140 B7
20 21 Visual Arts Ctr DN15 151 C7
20th Ave HU6 140 A7
21st Ave HU6 139 F6
22nd Ave HU6 140 A7
23rd Ave HU6 140 A6
24th Ave HU6 140 A7
25th Ave HU6 140 A6
26th Ave HU6 139 F7
27th Ave HU6 140 A6
28th Ave HU6 139 F7
29th Ave HU6 139 F6

3

30th Ave HU6 139 F7
31st Ave HU6 139 F6
32nd Ave HU6 139 F7
33rd Ave HU6 139 F6
34th Ave HU6 139 F7
36th Ave HU6 139 F7
37th Ave HU6 139 E6
38th Ave HU6 139 F7

4

4th Ave
Humberston DN36 114 F8
Kingston upon Hull HU6 140 B7
40th Ave HU6 139 F7

5

5th Ave HU6 139 F6

6

6th Ave HU6 140 A7

7

7th Ave HU6 140 B6

8

8th Ave HU6 140 A7

9

9th Ave HU6 140 B6

A

A W Nielsen Rd DN14 149 A4
Abber La LS24 24 A2
Abbey Dr E DN32 152 D2
Abbey Dr W DN32 152 D2
Abbey Gdns 32 DN7 92 D4
Abbey Gn 30 DN7 92 D4
Abbey La
Kingston upon Hull HU10 138 E2
Preston HU12 58 C1
Abbey Leisure Ctr YO8 148 C5
Abbey Pk Mews DN32 152 D2
Abbey Pk Rd DN32 152 D2
Abbey Pl 9 YO8 148 D5
Abbey Rd
Bridlington YO16 122 B2
Grimsby DN32 152 D2
Hatfield DN7 92 D4
Kingston upon Hull HU11 142 F6
Scunthorpe DN17 150 F2
Ulceby DN39 86 A1
Abbey Rise DN19 85 D8
Abbey St
Kingston upon Hull HU9 146 C7
York YO30 130 A7
Abbey Way DN7 92 D5
Abbey Wlk
Grimsby DN32 152 D3
Selby YO8 148 C5
Abbey Wlk Sh Ctr YO8 148 C6
Abbey Yd YO8 148 C5
Abbeyfield Rd DN7 92 C4
Abbeygate 12 DN31 152 D3
Abbot St YO31 156 C4
Abbot's Lodge* DN39 86 B5
Abbot's Rd YO8 148 E3
Abbots Cl HU8 141 E5
Abbots Gait YO32 127 F6
Abbots Rd DN17 150 F2
Abbots Wlk HU16 139 A5
Abbotsford Cl HU5 139 F3
Abbotsford Rd YO10 130 F3
Abbotsway
Grimsby DN32 152 D2
York YO31 130 E8
Abbotts Grange DN36 114 B7
Abbotts Way YO16 122 D4
Abelton Gr 33 YO32 13 E5
Abercorn St DN16 151 A6
Aberdeen St HU9 141 F3
Aberdovey Cl 3 HU7 57 A7
Aberford Wlk HU9 142 E1
Abingdon Garth 1 HU7 57 A5
Acacia Ave
Flixborough DN15 96 B7
19 Gainsborough DN21 117 B1
York YO32 127 E4
Acacia Ct DN16 151 B2
Acacia Dr HU8 141 D2
Acacia Way DN17 107 C6
Acadia Gr HU13 143 F1
Acaster Ave YO23 36 A3
Acaster La
Acaster Malbis YO23 133 B1
Acaster Selby YO23 36 A4
Accommodation Rd YO25 8 D6
Acer Gr DN17 150 C1
Acey La HU12 58 B1
Achille Rd DN34 102 B3
Acklam Dr HU18 134 D6
Acklam Gr DN32 153 B2
Acklam Rd HU12 72 D7
Ackworth St HU8 141 C1
Acland St
Gainsborough DN21 117 B1
4 Kingston upon Hull HU3 145 A6
Acomb Comm Rd DN7 92 F4
Acomb Prim Sch YO24 129 E3
Acomb Rd YO24 129 D3
Acomb Wood Cl YO24 132 C7
Acomb Wood Dr YO24 132 B7
Acorn Cl 6 Barlby YO8 49 B4
Bridlington YO16 123 B7
Acorn Gr HU8 141 E7
Acorn Way
24 Bottesford DN16 96 D1
Gateforth YO8 48 B1
Hessle HU13 143 B3
York YO24 132 D7
Acredykes 7 YO15 4 D3
Acres La
Scrayingham YO41 16 B8
Wroot DN9 104 D7
Acton Cl HU8 141 F5
Acton Ct 7 DN32 153 A5
Adam Smith St DN31 152 C5
Adam St DN14 149 D3
Adderbury Gr 5 HU5 140 D2
Addison Gdns HU8 141 D3
Addison Rd 10 HU12 58 D1
Addle La DN14 65 E7
Addlekeld YO42 30 A5
Adelaide Prim Sch HU3 145 D5
Adelaide Rd 6 DN6 76 E2
Adelaide St
Kingston upon Hull HU1 155 A1
3 York YO23 130 B2
Adeline St DN14 149 C5
Adeliza Garth 20 HU12 72 D7
Adelphi Cl HU8 141 F4
Adelphi Ct 4 DN36 114 A7
Adelphi Dr 7 DN33 113 E8
Adelphi St YO25 124 E4
Adlard Gr DN36 114 C7
Adlingfleet Rd DN17 81 E6
Adlington Cl 8 YO32 14 A7
Admiral Walker Rd HU17 154 A2
Admirals Croft HU1 155 A1
Admirals Mews 1 YO15 122 D2
Advent Ct 9 DN39 86 A1
Aegre Dr DN14 65 C4
Africa Cl 15 DN34 102 B2
Agar St YO31 156 C3
Agard Ave DN15 150 E7
Aike La YO25 33 A1
Ainshaw HU6 139 E8
Ainslie Rd HU12 72 D7
Ainslie St DN32 152 E2
Ainsty Ave YO24 132 F8
Ainsty Gr YO24 132 F8
Ainsty St DN14 149 E4
Ainsty View YO17 16 E8
Ainsworth Rd 16 DN40 87 B1
Ainthorpe Gr HU5 144 C7
Ainthorpe Prim Sch HU5 144 C8
Aintree Cl HU17 136 E6
Aintree Ct YO24 132 F8
Air St HU5 140 F2
Aire Cl 10 Brough HU15 68 D5
36 Immingham DN40 87 B1
Aire St Goole DN14 149 D3
Knottingley WF11 61 A3
Airedale HU7 140 E6
Airedale Cl 10 DN20 97 E4
Airedale Dr YO16 122 F7
Airedale Rd DN16 151 D1
Airedale Way DN31 152 D4
Airlie St HU3 145 B5
Airmyn Ave
Goole DN14 149 B5
1 Kingston upon Hull HU3 144 E6
Airmyn Pk Prim Sch DN14 64 E4
Airmyn Rd Airmyn DN14 64 D3
Goole DN14 149 B5
Aisne St HU5 145 A8
Ajax Cl Grimsby DN34 102 B2
Kingston upon Hull HU9 142 D5
Ajax Ct DN15 96 C7
Akeferry Rd
Haxey DN9 105 C1
Westwoodside DN9 105 B2
Akester Cl 4 HU17 137 B3
Alan Cres DN15 150 F6
Alaska St HU8 141 B1
Alba Cl DN17 150 D1
Albany St
Gainsborough DN21 117 B1
Kingston upon Hull HU3 145 D8
3 York YO26 129 F5
Albany Villas HU13 144 A1
Albatross Dr DN37 102 A4
Albemarle Cl 5 HU15 68 B5
Albemarle Rd
Bilton HU11 58 A3
2 Keyingham HU12 73 C4
York YO23 130 B2
Albemarle St 2 HU3 145 B5
Albert Aur Pools HU3 145 A7
Albert Ave HU3 145 A7
Albert Cl
4 Grimsby DN32 152 F5
1 York YO32 130 F8
Albert Dock HU1 145 E4
Albert Marson Ct DN16 151 B6
Albert Pl 3 DN32 152 F5
Albert Rd
Cleethorpes DN35 153 F2
Scunthorpe DN16 151 A1
Albert St
10 Bridlington YO15 122 E2
Brigg DN20 98 C2
Goole DN14 149 C2
5 New Holland DN19 70 E2
3 Thorne/Moorends DN8 93 B8
York YO10 156 C1
Albert St E DN32 152 F5
Albert St W DN32 152 F5
Albert Terr
Beverley HU17 154 A2
Kingston upon Hull HU7 141 D6
Welwick HU12 90 A7
Alberta Cres 7 DN17 96 C2
Albertine Ct 5 DN37 113 D7
Albery Way DN36 114 A8
Albina Garth 1 HU12 72 D7
Albion Ave YO26 129 B6
Albion Ct
Beverley HU17 137 B4
Kingston upon Hull HU4 144 B6
Albion Hill DN9 105 E6
Albion La HU10 138 A3
Albion St
Great Driffield YO25 124 F3
Grimsby DN32 152 F4
Kingston upon Hull HU1 155 A3
York YO1 156 B1
Albion Terr
Bridlington YO15 122 F3
Misterton DN10 116 D5
Albourne Ave DN15 151 A6
Albright Cl 31 YO42 29 A3
Alcelina Ct YO23 156 B1
Alcuin Ave YO10 131 A4
Alcuin Way YO10 131 B2
Aldam Dr DN9 94 F1
Aldborough Gr HU9 142 A2
Aldborough Way YO26 129 F5
Aldbro' St HU2 155 B3
Aldbrough La HU11 59 A6
Aldbrough Prim Sch HU11 47 C1
Aldbrough Rd
East Garton HU11 59 D7
Withernwick HU11 46 E3
Alden Cl DN40 87 C1
Aldenham Pk HU7 56 E5
Alder Cl 16 HU15 68 D5
Alder Gr 6 DN8 79 B2
Alder Hey Dr 9 HU9 142 A5
Alder View 22 DN33 102 C2
Alder Way YO32 127 D2
Alderley Ct YO32 127 E3
Alderley Edge 6 DN37 113 D6
Alderman Cogans CE Prim Sch HU9 141 F2
Aldermans Way 10 YO25 34 B2
Alderney Way 2 DN40 101 C8
Alders The 22 DN21 117 C1
Alderson Ct YO16 122 D2
Alderson Mews 5 HU9 146 C7
Aldersyde YO24 132 E7
Aldersyde Ct YO24 132 E7
Aldersyde Mews YO24 132 E7
Aldreth Gr YO23 130 C2
Aldrich Rd DN35 103 C2
Aldwark YO1 156 C3
Aldwych Croft 6 DN36 114 A7
Aldwych Ct HU5 144 E8
Alexander Ave YO31 127 E2
Alexander Rd DN16 151 B6
Alexandra Ct
4 Bridlington YO15 122 F3
York YO10 130 E4
Alexandra Dock DN31 152 D6
Alexandra Dock N DN31 152 C6
Alexandra Dr
1 Beverley HU17 55 E8
5 Bridlington YO15 122 F3
Alexandra Prom YO15 123 A3
Alexandra Rd
Cleethorpes DN35 153 F2
Grimsby DN31 152 D4
Hornsea HU18 134 D4
Kingston upon Hull HU5 140 C3
Scunthorpe DN16 151 B2
Strensall YO32 14 A6
Thorne/Moorends DN8 79 B2
Alexandra Rd N DN40 87 D3
Alexandra Rd S DN40 87 D2
Alexandra Ret Pk DN31 152 D5
Alexandra St
Goole DN14 149 D4
Kingston upon Hull HU3 145 D7
Thorne DN8 79 A1
Alexandra Wlk YO15 122 F3
Alfonso St 5 HU3 145 B5
Alfred Bean Hospl YO25 125 A6
Alfred Gelder St HU1 155 B2
Alfred St
Gainsborough DN21 117 B1
Grimsby DN31 152 D4
Kingston upon Hull HU3 145 D5
Alfreton Ct 1 DN15 150 B6
Alfriston Cl HU7 141 B6
Algarth Rd
Pocklington YO42 29 A4
York YO31 131 B7
Algarth Rise
Pocklington YO42 28 F4
York YO31 131 B7
Algernon St DN32 152 F1
Alison Garth 29 HU12 72 D7
Alkborough La DN15 82 D7
Alkborough Prim Sch DN15 82 C8
All Hallows Rd 3 HU17 55 B7
All Saints CE VC Inf Sch HU13 143 F2
All Saints Cl 4 HU13 69 F4
All Saints Ct 6 YO43 135 D4
All Saints' RC Sch YO24 156 A1
All Saints' St HU3 145 D8
All Saints VE VC Jun Sch HU13 143 F2
Allan St 2 YO30 130 C7
Allanby St DN15 151 A7
Allanhall Way HU10 143 B8
Allanson Dr HU16 139 D5
Allanson Gr YO24 129 E2
Allderidge Ave HU5 140 B3
Allen Cl YO10 131 A4
Allenby Ave DN34 152 A2
Allenby Cres LN11 121 D3
Allendale YO24 132 D8
Allerford Dr 8 HU7 57 A5
Allerthorpe Comm Nature Reserve* YO42 28 B2
Allerton Dr
1 Immingham DN40 87 C1
22 Poppleton YO26 12 F1
Allerton Prim Sch DN40 87 B1
Allestree Dr 2 DN33 113 E8
Alliance Ave HU3 144 F7
Alliance La HU3 144 F7
Allington Dr
Great Coates DN31 102 C5
York YO31 131 B6
Allinson Yd HU17 45 A7
Allison Cl DN17 107 D7
Allison La
14 Flamborough YO15 5 A2
Ulrome YO25 22 F4
Alloa Cl 2 HU6 140 B8
Allotment La YO25 124 E5
Allotment Wlk YO16 122 B1
Alma Cl HU10 143 D7
Alma Gr YO10 130 D2
Alma St
6 Kingston upon Hull HU9 146 B7
4 Withernsea HU19 74 F7
Alma Terr Selby YO8 148 C6
York YO10 130 D2
Almery Terr YO30 156 A3
Almond Cl
Great Driffield YO25 124 F2
Hambleton YO8 48 B1
Almond Gr Brigg DN20 98 B2
3 Kingston upon Hull HU3 145 D6
Scunthorpe DN16 151 B4
York YO32 127 D4
Almond Tree Ave DN14 63 C3
Almsford Dr YO26 129 C5
Almsford Rd YO26 129 C5
Alne Terr YO10 130 E2
Alness Dr YO24 132 B7
Alpha Ave HU17 136 D6
Alpha Ct DN8 92 F8
Alsenham Pk 9 HU7 56 E5
Alston Ave 4 HU8 141 B1
Althorpe & Keadby Prim Sch DN17 95 D5
Althorpe Sta DN17 95 D5
Altoft Cl
2 Brandesburton YO25 34 B2
12 Laceby DN37 101 F1
Alton Pk Mews YO25 22 C1
Alton Rd YO16 122 D7
Altyre Way DN36 103 B1
Alured Garth 9 HU12 72 D7
Alveston Rd DN17 150 D4
Alvin Wlk 9 YO41 27 B2
Alvingham Ave 25 DN35 103 C2
Alvingham Rd DN16 151 B3
Alvis Gr YO10 131 D4
Alwoodley Cl 1 HU8 142 B5
Alwyn Rd 19 DN8 93 B8
Alwyne Dr YO30 126 E1
Alwyne Gr YO30 126 E1
Amanda Cl HU6 139 E6
Amanda Dr DN7 92 D4
Ambaston Rd HU18 134 C5
Amber Ct YO31 156 C4
Amber St YO31 156 C4
Amberley Cl HU7 141 B6
Amberly St 4 YO26 129 E5
Ambler's La YO30 12 F7
Ambleside Ave YO10 131 B4
Ambrey Cl 16 YO14 2 F8
Ambrose Ave 1 DN7 92 E4
Ambrose St YO10 130 D1
Amcott Ave DN10 116 D4
Amcotts Rd 14 DN33 102 D1
Amen La YO43 53 D5
Amesbury Ave DN33 113 D8
Amethyst Ct 11 DN36 114 A8
Amethyst Rd HU9 142 C4
Amos Cl 9 DN33 113 D8
Amos Cres DN16 151 D3
Ampleforth Gr HU5 144 D8
Amsterdam Rd HU7 141 A5
Amwell Gn 8 DN7 92 D3
Amy Johnson Ave YO16 122 E6
Amy Johnson Ct HU1 155 A1
Amy Johnson Sch HU3 144 F5
Amy Johnson Way YO30 127 A3
Amy St DN14 149 C4
Anastasia Cl 1 DN21 117 B2
Ancaster Ave
Grimsby DN33 113 D8
Kingston upon Hull HU5 139 F3
Ancaster Ct DN16 151 A1
Ancholme Ave 10 DN40 87 B1
Ancholme Gdns 11 DN20 98 C2
Ancholme Rd DN16 151 D2
Ancholme Way DN20 98 B2
Anchor Cl 31 DN8 93 A8
Anchor Rd
Kingston upon Hull HU6 140 C8
Scunthorpe DN16 97 A3
Anchorage St 7 DN20 98 B2
Anchors Way 16 DN20 98 B2
Ancient La DN7 92 F3
Ancourt HU6 139 E6
Ancress Wlk YO23 156 A1
Ancroft Cl YO1 156 C1
Anderby Dr DN37 102 B4
Anderson Gr 6 YO24 129 F2
Anderson Rd
Goole DN14 149 A4
Scunthorpe DN16 151 C3
Anderson St
7 Great Driffield YO25 124 F3
Grimsby DN31 152 D3
Andersons Cl 17 HU12 72 D7
Andrew Dr 4 YO32 127 F1
Andrew La 3 HU12 72 C7
Andrew Marvell Sch HU9 142 D4
Andrew Paddock DN20 108 F5
Andrew Rd 11 DN36 114 D8
Andrew's Ct 16 YO42 28 F4
Andrews Rd DN18 84 A7
Andrews Way 8 DN40 87 B1
Angerstein Rd DN17 150 F1
Anglesey Dr DN40 101 C8
Angram Cl YO30 126 F1
Angram La YO19 49 A6
Angram Rd YO26 24 A5
Angus Dr YO25 124 D4
Anlaby Acre Head Prim Sch HU4 144 B7
Anlaby Ave 7 HU4 144 B6
Anlaby High Rd HU4 144 C6
Anlaby Inf Sch HU10 144 A6
Anlaby Jun Sch HU10 144 A6
Anlaby Pk Rd N HU4 144 B5
Anlaby Pk Rd S HU4 144 B2
Anlaby Rd HU3 155 A2
Anlafgate 7 HU10 143 F6
Anlary Rd HU1 155 A2
Ann Gr DN35 103 B2
Ann Watson St HU7 141 A4
Annan Cl YO24 132 C6
Annandale Rd
Kingston upon Hull HU9 142 E2
Willerby HU10 138 B1
Anne St
Kingston upon Hull HU1 155 A2
York YO23 130 C2

Annerley Dr YO16 123 A7
Annes Cres DN16 151 C3
Annesley St DN31 152 D5
Annie Med La HU15 53 F1
Annie Rd Ct HU17 137 C3
Annie Reed Rd HU17 137 C3
Annie St YO8 148 C6
Anningson La 6 DN36 114 A8
Annumhills Rd YO8 50 D7
Anserdam La HU15 52 C2
Anson Dr YO10 133 D8
Anson Rd HU9 142 B3
Antelope Rd DN18 70 A1
Anthea Dr YO31 127 E1
Antholme Cl HU7 141 C6
Anthony Way 1 DN41 101 D6
Anthony's Bank Rd DN36 103 E1
Antrim Way 4 DN33 102 E1
Antwerp Rd HU7 141 A5
Anvil Wlk DN15 82 F3
Apollo St 9 YO10 130 E3
Apollo Wlk HU8 141 F4
Appian Way DN31 152 A6
Appin Cl 7 HU7 57 A6
Apple Croft HU16 138 B8
Apple Garth
21 Hedon HU12 72 D7
15 Poppleton YO26 12 F1
Apple Tree Cl
Kingston upon Hull HU8 141 D4
1 Long Riston/Arnold HU11 45 C5
Apple Tree Ct 1 DN41 101 F5
Apple Tree Wlk HU16 139 D6
Appleby Cl DN17 150 F1
Appleby Ct 8 DN32 153 A5
Appleby Gdns DN20 97 D4
Appleby Glade YO32 127 D7
Appleby La
Broughton DN20 97 D4
Burstwick HU12 73 A7
Appleby Mill Rd DN16 151 E7
Appleby Pl 2 YO31 131 A5
Applecroft Rd
Selby YO8 148 A4
York YO31 131 B7
Appledore Cl HU9 146 C6
Applefields Sch YO31 131 B5
Applegarth 8 HU15 66 D7
Applegarth Cl DN35 153 D1
Applegarth La
Bainton YO25 31 E7
Bridlington YO16 122 D4
Applegarth Mews 3 HU16 139 B7
Applegarth Rd HU8 155 C3
Appleton Ct YO23 132 F3
Appleton Gdns 8 HU15 53 F1
Appleton Prim Sch HU5 139 E2
Appleton Rd
Bishopthorpe YO23 133 A3
Kingston upon Hull HU5 139 E3
Appleton Way DN16 151 C2
Appleyard Dr DN18 84 E8
Arables La HU12 74 C4
ARC* YO1 156 C2
Arcade The DN14 149 D4
Archbishop Cl HU9 142 D2
Archbishop Holgate's Sch YO10 131 B3
Archbishop of York CE Jun Sch YO23 133 A4
Archbishop Thurston CE VC Sec Sch HU9 142 D3
Archer Rd DN37 113 D6
Archway The YO43 135 D4
Arcon Dr HU4 144 D6
Arctic Corsair* HU1 155 C2
Arden Ct HU5 139 C2
Arden Rd HU17 154 C4
Arden Village 21 DN35 103 C1
Ardent Rd DN18 70 A1
Ardmore Cl HU9 142 B4
Arenhall Cl 2 YO32 127 C8
Argam Dikes*
Grindale YO25 3 B2
Rudston YO25 10 A7
Argam La YO25 2 F1
Argent Cl 8 HU6 140 B8
Arglam La YO43 51 F6
Argyle Ct DN15 151 A7
Argyle St Goole DN14 149 D4
Kingston upon Hull HU3 145 C7
York YO23 130 B1
Ariston St DN32 153 B3
Ark Royal HU11 142 E6
Arkley Cl 18 HU15 68 C5
Arkwright St 10 DN21 117 B1
Arkwright Way DN16 151 F2
Arlington Ave HU16 139 B6
Arlington Rd YO30 127 A1
Arlington St 2 HU3 145 D6
Armeria Dr 23 DN17 96 D1
Armour Rd DN16 151 E7
Armoury Rd YO8 148 B5
Armstrong Cl HU17 154 C2
Armstrong Pl E DN31 152 C5
Armstrong Pl W DN31 152 C5
Armstrong St DN31 152 C5
Armstrong Way
Beverley HU17 154 B2
Rawcliffe YO32 128 E3
Armthorpe La DN3 92 A3
Arncliffe Cl 1 HU7 56 F6
Arncliffe Way HU16 139 A5
Arnold Cl DN37 101 F2
Arnold Ct 9 DN32 153 A5
Arnold La
Kingston upon Hull HU3 145 B6
Riston HU11 45 C5
Arnold La W HU11 45 C4
Arnold St HU3 145 B6
Arnside Pl 2 YO10 130 F3
Arram Gr HU6 139 E5
Arram Rd HU17 43 D6
Arram Sta HU17 43 F7
Arran Cl
Immingham DN40 101 C8
Kingston upon Hull HU9 142 A4
19 New Waltham DN36 114 A8
Arran Pl YO31 130 D7
Arras Dr HU16 138 E6
Arreton Cl HU8 142 D6
Art Coll Mews DN32 152 F4
Arthur Lucan Ct HU9 142 C1
Arthur Pl 6 YO30 126 B5
Arthur Rd 12 DN21 117 B1
Arthur St
Grimsby DN31 152 C4
Kingston upon Hull HU3 145 A5
Withernsea HU19 74 F7
York YO10 130 E4
Arundel Cl
4 Gainsborough DN21 117 C1
Kingston upon Hull HU9 146 C8
Arundel Gr YO24 132 C7
Arundel Pl DN35 153 E1
Arundel Rd 5 DN6 76 E2
Arundel St 4 HU9 146 C8
Arundel Wlk DN34 152 A3
Ascot Rd 23 DN37 113 D6
Ascot Way YO24 129 D1
Ascott Cl
Beverley HU17 136 E7
Kingston upon Hull HU4 144 D5
Asenby Wlk HU5 139 D3
Asgard Way 5 DN33 102 D1
Ash Ave HU15 68 C6
Ash Cl Hessle HU13 143 C3
Newton on Derwent YO41 27 E4
Sproatley HU11 58 D5
York YO31 131 B7
Ash Ct 13 DN35 103 B1
Ash Dell DN14 149 E6
Ash Dene 7 HU17 55 D8
Ash Dr
Kingston upon Hull HU10 143 F8
Thorngumbald HU12 72 E5
Ash Gr 4 Aldbrough HU11 47 C1
Brigg DN20 98 B2
17 Gainsborough DN21 117 B1
Hutton Cranswick YO25 32 E6
Market Weighton YO43 135 D4
Messingham DN17 107 D7
Newland HU5 140 C3
1 Riccall YO19 48 F8
3 Scotter DN21 107 B3
Scunthorpe DN16 151 B3
Willerby HU10 138 D1
Ash Hill Cres DN7 92 D4
Ash Hill Mid Sch DN7 92 D4
Ash Hill Rd
20 Hatfield DN7 92 D4
Sykehouse DN14 78 A3
Ash La 8 Haxby YO32 13 E5
Melbourne YO42 39 A5
Ash St YO26 129 E4
Ash Tree Cl 5 DN40 87 C2
Ash Tree Dr
5 Haxey DN9 105 D2
Leconfield HU17 43 D6
Ash Tree Rd 13 DN8 93 A7
Ashberry Dr
Messingham DN17 107 D7
1 Scunthorpe DN16 151 B2
Ashbourne 7 DN37 113 D6
Ashbourne Ct DN15 150 B7
Ashbourne Way YO24 132 C8
Ashburnham Cl 4 DN6 76 F2
Ashburnham Rd 14 DN8 93 A8
Ashburnham Wlk 5 DN6 76 F2
Ashbury Ct HU6 140 A6
Ashby Cl Grimsby DN37 102 B4
Holton le Clay DN36 114 B5
Kingston upon Hull HU4 144 B7
Ashby High St DN16 151 A2
Ashby Hill DN37 113 C3
Ashby Inf Sch DN16 151 B2
Ashby La DN37 113 C4
Ashby Rd
Cleethorpes DN35 103 B2
Kingston upon Hull HU4 144 B4
Scunthorpe DN16 151 A2
Ashcombe Rd HU7 56 E5
Ashcourt Cl HU18 134 C5
Ashcourt Dr HU18 134 B5
Ashdale Pk 14 HU14 69 A5
Ashdale Rd 19 YO19 26 F7
Ashdene Cl HU10 143 E7
Ashdown Ave DN15 150 E8
Ashdown Cl DN20 98 D2
Ashdown Way DN10 116 C5
Ashendon Dr HU8 141 A2
Ashfield YO43 40 A1
Ashfield Ave 1 DN8 93 A7
Ashfield Ct Crowle DN17 94 D7
York YO24 132 E7
Ashfield Gr 6 DN7 92 C6
Ashfield Pk DN17 150 B2
Ashfield Rd Hatfield DN7 92 C4
Ashfield Rd *continued*
Thorne DN8 92 F7
Ashford Pl YO24 129 D2
Ashford Wlk HU9 142 E1
Ashgate Rd HU10 138 E2
Ashlea 1 DN10 116 C5
Ashlea Cl YO8 148 D4
Ashleigh Ct 13 DN41 101 F5
Ashleigh Dr 6 YO25 22 D1
Ashley Pk Cres YO31 131 B6
Ashley Pk Rd YO31 131 B7
Ashmeade Cl YO24 132 B8
Ashmole Wlk HU17 154 C4
Ashridge Dr DN32 153 B1
Ashthorpe HU6 139 F8
Ashton Ave YO30 130 B8
Ashton Cl HU6 139 F8
Ashtree Ave DN34 152 A2
Ashtree Cl DN9 94 E1
Ashtree Cres HU15 53 D3
Ashtree Dr YO8 48 D1
Ashville St
Bridlington YO16 122 D3
York YO31 130 D7
Ashwell Ave HU9 142 D1
Ashwood Cl 21 HU15 68 C5
Ashwood Dr 17 DN36 103 D1
Ashwood Glade YO32 127 C6
Ashworthy Cl 5 HU7 56 F5
Aske Mews HU5 139 D3
Askern & Campsall Sports Ctr DN6 76 F1
Askew Ave HU4 144 E4
Askham Bog Nature Reserve* YO23 132 C5
Askham Bryan Coll YO23 24 F2
Askham Bryan La YO23 132 A6
Askham Croft 1 YO24 129 B1
Askham Fields La YO23 24 F2
Askham Gr YO24 129 B2
Askham La
Askham Bryan YO24 132 A8
York YO24 129 B1
Askrigg Wlk HU5 139 D4
Aspall Wlk HU8 142 C7
Aspen Cl
3 Dunnington YO19 26 F7
Market Weighton YO43 135 D5
Selby YO8 48 D2
Aspen Ct
15 Cleethorpes DN35 103 B1
18 Gainsborough DN21 117 C1
Aspen Gr DN16 151 B4
Aspen Wlk 4 HU15 68 D5
Asphodel Cl 15 DN36 114 B8
Asquith Ave YO31 131 A5
Asquith St DN21 117 A1
Asterby Rd DN17 150 F1
Astley Cres 18 DN21 107 C3
Astley St HU3 144 F7
Aston Gn 4 DN7 92 D3
Aston Hall Dr 11 HU14 69 A5
Aston Rd HU10 143 F8
Astoria Cres HU8 141 F4
Astral Cl
Northfield HU13 143 F3
Sutton-on-Hull HU7 141 D7
Astral Gdns HU7 141 C7
Astral Rd HU13 143 F3
Astral Way HU7 141 C7
Atcherley Cl YO10 133 D8
Athelstan Rd HU17 154 B4
Athena Dr DN31 152 A6
Athenian Way DN37 102 C6
Atherton Way DN20 98 B2
Athol St HU3 144 F4
Atholl Ave HU13 143 E3
Atkinson Ave DN20 98 C3
Atkinson Dr 19 HU15 68 C6
Atkinson La 6 DN37 113 E6
Atkinsons Way DN15 96 C8
Atlanta Ct 2 HU8 142 B5
Atlas Rd
Scunthorpe DN17 150 F4
York YO30 127 A3
Atterby La LN8 119 F3
Atterwith La YO26 24 A7
Attlee Dr DN14 149 C5
Atwick Ct 2 HU9 142 B1
Atwick Rd
Bewholme YO25 35 A4
Hornsea HU18 134 B6
Atwood Cl 4 DN40 87 B2
Aubretia Dr 22 DN17 96 D1
Auburn Cl
Bridlington YO16 122 B5
Kingston upon Hull HU9 142 C1
Auburn Wlk YO16 122 B5
Auchinleck Cl YO25 124 B1
Auckland Ave HU6 140 C5
Auckland Gr DN8 79 C2
Auckland Rd
Grimsby DN31 152 F6
Scunthorpe DN15 150 F6
Aucuba Cl YO32 127 D2
Audax Cl YO30 127 A3
Audax Rd YO30 127 A3
Audern Rd DN16 96 D2
Audley St HU2 155 A4
Audus St 10 YO8 148 C5
Augusta Cl
Grimsby DN34 152 C2
Kingston upon Hull HU8 142 B6
Augusta Oaks DN34 152 C2
Augusta St DN34 152 B2
Augustinian Priory (site of)* YO42 30 B5
Augustus Dr 13 HU15 68 C5
Auster Rd YO30 127 B3
Austfield La LS25 61 B8
Austin Cres 17 DN17 96 C2
Austin Garth 5 DN37 101 F1
Autherd Garth 1 HU17 55 C8
Autumn View YO25 124 D5
Avenswood La 8 DN15 96 B7
Avenue Cannes DN15 96 B7
Avenue Clamart DN15 96 B7
Avenue Fontenay 17 DN15 96 B7
Avenue Lourdes 16 DN15 96 B7
Avenue Nozay DN20 97 E4
Avenue Rd YO30 156 A4
Avenue Rouen 15 DN15 96 B7
Avenue Terr YO30 156 A4
Avenue The
Blyton DN21 117 E5
Burton upon Stather DN15 82 B4
Campsall DN6 76 E1
East Ravendale DN37 113 C2
19 Gainsborough DN21 117 B1
Great Driffield YO25 124 F5
Grimsby DN37 102 B4
5 Haxby YO32 13 E5
Healing DN41 101 F5
Holme-on-Spalding-Moor YO43 51 E8
Kirk Ella HU10 143 C7
Nun Monkton YO26 12 A4
11 Pocklington YO42 29 A4
Rowley HU20 54 D6
Rufforth YO23 24 C6
Sutton-on-Hull HU7 141 E6
Thorne/Moorends DN8 79 B3
Watton YO25 32 D4
York YO30 130 A6
Avenue Vivian DN15 150 E8
Avenues Ct HU5 140 C1
Aviator Ct YO30 126 F3
Avocet Way YO15 11 B4
Avon Dr YO32 127 F6
Avon Rd DN16 151 C6
Avon St 2 HU8 141 C1
Avondale 1 HU4 144 B2
Awmand Gn HU16 138 F5
Awnhams La
Bishop Wilton YO42 16 D2
North Cave HU15 53 E4
Axdane HU6 139 E7
Axholme Ave DN17 94 C7
Axholme Ct HU9 146 B5
Axholme Dr 11 DN9 105 D6
Axholme Gn 11 DN8 93 B7
Axholme Line Nature Reserve* DN9 105 C4
Axholme Rd
Scunthorpe DN15 150 D6
2 Westwoodside DN9 105 A2
Axholme St DN14 149 E4
Axminster Cl HU7 141 A8
Aylesbury Gr HU5 144 D8
Aylesby Gdns 26 DN33 102 D2
Aylesby La DN37 101 F2
Aylesby Rd
Aylesby DN37 101 E2
Scunthorpe DN17 150 F1
Aylesford St 7 HU3 145 B5
Aylesham Ct YO32 127 E3
Ayots Gn 10 DN7 92 D3
Ayscough Ave DN41 101 E6
Ayscough Gr 3 LN7 111 B4
Ayscough St DN31 152 C4
Aysgarth Ave
Kingston upon Hull HU6 139 E4
Messingham DN17 107 D7
Aysgarth Rise YO16 122 E6

B

Babington Row HU9 146 C8
Bacchus La HU15 54 A1
Bacheler St HU3 145 B5
Bachelor Hill YO24 129 C2
Back Field La DN7 92 E4
Back La
Acaster Selby YO23 36 B3
Allerthorpe YO42 28 E2
Appleton Roebuck YO23 36 A5
Asselby DN14 64 D6
Barlby with Osgodby YO8 49 C4
Bilbrough YO23 24 D1
Burstwick HU12 73 A6
Burton Agnes YO25 10 A2
Burton Pidsea HU12 59 C2
Catwick HU17 45 C8
Copmanthorpe YO23 132 A2
Cottingwith YO42 38 C5
Drax YO8 63 F5
Driffield YO25 124 B5
East Garton HU11 59 E6
Ellerton YO42 38 C1
Elstronwick HU12 59 B3
Fangfoss YO41 28 C8
Garthorpe & Fockerby DN17 81 F6
11 Haxby YO32 13 D5
Hayton YO42 29 C1
Hemingbrough YO8 49 F1
Hirst Courtney YO8 62 F3
Holme-on-Spalding-Moor YO43 40 A1
Holtby YO19 26 E8
Back La *continued*
Kilham YO25 9 B3
Luttons YO17 7 B8
Newton-on-Ouse YO30 12 B6
North Duffield YO8 50 A7
Norton DN6 76 E2
Nunburnholme YO42 29 F3
Patrington Haven HU12 89 C8
2 Riccall YO19 49 A8
Searby cum Owmby DN38 110 D8
3 Seaton HU11 35 A1
Shiptonthorpe YO43 40 F6
Snaith & Cowick DN14 78 E8
Stainforth DN7 92 C6
Wilberfoss YO41 27 F5
3 Winteringham DN15 68 B1
Wold Newton YO25 2 A4
York YO26 129 A5
Back La S YO19 37 F7
Back O' Newton YO41 27 E3
Back Pk St YO8 148 D5
Back Rd HU12 72 A5
Back Side YO17 6 B5
Back Southgate HU18 134 C3
Back St Alkborough DN15 82 C8
Bainton YO25 31 E7
Burton Fleming YO25 2 E3
3 Easington HU12 90 F6
East/West Stockwith DN21 116 E5
Fridaythorpe YO25 18 B6
Langtoft YO25 8 D5
Laxton DN14 65 F4
Skerne & Wansford YO25 21 A2
Skipsea YO25 23 A2
Wold Newton YO25 2 A4
Back W View 2 YO30 130 B7
Back Westgate HU18 134 B4
Backcarr La YO25 21 C5
Backhouse St YO31 156 B4
Bacon Garth La HU16 139 A5
Bad Bargain La YO31 131 A5
Baden Cl 3 HU5 140 D2
Bader Way DN21 119 B8
Badger Hill Prim Sch YO10 131 B2
Badger La
Halsham HU12 74 B5
Walden Stubbs DN6 77 A3
Badger Paddock 5 YO31 127 E2
Badger Way 1 DN20 97 E4
Badger Wood Wlk YO10 131 D3
Badgers Wood HU16 138 F8
Badminton Cl YO16 122 F6
Baffam Gdns YO8 148 B2
Baffam La YO8 148 B2
Bagby Mews 2 HU5 139 D3
Baggaby Hill YO42 29 E4
Bagsby Rd DN9 106 B3
Baildon Cl 3 YO26 129 D4
Baildon Rd DN15 150 D8
Baile Hill Terr YO1 156 B1
Bailey La Hatfield DN7 92 E6
Kingston upon Hull HU16 139 D8
Warter YO42 30 B5
Baileywood La YO43 51 F8
Bainbridge Ave HU9 142 D2
Bainbridge Dr YO8 148 C4
Bainton Cl HU17 136 D5
Bainton Gr HU6 139 E6
Bainton Rd YO25 19 E2
Bakehouse La 5 YO25 9 C3
Baker Dr DN15 83 A5
Baker St
Kingston upon Hull HU2 155 A3
York YO30 130 C7
Bakers Cl DN38 99 B5
Bakersfield DN20 98 D4
Bakersfield Dr DN14 61 F3
Bakewell Cl HU9 142 D1
Bakewell Ct DN15 150 B7
Balder Ct 2 DN33 102 E1
Baldwin Ave DN16 96 D1
Balfour Pl 14 DN40 87 B1
Balfour St
23 Gainsborough DN21 117 B1
3 Kingston upon Hull HU9 146 C8
York YO26 129 F5
Balfour Way YO32 14 A6
Balham Ave HU8 141 E6
Balk Cl HU17 45 B8
Balk La Hook DN14 149 F6
Pollington DN14 77 F7
Riston HU11 45 C4
Sproatley HU11 58 D5
Balk Mews HU5 139 D3
Balk The
Bishop Wilton YO41 16 C2
Millington YO42 29 C7
Pocklington YO42 29 A3
Ballantyne Cl HU7 141 C4
Balldon Ct HU12 72 D7
Ballhall La YO42 38 E6
Balliol Dr DN16 96 D2
Balmoral Ave
Grimsby DN34 152 A3
Kingston upon Hull HU6 140 B6
Balmoral Cl 8 YO16 122 D6
Balmoral Dr HU17 136 E1
Balmoral Rd
2 Cleethorpes DN35 103 B2
25 Hatfield DN7 92 D4
Balmoral Terr 5 YO23 130 B1

Balne Croft La DN14 78 A6
Balne Hall Rd DN14 77 F5
Balne Moor Rd DN14 77 B6
Bamford Ave HU9 142 E1
Banbury Ct 16 DN32 153 A5
Banbury Rd DN16 151 D6
Bank End Rd DN9 104 A3
Bank L Ctr The HU6 139 F6
Bank La 15 LN7 111 B4
Bank Rd YO8 148 D6
Bank Side
Kingston upon Hull HU5 140 F2
Rawcliffe DN14 64 A2
Bank St
3 Hornsea HU18 134 C4
Kingston upon Hull HU3 145 C7
Bank Terr HU18 134 C2
Bank Wood Rd WF8 76 A6
Bankfield La DN14 64 A7
Banks Cl HU12 90 F6
Bankside Cl 3 YO26 12 F1
Bannisdale 6 YO24 132 C7
Bannister Cl 3 HU13 69 F4
Bannister Dr HU9 146 C7
Bannister St HU19 75 A7
Bantock Garth HU4 144 B4
Baptist Chapel La DN40 86 F2
Baptist Pl YO16 122 D4
Bar Convent Mus*
YO24 156 A1
Bar La YO1 156 A2
Barbara Cl 3 DN33 113 E8
Barbara Gr 4 YO24 129 F3
Barbarry Rd HU12 72 B7
Barberry Ct
24 Brough HU15 68 C5
3 Kingston upon Hull
HU3 145 C5
Barbers Dr YO23 132 B4
Barbican Ct YO10 156 C1
Barbican Mews YO10 130 E3
Barbican Rd YO10 156 C1
Barbican Way 7 DN36 114 A7
Barbriggs La YO25 22 E2
Barcroft St DN35 153 B4
Barden Ct 6 YO30 126 F1
Bardney Ave DN16 151 A3
Bardney Gdns 16 DN34 102 C2
Bardney Rd 14 YO14 2 F8
Bardshaw HU6 139 F8
Barf La YO41 16 D4
Barff Cl 10 YO8 48 D1
Barff Gr 6 YO8 48 B2
Barff La YO8 48 C1
Barff View YO8 62 D7
Barfhill Cswy YO25 32 F2
Barfield Rd YO31 130 F8
Bargate DN34 152 C2
Bargate Ave DN32 152 D1
Bargate Gr 3 HU5 144 D8
Barham Rd HU9 142 B4
Bark House La DN35 153 F1
Bark St DN35 153 F1
Barker Dr YO8 148 B6
Barker La YO1 156 A2
Barkers Mill 6 HU17 137 B3
Barkhouse La DN35 153 F1
Barkhouse Wood La
WF11 61 D6
Barking Cl HU8 142 A5
Barkston Ave YO26 129 B3
Barkston Cl 3 YO26 129 A3
Barkston Gr YO26 129 A3
Barkston Rd YO26 129 A3
Barkworth Cl HU10 143 D6
Barkworth Ct 3 DN37 113 D6
Barlby Bridge CP Sch
YO8 148 D5
Barlby By-pass 2 YO8 49 B4
Barlby CP Sch YO8 49 B4
Barlby Cres YO8 148 F7
Barlby High Sch YO8 49 B5
Barlby Rd YO8 148 E6
Barleigh Croft HU9 142 B3
Barleigh Rd HU9 142 B3
Barley Cl DN20 109 A5
Barley Garth
14 Brandesburton YO25 34 B2
Burton Pidsea HU12 59 C2
Barley Gate HU17 45 A8
Barley Hall* YO1 156 B3
Barley Rise
Bridlington YO16 123 A6
Strensall YO32 14 A6
Barley View YO32 127 C8
Barleycorn Yd YO1 156 C2
Barleyholme HU17 154 C2
Barlings Ave DN16 151 A3
Barlings Cl DN21 107 D4
Barlow CE VC Prim Sch
YO8 63 C7
Barlow Comm Nature
Reserve* YO8 63 B7
Barlow Comm Rd YO8 63 B8
Barlow Rd YO8 63 B6
Barlow St YO26 129 D4
Barmby Ave YO10 133 E8
Barmby Cl 4 YO30 126 F1
Barmby Ferry Rd 1 YO8 49 F1
Barmby La DN14 52 A3
Barmby Moor CE Prim Sch
YO42 28 D4
Barmby on the Marsh Prim
Sch DN14 64 B7
Barmby Rd YO42 28 E4
Barmouth Cl 4 HU7 57 A7
Barmouth Dr 20 DN37 102 C4
Barmston Cl HU17 137 B5
Barmston La HU17 56 C8
Barmston Rd HU17 137 B5
Barmston St HU2 155 B4
Barnard Ave DN20 98 B2
Barnard Way HU12 72 D6
Barnards Dr 9 HU15 53 F1
Barnes Cl HU17 137 B4
Barnes Cres DN15 150 E8
Barnes Gn DN21 107 C4
Barnet Cl HU8 142 A5
Barnet Dr DN36 114 B8
Barnet Gn 9 DN7 92 D3
Barnetby La DN20 98 F7
Barnetby Rd
1 Kingston upon Hull
HU13 144 A3
Scunthorpe DN17 150 F1
Barnetby Sta DN38 99 B4
Barnett Pl DN35 153 B3
Barnfield Way YO23 132 A2
Barnhill La DN14 64 F7
Barnoldby Rd DN37 113 D6
Barnsdale View DN6 76 E2
Barnside DN20 108 F5
Barnsley Rd DN8 79 B2
Barnsley St HU8 141 B1
Barnstaple Rd
Kingston upon Hull HU7 141 B7
Scunthorpe DN17 150 D3
Barnston Way 11 DN15 82 B4
Baron Ave 8 DN36 114 A8
Baroness Cl 7 HU6 140 B8
Baroness Ct 4 DN34 102 C3
Baroness Rd DN34 152 A3
Barons Cres YO23 132 B2
Baronwood Cres 7
YO25 22 D1
Barr La YO32 14 D4
Barra Cl HU8 141 F6
Barraclough's La DN18 69 E2
Barrett Ave 3 YO24 129 F3
Barrick Cl 7 DN19 85 D8
Barrier Bank DN14 78 E6
Barrington Ave HU5 139 F3
Barrington Garth DN14 61 F3
Barrow Blow Wells Nature
Reserve* DN19 70 D1
Barrow Ct 3 HU3 140 D1
Barrow Haven Reedbed
Nature Reserve*
DN18 70 B2
Barrow Haven Sta
DN19 70 C2
Barrow La HU13 143 D2
Barrow Rd
Barrow upon Humber
DN19 70 E1
Barton-upon-Humber
DN18 85 A8
New Holland DN19 70 E2
Barry Ave DN34 102 C2
Barstow Ave YO10 130 F3
Bartholomew Ave
DN14 149 B5
Bartindale Rd YO14 3 A5
Bartle Garth YO1 156 C3
Bartlett Ave HU17 154 A2
Bartlett Cl 9 HU12 58 D1
Barton Cl 4 YO31 127 E3
Barton Dr HU13 143 D1
Barton La DN19 85 C8
Barton Rd DN20 98 D3
Barton St
Barrow upon Humber
DN19 85 D8
Irby DN37 112 F7
Keelby DN41 101 A4
Wyham cum Cadeby
DN36 120 F7
Barton St Peter's CE Prim
Sch DN18 69 F1
Barton-on-Humber Sta
DN18 69 F1
Bartons Garth YO8 148 B2
Bartrams HU15 68 D6
Barwic Par YO8 148 E4
Barwick Par CP Sch
YO8 148 E4
Basic Slag Rd DN16 151 E6
Basil Dr HU17 154 A1
Baslow Rd DN15 150 B6
Bassett Cl
1 Broughton DN20 97 E3
Selby YO8 148 C3
Bassett Rd 2 DN35 103 D2
Bate La DN14 78 A4
Bateson Cl YO10 131 C1
Bath St DN32 153 A5
Baths Hall The DN15 150 F7
Bathurst St 8 HU3 145 D5
Batley Cl HU9 142 C2
Battersea Cl HU8 141 F5
Battery Rd HU12 72 A4
Battery St DN40 87 C1
Battle Gn DN9 105 D7
Battleflats Way YO41 15 D2
Batty La 7 DN14 65 A7
Bawtry Cl YO8 148 D3
Bawtry Rd Hatfield DN7 92 F3
Selby YO8 148 D3
Baxter Gate HU12 72 D7
Bay Prim Sch YO16 122 E4
Bay View Ave HU18 134 C6
Bayard St DN21 117 B1
Bayle Mus* YO16 122 D4
Baylegate 6 YO16 122 D4
Baynard Ave HU16 139 A6
Bayons Ave 13 DN33 113 D8
Baysdale HU7 140 F6
Baysdale Ave YO10 131 D3
Baysdale Rd DN16 151 D1
Baysgarth House Mus*
DN18 84 F8
Baysgarth L Ctr DN18 84 F8
Baysgarth Sch DN18 84 F8
Baysgarth View DN18 84 F7
Bayswater Ct HU8 141 E5
Bayswater Pl 2 DN33 113 D8
Baytree Ave DN34 152 A2
Beach Holt La DN37 101 D2
Beacon Ave
14 Barton-upon-Humber
DN18 84 E8
Cleethorpes DN35 153 D2
Beacon Cl 5 HU13 69 F4
Beacon Ct DN35 153 D2
Beacon Hill* DN10 116 A1
Beacon Hill Rd DN10 116 A1
Beacon La YO25 21 B8
Beacon Rd
Bridlington YO16 123 A6
Millington YO42 17 B1
Beacon View YO43 40 B1
Beaconsfield HU19 74 F6
Beaconsfield Mews
YO24 129 D3
Beaconsfield St
1 Kingston upon Hull
HU5 140 D2
York YO24 129 D3
Beaconthorpe Rd
DN35 153 E3
Beadlam Mews HU5 139 E4
Beadle Garth YO23 132 B2
Beaford Ct DN17 150 C4
Beagle Cl 12 DN20 97 E4
Beagle Croft YO41 15 C1
Beagle Ridge Dr YO24 129 C1
Beagle Spinney YO41 15 C1
Beal La Beal DN14 61 D4
Cridling Stubbs WF11 61 C1
Bealey's La YO25 32 B1
Beamsley Way 18 HU7 56 F5
Bean Gdns 3 DN14 78 C8
Bean St HU3 145 C6
Beanland La YO32 14 D2
Bean's Way YO31 131 B8
Bearwood Cl HU9 142 B6
Beatty Ave 18 DN33 113 E8
Beauchamp St DN16 151 B5
Beauchamp Wlk DN16 151 B6
Beauchief Gdns DN16 151 A4
Beaufort Ave HU18 134 C2
Beaufort Cl
Kingston upon Hull HU3 145 D6
York YO10 131 B3
Beaufort Cres 5 DN35 103 B1
Beaufort St 5 DN21 117 B2
Beaulah Villas 1 DN18 84 A7
Beaulahland 2 DN18 84 A7
Beaulieu Cl 1 YO32 127 F5
Beaulieu Ct
Bridlington YO16 122 F7
5 Kingston upon Hull
HU9 142 A3
Beaumonde 5 DN36 114 A5
Beaumont Ct
Goole DN14 149 B6
3 Kingston upon Hull
HU9 146 D7
Beaumont Pl YO8 148 A2
Beautiman Ct HU6 140 A5
Beaver Rd HU17 137 B4
Beaverdyke YO30 126 F1
Beccles Cl HU8 142 B6
Beck Bank HU16 139 C6
Beck Cl 6 Elvington YO41 27 B2
Keelby DN41 101 A4
Beck Farm Mews
DN37 113 B6
Beck Garth 12 HU12 72 D7
Beck Hill
6 Barton-upon-Humber
DN18 84 F8
14 Bridlington YO16 122 E2
1 Bridlington YO15 122 E2
Beck La Appleby DN15 83 D1
5 Barrow upon Humber
DN19 85 D8
Broughton DN20 97 E3
Easington HU12 90 F6
Redbourne DN21 108 F2
Scunthorpe DN16 96 D2
Wheldrake YO19 38 A8
Beck Rd
Cottingham HU16 138 E6
North Cave HU15 53 D2
Willerby HU10 138 D1
Beck Row YO41 16 D5
Beck Side
Barmby Moor YO42 28 D3
Great Driffield YO25 124 F4
Hibaldstow DN20 108 F5
Beck St HU12 90 F6
Beck View 14 YO42 29 A3
Beck View Rd HU17 137 C4
Beck Wlk 7 DN35 103 C1
Beckdale 4 HU7 141 A6
Beckett Ave DN21 117 C1
Beckfield La YO26 129 B5
Beckfield Pl YO26 129 B4
Beckhole Cl HU3 145 A6
Beckhythe Cl DN33 102 F1
Beckingham Rd DN10 116 D2
Beckington Cl 1 HU8 142 C7
Becklands Pk Ind Est
YO43 135 C4
Becks Cl 5 YO32 127 C8
Becks La DN21 107 A3
Beckside
Beverley HU17 154 C2
4 Brough HU15 68 D6
7 Elvington YO41 27 B2
Hornsea HU18 134 C3
Rothwell LN7 111 F2
Wilberfoss YO41 27 F6
Beckside Cl
4 Humberston DN35 103 C1
Kingston upon Hull HU6 140 B7
Beckside Ct HU17 137 C3
Beckside N HU17 154 C2
Beckwith Cl YO31 131 C7
Bedale Ave
Kingston upon Hull HU9 141 E1
York YO10 131 D4
Bedale Ct YO43 135 E3
Bedale Rd
Market Weighton YO43 135 E3
Scunthorpe DN16 151 D1
Bedale Wlk YO43 135 F4
Bede Ave YO30 130 B7
Bedern YO1 156 C3
Bedford Gr YO15 122 D1
Bedford Rd
Humberston DN35 103 D1
Kingston upon Hull
HU13 143 F3
Bedford St
Grimsby DN32 153 A5
Kingston upon Hull HU8 141 A1
Bedfords Fold 6 LS25 61 A7
Beech Ave
3 Airmyn DN14 64 E4
Beverley HU17 136 F6
Bishopthorpe YO23 133 A3
3 Flamborough YO15 5 A2
Flixborough DN15 96 A7
14 Gainsborough DN21 117 B1
14 Grimsby DN33 102 E2
Gunness DN15 95 E6
Kingston upon Hull HU8 141 C2
7 Preston HU12 72 C7
York YO24 129 F3
Beech Cl
4 Broughton DN20 97 D3
Burstwick HU12 73 A6
2 Elvington YO41 27 B2
Kilham YO25 9 B3
8 Kingston upon Hull
HU3 145 C5
Market Weighton YO43 135 D4
Sproatley HU11 58 C5
Beech Cres 7 DN7 92 C6
Beech Croft
Barlby with Osgodby YO8 49 B6
Driffield YO25 125 A5
Beech Ct
Bishopthorpe YO23 133 A3
6 Pocklington YO42 29 A4
Beech Dr
Bridlington YO16 123 A6
2 North Ferriby HU14 69 A4
11 Patrington HU12 74 D1
Beech Garth DN19 85 C7
Beech Glade YO31 127 F2
Beech Gr 1 Airmyn DN14 64 E4
Burton upon Stather
DN15 82 B5
Camblesforth YO8 63 C5
2 Flamborough YO15 5 A2
Goole DN14 149 D1
Holton le Clay DN36 114 B5
Nafferton YO25 125 E8
Newland HU5 140 C3
Northfield HU13 143 C3
Selby YO8 148 C5
1 Swanland HU14 69 C7
York YO26 129 C4
Beech Hill Rd HU14 69 C7
Beech Lawn HU10 143 E6
Beech Pk YO19 49 A8
Beech Pl 5 YO32 14 A6
Beech Rd Brough HU15 68 C6
Campsall DN6 76 E1
Beech Rise HU12 72 A4
Beech Tree Ave 21 DN8 93 B7
Beech Tree Cl 3 HU17 136 F7
Beech Tree La YO8 63 C5
Beech View
Hutton Cranswick YO25 32 E6
Walkington HU17 55 C8
Beech Way
10 Cleethorpes DN36 103 B1
23 Upper Poppleton YO26 12 F1
Beechcliffe Ave 1 HU6 140 C7
Beechdale HU16 139 C5
Beeches Ave 23 DN16 96 D2
Beeches The
Great Driffield YO25 125 A4
Pocklington YO42 29 A4
Skelton YO30 126 C4
Beechfield
Kingston upon Hull HU6 140 B6
Newton-on-Ouse YO30 12 B6
Beechfield Cl YO8 48 B1
Beechfield Ct DN34 152 C2
Beechfield Dr HU10 138 C2
Beechfield Rd DN7 92 C4
Beechlands 9 YO25 124 F3
Beechway DN16 151 B3
Beechwood HU18 134 D1
Beechwood Ave
25 Grimsby DN33 102 C2
Beechwood Ave *continued*
3 Immingham DN40 87 C1
Beechwood Cl 9 DN3 92 A1
Beechwood Cres 3
DN20 97 E4
Beechwood Dr
Scawby DN20 108 E8
3 Scotter DN21 107 C3
Beechwood Glade 7
YO24 129 B1
Beechwood La 10 YO25 124 F2
Beechwood The YO25 125 A3
Beechwood Views
HU12 60 B1
Beeford CE VC Prim Sch
YO25 22 C1
Beeford Gr HU6 139 F5
Beeford Rd YO25 22 F1
Beeforth Cl YO32 127 D5
Beeley Rd DN32 153 C2
Beel's Rd DN41 101 E8
Beelsby Rd DN37 112 C5
Beesby Dr 22 DN35 103 C2
Beesby Medieval Village*
DN36 120 E7
Beesby Rd DN17 150 E1
Beeson Gr DN31 152 C5
Beeson St DN31 152 C5
Beggar Hill DN21 107 D5
Beilby St HU3 144 F4
Belcombe Way 1 YO30 130 A7
Beldevere Pk HU18 134 C6
Belfry Ct HU8 142 B6
Belgrave Cl 6 Belton DN9 94 E1
Belton DN9 105 E8
Belgrave Dr
Goole DN14 149 F5
Hornsea HU18 134 C5
Kingston upon Hull HU4 144 D5
7 North Cave HU15 53 D3
Belgrave Rd
Bridlington YO15 122 D1
1 Grimsby DN33 102 D1
Belgrave Sq 1 DN15 151 B7
Belgrave St YO31 130 C7
Belgravia 8 DN14 149 C4
Bell Cl Haxby YO32 127 C8
Kingston upon Hull HU7 141 D5
Bell Gn DN14 78 B2
Bell Hall* YO19 36 E6
Bell La Cawood YO8 48 A7
Foggathorpe YO8 51 B7
Rawcliffe DN14 64 A2
Scunthorpe DN15 151 A6
Bell Mills YO25 125 A2
Bellamy Ct HU9 146 C7
Bellasize La HU15 66 C6
Bellasize Pk HU15 66 D8
Bellbutts View 1 DN21 107 B3
Bellcroft La HU12 72 E4
Bellcroft Rd HU12 72 F5
Bellcross La 7 DN14 65 B7
Belle Vue St YO10 130 E3
Belle Vue Terr
19 Thorne/Moorends DN8 93 A8
York YO10 130 E3
Belleisle Rd 12 DN34 102 B3
Bellfarm Ave YO31 130 E8
Bellfield Ave 5 HU8 142 A5
Bellfield Dr HU10 138 D1
Bellfield Prim Sch
HU8 142 A4
Bellground La YO30 12 D4
Bellhouse Way YO24 132 B8
Bellingham Rd DN16 151 D3
Bellmans Croft YO23 132 B2
Bells Rd HU12 72 B7
Bellwin Dr DN15 82 A1
Bellwood Cres 7 DN8 93 A8
Bellwood Dr YO24 132 B8
Belmont DN36 114 A5
Belmont Cl
18 Cleethorpes DN35 103 B2
3 York YO30 127 A1
Belmont St
Kingston upon Hull HU9 146 D8
Scunthorpe DN16 151 A2
Belper Ct
17 Cleethorpes DN32 153 A5
3 Scunthorpe DN15 150 B6
Belprin Rd HU17 137 B5
Belshaw La DN9 94 D1
Belt Rd The DN21 117 C2
Beltham Gn HU16 138 F4
Belthorn Rd 1 DN17 81 F1
Belthorpe La YO42 16 E1
Belton All Saints CE Prim Sch
DN9 94 E2
Belton Cl 4 HU8 142 B5
Belton Fields DN9 94 D1
Belton Gr 7 DN33 102 D2
Belton Rd Belton DN9 95 A1
Epworth DN9 105 E7
Sandtoft DN9 94 B3
Belvedere Cl YO15 11 B4
Belvedere Cres DN14 149 B6
Belvedere Dr
Kingston upon Hull
HU11 142 D6
Scunthorpe DN17 150 E3
7 Thorne/Moorends DN8 79 B2
Belvedere Gr YO15 11 B4
Belvedere Par YO15 11 B4
Belvedere Rd
Bridlington YO15 11 B4

Belvedere Rd *continued*
Kingston upon Hull HU13 .....143 F2
Belvoir Ave 8 YO41 .....27 B2
Belvoir Rd DN35 .....103 B1
Belvoir St HU5 .....145 C8
Belwood Dr DN9 .....94 E2
Bempton Cl YO16 .....122 E6
Bempton Cliffs Nature Reserve* YO15 .....4 D4
Bempton Cres YO16 .....122 E6
Bempton Dr YO16 .....122 E6
Bempton Gdns YO16 .....122 E6
Bempton Gr
Grimsby DN32 .....153 A1
Kingston upon Hull HU5 .....144 D8
Bempton La
Bempton YO16 .....4 B1
Bridlington YO16 .....122 D8
Bempton Oval YO16 .....122 E6
Bempton Prim Sch YO15 .....4 C4
Bempton Sta YO16 .....4 C2
Bemrose Gr YO16 .....122 E5
Bemrose Way DN31 .....152 C4
Bence The YO42 .....17 C3
Benedict Ave YO8 .....148 E4
Benedict Cl 2 HU4 .....144 A2
Benedict Rd HU4 .....144 A2
Beningborough Hall & Gdns* YO30 .....12 B5
Beningbrough La YO30 .....12 D5
Benjy La YO19 .....37 E7
Bennetland La HU15 .....66 C7
Bennett Dr DN15 .....83 A4
Bennett Rd
Cleethorpes DN35 .....153 D3
Scunthorpe DN16 .....151 C3
Benningholme La
HU11 .....45 D2
Bennymoor La YO8 .....49 C4
Benson Ct LN11 .....121 C4
Bentley Ct HU3 .....145 A5
Bentley Gr HU6 .....139 F4
Bentley La DN38 .....110 E7
Bentley St DN35 .....153 E2
Berea The DN34 .....152 C1
Beresford Ave
Hornsea HU18 .....134 D2
Kingston upon Hull HU6 .....140 D4
Beresford Terr YO23 .....130 C1
Beretun Gn 11 DN18 .....84 E8
Bergen Way HU7 .....140 D6
Berkeley Dr
3 Beverley HU17 .....136 E1
32 Hedon HU12 .....72 D7
Berkeley Ind Est DN15 .....150 C8
Berkeley Jun & Inf Sch
DN15 .....150 D8
Berkeley Rd DN35 .....103 D1
Berkeley St
1 Kingston upon Hull HU3 .....145 D8
Scunthorpe DN15 .....150 F8
Berkeley Terr YO26 .....129 E5
Berkshire Cl 4 HU17 .....55 F8
Berkshire St HU8 .....141 C1
Bermondsey Dr HU5 .....144 E8
Bermuda Ave HU11 .....45 D2
Bernadette Ave HU4 .....144 B5
Berners Rd 15 DN35 .....103 D1
Berridge La DN14 .....78 A6
Berriman's La YO25 .....9 B3
Berryman Way HU13 .....144 A3
Berwick Ct 5 DN40 .....87 C1
Beside the Seaside Mus* YO16 .....122 E2
Bessacarr Ave HU10 .....138 F1
Bessemer Way DN15 .....96 D7
Bessingby Gate YO16 .....122 A2
Bessingby Gr HU9 .....142 B2
Bessingby Hill YO16 .....122 B3
Bessingby Rd YO16 .....122 C2
Bessingby Rd Ret Pk
YO16 .....122 C2
Bessingby Way YO16 .....122 C1
Bestall Rd DN32 .....153 C2
Beswick & Walton CE VC Prim Sch YO25 .....32 D3
Beswick Hall* YO25 .....32 D3
Beswick Heads YO25 .....32 C3
Beswick Rd YO25 .....32 E2
Bethell Ct 6 HU12 .....72 D7
Bethell Wlk YO25 .....125 A3
Bethlehem St DN32 .....152 D3
Bethune Ave HU4 .....144 A3
Bethune Ave W HU13 .....144 A3
Bethune Pk Prim Sch
HU4 .....144 C3
Betony Cl 4 DN15 .....96 B7
Betteras Hill Rd LS25 .....61 A8
Betula Ct HU8 .....141 E7
Betula Way DN17 .....150 C1
Between Dikes Rd YO8 .....63 F8
Between Rivers La
DN14 .....78 E7
Beverley Balk YO41 .....15 B2
Beverley Cl DN36 .....114 A5
Beverley Cres DN32 .....153 A1
Beverley Ct
11 Healing DN41 .....101 F5
Scunthorpe DN17 .....150 D3
Beverley Dr HU17 .....136 D7
Beverley Gram Sch
HU17 .....136 D2
Beverley High Sch
HU17 .....154 A4
Beverley L Ctr HU17 .....154 C2
Beverley La YO43 .....41 E2
Beverley Minst*
HU17 .....154 B2
Beverley Minst CE Prim Sch
HU17 .....136 D3
Beverley Parklands
HU17 .....154 C1
Beverley Racecourse
HU17 .....136 B4
Beverley Rd
Beeford YO25 .....22 D1
Bishop Burton HU17 .....43 B2
Great Driffield YO25 .....124 E2
Hutton Cranswick YO25 .....20 E1
Kingston upon Hull HU3 .....155 A4
Kirkburn YO25 .....124 D1
Leven HU17 .....45 A7
Market Weighton YO43 .....135 E4
Middleton YO25 .....31 D4
Newbald YO43 .....53 F8
Northfield HU13 .....143 E3
Skidby HU16 .....138 C7
South Cave HU15 .....54 A2
Watton YO25 .....32 D5
Withernwick HU11 .....46 A3
Beverley Rd Baths
HU5 .....140 D2
Beverley St DN14 .....149 C2
Beverley St Nicholas Prim Sch HU17 .....154 C2
Beverley Sta HU17 .....154 B3
Beverley Swimming Pool
HU17 .....154 B4
Bewholme Gr
4 Kingston upon Hull HU9 .....142 B1
Kingston upon Hull HU9 .....147 B8
Bewholme La
Bewholme YO25 .....35 A8
Seaton HU11 .....35 A2
Skipsea YO25 .....23 A1
Bewholme Rd YO25 .....35 C5
Bewlay St YO23 .....130 C2
Bexhill Ave HU9 .....142 E2
Bexley Ct 18 DN32 .....153 A5
Bibbill La YO42 .....39 B5
Bibury Cl HU8 .....141 B2
Bickerton Cl HU6 .....139 F7
Bickleigh Gr 1 HU8 .....142 C6
Bideford Gr HU9 .....142 E1
Bielby Dr HU17 .....137 B3
Bigby Gr DN17 .....96 C2
Bigby High Rd DN20 .....98 C1
Bigby Hill DN38 .....99 C1
Bigby Rd 16 DN20 .....98 C2
Bigby St DN20 .....98 C2
Biggin Ave HU7 .....141 C8
Biggin Hill Prim Sch
HU7 .....141 C8
Billet La DN15 .....96 C8
Billet Mill App DN16 .....151 F3
Billet Mill Rd DN16 .....151 E5
Billinghay Ct 16 DN35 .....103 C2
Billings La YO25 .....34 E5
Bilsdale Cl YO30 .....126 E2
Bilsdale Cres 3 YO16 .....122 E7
Bilsdale Gr HU9 .....146 F8
Bilsdale Rd DN16 .....151 E1
Bilton Com Prim Sch
HU11 .....142 E6
Bilton Gr HU9 .....142 B2
Bilton Rd HU11 .....142 D6
Binbrook Garth 2 HU7 .....57 A5
Binbrook Way 16 DN37 .....102 C4
Birch Ave Brigg DN20 .....98 B2
Grimsby DN34 .....152 A2
Birch Cl Beverley HU17 .....136 F6
5 Bridlington YO16 .....123 A6
East Ella HU4 .....144 B7
7 Gilberdyke HU15 .....66 D7
Northfield HU13 .....143 B3
4 Thorpe Willoughby YO8 .....48 B1
York YO32 .....127 D3
Birch Copse YO24 .....129 D2
Birch Dr HU10 .....138 E1
Birch Gr 16 DN21 .....117 B1
Birch La 13 YO32 .....13 E5
Birch Lea 3 HU17 .....55 B8
Birch Leigh HU3 .....145 C6
Birch Mews DN14 .....149 E6
Birch Tree Cl DN3 .....92 A4
Birch Way 4 DN38 .....99 B4
Bircham Cres 3 DN21 .....119 C8
Birchdale DN18 .....84 E7
Birches The
5 Haxey DN9 .....105 B2
Hornsea HU18 .....134 D2
Birchfield DN14 .....149 F6
Birchfield Rd 6 DN9 .....105 D6
Birchin Way DN31 .....152 D5
Birchin Way Ind Est
DN31 .....152 B5
Birchwood Ave HU4 .....144 A7
Birchwood Cl 2 DN8 .....79 A1
Birchwood Pk DN14 .....149 C2
Birchwood Rd DN16 .....151 B1
Birchwood View 21
DN21 .....117 C1
Bird La Hensall DN14 .....62 D2
Kellington DN14 .....61 F4
Birdcroft La 3 DN10 .....116 D3
Birdforth Mews 5 HU5 .....139 D3
Birds Wood Nature Reserve*
DN9 .....104 F3
Birdsall Ave HU5 .....139 C2
Birdsall Cl HU16 .....138 E5
Birk La YO42 .....50 D8
Birkby Gr HU9 .....142 C2
Birkdale 14 DN37 .....113 D6
Birkdale Cl HU10 .....143 B8
Birkdale Dr 8 DN40 .....87 C2
Birkdale Gr 4 YO26 .....129 B5
Birkdale Rd DN17 .....96 B2
Birkdale Way HU9 .....146 D8
Birker La
Newton on Derwent YO41 .....27 D4
Wilberfoss YO41 .....27 F6
Birkin La WF11 .....61 B4
Birkin Rd YO8 .....61 F5
Birklands Dr HU8 .....141 E4
Birnam Ct HU6 .....140 B8
Birrel St 2 DN21 .....117 A1
Birstwith Dr YO26 .....129 E4
Birt Gr DN14 .....149 B6
Bishop Alcock Rd
HU5 .....139 D3
Bishop Blunt Cl 2
HU13 .....143 F1
Bishop Burton Coll
Bishop Burton HU17 .....43 A3
Broughton DN20 .....97 E3
Bishop Burton Rd
HU17 .....43 A4
Bishop Cockin Cl 1
HU4 .....144 A1
Bishop Ct
9 Gilberdyke HU15 .....66 D8
2 Selby YO8 .....148 B6
Bishop Gurdon Cl 4
HU13 .....143 F1
Bishop Kempthorne Clo 3
HU13 .....143 F1
Bishop La HU1 .....155 C2
Bishop La Staith HU1 .....155 C2
Bishop Temple Ct
HU13 .....143 F3
Bishop Wilton CE VC Prim Sch YO42 .....16 F2
Bishop's La LN8 .....120 A7
Bishop's Wlk DN34 .....152 C2
Bishopdike Rd YO8 .....48 A6
Bishopgate St YO23 .....156 B1
Bishophill Jun YO1 .....156 A1
Bishophill Senior YO1 .....156 B1
Bishops Croft HU17 .....154 A2
Bishops Ct YO1 .....156 B1
Bishopsfields Dr YO26 .....130 A5
Bishopsway YO10 .....131 C3
Bishopthorpe Inf Sch
YO23 .....133 A4
Bishopthorpe Pal*
YO23 .....133 B4
Bishopthorpe Rd
Bishopthorpe YO23 .....133 B5
Cleethorpes DN35 .....103 C2
Bisley Gr HU7 .....141 A7
Bismarck St YO26 .....129 E5
Bittern Cl HU4 .....144 D2
Black Bank DN17 .....106 F6
Black Dike La YO26 .....24 F8
Black Fen La YO8 .....148 C8
Black Syke La DN14 .....78 E2
Black Tup La HU11 .....45 C3
Blackburn Ave
Bridlington YO15 .....122 F3
Brough HU15 .....68 C5
Blackburn La WF11 .....61 B2
Blackdykes Rd DN9 .....106 B4
Blackfriargate HU1 .....155 C1
Blackhope Cl 14 HU7 .....57 A6
Blacklee Cl 4 YO32 .....14 B8
Blackmoor Rd DN9 .....105 D2
Blacksmith Hill DN15 .....67 E3
Blacksmiths Cl 1 DN19 .....85 C7
Blacksmiths Cnr HU12 .....90 F6
Blackthorn Cl
20 Gainsborough DN21 .....117 C1
8 Newport HU15 .....52 F1
7 Scunthorpe DN15 .....96 B7
Blackthorn Ct 4 HU3 .....145 D6
Blackthorn Dr
Healing DN37 .....102 B5
York YO31 .....127 E2
Blackthorn La HU10 .....143 F7
Blackthorns The 3
DN20 .....97 D4
Blacktoft La DN14 .....66 D3
Blackwater Way 27 HU7 .....56 F6
Blackwood La YO8 .....49 F7
Blackwood Rd YO8 .....49 E8
Bladon Rd YO16 .....122 E5
Bladons Wlk HU10 .....143 C8
Blaides Staithe HU1 .....155 C2
Blake Ave DN17 .....150 E3
Blake Cl HU2 .....155 A4
Blake Ct YO19 .....38 A8
Blake St YO1 .....156 B3
Blakeley Gr YO30 .....126 F3
Blakeney Lea DN35 .....103 C1
Blakeney Pl YO10 .....130 F3
Blakeys Crossing DN14 .....65 A7
Bland La YO26 .....129 A4
Blandford Cl HU7 .....141 B6
Blands Hill LN8 .....120 A5
Blanket Row HU1 .....155 B1
Blankney Ct 13 DN15 .....83 A5
Blanshards La 1 HU15 .....53 D3
Blatchford YO30 .....130 B8
Blatchford Mews
YO30 .....130 B8
Blaycourt HU6 .....139 E6
Blaydes St HU6 .....140 C4
Blaydon Gr 1 DN34 .....102 C2
Bleaberry La YO41 .....16 B5
Bleachfield YO10 .....130 F2
Blenheim Cl 15 DN7 .....92 D3
Blenheim Ct
Rawcliffe YO30 .....126 D3
Scunthorpe DN16 .....96 D1
Blenheim Dr DN14 .....149 E6
Blenheim Pl 4 DN35 .....103 C2
Blenheim Rd
Beverley HU17 .....136 E1
Bridlington YO16 .....122 E3
5 Moorland Prison DN7 .....104 A8
Blenheim St HU5 .....145 C8
Blenkin St HU9 .....146 B7
Bleriot Way YO30 .....127 A3
Blisland Cl 13 HU7 .....56 F5
Bloom Hill Gr 16 DN8 .....79 B2
Bloom La DN15 .....82 C1
Bloom Mill App Rd
DN16 .....97 A4
Bloomfield Ave HU5 .....144 C8
Bloomhill Cl 4 DN8 .....79 B2
Bloomhill Ct DN8 .....79 B2
Bloomhill Rd DN8 .....79 A2
Bloomsbury Ct 1 HU3 .....145 D6
Bloomsbury Gdn 16
DN33 .....102 D1
Blossom Gr HU8 .....141 D8
Blossom St YO24 .....156 A1
Blossom Way 21 DN40 .....87 B1
Blossom's La HU15 .....53 C3
Blow Row DN9 .....105 E6
Blucher La HU17 .....154 C2
Blue Bridge La YO10 .....130 D2
Blue Slates Cl YO19 .....38 A8
Bluebeck Dr YO30 .....129 E8
Bluebell Cl DN15 .....151 C7
Bluebell Ct 15 DN41 .....101 F5
Blueberry Cl YO25 .....124 E2
Blueberry Ct HU4 .....144 C4
Bluestone Bottoms
HU17 .....55 A6
Bluestone Cl DN32 .....153 A4
Bluestone La DN40 .....87 B1
Blundell Ave DN35 .....153 C4
Blundell Cl HU2 .....155 A4
Blyth Cl YO8 .....148 A5
Blyth Ct DN18 .....85 A8
Blyth St 2 HU9 .....146 B7
Blyth Way DN37 .....101 E2
Blythe Wlk 1 YO16 .....122 D4
Blythorpe HU6 .....139 F8
Blyton CE Sch DN21 .....117 F6
Blyton Rd
Gainsborough DN21 .....117 B2
Laughton DN21 .....117 E8
Boardman La 6 YO25 .....34 B2
Boardman Pk 7 YO25 .....34 B2
Boatcliffe Rd YO14 .....3 D7
Boating Dyke Way 12
DN8 .....93 A8
Boatswain Croft HU1 .....155 B1
Bodiam Way DN32 .....152 F4
Bodmin Cl DN17 .....150 D4
Bodmin Rd HU7 .....140 E8
Bog La YO24 .....132 B6
Boggle La HU11 .....58 D5
Bolam La YO16 .....4 C2
Boldron Mews 7 HU5 .....139 D3
Bolingbroke Rd
Cleethorpes DN35 .....103 D2
Scunthorpe DN17 .....96 C2
Bolsover Rd DN15 .....150 B6
Bolt The 3 YO16 .....122 D4
Boltby Mews HU5 .....139 E3
Boltby Rd YO30 .....126 F2
Bolton La
Bishop Wilton YO42 .....16 E1
Wilberfoss YO41 .....28 A5
Bomber Cty Aviation Mus*
DN21 .....119 D1
Bon Accord Rd HU13 .....143 E1
Bonby Gr
11 Grimsby DN33 .....102 D2
Scunthorpe DN17 .....150 F1
Bonby La YO8 .....37 E2
Bonby Rd DN20 .....84 C1
Bond St Hedon HU12 .....72 D7
Kingston upon Hull HU1 .....155 B3
Bondane HU6 .....139 E7
Bondgate YO8 .....148 B7
Bondville Model Village*
YO15 .....123 B6
Bondyke Cl HU16 .....138 E6
Bonington Ct 7 YO26 .....129 E4
Bonnyhale Rd DN17 .....94 E6
Bontoft Ave HU5 .....139 E1
Booth Ferry Rd DN14 .....64 F6
Booth Nooking La
DN15 .....68 A3
Bootham YO30 .....156 A3
Bootham Bar* YO31 .....156 B3
Bootham Cl 1 DN7 .....92 D4
Bootham Cres
Stainforth DN7 .....92 C6
York YO30 .....156 A4
Bootham La DN7 .....92 D5
Bootham Pk Ct YO31 .....156 B4
Bootham Pk Hospl
YO31 .....156 B4
Bootham Rd 12 DN7 .....92 C6
Bootham Row YO31 .....156 B3
Bootham Sch YO31 .....156 A3
Bootham Sq YO31 .....156 B3
Bootham Terr YO30 .....156 A3
Boothferry Prim Sch
DN14 .....149 B4
Boothferry Rd HU13 .....143 B2
Boothferry Rd Ave 14
DN14 .....65 B7
Boothgate DN14 .....65 A6
Boothgate Cl DN14 .....65 A6
Boothgate Dr DN14 .....65 A6
Boothwood Rd YO30 .....126 E2
Booty La DN14 .....76 F7
Bore Tree Baulk YO19 .....26 D6
Borman's La 3 DN36 .....114 B1
Borodales HU12 .....72 C7
Borough Rd YO16 .....122 C3
Boroughbridge Rd
YO26 .....129 D5
Borrowdale HU7 .....140 F6
Borrowdale Dr YO30 .....126 F1
Borthwick Cl 3 HU7 .....57 A6
Borwick Dr HU17 .....137 C4
Bos App Rd DN16 .....151 F3
Bossington Cl 10 HU7 .....57 A5
Boston Cl 6 DN15 .....83 A5
Boston Ct 20 HU7 .....56 F5
Bosville Wlk YO16 .....122 B4
Bosworth Cl 16 DN7 .....92 D3
Botany Bay DN3 .....92 B4
Botany Bay La DN3 .....92 B4
Bothwell Gr HU9 .....147 D8
Bottesford Ave DN16 .....151 B1
Bottesford Inf Sch
DN16 .....96 D2
Bottesford Jun Sch
DN16 .....96 D2
Bottesford La DN16 .....151 B1
Bottlings The 10 DN20 .....98 C2
Boughton Ave DN15 .....150 F8
Boulevard HU3 .....145 B5
Boulevard Ave DN31 .....152 B4
Boulevard Gdns DN31 .....152 B4
Boulevard Way DN31 .....152 B3
Boulevard Wlk DN31 .....152 B4
Boulsworth Ave HU6 .....140 C7
Boulton Gr HU9 .....141 E2
Boundary Rd
Bridlington YO15 .....122 C1
Grimsby DN33 .....113 E7
Bourn Mill Balk Rd
DN14 .....78 B8
Bourne St HU2 .....155 B3
Bournemouth St HU5 .....140 E2
Bournville DN14 .....149 C5
Bouthwaite Dr 13 YO26 .....129 E4
Bovill Cl DN31 .....152 C3
Bow Rd HU15 .....68 E6
Bow St YO15 .....122 D1
Bowers Ave DN34 .....152 B3
Bowes Ave YO31 .....130 E5
Bowes Wlk HU5 .....139 E3
Bowfield Cl 9 DN37 .....102 B4
Bowlalley La HU1 .....155 B2
Bowland La YO42 .....38 E2
Bowland Way YO30 .....127 A1
Bowling Gn Ct YO31 .....130 D8
Bowling Gn La
4 Crowle DN17 .....94 D8
Grimsby DN32 .....152 E3
9 Hunmanby YO14 .....2 F8
York YO31 .....156 C4
Bowling Gn Rd 4 DN21 .....117 A1
Bowling La DN35 .....153 E2
Bowman Way 26 DN40 .....87 B1
Bowmandale DN18 .....84 E8
Bowmandale Prim Sch
DN18 .....84 E7
Bowmont Way HU17 .....56 F6
Bowness Dr YO30 .....126 E1
Bownhill La HU12 .....59 A2
Bowthorpe La YO8 .....50 B4
Bowyers Cl YO23 .....132 C4
Boyes La HU12 .....73 C4
Boynton Ave YO16 .....122 B4
Boynton Cres 4 DN15 .....83 A5
Boynton Garth YO25 .....124 D3
Boynton La DN14 .....64 A1
Boynton Prim Sch
YO16 .....10 E7
Boynton St 1 HU3 .....145 C4
Brabbs Ave 2 DN7 .....92 E4
Bracken Cl
Gainsborough DN21 .....117 A2
York YO32 .....127 F4
Bracken Heen Cl 4 DN7 .....92 D4
Bracken Hill
Skirlaugh HU11 .....45 E2
2 York YO10 .....131 C3
Bracken La YO25 .....32 A5
Bracken Pk 20 DN33 .....113 E8
Bracken Pl 4 DN37 .....102 B3
Bracken Rd
Great Driffield YO25 .....124 D3
York YO24 .....132 F7
Brackendale Cl 1 HU7 .....141 B4
Brackenhill Ave YO8 .....148 A4
Brackenhill La YO8 .....148 A3
Brackenhill Rd DN9 .....105 E2
Brackenhills YO26 .....12 F1
Brackenholmes Rd
DN15 .....83 A2
Brackenwoods HU20 .....55 A4
Brackley Cl HU8 .....141 B2
Bracon DN9 .....94 F2
Bracon Cl DN9 .....94 E2
Bradford Ave
Cleethorpes DN35 .....103 C2
Kingston upon Hull HU9 .....142 E2
Bradford Rd 20 DN40 .....87 B1
Bradgate Pk 30 HU7 .....56 F5
Bradley & Dixon Woods Nature Reserve*
DN37 .....113 C8

Bradley Cres YO23 ......24 D6
Bradley Dr YO24 ....132 C8
Bradley La YO23 ....24 C5
Bradley Rd DN37 ....102 C1
Bradley St DN32 ....152 E4
Bradman Ct 3 DN32 ....153 A5
Bradwell Cl 3 DN18 ......84 E8
Braemar Ave HU6 ......140 B6
Braemar Ct YO25 ....34 C8
Braemar Rd DN35 ....103 C2
Braeside Gdns YO24 ....129 E3
Braeton La 5 DN33 .....113 F8
Braid Hill Way HU7 ......57 B5
Braids Wlk HU10 ....143 B8
Brailsford Cres YO30 ...130 A8
Braithegayte YO19 ....37 F8
Braithwaite La DN7 ......92 A7
Bramar Rd 26 DN7 ....92 D4
Bramble Dene YO24 ....132 D7
Bramble Garth 4 HU17 .136 F7
Bramble Hill HU17 .....136 E1
Bramble Way
24 Brigg DN20 ....98 B2
15 Humberston DN35 .....103 C1
Brambles 8 YO8 ....48 B1
Brambles The 2 DN19 ...85 C8
Bramhall St DN35 ....153 C3
Bramham Ave YO26 ....129 A3
Bramham Gr YO26 .....129 A3
Bramham Rd YO26 .....129 A2
Bramley Ave YO8 ....49 B5
Bramley Cl DN18 ....69 F1
Bramley Cres 8 DN16 ....96 D1
Bramley Ct 16 DN21 ....117 C1
Bramley Garth YO31 ....131 B6
Bramley Gr 6 DN21 .....107 C3
Brampton Way DN35 ....103 B2
Bramwith La DN7 ....92 A6
Brandesburton Hospl
YO25 ....34 B2
Brandesburton Prim Sch
YO25 ....34 B2
Brandesburton St
HU3 ....145 B7
Brandon Ct 4 HU8 .....141 C1
Brandon Gr YO32 ....128 E3
Brandon Rd DN15 ......150 D6
Brandon Way 24 HU7 .....56 F6
Brandsby Gr
Kingston upon Hull HU9 ...142 E3
York YO31 ....127 E2
Brankwell Cres 21 DN17 ..96 C2
Bransdale Gr HU9 ......146 F8
Bransdale Rd
Bridlington YO16 ....122 E7
Scunthorpe DN16 ....151 D1
Bransholme Dr YO30 ....127 A2
Bransholme Rd HU7 .....57 B5
Brant Rd DN15 ....150 E6
Brantingham Cl 5
HU16 ....138 E6
Brantingham Rd HU15 ...68 C7
Brantingham Wlk
HU5 ....139 C2
Branton Pl YO26 ....129 A3
Brats La LN8 ....120 B5
Bratt La YO42 ....29 E3
Bravener Ct YO30 ....12 B6
Bray Cl 11 DN33 ....102 D1
Bray Gate YO42 ....16 E2
Bray Rd YO10 ....133 F8
Brayton CE VC Sch
YO8 ....148 A2
Brayton Coll YO8 ....148 A3
Brayton Com Jun Sch
YO8 ....148 A2
Brayton Junc YO8 ......148 C1
Brayton La YO8 ....148 B1
Brazil St HU9 ....146 C8
Breamer La HU11 ....35 A2
Breary Cl YO24 ....129 F1
Breck La HU15 ....53 B3
Brecks La
Kirk Sandall DN3 ....92 A2
Strensall YO32 ....14 B7
York YO32 ....127 F4
Brecksfield YO30 ....126 C5
Breckstreet La YO42 ....39 C3
Brecon Dr 22 HU7 ....56 F6
Brecon St HU8 ....141 B1
Breeze La YO25 ....22 D1
Breezemount Ct 4 DN7 ..92 C6
Breighton Rd
Bubwith YO8 ....50 D6
Wressle YO8 ....50 C3
Bremerhaven Way 24
DN33 ....102 C2
Brendon Ave HU8 ......141 B3
Brent Ave HU8 ....142 B6
Brentwood Cl HU15 ......68 B6
Brentwood Cres YO10 ..131 C2
Brereton Ave DN35 .....153 C4
Brereton Cl HU17 ....136 E6
Bretel Wlk YO16 ....122 B4
Bretherdale HU7 ....140 F6
Brethergate DN9 ....105 B2
Brett St YO16 ....122 C3
Bretton Ave DN14 ......149 F5
Bretton Cl 5 DN7 ....92 D3
Brevere Rd HU12 ....72 D7
Brewery Gdns DN17 .....94 D8
Brewery Rd DN17 ....94 D8
Brewster Ave 17 DN40 ...87 C1
Breydon Ct 4 DN15 ......82 B4
Brian Ave
Cleethorpes DN35 ....103 B2
Scunthorpe DN16 ....151 C1
Waltham DN37 ....113 D6
Briar Ave YO26 ....129 B4
Briar Cl 4 Newport HU15 ..52 F1
South Killingholme DN40 ....86 F3
Briar Cliffe YO8 ....148 A3
Briar Dr YO31 ....127 F2
Briar Garth YO25 ....124 D3
Briar La
4 Grimsby DN33 ....113 D8
Healing DN41 ....101 F5
Briar Way DN15 ....96 B7
Briarfield Rd HU5 ....139 F2
Briars La DN7 ....92 C7
Briars The HU13 ....143 E3
Briarsfield YO42 ....28 D4
Briarwood Cl YO8 ....61 F7
Brick Dike La HU20 ......54 C5
Brick Kiln Balk YO16 ....122 A1
Brick Kiln La YO8 ....62 D6
Brick La DN40 ....86 E5
Brick Lands La YO8 ......62 F4
Brick Rd HU12 ....88 F6
Brickenhole La DN10 ...116 C3
Brickhill La YO8 ....63 F4
Bricknell Ave HU5 ......139 E3
Bricknell Prim Sch
HU5 ....139 F2
Brickyard La
Melton HU14 ....68 F4
Walkeringham DN10 ......116 B3
Wrawby DN20 ....98 C3
Bridge Cl Haxby YO32 ...127 C7
Kingston upon Hull HU9 ...146 D6
Bridge Cres DN14 ....64 C8
Bridge Ct YO8 ....148 D6
Bridge Gdns DN31 ......152 A5
Bridge Hill DN7 ....92 C6
Bridge La Cadney DN20 ..109 C6
5 Great Driffield YO25 ...124 F4
Horkstow DN18 ....83 F5
Pollington DN14 ....77 F6
Rawcliffe DN14 ....79 B8
York YO30 ....156 B4
Bridge Rd
Airmyn DN14 ....149 A8
Bishopthorpe YO23 ......132 F3
Broughton DN20 ....97 F5
South Cave HU15 ....53 F1
Bridge St
7 Bridlington YO15 ......122 E2
10 Brigg DN20 ....98 B2
Goole DN14 ....149 C3
Great Driffield YO25 ......124 E4
Pocklington YO42 ....29 A4
Thorne/Moorends DN8 .....93 A8
York YO1 ....156 B2
Bridgegate DN14 ....65 A7
Bridgegate Dr HU9 .....146 C6
Bridges Ct YO8 ....148 D6
Bridges La YO42 ....38 E4
Bridges Rd DN17 ....150 E3
Bridges The DN18 ....84 F8
Bridgeview Specl Sch
HU13 ....143 D1
Bridgewater Rd DN17 ..150 D4
Bridle Way 1 YO26 .....129 A3
Bridle Wlk YO8 ....148 C4
Bridles The
9 Goxhill DN19 ....86 A8
Kingston upon Hull HU3 ...144 F2
Bridlington & District Hospl
YO16 ....122 B3
Bridlington Ave HU2 ....155 B4
Bridlington Balk YO25 ...34 A8
Bridlington Bay Rd
YO16 ....10 E4
Bridlington Harbour Heritage
Mus* YO15 ....122 F2
Bridlington Leisure World
YO15 ....122 F2
Bridlington Rd
Barmston YO25 ....22 F6
Brandesburton YO25 ......34 C3
Flamborough YO15 ....4 F1
Hunmanby YO14 ....3 A7
Sledmere YO25 ....7 C4
1 Stamford Bridge YO41 ...15 D2
Ulrome YO25 ....23 A2
Wold Newton YO25 ....2 A4
Bridlington Sch YO16 ....122 C3
Bridlington Sports Ctr
YO16 ....122 B4
Bridlington St YO14 ......2 F8
Bridlington Sta YO15 ....122 D2
Bridport Cl HU7 ....141 C7
Bridport Wlk DN17 .....150 C4
Brier La YO8 ....64 A4
Briergate YO32 ....127 C7
Brierholme Carr Rd
DN7 ....92 F5
Brierholme Cl DN7 ......92 F5
Brierholme Ings Rd
DN7 ....92 F5
Brierley Cl
10 Howden DN14 ....65 A7
Snaith DN14 ....78 C8
Brigg Dr HU13 ....143 F3
Brigg Farm Ct YO8 ....63 D5
Brigg La YO8 ....63 D5
Brigg Prep Sch DN20 .....98 C1
Brigg Prim Sch DN20 ....98 C2
Brigg Rd
Barton-upon-Humber
DN18 ....84 E5
Broughton DN20 ....97 F3
Cadney DN20 ....109 C7
Grasby LN7 ....111 A6
Hibaldstow DN20 ....108 F6
Messingham DN17 ....107 D7
Brigg Rd *continued*
North Kelsey LN7 ....110 A5
Scunthorpe DN15 ....151 C7
South Kelsey LN7 ....110 A1
Wrawby DN20 ....98 D3
Brigg Sta DN20 ....98 C1
Briggate Dr DN17 ......107 D7
Briggs St YO31 ....130 C7
Brigham Ct HU17 ....154 B4
Brigham Gr HU9 ....142 B1
Brigham La
Brigham YO25 ....33 E8
Foston YO25 ....21 E1
Brighowgate DN34 .....152 D2
Bright Cres 7 YO15 .....122 F3
Bright St
Kingston upon Hull HU8 ...146 B8
York YO26 ....129 F5
Bright Wlk YO8 ....148 B6
Brighton St HU3 ....145 A3
Brigsley Rd DN37 ......113 D6
Brimington Rd HU10 ...138 F2
Brimley HU17 ....136 C5
Brind La DN14 ....50 F2
Brindlegate 4 YO42 .....29 A4
Brindley St HU9 ....141 E2
Brindleys La DN14 ....50 F3
Brinkworth Terr 1
YO10 ....130 E3
Brisbane St HU3 ....145 D5
Bristol Rd
Kingston upon Hull HU5 ...144 C8
Scunthorpe DN17 ....150 C5
Britannia Cres 7 DN34 ..102 B3
Britannia Ct 10 YO16 ....122 F2
Britannia Gdns 7 HU5 ..140 E2
Britannia Rd DN14 .....149 A2
Britannia Way DN14 ....149 B3
Britton Cl DN17 ....81 D3
Brixham Ct
5 Kingston upon Hull
HU3 ....145 A5
Waltham DN33 ....113 E7
Brixton Cl HU8 ....141 E5
Broach La Heck DN14 ....62 D1
Kellington DN14 ....61 F3
Broach Rd Heck DN14 ....77 D8
Hensall DN14 ....62 C1
Broad Acres YO32 ......127 C7
Broad Balk YO17 ....6 A5
Broad Highway YO19 ....37 F8
Broad La
Appleton Roebuck YO23 ....36 A6
6 Beal DN14 ....61 D4
Catton YO41 ....27 C7
Cawood YO8 ....48 A6
Gilberdyke HU15 ....66 C8
Howden DN14 ....65 B6
Rufforth YO23 ....129 A2
Sykehouse DN14 ....78 B4
Wistow YO8 ....48 A5
Broad La Cl 5 HU16 ....139 B7
Broad Manor YO42 ......29 A3
Broad Oak
Kingston upon Hull
HU11 ....142 D6
Sutton-on-the-Forest
YO61 ....13 D8
Broad Oak La 18 YO32 ....13 E5
Broadacre Pk 1 HU15 ....68 D5
Broadacre Prim Sch
HU7 ....56 F6
Broadacres
Carlton DN14 ....63 D3
Keyingham HU12 ....73 D4
Broadacres Ave DN14 ...63 D3
Broadacres Garth
DN14 ....63 D3
Broadbent Gate Rd
DN8 ....79 B1
Broadgate HU17 ....136 B1
Broadland Dr 4 HU9 ...142 A3
Broadlands YO19 ....38 A8
Broadlands Cl 33 DN7 ...92 D4
Broadley Ave HU10 .....143 D6
Broadley Cl 6 HU9 ......146 C7
Broadley Croft 3 HU15 ..68 D5
Broadley Way HU15 ......68 D5
Broadmanor
North Duffield YO8 ....50 A7
Pocklington YO42 ....29 A3
Broadstairs Cl 1 HU8 ...141 E7
Broadstone Cl HU7 .....141 C6
Broadstone Way YO30 ..126 E3
Broadwater Dr 34 DN7 ...92 D4
Broadwaters 1 HU7 ......56 E5
Broadway Goole DN14 ...149 D4
5 Grimsby DN34 ....102 B2
Hatfield DN7 ....92 C3
Hornsea HU18 ....134 D4
7 Keelby DN41 ....101 A5
Scunthorpe DN16 ....151 A2
York YO10 ....133 E8
Broadway Dr 9 HU9 ....142 A3
Broadway Gr 3 YO10 ...133 E8
Broadway Nook DN7 .....92 C3
Broadway The 8 HU9 ...142 A3
Broadway W YO10 ......133 D8
Brock Cl 11 DN33 ....102 E1
Brockadale Nature Reserve*
WF8 ....76 B4
Brockenhurst Ave
HU16 ....139 D6
Brockenhurst Rd 7 DN7 ..92 E4
Brockfield Pk Dr YO31 ..127 F2
Brockfield Rd YO31 .....127 E2
Brockle Bank Ct 9 HU12 .58 C1
Brocklesby Cl 5 HU13 ..144 A3
Brocklesby Junc
DN39 ....100 B8
Brocklesby Pk Sch
DN41 ....100 E4
Brocklesby Pl 11 DN34 ..102 C2
Brocklesby Rd
10 Grimsby DN34 ....102 C2
Scunthorpe DN17 ....150 F1
Ulceby DN39 ....100 B8
Brockley Cl HU8 ....141 E6
Brockton Cl HU3 ....144 F5
Broc-o-bank 1 DN6 .....76 E2
Bromley St
Kingston upon Hull HU2 ...155 B4
2 York YO26 ....129 F5
Brompton Cl HU5 ....139 E2
Brompton Ct 4 HU3 ....140 D1
Brompton Rd YO30 .....130 A7
Bromwich Rd HU10 .....143 F8
Bronte Ct HU6 ....140 C7
Bronte Wlk YO16 ....122 B4
Bronzegarth DN32 ......153 B1
Brook La DN20 ....98 A1
Brook St
Great Driffield YO25 ......124 F4
Hemswell DN21 ....119 A2
Kingston upon Hull HU2 ...155 A3
Selby YO8 ....148 C4
York YO31 ....156 B4
Brookdale Rd DN17 .....150 D2
Brooke Dr HU18 ....134 C2
Brooke St DN8 ....93 A8
Brookes Cl DN21 ....108 B1
Brookfield Cl
Carnaby YO16 ....10 E4
1 Kingston upon Hull HU7 ..56 F5
8 Thorne/Moorends DN8 ...93 A8
Brookfield Rd DN33 .....102 D1
Brookland Rd YO16 .....122 C4
Brooklands
2 Broughton DN20 ....97 E3
Kingston upon Hull HU7 ...141 C5
York YO10 ....131 D4
Brooklands Ave
Broughton DN20 ....97 D4
Cleethorpes DN35 ....103 D3
Brooklands Cl HU17 ....137 A6
Brooklands Pk HU16 ....139 A5
Brooklands Rd HU5 ....144 E8
Brooklyn Dr DN36 ......114 D8
Brooklyn St HU5 ....140 D3
Brookside 2 HU15 ....68 D6
Brookside Cl YO42 ....28 D3
Broom Gr DN16 ....151 B4
Broome Cl YO32 ....127 F5
Broome Way YO32 ......128 A5
Broomfield Way YO25 ...23 A6
Broomfleet Carr La
HU15 ....67 B7
Broomfleet Sta HU15 .....67 B6
Broomhead Cl 5 HU7 ...141 E7
Broomhill Cl 23 WF11 ....61 A2
Broomhill Cres 25 WF11 ..61 A2
Broomhill Dr 26 WF11 ....61 A2
Broomhill Gr 19 WF11 ....61 A2
Broomhill Pl 22 WF11 ....61 A2
Broomhill Sq 24 WF11 ....61 A2
Broomhill Wlk 21 WF11 ..61 A2
Broompark Rd DN14 ....149 E6
Broomston La DN9 .....104 F1
Brosley Ave DN3 ....92 A4
Brough Prim Sch HU15 ...68 C6
Brough Rd HU15 ....54 A1
Brough St DN14 ....149 D5
Brough Sta HU15 ....68 B5
Brougham Cl YO30 .....129 F8
Brougham St HU3 ......144 F7
Broughton Cl 3 HU9 ....142 A3
Broughton Inf Sch
DN20 ....97 E3
Broughton Jun Sch
DN20 ....97 E3
Broughton Way YO10 ...131 B4
Brow La Kilpin DN14 .....65 E7
Snaith DN14 ....78 B8
Brown Cow Rd YO8 ......63 C8
Brown Moor 22 YO41 .....15 D2
Brown St DN31 ....152 F7
Browney Croft YO10 ....156 C1
Browning Cl
3 Kingston upon Hull
HU3 ....145 D8
Scunthorpe DN17 ....150 E2
Browning Rd 20 YO42 ....29 A3
Brownlow St YO31 .....156 C4
Brownmoor La YO61 .....13 B8
Browns La 15 DN8 ....93 A8
Browns Orch DN32 .....152 D2
Bruce Cl 6 DN20 ....97 D3
Bruce St DN15 ....150 F7
Brucella Gr 12 HU3 .....145 A4
Brumby Comm La
DN17 ....150 C3
Brumby Comm Nature
Reserve* DN17 ....150 C3
Brumby Comp Sch
DN16 ....151 B5
Brumby Hall* DN17 .....150 F5
Brumby Hospl DN16 .....151 C4
Brumby House Dr
DN16 ....151 A4
Brumby Jun Sch
DN16 ....151 B4
Brumby Wood La
DN15 ....150 D6
Brumby's Terr 4 HU9 ...146 D7
Brumfield Ct HU17 .....154 C4
Brunel Cl
Grimsby DN32 ....152 F1
4 Scunthorpe DN16 ......96 D2
Brunel Ct 12 YO26 ......129 F5
Brunslow Cl HU3 ....144 E5
Brunswick Ave HU2 .....155 A4
Brunswick Cl 2 YO32 ....14 C8
Brunswick Gr 5 HU13 ..143 E2
Brunswick St YO23 .....130 B1
Brunton Way DN36 .....114 A7
Bryan Mere 3 HU17 ......43 A2
Bryony Ct YO8 ....148 B2
Bryson Cl DN8 ....79 B1
Bubwith Prim Sch YO8 ..50 D7
Buccaneer Way 16 HU15 ..68 C5
Buck Beck Way 12
DN36 ....103 B1
Buckfast Ct DN17 ......150 D4
Buckingham Ave DN15 ..96 C7
Buckingham Ct YO1 ....156 A1
Buckingham Gr 17
DN33 ....102 D1
Buckingham Prim Sch
HU8 ....141 C1
Buckingham St
5 Kingston upon Hull
HU8 ....141 C1
York YO1 ....156 B1
Buckingham St N
DN15 ....150 F8
Buckingham St S
DN15 ....150 F8
Buckingham Terr YO1 ..156 B2
Buckland Cl 3 HU8 .....142 C7
Buckle Cl YO8 ....50 A8
Buckle Ct YO8 ....148 B7
Buckrose Gr YO16 ......122 C3
Buckton Gate YO15 ....4 C3
Buddleia Cl DN41 ....101 F5
Bude Cl 2 DN36 ....114 A8
Bude Pk Prim Sch HU7 ..56 F5
Bude Rd HU7 ....140 F8
Budworth Pk 4 HU7 ......56 E5
Bugthorpe La YO41 ......16 D5
Bugthorpe La Town E
YO41 ....16 E5
Bull Alley La DN14 ....63 B3
Bull Balk YO41 ....27 E4
Bull Bank LN11 ....121 F7
Bull La Everingham YO42 ..40 C4
Huby YO61 ....13 B7
York YO10 ....130 F3
Bull Moor La YO60 ....15 A8
Bull Moor Rd DN7 ....93 A4
Bull Pasture 14 HU15 .....53 F1
Bull Ring La 11 DN31 ....152 D3
Buller St Grimsby DN32 ..153 A3
Selby YO8 ....148 B6
Bullfinch La 5 DN35 ....103 C1
Bullivant Rd DN7 ....92 E4
Bulmer La YO43 ....51 E8
Bulwick Ave DN33 ......113 E8
Bunkers Hill DN21 ......119 B1
Bunkers Hill Cl 11 DN36 .114 D4
Bunting Cl YO25 ....125 A5
Burbage Ave HU8 ......141 C4
Burcom Ave 7 DN36 ....114 D8
Burcott Garth HU4 .....144 B3
Burdale Cl
Great Driffield YO25 ......124 D3
Kingston upon Hull HU9 ...142 B3
Burden Cl HU17 ....154 C4
Burden Rd HU17 ....154 C4
Burden Rd Adult Ed Ctr
HU17 ....154 B5
Burden St HU1 ....155 A2
Burdike Ave YO30 ......130 A8
Burdock Rd DN16 ....96 E2
Burgar Rd DN8 ....93 A7
Burgate
4 Barton-upon-Humber
DN18 ....84 F8
North Newbald YO43 ......53 F7
Burgess Ct HU17 ....154 B4
Burgess Rd DN20 ....98 C2
Burgess Wlk YO24 .....132 C8
Burghley Cl LN7 ....111 A3
Burghley Rd DN16 ......151 D4
Burgon Cres DN15 ....83 B5
Burke St DN15 ....151 A8
Burke St N DN15 ....151 A8
Burlands La YO26 ....24 F7
Burleigh St HU8 ....146 C8
Burley Ave 18 DN35 .....103 C2
Burlington Ave YO10 ...130 F4
Burlington Cres DN14 ..149 D4
Burlington Gdns YO16 ..122 D3
Burlington Inf Sch
YO16 ....122 D5
Burlington Jun Sch
YO16 ....122 C5
Burlington Rd HU8 .....141 D5
Burlyn Rd 3 YO14 ....3 A8
Burma Dr HU9 ....147 B8
Burma Rd DN16 ....151 F6
Burn Est YO32 ....127 E4
Burn Hall Cl YO8 ....62 D7
Burn La YO8 ....62 D6
Burn Rd DN15 ....150 C7
Burnaby Cl HU17 ....136 E6
Burnbutts La YO25 ....32 C7
Burnby Cl HU5 ....139 C2
Burnby Hall Gdns*
YO42 ....29 A3
Burnby La YO42 ....29 A3

Burnet Dr 12 DN16 96 E2
Burnett's Yd LN7 111 C4
Burney Cl HU17 154 A4
Burnham Ave 4 HU12 73 A6
Burnham La DN39 85 E4
Burnham Rd
Barton-upon-Humber DN18 85 A6
Epworth DN9 105 E6
Kingston upon Hull HU4 144 B3
Owston Ferry DN9 106 A3
Scunthorpe DN15 150 D6
Burnham Reach 26 DN35 103 C1
Burnham Sq DN9 106 A3
Burnholme Ave YO31 131 B6
Burnholme Com Coll YO31 131 A5
Burnholme Dr YO31 131 A6
Burnholme Gr YO31 131 A5
Burniston Gr YO10 131 A4
Burniston Rd HU5 139 E2
Burns Cl 2 YO42 28 F4
Burns Ct YO24 132 B7
Burns Gr 31 DN33 102 D2
Burns St DN21 117 A1
Burnsall Dr YO26 129 E4
Burnsalls Rd 5 HU12 72 C7
Burnside DN20 97 D3
Burrells Cl 11 DN9 105 D2
Burrill Ave YO30 130 B8
Burrill Dr 13 YO32 13 D5
Burrill La HU15 68 B8
Burrill Mews 2 HU5 139 E3
Burringham Rd DN17 150 B1
Burrs The HU15 68 B5
Bursall Sq HU12 89 C8
Bursar Prim Sch DN35 153 E2
Bursar St DN35 153 E2
Bursea La YO43 52 A5
Burslem St HU2 155 A4
Burstall Hill YO16 122 B5
Burstall La HU12 90 C5
Burstall Wlk YO16 122 B5
Burstwick Com Prim Sch HU12 73 B6
Burton Agnes Balk YO25 9 F5
Burton Agnes CE VC Prim Sch YO25 10 A1
Burton Agnes Hall & Gdns* YO25 10 A2
Burton Agnes Hall* YO25 10 A2
Burton Ave YO30 130 B7
Burton Comm La LS25 61 A6
Burton Constable Hall* HU11 58 C7
Burton Ct YO30 156 A4
Burton Fields Cl 12 YO41 15 D2
Burton Fields Rd 4 YO41 15 D2
Burton Fleming Rd
Rudston YO25 9 F8
Wold Newton YO25 2 B3
Burton Gates HU17 55 B8
Burton Gn YO30 130 B8
Burton Gn Prim Sch YO30 130 B8
Burton La HU18 134 C2
Burton Pidsea Prim Sch HU12 59 D2
Burton Rd
Beverley HU17 136 C6
Flixborough DN15 82 B2
Hornsea HU18 134 D4
Kilham YO25 9 C3
Kingston upon Hull HU16 138 F5
Roos HU12 59 F2
Burton Stone La YO30 156 A4
Burton upon Stather Prim Sch DN15 82 B4
Burtree Ave YO30 126 B4
Burwell Dr DN33 102 D2
Bush Cl HU4 144 D3
Bushey Pk HU7 56 F5
Bushfield Rd DN16 151 B5
Bushfield Rd Inf Sch DN16 151 A5
Butcher La DN14 77 A6
Butcher Row HU17 154 A3
Butcher Terr YO23 130 C1
Butcher's La
Burton Fleming YO25 2 E3
Withernwick HU11 46 D3
Butchers Row HU11 45 A1
Butforth La DN19 85 E8
Butler Pl DN35 153 B3
Butlers La 23 YO15 5 A2
Butt Balk YO25 9 E1
Butt Fields La DN14 62 F1
Butt Hedge YO26 24 A5
Butt Hill 22 Haxby YO32 13 D5
Leconfield HU17 43 D6
Butt Hills* Riston HU11 45 C5
Routh HU17 44 F5
Wold Newton YO25 2 A3
Butt La Beverley HU17 154 A1
Laceby DN37 101 F2
North Cave HU15 53 E3
Nunburnholme YO42 29 E3
Snaith DN14 78 C8
Thwing YO25 9 A8
Tickton HU17 137 F8
Butt La *continued*
Warter YO42 30 A5
Wold Newton YO25 2 A3
Buttacre La YO23 24 D2
Butter Mkt
10 Caistor LN7 111 B4
8 Snaith DN14 63 C1
Butterbur Dr DN14 149 E7
Buttercrambe Rd YO41 15 C3
Buttercross Cl 3 DN41 101 E6
Buttercup Cl 1 HU9 146 D7
Butterfield Cl
2 Laceby DN37 101 F1
Snaith DN14 78 D8
Butterfly La YO16 10 F5
Butterfly Mdws HU17 136 E6
Buttermere Cres 3 DN36 114 C8
Buttermere Ct 9 YO8 148 B6
Buttermere Dr YO30 126 E1
Buttermere Rd DN14 149 D5
Buttermere Way DN32 152 F4
Butters Cl 20 YO32 13 D5
Butterwick Cl 23 DN35 103 C2
Butterwick Rd
Foxholes YO17 1 B1
Langtoft YO25 8 C7
Messingham DN17 107 A7
Buttfield La DN14 65 A6
Buttfield Rd
Howden DN14 65 A6
Kingston upon Hull HU13 143 E1
Buttle La 3 DN14 63 C1
Butts Cl
Bridlington YO16 122 D4
19 Stamford Bridge YO41 15 D2
Butts Hill YO14 3 C6
Butts La YO25 19 E2
Butts Rd DN18 69 F1
Butts The HU20 55 A4
Buxton Ct DN15 150 B6
Byass Ave YO16 122 E4
Bycroft Rd DN21 117 B3
Bydales La HU12 74 B3
Byedales 4 YO15 4 D3
Byfield Rd DN17 150 D2
Bygot Cl 1 HU17 43 D6
Byland Ave YO31 130 E8
Byland Ct 4 HU9 146 E8
Byram Pk Rd WF11 61 A4
Byrd Rd DN16 151 E2
Byron Ave 3 DN6 76 E1
Byron Cl DN17 150 E2
Byron Dr YO30 129 F8
Byron Gr DN33 102 E2
Byron St Goole DN14 149 C5
Kingston upon Hull HU8 141 D2
Bywell Wlk HU9 147 D8
Bywood Pl 5 DN37 102 B3

C

Cabourne Rd 34 DN33 102 D2
Caddle Rd 9 DN41 101 A4
Cadeby Medieval Village* DN36 120 F6
Cadeleigh Cl HU7 141 A8
Cadman Rd YO16 123 A7
Cadney Rd Bigby DN20 98 C1
Cadney DN20 109 C8
Cadogan St HU3 145 B5
Caedmon Cl YO31 131 A7
Caenby Rd
14 Cleethorpes DN35 103 C2
Scunthorpe DN17 150 E1
Cairnborrow 4 YO24 132 B7
Caistor Ave DN16 96 D2
Caistor By-pass LN7 111 B3
Caistor Dr DN33 102 D2
Caistor Joint CE & Methodist Prim Sch LN7 111 B4
Caistor Rd
Barton-upon-Humber DN18 85 A7
Laceby DN37 112 E8
Nettleton LN7 111 A3
North Kelsey LN7 110 D4
Rothwell LN7 111 E2
South Kelsey LN7 110 A1
Swallow LN7 112 A5
Caistor Yarborough Sch LN7 111 C4
Caithness Cl 1 YO30 126 E3
Calais Croft 7 HU17 43 A2
Calam Villas YO25 35 C5
Caldane HU6 139 E8
Caldbeck Cl 1 YO30 127 A1
Caldberg Mews 3 HU5 139 E3
Calder Ave YO26 129 B8
Calder Cl 35 DN40 87 B1
Calder Cres DN14 77 F6
Calder Dr DN14 78 B8
Calder Gn DN17 107 D7
Calder Gr HU8 142 C6
Calder Rd DN16 151 D2
Calder St 4 DN14 149 D4
Calderdale HU7 140 F6
Calderdale Cl 2 YO16 123 A7
Caledon Cl HU9 142 D5
Caledonia Pk HU9 146 B5
Calf Cl YO32 127 D8
Callas 6 HU17 43 A2
Calver Cres DN37 102 B4
Calvert Cl YO32 127 C7
Calvert La HU4 144 D7
Calvert Rd HU5 144 D8
Calvi Ct 2 DN32 153 A5
Cam Gr HU8 142 C6
Camargue Ave DN37 113 E7
Cambeak Cl 3 HU7 56 F5
Camberwell Way HU8 142 A5
Camblesforth CP Sch YO8 63 C4
Camborne Gr HU8 141 B3
Cambrian Cl 2 YO32 127 F3
Cambrian Way 2 DN36 114 A6
Cambridge Ave
Goole DN14 149 B5
Scunthorpe DN16 96 D2
Cambridge Gr HU9 141 F1
Cambridge Pk Sch DN34 152 A1
Cambridge Rd
Grimsby DN34 152 A1
Kingston upon Hull HU13 143 F3
Scunthorpe DN16 151 C2
Cambridge St
Bridlington YO16 122 D3
Cleethorpes DN35 153 F2
Kingston upon Hull HU1 155 A2
4 York YO24 130 A3
Camden St 1 HU3 145 B5
Camela La YO8 63 B6
Camelford Cl 12 HU7 56 F5
Camellia Cl YO25 124 D3
Cameron Gr YO23 130 C1
Camerton Gr HU9 141 F2
Camilla Cl HU9 155 C1
Camm La DN14 63 C3
Cammidge St 2 HU19 74 F7
Camp The (Earthworks)* YO11 2 C7
Campbell Ave
26 Scunthorpe DN16 96 D2
York YO24 129 E2
Campbell Ct HU9 142 A2
Campbell St 3 DN21 117 A1
Campbells Farm Ave DN15 95 E6
Campden Cres DN35 153 D3
Camperdown HU11 142 D6
Campey La YO42 39 B6
Campion Ave HU4 144 B2
Campions Cl 12 DN36 114 A5
Campions' La 6 DN36 114 B1
Campleshon Rd YO23 130 B1
Campsall Balk DN6 76 E1
Campsall Hall Rd 12 DN6 76 E1
Campsall Pk Rd 11 DN6 76 E1
Campsmount Sch DN6 76 D1
Canada Dr
Cherry Burton HU17 43 A5
Kingston upon Hull HU16 138 E5
Canada La LN7 111 C4
Canal Garth DN14 77 F6
Canal La
Barmby Moor YO42 28 F3
West Stockwith DN10 116 E5
Canal Rd
Cottingwith YO42 38 C5
Selby YO8 148 D4
Canal Side E HU15 52 E3
Canal Side W HU15 52 E2
Canal View Selby YO8 148 D3
2 Thorne/Moorends DN8 93 A7
Canberra Ave DN7 104 A8
Canberra St HU3 145 D5
Candlesby Rd 4 DN37 102 B4
Candy Bank DN9 104 B5
Canham Gr YO10 131 D3
Canham La YO25 35 C5
Canning St HU1 155 A2
Cannon Hall La DN14 61 F1
Cannon Oakes Ct DN36 114 B7
Cannon St HU2 155 B4
Canon Lee Sec Sch YO30 130 A8
Canon Peter Hall CE Prim Sch DN40 87 C1
Canongate HU16 139 B7
Canons Ct YO23 133 B2
Canopias Cl HU3 145 A4
Canterbury Cl
Beverley HU17 136 D1
9 Haxby YO32 13 D5
Scunthorpe DN17 150 D3
Canterbury Dr
Grimsby DN34 152 C2
2 Kingston upon Hull HU8 141 E7
Canterbury Rd 21 DN7 92 D4
Canton Villas 5 YO15 122 F4
Canty Nook DN38 110 E7
Capstan Rd HU6 140 C8
Capstan Way 13 DN8 93 A8
Captains Wlk HU1 155 A1
Carden Ave HU9 142 C2
Cardiff Ave DN36 114 A7
Cardigan Rd
Bridlington YO15 122 D1
Kingston upon Hull HU3 144 E6
Cardinal Ct 1 DN37 113 D7
Cardinals Cl 3 YO8 48 B8
Carentan Cl 6 YO8 148 B6
Carew St HU3 144 F7
Carey St YO10 130 D1
Carisbrooke Ave HU16 139 B6
Carisbrooke Cl 9 DN36 114 A8
Carisbrooke Manor La DN17 150 A1
Carl St YO23 130 C2
Carlam La HU7 57 A7
Carleton St 17 YO26 129 F5
Carlisle Rd 8 YO15 122 F3
Carlisle St
23 Gainsborough DN21 117 B1
Goole DN14 149 D4
16 York YO26 129 F5
Carlton 24 HU15 68 C6
Carlton Ave
Healing DN41 101 F5
Hornsea HU18 134 C5
York YO10 131 B3
Carlton Cl
Eggborough DN14 61 F1
22 Humberston DN35 103 D1
Carlton Ct HU17 154 A3
Carlton Dr HU11 47 B1
Carlton La HU11 47 B1
Carlton Rd
Aldbrough HU11 46 F1
Grimsby DN34 152 B2
5 Healing DN41 101 F5
Sutton upon Derwent YO41 27 C1
Carlton Rise 2 HU17 55 F8
Carlton St
Bridlington YO16 122 D3
Kingston upon Hull HU3 144 F4
13 Scunthorpe DN15 151 B7
Carlton Twrs* DN14 63 D2
Carlton View YO8 148 D4
Carlton-in-Snaith CP Sch DN14 63 C3
Carmelite St YO1 156 C2
Carmen Cres 1 DN36 114 A6
Carmires Ave YO32 13 F5
Carnaby Ave YO16 122 B2
Carnaby Cl HU17 43 D6
Carnaby Gr
Grimsby DN32 153 A1
Kingston upon Hull HU6 139 E5
Carnaby Ind Est YO15 10 E3
Carnegie St 6 HU3 145 A6
Carnforth Cres DN34 152 A1
Carnforth Par DN34 152 A1
Carnot St YO26 129 F5
Carnoustie 13 DN37 113 D6
Carnoustie Cl
Kingston upon Hull HU8 141 C3
1 York YO26 129 B4
Carol Dickson Ct 9 HU3 145 C5
Caroline Cl 5 YO24 129 F3
Caroline Pl HU2 155 B3
Caroline St HU2 155 B4
Carolines Pl HU16 138 B8
Carperby Mews 6 HU5 139 D3
Carr Cl Beverley HU17 154 C3
13 Hemingbrough YO8 49 F1
Carr Dike La HU15 67 C7
Carr Dyke Bank DN17 106 D5
Carr Dyke Rd DN17 95 D3
Carr Inf Sch YO26 129 C5
Carr Jun Sch YO26 129 C5
Carr La Appleby DN15 83 D2
Barlby with Osgodby YO8 148 F5
Barlow YO8 63 C7
Blyton DN21 117 A5
Bonby DN20 84 B1
Bridlington YO16 123 A8
Broughton DN20 97 F3
Burton Pidsea HU12 59 D1
Burton upon Stather DN15 82 D4
Eastrington DN14 51 F1
Escrick YO19 37 B5
Everingham YO42 40 A4
Garthorpe & Fockerby DN17 81 E4
Goole DN14 149 D6
Grimsby DN32 153 B3
Haxey DN9 105 E2
Healing DN41 101 F4
Hibaldstow DN20 109 A6
Horkstow DN18 83 F4
Hotham YO43 53 A4
Kingston upon Hull HU1 155 A2
Laxton DN14 65 F4
Leven HU17 44 E8
Long Drax YO8 63 F6
Luddington & Haldenby DN17 81 C1
Misterton DN10 116 C5
Nafferton YO25 21 C4
Newport HU15 52 E2
Newton on Derwent YO41 27 F4
Pocklington YO42 40 A8
Redbourne DN21 108 F3
Riston HU11 45 B5
Seaton Ross YO42 39 E4
Snaith & Cowick DN14 78 C7
Stallingborough DN41 101 E7
Tickton HU17 137 E3
Ulceby DN39 86 B3
Watton YO25 33 A4
West Butterwick DN17 106 C8
Wildsworth DN21 117 C8
Winterton DN15 83 D6
Wistow YO8 48 A3
Worlaby DN20 98 A7
York YO26 129 D5
Carr Rd
Burton Pidsea HU12 59 D1
Molescroft HU17 136 E8
North Kelsey LN7 109 E4
Carr Side La DN7 92 E2
Carr St
Kingston upon Hull HU2 155 B4
Selby YO8 148 F4
Carrbank La YO32 14 E3
Carrfield YO24 132 C8
Carrfields DN14 149 D6
Carrhouse Rd DN9 94 D1
Carrick Gdns YO24 129 E3
Carrington Ave
Hornsea HU18 134 C6
Kingston upon Hull HU16 139 B6
1 York YO26 129 E5
Carrington Dr
20 Humberston DN36 103 D1
Humberston DN36 114 D8
Carrington St 6 HU3 145 B5
Carrnock Ct 3 YO32 127 F1
Carroll Pl HU1 155 C3
Carron Cres YO24 132 B7
Carroway Cl 4 YO16 123 A7
Carrs Mdw Escrick YO19 37 B5
Withernsea HU19 74 F6
Carrside 5 DN9 105 D7
Carson Ave DN34 152 B2
Carson Rd DN21 117 B1
Carter Ave YO31 130 F5
Carter Dr HU17 136 E7
Carter La YO15 5 A2
Carter St DN14 149 C4
Cartergate DN31 152 D3
Cartledge Ave DN32 153 B2
Cartmel Ct HU9 142 B2
Cartmel Gr DN32 153 B2
Cartwright La HU17 154 A1
Carver Rd DN40 87 C1
Cary La 4 DN20 98 B2
Cassbrook Dr LN11 121 E8
Casson's Rd 1 DN8 93 A8
Casswell Cl 4 DN32 153 A5
Casswell Cres LN11 121 E8
Castella Dr DN16 151 D7
Castle Cl Cawood YO8 48 A8
1 Haxby YO32 13 D5
3 Leconfield HU17 43 D6
Castle Cres 16 YO15 5 A2
Castle Ct 9 DN18 84 F8
Castle Dr
1 Epworth DN9 105 E6
South Cave HU15 53 F2
Castle Earthworks* YO8 63 F4
Castle Gn HU16 138 E6
Castle Hill Caistor LN7 111 B4
8 Hunmanby YO14 2 F8
Owston Ferry DN9 106 A3
Castle Hill Hospl HU16 138 D5
Castle Hill La YO8 63 F5
Castle Hills* DN21 117 C2
Castle Hills GM Com Sch DN21 117 B1
Castle Keep DN20 108 F6
Castle Pk 9 HU11 47 C1
Castle Rd HU16 138 D5
Castle Rise 1 HU15 54 A2
Castle St Grimsby DN32 153 A4
Kingston upon Hull HU1 155 A1
Castle View YO25 23 A1
Castle Way HU13 69 F4
Castle Wlk YO1 156 C2
Castledyke Prim Sch DN18 69 E1
Castledyke S 10 DN18 84 F8
Castledyke W 10 DN18 69 E1
Castleford Ave 2 DN34 102 D2
Castleford Gr HU9 142 E2
Castlegate YO1 156 B2
Castlehill Rd HU7 141 D8
Castleton Ave 6 HU5 139 E3
Castleton Rd DN15 150 B6
Cat La Balne DN14 77 E5
Bilbrough YO23 24 D1
Catford Cl HU8 141 E5
Catfoss Rd YO25 35 A4
Cathcart Cl DN14 76 F7
Cathedral Cl 8 HU17 136 E1
Cathedral Ct
Hatfield DN7 92 C2
Scunthorpe DN16 151 A2
Catherine Gr 6 DN20 97 E3
Catherine McAuley Cl HU6 140 C5
Catherine St
13 Barton-upon-Humber DN18 69 F1
Grimsby DN32 152 E3
Kingston upon Hull HU2 155 B4
Catkin Rd DN16 96 D1
Catterick Mews 8 HU5 139 D3
Catterton La LS24 24 A1
Cattistock Rd 27 DN35 103 C2
Cattle Rd DN10 116 A5
Catton La YO42 28 F4
Catwick Heads HU11 45 E8
Catwick La
Brandesburton YO25 34 C2
Catwick HU17 45 D8
Caughey St HU3 145 D7
Causeway Ings La HU12 73 E7
Causewy The HU17 154 B3
Cave Cres HU16 138 E5
Cave Rd HU15 68 B6
Cave St HU5 140 D1
Cave Terr 1 HU5 140 D1
Cavendish Cl 14 DN35 103 D1
Cavendish Dr 2 HU17 136 E1

Cavendish Gr YO10 .....131 D3
Cavendish Pk 8 HU15 ....68 C5
Cavendish Prim Sch
HU8 ....141 E4
Cavendish Rd
Kingston upon Hull HU8 ...141 D5
9 Scunthorpe DN16 ......96 D2
Cavendish Sq HU3 .....140 D1
Cavendish Way DN32 ...152 F3
Cave's La DN10 ....116 B3
Cavill Dr 12 DN14 ....65 B7
Cavill Pl HU3 ....145 D5
Cawood CE VA Prim Sch
YO8 ....48 B8
Cawood Cl HU11 ....45 D2
Cawood Cres HU11 ......45 D2
Cawood Dr HU11 ....45 D2
Cawood Rd
Stillingfleet YO19 ....36 D3
Wistow YO8 ....48 C7
Cawthorn Cl YO25 ......125 A3
Cawthorne Dr HU4 .....144 C3
Caxton Ave YO26 ....129 D6
Cayley Cl YO30 ....126 F1
Cayley Rd HU10 ....143 F6
Cayton Rd HU8 ....141 D4
Cecil Cl 10 DN21 ....107 C3
Cecil Rd 7 YO14 ....3 A8
Cecil St
24 Gainsborough DN21 ...117 B1
Goole DN14 ....149 E4
Kingston upon Hull HU3 ...144 F5
Cecile Cres DN15 ....150 E7
Cecilia Pl 3 YO24 ......130 A3
Cedar Ave
Flixborough DN15 ....96 A7
Kingston upon Hull
HU16 ....139 A6
Cedar Cl
11 Cleethorpes DN35 .....103 B1
Gainsborough DN21 ......117 A2
Hambleton YO8 ....48 B1
Hornsea HU18 ....134 D1
Kingston upon Hull
HU10 ....143 D7
Scawby DN20 ....108 F8
7 Scotter DN21 ....107 C3
Wawne HU7 ....56 F8
Cedar Cres YO8 ....48 D2
Cedar Ct
Bridlington YO16 ....123 A8
8 Hedon HU12 ....72 C7
Cedar Dr 2 DN40 ....87 C2
Cedar Glade YO19 ....26 E7
Cedar Gr
2 Aldbrough HU11 ....47 C1
Stainforth DN7 ....92 D6
York YO31 ....131 B7
Cedar Gr The HU17 .....136 C6
Cedar Rd 2 DN8 ....79 B1
Cedarwood 5 HU15 ....66 D7
Cedarwood Cl 8 YO24 ...129 B1
Cedarwood Dr HU4 .....144 B7
Cedric Rd DN3 ....92 A1
Celandine Cl 8 HU5 ....139 D1
Celery Bank DN14 ....66 A4
Celtic Cl YO26 ....129 B5
Cemetery Cres 7 DN37 .101 F1
Cemetery La
North Kelsey LN7 ....110 A5
Pocklington YO42 ....29 A3
Cemetery Rd
Hatfield DN7 ....92 F4
Laceby DN37 ....101 F1
Scunthorpe DN16 ....151 B5
Winterton DN15 ....83 B5
York YO10 ....156 C1
Centenary Rd DN14 ....149 B5
Central Ave
Beverley HU17 ....154 A2
Ulrome YO25 ....23 B3
Central Parade DN34 ...152 A3
Central Promenade
DN35 ....153 F2
Central St HU2 ....140 F1
Central Way DN16 .....151 D6
Centurion Pk YO30 .....127 B2
Centurion Way
Brough HU15 ....68 C5
Clifton YO30 ....127 B3
Centurion Wlk YO43 ....135 E4
Century Rd HU12 ....72 A8
Ceylon St HU9 ....147 C7
Chadcourt HU6 ....139 E6
Chadwell Springs
DN37 ....113 C6
Chaffinch Cl DN15 ....96 B7
Chaffinch Dr 14 DN35 ...103 C1
Chaldon Cl 4 YO32 ......14 A6
Chalfont Cl HU13 ......143 D2
Chalfonts YO24 ....129 F1
Chaloner's Cres YO24 ..132 D7
Chaloner's Rd YO24 ....132 D8
Chamberlain Cl HU7 ....141 D6
Chamberlain Ct HU7 ....141 D7
Chamberlain Gdns
HU8 ....141 C3
Chamberlain Rd HU8 ...141 B3
Chamberlain St HU7 ....141 D6
Chambers La 1 HU18 ...134 C4
Chamomile Cl 17 DN16 ...96 E2
Champney Rd HU17 ....154 A2
Chancel Rd DN16 ....96 D2
Chancel Wlk 8 DN20 .....97 E3
Chancery Ct
Kingston upon Hull HU5 ...144 E8
York YO24 ....129 C3
Chancery La 2 DN17 .....94 D7
Chancery Rise YO24 ....129 F3
Chancewaters 5 HU7 .....56 E5
Chandlers Cl 2 DN36 ...114 A7
Chandlers Ct HU9 ......146 C6
Chandos Rd DN17 ......150 F3
Channel Rd HU12 ....89 B6
Chanterlands Ave
HU5 ....140 A1
Chantreys Dr 13 HU15 ....68 C6
Chantry Ave 14 YO26 .....12 F1
Chantry Cl
Grimsby DN31 ....152 C3
York YO24 ....132 C8
Chantry Ct YO16 ....122 D4
Chantry Gap 11 YO26 .....12 F1
Chantry Gr 13 YO26 ....12 F1
Chantry La
Beverley HU17 ....154 B2
Bishopthorpe YO23 ....133 B4
Etton HU17 ....43 A6
Grimsby DN31 ....152 C3
Rimswell HU12 ....74 C5
Chantry Mdws 1 YO25 .....9 C3
Chantry Way 13 HU14 ....69 B7
Chantry Way E 9 HU14 ...69 B7
Chapefield Rd DN19 ......86 B7
Chapel Balk Rd YO8 ......49 F1
Chapel Baulk DN9 ......104 E1
Chapel Cl
Barrow upon Humber
DN19 ....85 D7
2 Kingston upon Hull
HU4 ....144 A1
7 Misterton DN10 ....116 C5
12 Preston HU12 ....58 C1
Rawcliffe DN14 ....64 A1
Skidby HU16 ....138 A8
Skirlaugh HU11 ....45 E2
4 Westwoodside DN9 ....105 B2
Chapel Cnr YO43 ....135 D4
Chapel Ct
Alkborough DN15 ....82 C8
7 Hibaldstow DN20 ......108 F5
Scunthorpe DN15 ....151 B8
Chapel Fields
Coniston HU11 ....57 F6
Holme-on-Spalding-Moor
YO43 ....40 A1
Chapel Fields Rd
YO26 ....129 A3
Chapel Garth
Broomfleet HU15 ....67 B5
11 Gilberdyke HU15 ....66 D8
Holme-on-Spalding-Moor
YO42 ....40 A1
Ottringham HU12 ....73 E3
Skipsea YO25 ....23 A1
3 Tetney DN36 ....114 D4
Chapel Haddlesey CE VC
Prim Sch YO8 ....62 B5
Chapel Hill 1 HU15 ....68 E6
Chapel Hill La HU15 .....68 E6
Chapel Hill Rd YO42 .....29 A4
Chapel La
Ashby cum Fenby DN37 ...113 D3
Askham Bryan YO23 ....24 F3
Barmston YO25 ....23 A6
Barnoldby le Beck DN37 ...113 B6
14 Barton-upon-Humber
DN18 ....69 E1
Brayton YO8 ....148 B1
Broughton DN20 ....97 E3
Elsham DN20 ....98 F7
10 Gainsborough DN21 ...117 A2
Habrough DN40 ....100 E8
Horkstow DN18 ....84 A5
Keadby with Althorpe
DN17 ....95 C6
13 Keyingham HU12 ....73 C4
Kilham YO25 ....9 B3
Kingston upon Hull HU1 ...155 C2
Langtoft YO25 ....8 D5
Laxton DN14 ....65 F4
Little Smeaton WF8 ....76 B3
Ludborough DN36 ....121 B6
Middleton YO25 ....31 C4
8 Misterton DN10 ....116 C5
Northorpe DN21 ....118 D8
Ottringham HU12 ....73 E3
Rawcliffe DN14 ....64 A2
Reighton YO14 ....3 E5
3 Riccall YO19 ....37 A1
Scawby DN20 ....108 E8
Skeffling HU12 ....90 C6
Swallow LN7 ....112 B5
Sykehouse DN14 ....78 A4
18 Thorne/Moorends DN8 ...93 A8
Utterby LN11 ....121 C4
1 Wawne HU7 ....56 E7
West Ella HU10 ....69 C8
West/East Butterwick
DN17 ....95 D1
Whitton DN15 ....67 E3
Winterton DN15 ....83 A5
Wrawby DN20 ....98 D4
Chapel La Staith HU1 ...155 C2
Chapel Mdws 8 HU15 ....66 D8
Chapel Mews 3 HU15 .....68 C6
Chapel Rd
Broughton DN20 ....97 E3
Habrough DN40 ....100 E8
Tetney DN36 ....114 D4
Chapel Row YO10 ......156 C1
Chapel St
2 Amcotts DN17 ....81 F1
Barmby Moor YO42 ....28 D3
Bridlington YO15 ....122 E2
13 Caistor LN7 ....111 B4
Chapel St *continued*
5 Crowle DN17 ....94 D8
6 Epworth DN9 ....105 E6
6 Flamborough YO15 ....5 A2
Goole DN14 ....149 D3
Goxhill DN19 ....86 A8
Hillam LS25 ....61 B7
Kingston upon Hull HU1 ...155 A2
Lockington YO25 ....32 B2
North Kelsey LN7 ....110 A4
Scunthorpe DN15 ....151 B7
Chapel Terr YO24 ......129 C3
Chapel Way 21 DN20 .....98 C2
Chapel Wlk 4 YO19 ....37 A1
Chapelry Garth 28 HU12 ..72 D7
Chapman Ave DN17 ....150 D2
Chapman Cl 1 YO32 ......14 C8
Chapman Ct DN31 ......152 D4
Chapman Gr DN35 ......153 F1
Chapman Rd DN35 .....153 D3
Chapman St HU8 ....155 C4
Chapman's La YO30 ......12 E7
Chapmans Ct YO24 .....132 D6
Chapter House St YO1 ..156 B3
Chapter Wk DN20 ....97 E3
Charing Cl HU3 ....145 C8
Chariot St HU1 ....155 A2
Chariot Way 6 YO25 .....19 B6
Charles Ave
Grimsby DN33 ....102 E1
Laceby DN37 ....101 E1
17 New Waltham DN36 ...114 A7
15 Scotter DN21 ....107 C3
Charles Ct 7 DN8 ....79 B1
Charles Dr DN14 ....149 B6
Charles Hume Ct
DN32 ....153 B4
Charles Lovell Way
DN17 ....150 D4
Charles Moor YO31 .....130 F7
Charles St
Cleethorpes DN35 ....153 F1
30 Gainsborough DN21 ...117 B1
22 Hedon HU12 ....72 D7
Kingston upon Hull HU2 ...155 B3
Selby YO8 ....148 B6
Charles Wesley Dr
YO8 ....148 B2
Charlestown Way
HU9 ....146 C6
Charlotte St HU1 ....155 C3
Charlotte St Mews
HU1 ....155 B3
Charlton St
Grimsby DN31 ....152 C4
York YO23 ....130 C2
Charnock Ave HU9 .....142 A4
Charnwood Cl 29 HU7 ....56 F6
Charter Ave DN14 ....64 A1
Charter's La 4 YO25 .....34 B2
Charterfield HU11 ......142 D6
Charterhouse Dr 3
DN16 ....96 E2
Charterhouse La HU2 ..155 B3
Charterhouse The*
HU2 ....155 C3
Charters The YO8 ....49 B5
Chase Hill Rd DN40 .....86 E5
Chase Side Ct YO24 ....132 E8
Chase Specl Sch DN7 ....92 D4
Chase The
Driffield YO25 ....125 A4
2 Snaith DN14 ....78 C8
Chatham St HU3 ....144 F7
Chatsworth Cl
Beverley HU17 ....154 A1
5 Bridlington YO16 ......122 D6
Chatsworth Dr
Goole DN14 ....149 B6
16 Haxby YO32 ....13 F5
Chatsworth Pl 1 DN35 ...103 B2
Chatsworth St HU5 .....145 B8
Chatsworth Terr 4
YO26 ....129 E4
Chatsworth Way 12
DN9 ....105 D2
Chatterton Cres DN15 ....96 D7
Chaucer Ave DN17 .....150 D3
Chaucer St
Kingston upon Hull HU8 ...141 C2
7 York YO10 ....130 E3
Chaumont Way 1 YO32 ...14 D2
Chaytor Cl 16 HU12 ......72 D6
Cheadle Cl
Kingston upon Hull HU2 ...155 A4
Sculcoates HU2 ....140 E1
Cheapside
Kingston upon Hull HU8 ...155 C4
Waltham DN37 ....113 E5
Cheapside Rd DN37 ....113 F4
Cheapsides La HU15 ....66 D8
Checker La YO19 ....49 A7
Cheesemans Cl 9
DN37 ....113 E6
Cheesemans La 8
DN37 ....113 E6
Chelkar Way YO30 .....126 F1
Chellsway HU19 ....74 F6
Chelmer Rd HU8 ....142 B5
Chelmsford Ave DN34 ..152 A1
Chelmsford Cl 6 HU9 ...142 E1
Chelmsford Pl DN34 ...152 B2
Chelsea Cl HU8 ....141 F5
Chelsea Ct 3 HU16 .....138 F5
Chelsea Wlk 1 DN35 ...103 D1
Cheltenham Ave HU7 ...141 A8
Cheltenham Cl 8 DN16 ...96 E2
Cheltenham Way
DN35 ....103 C1
Chelwood Dr 30 DN33 ...102 D2
Chelwood Rd DN17 .....150 F3
Chelwood Wlk 12 YO26 ..129 E4
Chepstow Gr DN34 .....152 A1
Chequers The DN15 ....150 E7
Cheriton Cl 14 HU7 ......56 F5
Cherry Burton CE VC Prim
Sch HU17 ....43 B5
Cherry Cl
Great Driffield YO25 .....124 F2
Hornsea HU18 ....134 D1
Cherry Cobb Sands Rd
HU12 ....87 F8
Cherry Cres YO43 ....40 A1
Cherry Ct 16 HU15 ....66 D8
Cherry Dale 11 DN35 ....103 B2
Cherry Dr
Holme-on-Spalding-Moor
YO43 ....40 A1
Nafferton YO25 ....125 F6
Cherry Garth
Beverley HU17 ....154 C3
Kingston upon Hull HU3 ...145 A5
Lund YO25 ....31 F2
York YO31 ....131 B5
Cherry Gr 5 Belton DN9 ...94 E1
Belton DN9 ....105 E8
16 Poppleton YO26 ....12 F1
Scunthorpe DN16 ....151 B2
Cherry Hill La YO23 ....156 B1
Cherry Hill Pk HU12 .....74 B8
Cherry Holt 7 LN7 ......111 B4
Cherry La
Barrow upon Humber
DN19 ....85 D8
Kingston upon Hull HU8 ...141 C4
Wootton DN39 ....85 E2
York YO24 ....132 F8
Cherry Mount 1 DN16 ....96 E2
Cherry Orch
16 Epworth DN9 ....105 E6
2 Haxby YO32 ....127 D8
Cherry Orch Mews 12
YO42 ....29 A4
Cherry Paddock
4 Haxby YO32 ....127 D8
Kexby YO41 ....15 C2
Cherry Rd 4 YO14 ....3 A8
Cherry St YO23 ....156 B1
Cherry Tree Ave
1 Brigg DN20 ....98 B2
Kingston upon Hull HU8 ...141 C2
Newton-on-Ouse YO30 .....12 B6
9 Withernsea HU19 ....75 A6
York YO32 ....127 D4
Cherry Tree Cl
Bilton HU11 ....58 A3
13 Brayton YO8 ....48 D1
Cherry Tree Cres
DN34 ....102 C4
Cherry Tree Crossing
HU17 ....154 B3
Cherry Tree Ct 12 YO8 ....49 B4
Cherry Tree Dr
Hatfield DN7 ....92 D5
3 Thorne/Moorends DN8 ...79 A1
Cherry Tree Gr DN7 .....92 C5
Cherry Tree La
Beverley HU17 ....154 B3
31 Hedon HU12 ....72 D7
Cherry Tree Rd 18
DN21 ....117 C1
Cherry Tree Rise
DN21 ....107 D4
Cherry Tree Terr
HU17 ....154 C3
Cherry Tree Wlk 7 YO8 ...49 B4
Cherry Trees HU16 .....138 A7
Cherry Tree's Bsns Pk
DN31 ....152 A6
Cherry Way
Messingham DN17 ....107 D7
Nafferton YO25 ....125 F6
Cherry Wood Cres
YO19 ....133 E5
Chesham Gr DN14 ......149 B6
Cheshire Ave YO32 ......14 A6
Cheshire Cl
Kingston upon Hull HU5 ...139 D1
6 Rawcliffe YO32 ....128 E4
Chesney Dr DN16 ....96 D2
Chesney Fields 4 YO24 .129 D1
Chesnut Ave HU5 ......140 C2
Chesnut Way 6 DN19 ....86 A8
Chessingham Gdns
YO24 ....132 E6
Chessingham Pk YO19 ...26 F6
Chesswick Ave DN17 ....95 D5
Chesswick Cres DN17 ...95 D5
Chester Ave HU17 ......136 E1
Chester Ct Rd YO8 ......63 A6
Chester Grange DN33 ...102 F1
Chester Pl DN35 ....153 C1
Chester Rd HU5 ....139 B1
Chester Wlk DN34 .....152 A1
Chesterfield Rd DN15 ...150 B6
Chesterholme HU11 ....142 E6
Chestnut Ave
2 Airmyn DN14 ....64 E4
Beverley HU17 ....136 F6
15 Gainsborough DN21 ...117 B1
Goole DN14 ....149 B3
Great Driffield YO25 .....124 F2
Grimsby DN31 ....152 B3
Hedon HU12 ....72 C8
10 Hemingbrough YO8 .....49 F1
Chestnut Ave *continued*
Hessle HU13 ....143 E1
Immingham DN40 ....87 D2
Kirk Ella HU10 ....143 E8
Stainforth DN7 ....92 D6
3 Thorne/Moorends DN8 ...93 B7
2 Thorngumbald HU12 ....72 E5
Withernsea HU19 ....75 A5
York YO31 ....130 F6
Chestnut Cl
Beverley HU17 ....136 F6
Bridlington YO15 ....123 B7
6 Burstwick HU12 ....73 A6
4 Scotter DN21 ....107 C3
Snaith DN14 ....78 B8
17 Waltham DN37 ....113 D6
Chestnut Cres YO43 .....40 A1
Chestnut Croft 7 YO8 ....49 F1
Chestnut Ct
9 Hemingbrough YO8 .....49 F1
York YO32 ....127 F5
Chestnut Dr
15 Gilberdyke HU15 ....66 D8
8 Hemingbrough YO8 .....49 F1
Holme-on-Spalding-Moor
YO43 ....40 A1
Messingham DN17 ....107 D7
Chestnut Garth
Burton Pidsea HU12 ....59 C2
4 Hemingbrough YO8 .....49 F1
Roos HU12 ....60 A1
Chestnut Gn 10 LS25 .....61 A8
Chestnut Gr
Acomb YO26 ....129 C4
8 Barnetby le Beck DN38 ..99 B4
5 Broughton DN20 ....97 E4
Huntington YO32 ....127 E4
Kingston upon Hull HU8 ...141 B2
Sproatley HU11 ....58 D5
Chestnut Mews YO8 .....48 A8
Chestnut Pk YO41 ....28 C8
Chestnut Rd
Cawood YO8 ....48 A8
Waltham DN37 ....113 D6
Chestnut Rise
Barrow upon Humber
DN19 ....85 C8
6 Hemingbrough YO8 .....49 F1
Chestnut View YO42 .....29 B3
Chestnut Way DN16 ....151 B3
Chestnut Wlk DN41 .....102 A5
Chestnuts The
6 Haxby YO32 ....127 C8
Hensall DN14 ....62 D2
Chevering Pk 8 HU7 .....56 E5
Cheverton Ave 19 HU19 ...75 A6
Cheviot Ave DN14 ......149 D5
Cheviot Cl
3 Thorne/Moorends DN8 ..93 A7
1 York YO32 ....127 F3
Cheviotdale HU7 ....140 F6
Chevy Chase HU11 .....142 E6
Cheyne Garth HU18 ....134 A4
Cheyne Wlk HU18 ......134 A4
Chichester Dr 19 LN7 ...111 B4
Chichester Rd DN35 ...103 C2
Chiltern Cres DN17 ....150 D4
Chiltern Dr 19 DN37 ...113 D6
Chiltern Prim Sch
HU3 ....145 B5
Chiltern Rd DN14 ......149 D5
Chiltern Way
26 Grimsby DN33 ....113 E8
York YO32 ....127 F5
Chilterns The HU9 .....142 D2
Chilton Cl 19 DN40 ......87 B1
Chilton Rise HU10 .....138 B1
Chilvers Ct 4 YO8 .....148 A1
Chimes Rd YO8 ....148 C6
Chimes The 9 YO8 .....148 C6
Chimney Field Rd HU12 ..74 B6
Chingford Ave 1 DN34 ..102 D2
Chingford Wlk HU9 .....142 E1
Chippendale Cl 2
DN36 ....114 D8
Chiswick Cl 3 HU8 .....142 A5
Cholmley St HU3 ......145 B5
Christine Pl 4 DN33 ....113 F8
Chrystals Rd HU18 .....134 D5
Chrystals Wlk HU18 ....134 D5
Chudleigh Rd 1 YO26 ...129 F5
Church Acres DN14 ......65 D1
Church Ave
Humberston DN36 ....114 C8
6 North Ferriby HU14 .....69 A4
6 Selby YO8 ....148 D5
Church Balk
Dunnington YO19 ....26 E7
Thorne/Moorends DN8 .....93 B8
Church Cl
Askham Bryan YO23 ....24 F3
Bonby DN20 ....84 C2
Bridlington YO16 ....122 D4
4 Bubwith YO8 ....50 D7
25 Flamborough YO15 ......5 A2
Goole DN14 ....149 E2
Grimsby DN32 ....153 B1
Kingston upon Hull HU7 ...141 D6
Laxton DN14 ....65 F4
1 Market Weighton
YO43 ....135 D4
8 Thorne/Moorends DN8 ...93 B8
5 Wetwang YO25 ....19 B5
Wheldrake YO19 ....38 A7

Church Cres
Owston Ferry DN9 ... 106 A3
4 Wawne HU7 ... 56 E7
Church Ct
Great Driffield YO25 ... 124 E4
Scunthorpe DN15 ... 151 B8
Church Dike La YO8 ... 63 F5
Church Dr Leven HU17 ... 45 A8
6 Misterton DN10 ... 116 C5
Church End YO8 ... 48 B8
Church Farm Cl YO23 ... 24 C6
Church Field Rd DN6 ... 76 E1
Church Fields DN15 ... 83 A5
Church Gate 21 HU12 ... 72 C7
Church Gn
Beverley HU17 ... 136 B6
5 Bridlington YO16 ... 122 D4
3 Elvington YO41 ... 27 C2
Church Hill
Grasby DN38 ... 110 E7
10 Hunmanby YO14 ... 2 F8
Reighton YO14 ... 3 C6
Riby DN37 ... 101 B2
3 Selby YO8 ... 148 D5
South Cave HU15 ... 53 F2
Stillingfleet YO19 ... 36 D3
Whitton DN15 ... 67 E3
8 Wistow YO8 ... 48 D6
Church Hill Rd YO25 ... 31 C4
Church La Appleby DN15 ... 83 C1
Atwick YO25 ... 35 C5
Aylesby DN37 ... 101 E2
Barnetby le Beck DN37 ... 113 B6
1 Beeford YO25 ... 22 D1
Beswick YO25 ... 32 B4
Bilton HU11 ... 142 F6
Bishop Burton HU17 ... 43 B2
Bishopthorpe YO23 ... 133 A4
Blyton DN21 ... 117 F5
Bonby DN20 ... 84 C2
Bradley DN37 ... 102 C1
Brandesburton YO25 ... 34 B2
Bridlington YO15 ... 123 B7
Brigsley DN37 ... 113 D4
3 Brough HU15 ... 68 C7
Broughton DN20 ... 97 E3
6 Buckton/Bempton YO15 ... 4 D3
Burstwick HU12 ... 73 A7
Cadney DN20 ... 109 D6
Carlton DN14 ... 63 C3
Carnaby YO16 ... 10 D5
Catton YO41 ... 27 D8
Catwick HU17 ... 45 C8
Corringham DN21 ... 118 B2
Driffield YO25 ... 124 B4
Dunnington YO19 ... 26 E7
4 Elvington YO41 ... 27 C2
Fishlake DN7 ... 92 D8
24 Flamborough YO15 ... 5 A2
Fotherby LN11 ... 121 D2
Fridaythorpe YO25 ... 18 B7
Garton YO25 ... 124 B4
Gateforth YO8 ... 61 F8
Great Driffield YO25 ... 124 E4
Great Limber DN37 ... 100 D3
12 Grimsby DN33 ... 102 E1
Grimsby DN32 ... 152 D3
17 Haxby YO32 ... 13 E5
Haxey DN9 ... 105 C2
Hedon HU12 ... 72 C7
Hensall DN14 ... 62 C1
Hollym HU19 ... 75 A4
Holton le Clay DN36 ... 114 A5
Hook DN14 ... 149 F7
Hotham YO43 ... 53 D5
Humberston DN36 ... 114 D8
Hutton Cranswick YO25 ... 32 E8
Immingham DN40 ... 86 E4
Irby DN37 ... 112 D7
Keadby with Althorpe
DN17 ... 95 D4
Kellington DN14 ... 61 E3
Keyingham HU12 ... 73 C4
2 Kilham YO25 ... 9 C3
Kirk Ella HU10 ... 143 C8
Laceby DN37 ... 101 F1
Langtoft YO25 ... 8 C1
Lockington YO25 ... 32 B1
Luddington & Haldenby
DN17 ... 81 D4
Marfleet HU9 ... 147 C8
Marsh Chapel DN36 ... 115 B1
Millington YO42 ... 29 D6
3 Misterton DN10 ... 116 C5
4 Monk Fryston LS25 ... 61 A8
Moor Monkton YO26 ... 12 B2
Nether Poppleton YO26 ... 126 B3
New Earswick YO32 ... 127 F5
4 North Cave HU15 ... 53 D3
North Frodingham YO25 ... 33 F8
North Kelsey LN7 ... 110 A4
North Thoresby DN36 ... 114 B1
Nunburnholme YO42 ... 29 E2
Patrington HU12 ... 74 D1
Poppleton YO26 ... 126 A3
Rudston YO25 ... 9 F6
Saxby All Saints DN20 ... 84 B3
Scawby DN20 ... 98 A1
Scotter DN21 ... 107 C3
19 Scunthorpe DN16 ... 96 D2
Scunthorpe DN15 ... 150 F6
Seaton Ross YO42 ... 39 E4
4 Selby YO8 ... 148 D5
Sigglesthorne HU11 ... 45 F8
Skelton YO30 ... 126 B5
Church La *continued*
Skirlaugh HU11 ... 45 E2
2 Snaith DN14 ... 63 C1
Sproatley HU11 ... 58 D5
Stallingborough DN41 ... 101 D6
10 Stamford Bridge YO41 ... 15 D2
Strensall YO32 ... 14 A7
Swinefleet DN14 ... 65 D1
Tetney DN36 ... 114 D3
Thorngumbald HU12 ... 72 E5
Thwing YO25 ... 2 A1
Twin Rivers DN14 ... 81 A8
Ulceby DN39 ... 86 A1
Utterby LN11 ... 121 C3
Waithe DN36 ... 114 A3
4 Waltham DN37 ... 113 E6
Watton YO25 ... 32 D4
Wetwang YO25 ... 19 B6
Wheldrake YO19 ... 38 A7
Withernwick HU11 ... 46 D3
York YO1 ... 156 B2
Church La Staith HU1 ... 155 C2
Church Mews
Barlby YO8 ... 49 A5
2 York YO26 ... 129 C3
Church Mount
Kingston upon Hull HU7 ... 141 D6
9 North Newbald YO43 ... 53 F7
Church Rd
Beverley HU17 ... 136 B6
33 Dunswell HU7 ... 56 F6
Laughton DN21 ... 117 F8
North Ferriby HU14 ... 69 A4
Rimswell HU19 ... 74 D7
Skeffling HU12 ... 90 D6
Stainforth DN7 ... 92 C6
Stamford Bridge YO41 ... 15 D2
Thornton YO42 ... 39 B7
Wawne HU7 ... 56 E7
York YO10 ... 131 D4
Church Rise Holtby YO19 ... 14 F1
Skidby HU16 ... 138 A8
Church Row HU8 ... 155 C4
Church Side
Alkborough DN15 ... 82 C8
Appleby DN15 ... 83 D2
Goxhill DN19 ... 86 A7
Grasby DN38 ... 110 E7
2 Market Weighton
YO43 ... 135 D4
West Halton DN15 ... 82 E7
16 Winterton DN15 ... 83 A5
Church Sq 3 DN15 ... 151 B7
Church St
7 Aldbrough HU11 ... 47 C1
Amcotts DN17 ... 81 F1
Bainton YO25 ... 31 E7
Beckingham DN10 ... 116 D1
6 Brough HU15 ... 68 D6
Bubwith YO8 ... 50 D7
Burton Pidsea HU12 ... 59 D1
14 Caistor LN7 ... 111 B4
Copmanthorpe YO23 ... 132 B2
Dunnington YO19 ... 26 E7
Elsham DN20 ... 98 F7
2 Epworth DN9 ... 105 E6
Fishlake DN7 ... 92 D8
19 Flamborough YO15 ... 5 A2
Gainsborough DN21 ... 117 B1
Goole DN14 ... 149 D4
5 Goxhill DN19 ... 86 A8
Great Driffield YO25 ... 124 D4
Grimsby DN32 ... 152 F5
Haxey DN9 ... 105 C2
Hemswell DN21 ... 119 A1
Hibaldstow DN20 ... 108 F5
Huggate YO42 ... 18 C2
Hutton Cranswick YO25 ... 32 E8
4 Kilham YO25 ... 9 C3
Kingston upon Hull HU7 ... 141 E6
Anlaby HU10 ... 143 E6
Kirton in Lindsey DN21 ... 108 B1
Messingham DN17 ... 107 D7
Misterton DN10 ... 116 C5
Nettleton LN7 ... 111 B3
North Cave HU15 ... 53 D3
North Kelsey LN7 ... 110 A4
Owston Ferry DN9 ... 106 A3
Scawby DN20 ... 108 E8
South Cave HU15 ... 53 F1
Thorne/Moorends DN8 ... 93 A8
Willoughton DN21 ... 119 B4
York YO1 ... 156 B2
Church View
12 Airmyn DN14 ... 64 E4
Alkborough DN15 ... 82 C8
8 Barton-upon-Humber
DN18 ... 84 F8
4 Beckingham DN10 ... 116 D1
Beverley HU17 ... 154 C3
4 Brough HU15 ... 68 C7
Grimsby DN34 ... 102 C4
Norton DN6 ... 76 E1
Ottringham HU12 ... 73 E3
7 Patrington HU12 ... 74 D1
1 Waltham DN37 ... 113 E6
Church View Cl DN9 ... 94 E1
Church Wlk
Bridlington YO16 ... 122 D5
Holton le Clay DN36 ... 114 A5
Owston Ferry DN9 ... 106 A3
5 Wistow YO8 ... 48 D6
Churchfield Dr 28 YO32 ... 13 E5
Churchfield La DN6 ... 76 C4
Churchfield Rd DN16 ... 151 B1
Churchfields HU17 ... 137 E8
Churchill Ave
Brigg DN20 ... 98 C2
Churchill Ave *continued*
Burstwick HU12 ... 73 A7
Hatfield DN7 ... 92 F4
Hutton Cranswick YO25 ... 32 E7
10 Keelby DN41 ... 101 A5
Kingston upon Hull
HU16 ... 138 F6
Churchill Rise HU12 ... 73 A7
Churchill St HU9 ... 146 D7
Churchill Way DN32 ... 152 F3
Churchill Wlk DN14 ... 149 C5
Churchside 4 DN19 ... 85 D8
Churchthorpe LN11 ... 121 E8
Churchtown DN9 ... 94 E1
Cinder La
Upper Poppleton YO26 ... 129 A7
York YO26 ... 130 A4
Cinder Mews YO26 ... 130 A5
Cinema St HU18 ... 134 C4
Circle The 4 HU13 ... 143 E2
Cissplatt La DN41 ... 101 A5
Citadel Ct HU17 ... 154 B3
Citadel Way HU9 ... 155 C2
Cladshaw HU6 ... 139 F8
Clanthorpe HU6 ... 139 F8
Clapham Ave HU8 ... 141 E5
Clare Ave DN17 ... 150 D3
Clare Ct Beverley HU17 ... 137 B4
Grimsby DN34 ... 152 A1
Clare Gr HU9 ... 142 A1
Claremont Ave HU6 ... 140 D4
Claremont Rd DN32 ... 153 D2
Claremont Terr YO31 ... 156 B4
Clarence Ave
Bridlington YO15 ... 122 D1
Kingston upon Hull HU8 ... 141 E4
Clarence Cl 25 DN40 ... 87 B1
Clarence Ct HU2 ... 155 A3
Clarence Rd 1 YO15 ... 122 F2
Clarence St
Kingston upon Hull HU9 ... 155 C2
York YO31 ... 156 B4
Clarendon Ct YO31 ... 130 C7
Clarendon Rd
6 Grimsby DN34 ... 102 C2
Scunthorpe DN17 ... 150 F3
Clarendon St HU3 ... 145 D7
Clark Ave DN34 ... 152 A3
Clark's La YO43 ... 53 D6
Clarke Cres 9 YO15 ... 4 D3
Clarke St DN15 ... 151 A7
Clarkes Rd DN40 ... 86 E4
Clarks La 10 HU12 ... 74 D1
Clarks Terr YO31 ... 130 F6
Clarksons Dr DN41 ... 101 E6
Clarondale HU7 ... 140 E7
Clavering St DN31 ... 152 B5
Claxby Rd DN17 ... 150 F1
Clay Bank Rd DN8 ... 93 C6
Clay Hill YO41 ... 16 C3
Clay La Bubwith YO8 ... 50 C5
Camblesforth YO8 ... 63 C6
Cliffe YO8 ... 49 D4
Holton le Clay DN36 ... 114 A6
Kirton in Lindsey DN21 ... 118 F8
Market Weighton YO43 ... 135 B5
Millington YO42 ... 29 C6
Scotter DN21 ... 107 C4
Clay Pl 3 YO24 ... 129 D1
Clay St HU8 ... 141 A3
Clayden St DN31 ... 152 B5
Clayfield Cl 18 YO42 ... 29 A3
Clayfield La
Pocklington YO42 ... 29 A4
Shipton Thorpe YO43 ... 40 F6
Clayfield Rd
Pocklington YO42 ... 29 A3
Scunthorpe DN15 ... 96 C7
Claygate YO31 ... 131 B6
Claymore Cl DN35 ... 153 E2
Claypit La DN14 ... 63 C3
Clear View Cl HU8 ... 141 F6
Clearwaters 6 HU7 ... 56 E5
Cleatham Rd DN21 ... 108 A3
Cleaves Ave HU15 ... 54 A2
Clee Cres DN32 ... 153 C1
Clee Ness Dr 16 DN36 ... 103 D1
Clee Rd DN35 ... 153 D2
Clee Village DN32 ... 153 C2
Cleefields Cl DN32 ... 153 B1
Cleethorpe Rd DN32 ... 153 A5
Cleethorpes Coast Light Rly*
DN35 ... 103 E2
Cleethorpes Ctry Pk*
DN35 ... 103 C1
Cleethorpes Discovery Ctr*
DN35 ... 103 D2
Cleethorpes L Ctr
DN35 ... 103 D2
Cleethorpes Sta DN35 ... 153 F3
Cleeton La YO25 ... 23 A2
Cleeton Way YO16 ... 122 B6
Cleeve Dr 12 HU7 ... 57 A5
Cleeve Prim Sch HU7 ... 57 A5
Cleeve Rd HU12 ... 72 D6
Clematis Ave DN41 ... 101 F5
Clematis Cl YO25 ... 124 D3
Clematis Way DN16 ... 96 E2
Clement St 4 YO23 ... 156 B1
Clementhorpe YO23 ... 156 B1
Clementhorpe La HU15 ... 66 D8
Clementhorpe Rd
HU15 ... 66 D8
Clerke St DN35 ... 153 B4
Clevedon Rd DN17 ... 150 D4
Cleveland Cl Hook DN14 ... 65 B5
4 Immingham DN40 ... 87 B1
Scunthorpe DN17 ... 150 D4
Cleveland Gdns DN31 ... 152 B5
Cleveland St
Grimsby DN31 ... 152 B5
Kingston upon Hull HU8 ... 155 C4
York YO24 ... 130 A4
Cleveland Terr YO32 ... 127 F4
Cleveland Way
41 Hatfield DN7 ... 92 D4
York YO32 ... 127 F3
Cliff Ave DN15 ... 82 F5
Cliff Closes Rd DN15 ... 150 D6
Cliff Dr
Burton upon Stather
DN15 ... 82 B5
3 Kingston upon Hull HU13 ... 69 E4
Cliff Gdns DN15 ... 150 E6
Cliff Gr DN18 ... 84 E8
Cliff Hill Rd DN6 ... 76 D2
Cliff La Bempton YO15 ... 4 D4
Mappleton HU18 ... 47 A6
Waddingham DN21 ... 119 F6
Cliff Rd Atwick YO25 ... 35 D5
Bridlington YO15 ... 123 B6
Hessle HU13 ... 69 E4
Hornsea HU18 ... 134 C6
Snitterby DN21 ... 119 F5
Winteringham DN15 ... 83 A8
Cliff St Bridlington YO15 ... 122 F2
Scunthorpe DN16 ... 151 C6
Cliff The DN15 ... 150 D7
Cliff Top La 2 HU13 ... 69 E4
Cliffe La YO43 ... 52 D8
Cliffe Rd
Market Weighton YO43 ... 135 D1
Newbald YO43 ... 53 C7
Cliffe VC Prim Sch YO8 ... 49 E2
Clifford Ave HU8 ... 141 E4
Clifford St
Hornsea HU18 ... 134 C5
York YO1 ... 156 B2
Clifford's Twr* YO1 ... 156 B1
Clifton YO30 ... 156 A4
Clifton Ct 27 DN8 ... 93 A8
Clifton Dale YO30 ... 130 A6
Clifton Gdns DN14 ... 149 B4
Clifton Gn YO30 ... 130 A6
Clifton Gn Jun Sch
YO30 ... 130 B7
Clifton Gn Sch YO30 ... 130 B7
Clifton Moor Gate
YO30 ... 127 A2
Clifton Moor Ind Pk*
YO30 ... 127 A4
Clifton Moor Ret Pk
YO30 ... 126 E3
Clifton Moor Sh Ctr
YO30 ... 126 F3
Clifton Moorgate
YO30 ... 127 B3
Clifton Pk Ave YO30 ... 129 E8
Clifton Pl 3 YO30 ... 130 A7
Clifton Prep Sch
YO30 ... 156 A4
Clifton Prim Sch HU2 ... 155 A4
Clifton Rd DN34 ... 152 A2
Clifton St
Hornsea HU18 ... 134 C5
Kingston upon Hull HU2 ... 155 A4
Clifton Terr HU5 ... 140 E1
Clifton Without Jun Sch
YO30 ... 129 F8
Clive Gr YO24 ... 129 F2
Clive Sullivan Way
HU4 ... 144 C1
Clixby Cl DN35 ... 103 D2
Clixby La DN38 ... 110 E7
Clockmill La YO42 ... 29 A4
Cloeberry Way 14 HU12 ... 72 C7
Cloister Cl DN17 ... 150 F2
Cloister Wk DN20 ... 97 E3
Cloisters The
6 Grimsby DN37 ... 102 B4
15 Hemingbrough YO8 ... 49 F1
Humberston DN36 ... 114 D8
Wilberfoss YO41 ... 27 F6
York YO31 ... 156 C3
Cloisters Wlk YO31 ... 156 C3
Close The Cawood YO8 ... 48 A7
Goxhill DN19 ... 71 A1
Great Driffield YO25 ... 124 F5
Grimsby DN34 ... 152 C3
Kingston upon Hull
HU10 ... 138 F1
4 Leven HU17 ... 45 A8
5 Market Weighton YO43 ... 135 E4
Norton DN6 ... 76 E2
12 Patrington HU12 ... 74 D1
Riccall YO19 ... 49 A8
Scunthorpe DN16 ... 151 B6
Sutton-on-Hull HU7 ... 141 D6
8 Withernsea HU19 ... 75 A6
York YO30 ... 129 F8
Clouds La Belton DN9 ... 95 B1
West Butterwick DN17 ... 106 C8
Clough Garth HU12 ... 72 D8
Clough La DN6 ... 77 B2
Clough Rd HU5 ... 140 F3
Cloughton Gr HU5 ... 139 E2
Clovelly Gdns 3 HU5 ... 140 E1
Clover Bank View HU6 ... 56 E5
Cloverley Cl YO41 ... 15 C2
Cloverley Rd 6 YO16 ... 123 A6
Clowes Ct 4 HU13 ... 143 E1
Clumber Pl DN35 ... 153 E1
Clumber St HU5 ... 145 C8
Clyde St Grimsby DN32 ... 152 F4
Kingston upon Hull HU3 ... 144 F5
Clyfton Cres DN40 ... 87 B1
Coach House Garth
YO42 ... 28 D3
Coach House Gdns
DN20 ... 108 E8
Coachings The 4 HU13 ... 69 E4
Coal Pit La WF8 ... 76 A2
Coal Shore La LN11 ... 115 E1
Coastguard Hill YO14 ... 3 E5
Coates Ave DN15 ... 83 A5
Coates Marsh La DN14 ... 63 B2
Cobble Ct Mews YO24 ... 156 A1
Cobble La DN14 ... 51 F1
Cobbler Hill DN14 ... 149 B6
Cobcroft La WF11 ... 76 B8
Cobdale La YO42 ... 29 F7
Cobden St HU3 ... 144 F7
Cobden St N End
DN32 ... 152 F4
Cober Gr HU8 ... 142 C7
Cobham Way YO32 ... 128 E3
Cochrane St YO8 ... 148 D3
Cock Pit Cl HU10 ... 143 C6
Cockerell La YO25 ... 22 B4
Cocketts La DN20 ... 108 F5
Cockret Cl 8 YO8 ... 148 B6
Cockret Ct YO8 ... 148 B7
Cockret Rd YO8 ... 148 B7
Cockthorne La DN15 ... 83 C7
Coda Ave YO23 ... 133 B3
Coelus St HU9 ... 155 C3
Coeside YO24 ... 132 B7
Cogan St HU1 ... 155 A1
Coggan Cl YO23 ... 130 B2
Coggan Way YO23 ... 132 F4
Cohort Cl 10 HU15 ... 68 C5
Coke Oven Ave DN16 ... 151 F6
Cold Harbour La LN11 ... 121 F4
Cold Harbour Rd HU17 ... 43 A1
Cold Harbour View 5
HU17 ... 43 A2
Coldstream Cl 4 HU8 ... 142 C5
Cole St
Scunthorpe DN15 ... 151 B6
York YO31 ... 156 B4
Coleby Rd DN15 ... 82 E7
Coledale Cl 2 YO30 ... 126 F1
Coleford Gr HU7 ... 141 A7
Coleford Prim Sch
HU7 ... 141 A7
Colemans Rd HU12 ... 72 C7
Colenso St
Kingston upon Hull HU3 ... 145 A5
York YO23 ... 156 B1
Coleridge Ave DN17 ... 150 D3
Coleridge St HU8 ... 141 D2
Colin Ave DN32 ... 153 B2
Colin Rd DN16 ... 151 C6
Colins Wlk DN21 ... 107 C4
Coll of Ripon & York St John
York YO31 ... 130 E6
York YO31 ... 156 B3
Coll of Ripon YO31 ... 130 E5
College Ave 31 DN33 ... 113 E8
College Cl DN15 ... 82 C8
College Farm Cl DN14 ... 77 A8
College Gdns
32 Grimsby DN33 ... 113 E8
Hornsea HU18 ... 134 B5
College Gr HU9 ... 141 F1
College of Law YO23 ... 133 B7
College Rd
Barrow upon Humber
DN19 ... 85 E7
Copmanthorpe YO23 ... 132 A3
Thornton Curtis DN39 ... 86 B6
College St
Cleethorpes DN35 ... 153 E2
Grimsby DN34 ... 152 C2
Kingston upon Hull HU2 ... 155 A3
York YO1 ... 156 B3
Colleridge Gr 4 HU17 ... 55 E8
Colleys HU19 ... 75 A5
Colleywell Cl 3 DN9 ... 105 A2
Collier Cl 10 HU14 ... 69 A4
Collier Hag La YO23 ... 24 B3
Collier Rd 16 DN40 ... 87 C1
Collier St HU1 ... 155 A2
Colliergate YO1 ... 156 B2
Collin Ave HU9 ... 142 C2
Collingwood Ave
YO24 ... 129 F2
Collingwood Cres 12
DN34 ... 102 B2
Collingwood Prim Sch
HU3 ... 145 C7
Collingwood Rd 3 YO15 ... 4 C3
Collingwood St HU3 ... 145 D7
Collinson Ave DN15 ... 150 C7
Collinson La HU15 ... 67 A8
Collum Ave DN16 ... 151 B3
Collum Gdns DN16 ... 151 B2
Collum La DN16 ... 151 B2
Collynson Cl 1 HU10 ... 143 E8
Colonel's Wlk DN14 ... 149 D5
Colonial St HU2 ... 145 D7
Colonsay Ct 20 DN36 ... 114 A8
Colson Pl DN35 ... 153 B3
Coltman Ave HU17 ... 154 C4
Coltman Cl HU17 ... 136 F7
Coltman St HU3 ... 145 C5
Colton St 3 Brigg DN20 ... 98 B2
Misterton DN10 ... 116 C5
Coltsfoot Cl 5 DN15 ... 96 B7
Coltsfoot Dr DN37 ... 113 D7
Columbia Rd DN32 ... 153 A3
Columbus Way DN33 ... 102 C2
Colville Ave HU4 ... 144 B6
Colwall Ave HU5 ... 139 D2

Colwyn Cl 5 HU7 57 A7
Combe St DN35 153 C4
Comber Pl 5 DN32 152 F5
Comberdale Hill Swinescaif Rd HU15 54 B3
Comforts Ave DN15 151 A6
Commerce La HU1 145 D4
Commercial Rd
Kingston upon Hull HU1 155 A1
Scunthorpe DN16 151 C7
Commodore Croft HU1 155 B1
Common Croft La YO26 12 E1
Common Hill YO43 53 C5
Common La
Barnby Dun with Kirk Sandall DN3 92 B4
Beal DN14 61 D3
Burn YO8 62 E7
Catton YO41 27 E8
Dunnington YO19 26 F5
Fangfoss YO41 16 B1
Knottingley WF11 61 B1
North Cave HU15 53 B2
Norton DN6 76 E2
1 Seaton HU11 35 A1
Sutton upon Derwent YO41 38 C8
Temple Hirst YO8 62 F4
Thorganby YO19 37 F5
Thornton YO42 39 B8
Twin Rivers DN17 81 B6
Walden Stubbs DN6 76 F4
Warthill YO19 14 F2
Wawne HU7 56 F7
Welton HU15 68 D4
York YO10 131 B1
Common La W HU15 53 B2
Common Mid Rd DN17 94 C8
Common Rd
Broughton DN20 97 E4
Dunnington YO19 26 F7
Rowley HU20 54 F5
Skipwith YO8 37 E1
South Cave HU15 67 C7
Commonside
Crowle DN17 94 C8
Westwoodside DN9 105 A2
Compass Rd HU6 140 C8
Compton Dr
Grimsby DN34 152 C3
Keyingham HU12 73 C3
Compton St YO30 130 A6
Comrie Dr 16 YO42 29 A3
Concast Rd DN16 97 A3
Concorde Pk YO30 127 A3
Coney St YO1 156 B2
Coneycroft 10 YO19 26 F7
Coneygarth La YO19 26 E5
Conference Ct 10 DN16 96 D1
Conifer Cl
6 Kingston upon Hull HU4 144 C7
Scunthorpe DN17 150 C1
6 York YO32 127 D3
Conifers Cl 2 YO8 48 D1
Coningham Ave 1 YO30 126 E2
Coningsby Dr DN34 152 A1
Coningsby Rd DN17 150 D1
Conington Ave HU17 137 B4
Conisborough Ave 2 DN36 113 F7
Coniston Ave DN33 113 D8
Coniston Cl 1 YO30 126 E1
Coniston Cres 19 DN36 103 C1
Coniston Dr YO10 131 B4
Coniston La
Coniston HU11 58 A5
Swine HU11 57 E6
Coniston Way DN14 149 E5
Connaught Ave DN32 152 D1
Connaught Rd 9 DN21 117 B1
Connaught Way YO32 127 F6
Consort Ct HU9 146 B5
Constable Ave HU11 58 A4
Constable Cl
18 Flamborough YO15 5 A2
Sproatley HU11 58 D5
Constable Garth 5 HU12 72 D7
Constable Prim Sch HU3 145 C5
Constable Rd
Flamborough YO15 5 A2
Hornsea HU18 134 D5
Hunmanby YO14 3 A8
Constable St HU3 145 C5
Constantine Ave YO10 131 A4
Constitution Hill HU17 136 A6
Constitutional Ave DN35 153 C4
Convamore Rd DN32 152 F2
Convent Ct HU5 140 D1
Convent La HU3 145 D6
Conway Ave DN34 152 A3
Conway Cl
Kingston upon Hull HU3 145 B5
2 York YO30 126 E3
Conway Sq DN15 150 E7
Conyard Rd DN35 153 E3
Conyers Ave DN33 102 E1
Cookbury Cl 6 HU7 56 F5
Cookridge Dr 11 DN7 92 D4
Cooks La Grimsby DN37 102 B5
Nettleton LN7 111 A3
Coomb Briggs Prim Sch DN40 87 B1
Coombs Yd HU17 154 A3
Cooper La DN37 101 E1
Cooper Rd DN32 153 A3
Cooper St
Beverley HU17 154 B4
Kingston upon Hull HU2 155 B4
Coopers Dr YO23 132 B3
Coopers Mdw 3 HU11 45 C5
Copandale Rd HU17 154 A4
Cope St DN32 153 A4
Copenhagen Rd HU7 140 F5
Copmanthorpe La YO23 132 E3
Copmanthorpe Prim Sch YO23 132 B3
Copmanthorpe Sports Club YO23 132 B2
Copper Beech Cl
6 Swanland HU14 69 B6
Upper Poppleton YO26 24 F8
Copper Beech Dr DN14 77 A8
Copper Beech Wlk 24 DN16 96 D2
Copper Beeches The 2 YO19 26 E7
Coppergate
Nafferton YO25 125 F7
1 Riccall YO19 36 F1
York YO1 156 B2
Coppergate Sh Ctr YO1 156 B2
Coppergate Wlk YO1 156 B2
Coppice Ave DN7 92 D3
Coppice Cl 10 YO32 13 E5
Coppice Gr 39 DN7 92 D3
Coppice La 1 DN7 92 D3
Coppice Side HU4 144 C6
Coppice The
Bishopthorpe YO23 132 F4
Brayton YO8 48 C1
Coppleflat La
Rowley HU17 55 D6
Walkington HU17 43 C1
Copse Cl 1 DN40 87 C2
Copse Mead YO25 124 D5
Copse Rd DN16 151 B1
Copse The
Beverley HU17 137 B3
Bigby DN20 98 D1
28 Grimsby DN33 113 E8
Copwood Gr 7 YO32 127 C8
Coral Dr 2 DN37 113 D7
Corban La YO32 13 B6
Corban Way 21 YO32 13 D5
Corbridge Cl 2 HU9 142 E1
Corby Pk HU14 69 A5
Corby Rd DN16 151 C6
Cordeaux Cl DN21 107 C4
Cordella Cl 1 HU3 145 A5
Coriander Cl HU17 154 A1
Corinthian Ave DN34 152 B2
Corinthian Way HU9 146 D6
Corlett Ct YO24 132 C8
Cormorant Cl 2 HU7 141 D8
Cormorant Dr 1 DN37 102 B4
Cornaught Ct YO10 133 D8
Cornborough Av YO31 130 F6
Cornelius Cswy YO8 49 E8
Cornelius Wlk YO43 135 E4
Corner Cl 17 YO32 13 D5
Cornfield Cl 5 DN33 113 D8
Cornfield Cres YO16 122 B2
Cornflower Cl 17 DN41 101 F5
Cornhill Dr DN18 85 A8
Cornlands Rd YO24 129 B1
Cornley Rd DN10 116 A6
Cornmill Cl YO8 48 B8
Cornwall Dr YO10 133 E8
Cornwall Rd
2 Keadby DN17 95 D6
Scunthorpe DN16 151 C1
Cornwall St
7 Kirton in Lindsey DN21 108 B1
New Village HU16 139 C6
Stoneferry HU8 141 A1
Cornwell Cl 5 DN33 102 E2
Cornwood Way 11 YO32 127 C8
Corona Dr
Kingston upon Hull HU8 141 C4
8 Thorne/Moorends DN8 79 A1
Coronation Cl HU17 154 C3
Coronation Cotts DN35 153 F1
Coronation Cres 10 DN9 105 D6
Coronation Gdns 4 DN20 97 E3
Coronation Rd
Cleethorpes DN35 153 F1
Stainforth DN7 92 C6
7 Ulceby DN39 86 A1
Coronation Rd N HU5 139 C2
Coronation Rd S HU5 139 B1
Coronation St 10 DN14 149 C4
Coronet Cl 5 HU6 140 B8
Corporation Rd
Beverley HU17 154 A3
Grimsby DN31 152 C5
Kingston upon Hull HU9 147 A7
Scunthorpe DN15 151 A7
Corpslanding Rd YO25 33 A7
Corran Garth 6 HU4 144 A3
Corringham CE Prim Sch DN21 118 B2
Corringham Rd DN21 117 D1
Corsair Gr 4 HU3 145 A4
Corunna Ct 5 YO8 148 D5
Cosford Garth 5 HU7 57 A5
Cosgrove St DN35 153 F2
Cosmo Ave YO31 131 A5
Costello Stadium HU4 144 C5
Cotham Gdns 6 DN41 101 A4
Cotness La DN14 65 F3
Cotswold Ave DN14 149 D5
Cotswold Dr 20 DN37 113 D6
Cotswold Rd DN8 93 A7
Cotswold Way YO32 128 A5
Cotswolds The HU9 142 D2
Cottage Beck Rd DN16 151 B6
Cottage Cl DN20 108 F5
Cottage Dr HU10 143 B8
Cottage Field 1 HU17 43 A2
Cottage Mews HU17 154 B3
Cottage Yd La DN36 114 C7
Cottam La YO25 8 C5
Cottam Wlk HU11 139 A5
Cotterdale HU7 140 E7
Cotterdale Gdns LS25 61 A6
Cottesmore Rd
Cleethorpes DN35 103 C1
6 Kingston upon Hull HU13 144 A2
Cottingham Bacon Garth Cty Prim Sch HU16 139 A5
Cottingham Croxby Prim Sch HU5 139 D4
Cottingham Gr 2 HU6 139 F4
Cottingham High Sch HU16 138 E8
Cottingham Playsport HU16 139 A7
Cottingham Rd HU5 139 E4
Cottingham St DN14 149 C1
Cottingham Sta HU16 139 B6
Cottom La YO42 38 C2
Coulam Pl 8 DN36 114 D8
Coulbeck Dr DN35 153 D1
Coulman Rd 4 DN8 93 B8
Coulman St 5 DN8 93 B8
Coulson Cl
Hibaldstow DN20 109 A5
5 Strensall YO32 14 C8
Coulson Dr HU13 143 F2
Coultas Ct 3 HU3 145 A6
Council Ave HU4 144 E3
Council Terr 9 DN18 69 E1
Council Villas DN19 85 F8
Count De Burgh Terr 4 YO23 130 B1
Countess Cl*
Alkborough DN15 82 B8
6 Kingston upon Hull HU6 140 B8
County Rd N HU5 139 E1
County Rd S 2 HU5 144 C8
Couper Gr DN14 149 D1
Coupland Gdns 2 HU5 140 E2
Coupland Rd 1 YO8 148 C6
Courcey Gr YO26 129 C4
Court Dr YO8 148 A4
Court Gdns 8 DN14 78 C8
Courtland Rd HU6 139 E6
Courtney St HU8 146 B8
Courtneys Selby YO8 148 B4
Wheldrake YO19 38 A8
Courtneys The YO8 148 B4
Courtpark Rd HU6 139 F7
Courts Cl 7 DN14 64 E4
Courtway Rd HU6 139 E7
Courtyard The YO23 133 B4
Cove Rd DN9 104 F3
Coventry Ave DN34 152 A1
Coventry Cl DN17 150 D3
Coventry Rd
Kingston upon Hull HU5 139 C1
12 Thorne/Moorends DN8 93 B8
Coverdale HU7 140 F7
Coverdale Garth 2 YO16 122 E7
Covert Rd DN16 151 B1
Covert The
Kingston upon Hull HU16 139 C5
York YO24 132 F7
Covington 21 HU15 68 C6
Covin's La LN11 121 F8
Cow La Knottingley WF11 61 A2
Twin Rivers DN17 81 C6
Womersley DN6 76 D6
Cow Marsh La DN36 114 E5
Cow Pasture La YO42 38 C3
Cow Wold Rd HU17 42 E1
Cowden Gr 2 HU9 142 A2
Cowden La HU11 46 E4
Cowgate HU15 68 D6
Cowick CE VC Prim Sch DN14 78 E8
Cowick Rd Fishlake DN8 78 F1
Snaith DN14 78 C8
Cowie Dr YO8 148 D5
Cowlings Cl 16 YO14 3 A8
Cowper Ave DN17 150 D3
Cowper La YO23 36 C8
Cowslams La YO25 21 E1
Cowton La YO14 3 C6
Cox La 1 DN17 94 D8
Cox's Ct DN20 109 A5
Cox's Hill DN21 117 B1
Coxlea Gr YO31 131 B6
Coxwold Gr HU4 144 E5
Crab Tree La
Coniston HU11 57 F7
Kirk Smeaton WF8 76 A1
Crabley La HU15 67 E7
Crabtree Gr 1 YO32 127 D3
Crabtree La YO25 32 B4
Crabtree Rd DN7 92 C4
Crackle Hill 6 DN9 105 B2
Cradley Rd HU5 139 C3
Cragston Ave 19 DN33 102 E2
Craig Cl 5 DN20 97 D3
Craik Hill Ave 18 DN40 87 C1
Craikewells YO15 5 A3
Craithie Rd 11 DN35 103 C2
Crake Ave DN33 102 E1
Crake Wells HU17 55 C8
Crakedale Rd DN15 83 B5
Crampin Rd DN35 153 E3
Cranbeck Cl YO16 122 B1
Cranberry Way HU4 144 C4
Cranbourne Cl 23 DN35 103 C1
Cranbourne St HU3 145 C8
Cranbrook Ave
Kingston upon Hull HU6 140 B6
York YO26 129 C5
Cranbrook Rd YO26 129 C5
Cranbrooks The YO19 37 F8
Crane Rd HU9 146 C6
Cranfield Pl 4 YO24 132 C8
Cranham Gr HU7 141 A7
Cranidge Cl 2 DN17 94 D8
Cranswick Cl 8 HU17 43 E6
Cranswick Gr HU9 142 B1
Cranwell Cl 6 DN21 119 C8
Cranwell Dr 10 DN37 102 C5
Cranwell Rd YO25 124 E4
Cranwell St YO25 124 E4
Crapple La DN21 107 C2
Crathorne Rd HU17 154 C4
Craven Garth 5 DN14 61 D4
Craven Prim Sch HU9 146 C8
Craven Rd
Cleethorpes DN35 153 B3
Hatfield DN7 92 C4
Craven St N HU9 146 C8
Craven St S HU9 146 D7
Crawley Way YO31 131 B6
Crawshaw Ave HU17 136 E6
Craycroft Rd DN9 105 B3
Crayford Cl 7 HU9 142 E1
Crayke The YO16 122 F7
Crescent St
Grimsby DN31 152 C3
Kingston upon Hull HU16 139 A6
Crescent The
Beckingham DN10 116 E1
9 Bridlington YO15 122 F2
Brough HU15 68 D6
Burton Fleming YO25 2 E3
Hatfield DN7 92 C5
Holton le Clay DN36 114 A5
Hornsea HU18 134 D3
Huggate YO42 18 C2
Kelfield YO19 36 D1
Kexby YO41 27 C5
2 Kirk Sandall DN3 92 A1
18 Patrington HU12 74 D1
6 Riccall YO19 48 F8
Stamford Bridge YO41 15 D2
York YO10 131 C1
York YO24 156 A1
Cressey St DN31 152 E5
Cresswell Cl HU2 155 A4
Cresta Dr 10 DN17 96 C2
Cresta The DN34 152 C1
Creyke Cl 6 HU16 139 B7
Creyke La 7 HU15 68 D6
Creyke View DN14 64 A1
Crichton Ave YO30 130 B8
Cricklewood Wlk HU8 141 E6
Cridling Gdns DN6 76 F2
Cridling Pl 5 DN35 103 B2
Crinan Ct 3 YO32 127 F6
Crinan Dr 1 HU6 140 B8
Crispin Cl 5 HU4 144 A2
Crispin Way DN16 96 D1
Croft Ave 8 WF11 61 A3
Croft Cl
Eastrington DN14 51 F1
Market Weighton YO43 135 D3
Swanland HU14 69 B7
Croft Ct YO23 133 A4
Croft Dr HU10 143 C5
Croft Farm Cl YO23 132 B3
Croft La DN17 96 C1
Croft Lodge DN9 94 E1
Croft Pk HU14 69 A5
Croft Rd
Camblesforth YO8 63 D4
Finningley DN10 104 A1
Croft The
Beverley HU17 136 C7
Kingston upon Hull HU7 140 E8
Knottingley WF11 61 A3
22 Thorne/Moorends DN8 93 B7
1 West/East Butterwick DN17 106 D8
Croft View
Bransholme HU7 141 C7
Kirk Ella HU10 143 C6
Market Weighton YO43 135 D3
Croft's La DN9 106 B3
Crofters Dr HU16 139 C5
Croftlands 7 WF11 61 A3
Crofts La Hollym HU19 74 F4
Stainforth DN7 92 B6
Crofts The
9 Humberston DN36 114 C8
Scunthorpe DN16 151 B6
Ulrome YO25 23 A3
Croftside 1 YO26 129 B3
Croftway
Camblesforth YO8 63 C5
Selby YO8 148 C4
2 York YO26 129 B3
Cromarty Cl HU9 142 A3
Crombie Ave YO30 130 B7
Cromer Ave DN34 152 A1
Cromer St
4 Kingston upon Hull HU5 140 D2
York YO30 130 B7
Cromford St 18 DN21 117 B1
Crompton Terr YO32 127 D6
Cromwell Ave
Grimsby DN31 152 C3
Scunthorpe DN16 151 B5
Cromwell Cl 2 HU3 145 D8
Cromwell Ct 1 HU10 143 E7
Cromwell Rd
Cleethorpes DN35 103 D2
Grimsby DN31 152 A4
35 Hedon HU12 72 D7
York YO1 156 B1
Cromwell View 25 LN7 111 B4
Crook Hill HU15 68 C8
Crook La HU11 58 D7
Crook Mill Rd DN40 86 D5
Crook Tree La DN7 92 F5
Crooked Billet St 5 DN21 117 A2
Crookes Broom Ave DN7 92 D4
Crookes Broom La DN7 92 D4
Crookland La YO32 13 F5
Croom Medieval Village* YO25 7 B4
Croome Dale La YO17 7 C6
Croome Rd YO25 7 B4
Cropton Rd HU5 139 E2
Crosby Ave DN15 96 C7
Crosby Prim Sch DN15 151 A8
Crosby Rd
Grimsby DN33 102 D1
Scunthorpe DN15 151 B8
Crosland Rd DN37 102 B4
Cross Carr Rd DN20 109 A5
Cross Coates Rd DN34 152 A2
Cross Gate YO43 41 E6
Cross Gates YO25 21 F8
Cross Gordon St 1 DN14 149 C4
Cross Hill
5 Brandesburton YO25 34 B2
Driffield YO25 124 E4
Haxey DN9 105 C3
Hayton YO42 40 C8
Cross Hills La YO8 148 A5
Cross La
Alkborough DN15 82 C8
3 Amcotts DN17 81 F1
Flaxton YO60 14 E8
Flixborough DN15 82 A2
Fulford YO19 133 F5
Hutton Cranswick YO25 32 F6
Leven HU17 44 F7
North Frodingham YO25 33 F7
North Kelsey LN7 110 B5
Cross Rd Hatfield DN7 93 B4
North Frodingham YO25 33 F7
Ulceby DN39 86 B3
Cross Slack 8 DN17 94 D8
Cross St
8 Aldbrough HU11 47 C1
3 Barrow upon Humber DN19 85 D8
Beverley HU17 154 A2
Bridlington YO15 122 F2
18 Brigg DN20 98 C2
Cleethorpes DN35 153 E2
Crowle DN17 94 D8
35 Gainsborough DN21 117 B1
Garthorpe & Fockerby DN17 81 E6
Goole DN14 149 D3
Grimsby DN31 152 F6
Hatfield HU11 46 C6
Kingston upon Hull HU1 155 A2
2 Scunthorpe DN15 151 B8
Skipsea YO25 23 A2
3 Waltham DN37 113 E6
West Halton DN15 82 E8
5 York YO24 129 C3
Cross St W DN14 149 B4
Cross Tree Rd DN17 107 D7
Crossbeck Rd 2 DN16 96 D2
Crossfield Cres YO19 133 E6
Crossfield Rd HU13 143 E3
Crosshill La DN14 77 E6
Crossings The 13 DN14 64 E4
Crosskill Cl HU17 154 C4
Crosslands La HU15 53 B3
Crosslands Rd 2 YO10 133 E8
Crossmoor Bank DN14 80 C5
Crossmoor La YO32 13 E6
Crossway The
Grimsby DN34 102 B2
2 York YO31 130 E8
Crossways
10 Stainforth DN7 92 C6
York YO10 131 C2
Crosswood Cl 6 HU7 57 A7
Crow Croft La DN14 78 A5

- Crow Hill Ave DN35 153 E2
- Crow Tree Bank DN8 93 D4
- Crowberry Dr DN16 151 D1
- Crowland Ave
  - Grimsby DN34 102 C2
  - Scunthorpe DN16 151 A3
- Crowland Cl 2 HU8 142 C7
- Crowland Rd 9 DN17 94 D7
- Crowle Bank Rd DN17 95 C4
- Crowle Dr DN33 102 D2
- Crowle Prim Sch DN17 94 C7
- Crowle Rd DN17 80 F2
- Crowle St HU9 146 D7
- Crowle Sta DN17 94 E6
- Crowle Waste or Moors Nature Reserve* DN17 94 B8
- Crown Gdns 21 DN21 107 C3
- Crowther Cl HU17 137 A6
- Crowther Way 5 HU14 69 B7
- Croxby Ave DN33 113 E8
- Croxby Gr 14 DN33 113 E8
- Croxton Rd
  - Croxton DN39 99 F7
  - Kirmington DN39 100 A5
- Cruckley Animal Farm* YO25 21 E1
- Cruckley La YO25 21 E1
- Crudhall La YO42 40 A8
- Crummock 3 YO24 132 C7
- Crumpton Rd YO43 135 C3
- Crystal St HU3 145 C7
- Cuckoo La DN7 92 E6
- Cudworth Gr 1 HU8 141 B1
- Cullen Cl HU8 141 C5
- Cullingworth Ave 2 HU6 140 C7
- Cumberland Ave DN32 152 D1
- Cumberland Cl
  - Goole DN14 149 A4
  - 6 Strensall YO32 14 B6
- Cumberland Rd DN35 103 D1
- Cumberland St
  - Kingston upon Hull HU2 155 C4
  - York YO1 156 B2
- Cumbrian Ave 4 YO32 14 B6
- Cumbrian Way HU7 56 F7
- Cundall Cl
  - Kingston upon Hull HU9 141 E1
  - 6 Strensall YO32 14 C8
- Cunningham Rd 3 DN7 104 A8
- Cupid's Alley YO17 6 B6
- Cupola Way DN15 96 C8
- Curlew Cl
  - Beverley HU17 136 E6
  - Driffield YO25 125 A5
  - Kingston upon Hull HU7 141 D8
- Curlew Glebe 8 YO19 26 E7
- Curlew Gn YO15 11 B4
- Curry Rd DN34 102 C4
- Curson Terr YO8 49 E3
- Curzen Cres 5 DN3 92 A2
- Curzon Ave DN35 153 D1
- Curzon Ct 3 DN35 103 B2
- Curzon St
  - 4 Gainsborough DN21 117 B1
  - Kingston upon Hull HU3 144 F7
- Curzon Terr YO23 130 B1
- Cushman Cres 10 DN40 87 C1
- Custance Wlk YO23 156 A1
- Cuthbert Ave 6 DN38 99 B4
- Cuxwold Rd
  - Scunthorpe DN16 151 C4
  - Swallow LN7 112 B5
- Cycle St 4 YO10 131 A3
- Cygnet St YO23 156 A1
- Cynthia Rd DN32 153 C1
- Cyprus St HU9 147 B8
- Cyrano Way DN37 102 B4
- Cyril Cooper Ct DN32 152 E2

D

- Dacre Lakeside Pk* YO25 34 B1
- Dagger La HU1 155 B2
- Daggett La YO25 21 F8
- Daggett Rd DN35 103 D2
- Dairy House La HU12 73 A8
- Dairycoates Ave HU3 145 A4
- Dairycoates Rd HU4 144 E3
- Daisyfield Dr HU9 142 D6
- Dalby Gr HU9 142 B2
- Dalby Mead YO32 127 F1
- Dale Cl Selby YO8 148 C3
  - 5 Swanland HU14 69 B7
- Dale Dike Gr YO30 126 F2
- Dale Garth YO43 135 E5
- Dale Gate HU17 43 A1
- Dale Pit Rd DN7 92 F3
- Dale Pk Ave DN15 83 A5
- Dale Rd
  - Brantingham HU15 68 C8
  - Bridlington YO16 122 D4
  - Elloughton-cum-Brough HU15 68 C6
  - Swanland HU14 69 B7
  - Welton HU15 68 E6
- Dale St
  - Scunthorpe DN15 151 A8
  - York YO23 156 A1
- Dale St N DN15 150 F8
- Dale View 27 DN33 102 C2
- Dale's La YO31 130 F6
- Dalehouse Dr 2 HU10 143 F6
- Dales Prim Sch The HU7 56 F6
- Dales The
  - Kingston upon Hull HU9 142 D2
  - Scunthorpe DN17 96 C2
  - Willerby HU16 138 D6
- Dalesway HU10 143 B6
- Dalguise Gr YO31 156 C4
- Dalkeith Cl 16 HU7 57 A6
- Dallisons Rd DN20 109 A5
- Dalmais Cl 1 YO42 28 F4
- Dalmally Cl YO24 132 B6
- Dalmatian Way DN20 97 E4
- Dalsetter Rise HU8 141 F6
- Dalton Cl YO25 124 D3
- Dalton Hill YO19 38 A8
- Dalton La HU12 73 F6
- Dalton St HU8 141 A1
- Dalton Terr YO24 130 A3
- Dalwood Cl HU7 141 B8
- Dam Bank YO8 148 C6
- Dam Gn La HU15 68 C7
- Dam Hill YO23 24 B4
- Dam La Ottringham HU12 73 D2
  - Selby YO8 48 B3
  - Thornton Curtis DN39 85 E4
- Dam Rd DN18 69 E1
- Dame Kendal Gr 29 DN33 102 D2
- Damson Cl YO26 129 E4
- Damson Garth YO25 31 F2
- Danby Cl HU8 141 E7
- Danby Rd DN17 107 D7
- Dancing La Riston HU11 45 C5
  - Swine HU11 57 D7
- Dane Ave
  - Thorpe Willoughby YO8 48 B1
  - York YO26 129 C5
- Dane Cl 13 DN20 97 E4
- Dane Pk Rd HU6 139 E7
- Dane's Graves (Tumuli)* YO25 8 D2
- Danebury Cres YO26 129 C4
- Danebury Ct YO26 129 C4
- Danebury Dr YO26 129 C4
- Danes Croft
  - Bridlington YO16 122 D5
  - 2 York YO10 133 D8
- Danes Ct 5 YO19 49 A8
- Danes Dr HU13 69 F4
- Danes' Dyke* YO15 4 F2
- Danes Dyke Nature Reserve* YO15 123 E8
- Danes Hills (Tumuli)* YO8 37 E2
- Danes Rd DN21 117 C1
- Danescroft YO8 148 C2
- Danesfield Ave DN37 113 E7
- Danesfort Ave YO24 129 D2
- Danesgate YO26 129 C4
- Danesmead YO10 133 D8
- Danesway HU17 136 D6
- Daneswell Cl 3 YO41 15 D2
- Dansom La HU8 141 B1
- Dansom La S HU8 146 B8
- Danson Cl DN18 85 A8
- Danthorpe Rd HU11 59 B4
- Danube Rd HU5 144 C8
- Danum Cl 14 DN8 93 B8
- Danum Dr YO10 133 E8
- Danum Rd
  - 2 Hatfield DN7 92 D3
  - Scunthorpe DN17 150 F4
  - York YO10 133 E8
- Dar Beck Rd DN21 107 C4
- Darbie Cl YO32 127 D4
- Darby Rd DN15 82 B4
- D'arcy Rd YO8 148 E4
- Darfield Cl YO32 14 B8
- Dark La 5 Amcotts DN17 81 F1
  - Paull HU12 72 D4
- Darley Cl Kilham YO25 9 B3
  - 7 Stamford Bridge YO41 15 D2
- Darling La YO23 36 C8
- Darlington Gr DN8 79 B2
- Darnborough St YO23 156 B1
- Darnbrook Wlk YO31 131 B5
- Darneley Ct HU18 134 D6
- Darnholm Ct 14 HU8 141 E7
- Darnholme Cres DN17 107 D7
- Darrismere Villas 4 HU3 145 A5
- Dart Gr HU8 142 B5
- Dartford Wlk HU9 142 E1
- Dartmouth Rd DN17 150 D5
- Dartmouth Wlk HU4 144 A3
- Darwin Cl YO31 127 E1
- Darwin Ct DN34 102 C3
- Darwin Dr YO25 125 A3
- Darwin Rd YO16 122 E6
- Darwin St 4 DN21 108 B1
- Datchet Garth 3 HU4 144 B2
- Daubney St DN35 153 B4
- Dauby La YO41 27 B3
- Davenport Ave HU13 143 D1
- Davenport Dr DN35 153 D1
- Davey Cl YO25 124 E4
- David Lister Sch HU9 141 E1
- David Pl DN36 114 A7
- David St DN32 152 F1
- David's Cl HU16 138 B8
- Davidstow Cl HU7 140 F8
- Davie Pl DN35 153 B3
- Daville Cl HU5 139 B1
- Davisons Ave DN31 152 D4
- Davis's Cl HU10 143 C8
- Davy Ave DN15 150 E8
- Davy Cres 2 DN20 98 C3
- Davygate YO1 156 B2
- Daw La YO23 36 A5
- Dawes La 1 DN15 151 C7
- Dawlish Rd DN33 113 E7
- Dawnay Dr HU10 144 A6
- Dawnay Garth
  - Shipton YO30 12 E5
  - 2 Snaith DN14 63 B1
- Dawnay Rd HU11 58 A4
- Dawnhill La DN21 119 B2
- Dawson City Claypits Nature Reserve* DN19 71 C4
- Dawson Dr HU6 140 D8
- Day Cl Keadby DN17 95 D6
  - Wrawby DN20 98 E4
- Daysfoot Ct 8 YO10 130 E3
- Dayton Rd HU5 139 D1
- De Aston Sq DN15 150 E7
- De Grey Ct YO30 156 A4
- De Grey Pl 2 YO23 133 B3
- De Grey St
  - Kingston upon Hull HU5 140 C2
  - York YO31 156 B4
- De Grey Terr YO30 156 A4
- De La Pole Ave HU3 144 F7
- De Lacy La DN35 153 F2
- De Lacy Way DN15 83 A5
- De Mowbray Ct YO23 24 D3
- Deacon Ct 3 YO8 148 B6
- Deacon Dr DN15 150 B6
- Deacons Ct YO23 132 B2
- Dead La Bainton YO25 31 E7
  - Foggathorpe YO8 51 A8
  - Kirkburn YO25 20 A2
  - Lockington YO25 32 B2
- Deal Cl HU8 141 E8
- Dealtry Ave 1 YO32 127 C8
- Dean La YO43 53 D4
- Dean Pk Ind Est HU17 137 C4
- Dean Rd DN17 150 E2
- Deane Rd 12 DN40 87 C1
- Deangate YO1 156 B3
- Deanhead Gr 7 YO30 126 E2
- Deans Cl
  - Bishopthorpe YO23 132 F4
  - 5 Misterton DN10 116 C5
- Dean's La 7 YO42 29 A3
- Deansgate DN34 152 C2
- Deansgrove DN32 152 D3
- Dearne Ct 9 HU15 68 D5
- Dearne Gr 1 HU8 141 C1
- Deaton La DN36 114 A7
- Debdhill Rd DN10 116 C6
- Deben Gr HU8 142 C7
- Dee Cl YO24 132 B7
- Dee St 6 HU3 145 B4
- Deene Cl 8 DN34 102 B2
- Deep The (Aquarium & Marine Research Ctr)* HU9 155 C1
- Deepdale 5 YO24 132 D8
- Deepdale Cl YO16 122 E7
- Deepdale Gr 2 HU9 146 E8
- Deepfurrows La YO41 27 D3
- Deeping Way YO8 148 A6
- Deer Hill Gr YO30 126 F3
- Deer Pk Ct 1 LS25 61 A8
- Deer Pk Way 6 HU17 55 F8
- Deerhurst Gr HU7 141 A7
- Deerstone Way 22 YO19 26 F7
- Defender Dr DN37 102 A4
- Deira Ct YO25 124 F5
- Del Pyke YO31 156 C4
- Delamere Cl 6 YO32 13 D5
- Delamere Ct 24 DN35 103 C1
- Delamere Wlk DN14 149 F5
- Delhi St HU9 147 B7
- Delius Cl HU4 144 B4
- Dell The Beverley HU17 137 B2
  - 9 Broughton DN20 97 D3
  - Scunthorpe DN17 150 D1
  - 5 Skelton YO30 126 B5
- Delwood YO10 133 D7
- Dempster Ave DN14 149 C1
- Denaby Ct HU8 146 B8
- Denby Cl DN15 150 D8
- Denby Dr DN36 103 B2
- Dene Cl Dunswell HU6 56 D5
  - Hensall DN14 62 C2
- Dene Pk Sports Club HU6 56 D5
- Dene Rd Grimsby DN32 102 F2
  - Kingston upon Hull HU16 138 F6
- Dene St HU9 141 D1
- Dene Wlk DN14 149 F6
- Denehall Rd DN3 92 A2
- Denesway HU13 143 D2
- Denholme Ave 3 HU6 140 C7
- Denison Rd
  - Pocklington YO42 29 A4
  - Selby YO8 148 E4
- Denmark Ct 7 HU9 146 C7
- Denmark Rise 5 HU15 53 D3
- Dennett Rd HU17 137 B5
- Dennis St YO1 156 C2
- Dennison St YO31 156 C4
- Dent Rd HU5 139 D3
- Denton La YO43 53 D6
- Denton St HU17 137 B3
- Denton's Way DN20 109 A5
- Denver Rd 6 DN6 76 F2
- Deramore Dr YO10 131 C3
- Deramore Dr W YO10 131 C3
- Derby Cl DN32 153 A5
- Derby Rd DN15 150 B6
- Derby St HU3 145 D8
- Derringham Ave 5 HU4 144 B6
- Derringham St HU3 145 C7
- Derry Way 27 DN33 113 E8
- Derrymore Rd HU10 138 C2
- Derrythorpe Rd DN17 95 D4
- Derwent Ave
  - 18 North Ferriby HU14 69 A4
  - York YO31 130 F4
- Derwent Cl
  - Elvington YO41 27 B3
  - Kingston upon Hull HU6 139 D6
  - 2 Stamford Bridge YO41 15 D2
- Derwent Cres DN14 65 B7
- Derwent Ct YO41 27 C2
- Derwent Dr 4 Barlby YO8 49 B5
  - 12 Humberston DN36 103 C1
  - 9 Kirk Sandall DN3 92 A2
  - Wheldrake YO19 37 F7
- Derwent Est YO19 26 E7
- Derwent Gdns YO16 122 E7
- Derwent Inf Sch YO10 131 B4
- Derwent Jun Sch YO10 131 B4
- Derwent Pk YO19 38 A8
- Derwent Rd
  - Goole DN14 149 D1
  - 1 Howden DN14 65 B7
  - Scunthorpe DN16 151 D2
  - York YO10 133 D8
- Derwent St HU8 141 B1
- Derwent Wlk YO32 127 F5
- Desmond Ave
  - 4 Hornsea HU18 134 C4
  - Kingston upon Hull HU6 140 D4
- Despatch Rd DN16 97 A5
- Detuyll St W DN15 96 C7
- Deveron Way YO24 132 B7
- Devon Pl YO10 130 F3
- Devon St
  - Cottingham HU16 139 C7
  - Gipsyville HU4 144 F3
- Devonshire Ave DN32 102 E2
- Devonshire Dr DN14 149 B5
- Devonshire Rd DN17 150 F2
- Dewberry Ct HU4 144 D4
- Dewsbury Ave DN15 150 C8
- Dewsbury Ct YO1 156 A1
- Dewsbury Terr YO1 156 A1
- Deyne Ave DN15 151 A7
- Diadem Gr HU9 142 C5
- Dial Sq DN31 152 E3
- Diamond St YO31 156 C4
- Diana Princess of Wales Hospl DN33 102 E2
- Diana St DN15 96 D7
- Dibsdane HU6 139 E8
- Dick La DN14 65 E7
- Dickens Cl 1 YO32 127 F1
- Dickey La YO8 48 D5
- Dickinson Cl DN20 108 F5
- Dickinson's La DN36 114 B1
- Dickson Rd 4 YO24 129 B1
- Didscourt HU6 139 E6
- Digby Garth HU7 57 A5
- Digby Gdns DN34 152 A1
- Digby St DN15 150 F8
- Dijon Ave YO24 129 C2
- Dike Ray Cl YO32 127 C7
- Dikelands Cl 19 YO26 12 F1
- Dikelands La YO26 12 F1
- Dill Dr HU17 154 B1
- Dilys Gr 5 YO26 129 E4
- Dimlington Bglws 5 HU12 90 F6
- Dimlington Rd HU12 90 F6
- Dimmer Dales Rd HU12 90 D5
- Dingley Cl HU6 140 B6
- Dinostar* HU1 155 B1
- Dirty La DN7 92 D8
- Disraeli Cl YO32 127 E1
- Distaff La 33 HU12 72 C7
- Ditmas Ave 9 HU4 144 B6
- Division Rd 1 HU3 145 B4
- Dixon Ave
  - Broughton DN20 97 D3
  - Grimsby DN32 102 F2
- Dixon Cl Beverley HU17 154 A3
  - 4 Brigg DN20 98 C2
  - Market Weighton YO43 135 D2
  - 4 Tetney DN36 114 D4
- Dixon Ct
  - Kingston upon Hull HU16 139 A5
  - Selby YO8 148 B6
- Dixon Gdns YO8 148 B6
- Dixon La YO1 156 C1
- Dixons Yd YO1 156 C2
- Dobella Ave DN14 64 A1
- Dobella La DN14 79 B8
- Dock Office Row HU1 155 C3
- Dock St Goole DN14 149 C2
  - Kingston upon Hull HU1 155 B2
- Dodgson Terr YO26 129 D4
- Dodswell Gr HU9 147 E8
- Dodsworth Ave YO31 130 E7
- Dodthorpe HU6 140 A8
- Doe Pk YO30 126 F2
- Doe Pk La YO41 16 B4
- Dog & Duck La
  - Beverley HU17 154 A3
  - 12 Gainsborough DN21 117 A2
- Dog & Duck Sq 13 YO15 5 A2
- Dog Kennel La HU17 43 C3
- Doherty Wlk YO24 132 C8
- Dolby Vale 28 DN34 102 C2
- Dole Rd DN17 80 B1
- Dolegate YO41 15 F4
- Doll La 2 DN20 98 F7
- Dollyth Howe* YO17 6 F6
- Dolman Cres 11 DN17 96 C2
- Dolphin St DN35 153 F2
- Dominican Wlk HU17 154 B2
- Dominion Cl 9 DN36 114 A7
- Don Ave YO24 132 E8
- Don St DN14 149 D1
- Doncaster Rd
  - Brayton YO8 148 B3
  - Gunness DN15 95 E6
  - Hatfield DN7 92 D3
  - Haxey DN9 104 F2
  - North Elmsall WF8 76 A1
  - Scunthorpe DN15 150 A7
  - Stainforth DN7 92 B6
- Doncaster St HU3 145 B6
- Donna Fields YO25 9 F6
- Donnington Gdns DN15 150 F7
- Donnington St DN32 152 F3
- Donville Rd DN17 81 A3
- Dooks Cl DN21 107 C1
- Doon Garth HU4 144 A3
- Dorado Cl 2 HU3 145 A5
- Dorchester Prim Sch HU7 141 B6
- Dorchester Rd
  - Kingston upon Hull HU7 141 B7
  - Scunthorpe DN17 150 C4
- Doriam Ave YO31 127 F2
- Doriam Dr YO31 127 F2
- Dorking Cl HU8 142 A4
- Dornoch Dr HU8 141 C3
- Dorothy Ave
  - Thorne/Moorends DN8 92 F8
  - 6 Waltham DN37 113 E7
- Dorr La DN14 78 A8
- Dorrington Cl 23 YO42 29 A3
- Dorset Ave HU11 45 E2
- Dorset Cl E 2 DN15 82 B4
- Dorset Cl W 1 DN15 82 B4
- Dorset St HU4 144 F3
- Dorsey Way 5 HU15 68 C7
- Dot Hill Cl 3 YO43 53 F7
- Double Bridges Rd DN8 93 B6
- Double Dike* HU20 54 E5
- Doughty Cl 2 DN37 113 E7
- Doughty Rd DN32 152 E3
- Douglas Ave DN34 152 A4
- Douglas Rd
  - Cleethorpes DN35 153 D4
  - Kingston upon Hull HU8 142 C6
- Douglas St 3 YO8 148 C5
- Dove Cl HU12 74 A8
- Dove Cote Gdns DN14 62 D2
- Dove La HU12 74 B8
- Dove St YO23 156 A1
- Dovecote Garth 5 YO41 27 B2
- Dovecote Mdws DN20 98 D3
- Dovedale Cl DN15 83 A6
- Dovedale Ct YO16 122 F7
- Dovedale Dr 18 DN33 113 E8
- Dovedale Gr 1 HU9 146 E8
- Dovedale Rd DN16 151 D1
- Dover St Grimsby DN31 152 C4
  - Kingston upon Hull HU3 145 C8
- Dower Chase YO19 37 A6
- Dower Pk YO19 37 B6
- Dower Rise 11 HU14 69 B7
- Downe Cl DN14 78 D7
- Downe St YO25 124 E4
- Downfield Ave HU6 140 B8
- Downhill Dr 7 HU7 57 B5
- Downing Cl 7 DN34 102 C3
- Downing Cres 11 DN16 96 D2
- Downing Gr HU9 142 A1
- Downland Cres WF11 61 A1
- Downs Cres HU5 139 D2
- Dowse Ave DN15 150 E8
- Dowsons La DN14 78 E8
- Dr Anderson Ave 9 DN7 92 C6
- Dragon La YO16 122 C5
- Dragonby Rd 3 DN17 96 C2
- Drain Bank HU15 67 B8
- Drain La
  - Gilberdyke HU15 52 D2
  - Holme-on-Spalding-Moor YO43 51 F8
- Drake Ave DN32 153 B2
- Drake St 2 YO23 156 B1
- Drakes Cl YO32 127 F5
- Draper's La 17 HU12 72 C7
- Drapers Croft YO23 132 B4
- Drax CP Sch YO8 63 F5
- Dray Dr HU17 43 E5
- Draycot LN7 111 A2
- Draycott Ave HU18 134 C5
- Drayton Cl 5 HU8 142 C5
- Dressay Gr HU8 141 F7
- Drew Ave DN32 102 F2
- Drewry La 7 DN9 105 A2
- Drewton Ct 8 DN14 65 A7
- Drewton La HU15 54 A4
- Driffield Bsns Ctr YO25 124 F2
- Driffield CE VC Inf Sch YO25 124 E4
- Driffield Cl HU16 138 E6
- Driffield Jun Sch YO25 124 F5
- Driffield Rd
  - Beverley HU17 136 C6
  - Huggate YO42 18 C1
  - Kilham YO25 9 C2

Driffield Rd *continued*
Langtoft YO25 8 C4
Molescroft HU17 136 B8
Nafferton YO25 125 E7
Skerne & Wansford YO25 21 A2
Driffield Sch YO25 125 A5
Driffield Showground* YO25 124 D2
Driffield Spellowgate YO25 124 B7
Driffield Sports Ctr YO25 125 A5
Driffield Sta YO25 124 F3
Driffield Terr YO24 130 A2
Driffil Way DN15 83 A4
Drill Hall La 28 DN21 117 B1
Dring La DN21 118 A7
Dringfield Cl 2 YO24 132 D8
Dringhouses Prim Sch YO24 132 F8
Dringhouses Sports Club YO24 132 F8
Dringshaw HU6 139 F8
Dringthorpe Rd YO24 132 F7
Drive The
Cherry Burton HU17 43 A4
Kirk Sandall DN3 92 A1
Waltham DN37 113 E6
Drome Rd YO23 132 C2
Dronfield Ct DN15 150 B7
Drove La HU7 44 E1
Drovers Rise 1 HU15 68 C6
Drummer's Well* YO25 21 F8
Drummond Ct 5 HU7 57 B5
Drummond View YO23 133 B4
Drury Cl 1 DN37 113 D6
Drury La 3 DN36 114 A7
Drydales HU10 143 C6
Dryden Rd DN17 150 D2
Dryden St HU8 141 C2
Dryham La HU15 53 C3
Dryhurst Cl 9 DN6 76 F2
Drypool Way HU9 146 B6
Duchess St DN32 152 D2
Duck La YO12 1 A8
Duckthorpe La DN36 115 B2
Duddon Gr HU8 142 B6
Dudley Mews YO31 156 C4
Dudley Pl DN35 103 B2
Dudley Rd 28 Brigg DN20 98 C2
Scunthorpe DN16 151 E2
Dudley St
Grimsby DN34 152 C3
York YO31 156 C4
Dudley Wlk HU4 144 B3
Duesbery St HU5 145 C8
Duesbury Cl HU17 154 A3
Dugard Rd DN32 153 B3
Duggleby Howe* YO17 6 C5
Duke St Grimsby DN32 153 A5
13 Stainforth DN7 92 C6
Duke's La YO25 2 A1
Dukes Wharf YO23 156 B1
Dulverton Cl 4 HU7 56 F5
Dumfries Wlk HU8 142 C7
Dunbar Ave 5 DN36 114 A7
Dunbar Cl 6 DN21 117 C1
Dunce Mire Rd LS25 61 A8
Duncombe Ct HU12 72 E7
Duncombe Dr
Great Driffield YO25 124 D3
Strensall YO32 14 B8
Duncombe Gdns DN32 152 F5
Duncombe La YO32 14 B8
Duncombe Pl YO1 156 B3
Duncombe St DN32 152 F4
Dundas St YO1 156 C2
Dundee St HU5 145 A8
Dunelm Cl 3 HU8 141 C1
Dunelm Cres 18 DN8 79 B2
Dunflat Gate HU17 55 D6
Dunflat La HU20 55 B5
Dunflat Rd HU17 55 D6
Dunhill Rd DN14 149 B4
Dunkeld Dr 4 HU6 140 B8
Dunken Hill Highgate HU17 42 F4
Dunlin Cl HU7 141 D8
Dunlop Way DN16 151 E3
Dunmires La DN14 80 E8
Dunmow Cl 1 HU8 142 C5
Dunmow St DN31 152 B5
Dunnington CE Prim Sch YO19 26 E7
Dunnington La
Beeford YO25 34 D7
Skipsea YO25 22 F1
Dunnock Cl
7 Kingston upon Hull HU8 141 D7
26 Yaddlethorpe DN17 96 D1
Dunn's La 6 YO25 124 F4
Dunns Paddock 3 DN20 98 F7
Dunscombe Pk HU8 141 B2
Dunstall St DN15 151 A7
Dunstan Dr
30 Canal Side DN8 93 A8
28 Thorne/Moorends DN8 93 A8
Dunstan Hill DN21 108 B1
Dunstan Villas 17 DN21 108 B1
Dunster Rd DN21 117 C1
Dunston Dr HU13 143 D1
Dunston Rd HU4 144 D7
Dunsville Cty Prim Sch DN7 92 D3
Dunswell Cl HU6 140 A7
Dunswell La HU6 56 C6
Dunswell Prim Sch HU6 56 D6
Dunswell Rd
Cottingham HU16 56 B6
Kingston upon Hull HU16 139 C8
Dunvegan Rd HU8 141 F6
Durban Rd DN32 153 B3
Durban St HU8 155 C3
Durham Ave
Grimsby DN34 152 A3
10 Thorne/Moorends DN8 93 A8
Durham Cl 18 YO8 49 F1
Durham Mews HU17 154 A1
Durham Rd
Cleethorpes DN35 153 C1
Hatfield DN7 92 D4
Durham St HU8 141 C1
Durlston Dr YO32 14 A7
Dursley Ave 1 DN36 113 F7
Dyer La HU17 154 A3
Dyke Cl 2 HU13 69 F4
Dyke Rd DN36 115 C5
Dykelands Cl YO19 37 F7
Dykes La YO23 132 A1
Dymoke Dr DN37 102 B3
Dyon La YO8 50 B3
Dyon Rd YO8 50 D7

E

Eadon Pl DN14 78 B8
Eagle Bsns Ctr HU2 155 C4
Eagle Terr HU8 155 C4
Ealand Rd DN17 95 C6
Ealdane HU6 139 E8
Ealing Cl HU8 141 F5
Earfit La YO23 36 A8
Earl Ave DN36 114 A8
Earl St Grimsby DN31 152 C3
Scunthorpe DN16 151 B6
Earle St YO31 156 C4
Earle's Rd
Kingston upon Hull HU9 146 D7
North Cotes DN36 115 C5
Earlescourt HU6 139 E7
Earls Wlk DN16 151 B6
Earlsborough Terr YO30 156 A3
Earlsgate Gdns DN15 82 F5
Earlsgate Rd DN15 83 A5
Earsham Cl HU8 142 C6
Earswick Chase YO32 127 F7
Earswick Village YO32 127 F7
Easby Ct HU5 139 C2
Easedale Ave HU9 142 D3
Easenby Ave HU10 143 C6
Easenby Cl 3 HU14 69 C7
Easington CE VC Prim Sch HU12 90 F5
Easington Rd
Easington HU12 91 B2
Skeffling HU12 90 E6
Eason Rd
8 Grimsby DN33 102 D1
York YO24 132 E8
Eason View YO24 132 E8
East Acridge 7 DN18 84 F8
East Back Side YO25 10 C3
East Bank DN7 92 C7
East Boundary Rd DN16 151 F6
East Carr Rd
Keyingham HU12 73 D5
Kingston upon Hull HU8 141 F7
East Cl HU17 136 D6
East Comm La
Scunthorpe DN16 151 B4
Selby YO8 148 F4
East Cross St 15 DN21 108 B1
East Dale Dr DN21 108 B2
East Dale Rd HU14 68 E5
East Dock Rd DN40 87 E2
East Ella Dr HU4 144 C6
East End
Humberside Airport DN39 100 A6
Walkington HU17 55 C8
East End Cl DN33 102 E1
East End Rd HU12 58 D1
East Ferry Rd
Laughton DN21 106 D1
Wildsworth DN21 117 A8
East Field Rd DN7 92 C8
East Gate Rudston YO25 9 F6
Thorne/Moorends DN8 79 B2
East Gate N YO25 124 E5
East Gate S YO25 124 F4
East Gn DN17 107 D7
East Gr
Barton-upon-Humber DN18 69 F1
Kingston upon Hull HU4 144 D4
East Halton Prim Sch DN40 86 D6
East Halton Rd DN40 86 E3
East Hann La DN19 70 E1
East Hull Pools HU9 146 C8
East La Beverley HU17 136 D5
Corringham DN21 118 B2
Sigglesthorne HU11 45 F8
Stainforth DN7 92 C6
East Lambwath Rd HU11 46 D3
East Lound Rd
Haxey DN9 105 D2
East Lound Rd *continued*
Owston Ferry DN9 106 A3
East Marsh Rd DN19 71 C3
East Mid Mere Rd DN40 86 F4
East Moor Gdns YO19 133 F5
East Mount 8 HU14 69 A4
East Mount Ave HU8 142 B5
East Mount Rd YO24 156 A1
East Newton Rd HU11 47 D1
East Parade Brigg DN20 98 C2
Goole DN14 149 D3
York YO31 130 F6
East Pk HU17 45 B8
East Pk Ave HU8 141 E3
East Ravendale CE Prim Sch DN37 113 B2
East Rd
Bridlington YO15 122 D1
Keadby with Althorpe DN17 95 C6
East Riding Bsns Pk HU17 137 C3
East Riding Coll Beverley Campus HU17 136 C5
East Riding Coll Bridlington Campus YO16 122 D4
East Riverside DN40 87 E3
East Scar YO15 5 A3
East St
Dalton Holme HU17 31 E1
Grimsby DN32 152 E3
Hibaldstow DN20 108 F5
Kilham YO25 9 C3
5 Kingston upon Hull HU9 146 B7
Leven HU17 45 A8
Roxby cum Risby DN15 83 A4
East St Mary's Gate 3 DN31 152 D3
East View
7 Campsall DN6 76 E1
10 Knottingley WF11 61 A2
East Way YO31 127 E2
East Wlk DN15 151 B7
East Yorkshire Coll YO16 122 D4
East Yorkshire Hospl (Artificial Limb Unit) HU2 155 B3
Eastbourne Gr YO31 130 F5
Eastbourne Rd HU18 134 D4
Eastbourne St HU3 145 A5
Eastbourne Way 12 DN33 113 E8
Easterfield Ct 10 YO25 124 F4
Eastern Ave DN21 117 C1
Eastern Inway DN34 152 A1
Eastern Terr YO31 130 E6
Eastfield
5 Humberston DN36 114 D8
Hunmanby YO14 2 F8
Eastfield Ave
Grimsby DN33 113 E8
Haxby YO32 127 C7
Eastfield Cl
3 Beverley HU17 137 A6
North Frodingham YO25 34 A8
Eastfield Cres YO10 131 C2
Eastfield Ct YO10 131 C2
Eastfield Est HU12 60 B1
Eastfield Inf & Jun Schools DN40 87 C1
Eastfield La
Dunnington YO19 26 F8
Kellington DN14 61 F4
Rise HU11 45 F6
Eastfield Prim Sch HU4 144 D6
Eastfield Rd
Barton-upon-Humber DN18 84 F7
Brandesburton YO25 34 C2
Bridlington YO16 122 E5
Brigg DN20 98 C2
Easington HU12 91 A5
Epworth DN9 105 E6
Fangfoss YO41 28 D7
Great Driffield YO25 124 E5
1 Keelby DN41 101 A5
Keyingham HU12 73 D4
Kingston upon Hull HU4 144 D6
Market Weighton YO43 135 E3
Messingham DN17 107 D7
North Killingholme DN40 86 F4
Scunthorpe DN16 151 C1
Eastfield Rise 4 DN36 114 A5
Eastgate Beverley HU17 154 B2
2 Goole DN14 149 D4
Grimsby DN32 152 E4
4 Hornsea HU18 134 B4
Kingston upon Hull HU13 143 E2
Lund YO25 31 F2
Nafferton YO25 125 F7
North Newbald YO43 53 F7
Patrington HU12 74 D1
Scotton DN21 107 C2
Eastgate Ct HU18 134 C5
Eastgate View HU18 134 B4
Easthall Rd LN7 110 B4
Eastholme Cl YO25 124 F5
Eastholme Dr YO30 126 E1
Eastholme Gdns 9 DN15 82 B4
Eastholme La HU12 73 C7
Easthorpe Dr YO26 126 A1
Eastland Ave YO24 129 E2
Eastlands YO25 125 F7
Eastlands Rd YO25 19 E2
Eastmount Recn Ctr HU8 142 B6
Eastoft CE Prim Sch DN17 81 A3
Eastoft Rd Crowle DN17 94 D8
Luddington & Haldenby DN17 81 C3
Easton Ave HU8 141 A2
Easton Rd YO16 122 A4
Easton Wlk YO16 122 B4
Eastrington Ponds Nature Reserve* DN14 65 E8
Eastrington Prim Sch DN14 51 F1
Eastrington Sta DN14 66 A8
Eastside Rd
Grimsby DN31 152 F5
Scunthorpe DN16 151 F6
Eastville Rd 10 DN33 102 D2
Eastward Ave YO10 133 E7
Eastwold 2 YO43 53 F7
Eastwood Ave DN32 102 E2
Eastwood Ct DN15 150 B6
Eastwood Dr 8 DN20 97 E4
Eaton Ct Grimsby DN34 152 C2
7 York YO24 132 B8
Eaton Rd 13 DN40 87 C1
Ebberston Gr 5 HU5 139 E3
Ebor Ave HU18 134 D2
Ebor Cl HU8 142 B6
Ebor Ct 7 YO8 148 C6
Ebor Ind Est YO31 156 C3
Ebor Manor 1 HU12 73 C4
Ebor Prep Sch YO30 130 A7
Ebor St Selby YO8 148 C5
York YO23 156 B1
Ebor View YO43 135 E4
Ebor Way YO26 126 A2
Ebsay Dr YO30 127 A1
Eccles Cl YO30 126 D2
Eccles Ct DN20 98 D4
Ecclesfield Ave HU9 142 D1
Eccleston Rd DN3 92 A3
Eddlemere La YO25 32 E7
Eden Ave YO8 148 D3
Eden Cl Beverley HU17 136 D5
York YO24 132 C7
Eden Dene DN16 151 D1
Eden Dr HU8 141 C3
Eden Field Rd 12 DN3 92 A2
Eden Gdns YO15 4 D2
Eden Gr Rd 1 DN3 92 A1
Eden Rd HU17 136 D5
Eden Rise HU10 138 C2
Edencroft Dr 14 DN3 92 A2
Edendale HU7 140 F6
Edenfield Ave HU18 134 C2
Edenthorpe Hall Prim Sch DN3 92 A1
Edgar Cl DN21 107 C4
Edgar St HU3 145 D5
Edgbaston Ave 27 DN17 96 C2
Edge Ave DN33 102 E1
Edgecliffe Villas 4 YO15 122 F4
Edgecumbe St HU5 140 C2
Edgemere DN15 150 B7
Edgeware Ave 1 HU9 141 F1
Edgware Rd YO10 130 E2
Edinburgh Dr 4 DN36 114 A6
Edinburgh Rd 3 DN17 95 D6
Edinburgh St
Goole DN14 149 C4
Kingston upon Hull HU3 145 A5
Edison Gr HU9 141 E2
Edith Cavell Ct 4 HU5 139 F4
Edmonds Way DN31 152 D4
Edmund Cl DN21 118 A1
Edmund Wilson Swimming Baths YO24 129 D1
Edward Collins Sq 2 HU9 146 C7
Edward Ct 6 DN8 79 B1
Edward Heneage Prim Sch DN32 152 F3
Edward Rd 11 DN21 117 B1
Edward St
Beverley HU17 154 B3
Cleethorpes DN35 153 E1
Grimsby DN32 152 F3
Kingston upon Hull HU13 143 F1
1 Pocklington YO42 29 A4
6 Withernsea HU19 74 F7
Edwardian Dr YO15 122 C1
Edwards Rd DN15 150 F8
Edwins Garth YO43 135 F6
Eelmere La HU11 47 A5
Egginton Cl HU10 143 C7
Egginton St HU2 155 B3
Eglins Rd DN8 79 C1
Eglinton Ave HU8 141 F3
Egremont Cl 11 YO41 15 D2
Egrom's La HU19 75 A5
Egton Ave DN17 107 D7
Egton St HU8 155 C4
Egypt St HU9 147 B7
Eighth Ave
Bridlington YO15 122 F4
Fixborough Stather DN15 82 A1
York YO31 130 F5
Eildon Hills Cl HU7 57 B5
Elba St HU9 147 C7
Elderberry Dr HU4 144 D4
Elderberry Way 4 DN35 103 B1
Elderwood Ct 6 HU3 145 D5
Eldon Dr 11 HU12 58 C1
Eldon Gr
Kingston upon Hull HU5 140 D2
Thorne/Moorends DN8 79 C2
Eldon St YO31 156 C4
Eldon Terr YO31 156 C4
Eldwick Cl YO30 126 F2
Eleanor Ct HU9 142 B2
Eleanor St DN32 152 F4
Elgar Cl YO31 127 E1
Elgar Rd HU4 144 B4
Elizabeth Ave 6 DN3 92 A2
Elizabeth Cl
Bridlington YO15 122 C1
4 Gainsborough DN21 117 B2
14 Grimsby DN33 113 D8
Scotter DN21 107 C4
Elizabeth Ct 7 YO8 148 B6
Elizabeth Dr YO25 124 D3
Elizabeth St DN15 151 A8
Ella Ct HU10 143 C8
Ella Pk HU10 143 D7
Ella St HU5 140 B2
Ellen Way 9 DN36 113 F8
Ellerbeck Ct HU7 141 D7
Ellerburn Ave HU6 140 A7
Ellerburn Dr 3 YO16 122 C5
Ellerby Gatehouse* HU11 46 A1
Ellerby Gr HU9 141 F2
Ellerby Rd HU11 45 F2
Ellerington La HU17 42 F6
Ellerker La HU15 53 F1
Ellerker Rd HU17 154 A2
Ellerker Rise HU10 138 D2
Ellerker Wold La HU15 54 B1
Ellesmere Ave HU8 142 A4
Ellesmere Gr DN7 92 D6
Ellesmere Rise DN34 102 B2
Ellifoot La HU12 73 B7
Ellingham Cl HU8 142 B6
Elliot Ct YO10 133 D7
Elliot Way YO43 135 D3
Ellis Cl 4 HU12 58 D1
Ellis St HU9 146 C8
Ellis Way DN31 152 E4
Ellison Ave DN16 96 D1
Ellison St DN8 93 A7
Elliston Inf Sch DN35 153 D4
Elliston Jun Sch DN35 153 C4
Elliston St DN35 153 C3
Ellmore La LN7 110 B4
Elloughton Dale HU15 68 D8
Elloughton Gr 4 HU16 138 E6
Elloughton Prim Sch HU15 68 C7
Elloughton Rd HU15 68 C5
Ellwood Ct YO10 130 D2
Elm Ave 15 Brough HU15 68 C6
Burstwick HU12 73 A6
Cleethorpes DN35 153 E2
Goole DN14 149 B4
Grimsby DN34 152 A2
Kingston upon Hull HU8 141 C2
Elm Cl HU17 136 D5
Elm Dr HU17 43 A5
Elm End 9 YO32 13 E5
Elm Garth HU12 60 B1
Elm Gdns DN35 153 E2
Elm Gr 1 Aldbrough HU11 47 C1
Healing DN41 102 A5
Scunthorpe DN16 151 B4
York YO31 127 F2
Elm La Goxhill DN19 71 A1
Laceby DN37 101 E1
Elm Rd
Cleethorpes DN35 153 E2
Great Driffield YO25 124 F2
Waltham DN37 113 E6
Elm St
Kingston upon Hull HU5 140 D2
Selby YO8 148 D6
Elm Terr HU5 140 D2
Elm Tree Ave
9 Poppleton YO26 12 F1
5 Thorngumbald HU12 72 E5
Elm Tree Cl
Keyingham HU12 73 C4
6 Thorngumbald HU12 72 E5
Elm Tree Ct
Cottingham HU16 139 B6
Kingston upon Hull HU9 142 C1
Elm Tree Farm Rd 1 HU12 73 A6
Elm Tree Gr 4 DN8 93 B7
Elm Way Brigg DN20 98 B2
Messingham DN17 107 C7
Elma Ave YO16 122 D2
Elma Gr 3 YO30 126 E2
Elma Villas 3 YO16 122 D2
Elmbridge Par 3 HU9 142 E1
Elmdale 16 DN18 84 E8
Elmfield HU6 140 B6
Elmfield Ave YO31 130 F8
Elmfield Dr
16 Brandesburton YO25 34 B2
Kingston upon Hull HU16 139 A6
Elmfield Terr YO31 130 F7
Elmhirst Rd DN8 93 B8
Elmlands Gr YO31 130 F8
Elmpark Vale YO31 131 A8
Elmpark View YO31 131 A8
Elmpark Way YO31 131 A8
Elms Cl 2 YO19 36 F1

Elms Dr HU10 ... 143 C8
Elms The
4 Gilberdyke HU15 ... 66 D7
Stockton on the Forest YO32 ... 14 D2
Elmsall Dr HU17 ... 136 C6
Elmswell Spellowgate YO25 ... 20 B6
Elmswood HU13 ... 143 C2
Elmtree Ave 9 HU14 ... 69 A4
Elmtree Gdns 3 YO26 ... 129 C3
Elsenham Rd DN31 ... 152 B5
Elsham Dr DN37 ... 113 D6
Elsham Gr 21 DN33 ... 102 D2
Elsham Hall Ctry & Wildlife Pk* DN20 ... 98 F6
Elsham Rd DN20 ... 98 D7
Elsham Rise HU13 ... 143 D1
Elsham Wold Ind Est DN20 ... 99 A8
Elsie St DN14 ... 149 C5
Elsiemere Wlk 6 HU4 ... 144 B6
Elsternwick Ave HU8 ... 141 B2
Elston Cl
Kingston upon Hull HU6 ... 140 D6
York YO30 ... 130 A8
Elston Pl YO8 ... 148 C6
Elvaston Ave HU18 ... 134 C5
Elvaston Pk 10 HU7 ... 56 E5
Elveley Dr HU10 ... 143 A7
Elvington CE Prim Sch YO41 ... 27 B3
Elvington Cl HU6 ... 140 A6
Elvington Cres HU17 ... 43 D5
Elvington Ind Est YO41 ... 27 A3
Elvington La YO19 ... 26 E5
Elvington Pk YO41 ... 27 A3
Elvington Terr YO10 ... 130 E4
Elwell Ave HU17 ... 154 A2
Elwes St 9 DN20 ... 98 C2
Elwick Gr YO10 ... 131 C4
Elwyn Pl 2 DN35 ... 103 B1
Elwyn Way 40 HU12 ... 72 D7
Embankment The YO25 ... 124 B3
Emberton Pk 12 HU7 ... 56 F6
Embleton Dr 1 YO30 ... 126 F1
Emerald Gr 8 HU3 ... 145 A4
Emerald St YO31 ... 156 C4
Emerson Ave DN7 ... 92 C5
Emfield Gr DN33 ... 113 E7
Emfield Rd DN33 ... 113 D8
Emily Mews YO10 ... 130 E4
Emily St 8 HU9 ... 146 C7
Eminson Cl DN21 ... 107 C4
Emmanual Rd DN16 ... 151 F2
Emmanuel Ct
Grimsby DN34 ... 152 A2
Scunthorpe DN16 ... 151 B2
Emmanuel Dr 18 DN16 ... 96 D2
Emmerson St 2 YO31 ... 130 E5
Emmery Cl DN20 ... 97 D4
Emmott Rd HU6 ... 140 C7
Empringham St 5 HU9 ... 146 D7
Empson Ave DN14 ... 149 B6
Empson Terr HU17 ... 154 A2
Emsdale Wlk YO16 ... 122 B4
Ena St HU3 ... 145 B6
Enclosure Gdns 1 YO10 ... 131 B1
Endcliffe Ave DN17 ... 96 C1
Endeavour Cres 3 HU9 ... 142 B1
Endeavour High Sch HU3 ... 140 E1
Enderby Rd DN17 ... 150 D1
Enderby Rd Inf Sch DN17 ... 96 C2
Endfields Rd 1 YO10 ... 133 E8
Endike La HU6 ... 140 A6
Endike Prim Sch HU6 ... 140 C6
Endsleigh Holly Child RC VA Prim Sch HU6 ... 140 C4
Endsleigh St HU3 ... 145 A7
Endyke La HU16 ... 139 D6
Endymion St HU8 ... 141 B1
Enfield (New Waltham) Prim Sch DN36 ... 114 A7
Enfield Ave DN36 ... 114 A7
Enfield Cres 1 YO24 ... 130 A3
Enfield Mews HU17 ... 154 B3
Engine La HU11 ... 58 D7
Engine St 19 DN20 ... 98 B2
England Rd HU11 ... 142 F7
English Cl HU3 ... 145 E4
English Martyrs' RC Prim Sch YO24 ... 129 F3
English St HU1 ... 155 A1
Ennerdale HU7 ... 140 E7
Ennerdale Ave YO31 ... 131 B5
Ennerdale Cl 13 DN36 ... 103 C1
Ennerdale Leisure Ctr HU7 ... 140 E6
Enstone Garth 20 HU7 ... 57 A5
Enterprise Pk HU17 ... 137 B3
Enterprise Rd LN7 ... 111 A4
Enterprise Way
Bridlington YO16 ... 122 C2
Grimsby DN32 ... 153 A2
Winterton DN15 ... 82 F5
Ephams La DN41 ... 101 E7
Epping Cl HU8 ... 141 E6
Eppleworth Rd HU16 ... 138 D6
Epworth L Ctr DN9 ... 105 D6
Epworth Prim Sch DN9 ... 105 D6
Epworth Rd Hatfield DN7 ... 92 F4
Haxey DN9 ... 105 D3
Owston Ferry DN9 ... 106 A4
Epworth Rd W 9 DN7 ... 92 E4
Epworth St HU5 ... 140 D1
Epworth Turbary Nature Reserve* DN9 ... 105 B6
Eric Bielby Cl HU17 ... 154 B3
Ermine St Appleby DN15 ... 97 D8
Winteringham DN15 ... 83 B8
Ernest Hill Ct 1 HU5 ... 140 A2
Ernest Kirkwood Cl 4 HU5 ... 139 D1
Eryholme Cres DN15 ... 150 F7
Escart Ave DN32 ... 153 B2
Escrick CE VC Prim Sch YO19 ... 37 A5
Escrick Ct YO19 ... 37 B5
Escrick Pk Gdns YO19 ... 37 B5
Escrick St YO10 ... 156 C1
Escrick Terr YO10 ... 156 C1
Esk Dr YO26 ... 129 B8
Eskdale Ave
2 Kingston upon Hull HU9 ... 141 E1
York YO10 ... 131 C3
Eskdale Dr YO16 ... 122 F8
Eskdale Way 12 DN37 ... 102 B4
Eske Cl HU17 ... 44 C5
Eske La HU17 ... 44 C5
Eskham Cl 19 DN35 ... 103 C2
Eskholme La DN14 ... 78 B4
Eskwood Wlk DN14 ... 149 F6
Esmond St HU6 ... 140 D5
Esplanade
Bridlington YO15 ... 122 F2
Hornsea HU18 ... 134 D5
York YO26 ... 156 A2
Esplanade Ct YO30 ... 156 A3
Essex Dr 7 DN15 ... 82 B4
Essex St HU4 ... 144 E3
Estate Ave DN20 ... 97 D3
Estate Rd No 1 DN31 ... 152 A6
Estate Rd No 2 DN31 ... 152 A5
Estate Rd No 3 DN31 ... 102 C5
Estate Rd No 4 DN31 ... 102 C5
Estate Rd No 5 DN31 ... 152 A6
Estate Rd No 6 DN37 ... 102 C5
Estate Rd No 7 DN37 ... 102 C5
Estate Rd No 8 DN37 ... 102 C5
Estcourt Prim Sch HU9 ... 146 D8
Estcourt St
Goole DN14 ... 149 D4
Kingston upon Hull HU9 ... 146 D8
Estcourt Terr DN14 ... 149 D4
Estuary Way DN31 ... 152 B6
Ethel Ct 5 DN15 ... 151 B7
Ethelstone Rd DN34 ... 152 A3
Etherington Cl 5 HU12 ... 73 C4
Etherington Ct HU17 ... 137 B3
Etherington Dr HU6 ... 140 D5
Etherington La YO25 ... 124 E4
Etherington Rd HU6 ... 140 C5
Etive Pl YO24 ... 132 B7
Eton Dr 7 Haxby YO32 ... 13 D5
Scunthorpe DN17 ... 96 C2
Eton Rd DN14 ... 149 B5
Eton St HU3 ... 145 C4
Etton Cl HU16 ... 138 E5
Etton Dikes HU17 ... 43 A6
Etton Gr HU6 ... 139 F5
Etton Rd HU17 ... 43 A5
Etty Ave YO10 ... 131 A4
Etty Cl 24 YO41 ... 15 D2
Europa Bsns Pk DN31 ... 152 A6
Europa Way Brigg DN20 ... 98 B2
Immingham DN41 ... 87 E1
Europarc Innovation Ctr DN37 ... 102 B6
Eva Ave YO30 ... 126 D2
Evelyn Cres YO30 ... 130 B7
Evelyn Gr N DN32 ... 153 B2
Evelyn Gr S DN32 ... 153 B2
Evendine Ct 2 DN36 ... 114 B5
Ever Thorpe Cl 5 HU3 ... 145 C5
Everest Rd DN16 ... 151 C1
Evergreen Dr HU6 ... 56 D5
Evergreen Way 1 YO8 ... 48 D1
Everingham La YO42 ... 40 A7
Everingham Wlk HU5 ... 139 C2
Eversfield Cl 21 HU7 ... 56 F5
Everthorpe Rd HU15 ... 53 D3
Evesham Ave DN34 ... 102 C3
Evesham Croft 1 YO16 ... 122 D5
Exchange Pl 6 DN20 ... 98 B2
Exchange St
Great Driffield YO25 ... 124 E4
Kingston upon Hull HU5 ... 140 E2
Exeter Ct 11 DN34 ... 102 B2
Exeter Gr HU9 ... 142 A2
Exeter Rd DN15 ... 150 F7
Exeter St HU16 ... 139 C7
Exhibition Sq YO1 ... 156 B3
Exmoor Ave DN15 ... 96 B8
Exmoor Rd DN17 ... 150 C4
Exmouth St HU5 ... 140 C3
Exton Cl HU7 ... 56 F5
Eyre Ave DN16 ... 151 B1
Eyre Cl YO8 ... 148 A2

F

Faber Cl YO23 ... 132 B3
Faber St YO31 ... 130 E5
Faceby Wlk HU5 ... 139 E3
Fair Pl HU18 ... 134 B4
Fair View Ave DN35 ... 153 E2
Fairbourne Cl 1 HU7 ... 57 A7
Faircourt HU6 ... 139 E7
Fairfax 15 YO41 ... 15 D2
Fairfax Ave
Kingston upon Hull HU5 ... 139 F3
Selby YO8 ... 148 B4
Fairfax Croft YO23 ... 132 B2
Fairfax Dr HU12 ... 72 C8
Fairfax House* YO1 ... 156 C2
Fairfax Rd DN34 ... 152 B3
Fairfax St YO1 ... 156 B1
Fairfield Goole DN14 ... 149 F6
North Cave HU15 ... 53 D2
Rawcliffe DN14 ... 79 B8
Fairfield Ave
Grimsby DN33 ... 113 E8
Kingston upon Hull HU10 ... 138 C1
Fairfield Cl
5 Broughton DN20 ... 97 E3
Nafferton YO25 ... 125 F7
Fairfield Croft 8 DN9 ... 105 E6
Fairfield Ct 4 DN35 ... 103 D1
Fairfield Dr
25 Barton-upon-Humber DN18 ... 84 F8
Messingham DN17 ... 107 D7
Fairfield La LS25 ... 61 A6
Fairfield Pit Nature Reserve* DN19 ... 70 D3
Fairfield Prim Sch DN33 ... 113 E8
Fairfield Rd
Bridlington YO15 ... 122 D1
Grimsby DN33 ... 113 E8
Kingston upon Hull HU5 ... 139 F3
Scunthorpe DN15 ... 150 C8
Fairfield View 5 HU15 ... 68 D5
Fairfields 21 DN21 ... 108 B1
Fairfields Dr YO30 ... 126 B5
Fairholme La HU7 ... 56 F7
Fairisle Rise 5 DN40 ... 101 C8
Fairlawn HU17 ... 136 C6
Fairmont Cres DN16 ... 151 B6
Fairmont Rd DN32 ... 153 A3
Fairtree Wlk 21 DN8 ... 93 A8
Fairway Selby YO8 ... 148 A4
Waltham DN37 ... 113 E7
York YO30 ... 130 A8
Fairway Ave DN21 ... 117 B2
Fairway Ct DN35 ... 103 E1
Fairway Dr 18 YO26 ... 12 F1
Fairway The
Kingston upon Hull HU10 ... 143 A8
Thorne/Moorends DN8 ... 79 B2
Fairways The
Kingston upon Hull HU8 ... 142 A6
Scunthorpe DN15 ... 150 B6
Falcon Cl 10 YO32 ... 13 F5
Falcon Ct HU4 ... 144 D2
Falconer St 1 YO24 ... 129 F3
Falconers The DN21 ... 108 F2
Falkirk Cl 7 HU7 ... 57 A7
Falkland Rd HU9 ... 142 D1
Falkland St YO1 ... 156 B1
Falkland Way DN18 ... 69 F1
Fallowfield Rd DN33 ... 113 D8
Falmouth St HU5 ... 140 C3
Falsgrave Cres YO30 ... 130 B7
Falsgrave Gr HU4 ... 144 D7
Fangfoss Pottery* YO41 ... 28 C8
Fannystone Rd DN34 ... 152 B3
Far Bank La DN7 ... 92 C8
Far Comm Rd DN7 ... 93 A4
Far Field Cl 15 DN3 ... 92 A2
Far Field Rd DN3 ... 92 A2
Far Ings La DN18 ... 69 C1
Far Ings National Nature Reserve* DN18 ... 69 D2
Far Ings Rd DN18 ... 69 D1
Far La YO25 ... 35 A5
Faraday St HU9 ... 141 E2
Farbridge La HU12 ... 72 C6
Fardell Rd DN16 ... 151 D3
Farebrother St DN32 ... 152 E1
Farfield YO26 ... 129 C6
Farfield La YO19 ... 26 E8
Farfield lane YO19 ... 14 E1
Faringdon Rd DN31 ... 153 A6
Farlington Cl HU9 ... 142 C5
Farm Cl
4 Edenthorpe DN3 ... 92 A1
Gunness DN15 ... 95 E6
Farm Ct YO43 ... 135 C5
Farm La 2 DN17 ... 106 D8
Farm Way YO8 ... 148 B7
Farmers Way YO23 ... 132 B3
Farmhouse Mews 11 DN36 ... 114 A7
Farmlands Rd 1 YO24 ... 132 D8
Farms La DN14 ... 66 A8
Farmstead Rise YO32 ... 127 D7
Farndale Ave
Kingston upon Hull HU9 ... 141 E1
York YO10 ... 131 D4
Farndale Cl 1 YO32 ... 13 F5
Farndale Rd 1 YO16 ... 122 E7
Farndale St YO10 ... 130 D2
Farndale Way
2 Grimsby DN31 ... 152 D4
1 Winterton DN15 ... 83 A5
Farnella Cl HU3 ... 145 A5
Faroes Cl 1 HU9 ... 142 A3
Farrand Rd HU12 ... 72 C7
Farrar St YO10 ... 130 E3
Farriers Croft 2 YO23 ... 132 B3
Farriers Fold 13 DN9 ... 105 D2
Farriers Wlk HU17 ... 45 A8
Farringdon St 2 HU5 ... 140 E1
Farrishes La DN18 ... 84 A8
Farrows Pond DN19 ... 71 A1
Farthing Ave DN15 ... 150 E8
Farthing Dr 2 HU7 ... 56 E5
Farthing La YO25 ... 125 C4
Fauconberg Ave 6 DN33 ... 102 E1
Faulding La DN40 ... 86 F2
Faulding Way DN37 ... 102 B4
Faversham Ave HU4 ... 144 B6
Fawcett Cl HU5 ... 140 D1
Fawcett Gdns 9 YO25 ... 124 F4
Fawcett St
26 Gainsborough DN21 ... 117 B1
York YO10 ... 156 C1
Fawkes Dr YO26 ... 129 C4
Fawley Cl HU5 ... 140 E3
Faxfleet La DN14 ... 67 A3
Feasegate YO1 ... 156 B2
Feather La 5 DN19 ... 85 C7
Featherbed La YO42 ... 29 C4
Felbridge Cl 1 HU9 ... 142 E2
Feldane HU6 ... 139 E8
Fellbrook Ave YO26 ... 129 B4
Felstead Rd DN34 ... 102 C3
Fen La DN36 ... 114 D1
Fen Wlk DN36 ... 115 C5
Fenby Cl 3 DN37 ... 102 B3
Fenchurch St 1 HU5 ... 140 E1
Fenland Rd 12 DN8 ... 93 B7
Fenners Ave 29 DN17 ... 96 C2
Fenton St DN15 ... 151 B7
Fenwick Comm La DN6 ... 77 D2
Fenwick Ct DN36 ... 114 A5
Fenwick La DN6 ... 77 B1
Fenwick Rd 10 DN33 ... 102 D1
Fenwick St YO23 ... 130 C2
Fenwick's La YO10 ... 133 D7
Feoffee La YO42 ... 28 C5
Ferens Art Gall* HU1 ... 155 B2
Ferens Ave HU6 ... 140 B4
Ferens Ct 2 HU9 ... 141 D1
Ferens Gdns HU16 ... 138 F8
Ferensway HU2 ... 155 A3
Ferguson Rd 2 HU17 ... 55 B7
Ferguson Way YO32 ... 127 F1
Fern Cl Driffield YO25 ... 124 D2
Kingston upon Hull HU2 ... 155 A4
York YO32 ... 128 A4
Fern Croft 18 DN9 ... 105 E6
Fern Ct HU13 ... 144 A1
Fern St YO31 ... 156 C4
Fernbank 1 DN9 ... 105 D7
Ferndale Ave HU10 ... 138 D1
Ferndale Dr DN8 ... 79 B1
Ferndale Gr DN14 ... 149 C6
Ferndale Rd YO8 ... 148 C4
Ferndale Terr 11 YO15 ... 122 E2
Ferndown DN37 ... 102 B5
Ferndown Dr DN40 ... 87 C2
Fernhall Cl 17 DN3 ... 92 A2
Fernhill 5 DN37 ... 102 B4
Fernhill Rd HU5 ... 139 D3
Fernland Cl 15 HU15 ... 68 C5
Fernlea Cl YO8 ... 148 D4
Fernley Gn Cl 6 WF11 ... 61 A2
Fernway YO10 ... 131 C3
Ferriby Gr HU6 ... 139 F5
Ferriby High Rd HU14 ... 69 B5
Ferriby La DN33 ... 102 E1
Ferriby Rd
Barton-upon-Humber DN18 ... 84 E8
Hessle HU13 ... 143 B1
Scunthorpe DN17 ... 150 E1
Ferriby Sta HU14 ... 69 A4
Ferries St HU9 ... 146 D7
Ferry Cl 11 YO8 ... 49 F1
Ferry Farm Cl 2 YO19 ... 36 D8
Ferry La Airmyn DN14 ... 149 A8
Bishopthorpe YO23 ... 133 B4
Bubwith YO8 ... 50 C5
Goole DN14 ... 65 B5
Snaith & Cowick DN14 ... 63 C1
Thorganby YO19 ... 38 B5
Winteringham DN15 ... 68 B1
Woodmansey HU17 ... 56 C7
Ferry Mdw Pk 24 HU7 ... 56 F5
Ferry Rd
Barrow upon Humber DN19 ... 70 C1
Fishlake DN8 ... 78 F1
Goxhill DN19 ... 85 F8
Haxey DN9 ... 105 D1
Keadby with Althorpe DN17 ... 95 D4
Kilpin DN14 ... 65 B5
Kingston upon Hull HU13 ... 143 E1
Scunthorpe DN15 ... 150 D8
South Cave HU15 ... 53 E1
Wawne HU7 ... 56 D8
Wold Haven YO42 ... 29 A3
Ferry Rd E DN19 ... 85 C8
Ferry Rd W DN15 ... 96 A7
Ferry View
Keyingham HU12 ... 73 C4
Thorngumbald HU12 ... 72 E5
Ferryman Pk HU12 ... 72 A5
Fetherston Cl 19 YO42 ... 29 A3
Fetter La YO1 ... 156 B2
Feversham Cres 4 YO31 ... 130 C7
Fewson Garth 26 HU12 ... 72 D7
Fewster Way YO10 ... 156 C1
Fewston Dr 9 YO30 ... 126 F1
Field Ave YO8 ... 48 B1
Field Cl 10 Laceby DN37 ... 101 F1
Snaith DN14 ... 78 C8
Field Head
Laceby DN37 ... 101 E1
Wilberfoss YO41 ... 27 F6
Field La Eastoft DN17 ... 81 A4
Gowdall DN14 ... 77 F8
Hambleton YO8 ... 48 B1
Hensall DN14 ... 62 D2
Heslington YO10 ... 131 C2
Morton DN21 ... 116 F3
Rawcliffe DN14 ... 64 A1
Thornton YO42 ... 39 A8
Wistow YO8 ... 48 C7
Wroot DN9 ... 104 D5
Field La Sports Ctr YO8 ... 48 B1
Field Rd
Bridlington YO16 ... 122 C4
Crowle DN17 ... 94 D7
Stainforth DN7 ... 92 C6
Thorne/Moorends DN8 ... 93 A8
West Haddlesey YO8 ... 62 A5
Field Side DN8 ... 93 A8
Field St HU9 ... 146 B7
Field The DN32 ... 153 C2
Field View YO31 ... 130 C7
Fieldend La HU12 ... 59 B2
Fieldfare YO25 ... 125 B5
Fieldhouse Rd 7 DN36 ... 103 D1
Fielding Way 19 DN21 ... 117 C1
Fields Cl 2 DN9 ... 105 D7
Fields Cl Rd HU12 ... 73 E4
Fields Rd DN9 ... 105 E2
Fieldside Blyton DN21 ... 117 F5
Crowle DN17 ... 94 D7
Epworth DN9 ... 105 D6
Fieldside Garth HU6 ... 56 D5
Fifth Ave
Bridlington YO15 ... 123 A4
Flixborough Stather DN15 ... 82 A1
Goole DN14 ... 149 C5
Scunthorpe DN17 ... 150 B2
York YO31 ... 130 F4
Fifth Ave Prim Sch HU6 ... 140 A6
Fiftyeights Rd DN10 ... 104 B2
Figham Rd HU17 ... 137 B3
Figham Springs Way HU17 ... 154 B1
Fildes St DN31 ... 152 D3
Filey Rd Grimsby DN32 ... 153 A1
Hunmanby YO14 ... 3 A8
Filey Terr YO30 ... 130 C7
Fillingham Cres
Cleethorpes DN35 ... 103 C2
Gunness DN15 ... 150 B7
Fimber Ave HU16 ... 139 A5
Finch Croft 5 HU7 ... 141 D7
Finch Pk HU17 ... 136 D5
Finchcroft La HU17 ... 43 B2
Finchley Cl HU8 ... 141 F5
Finchley Ct DN31 ... 152 A4
Findlay Cres DN36 ... 114 A7
Findon Cl 28 HU7 ... 56 F6
Fingall Mews 1 HU5 ... 139 D3
Finkle La DN18 ... 69 F1
Finkle St
2 Bishop Burton HU17 ... 43 A2
Hensall DN14 ... 62 D2
Kingston upon Hull HU2 ... 155 B1
Kingston upon Hull HU16 ... 139 A6
Market Weighton YO43 ... 135 D4
2 North Cave HU15 ... 53 D3
Selby YO8 ... 148 C5
Stainforth DN7 ... 92 C7
Finningley Garth 14 HU7 ... 57 A5
Finnley's La DN14 ... 78 C7
Finsbury Ave YO23 ... 130 C1
Finsbury Dr 7 DN33 ... 102 D1
Finsbury St YO23 ... 130 C1
Fir Cl 11 Brough HU15 ... 68 D5
Scunthorpe DN16 ... 96 D2
Fir Heath Cl 5 YO24 ... 129 C1
Fir Tree Cl YO8 ... 48 B2
Fir Tree Dr 11 DN6 ... 76 E2
Fir Tree La YO8 ... 48 B2
Fir Tree Way YO8 ... 48 B2
Fir Trees HU10 ... 143 D6
Fir Trees The YO8 ... 48 B2
Firbank Cl 9 YO32 ... 14 A7
Fircroft Way DN34 ... 152 A3
Firethorn Cl 3 HU3 ... 145 D5
Firsby Cres DN33 ... 102 D1
First Ave
Bridlington YO15 ... 122 F4
Flixborough DN15 ... 82 A1
3 Goole DN14 ... 149 C4
Grimsby DN33 ... 102 E2
Scunthorpe DN17 ... 150 C2
York YO31 ... 130 F6
First Comm La YO8 ... 48 D4
First La
Kingston upon Hull HU10 ... 144 A5
South Cave HU15 ... 54 A2
Firth Field Rd DN7 ... 92 F4
Firth La DN9 ... 104 D5
Firtholme Rd HU12 ... 91 A4
Firtree Cl
4 Earswick YO32 ... 127 F7
York YO24 ... 129 E3
Firtree Dr DN20 ... 98 F7
Firwood Whin 5 YO32 ... 127 F3
Fish Dock Rd DN31 ... 152 F6

Fish La HU15 .....52 D2
Fish St HU1 .....155 B1
Fishemore Ave HU13 ...143 F2
Fisher Cl HU10 .....138 D2
Fisher La YO25 .....22 E5
Fisher Pl DN35 .....153 D3
Fisher Sq HU17 .....154 A2
Fishergate YO10 .....156 C1
Fishergate Prim Sch
YO10 .....156 C1
Fisherman's Wharf
DN31 .....152 D4
Fishermans Wlk 2 HU3 .145 C4
Fishlake Nab DN7 .....92 C7
Fishpond Hill YO42 .....29 C4
Fishwick Ave 5 HU13 ...143 E1
Fiskerton Cl 20 DN34 ...102 C2
Fiskerton Way DN31 ....102 C6
Fitling Rd HU11 .....59 B5
Fitties La DN36 .....115 C5
Fitzroy St HU5 .....140 D2
Fitzwilliam Mews 2
DN35 .....103 C1
Five Rivers DN14 .....149 C5
Flaen Cl YO15 .....5 A2
Flaen Rd YO15 .....5 A2
Flag Wlk 1 HU6 .....140 C8
Flag Yd YO16 .....122 C4
Flamborough CE VC Prim
Sch YO15 .....5 A2
Flamborough Cliff Nature
Reserve* YO15 .....5 C4
Flamborough Head Nature
Reserve* YO15 .....5 D2
Flamborough Outer Headland
Nature Reserve* YO15 ...5 D2
Flamborough Rd
Bempton YO15 .....4 E1
Bridlington YO15 .....122 F4
Flarepath The DN20 .....99 A8
Flashley Carr La DN6 ....77 F1
Flat La YO42 .....28 D4
Flatgate DN14 .....65 B7
Flavian Gr YO30 .....129 F8
Flaxdale Ct HU5 .....139 E1
Flaxley Ct YO8 .....148 B5
Flaxley Rd YO8 .....148 A7
Flaxman Ave YO10 .....131 A4
Flaxman Croft YO23 ....132 B3
Flaxmill Wlk 2 HU15 .....66 D7
Flaxton Rd
Kingston upon Hull HU5 ...139 D1
Strensall YO32 .....14 B7
Fleet Garth 11 HU12 .....72 D7
Fleet La DN14 .....64 A7
Fleetgate 11 DN18 .....69 E1
Fleets Cl DN7 .....92 C7
Fleetway DN36 .....115 A3
Fleetwood Cl 4 DN33 ...113 E8
Fleming Ave 3 YO31 ....130 E5
Fleming Wlk
Cottingham HU16 .....139 A4
Gipsyville HU4 .....144 D2
Flemingate HU17 .....154 C2
Flemingdale HU7 .....140 F7
Fletcher Cl
Kingston upon Hull
HU13 .....143 E2
6 Scunthorpe DN15 .....96 B7
Fletcher Ct 14 YO32 .....13 E5
Fletcher Gate HU12 .....72 C7
Fletcher Rd DN34 .....102 C4
Fletcher's Croft YO23 ...132 C3
Flinton Gr HU9 .....142 A1
Flinton Rd
Aldbrough HU11 .....58 F8
Humbleton HU11 .....59 A7
Flinton St HU3 .....145 B3
Flixborough Rd DN15 ....82 A4
Floral Hall HU18 .....134 D5
Florence Ave HU13 .....143 F1
Florence Gr YO30 .....126 D2
Florence Nightingale 3
HU5 .....139 F4
Florence St DN32 .....152 E1
Florin Dr 3 HU7 .....56 E5
Flottergate Mall 8
DN31 .....152 D3
Flour Sq DN31 .....152 E5
Fog La YO42 .....38 E4
Folk Mus* HU18 .....134 C4
Folkestone St HU5 .....140 D2
Folks Cl 13 YO32 .....13 F5
Folkton Ave HU16 .....139 A4
Follies The DN15 .....97 E7
Folly La LN7 .....110 C5
Football Gn HU18 .....134 C3
Forber Ave HU9 .....142 C2
Forbes Ave HU6 .....140 C8
Ford Cl HU17 .....136 F4
Ford La DN20 .....108 F5
Ford's Ave 9 DN41 .....101 F5
Fordlands YO8 .....48 B2
Fordlands Cres YO19 ....133 E5
Fordlands Rd YO19 .....133 E6
Fordon La Willerby YO12 ...1 E7
Wold Newton YO25 .....2 A6
Foredyke Ave HU7 .....141 A4
Foredyke Prim Sch
HU9 .....142 A1
Forest Cl 27 YO32 .....13 E5
Forest Dr DN36 .....103 D1
Forest Gr YO31 .....130 F6
Forest La Fulford YO19 ....26 A2
Strensall YO32 .....14 A8
Forest of Galtres Prim Sch
YO30 .....12 F5
Forest Way
24 Humberston DN36 .....103 D1
York YO31 .....130 F6
Forester Way HU4 .....144 D3
Forester's Wlk YO24 .....129 B1
Foresters Way YO16 .....123 A7
Foresters Wlk YO41 .....15 C1
Forestgate YO32 .....127 C7
Forge Cl
Huntington YO32 .....128 A2
Melbourne YO42 .....39 B6
South Kelsey LN7 .....110 A1
8 Thorngumbald HU12 ....72 E5
Wheldrake YO19 .....38 A7
Forge Cres 3 DN39 .....86 A1
Forge La YO19 .....37 A7
Forge Pl HU16 .....138 B7
Forge The YO25 .....124 E3
Forge Way 3 DN36 .....114 A6
Forkedale DN18 .....84 E8
Formby Cl HU6 .....139 E5
Forrester St 20 DN20 .....98 B2
Forrester's Cl 3 DN6 .....76 E2
Forster St 25 DN21 .....117 B1
Forsythia Ave 14 DN41 ...101 F5
Forsythia Dr DN33 .....102 E1
Fort Paull Battery*
HU12 .....72 B4
Fort Terr 6 YO15 .....122 F2
Forth St YO26 .....129 F6
Fortuna Way 2 DN37 ...102 B4
Fortune Cl HU8 .....141 F4
Forty Acre HU10 .....143 F7
Forty Foot La DN39 .....99 F6
Forty Stps HU10 .....143 F7
Fortyfoot YO16 .....122 F4
Fortyfoot Ct YO16 .....122 E4
Fortyfoot Gr 1 YO16 ....122 F4
Forum Ctr* YO15 .....122 F2
Fosham Rd HU11 .....46 D2
Foss Bank YO31 .....156 C3
Foss Ct YO31 .....127 E1
Foss Field La YO23 .....36 B8
Foss Garth YO41 .....27 F5
Foss Gr HU8 .....142 B6
Foss Islands Rd YO31 ...156 C3
Foss Wlk YO26 .....129 B8
Fossdale Cl HU8 .....141 E6
Fosse Hill Jet Ski Ctr*
YO25 .....34 C1
Fossgate YO1 .....156 C2
Fossland View 4 YO32 ....14 A7
Fossway
Stamford Bridge YO41 .....15 D1
York YO31 .....130 D7
Foster Gate YO8 .....148 D4
Foster Rd 9 DN8 .....93 A8
Foster St HU8 .....141 A2
Fostergate YO8 .....48 A8
Foston Gr
Kingston upon Hull HU9 ...142 A1
4 York YO31 .....130 F8
Foston La Beeford YO25 ...22 B1
North Frodingham YO25 ....21 F1
Fotherbie Garth 11 HU12 .72 C7
Fotherby Rd 4 DN17 .....96 C2
Fotherby St DN31 .....152 E5
Fotherby Wlk HU17 .....154 C4
Fothergill Dr 16 DN3 .....92 A2
Foundry Garth HU12 .....59 D1
Foundry La 5 WF11 .....61 A2
Foundry Sh Ctr The
DN15 .....151 B7
Fountain Cl
Kingston upon Hull HU2 ...155 A4
Northfield HU13 .....143 C3
6 Waltham DN37 .....113 D7
Fountain Ct DN40 .....87 D1
Fountain Hill DN10 .....116 B3
Fountain Hill Rd DN10 ...116 B4
Fountain Rd HU2 .....140 E1
Fountain Rd Ind Est
HU2 .....155 C4
Fountain St
16 Caistor LN7 .....111 B4
Kingston upon Hull HU3 ...145 D6
Fountains Ave YO16 ....122 D7
Fountains Way HU15 .....53 D3
Fountayne Rd 13 YO14 .....2 F8
Fountayne St
Goole DN14 .....149 E5
York YO31 .....130 C7
Four Acre Cl HU10 .....143 C6
Fourth Ave
Bridlington YO15 .....123 A4
Fixborough Stather DN15 ...82 A1
Goole DN14 .....149 C4
Scunthorpe DN17 .....150 C2
York YO31 .....130 E5
Fourways 9 DN36 .....114 D4
Fowler Ct 3 DN15 .....83 A5
Fowler Rd DN16 .....151 C3
Fox Covert
Hibaldstow DN20 .....108 F5
York YO31 .....127 F2
Fox Covert La DN10 .....116 D4
Fox Covert Rd WF8 .....76 C1
Fox Ct DN17 .....94 D8
Fox Garth YO26 .....126 A3
Fox Glade YO41 .....15 C2
Fox Hill (Tumulus)*
YO25 .....21 D8
Fox Hill La YO8 .....148 A3
Fox La
Chapel Haddlesey YO8 .....62 C5
Hambleton LS25 .....61 D8
Laxton DN14 .....65 E3
Thorpe Willoughby YO8 .....48 B1
Fox St DN15 .....150 F7
Foxcroft 3 YO32 .....127 C7
Foxdale Ave YO8 .....48 B1
Foxglove Cl
22 Brigg DN20 .....98 B2
16 Kingston upon Hull HU7 ..56 F5
Foxglove Gdns 5 DN34 ..102 C3
Foxhill DN37 .....102 B4
Foxhill Cl HU9 .....142 E2
Foxhill La YO8 .....148 A3
Foxhill Rd DN8 .....93 B7
Foxhills Ind Pk DN15 .....96 C8
Foxhills Rd DN15 .....96 C7
Foxhills Tech Coll
DN15 .....96 C7
Foxholme Rd HU7 .....141 D7
Foxthorn Paddock
YO10 .....131 D3
Foxton Cl YO24 .....132 C8
Foxwood La 3 YO24 ....129 C1
Foynes Gn 6 HU8 .....142 C5
Frampton Cl HU7 .....141 B6
Frances Ct 8 DN37 .....113 D7
Frances St
Scunthorpe DN15 .....151 A7
York YO10 .....130 D1
Francis Askew Prim Sch
HU4 .....144 E4
Francis Ave 10 HU19 .....75 A6
Francis Ct 7 YO8 .....48 B2
Francis St HU2 .....155 B3
Francis Terr YO25 .....124 E5
Francis Way 3 HU12 .....74 D1
Frank Walsham Ct
DN32 .....153 A4
Frankland Cl DN20 .....98 E3
Frankland Pl DN35 .....153 D3
Franklin Cres DN16 .....151 E2
Franklin Rd DN21 .....107 C4
Franklin Sixth Form Coll
DN34 .....152 B1
Franklin St HU9 .....146 C8
Franklin Way DN38 .....99 F5
Fraser St DN32 .....152 F3
Frazer Ct YO30 .....129 E8
Frederic St YO30 .....156 A3
Frederick Gough Sch
DN16 .....96 E2
Frederick Holmes Specl Sch
HU6 .....140 A5
Frederick St
Cleethorpes DN35 .....153 E2
Goole DN14 .....149 E5
Grimsby DN31 .....152 D4
Frederick Ward Way
DN31 .....152 D3
Freehold St HU3 .....145 D7
Freeman Ave 4 HU15 .....68 C5
Freeman Ct DN36 .....114 B5
Freeman St DN32 .....152 F4
Freeman Way 1 DN32 ..152 F5
Freemans La DN20 .....84 C2
Freeport Hornsea Outlet
Village HU18 .....134 C1
Freeport Wharf DN31 ...152 E4
Freeschool La or Gr
DN14 .....52 A2
Freeston St DN35 .....153 B4
Freetown Ct HU6 .....140 B5
Freetown Way HU2 .....155 A3
Freightliner Rd HU3 .....144 F2
Fremantle Ave HU9 .....142 D2
Frensham Cl 9 HU7 .....56 F6
Fresh Fields 12 HU15 .....68 C5
Freshney Bog Nature
Reserve* DN34 .....102 B3
Freshney Dr DN31 .....152 C4
Freshney Pl 9 DN31 .....152 D3
Freshney Places Sh Ctr
DN31 .....152 D3
Friar's Wlk YO31 .....130 E8
Friargate YO1 .....156 B2
Friargate Theatre
YO1 .....156 B2
Friars Cl YO19 .....26 D7
Friars La HU17 .....154 B2
Friars Mdw YO8 .....148 C8
Friars Rd DN17 .....150 E2
Friary Ct 5 HU3 .....140 D1
Friendship Ct 2 YO8 ...148 C6
Frith Mews 4 YO8 .....148 C6
Frobisher Ave DN32 .....153 B2
Frodingham Footpath 2
DN15 .....151 B7
Frodingham Inf Sch
DN15 .....151 B6
Frodingham La HU12 .....74 D4
Frodingham Rd
Brandesburton YO25 .....34 B4
Scunthorpe DN15 .....151 A8
Frodingham S Rd
DN16 .....151 E5
Frodsham St HU9 .....147 B7
Froebel House Sch
HU17 .....136 C6
Frome Rd HU8 .....142 C7
Front La HU12 .....59 A3
Front St
Alkborough DN15 .....82 C8
Burton Fleming YO25 .....2 E3
East Stockwith DN21 .....116 E5
Elsham DN20 .....98 F7
Gainsborough DN21 .....117 A2
Grasby DN38 .....110 E7
Langtoft YO25 .....8 C5
Laxton DN14 .....65 E4
Lockington YO25 .....32 B2
Middleton YO25 .....31 C4
Front St *continued*
Naburn YO19 .....36 D8
Ulceby DN39 .....86 A1
Wold Newton YO25 .....2 A4
York YO24 .....129 C3
Froscoles Cl 6 HU15 .....53 D3
Frusher Ave 7 DN33 ....102 E2
Fryston 11 HU15 .....68 C6
Fryston Comm La LS25 ..61 A8
Fuchsia Croft DN15 .....150 F6
Fuchsia Dr HU4 .....144 B2
Fulbeck Rd DN16 .....151 C2
Fulford Cres
Kingston upon Hull
HU10 .....144 A8
3 New Holland DN19 .....70 E2
Fulford Cross YO10 .....130 D1
Fulford Gr HU9 .....142 E2
Fulford Mews YO10 .....133 E6
Fulford Pk YO10 .....133 D7
Fulford Rd YO10 .....133 D8
Fulford Sch YO10 .....133 E7
Fulfordgate YO10 .....133 E7
Fulham La DN14 .....76 E7
Fulham Pk 2 DN33 .....102 D1
Fuller St DN35 .....153 D4
Fulmar Cl HU7 .....141 D8
Fulstow Cty Prim Sch
LN11 .....121 E8
Fulstow Gr 22 DN33 ....102 D2
Furlong Rd 23 YO41 .....15 D2
Furness Cl 8 HU7 .....57 A7
Furness Dr YO30 .....126 E1
Furniss Ct 25 DN18 .....84 E8
Furnwood 2 YO32 .....127 D7
Furze Rd HU12 .....60 B2
Fussey Gdns DN20 .....84 C1
Fylingdales Ave 6
YO30 .....126 E1

G

Gable Pk YO23 .....24 C6
Gables Cl 8 DN14 .....61 D4
Gadwall Cl 2 HU15 .....52 F1
Gain Hills Balk YO16 .....10 D4
Gainas Ave DN21 .....117 B1
Gainford Gr HU9 .....142 E2
Gainford Rd DN8 .....79 B2
Gainford Sq 18 DN8 .....79 B2
Gainsborough Cl YO32 ...14 B8
Gainsborough La
DN20 .....108 F8
Gainsborough Rd
Blyton DN21 .....117 E4
20 Kirton in Lindsey DN21 .108 B1
Scotter DN21 .....107 B3
Gainsthorpe Rd E
DN21 .....108 D4
Gainsthorpe Rd W
DN21 .....108 C4
Gale Farm Ct 6 YO24 ...129 C3
Gale La Thorganby YO19 ...37 F4
York YO24 .....129 C2
Gale The YO19 .....36 D4
Galecarr La YO42 .....39 E6
Galegate YO43 .....53 E7
Galfrid Rd HU11 .....142 F7
Gallagher Ret Pk
DN15 .....150 A7
Gallands Cl HU14 .....69 A7
Galleon Ct HU9 .....145 C6
Galley Ct HU9 .....146 C6
Galliard Cl 11 HU3 .....145 A4
Galligap La YO10 .....131 C4
Gallops The YO24 .....132 B8
Galloway Ct 4 YO25 .....124 F4
Galloway La 3 YO25 ....124 F4
Gallows Bridge Rd
HU11 .....59 A7
Gallows Hill* YO25 .....9 A2
Gallows La HU17 .....136 D5
Galmanhoe La YO30 .....156 A3
Galtres Ave YO31 .....131 B7
Galtres Gr YO30 .....129 F7
Galtres Rd YO31 .....131 B7
Gandhi Wy HU1 .....155 C2
Ganstead Gr HU9 .....142 A2
Ganstead La HU11 .....142 D6
Gant Wlk 7 YO8 .....148 D5
Ganton Ave HU16 .....139 A5
Ganton Ct 3 HU8 .....142 B5
Ganton Hill YO12 .....1 B7
Ganton Pl YO24 .....132 E7
Ganton Rd YO25 .....1 C4
Ganton Specl Sch
HU10 .....144 A7
Ganton Way HU10 .....143 F8
Gap Cres YO14 .....3 D7
Gap Rd YO14 .....3 D8
Garbett Way 1 YO23 ....133 B3
Garburn Gr 3 YO30 .....126 E1
Garbutt Cl 2 HU12 .....58 D1
Garbutt Gr YO26 .....129 D5
Garbutt Pl 3 DN35 .....103 D2
Garden Dr DN36 .....114 A8
Garden Flats La YO19 ....26 E7
Garden La 11 WF11 .....61 A3
Garden Pl YO1 .....156 C2
Garden St 14 Brigg DN20 ..98 C2
Grimsby DN32 .....152 D3
York YO31 .....156 B4
Garden Wlk 12 YO15 .....122 E2
Gardeners Cl 8 YO23 ...132 B3
Gardeners Row YO25 .....7 B3
Gardenia Dr 21 DN17 .....96 D1
Gardens The HU3 .....145 C5
Gardham La YO25 .....35 A6
Gardham Rd HU17 .....42 E5
Gare La DN14 .....66 A6
Garends Rd 4 YO15 .....5 A2
Garfield Cl HU9 .....142 D1
Garfield St 21 DN21 .....117 B1
Garfield Terr YO26 .....129 F5
Garibaldi St DN32 .....152 F5
Garland Cl HU9 .....142 C4
Garland St 2 YO26 .....129 E4
Garlands The YO30 .....130 A8
Garman Carr La YO8 ....48 D6
Garner St DN32 .....152 E2
Garnet Gr 6 HU3 .....145 A4
Garnet Terr YO26 .....129 E5
Garnett St DN35 .....153 D4
Garrick Cl Brayton YO8 ...148 B1
Kingston upon Hull HU8 ...141 F4
15 Pocklington YO42 .....29 A3
Garrick La 21 DN36 .....114 A8
Garrison Rd HU9 .....155 C1
Garrison St YO15 .....122 F2
Garrow Hill YO10 .....130 F2
Garrow Hill Ave YO10 ...131 A3
Garroway Way YO10 .....26 A4
Garrowby Hill YO41 .....16 F3
Garrowby Rd YO42 .....16 F2
Garrowby St YO41 .....16 E3
Garrowby View 5 YO41 ..15 D2
Garrowby Wlk HU5 .....139 C2
Garth Ave
Kingston upon Hull HU11 ...58 A3
4 North Duffield YO8 .....50 A7
Garth Cl 6 YO8 .....48 D6
Garth Ct YO32 .....128 A4
Garth End YO32 .....127 F4
Garth Ends Rd HU17 .....43 A2
Garth Glebe 8 YO8 .....49 B5
Garth La Goole DN14 .....65 C4
Grimsby DN31 .....152 D4
Garth Mill 1 DN14 .....61 D4
Garth Morrell YO8 .....148 C2
Garth Rd YO32 .....127 F4
Garth Terr YO30 .....130 B7
Garth The HU16 .....139 A5
Garth's End YO10 .....133 E8
Garthends La
3 Hemingbrough YO8 .....49 F1
Mappleton HU11 .....47 B5
Garthorpe Rd
Luddington & Haldenby
DN17 .....81 C4
Twin Rivers DN14 .....81 E7
Garths End 20 Haxby YO32 .13 F5
Pocklington YO42 .....29 A4
Garths End La YO42 .....29 A8
Garthway
18 Holton le Clay DN36 ...114 A5
4 York YO32 .....127 D3
Garton Balk YO25 .....20 D8
Garton Gr
Grimsby DN32 .....153 A1
3 Kingston upon Hull
HU4 .....144 C7
Garton Hill YO25 .....19 E7
Garton Rd HU11 .....47 C1
Garton Slack YO25 .....19 D6
Garton-on-the-Wolds CE VC
Prim Sch YO25 .....20 A6
Garvey Way 34 HU12 .....72 D7
Gas House La 13 DN14 ....65 B7
Gascoigne Wlk YO23 ....156 B1
Gashouse La DN9 .....106 B3
Gate La 11 DN33 .....102 E1
Gate Way DN31 .....152 C6
Gateforth New Rd YO8 ..62 A8
Gatehead La YO42 .....38 D7
Gatehouse* DN39 .....86 B5
Gatehouse Rd DN19 .....85 F7
Gatehowe Rd YO17 .....17 A7
Gateland Cl YO32 .....127 C7
Gateland Field La DN14 ..64 B6
Gatesby Rd DN14 .....149 C6
Gatewood La DN7 .....92 E1
Gatherums The DN35 ....153 E1
Gatwick Garth 15 HU7 ....57 A5
Gaufer Hill YO43 .....41 D3
Gautry La DN9 .....106 B4
Gay Mdws YO32 .....14 D2
Gayles Mews 3 HU5 ....139 D3
Gayton Rd DN35 .....103 D2
Gedney Cl 8 DN37 .....102 B4
Gee St HU3 .....145 C5
Geeseness La DN14 .....78 D2
Geldof Rd YO32 .....127 F1
Gembling La YO25 .....22 A4
Gembling Prim Sch
YO25 .....22 A3
Gemel Rd HU12 .....59 C2
Gemsbok Way 3 HU4 ....144 D2
General La YO42 .....38 E6
Genesis Way DN31 .....102 B6
Geneva Sq DN8 .....79 C2
Geneva Way HU7 .....141 B5
George Ave DN17 .....95 D5
George Butler Cl 16
DN37 .....101 F1
George Cayley Dr
YO30 .....127 A3
George Ct YO31 .....156 C3
George Hudson St
YO1 .....156 B2
George Janney Ct
DN32 .....153 A5
George La HU17 .....55 D8

George Mews 8 LN7 111 B4
George Odey Ct HU17 154 B2
George St
2 Barton-upon-Humber DN18 84 F8
Beverley HU17 154 B3
Bridlington YO15 122 C1
Broughton DN20 97 D3
Cleethorpes DN35 153 E1
Cottingham HU16 139 A7
Gainsborough DN21 117 A1
Great Driffield YO25 124 E4
Grimsby DN31 152 D3
28 Hedon HU12 72 C7
Keadby DN17 95 D5
Kingston upon Hull HU1 155 B2
11 Kirton in Lindsey DN21 108 B1
Pocklington YO42 29 A4
Scunthorpe DN15 151 A8
4 Selby YO8 148 D6
Snaith DN14 63 C1
7 Wistow YO8 48 D6
3 Withernsea HU19 74 F7
York YO1 156 C1
George Terr 1 YO8 49 B4
Georgian Mews
Bridlington YO15 122 C1
4 Great Driffield YO25 124 F3
Georgian Way YO15 122 C1
Georgina Ct 8 DN18 84 E8
Gerard Ave YO31 131 A5
Germain Rd YO8 148 E4
German Nook La HU17 56 D8
Germany La YO19 133 E6
Gershwin Ave HU4 144 B4
Gertrude St DN32 152 E1
Gervase St DN15 151 A7
Giant Hill* HU11 57 D6
Gibraltar La DN37 101 F1
Gibraltar Way HU7 56 E5
Gibson La 36 Hedon HU12 72 D7
Welton HU14 68 E4
Gibson Rd 4 DN7 104 A8
Gibson St YO25 124 E5
Gifford Cl HU7 57 A6
Gilberdyke Prim Sch HU15 66 D8
Gilberdyke Sta HU15 66 D7
Gilbert St YO16 122 D3
Gilbey Rd DN31 152 B5
Gilcross Rd HU12 90 C6
Gildane HU6 139 E8
Giles Ave YO31 131 A5
Giles St DN35 153 E2
Gillamoor Ave YO31 131 B5
Gillamoor Cl 16 HU8 141 E7
Gillann St 15 WF11 61 A2
Gillatts Cl DN20 98 D4
Gillett St HU3 145 B4
Gilliatt St DN15 151 A7
Gilling Mews 4 HU5 139 D3
Gillingwood Rd YO30 126 F3
Gillshill Prim Sch HU8 141 D5
Gillshill Rd HU8 141 D4
Gillus La 5 YO15 4 D3
Gillyon Cl 3 HU17 137 B3
Gipsey Cnr YO19 26 E3
Gipsy La
Holton le Moor LN7 110 C1
Owston Ferry DN9 116 F8
Girton Cl 5 DN16 96 D2
Girvan Cl YO24 132 B7
Gisburn Rd HU13 143 F2
Givendale Gr 3 YO10 131 C4
Givendale Hill YO42 29 C6
Givendale La YO42 29 A8
Glade Rd YO19 37 B2
Glade The
Beverley HU17 137 B3
Escrick YO19 37 A6
York YO31 131 B7
Gladstone Dr DN16 151 C5
Gladstone St
Hessle HU13 143 E1
Kingston upon Hull HU3 145 C6
York YO24 129 D3
York YO31 156 C4
Gladstone Terr 6 YO15 122 F3
Glaisby Ct YO31 131 A6
Glaisdale YO24 132 D7
Glaisdale Cl YO16 122 F7
Glaisdale Gr HU9 146 F8
Glaisdale Rd DN16 151 E1
Glamis Rd HU13 143 F2
Glanford Gr 6 DN19 85 D8
Glanford Rd
23 Brigg DN20 98 C2
Scunthorpe DN17 96 C2
Glanford Way DN15 150 B7
Glanville Ave DN17 150 F4
Glanville Cres DN17 150 F4
Glasgow St HU3 145 A5
Glass House Row HU8 141 A1
Glebe Ave
Full Sutton YO41 16 A2
York YO26 129 D5
Glebe Cl
Burton upon Stather DN15 82 A5
5 Holton le Clay DN36 114 A6
3 Strensall YO32 14 B7
2 Wawne HU7 56 E7
Glebe Farm HU7 56 E7
Glebe Gdns YO25 22 D1
Glebe Lands The 4 YO43 135 E4
Glebe Rd Brigg DN20 98 C2
Campsall DN6 76 E1
Cleethorpes DN35 153 E2
Grimsby DN33 102 F1
Humberston DN36 114 C8
Kingston upon Hull HU7 141 A4
Scunthorpe DN15 151 B8
Thorne/Moorends DN8 93 B8
Wawne HU7 56 E7
Glebe Way
Barton-upon-Humber DN18 85 A8
26 Haxby YO32 13 E5
Glebelands HU12 59 D2
Glen Almond HU11 142 D6
Glen Ave YO31 130 E5
Glen Cl YO10 133 E6
Glen Cres YO42 39 A7
Glen Hall Rise 11 DN19 85 C8
Glen Rd YO31 130 E5
Glen The
Beverley HU17 137 B2
Kingston upon Hull HU10 138 B1
Glencoe Cl 22 DN7 92 D4
Glencoe St
Kingston upon Hull HU3 144 F6
1 York YO30 130 B7
Glencourt HU6 139 E6
Glendale Cl HU10 138 C1
Gleneagles 15 DN37 113 D6
Gleneagles Cres 4 DN19 70 E2
Gleneagles Pk HU8 141 F6
Glenfell Cl HU8 141 D5
Glenfield Ave YO43 135 D4
Glenfield Dr HU10 138 B1
Glenfield Rd DN37 102 B4
Glenham Dr HU10 143 E7
Glenholme Ct YO25 32 E7
Glenridding YO24 132 D7
Glenrock Pk HU15 68 B6
Glenville Cl YO25 33 F8
Glenwood Cl HU8 141 C3
Glenwood Dr 2 HU4 144 B6
Glews Hollow Bsns Enterprise Pk DN14 149 B2
Glimpse The YO16 123 A7
Globe Mews HU17 154 A3
Gloria Way 3 DN37 102 B4
Glossop Rd DN15 150 B6
Gloucester Ave
Grimsby DN34 102 D2
Scunthorpe DN16 151 B3
Gloucester Rd HU10 138 E2
Gloucester St HU4 144 E3
Glover Rd DN17 150 E4
Glovers Ave DN17 95 D4
Goathead La DN14 78 E8
Goathland Cl HU3 145 A6
Goble Cl DN18 85 A8
Godbold Cl HU17 154 C3
Goddard Ave HU5 140 B2
Goddard Cl 9 DN18 84 E8
Godfrey Rd 11 DN8 93 A8
Godman's La HU10 143 B8
Godnow Rd DN17 94 C6
Godwinsway 18 YO41 15 D2
Gold Thread La 5 YO8 48 B8
Goldcrest Cl
1 Kingston upon Hull HU7 141 D8
Scunthorpe DN15 96 B7
Golden Ct 10 HU9 142 A3
Golden Gr HU11 142 D6
Goldgarth DN32 153 A1
Goldings The DN9 105 D2
Golf Links Dr HU15 68 B6
Golf Links Rd HU6 139 E5
Gollands La DN9 105 B2
Goodfell Rd HU17 137 A6
Goodhand Cl DN18 85 A8
Goodhart Rd HU7 141 B8
Goodmanham Rd
Market Weighton YO43 135 D5
Middleton YO25 31 C3
Goodmanham Way 6 HU16 138 E6
Goodramgate YO1 156 B2
Goodrich Cl HU3 140 E1
Goods Yd The YO8 148 D5
Goodwin Par 1 HU3 145 D5
Goodwood DN17 96 B2
Goodwood Cl HU17 136 E6
Goodwood Gr YO24 129 F1
Goole & District Hospl DN14 149 C6
Goole Coll DN14 149 B4
Goole L Ctr DN14 149 D3
Goole Musuem* DN14 149 D4
Goole Rd Goole DN14 65 C3
Swinefleet DN14 80 C8
Goole Sta DN14 149 C4
Gooseacre DN17 107 D7
Goosenook La HU17 45 A8
Gordan Pk HU16 139 C6
Gordon Gdns DN33 113 E8
Gordon Rd YO16 122 C4
Gordon St Goole DN14 149 C4
4 Kingston upon Hull HU3 145 B5
York YO10 130 E3
Gordons Terr YO25 124 E4
Gore La DN14 77 B5
Goring Pl DN35 153 D3
Gormire Ave 2 YO31 127 E2
Gorse Cl Hatfield DN7 92 C3
Selby YO8 148 C2
Gorse Hill 1 YO19 26 F7
Gorse Paddock YO32 127 F2
Gorsedale HU7 140 E7
Gorton Rd HU10 143 E7
Gorton St DN31 152 F6
Gosport Rd DN34 152 A2
Gosport Wlk HU4 144 A4
Gossips Wood Rd DN14 79 B8
Gothenburg Way HU7 140 E6
Goths La HU17 154 B4
Gott Cl YO25 124 C2
Gouldesborough Ct 2 HU5 140 C3
Goulding Ct HU17 154 A3
Goulton St HU3 145 B3
Gouthwaith Cl YO30 126 F2
Government House Rd YO30 130 A6
Government St 1 DN14 149 D4
Gowdall Broach DN14 77 E8
Gowdall La
Pollington DN14 77 F7
Snaith & Cowick DN14 63 B1
Gowdall Rd DN14 62 E2
Gowdall Way 1 DN14 65 A7
Gower Rd
Kingston upon Hull HU4 144 B3
York YO24 132 E8
Gowthorpe YO8 148 C5
Gowthorpe La DN14 66 E4
Goxhill Airport DN19 86 B8
Goxhill Gdns 17 DN34 102 C2
Goxhill Prim Sch DN19 86 A8
Goxhill Rd DN19 85 E8
Goxhill Sta DN19 85 F8
Grafton St
Grimsby DN32 153 A5
Kingston upon Hull HU5 140 C2
Gragdale Cl HU8 141 E7
Graham Ave HU4 144 C2
Graingers Rd HU18 134 D3
Grains Gate LN11 115 E1
Grainsby Ave
Cleethorpes DN35 103 B2
Holton le Clay DN36 114 B5
Grainsby Healing* DN36 113 F3
Grainsby La
Grainsby DN36 113 E1
Tetney DN36 114 D3
Graizelound Fields Rd DN9 105 D1
Grammar Sch La DN20 98 C3
Grammar Sch Rd
Brigg DN20 98 C2
Kingston upon Hull HU5 139 E2
Grammar Sch Rd S 7 DN20 98 C2
Grammar Sch Wlk DN16 96 E2
Grammar Sch Yd HU1 155 B1
Grampian Cl 4 YO32 127 F5
Grampian Way
23 Grimsby DN33 113 E8
Kingston upon Hull HU7 57 A6
Thorne/Moorends DN8 93 A7
Granary Cl DN21 117 A3
Granary Croft 7 DN9 105 D2
Granary Ct YO1 156 B3
Grandale HU7 140 E7
Grange Ave
12 Barton-upon-Humber DN18 84 E8
Hatfield DN7 92 D4
14 Laceby DN37 101 F1
Misterton DN10 116 D5
Grange Cl
2 Buckton/Bempton YO15 4 C3
Full Sutton YO41 16 A2
5 Hatfield DN7 92 D4
Kingston upon Hull HU2 155 B4
Misterton DN10 116 D4
Skelton YO30 126 B5
Grange Cres
Kingston upon Hull HU10 143 E6
Tickton HU17 137 F8
Grange Dr
Kingston upon Hull HU16 139 A7
Misterton DN10 116 D4
Grange Farm Cl YO8 49 B5
Grange Farm La 20 DN36 114 A7
Grange Field DN20 98 D8
Grange Garth YO10 130 D2
Grange Gr 3 DN8 79 B2
Grange Ind Est DN15 151 D4
Grange Ind Est The DN14 149 B4
Grange Jun & Inf Sch DN34 102 C3
Grange La
Covenham St Bartholomew LN11 121 F6
Molescroft HU17 137 A7
North Kelsey LN7 110 A3
Rufforth YO26 129 A2
Utterby LN11 121 C4
Grange La Inf Sch DN16 151 D1
Grange La Jun Sch DN16 151 D1
Grange La N DN16 151 D3
Grange La S DN16 151 D1
Grange Pk
1 Brough HU15 68 C5
Gainsborough DN21 117 A3
2 Kirk Sandall DN3 92 A2
Swanland HU14 69 B6
Grange Pk La HU10 138 B2
Grange Rd
3 Bridlington YO16 122 D5
8 Campsall DN6 76 E1
Gainsborough DN21 117 D1
Garthorpe & Fockerby DN14 81 E8
Goole DN14 149 B4
7 Leconfield HU17 43 D6
North Frodingham YO25 34 B6
Snaith DN14 78 C8
Thorne/Moorends DN8 79 B2
Thorngumbald HU12 72 F5
Grange St YO10 130 D2
Grange Way HU17 136 E7
Grange Wlk
Grimsby DN34 152 A2
Misterton DN10 116 D5
Grangeland Wlk YO42 28 E3
Granger Ave YO26 129 C4
Granger's Yd 8 HU18 134 C4
Grangeside Ave HU6 139 F5
Gransmoor La YO25 22 A5
Gransmoor Rd YO25 22 D5
Grant St
Cleethorpes DN35 153 E3
Grimsby DN31 153 B5
Grantchester Cl HU5 139 C1
Grantham Ave
Grimsby DN33 102 E1
11 Kingston upon Hull HU7 56 F6
Grantham Dr YO26 129 E4
Grantley Gr HU9 142 C2
Grants Ave YO10 133 E8
Granville St
Grimsby DN32 152 F2
1 Kingston upon Hull HU3 145 A6
Granville Terr 4 YO10 130 E3
Grape La YO1 156 B3
Grasby All Saints CE Prim Sch DN38 110 E8
Grasby Cres DN37 102 B4
Grasby Rd
Great Limber DN37 100 C3
Kingston upon Hull HU8 142 A4
North Kelsey LN7 110 D5
Scunthorpe DN17 150 E1
Grasby Wold La DN38 110 F8
Grasmere Cl
Gainsborough DN21 117 C1
Goole DN14 149 D5
Grasmere Dr YO10 131 B4
Grasmere Gr
Bridlington YO16 122 E7
11 Humberston DN36 103 C1
5 York YO30 126 F1
Grassam Cl 3 HU12 58 D1
Grassdale Pk 3 HU15 68 B5
Grassholme YO24 132 C7
Grassington Cl 11 HU7 57 A6
Grassmoor Ct 2 DN15 150 B6
Gravel Pit Hill DN20 109 D6
Gravel Pit La DN39 100 A6
Gravel Pit Rd
Barton-upon-Humber DN18 84 D8
Scotter DN21 107 C4
Gravelhill La DN14 76 F7
Gravelholes La DN10 116 C4
Gravelpit La
Kirkburn YO25 19 F1
Sancton YO43 41 E2
Graves La YO42 39 B6
Gray Friars DN37 102 B4
Gray Rd DN17 150 D2
Gray St Goole DN14 149 C5
York YO23 156 A1
Grayburn Ct HU17 154 A3
Grayburn La HU17 154 A2
Grayingham Rd 19 DN21 108 B1
Grayling Cl 15 DN37 102 B4
Grays Croft HU12 59 C2
Grayshon Dr YO26 129 B5
Greame Rd YO16 123 A5
Great Barn St 4 YO16 122 D5
Great Cl YO8 48 B8
Great Coates Prim Sch DN37 102 B5
Great Coates Rd
Grimsby DN37 102 B4
Healing DN41 101 F5
Great Coates Sta DN37 102 B5
Great Field La HU9 147 C8
Great Gutter La HU10 55 C1
Great Gutter La E HU10 138 C2
Great Gutter La W HU10 138 A2
Great Hatfield Rd HU11 46 D4
Great Mdw Rd YO16 122 E5
Great N Way YO26 129 B8
Great Pas St HU1 155 A1
Great Thornton St HU3 145 D6
Great Union St HU9 155 C3
Grebe Rd HU15 52 F1
Greek St HU3 144 F5
Green Acres HU10 143 C6
Green Balk YO42 17 D1
Green Bank DN8 93 D6
Green Cl
Kingston upon Hull HU6 139 F6
York YO30 130 A8
Green Dike YO32 127 C8
Green Dikes La YO25 8 F1
Green Dykes La YO10 130 F3
Green Hill 10 DN35 103 B2
Green Hills YO60 15 B7
Green Island HU9 142 E5
Green La Acomb YO24 129 D2
Appleton Roebuck YO23 36 B6
Barmby on the Marsh DN14 64 A6
Barrow upon Humber DN19 85 D8
Barton-upon-Humber DN18 84 F8
Belton DN9 94 D2
Bishopthorpe YO24 133 A6
Brigsley DN37 113 D4
Broughton DN20 97 E3
Buckton/Bempton YO15 4 D3
Cottingham HU16 138 E6
Cottingwith YO42 38 C5
Fimber YO25 18 F6
Hatfield DN7 92 E1
Heck DN14 77 D8
Kingston upon Hull HU2 155 B4
Langtoft YO25 8 D5
Moor Monkton YO26 24 A8
Nafferton YO25 125 D7
North Duffield YO8 49 F8
North Kelsey LN7 110 A4
Pilham DN21 118 A4
Rawcliffe YO30 127 A1
Selby YO8 148 A3
Skidby HU10 138 B4
South Cave HU15 53 D1
Sutton Ings HU13 144 A1
Swine HU11 57 E7
Tibthorpe YO25 19 D2
Tickton HU17 137 F8
Weaverthorpe YO25 8 A8
Wetwang YO25 18 D5
Wigginton YO32 13 D5
Wressle DN14 64 D8
Green Marsh Rd HU12 72 E4
Green Mdws YO31 131 A7
Green Rd
Gringley on the Hill DN10 116 A1
15 Hedon HU12 72 C7
Green Sward YO31 131 A8
Green The
Barmby Moor YO42 28 D3
5 Brough HU15 68 D6
20 Dunnington YO19 26 F7
Great Driffield YO25 125 A4
Lund YO25 31 F3
7 Market Weighton YO43 135 D4
Rawcliffe DN14 64 A1
20 Scotter DN21 107 C3
1 Skelton YO30 126 B5
Sproatley HU11 58 D5
1 Swanland HU14 69 B7
20 Thorne/Moorends DN8 93 A8
Wistow YO8 48 D6
York YO26 129 C3
Green Top Fst Sch DN8 93 A7
Green Way YO32 127 F4
Green Ways 2 YO8 48 D6
Greenacre Cl
Dunsville DN7 92 D2
Pocklington YO42 29 B3
Greenacre Pk
Gilberdyke HU15 66 D8
Hornsea HU18 134 C1
Greenacres
4 Swanland HU14 69 C7
York YO32 127 F4
Greenacres Cl 8 YO8 48 D1
Greenacres Cres 7 YO8 48 D1
Greenacres Dr 4 YO8 48 D1
Greenacres Gr 3 YO8 48 D1
Green's Rd DN7 92 C3
Greencliffe Dr YO30 130 A6
Greencroft Ct 14 YO19 26 F7
Greencroft La 17 YO19 26 F7
Greendale Ct HU16 138 E5
Greenfield Cl 6 DN3 92 A3
Greenfield Dr
6 Brayton YO8 48 D1
Hibaldstow DN20 109 A5
Greenfield Garth HU6 56 D5
Greenfield La YO25 31 C4
Greenfield Pk Dr YO31 131 A7
Greenfield Rd
Bridlington YO16 122 B2
Middleton-on-the-Wolds YO25 31 C4
Greenfields DN14 77 F6
Greenfinch Dr 8 DN35 103 C1
Greengales Ct YO19 38 A8
Greengales La YO19 38 A8
Greengarth DN17 96 C1
Greengate DN9 105 E6
Greengate La Cliffe YO8 49 F6
2 Goxhill DN19 86 A8
Greengate Rd WF8 76 C1
Greenhill 8 DN20 97 D3
Greenhill Rd DN9 105 C2
Greenhoe Rd DN17 96 B2
Greenhow Cl HU8 141 E7
Greenland La DN14 78 F7
Greenlands YO25 124 F5

Greenlands Ave 18 DN36 114 A7
Greenlands La YO8 48 C3
Greenoak La DN14 66 B7
Greens Cl 11 DN15 151 B7
Greens La
Burstwick HU12 73 B8
Burton Pidsea HU12 59 C1
Wawne HU7 56 E7
Greensborough Ave 3 YO26 129 B5
Greenshaw Dr YO32 127 C8
Greenshaw La HU12 74 D1
Greenside
18 Dunnington YO19 26 F7
8 Flamborough YO15 5 A2
Greenside Cl 24 YO19 26 F7
Greenside Wlk 23 YO19 26 F7
Greenstiles La HU14 69 C7
Greenway
8 Barton-upon-Humber DN18 69 F1
10 Waltham DN37 113 E6
Greenway The
2 Haxby YO32 127 C7
Hornsea HU18 134 C2
1 Kingston upon Hull HU4 144 C6
Greenways
Great Driffield YO25 124 F5
2 North Ferriby HU14 69 A5
Greenways Cl YO16 122 F6
Greenways Dr 1 YO8 48 D6
Greenways Wlk YO16 122 F6
Greenwich Ave HU9 142 C4
Greenwood Ave
Beverley HU17 154 C3
Kingston upon Hull HU6 139 E5
Greenwood Gdns HU17 136 F7
Greenwood Gr YO24 132 C8
Greetham's La DN32 153 B1
Greet's Hill YO17 16 E7
Gregory Cl YO30 126 C5
Grenley St 8 WF11 61 A2
Grenville Bay HU11 142 D6
Grenwich Cl 5 YO30 126 E3
Gresley Ct 3 YO26 129 B4
Gresley Way DN40 87 D2
Greville Rd HU12 72 D7
Grey St
Gainsborough DN21 117 A1
Kingston upon Hull HU2 145 D7
Greyfriars Cres HU17 154 A1
Greyfriars Rd DN20 97 E3
Greygarth Cl 14 HU7 56 F6
Greystoke Rd YO30 126 E1
Greystone Ave HU4 144 E7
Greystone Ct YO32 127 C7
Greystones Rd DN21 117 A2
Griffin Prim Sch HU9 142 C3
Griffin Rd HU9 142 C3
Griffiths Way 18 HU12 73 C4
Grime St DN31 152 E4
Grimsby Coll DN34 152 C1
Grimsby Docks DN32 152 F5
Grimsby L Ctr DN34 152 A4
Grimsby Maternity Hospl DN33 102 E2
Grimsby Rd
Caistor LN7 111 C4
Cleethorpes DN35 153 D4
Fotherby LN11 121 D1
Humberston DN36 103 B1
Laceby DN37 101 F1
Swallow LN7 112 B6
Waltham DN37 113 E7
Grimsby Town Football Club DN35 153 C5
Grimsby Town Sta DN32 152 D3
Grimscott Cl 2 HU7 56 F5
Grimston Bar YO19 131 F4
Grimston Rd
12 Hunmanby YO14 3 A8
5 Kingston upon Hull HU10 143 F6
Grimston St HU1 155 B3
Grimthorpe Hill YO42 29 B7
Grimwith Garth YO30 126 F2
Grindale La YO16 122 A7
Grindale Rd
Bempton YO16 4 A3
Grindale YO16 3 F2
Grindell St HU9 146 D8
Gringley Rd DN10 116 B4
Grinsdale Rise YO25 125 F7
Grizedale HU7 140 F7
Grosmont Cl HU8 141 E7
Grosvenor Ave DN14 149 A5
Grosvenor Cres 1 DN32 152 D3
Grosvenor Ct DN7 92 D8
Grosvenor House YO30 156 A4
Grosvenor Pk YO30 156 A4
Grosvenor Pl HU17 136 D2
Grosvenor Rd
Hornsea HU18 134 D4
York YO30 156 A4
Grosvenor St
Grimsby DN32 152 D2
Kingston upon Hull HU3 145 D8
Grosvenor St N DN15 151 A8
Grosvenor St S DN15 151 A8
Grosvenor Terr YO30 156 A4
Grove Cl HU17 154 B4
Grove Cres DN32 153 C3
Grove Ct YO25 124 F3
Grove Gdns 12 YO26 12 F1
Grove Hill HU13 143 E1
Grove Hill Ind Est HU17 137 C4
Grove House View HU5 140 D3
Grove La DN37 113 E6
Grove Pk 7 Barlby YO8 49 B5
Beverley HU17 154 A4
Misterton DN10 116 C5
Grove Rd DN7 92 D8
Grove St
Kingston upon Hull HU5 140 D1
Kirton in Lindsey DN21 108 A1
Grove Terr La YO31 156 C4
Grove The
Barrow upon Humber DN19 85 D8
Beckingham DN10 116 D1
Kellington DN14 62 A3
York YO24 132 E6
Grove View YO30 130 A6
Grove Wharf* DN15 95 E7
Grove Wood Rd DN10 116 C5
Grove Wood Terr DN10 116 C5
Grovehill HU17 137 C4
Grovehill Rd HU17 154 C3
Grovenor Ct 11 DN35 103 D1
Groves Ct YO31 156 C3
Groves La YO31 156 C3
Groves The
Great Driffield YO25 125 A3
Kingston upon Hull HU4 144 B2
Grundale HU10 143 C6
Grundell's Yd 4 YO16 122 D4
Grundill La
Hatfield HU11 46 A8
Seaton HU11 35 A1
Guardians Rd 2 HU12 74 D1
Guernsey Gr 1 DN40 101 C8
Guest Field HU11 47 B1
Guildford Ave HU8 141 D4
Guildford Cl HU17 136 E1
Guildford St 20 DN32 153 A5
Guildhall Rd HU1 155 B2
Guilicarr La LN7 109 E4
Guisefield Rd 5 DN9 105 D6
Gull Nook YO15 5 A2
Gullane Dr HU6 56 D5
Gunby Pl 9 DN35 103 C2
Gunby Rd Bubwith YO8 50 D5
Scunthorpe DN17 150 E1
Gunbywood Rd YO8 50 D6
Gunness & Burringham CE Prim Sch DN17 95 E5
Gunness La DN15 95 F8
Gunthorpe Rd DN9 116 F8
Gurnell St DN15 151 A8
Gurth Ave DN3 92 A1
Gus Walker Dr YO42 29 B4
Guy Garth 3 HU12 72 D7
Guy's Cres 8 HU9 142 A5
Gypsey Rd YO16 122 B4

H

Habrough La DN39 100 C6
Habrough Rd
Immingham DN40 87 A1
South Killingholme DN40 86 E2
Habrough Sta DN40 100 E8
Hackforth Wlk HU5 139 D4
Hackness Gr 2 HU5 144 D8
Haddlesey Rd WF11 61 D5
Haddon Cl YO24 129 C2
Haddon Rd YO16 122 D7
Haddon St HU3 144 F4
Hadds La DN8 78 F3
Hadds Nook Rd DN8 78 F2
Hadleigh Cl 4 HU3 140 E1
Hadleigh Ct DN15 151 A8
Hadleigh Gn 4 DN17 95 D4
Hadleigh Rd DN40 87 C1
Hadrian Ave YO10 131 B3
Hag La YO42 38 C4
Hagg La Belton DN17 94 E3
Cottingwith YO42 38 E8
Dunnington YO19 26 F6
Hemingbrough YO8 49 F3
Haggs La Fenwick DN6 77 D2
Kingston upon Hull HU10 138 E3
Hague Pk La 12 YO25 124 F4
Haig Ave DN16 151 B5
Haig Rd DN8 79 B2
Haig St YO8 148 B6
Haigh Ct DN32 102 F2
Haigh La DN14 77 A6
Haigh St DN35 103 D3
Haile Rd DN36 103 D1
Hailgate DN14 65 A7
Hailgate Cl 8 DN14 65 B7
Hainton Ave DN32 152 F2
Haith's La DN36 114 B1
Haldane Ct HU4 144 D2
Haldane St DN21 117 A1
Hale Hill La DN7 92 E3
Hales Cl 3 DN16 96 D1
Hales Cres 12 HU12 72 C7
Hales Entry HU9 146 C6
Hales La YO8 63 E5
Haley's Terr YO31 130 D8
Half Acre Wood 1 DN17 95 D4
Halfacres La YO42 40 A6
Halifax App DN20 99 A8
Halifax Ave DN14 149 C6
Halifax Cl
Full Sutton YO41 16 A2
8 Pocklington YO42 28 F4
Halifax Ct 7 YO30 127 A1
Halifax Way
Elvington YO41 27 A3
Pocklington YO42 28 E3
Halkon Cl DN17 81 D3
Hall Cl 5 Airmyn DN14 64 E4
Cawood YO8 36 D1
Nafferton YO25 125 E7
7 Snaith DN14 78 C8
Hall Ct DN17 81 A3
Hall Farm Cl 4 YO19 48 F8
Hall Farm Ct YO42 16 F2
Hall Gdns
Rawcliffe DN14 64 B2
Winterton DN15 83 B5
Hall La Elsham DN20 98 F7
Stainforth DN7 92 A6
Hall Mdw DN20 84 C2
Hall Pk Swanland HU14 69 C6
Wistow YO8 49 A5
York YO10 131 B1
Hall Pk Rd YO14 2 F8
Hall Rd Goole DN14 149 D1
Hornsea HU18 134 D5
Kingston upon Hull HU6 139 E5
Market Weighton YO43 135 D4
Sproatley HU11 58 D5
Hall Rd Prim Sch HU6 139 F4
Hall Rise 12 Haxby YO32 13 F5
Messingham DN17 107 D7
Hall Spinney The 5 DN14 65 B7
Hall St HU2 145 D7
Hall View DN17 107 D7
Hall Way DN38 99 F5
Hall Wlk 1 Brough HU15 68 D6
Kingston upon Hull HU16 139 B6
Walkington HU17 55 B8
Halladale Cl 1 YO24 132 B7
Hallard Way 7 YO32 14 B7
Hall's Rd DN10 116 A2
Hallbrook Ct 4 DN16 96 D1
Hallcroft 1 DN39 86 A1
Hallcroft La YO23 132 A3
Hallcroft Rd 1 DN9 105 D2
Haller St HU9 146 E8
Hallfield Rd YO31 130 E5
Hallgarth DN36 115 B2
Hallgarth Ave DN16 151 B6
Hallgarth Way HU17 154 B2
Hallgate
Kingston upon Hull HU16 139 A6
10 Pocklington YO42 29 A4
Hallgate Jun & Inf Sch HU16 139 B7
Halliwell Cl HU9 147 E8
Halls La 18 Keelby DN41 101 A4
North Kelsey LN7 110 A4
Hallytreeholme Rd YO25 33 E3
Haltemprice L Ctr HU10 143 E7
Haltemprice St HU3 144 F5
Halton Cl 5 DN21 119 C8
Halton Pl DN35 103 B2
Halton Way DN34 102 D2
Halyard Croft HU1 155 B1
Halycon Ave 1 HU13 143 E2
Hambledon Cl HU7 141 B6
Hambleton Ave YO10 131 C4
Hambleton Terr YO31 130 C7
Hambleton View 10 YO32 13 D5
Hambleton Way YO32 127 F3
Hambling Dr HU17 136 E7
Hamburg Rd HU7 141 A5
Hamden Rd YO42 28 E3
Hamerton Cl 11 YO14 3 A8
Hamerton Rd 10 YO14 3 A8
Hamilton Cl 7 DN34 102 B2
Hamilton Dr
Kingston upon Hull HU8 141 F6
York YO24 129 E2
Hamilton Dr E YO24 129 F2
Hamilton Dr W YO24 129 D2
Hamilton Hill Rd YO25 23 A6
Hamilton Rd
Bridlington YO15 122 D2
Scunthorpe DN17 150 F4
Hamilton St DN32 153 B5
Hamilton Way YO24 129 E2
Hamish Wlk 27 DN40 87 B1
Hamlet The 8 DN14 61 F2
Hamling Way HU4 144 D2
Hamlyn Ave HU4 144 E7
Hamlyn Dr HU4 144 E6
Hammersike Rd YO8 48 A4
Hammersmith Rd 1 HU8 141 F5
Hammerton Cl 3 YO26 129 B3
Hammerton Rd 25 DN17 96 C2
Hammond Rd HU17 154 C4
Hamont Rd DN32 153 B3
Hampden Cres 1 DN7 104 A8
Hampden St YO1 156 B1
Hampshire St HU4 144 E3
Hampson Gdns
19 Kirk Sandall DN3 92 A2
York YO30 130 B8
Hampstead Ct 6 HU3 140 D1
Hampstead Pk 6 DN33 102 D1
Hampston Cl HU6 140 A7
Hampton Cl 18 DN35 103 C1
Hampton Gdns YO30 130 C8
Hampton Rd
Hatfield DN7 92 C4
Scunthorpe DN16 151 B4
Hancock La HU15 52 F3
Handel House Prep Sch DN21 117 B1
Handley Cl YO30 127 A2
Hands on History Mus* HU1 155 B2
Hanger La DN14 63 B3
Hankins La YO42 38 D1
Hanley Rd HU5 139 D3
Hanover Ct
Beverley HU17 154 C3
Kingston upon Hull HU1 155 A2
Hanover Gdns DN16 151 C2
Hanover Grange YO16 122 D4
Hanover Sq HU1 155 B2
Hanover St E 5 YO26 129 F5
Hanover St W 7 YO26 129 F5
Hansard Cres
6 Caistor LN7 111 B4
5 Gilberdyke HU15 66 D8
Hansard Dr 6 HU15 66 D8
Hansom Pl YO31 130 C7
Hanson Cl YO43 135 D3
Hanson Way DN32 153 B4
Ha'penny Bridge Way HU9 146 B5
Harborough Cl 20 YO14 2 F8
Harbour Rd YO15 122 F2
Harbour Way HU9 146 C6
Harcourt Cl
Bishopthorpe YO23 133 A4
Wheldrake YO19 37 F7
Harcourt Dr HU9 146 C8
Harcourt St YO31 130 E5
Hardane HU6 139 E8
Harden Cl YO30 126 F2
Hardenshaw La YO8 63 B4
Hardington Cl HU8 142 B7
Hardisty Mews YO26 130 A4
Hardmoor La YO43 53 C5
Hardrada Way 3 YO41 15 D1
Hardwick St HU5 145 B8
Hardy Rd DN17 150 D2
Hardy St
Kingston upon Hull HU5 140 C3
Selby YO8 148 E4
Hardy's Rd DN35 103 C2
Hardys Rd 4 HU12 72 C7
Hare St DN32 152 F2
Harewood HU17 136 B6
Harewood Ave
Bridlington YO16 122 D6
Kingston upon Hull HU9 142 A3
4 Kirk Sandall DN3 92 A2
Harewood Cl
Rawcliffe YO30 126 D2
5 Wigginton YO32 13 D5
Harewood Gr 17 DN35 103 C1
Harewood Way YO10 131 A2
Harfry Wlk DN14 149 F6
Hargrave St DN31 152 B5
Hargreave Cl HU17 136 E6
Hargreaves Way DN15 96 D7
Hariff La HU12 73 B4
Harington Ave YO10 130 F4
Harker St 12 WF11 61 A2
Harland La YO25 124 E4
Harland Rd
Bridlington YO16 122 F5
6 Brough HU15 68 C6
Harland Way HU16 138 E8
Harlech Cl 1 HU7 57 A6
Harlech Way DN32 152 F4
Harleigh Ave HU7 141 A5
Harlequin Dr 15 HU7 56 F5
Harleston Cl 5 HU8 142 B5
Harlestone Ct 8 DN34 102 B3
Harley St HU2 155 A4
Harlow Cl
2 Kingston upon Hull HU8 142 C6
1 York YO24 129 F2
Harlow Rd YO24 129 F2
Harlow St DN31 152 B5
Harlthorpe Gn YO8 51 A8
Harneis Cres DN37 101 F1
Harold Ct YO24 129 D3
Harold St
Grimsby DN32 153 A4
Selby YO8 148 F4
Harolds Way 1 YO41 15 D1
Harome Gr HU4 144 C7
Harpenden Cl 12 DN7 92 D3
Harpendon Dr 6 DN7 92 D3
Harper Cl YO42 29 A3
Harper St
8 Great Driffield YO25 124 F4
2 Selby YO8 148 C5
Harpham Gr HU9 142 A1
Harpham La YO25 9 D2
Harpham Rd DN36 115 B2
Harpings Rd HU5 139 F1
Harpswell Hill DN21 119 B1
Harpswell La DN21 118 F1
Harrier Rd 2 DN18 69 F1
Harrington Ct 33 HU12 72 D7
Harrington Pl DN16 151 A1
Harrington Rd YO16 122 B2
Harrington St DN35 153 B5
Harris St HU3 144 F5
Harrison Cl
Sproatley HU11 58 D5
Winteringham DN15 83 B8
Harrison St
Grimsby DN31 152 C3
York YO31 130 F6
Harrow Cl 12 DN21 117 C1
Harrow Gdns 12 DN17 96 C2
Harrow Glade 5 YO30 127 A1
Harrow St HU3 145 B4
Harrowdyke 10 DN18 84 E8
Harry Moor La YO8 48 B2
Harry's Ave HU8 141 B3
Harrybeck La YO43 53 D4
Harrys Dream 3 DN20 97 E3
Harsell La HU11 34 F2
Harswell La
Everingham YO43 40 D5
Holme-on-Spalding-Moor YO42 40 C2
Hart Dr 26 YO42 29 A3
Hart Hill Cres YO41 16 A2
Hart La DN15 83 B5
Hart St DN35 153 C4
Hartendale Cl 22 YO15 5 A2
Hartford Wlk HU8 142 C7
Harthill Ave HU17 43 D6
Harthill Dr HU3 145 C5
Hartland Cl HU7 140 F8
Hartley Bridge HU9 146 C6
Hartley Ct YO15 122 D1
Hartley St HU18 134 D5
Hartoft Rd HU5 139 E2
Hartoft St YO10 130 D2
Harts Cl HU18 134 B4
Hartshead Ave DN15 150 C7
Hartshead Wlk YO16 122 B4
Hartsholme Pk 27 HU7 56 F5
Harvest Ave 19 DN18 84 E8
Harvest Cl 18 DN3 92 A2
Harvest Cres 4 DN37 113 D6
Harvest Rise 1 DN19 85 C8
Harvester Cl DN9 105 F6
Harwood Dr 1 HU4 144 B6
Hase Wlk HU13 143 E1
Haslemere Ave YO15 122 E3
Hassacarr La YO19 26 F6
Hastings Ave 1 HU5 140 E2
Hastings Cl 4 YO30 127 A1
Hastings Gr HU4 144 E7
Hastings Wlk YO16 122 C2
Hatcliffe Cl 20 DN33 102 D2
Hatfield & Stainforth Sta DN7 92 C5
Hatfield Cl 3 YO30 126 E3
Hatfield Crookesbroom Prim Sch DN3 92 A1
Hatfield La
Barnby Dun DN3 92 A4
Edenthorpe DN3 92 A1
Hatfield Manor CE VA Jun Sch DN7 92 E4
Hatfield Pl DN14 149 C1
Hatfield Rd DN7 93 A6
Hatfield Sheep Dip La Prim Sch DN7 92 D4
Hatfield Travis CE Inf Sch DN7 92 E4
Hatfield Visual Arts Coll DN7 92 D4
Hatfield Wlk
Kingston upon Hull HU8 141 C1
York YO24 132 B8
Hatfield Woodhouse Prim Sch DN7 93 A3
Hatfield Wr Pk* DN7 92 E5
Hathersage Ct DN15 150 B6
Hathersage Rd HU7 141 C4
Hatkill La YO41 16 B1
Hatters Cl YO23 132 B3
Hatton Gr 32 DN33 102 D2
Haugh La YO8 61 F8
Haughton Rd YO30 130 C7
Hauling La YO23 36 C8
Hauxwell Gr 6 HU8 142 A5
Havelock Cres YO16 122 D3
Havelock Mews DN32 153 C2
Havelock Pl YO16 122 D3
Havelock Sch DN32 153 C2
Havelock St
Bridlington YO16 122 D3
Kingston upon Hull HU3 145 A4
Haven Ave
2 Brough HU15 68 B5
Grimsby DN31 152 C4
Haven Basin Rd HU12 72 C6
Haven Cl DN21 117 F5
Haven Garth
1 Brough HU15 68 B5
2 Hedon HU12 72 D7
Haven Gdns DN31 152 A5
Haven Rd
Barton-upon-Humber DN18 69 E1
North Killingholme DN40 87 A6
Patrington HU12 89 C8
Haven Staithes 24 HU12 72 C7
Haven Terr DN31 152 C4
Haven The
Kingston upon Hull HU9 146 B6
Selby YO8 148 D5
2 Walkington HU17 55 D8
Haverah Ct YO30 126 F1
Havercroft Rd 15 YO14 3 A8
Haverflats Cl 3 HU5 139 F1
Haverstoe Pl 7 DN35 103 B2
Hawdon Ave YO8 148 D5
Hawerby Rd DN37 101 F1

Hawes Wlk HU5 139 D3
Hawke Garth 5 YO14 3 A8
Hawkesbury St HU8 141 E3
Hawkins Gr DN32 153 B2
Hawkins Way 3 DN40 86 E3
Hawkshead Cl 3 YO24 132 B8
Hawling Rd YO43 135 C2
Haworth Cl DN15 150 D8
Haworth St HU6 140 C4
Haworth Wlk YO16 122 B4
Hawse Rd YO8 63 E8
Hawthorn Ave
2 Brigg DN20 98 C2
Gainsborough DN21 117 B1
1 Immingham DN40 87 D2
Kingston upon Hull HU3 144 F5
Hawthorn Cl
Healing DN41 101 F6
5 Newport HU15 52 F1
Wootton DN39 85 E2
Hawthorn Ct 1 HU3 144 F6
Hawthorn Dr
Wilberfoss YO41 27 E5
Wistow YO8 49 A5
Hawthorn Garth DN14 61 F4
Hawthorn Gate 17 DN18 84 F8
Hawthorn Gr
Gainsborough DN21 117 B1
York YO31 130 E5
Hawthorn Pl YO32 127 E4
Hawthorn Rise 6 DN19 85 C8
Hawthorn Spinney
YO32 127 E3
Hawthorn St 1 YO31 130 E5
Hawthorn Terr
Goole DN14 149 F5
York YO32 127 D4
Hawthorn Terr Cent 2
YO32 127 D3
Hawthorn Terr N
YO32 127 D4
Hawthorn Terr S
YO32 127 D3
Hawthorn Way 9 HU15 66 D7
Hawthorne Ave
Cleethorpes DN35 153 D4
29 Grimsby DN33 113 E8
Hatfield DN7 92 C2
12 Haxby YO32 13 E5
Kingston upon Hull
HU10 138 D1
5 New Waltham DN36 113 F7
Scunthorpe DN17 150 F4
4 Thorne/Moorends DN8 79 A1
Hawthorne Cl
10 Thorpe Willoughby YO8 48 B2
12 Winterton DN15 83 A5
Hawthorne Cres DN17 150 F4
Hawthorne Dr YO43 40 A1
Hawthorne Garth
HU17 136 F7
Hawthorne Gdns DN19 86 A8
Hawthorne Gr
5 Thorne/Moorends DN8 79 A1
York YO31 130 E5
Hawthorne Mews YO32 14 A8
Hawthorne Rd DN8 79 A1
Hawthorne Rise HU13 143 B3
Hawthorns 3 Riccall YO19 48 F8
2 Riccall YO19 48 F8
Hawthorns The
12 Kingston upon Hull
HU8 141 E7
5 Long Riston/Arnold
HU11 45 C5
Hawton Cl 1 DN21 117 C1
Haxby Moor Rd
Haxby YO32 13 F7
Towthorpe YO32 14 A7
Haxby Rd Clifton YO31 127 D1
New Earswick YO32 127 D6
York YO31 156 B4
Haxby Rd Prim Sch
YO31 130 D7
Haxey CE Prim Sch
DN9 105 D3
Haxey Gate Rd DN10 116 C7
Haxey Grange 8 DN9 105 D2
Haxey La DN9 105 D2
Haxey Rd DN10 116 C6
Hayburn Ave HU5 139 F2
Haycroft Ave DN31 152 C3
Haycroft St DN31 152 C3
Haydock Garth 6 HU7 57 A5
Haydon Cl HU10 143 D8
Hayes La DN7 78 D1
Hayfield Cl
Barnby Dun DN3 92 A4
9 Haxey DN9 105 D2
Hayforth Cl YO30 127 A2
Hayling Mere 29 DN35 103 C1
Haymarket Cl HU8 141 F4
Haymer Dr HU12 72 D7
Haynes Cl 2 DN8 93 B7
Haynes Gdns 15 DN8 93 B8
Haynes Gn 9 DN8 93 B8
Haynes Gr 1 DN8 93 B7
Haynes Rd DN8 93 B8
Hays Cl 3 DN36 114 A5
Hayton Cl DN15 83 A5
Hayton Gr HU4 144 D4
Hayton's La DN15 83 D2
Hayward Cl 3 HU17 55 D8
Hazel Ave HU19 75 A5
Hazel Cl
Great Driffield YO25 124 E3
Messingham DN17 107 C7
York YO32 127 D2
Hazel Cres 12 HU15 66 D7
Hazel Croft 5 DN40 87 B1
Hazel Ct YO31 130 E4
Hazel Garth YO31 131 B7
Hazel Gr Goole DN14 149 D1
2 Kingston upon Hull
HU3 145 D5
20 Yaddlethorpe DN17 96 D1
Hazel Old La DN14 62 C2
Hazel Rd DN7 92 C5
Hazelbarrow Dr HU10 143 F7
Hazelmere Ct YO32 127 E3
Hazelnut Gr YO30 127 B2
Hazelwood Ave YO10 131 D4
Hazing La DN14 77 B6
Headingley Ave 20 DN17 96 C2
Headingley Rd 7 DN6 76 E2
Headland Cl 30 YO32 13 E5
Headland View HU18 134 D5
Headlands Cl YO16 122 F6
Headlands Dr
Aldbrough HU11 47 C1
Bridlington YO16 122 F6
Kingston upon Hull
HU13 143 C2
Headlands Lower Sch
YO16 122 E4
Headlands Prim Sch
YO32 127 D8
Headlands Rd HU11 47 C1
Headlands Sch & Com
Science Coll YO16 122 F5
Headlands Wlk YO16 122 E6
Headley Cl 2 YO30 127 B1
Heads La HU13 143 C1
Healey Gr YO31 130 F8
Healey Rd DN16 151 C4
Healing Prim Sch
DN41 101 F5
Healing Rd DN41 101 D6
Healing Sch DN41 101 F5
Healing Sta DN41 101 F6
Heanor Ct DN15 150 B7
Heapham Rd DN21 117 C1
Hearfield Terr HU13 143 E1
Heater Cnr HU17 31 F1
Heath Cl 2 YO24 129 F2
Heath Croft YO10 133 F7
Heath Moor Dr YO10 133 F8
Heath Ride YO32 14 B8
Heathcote St HU6 140 D4
Heather Bank
13 Stamford Bridge YO41 15 D2
York YO10 131 C4
Heather Cl
7 Kingston upon Hull
HU5 139 D1
Selby YO8 148 C3
York YO32 128 A4
Heather Croft 4 YO31 127 E2
Heather Garth YO25 124 E2
Heather Gr 1 DN16 96 F2
Heatherdale Cl 9 DN33 113 E8
Heathfield Cl 8 DN3 92 A3
Heathfield Ct DN34 152 B1
Heathfield Rd 1 YO10 131 A3
Hebden Ave HU8 142 C5
Hebden Rd DN15 150 C8
Hebdon Rise 2 YO26 129 D4
Heber St DN14 149 C2
Hebrides Cl HU9 142 A3
Heck & Pollington Lake
DN14 77 E7
Heck La DN14 77 C7
Heckdyke La DN10 116 F7
Hedgerow Cl 4 DN19 85 C8
Hedgerow La 24 DN20 98 C2
Hedley Cl 7 HU15 53 F1
Hedon Mus* HU12 72 C7
Hedon Prim Sch HU12 72 C7
Hedon Rd HU9 146 B6
Heigholm La YO25 34 A1
Heigholme La HU17 44 F8
Height Lands La YO23 24 D6
Heimdal Rd DN33 102 E1
Helen Cres 9 DN40 87 B1
Helene Gr DN32 153 B3
Heliport HU15 68 C4
Hellyer Cl HU14 69 A5
Hellyers Ct HU4 144 D2
Helm Dr HU9 146 C6
Helms Ave 6 HU12 58 C1
Helmsdale YO24 132 C6
Helmsley Gr
16 Haxby YO32 13 D5
Kingston upon Hull HU5 144 C7
Helperby Wlk HU5 139 E3
Helsinki Rd HU7 140 F5
Helston Wlk DN17 150 C4
Helvellyn Cl 10 HU7 57 A6
Hemble Way HU7 56 F5
Hemingbrough CP Sch
YO8 49 F1
Hemlock Ave YO31 127 E1
Hemmingway Wlk
HU13 143 E3
Hempbridge Cl YO8 148 A5
Hempbridge Rd YO8 148 A5
Hempdyke Rd DN15 150 E8
Hempland Ave YO31 130 F6
Hempland Dr YO31 131 A7
Hempland Jun Sch
YO31 131 B6
Hempland La YO31 131 A7
Hempland Prim Sch
YO31 131 A6
Hemswell Ave HU9 147 D8
Hemswell Dr 6 DN37 102 C4
Hemswell La DN21 119 A1
Henderson Ave DN15 150 F8
Henderson Ave Prim Sch
DN15 150 F8
Henderson Cres DN15 150 F8
Henderson St DN31 153 A6
Henderson Way DN15 83 A5
Hendon Garth YO30 127 A1
Heneage Rd DN32 152 F2
Hengate HU17 154 A3
Henley Ct 6 DN21 117 B1
Henley Dr HU9 141 E1
Henlow Cl 4 DN21 119 C8
Henry Boot way HU4 144 B1
Henry Ct 8 DN8 79 B1
Henry St Goole DN14 149 B4
Grimsby DN31 152 C4
Scunthorpe DN15 150 F7
Henry Verone Ct HU2 155 B1
Hensall CP Sch DN14 62 C1
Hensall Sta DN14 62 C1
Henwick Hall La YO8 148 C1
Hepscott Wlk HU8 142 D6
Hepworth's La DN14 63 C2
Herbert St 6 YO10 130 E3
Herberts Way YO31 130 F7
Herdsman Dr YO23 132 C3
Herdsman Rd 3 YO24 132 D8
Herdwick Cl 1 YO30 127 B1
Hereford Ave DN34 152 C1
Hereford Cl 4 HU17 136 E1
Hereford Rd YO42 28 E3
Hereford St HU4 144 E3
Hereford Tech Sch The
DN34 152 B1
Hereward Pl DN16 151 E3
Herman Wlk YO24 132 C8
Hermes Cl HU9 142 C4
Hermitage Rd YO16 122 C4
Hermitage The 5 DN8 79 B2
Heron Ave YO24 132 C8
Heron Cl Grimsby DN32 103 A2
16 Hedon HU12 72 C7
10 Scunthorpe DN15 96 B7
Heron Holt 1 DN20 97 D4
Heron Mews YO15 11 B4
Heron Rise YO32 127 F5
Heron St HU3 145 B5
Heron Way 6 DN36 114 A6
Herrick Rd DN17 150 D3
Herriot Way DN15 150 C7
Hersey Rd 24 LN7 111 B4
Hertfordshire Cl 2
HU5 139 D1
Hesketh Bank YO10 131 D3
Hesketh Dr DN3 92 A2
Heslerton Ave HU16 139 A4
Heslin Cl 8 YO32 127 C8
Heslington Croft YO10 133 F7
Heslington Ct 2 YO10 131 B1
Heslington La
Heslington YO10 131 A1
York YO10 130 F3
Heslington Rd YO10 130 E3
Hessay Pl 2 YO26 129 A3
Hessle High Sch
HU13 143 C2
Hessle Lower Sch
HU13 143 E3
Hessle Mount Sch
HU13 143 C3
Hessle Penshurst Prim Sch
HU13 143 F3
Hessle Rd HU1 155 A1
Hessle View 22 DN18 84 E8
Hessleskew La YO43 42 A4
Hetherton St YO30 156 A3
Hewde La DN15 83 A8
Hewitt's Ave DN36 114 A8
Hewitt's Cir DN36 103 B1
Hewitts Manor 3 DN35 103 B1
Hewley Ave YO10 131 A4
Heworth YO31 131 A6
Heworth CE Prim Sch
YO31 130 F6
Heworth Gn YO31 156 C4
Heworth Hall Dr YO31 130 F6
Heworth Mews YO31 130 E6
Heworth Pl YO31 130 F6
Heworth Rd YO31 130 F6
Heworth Village YO31 131 A6
Hewson Rd DN36 114 D8
Hewson St DN17 107 D7
Hey St DN35 153 F1
Heythrop Rd DN35 103 C2
Hibaldstow Cl 21 DN34 102 C2
Hibaldstow Prim Sch
DN20 109 A5
Hickleton Cl HU8 141 C1
Hickman Cres DN21 117 B2
Hickman Gr DN21 117 E5
High Bridge Rd DN8 93 C7
High Brighton St 13
HU19 75 A6
High Burgage 2 DN15 68 B1
High Catton Rd YO41 27 D8
High Croft 7 YO14 2 F8
High Eggborough La
DN14 62 A1
High Farm Ct HU11 142 F7
High Field YO10 131 D4
High Field Rd DN20 98 D3
High Garth DN17 96 C1
High Gn YO16 122 D5
High Hazel Rd DN8 79 B2
High La Carnaby YO25 10 C3
Sutton upon Derwent
YO41 27 D3
High Levels Bank
Belton DN8 94 A4
Hatfield DN8 93 A6
High Leys Rd DN17 96 C2
High Mdw Gowdall DN14 63 A1
Selby YO8 148 B6
High Mdws HU10 143 C8
High Moor La YO30 12 C8
High Newbiggin St
YO31 156 B3
High Oaks YO31 131 B7
High Ousegate YO1 156 B2
High Peter La YO25 20 D7
High Petergate YO1 156 B3
High Rd
Elloughton-cum-Brough
HU15 68 D6
North Cave HU15 53 E3
High Ridge Sch Specialist
Sports Coll DN15 150 E7
High Risby Medieval
Village* DN15 83 A1
High Row YO41 16 D4
High Sewerby Rd
YO15 123 C7
High Side YO25 34 A8
High St Airmyn DN14 64 E3
Aldbrough HU11 47 C1
Barmby on the Marsh
DN14 64 A7
Barrow upon Humber
DN19 85 D8
Barton-upon-Humber
DN18 69 E1
Beckingham DN10 116 D1
Belton DN9 94 E1
Blyton DN21 117 F5
Boynton YO16 10 D7
Bridlington YO16 122 C4
Broughton DN20 97 D3
Buckton/Bempton YO15 4 C3
Burringham DN17 95 D4
Burton upon Stather
DN15 82 B4
Caistor LN7 111 B4
Carlton DN14 63 C2
Cawood YO8 48 B8
Cleethorpes DN35 153 E2
Corringham DN21 118 A1
Cottam YO25 7 E5
4 Crowle DN17 94 D7
Easington HU12 90 F6
East Butterwick DN17 106 D8
East Ferry DN21 106 B2
Eastoft DN17 81 A3
Eastrington DN14 65 F8
Epworth DN9 105 E6
7 Flamborough YO15 5 A2
Flixborough DN15 82 B1
Garthorpe & Fockerby
DN17 81 E5
Goole DN14 65 C4
Great Limber DN37 100 D3
Gringley on the Hill
DN10 116 A1
Hatfield DN7 92 C2
Haxey DN9 105 D2
Holme-on-Spalding-Moor
YO43 40 A1
Humberside Airport
DN39 100 A6
Kilham YO25 9 A8
Kingston upon Hull HU1 155 C1
Kirby Grindalythe YO17 6 D8
Kirton in Lindsey DN21 108 B1
Laceby DN37 101 F1
Langtoft YO25 8 C8
Luddington & Haldenby
DN17 81 C4
Market Weighton YO43 135 D4
Messingham DN17 107 D7
Misterton DN10 116 C5
Nafferton YO25 125 E7
Nettleton LN7 111 C2
North Ferriby HU14 69 A5
North Kelsey LN7 110 A4
North Thoresby DN36 114 A1
14 Norton DN6 76 E1
Owston Ferry DN9 106 B3
Rawcliffe DN14 64 A1
Redbourne DN21 108 F2
Roxby cum Risby DN15 82 E1
Sancton YO43 41 D2
Scotter DN21 107 C3
Scotton DN21 107 C1
Scunthorpe DN15 151 A7
Snaith DN14 63 B1
South Ferriby DN18 84 A7
Swinefleet DN14 65 D1
Ulceby DN39 86 A1
Walkeringham DN10 116 C3
Waltham DN37 113 E6
West/East Butterwick
DN17 95 D1
Wharram YO17 6 A6
Winterton DN15 83 A5
Withernwick HU11 46 D3
Wootton DN39 85 E2
Wroot DN9 104 D6
High St E DN15 151 C7
High St W DN21 107 C4
High Stile HU17 45 B8
High Thorpe Cres
DN35 103 B2
High Trees Mount
HU7 141 E6
Higham Cl HU8 141 E7
Higham Way HU15 68 D5
Highcliff Gdns DN15 150 E7
Highcliffe Ct YO30 130 A6
Highcourt HU6 139 E7
Highcroft HU17 43 A5
Highdales HU10 143 C8
Highfield
Kingston upon Hull HU7 141 D6
Pollington DN14 77 F7
Withernsea HU19 75 A6
Highfield Ave
Great Driffield YO25 124 E6
Grimsby DN32 152 E1
22 Immingham DN40 87 B1
Scunthorpe DN15 150 E7
Highfield Cl
Barnby Dun DN3 92 A4
Fangfoss YO41 28 C8
Gainsborough DN21 117 C1
Kingston upon Hull HU7 141 D6
5 North Thoresby DN36 114 B1
Wold Newton YO25 2 A4
Highfield Cres
Barlby with Osgodby YO8 49 B5
15 Barton-upon-Humber
DN18 84 F8
Kingston upon Hull
HU11 142 F7
9 Thorne/Moorends DN8 79 A1
2 Westwoodside DN9 105 B2
Highfield Ct YO8 148 B1
Highfield Dr 1 DN21 108 B1
Highfield Gr 4 DN20 98 C3
Highfield La
Fangfoss YO41 16 B1
Womersley DN6 76 D5
Highfield Rd
Beverley HU17 136 F6
North Thoresby DN36 114 B1
Highfield Rise 1 HU12 58 D1
Highfield View 3 YO8 49 B4
Highfield Way HU14 69 A4
Highfields
10 Barrow upon Humber
DN19 85 C8
Crowle DN17 94 D8
South Cave HU15 54 A2
Highgate Balne DN14 77 D6
Beverley HU17 154 B2
Cherry Burton HU17 42 E4
Cleethorpes DN35 153 E1
Highgate Cl HU8 142 A5
Highgrove DN17 107 D7
Highgrove Cl 7 YO30 126 E3
Highgrove Way HU7 56 F6
Highland Tarn 31 DN40 87 B1
Highlands Ave 5 YO32 14 B7
Highlands Prim Sch
HU7 57 A6
Highmoor Cl YO24 132 D8
Highmoor Rd YO24 132 D8
Highthorn Rd YO31 127 E2
Highwood YO25 124 E6
Higrove Way 32 HU7 56 F6
Hilary Gr HU4 144 B2
Hilary Rd 11 DN33 113 E8
Hilbeck Gr YO31 131 B6
Hilbra Ave YO32 127 D6
Hilda St Goole DN14 149 C5
Grimsby DN32 153 A4
6 Selby YO8 148 C5
3 York YO10 130 E3
Hilderthorpe Inf Sch
YO15 122 C1
Hilderthorpe Jun Sch
YO15 122 C1
Hilderthorpe Rd YO15 122 D2
Hildyard Cl
19 Hedon HU12 72 D7
1 Kingston upon Hull
HU10 143 F6
Hildyard St DN32 153 A4
Hiles Ave DN15 83 A5
Hill Brow HU10 143 B6
Hill Crest YO19 14 F1
Hill Crest Gdns YO24 129 F1
Hill Field YO8 148 B8
Hill Rd DN21 118 B1
Hill Rise Brough HU15 68 C6
Market Weighton YO43 135 E4
Hill Rise Cl YO43 135 E4
Hill Rise Dr YO43 135 E4
Hill St Bridlington YO16 122 D3
Kingston upon Hull HU8 141 A2
York YO24 129 E3
Hill The DN20 98 D8
Hill Top La DN21 117 E5
Hill Top Pl DN34 102 B2
Hill Top Rd 4 YO8 48 D6
Hill Top View HU11 57 F6
Hill View YO31 131 C7
Hillam Comm La LS25 61 B7
Hillam H Cl 5 LS25 61 A7
Hillam Hall La 4 LS25 61 A7
Hillam Hall View 3 LS25 61 A7
Hillam La LS25 61 A7
Hillam Rd YO8 61 F8
Hillary Garth 9 YO26 129 E4
Hillary Rd DN16 151 B1
Hillary Way DN37 102 C4
Hillcrest Beverley HU17 136 C6
8 Monk Fryston LS25 61 A8
Hillcrest Ave
Kingston upon Hull
HU13 143 C2

Hillcrest Ave *continued*
Poppleton YO26 126 A2
Hillcrest Dr
Beverley HU17 136 D6
Burton upon Stather
DN15 82 A4
Hillerby La HU18 134 B4
Hillfield Dr HU11 45 D2
Hillfoot Dr 22 DN17 96 C2
Hillgarth Ct 4 YO41 27 B2
Hillman Rd HU13 143 F3
Hills Dr 6 DN36 114 D4
Hillsborough Terr 5
YO30 130 C7
Hillside Cl
Bootham Stray YO30 127 B2
9 Monk Fryston LS25 61 A8
Hillside Cres DN38 99 B5
Hillside Dr DN18 84 E8
Hillside Gdns YO25 8 D5
Hillside Rd DN20 97 E4
Hillside Way YO17 7 B8
Hillsmere Gr 5 DN15 83 A5
Hillstead Cl 5 DN36 114 D4
Hillsway Cl HU8 141 D4
Hillsyde Ave DN10 116 C5
Hilltop Ave DN15 150 E8
Hilston Gr HU9 142 B1
Hilton Ave DN15 150 B7
Hilton Cl DN9 94 E2
Hilton Ct DN35 103 D1
Hinch Garth HU12 60 B1
Hinderwell St HU5 140 C1
Hindon Wlk DN17 150 C4
Hinkler St DN35 153 E1
Hinkley Dr 2 DN40 87 B2
Hinman Wlk DN15 151 B7
Hinsley La DN14 63 C2
Hinton Ave 1 YO24 132 C8
Hirncroft Cl 10 HU8 141 E7
Hirst Courtney & Temple
Hirst CP Sch YO8 62 E3
Hirst Rd YO8 63 A3
Hive La DN14 52 B1
Hob Moor Com Prim Sch
YO24 129 D2
Hob Moor Dr YO24 129 E2
Hob Moor Jun Sch
YO24 129 E2
Hob Moor Oaks Sch
YO26 129 C6
Hobb La 14 DN21 107 C3
Hobgate YO24 129 D3
Hobman La YO25 32 E7
Hobmoor Terr YO24 129 F1
Hobson Cl YO23 132 B1
Hobson Ct HU17 154 B4
Hobson Rd 5 HU15 68 C6
Hobson Way DN41 101 F8
Hodder Gr HU8 142 C6
Hoddesdon Cres 13 DN7 92 D3
Hoddy Cows La YO15 4 C3
Hodge Ct 3 HU9 146 C7
Hodge La WF8 76 B3
Hodgson Ave HU17 154 B4
Hodgson La Roos HU12 60 A1
Upper Poppleton YO26 24 F8
Hodgson St HU8 155 C3
Hodgson's Fields Nature
Reserve* HU12 90 D7
Hodsow Fields YO42 28 E4
Hodsow La YO42 28 F3
Hogg La HU10 143 B8
Hoggard La DN14 81 E8
Hogsea La HU12 60 B4
Holbeck Pl 17 DN40 87 B1
Holborn St HU8 146 B7
Holbrook Cl 2 HU7 141 B4
Holburns Croft 3 YO10 131 B1
Holcombe Cl HU8 142 B7
Holcroft Garth 10 HU12 72 D7
Holden Gdns YO8 48 D2
Holderness Com Coll
HU18 134 C4
Holderness Cres
HU17 154 B3
Holderness Rd HU9 146 C8
Holgate Bridge Gdn 7
YO24 130 A3
Holgate Cl 2 HU17 137 B3
Holgate Lodge Dr
YO26 129 E4
Holgate Pl 12 HU14 69 B7
Holgate Rd
Scunthorpe DN16 151 D4
York YO24 156 A1
Holland Ave
Crowle DN17 94 D8
Scunthorpe DN15 150 E8
Holland St HU9 146 C8
Holles St DN32 152 E3
Hollicarrs Cl YO19 37 A2
Hollies The
Barlby with Osgodby YO8 49 C4
Beverley HU17 137 A7
Hornsea HU18 134 D2
Kingston upon Hull
HU10 138 E2
Snaith & Cowick DN14 78 C8
Hollin Bridge La DN7 93 A3
Hollingsworth Ave 12
DN40 87 B1
Hollingsworth Cl 14
DN35 103 B1
Hollingsworth La 22
DN9 105 E6
Hollis Cres YO32 14 B6
Hollowgate Hill DN21 119 A3
Hollows The 9 YO16 122 C5
Holly Bank Gr 3 YO24 129 F2
Holly Bank Rd YO24 129 F2
Holly Cl
Acaster Malbis YO23 36 C8
Full Sutton YO41 16 A2
18 Scunthorpe DN16 96 E2
Stallingborough DN41 101 D6
Holly Dr HU16 138 E5
Holly Gr
11 Gilberdyke HU15 66 D7
Selby YO8 148 B3
8 Thorpe Willoughby YO8 48 B2
Holly Hill HU15 68 E6
Holly Rd 11 DN8 79 B1
Holly Terr YO10 130 D1
Holly Tree Croft 2 YO19 26 F7
Holly Tree Garth YO32 14 E3
Holly Tree La
Dunnington YO19 26 F7
Haxby YO32 127 D8
Holly Wlk 10 DN8 79 B1
Hollybush Way HU17 136 D4
Hollycroft YO25 23 A6
Hollygarth La DN14 61 D4
Hollym Rd
Patrington HU19 74 F3
Withernsea HU19 75 A5
Hollyrood Rd YO30 126 E3
Hollytree Ave 2 HU4 144 B7
Hollywood YO8 148 B7
Holm Garth Dr HU8 142 B4
Holm Rd DN9 105 B2
Holme Ave DN36 114 A7
Holme Church La
HU17 154 C2
Holme Cl 19 Brigg DN20 98 C2
Holme-on-Spalding-Moor
YO43 40 A1
Paull HU12 72 A5
Holme Cres HU16 138 E6
Holme Ct YO43 135 D4
Holme Dene DN9 105 C2
Holme Dr DN15 82 B5
Holme Farm Cl DN37 102 B5
Holme Gdns 11 DN7 92 C6
Holme Hall Ave DN16 96 D2
Holme Hill La YO10 26 C4
Holme Ind Est YO43 52 C6
Holme La Holme DN16 96 E2
Messingham DN17 107 D8
Scunthorpe DN16 96 D2
Selby YO8 148 D6
Holme on Spalding Moor
Prim Sch YO43 40 A1
Holme Rd YO43 135 B3
Holme St DN32 152 E3
Holme Valley Prim Sch
DN16 96 E2
Holmefield Cl 3 YO8 148 A1
Holmefield Ct 2 YO8 148 A1
Holmefield La YO10 131 A1
Holmes Dr 2 YO19 37 A1
Holmes House* YO8 50 B3
Holmes Ind Est YO8 148 D6
Holmes La Bilton HU11 58 A4
Roxby cum Risby DN15 83 D5
Holmes Pk DN14 51 F1
Holmes The YO8 148 C6
Holmfirth Rd DN15 150 C8
Holmpton Gr HU9 142 B1
Holmpton Rd
Patrington HU12 74 E1
Withernsea HU19 75 A5
Holms La YO43 53 E7
Holmshaw Cl 18 DN3 92 A2
Holray Pk DN14 63 C2
Holroyd Ave YO31 131 A5
Holstein Dr 2 DN16 96 D1
Holt The DN21 117 C1
Holtby Cl HU9 142 C5
Holtby Gdns HU18 134 C6
Holtby La Holtby YO19 14 D1
Stockton-on-the-Forest
YO32 128 F2
Holtby's Yd YO16 122 C4
Holton Ct 8 DN36 114 A5
Holton le Clay Jun Sch
DN36 114 B5
Holton Mount 7 DN36 114 A5
Holton Rd
Holton le Moor LN7 110 F1
Tetney DN36 114 C5
Holwell Rd HU7 141 A5
Holwick Mews HU5 139 D4
Holy Family CP Sch
DN7 92 D6
Holy Family RC High Sch
DN14 63 C3
Holy Name RC Prim Sch
HU6 139 E7
Holy Well* DN15 83 C4
Holy Well La LN11 121 D4
Holydyke DN18 84 E8
Holyoake Rd DN32 153 C2
Holyroad Dr DN15 96 B7
Holyrood Ave YO15 122 F3
Home Beat Dr DN20 97 C3
Home Cl HU4 144 C5
Home Gn HU16 139 A5
Home Paddock 5 DN37 113 E6
Home St DN15 151 B8
Homefield Ave 8 DN33 102 E2
Homefield Cl YO23 132 A2
Homestead Cl
Eggborough DN14 62 A2
2 York YO32 127 F1
Homestead Garth 3
DN7 92 D4
Homestead Rd HU12 72 F5
Homethorpe HU6 140 A8
Honey Pot 5 YO8 50 D7
Honeypots La HU12 59 A2
Honeysuckle Cl
20 Brough HU15 68 C5
Selby YO8 148 C2
Honeysuckle Ct
24 Bottesford DN16 96 E2
Humberston DN35 103 C1
Honeysuckle Farm*
HU18 35 C3
Honeysuckle Pl 15 HU15 68 D5
Honiton Rd HU7 141 A8
Hood Gr DN14 149 B6
Hood Rd DN17 150 D2
Hood St HU8 155 C4
Hook CE VC Prim Sch
DN14 65 B4
Hook La DN14 149 C8
Hook Pasture La
DN14 149 C1
Hook Rd DN14 149 E4
Hooks La Holmpton HU19 75 B2
Thorngumbald HU12 72 E4
Hoop End DN36 114 D4
Hop Hills La DN7 92 D5
Hope St
Cleethorpes DN35 103 D3
Grimsby DN32 152 F4
York YO10 156 C1
Hopewell Rd HU9 142 C3
Hopfield DN20 109 A5
Hopgarth DN9 105 D2
Hopgrove La N YO32 128 C3
Hopgrove La S YO32 128 E3
Hopkins Ave DN17 151 A3
Hopkins St HU9 142 A3
Hopwood Cl HU3 145 D8
Hopwood La HU15 52 F1
Horbury Ave HU9 142 B2
Horbury Cl DN15 150 D8
Hords La YO25 21 D4
Horkstow Rd DN18 84 A6
Hornbeam Ave DN16 151 A1
Hornbeam Cl YO30 127 B2
Hornbeam Dr HU16 139 C5
Hornbeam Wlk HU16 139 B5
Hornby Gr HU9 142 C3
Horner St YO30 130 B7
Hornsby Cres DN15 96 C7
Hornsea & District War Meml
Hospl HU18 134 C5
Hornsea Bridge Ind Est
HU18 134 C2
Hornsea Burton Prim Sch
HU18 134 C4
Hornsea Burton Rd
HU18 134 D3
Hornsea Leisure Ctr
HU18 134 D4
Hornsea Par 5 HU9 146 C8
Hornsea Rd
Aldbrough HU11 47 B2
Atwick HU18 134 A8
Hatfield HU11 46 D6
Leven HU17 45 B8
Seaton HU11 35 B1
Skipsea YO25 23 B1
Hornsea Sch & Language Coll
HU18 134 B4
Hornsey Garth 25 YO32 13 E5
Hornsey Hill Rd DN21 106 D1
Horse Carr La YO25 10 B1
Horse Fair Gn 21 DN8 93 A8
Horse Mkt 17 LN7 111 B4
Horsefair La YO25 124 B5
Horsefair The YO25 124 C5
Horsegate Field Rd
DN19 86 A8
Horseman Ave YO23 132 A3
Horseman Cl 2 YO23 132 A3
Horseman Dr YO23 132 A3
Horseman La YO23 132 A3
Horseshoe Cres YO43 40 A1
Horseshoe Dr YO15 123 C6
Horseshoe The
Great Driffield YO25 124 E3
York YO24 132 E7
Horsfield Way YO19 26 F7
Horsforth Ave YO15 122 D1
Horsman Ave YO10 156 C1
Horstead Ave DN20 98 C3
Hospital Fields Rd
YO10 130 D1
Hospital Hill 4 YO25 10 A2
Hospital La YO8 48 B4
Hospitium The* YO1 156 A3
Hotham Ave YO26 129 B2
Hotham Dr HU5 144 B8
Hotham Rd
Hutton Cranswick YO25 32 E7
Kingston upon Hull HU5 144 A8
North Cave YO43 53 D4
Hotham Rd N HU5 139 E3
Hotham Rd S HU5 144 B8
Hotham Sq HU17 137 B4
Hotham St HU9 146 D7
Hothams Ct YO1 156 C2
Hotspur Rd 1 DN21 117 B1
Hotton Cl HU9 142 C1
Houghton La YO43 41 C1
Houghton Wlk HU5 139 C2
Houndale La YO25 125 E8
Houndsway 6 YO24 132 B8
Houps Rd 10 DN8 93 B8
Hourne Ct HU13 143 E2
Hourne The HU13 143 E2
House Ct DN16 96 E2
Housemartin Dr 4 HU8 141 D8
Houston Dr HU5 140 D3
Hove Rd HU5 139 D1
Hovedene Dr DN14 65 A6
Hovingham Cl 17 HU8 141 E7
Howard Dr YO30 126 E2
Howard Gr DN32 153 B2
Howard Link YO30 126 D2
Howard Rd YO32 14 B6
Howard St YO10 130 D2
Howdale Rd HU8 141 E7
Howden CE Jun & Inf Sch
DN14 65 B7
Howden Croft Hill
HU15 68 A8
Howden La YO19 133 E1
Howden Marsh Nature
Reserve* DN14 65 A7
Howden Rd 4 Barlby YO8 49 B4
Eastrington DN14 65 F8
Holme-on-Spalding-Moor
YO43 51 F6
Howden Sch DN14 65 B7
Howdens Hill DN15 151 A6
Howdenshire Way
DN14 64 F6
Howe Hill* DN39 85 D2
Howe Hill Cl YO26 129 E4
Howe Hill Rd YO26 129 E4
Howe La Goxhill DN19 85 F8
Kirby Underdale YO41 17 A5
Nafferton YO25 125 F7
Howe St YO24 129 D3
Howes La YO25 33 E8
Howes Rd 8 YO14 3 A8
Howgate La YO43 41 A8
Howl Gate YO41 27 E8
Howl La YO25 32 E8
Howlett Rd 4 DN35 103 D2
Howsham Cl HU9 142 D5
Howsham La DN38 110 C8
Howville Ave DN7 92 F3
Howville Rd DN7 92 F3
Hoylake Cl HU6 139 E5
Hoylake Dr 6 DN40 87 C2
Hoylake Rd DN17 96 B2
Hubert St
1 Withernsea HU19 74 F7
2 York YO23 130 B1
Huby Ct YO10 130 E3
Hucknall Garth 16 HU7 57 A5
Huddleston Rd DN32 153 B3
Hudson Ave DN15 96 C7
Hudson Cl YO41 15 D2
Hudson Cres 2 YO30 130 A7
Hudson Ct
Kingston upon Hull
HU13 143 D1
Market Weighton YO43 135 D4
Hudson Gdns 2 HU5 140 D1
Hudson St
Kingston upon Hull HU3 145 D8
6 York YO30 130 C7
Hudson's La YO25 31 B7
Huggate Dikes* YO42 17 F2
Huggate Hill YO17 17 E7
Huggate La YO25 18 B5
Huggin Carr Rd DN7 92 F1
Hugh Field La YO8 50 A8
Hugh Field N La YO8 38 A1
Hugh Hill La DN7 92 D6
Hulberry Cl 11 DN41 101 A4
Hull & E Riding Hospl
HU10 143 E5
Hull & E Riding Mus*
HU1 155 C2
Hull Arena HU1 145 E4
Hull Bridge Rd
Beverley HU17 154 B4
Tickton HU17 137 C7
Hull City AFC HU4 144 E5
Hull Coll (Local History Unit)
HU9 146 B8
Hull Coll East Ella HU3 144 F7
Kingston upon Hull HU1 155 C3
Hull Coll of F Ed HU1 155 C3
Hull Coll Pk St Ctr
HU2 145 D7
Hull Coll Sch of Art & Design
HU2 155 C3
Hull Gram Sch HU5 140 C3
Hull High Sch HU10 143 C5
Hull Maritime Mus*
HU1 155 B2
Hull Maternity Hospl
HU9 147 A8
Hull New Theatre
HU2 155 B3
Hull Nuffield Hospl
HU5 140 B1
Hull Rd Aldbrough HU11 59 B7
Beverley HU17 137 B3
Cliffe YO8 49 E2
Coniston HU11 57 F5
Easington HU12 90 E6
Hatfield HU11 46 C5
Hemingbrough YO8 50 B1
Hornsea HU18 134 B1
Howden DN14 65 B7
Keyingham HU12 73 C4
Marfleet HU12 147 F6
Northfield HU13 143 F1
Osbaldwick YO10 131 D3
Preston HU12 72 A7
Rimswell HU19 74 E6
Hull Rd *continued*
Woodmansey HU17 137 B2
York YO10 131 B3
Hull Rd Ave 4 DN14 65 B7
Hull Royal Infmy HU3 145 C6
Hull Sta HU1 155 A2
Hull Trinity Ho Sch
HU1 155 B2
Hull Truck Theatre*
HU2 145 D7
Humber Bank S DN31 153 A6
Humber Bridge Ctry Pk*
HU13 69 D4
Humber Bridge Ind Est
DN18 70 A1
Humber Bridge Rd
DN31 153 A5
Humber Cres
5 Brough HU15 68 C5
Scunthorpe DN17 150 F2
Humber Dock St HU1 155 B1
Humber Dr 5 YO32 14 B6
Humber La
Patrington HU12 74 D1
Skeffling HU12 90 D5
Welwick HU12 90 A7
Humber Pl HU1 155 B1
Humber Rd
Barton-upon-Humber
DN18 69 E1
North Ferriby HU14 69 A4
South Killingholme DN40 86 F3
Humber Side La
Easington HU12 90 F4
Welwick HU12 89 F6
Humber Side Rd HU12 90 B6
Humber St
Cleethorpes DN35 153 F1
Goole DN14 149 D1
Grimsby DN31 153 A5
Kingston upon Hull HU9 155 C1
Market Weighton YO43 135 F4
Humber Terr DN31 152 C4
Humber View
Barton-upon-Humber
DN18 84 E8
Kingston upon Hull
HU13 143 C2
5 Swanland HU14 69 B6
Humberdale Cl 4 HU14 69 B6
Humberdale Dr HU14 69 C5
Humberside Int Airport
DN38 99 F5
Humberston Ave 13
DN36 114 D8
Humberston CE Prim Sch
DN36 114 D8
Humberston Cloverfields
Prim Sch DN36 114 C8
Humberston Rd DN36 103 B1
Humberston Sch The
DN36 114 C8
Humberstone Rd
DN32 153 A2
Humberville Rd DN40 87 C1
Humbleton Rd
East Garton HU12 59 C6
Elstronwick HU12 58 E3
Hume Brae DN40 87 B1
Hume St DN31 152 C3
Hund Oak Dr DN7 92 D4
Hungate
13 Barton-upon-Humber
DN18 69 E1
York YO1 156 C2
Hungate Ct
11 Hunmanby YO14 2 F8
Market Weighton YO43 135 D5
Hungate La YO14 2 F8
Hunger Hills Balk YO25 10 C4
Hungerhills Dr HU11 58 A4
Hunmanby Prim Sch
YO14 2 F8
Hunmanby Rd
Burton Fleming YO25 2 E3
Reighton YO14 3 C6
Hunmanby Sta YO14 3 A7
Hunsley Ave 3 HU5 139 B1
Hunsley Cres DN32 103 A2
Hunsley Dr DN41 101 E6
Hunsley Rd HU17 55 A7
Hunt Ct YO31 156 C3
Hunt Rd DN16 151 C1
Huntcliffe Sch DN21 108 C1
Hunter Cl
1 Patrington HU12 74 D1
5 Preston HU12 58 D1
Hunter Gr HU3 145 A4
Hunter Rd HU15 68 C6
Hunter's Croft DN9 105 D3
Hunters Cl
Dunnington YO19 26 E7
10 Haxby YO32 127 C8
Hunters Gate DN37 102 B5
Hunters Way
Selby YO8 148 B4
York YO24 132 F7
Hunters Wlk YO8 63 D7
Hunters Wood Way 21
YO19 26 F7
Huntingdon Cres 5
DN15 82 B4
Huntingdon St HU4 144 E3
Huntington Mews
YO31 130 D7

Huntington Prim Sch YO32 127 F4
Huntington Rd YO31 156 C4
Huntington Sec Sch YO32 127 E3
Huntington Sports Club YO32 128 A5
Huntley Dr HU5 140 A1
Hunts Cl 7 DN20 97 E4
Hunts La DN20 108 F5
Huntsman's Wlk YO24 129 B1
Huntsmans Chase 8 DN36 113 F8
Huntsmans La YO41 15 C2
Hurford Pl DN37 113 E7
Hurley Cl HU8 141 F3
Hurlstone Cl 20 DN3 92 A2
Hurn Cl HU8 141 E6
Hurns La YO30 126 A7
Hurricane Way YO30 126 E3
Hurst La DN17 96 C2
Hurst's Yd YO1 156 C2
Hurstlea Dr 19 DN36 103 D1
Hurton's La LN11 121 F6
Hushells La DN14 78 C2
Hustler Rd YO16 122 F5
Hutch La DN14 66 C3
Hutchinson Rd DN35 153 D3
Hutchinson St 1 YO8 148 B6
Huteson La DN15 82 C8
Hutt St HU3 145 D7
Hutton Balk YO25 32 D8
Hutton Cl
Kingston upon Hull HU5 139 E2
Poppleton YO26 126 A2
Hutton Cranswick Com Prim Sch YO25 32 E7
Hutton Rd
Grimsby DN31 153 A6
Hutton Cranswick YO25 32 E7
Hutton St YO26 24 A5
Huzzard Cl 5 HU17 55 D8
Hyde Pk Cl 18 DN33 102 D1
Hykeham Cl 17 HU7 56 F6
Hymers Ave HU3 145 B7
Hymers Cl 11 YO25 34 B2
Hymers Coll HU3 145 B7
Hyperion St HU9 155 C3
Hyrst Gr YO31 130 E6
Hytec Way 7 HU15 68 B5

I

Icehouse Rd HU3 145 D6
Icelandic Cl HU3 145 C5
Idas Cl HU9 155 C1
Idle Bank Epworth DN9 94 A2
Haxey DN9 104 F4
Ikin Way YO32 127 F6
Ilchester Cl HU7 141 B5
Ilford Rd HU5 139 C1
Ilkeston Ave DN14 149 B5
Ilkeston Ct DN15 150 B7
Ilthorpe HU6 140 A8
Ilton Garth YO30 127 A2
Immingham Dock DN40 87 D3
Immingham Medieval Village* DN40 87 B2
Immingham Mus* DN40 87 C1
Immingham Sch The DN40 87 C1
Immingham Sports Ctr DN40 87 C1
Immingham Swimming Pool DN40 87 C1
Impala Way HU4 144 D2
Imperial Ave DN35 153 C4
Imperial Ct 12 HU9 142 A3
Ing Nook Rd HU15 52 C2
Inghams La 12 DN36 114 D4
Inghams Rd DN36 114 D4
Ingland Ct HU9 142 B1
Ingleborough Ave YO10 131 B4
Ingleby Cl HU8 141 F7
Ingleby Rd DN17 107 D7
Inglefield Cl 7 HU17 55 E8
Inglemire Ave HU6 140 C5
Inglemire La HU6 139 E5
Inglenook Dr 1 DN8 93 B8
Ingleton Ave HU4 144 C6
Ingleton Wlk 3 YO31 131 A5
Inglewood Dr 4 HU4 144 B5
Ingmires 3 HU15 68 D6
Ingram Ave HU11 142 F6
Ingram Cres DN7 92 C4
Ingram Gdns DN20 108 E8
Ingram Gr DN7 92 C4
Ingram Pl DN35 103 B2
Ingram Rd DN7 92 C3
Ingrish La YO23 24 C1
Ings Ct DN14 61 F4
Ings Dr YO43 53 F7
Ings La Beal DN14 61 D4
Bishop Wilton YO42 16 D2
Brough HU15 68 C5
Carlton DN14 63 E2
Cawood YO8 48 D8
Cottingwith YO42 38 C5
Dunswell HU6 56 D2
Ellerker HU15 67 F8
Hensall DN14 62 D2
Ings La *continued*
Hibaldstow DN20 109 A5
Immingham DN40 87 D1
Kellington DN14 61 F4
Keyingham HU12 73 C4
Kirk Bramwith DN7 92 C7
Nether Poppleton YO26 126 B1
North Coates DN36 115 A3
North Ferriby HU14 69 A4
Patrington HU12 74 C1
Riccall YO19 48 E8
Riston HU11 45 C2
South Cave HU15 67 E7
Spaldington DN14 51 C4
Thorganby YO19 38 B5
Utterby LN11 121 E4
Walkerith DN21 116 F3
Waltham DN37 113 E6
West Stockwith DN10 116 F6
Wheldrake YO19 38 B7
Whitton DN15 67 E3
Winterton DN15 83 D7
Wistow YO8 49 A6
York YO10 131 A1
Ings Prim Sch HU8 141 F4
Ings Rd Cliffe YO8 49 D2
Kingston upon Hull HU7 141 D5
Kirton in Lindsey DN21 107 F1
Molescroft HU17 136 D7
Snaith DN14 63 C1
Thorganby YO19 38 B4
Wilberfoss YO41 27 E6
Ings View YO30 126 D2
Inman Terr YO26 129 D4
Inmans Prim Sch HU12 72 D7
Inmans Rd HU12 72 D7
Innescourt HU6 139 E7
Innovation Cl YO10 131 B2
Innovation Way
Great Coates DN31 102 B6
York YO10 131 B2
Innsworth Garth 17 HU7 57 A5
Inrea Hill YO42 29 F5
Intake Ave YO30 130 C8
Intake Hill YO43 135 C8
Intake La
Acaster Malbis YO23 36 C7
Beal WF11 61 D5
Dunnington YO19 26 F7
Heck DN14 77 C8
West Haddlesey YO8 61 F6
Intakefield Rd YO8 50 D7
Intakes La YO42 39 A6
Intax Farm Mews DN32 152 F2
Inverewe Way 2 HU16 138 F5
Inverness Rd 24 DN7 92 D4
Invicta Ct YO24 132 B8
Iona Cl
8 Gainsborough DN21 117 C1
Kingston upon Hull HU8 141 E7
Iona Dr DN36 114 D8
Iona Rd YO16 122 F4
Irby Ct 8 DN35 103 B2
Irby Rd DN17 150 E1
Ireland Wlk HU4 144 B4
Irvine Rd DN16 151 C1
Irvine Way YO24 132 B7
Irwin Ave YO31 130 E6
Isaac Newton Sch HU9 142 D1
Isaac's Hill DN35 153 E2
Isis Ct HU9 146 B5
Island Carr Rd DN20 98 B2
Island Rd DN17 81 E6
Isle Cl DN17 94 D8
Isledane HU6 139 E8
Itlings La HU13 143 F1
Itterby Cres DN35 103 B2
Ivanhoe Rd DN16 151 C5
Iver Cl YO26 129 C5
Iveson Cl 27 HU12 72 C7
Ivy Cl DN7 92 E4
Ivy Farm Ct 6 DN41 101 F5
Ivy La Grainthorpe LN11 115 E1
Hedon HU12 72 C7
Snaith & Cowick DN14 78 D8
Ivy Mdw HU12 59 C2
Ivy Pk Rd DN14 149 E6
Ivy Pl YO32 127 D3
Ivy Rd DN8 79 A1
Ivybridge Wlk 5 HU9 142 E1

J

Jack Rd YO43 53 C8
Jack Row La DN7 92 B8
Jack Taylor La HU17 137 B4
Jackey La HU11 58 B8
Jacklin La DN17 81 C3
Jacklins App DN16 96 D2
Jackson La YO41 27 E4
Jackson Mews 7 DN40 87 B1
Jackson Rd DN15 150 E7
Jackson St Goole DN14 149 C4
Grimsby DN31 152 C4
Kingston upon Hull HU3 145 D4
York YO31 156 C4
Jackson's Pl DN36 103 B1
Jackson's Wlk YO23 24 D3
Jacksonville DN14 149 C5
Jacobi Cl YO30 130 A7
Jacques' La YO8 49 E4
Jade Gr 1 HU3 145 A4
Jalland St HU8 141 C1
James Backhouse Pl YO24 129 E3
James Cl 1 HU19 75 A6
James Ct 5 DN8 79 B1
James Nicholson Way YO30 127 A2
James Nicolson Link YO30 127 A2
James Niven Ct 1 HU9 141 D1
James Pl DN39 86 B1
James Reckitt Ave HU8 141 B1
James St 21 Brigg DN20 98 B2
Goole DN14 149 D2
Grimsby DN31 152 C4
Selby YO8 148 C5
York YO10 130 E4
James Way 29 DN40 87 B1
Jameson Rd YO16 122 C4
Jameson St HU1 155 A2
Jamieson Terr YO23 130 B1
Janton Ct 23 DN36 114 A8
Japan Rd DN21 117 A1
Japonica Hill 8 DN40 87 C1
Jaque's Bank DN8 94 A5
Jarratt Hill La HU15 67 C8
Jarratt St HU1 155 B3
Jasmine Cl
10 Snaith DN14 63 C1
York YO32 127 D2
Jasmine Ct 8 DN19 86 A8
Jasmine Gr 17 HU7 56 F5
Jasmine Way DN40 87 C1
Jason Cl YO16 122 E6
Jason Garth 1 HU7 57 B5
Jaywick Cl YO32 14 B8
Jedwell Cl YO32 127 D5
Jefferson Cl Goole DN14 65 C4
Molescroft HU17 136 E6
Jefferson Dr HU15 68 C6
Jefferson St DN14 149 C4
Jeffrey La DN9 94 E1
Jellicoe Ct DN16 151 C5
Jendale HU7 140 F8
Jenkings Cl 30 YO42 29 A3
Jenkinson La YO25 32 D8
Jenner Ct DN35 153 B4
Jenner Pl DN35 153 B4
Jennifer Gr 4 YO24 129 F2
Jenning St HU8 155 C4
Jenny Brough La HU13 143 B3
Jenny Brough Mdws HU13 143 B3
Jenny Cl HU13 143 B3
Jenny La DN14 77 B5
Jenthorpe HU6 140 A8
Jericho La DN40 86 D7
Jervis Ct YO41 27 C1
Jervis Rd
Kingston upon Hull HU9 142 D5
York YO24 132 E8
Jesmond Ave 28 DN17 96 C2
Jesmond Gdns HU9 141 D1
Jesmond Rd HU16 139 C6
Jetcourt HU6 139 E7
Jevans Ct 2 YO25 124 F4
Jewbury YO31 156 C3
Jewison La
Bempton YO16 4 D1
Flamborough Maltings YO15 123 B8
Jill Gr HU13 143 F1
Jipdane HU6 139 F8
Jobsons Cl 11 HU15 53 F1
Joby La HU17 43 A2
Jockey La YO32 127 F2
John Bull World of Rock* YO15 10 F3
John Coupland Hospl DN21 117 A2
John Gray Ct HU10 138 D1
John Harrison CE Prim Sch DN19 85 C8
John Harrison's Cl 1 DN19 85 D8
John Leggott Coll DN17 150 E4
John Newton Way HU7 56 E5
John St
Kingston upon Hull HU2 155 B3
Scunthorpe DN15 151 B7
Selby YO8 148 D6
York YO31 130 E6
Johnny Moor Long La DN14 79 B6
Johnson Cl DN9 94 E2
Johnson Dr
21 Bottesford DN16 96 E2
Scotter DN21 107 C4
Johnson St
Cleethorpes DN35 153 B4
Selby YO8 148 B6
Johnson's La DN17 94 C7
Johnston Ct HU17 136 D7
Johnston's Rd DN7 92 E7
Joiners La YO25 19 B6
Jonquil Ave 16 DN16 96 E2
JORVIK* YO1 156 C2
Jorvik Cl YO26 129 C5
Joscelyn Ave HU7 141 B5
Joseph Ogle Cl 6 DN36 113 F8
Joseph Rowntree Sec Sch YO32 127 E5
Joseph St DN31 152 C4
Jowland Winn La YO8 63 A4
Jubbergate YO1 156 B2
Jubilee Ave YO16 122 D4
Jubilee Cres 34 DN21 117 B1
Jubilee Ct YO32 127 D8
Jubilee Gr 8 YO16 122 D5
Jubilee La HU12 59 C2
Jubilee Rd YO8 48 D6
Jubilee Sq HU2 155 B3
Jubilee Terr YO26 129 F5
Jubilee Way 8 DN15 151 B7
Jubilee Wlk YO16 122 D5
Julia Ave YO32 128 B2
Julian Cl HU4 144 A7
Julian St DN32 153 A3
Julian's Bower (Maze)* DN15 82 C8
Julian's Wlk 8 HU10 143 F6
Junction Rd DN7 92 C6
Junella Cl HU3 145 A4
Jungle The* DN35 103 D2
Juniper Chase HU17 136 D4
Juniper Cl Crosby DN15 96 B7
York YO32 127 D3
Juniper Way DN33 102 E1
Justice Hall La 3 DN17 94 D8
Justice La DN14 81 B8
Jute Rd YO26 129 B5
Jutland Ct 13 DN36 114 A8

K

Karelia Ct HU4 144 B5
Karen Ave 10 DN41 101 A4
Kathleen Ave
Cleethorpes DN35 153 D4
Scunthorpe DN16 151 B1
Kathleen Gr DN32 153 C3
Kathleen Rd HU8 141 B2
Kathleen Rice Cl DN32 153 A4
Kathryn Ave YO32 128 A2
Katrine Cl HU7 141 D5
Kay Kendall Ct 16 HU19 75 A6
Kaye Dr YO8 49 B4
Kaymile Cl 15 DN36 114 A7
Kealholme Rd DN17 107 D7
Keats Ave DN17 150 D3
Keats Cl YO30 129 F8
Keb La DN15 83 D2
Keble Cl YO23 133 B3
Keble Dr YO23 133 A2
Keble Gdns YO23 133 B2
Keble Pk Cres YO23 133 A2
Keble Pk N YO23 133 A3
Keble Pk S YO23 133 A2
Keddington Rd 13 DN17 96 C2
Kedrum Rd HU9 141 F1
Keel Ct HU17 137 B3
Keel Rd HU6 140 C8
Keelby CP Sch DN41 101 A5
Keelby Rd
Scunthorpe DN17 150 F1
Stallingborough DN41 101 C6
Keeper's Hill YO25 7 A1
Keeper's Way 2 DN9 94 E1
Keepers Way 11 YO19 26 F7
Keir Hardie Wlk 13 DN32 152 D3
Keirhardie Wlk 4 DN32 152 E3
Keith Ave YO32 128 A4
Keith Cres DN37 101 E1
Kelberdale Cl 30 HU7 56 F6
Keldale 4 YO32 13 F5
Keldgarth YO25 32 F6
Keldgate HU17 154 A2
Keldgate Cl HU17 154 A2
Keldgate Rd
Beverley HU17 136 C2
Cottingham HU16 138 D7
Keldmarsh Nature Reserve* HU17 154 B1
Keldspring La YO42 28 E4
Kelfield Rd 9 YO19 48 F8
Kelgate Cl 11 HU8 141 E7
Kelham Rd DN32 153 D2
Kelk La YO25 22 B6
Kelleythorpe Ind Est YO25 124 B3
Kellington La DN14 61 F2
Kellington Prim Sch DN14 61 F3
Kelsey Ave DN15 150 B7
Kelsey Cl YO43 135 D2
Kelsey Dr 3 HU12 73 C4
Kelsey La DN17 95 D4
Kelsey Rd LN7 110 D1
Kelstern Ct DN34 152 A1
Kelston Dr 2 HU13 144 A3
Kelvin Hall Sch HU5 139 E3
Kelvin St HU9 141 E2
Kemp Rd
Grimsby DN31 153 A7
North Ferriby HU14 69 B6
Kempton Cl
Beverley HU17 136 E6
2 York YO24 129 D1
Kempton Dr DN7 92 C2
Kempton Rd HU3 144 E6
Kendal Cl 6 YO19 26 F7
Kendal Ct DN16 151 C2
Kendal Rd DN40 87 D1
Kendal Way HU4 144 C7
Kendale Rd DN16 151 E4
Kendale View YO25 124 E6
Kendon Gdns DN8 93 B8
Kendrew Cl 3 YO32 127 F3
Kenerdales La YO43 53 E8
Kenford Ct 1 DN36 114 A8
Kenilworth Ave HU5 139 F3
Kenilworth Rd
6 Cleethorpes DN35 103 B2
Kenilworth Rd *continued*
Scunthorpe DN16 151 C5
Kenlay Cl YO32 127 D4
Kenmar Rd DN37 101 F1
Kenmore Dr HU6 56 D5
Kennedy Cl DN20 98 D2
Kennedy Dr
Goole DN14 149 D5
32 Haxby YO32 13 E5
Kennedy Way Sh Ctr DN40 87 C1
Kennet Rd HU8 142 C6
Kenneth Ave 5 DN7 92 C6
Kennington Wlk HU16 139 D6
Kenrick Pl 5 YO26 129 B5
Kensal Rise YO10 130 D2
Kensington Ct 1 YO24 132 F8
Kensington Gdns 14 DN14 65 A7
Kensington Pl 3 DN33 113 F8
Kensington Rd
Rawcliffe YO30 126 D2
Scunthorpe DN15 150 B7
Kensington St YO23 130 B1
Kent Cl HU9 146 C7
Kent Dr DN20 109 A5
Kent Rd
Bridlington YO16 122 A2
Goole DN14 149 B4
Kingston upon Hull HU16 139 A5
Selby YO8 148 A6
Kent Sq YO16 122 A2
Kent St Grimsby DN32 152 F5
York YO10 156 C1
Kentmere Cl 2 HU7 57 A7
Kentmere Dr YO30 126 F1
Kents Gdns 14 DN8 79 B2
Kenwardly Rd HU10 143 E8
Kenwood HU19 75 A5
Kenya Dr 3 DN17 96 C1
Kenyon Cl 28 DN8 93 A8
Keppel Dr YO16 123 A8
Kerdane HU6 139 F8
Kerries Wlk DN17 150 C2
Kerrside YO30 129 E8
Kerry Dr HU10 143 C6
Kerry Pit Way HU10 143 C6
Kerver La YO19 26 F7
Kesgrave St DN31 153 A5
Kesteven Ct 6 DN40 100 E8
Kesteven Gr 9 DN17 94 D8
Kesteven Way HU7 56 F5
Kestrel Ave HU7 141 D8
Kestrel Cl YO25 125 A5
Kestrel Dr YO15 123 B7
Kestrel Rd DN17 150 E2
Kestrel Wood Way YO31 127 F2
Keswick Gdns HU6 139 E6
Keswick Way 5 YO32 127 F5
Kettering Rd DN16 151 C6
Kettlebridge La DN40 86 D6
Kettleby La DN20 98 E3
Kettleby View DN20 98 D2
Kettlestring La YO30 127 A3
Kettlethorpe Hill HU15 53 F4
Kettlewell Cl 2 HU7 56 F6
Kettlewell St DN32 152 E1
Ketwell La 19 HU12 72 C7
Kew Rd DN35 153 E2
Kexby Ave YO10 130 F3
Kexby Bridge* YO41 27 C6
Kexby Stray YO41 27 A5
Key Way YO19 133 F5
Keyholme La DN36 115 D2
Keyingham Inf Sch HU12 73 D4
Keyingham Jun Sch HU12 73 C3
Keyingham Rd HU12 73 D3
Keynes Pk 22 HU7 56 F5
Keyworth Dr 5 LN7 111 B4
Kidd La Brough HU15 68 D6
Melbourne YO42 39 A6
Kiddier Ave 12 DN33 113 D8
Kidhill La HU11 45 B2
Kilburn Ave HU2 155 A4
Kilburn Rd YO10 130 D2
Kildale Cl HU8 141 E6
Kilham CE VC Prim Sch YO25 9 C3
Kilham La Kilham YO25 9 E5
Thwing YO25 9 B8
Kilham Rd YO25 8 D5
Kilkoy Dr 4 HU7 56 F6
Killingholme CE Prim Sch DN40 86 E3
Killingholme Haven Pits Nature Reserve* DN40 87 A6
Killingholme Rd DN40 86 F1
Killingwoldgraves La HU17 43 C2
Kiln Beck Bsns Pk HU17 137 C3
Kiln La 17 Brigg DN20 98 B2
Patrington HU12 74 D1
Stallingborough DN41 101 D8
Kiln La Ind Est DN40 101 E8
Kiln La Trading Est DN40 87 F1
Kilnhouse La HU12 60 C2
Kilnsea Gr HU9 141 F2
Kilnwick Ave HU5 139 C2
Kilnwick Garth 2 YO42 29 A3
Kilnwick La YO25 32 B2

Kilnwick Percy Hill YO42 ....29 D4
Kilnwick Rd YO42 ....29 B4
Kilpin Broad La DN14 ....65 E6
Kilton Ct 12 HU8 ....141 D7
Kilvin Dr HU17 ....137 A6
Kimberley St HU3 ....145 C7
Kimberlows Wood Hill 3 YO10 ....131 C3
Kimmeridge Cl HU7 ....141 B6
Kinbrace Dr YO24 ....132 B7
Kinderscout Cl 15 HU7 ....56 F6
King Charles Cl HU10 ....143 E7
King Edward Cres 9 DN8 ....79 B1
King Edward Fst Sch DN8 ....93 B8
King Edward Rd DN8 ....93 A8
King Edward St
Belton DN9 ....94 E2
Grimsby DN31 ....152 E5
Kingston upon Hull HU1 ....155 A3
12 Kirton in Lindsey DN21 ....108 B1
Scunthorpe DN16 ....151 A5
King Edwards Terr 4 HU15 ....68 B5
King George V Athletic Stadium DN32 ....153 B1
King Georges Ct DN7 ....92 C5
King Rudding Cl 6 YO19 ....49 A8
King Rudding La YO19 ....49 B8
King St
1 Barton-upon-Humber DN18 ....84 F8
Bridlington YO15 ....122 E2
6 Cawood YO8 ....48 B8
Cottingham HU16 ....139 B6
East Halton DN40 ....86 D7
Goxhill DN19 ....86 A8
Great Driffield YO25 ....124 F4
1 Hornsea HU18 ....134 C3
19 Keelby DN41 ....101 A4
Kingston upon Hull HU1 ....155 B2
Sancton YO43 ....41 E2
Scunthorpe DN15 ....151 B8
Thorne/Moorends DN8 ....93 A8
Winterton DN15 ....83 A5
17 Withernsea HU19 ....75 A6
Woodmansey HU17 ....137 D1
York YO1 ....156 B2
King's Ave DN20 ....98 C2
King's Bench St HU3 ....145 B5
King's Cl 7 DN7 ....92 D4
King's Cross Cl 2 HU3 ....145 C6
King's Cswy
Reedness DN14 ....80 E8
Swinefleet DN14 ....65 D1
King's Mill Rd YO25 ....124 D3
King's Pl 29 HU12 ....72 C7
King's Rd
Barnetby le Wold DN38 ....99 B5
Cleethorpes DN35 ....103 D2
King's Sq
Beverley HU17 ....154 B3
York YO1 ....156 C2
King's Staith YO1 ....156 B2
Kingerby Rd DN17 ....150 E1
Kingfisher HU7 ....141 D6
Kingfisher Cl
Kingston upon Hull HU7 ....141 D8
1 Leven HU17 ....45 A8
Scunthorpe DN15 ....96 B7
Kingfisher Dr YO15 ....11 B4
Kingfisher Rise HU7 ....141 E6
Kings Acre YO31 ....131 B6
Kings Cl 5 Barlby YO8 ....49 B5
24 Pocklington YO42 ....29 A3
Kings Croft 3 DN17 ....94 E6
Kings Ct Scawby DN20 ....108 F8
Scunthorpe DN15 ....151 B8
York YO1 ....156 B2
Kings Ct Rd 4 DN8 ....79 B1
Kings Garth YO25 ....125 F7
Kings Lea YO8 ....50 A8
Kings Leigh 1 HU3 ....145 C6
Kings Mdw YO25 ....124 D4
Kings Mead
Great Driffield YO25 ....124 D4
Woodmansey HU17 ....137 D1
Kings Mews DN35 ....103 E1
Kings Mill Cl YO25 ....124 D4
Kings Mill Pk YO25 ....124 D4
Kings Mill Sch YO25 ....124 E4
Kings Moor Rd YO32 ....14 D2
Kings Rd DN40 ....87 D1
Kingsbury Way 7 HU7 ....56 F6
Kingsclere YO32 ....127 F6
Kingscott Cl 10 HU7 ....56 F5
Kingsdale DN17 ....96 C1
Kingsgate
Bridlington YO15 ....122 D1
Carnaby YO15 ....10 F2
Cleethorpes DN32 ....153 A3
Kingsland Terr 11 YO26 ....129 F5
Kingsley Ave HU9 ....141 E2
Kingsley Cl 6 HU15 ....68 B5
Kingsley Dr HU10 ....138 D1
Kingsley Gr 4 DN33 ....102 E2
Kingsport Cl HU3 ....145 A7
Kingsthorpe YO24 ....129 D2
Kingston Ave
Grimsby DN34 ....152 A2
Kingston upon Hull HU13 ....143 F1
Kingston Cl
Hilderthorpe YO15 ....11 B4
8 Humberston DN35 ....103 D1
Kingston Cres YO15 ....11 B4
Kingston Rd
Bridlington YO15 ....11 B4
Kingston upon Hull HU10 ....138 D1
Scunthorpe DN16 ....151 A3
Kingston Ret Pk HU1 ....155 A1
Kingston Rise HU10 ....138 C1
Kingston Sq HU2 ....155 B3
Kingston St
Goole DN14 ....149 C2
Kingston upon Hull HU1 ....155 B1
Kingston View 27 DN18 ....84 F8
Kingston Way HU7 ....140 F5
Kingston Wharf HU1 ....155 A1
Kingsway 2 Brigg DN20 ....98 B2
Cleethorpes DN35 ....103 D3
Goole DN14 ....149 D4
Kingston upon Hull HU16 ....139 B5
Scunthorpe DN15 ....150 C7
14 Stainforth DN7 ....92 C6
6 Stamford Bridge YO41 ....15 D2
Kingsway N YO30 ....130 B7
Kingsway Prim Sch DN14 ....149 E5
Kingsway Sta DN35 ....103 D2
Kingsway W YO24 ....129 D1
Kingswood Gr YO24 ....129 D3
Kingswood High Sch HU7 ....57 A5
Kingswood Ret Pk HU7 ....56 E5
Kingtree Ave HU16 ....139 B6
Kinloch Way 28 DN40 ....87 B1
Kinloss Garth 2 HU7 ....57 B5
Kinloss Prim Sch HU7 ....57 B5
Kinsbourne Gn 37 DN7 ....92 D4
Kinsley Wlk 7 DN15 ....151 B7
Kinthorpe HU6 ....140 A8
Kiplin Dr 14 DN6 ....76 E2
Kipling Ave DN17 ....150 D3
Kipling Cl YO25 ....31 C4
Kipling Cotes Medieval Village* YO25 ....30 D2
Kipling Wlk 1 HU4 ....144 D2
Kiplingcotes La YO43 ....42 A5
Kiplingcotes Chalk Pit Nature Reserve* YO43 ....41 F6
Kiplingcotes Racecourse* YO25 ....30 E1
Kiplington Cl HU3 ....145 A7
Kir Cres YO24 ....129 C3
Kirby Cl YO43 ....135 E2
Kirby Dr HU16 ....139 B6
Kirby La YO25 ....7 A4
Kirk Balk YO17 ....16 E8
Kirk Balk La YO60 ....15 B7
Kirk Cl HU7 ....141 D6
Kirk Croft HU16 ....139 A6
Kirk Gate DN37 ....113 E6
Kirk La Sykehouse DN14 ....78 B4
Walkington HU17 ....55 B7
Kirk Rd 2 HU12 ....58 C1
Kirk Rise HU10 ....143 C7
Kirk Smeaton CE VC Prim Sch WF8 ....76 B3
Kirk View 1 YO26 ....129 C3
Kirkby Ave YO8 ....148 B7
Kirkby Cl DN14 ....149 C5
Kirkby Rd
Scunthorpe DN17 ....96 C2
Selby YO8 ....148 B7
Kirkby St HU2 ....155 B4
Kirkcroft YO32 ....127 C8
Kirkdale Rd YO10 ....131 D4
Kirkden Paddocks DN9 ....94 C2
Kirkfield Rd HU19 ....75 A6
Kirkgate
Bridlington YO16 ....122 D4
8 Pocklington YO42 ....29 A4
Kirkgate Mews YO16 ....122 D5
Kirkham Ave 1 YO31 ....130 E8
Kirkham Cl HU13 ....143 F2
Kirkham Ct DN14 ....149 E6
Kirkham Dr HU5 ....140 B2
Kirkham Rd YO16 ....122 D7
Kirkholme Way HU17 ....137 B4
Kirkhouse Gn Rd DN7 ....92 A8
Kirkland Cl YO8 ....148 D4
Kirkland St YO42 ....29 A4
Kirklands YO32 ....14 B6
Kirklands La YO41 ....16 C2
Kirklands Rd HU5 ....144 E8
Kirkside 2 DN37 ....113 E6
Kirkstead Cres DN33 ....102 D2
Kirkstead St HU8 ....141 A2
Kirkstone Dr YO31 ....131 A6
Kirkstone Rd HU5 ....139 D2
Kirkway HU10 ....143 B7
Kirkwell YO23 ....133 A4
Kirman Cres 18 DN17 ....96 C2
Kirmington CE Prim Sch DN39 ....100 A6
Kirmington Gdns DN34 ....152 A2
Kirncroft Cl 16 HU12 ....73 C4
Kirton La DN7 ....92 E6
Kirton La Prim Sch DN7 ....92 D7
Kirton Lindsey Prim Sch DN21 ....108 A1
Kirton Lindsey Sta DN21 ....108 B2
Kirton Rd Blyton DN21 ....117 F6
Holme DN16 ....97 B2
Kirton in Lindsey DN21 ....108 A3
Messingham DN17 ....107 E6
Scawby DN20 ....108 C8
Scotton DN21 ....107 D2
Kishorn Ct 30 DN40 ....87 B1
Kissing Gate HU12 ....59 D2
Kitchen Dr YO8 ....148 D4
Kitchen La HU17 ....154 A1
Kitchener Cl YO8 ....148 B5
Kitchener St Selby YO8 ....148 B6
York YO31 ....130 D7
Kitemere Pl 2 YO24 ....132 B8
Kitty Garth YO19 ....38 A7
Kitty Hill (Tumulus)* YO41 ....16 E3
Knapton Ave 7 HU5 ....139 E3
Knapton Cl 1 YO32 ....14 B6
Knapton Ct LN7 ....111 C4
Knapton La YO26 ....129 B4
Knavesmire Cres YO23 ....130 B1
Knavesmire Prim Sch YO23 ....130 B1
Knavesmire Rd YO23 ....130 A1
Knedlington Rd DN14 ....65 A6
Knight St DN32 ....153 B2
Knight's Ct 16 DN16 ....96 D2
Knightly Way HU7 ....56 E5
Knights Cl Belton DN9 ....94 E2
8 Laceby DN37 ....101 F1
Knights Ct HU17 ....154 B2
Knights Way HU17 ....154 B3
Knightsbridge 7 DN36 ....114 A8
Knightsbridge Ct 7 HU3 ....140 D1
Knightsbridge Rd DN17 ....107 D7
Knightscourt HU6 ....139 E7
Knole Pk HU7 ....56 F5
Knoll St DN35 ....153 F2
Knoll The YO24 ....129 B2
Knottingley High Sch WF11 ....61 A2
Knowle Rd 25 HU7 ....56 F5
Knowles Ave HU6 ....140 C8
Knowsley Ave HU16 ....139 A7
Kyffin Ave HU9 ....142 D2
Kyle Cl HU8 ....142 C6
Kyle Way YO26 ....129 B8
Kyme St YO1 ....156 B1

L

Labrador Dr 11 DN20 ....97 E4
Laburnham Ave 21 DN37 ....113 D6
Laburnham Cl 22 DN37 ....113 D6
Laburnum Ave
18 Gainsborough DN21 ....117 B1
Gunness DN15 ....95 E6
Hutton Cranswick YO25 ....32 E7
Kingston upon Hull HU8 ....141 C2
11 Thorne/Moorends DN8 ....79 B2
Laburnum Cl
Rufforth YO23 ....24 C6
7 Snaith DN14 ....63 C1
3 Thorpe Willoughby YO8 ....48 B1
Laburnum Ct
4 Bridlington YO16 ....123 A6
Kingston upon Hull HU13 ....143 D1
Laburnum Dr
Beverley HU17 ....137 A7
Grimsby DN34 ....102 C4
3 Kingston upon Hull HU4 ....144 B7
Laburnum Garth 6 YO31 ....130 F8
Laburnum Gr
Burton upon Stather DN15 ....82 B5
10 Crowle DN17 ....94 D7
Scunthorpe DN16 ....151 B3
Stillingfleet YO19 ....36 D4
Laburnum Wlk 17 HU15 ....66 D8
Laceby Acres Prim Sch DN34 ....102 B3
Laceby Rd
Grimsby DN34 ....102 C2
Scunthorpe DN17 ....150 E1
Lady Anne Ct YO1 ....156 B1
Lady Frances Cres DN35 ....153 C1
Lady Hamilton Gdns YO24 ....129 E2
Lady Mill Garth YO30 ....130 B8
Lady Peckitts Yd YO1 ....156 B2
Lady Rd YO30 ....130 B7
Lady Wortley Pl YO23 ....133 B6
Lady's Well* YO43 ....135 F7
Ladybower Cl 4 HU7 ....141 E7
Ladygate HU17 ....154 A3
Ladyside Cl 17 HU7 ....57 A6
Ladysmith Ind Est DN32 ....153 A2
Ladysmith Mews 13 YO32 ....14 A7
Ladysmith Rd
Grimsby DN32 ....152 F3
Kingston upon Hull HU10 ....138 E1
Ladywell Gate 3 HU15 ....68 E6
Laforey Rd DN37 ....102 C6
Lagoon Dr HU7 ....141 D8
Lagoon Rd DN17 ....150 B2
Lairgate HU17 ....154 A2
Lairs La YO42 ....30 A5
Lake Dr HU8 ....141 E3
Lake View HU8 ....141 E3
Lakeside
Acaster Malbis YO23 ....36 C7
Lakeside *continued*
Great Coates DN31 ....102 B6
Lakeside Dr DN17 ....150 C1
Lakeside Gr
Kingston upon Hull HU4 ....144 D4
1 Strensall YO32 ....14 B8
Lakeside Parkway DN16 ....151 F1
Lakeside Prim Sch YO30 ....126 F2
Lakeside Ret Pk DN16 ....151 F1
Lakeside Sta DN35 ....103 E2
Laking La YO25 ....2 A3
Lalrgate Pl 20 DN36 ....103 C1
Lamb Inn Rd 9 WF11 ....61 A2
Lamb La Newport HU15 ....67 B8
Roos HU12 ....60 A1
Lambert Ave 16 HU15 ....68 C6
Lambert Cl YO43 ....135 E3
Lambert Ct YO1 ....156 B1
Lambert Pk Rd 23 HU12 ....72 C7
Lambert Rd
Bridlington YO16 ....122 F5
Grimsby DN32 ....152 E2
Lambert St HU5 ....140 D2
Lambourn Ct 25 DN35 ....103 C1
Lambourne Rise 7 DN16 ....96 D1
Lambton St HU5 ....140 C3
Lambwath La HU11 ....46 A3
Lambwath Prim Sch HU8 ....141 F5
Lambwath Rd HU8 ....141 C4
Lambwell Hill HU15 ....54 E2
Lamel St YO10 ....131 A3
Lamorna Ave HU8 ....141 B3
Lamplugh Cres YO23 ....133 B3
Lamplugh La 7 YO15 ....122 F4
Lamplugh Rd YO15 ....122 F4
Lamplugh Sq 6 YO15 ....122 F4
Lampton Gr DN32 ....152 D2
Lanark St 3 HU5 ....145 B8
Lancar Cl 18 YO32 ....13 D5
Lancaster App DN40 ....86 D4
Lancaster Ave DN31 ....152 B3
Lancaster Ct 13 DN33 ....102 D1
Lancaster Dr
Kingston upon Hull HU8 ....141 D4
2 Moorland Prison DN7 ....104 A8
Lancaster Gate DN36 ....114 A4
Lancaster Rd
Carnaby YO25 ....10 D2
Gringley on the Hill DN10 ....116 A1
Pocklington YO42 ....28 E3
Scunthorpe DN16 ....151 A1
Lancaster Way YO30 ....127 A1
Lancelot Ct HU9 ....146 C6
Lancing Way 24 DN33 ....113 E8
Land Dike LN11 ....115 A1
Land Ends Rd DN8 ....78 F1
Land of Gn Ginger HU1 ....155 B2
Landalewood Rd YO30 ....126 F2
Landau Cl YO30 ....129 F8
Landeck Ave DN34 ....152 B2
Landing La
Asselby DN14 ....64 D6
Barlby with Osgodby YO8 ....148 F8
Broomfleet HU15 ....67 A7
Gilberdyke HU15 ....52 D1
Haxby YO32 ....127 E7
Hemingbrough YO8 ....63 F8
Newport HU15 ....52 E1
Riccall YO19 ....48 F8
York YO26 ....129 E6
Landing Rd YO8 ....62 A7
Landings The 21 YO32 ....13 F5
Landor Ave DN17 ....150 D3
Landress La HU17 ....154 A2
Lane The YO41 ....15 B2
Laneham St DN15 ....151 A7
Lanes The 7 DN36 ....114 D4
Lang Ave YO10 ....131 A4
Lang Rd
Bishopthorpe YO23 ....132 F4
York YO32 ....127 F6
Langdale Ave
Beverley HU17 ....154 B3
Grimsby DN33 ....113 D8
Kingston upon Hull HU5 ....139 E2
York YO31 ....131 B6
Langdale Cres HU16 ....139 A5
Langdale Dr 4 HU12 ....73 C4
Langdale Gr YO8 ....148 B3
Langdale Mews YO16 ....122 E7
Langdale Rd YO43 ....135 E4
Langford Wlk 1 HU4 ....144 B7
Langham Rd 13 HU12 ....72 E5
Langholm Cl HU17 ....136 D5
Langholme Dr YO26 ....129 C6
Langholme La DN9 ....116 B8
Langley Ct 1 YO32 ....127 F6
Langley Dr DN16 ....96 D1
Langley Garth
11 Driffield YO25 ....124 F4
Great Driffield YO25 ....124 F4
Langley Pk 25 HU7 ....56 F5
Langley Pl 5 DN35 ....103 D2
Langleys Rd 6 DN6 ....76 E1
Langrick Ave 9 DN14 ....65 B7
Langrickgate La YO42 ....38 C5
Langsett Gr YO30 ....126 F3
Langsett Rd HU7 ....141 D7
Langthorpe Rd HU11 ....45 F2
Langtoft Gr HU6 ....139 F5
Langtoft Prim Sch YO25 ....8 C5
Langton Cl 16 DN33 ....102 D2
Langton Ct 1 YO32 ....14 A6
Langton Dr DN33 ....102 D2
Langton Rd DN36 ....114 B5
Langtree Cl HU7 ....140 F8
Langwith Stray YO10 ....26 C2
Lansdown Link 17 DN35 ....103 C2
Lansdown Rd
Goole DN14 ....149 A5
13 Immingham DN40 ....87 B1
Lansdown Way 7 YO32 ....13 F5
Lansdowne Ave DN33 ....102 E2
Lansdowne Cres 9 YO15 ....122 F3
Lansdowne Rd YO15 ....122 F2
Lansdowne St HU3 ....145 C6
Lansdowne Terr 5 YO10 ....130 E3
Lanshaw Croft YO30 ....126 F1
Lanyon Cl HU7 ....141 C7
Laporte Rd DN40 ....87 E2
Lapwing Cl HU7 ....141 D8
Lapwing Rd YO25 ....125 B5
Larard Ave 2 HU6 ....140 C8
Larch Cl
2 Immingham DN40 ....87 D2
Kingston upon Hull HU5 ....140 D2
Larch Ct 11 DN21 ....117 C1
Larch Dr HU12 ....72 E5
Larch Gr Scawby DN20 ....108 F8
Scunthorpe DN16 ....151 B3
Larch Rd 6 DN35 ....103 B1
Larchfield YO31 ....131 C7
Larchmont Cl 7 HU15 ....68 C6
Larden Ave 1 DN33 ....113 E8
Lark Rise 2 DN21 ....107 B3
Larkfield Cl 1 YO23 ....132 A3
Larkfield Rd YO8 ....148 A4
Larkspur Ave DN41 ....101 F5
Larmour Rd DN37 ....102 B4
Larne Rd HU9 ....142 B4
Larsen Pk DN14 ....149 A3
Larsen Rd DN14 ....149 A3
Lascelles Ave HU19 ....74 F6
Lasenby Cl YO32 ....127 D5
Lashbrook Garth HU4 ....144 B4
Lastingham 12 HU15 ....68 C6
Lastingham Cl HU6 ....139 F6
Lastingham Terr YO10 ....130 D2
Laughton Endowed CE Prim Sch DN21 ....117 E8
Laughton Rd
Beverley HU17 ....154 B4
Blyton DN21 ....117 B4
Laundry La YO25 ....124 E5
Laura St DN14 ....149 C5
Laurel Ave DN8 ....79 B2
Laurel Cl
10 Gainsborough DN21 ....117 C1
Gateforth YO8 ....48 B1
3 Grimsby DN33 ....102 E1
Kingston upon Hull HU4 ....144 B7
Laurel Way 19 DN16 ....96 E2
Laurels Cl 1 DN40 ....100 E8
Laurels The YO42 ....28 D3
Laurence Gr YO8 ....148 D3
Laurier St DN35 ....153 D4
Laurold Ave DN7 ....93 A3
Lauty La HU11 ....45 C5
Lavender Cl 23 HU7 ....56 F5
Lavender Gr
10 New Waltham DN36 ....113 F8
York YO26 ....129 E5
Lavender Way DN15 ....151 B6
Lavender Wlk
Beverley HU17 ....154 A1
1 Kingston upon Hull HU4 ....144 C7
Lavenham Rd DN33 ....113 D8
Laveracks Ind Est YO41 ....27 B3
Lawn La DN6 ....77 E3
Lawns The
Beverley HU17 ....136 C6
Bridlington YO16 ....122 E7
Grimsby DN34 ....152 C2
Kirk Ella HU10 ....143 D7
Sutton-on-Hull HU7 ....141 D6
Lawnsgarth HU16 ....139 A7
Lawnswood HU13 ....143 D2
Lawnswood Cl HU7 ....141 D5
Lawnswood Dr YO30 ....129 F8
Lawnway YO31 ....131 A7
Lawrence Ave
Bewholme YO25 ....34 E3
Kingston upon Hull HU8 ....141 F3
Lawrence St
Grimsby DN31 ....152 C4
York YO10 ....130 E3
Lawson Ave
Grimsby DN31 ....152 B3
Kingston upon Hull HU16 ....139 B7
Lawson Cl
Kingston upon Hull HU6 ....140 B5
1 Walkington HU17 ....55 B7
Lawson Rd
Bridlington YO16 ....122 D4
York YO24 ....132 F7
Lawsons Cl YO14 ....2 F7
Laxthorpe HU6 ....140 A8
Laxton Garth HU10 ....138 B1
Laxton Gr 5 DN16 ....96 D1
Layerthorpe YO31 ....156 C3
Lea Cres HU16 ....139 A5
Lea Croft 2 YO43 ....135 E4

Lea Dr DN32 .... 102 F2
Lea Field Rd YO25 ...... 31 E6
Lea Garth DN17 .... 107 D7
Lea The HU15 .... 54 A2
Lea Way YO32 .... 128 A4
Leaburn Rd DN17 ...... 107 D7
Lead Mill La YO1 .... 156 C1
Leadhills Way 6 HU7 .... 57 B5
Leadley Croft YO23 ..... 132 A1
Leads Rd HU7 .... 141 C6
Leake St YO10 .... 130 E3
Lealholm Ct 11 HU8 ..... 141 D7
Leame Cl HU3 .... 145 A7
Leamington Cl DN16 ..... 151 C5
Leamington Ct DN16 ..... 151 C5
Leander Rd HU9 .... 142 B3
Learmans Way YO23 ..... 132 C3
Learning La DN14 .... 61 F1
Leas Cl DN37 .... 113 E7
Leas Jun & Inf Sch The
DN37 .... 113 E7
Leas La HU11 .... 34 F1
Lease La DN40 .... 86 D6
Leases The HU17 .... 154 A2
Leatherdog La HU15 ..... 52 E1
Leathley Cl 1 HU17 ..... 136 E1
Leavens La HU15 .... 52 D2
Leconfield Cl HU9 ...... 142 D1
Leconfield Prim Sch
HU17 .... 43 D6
Ledbury Dr 10 DN36 ..... 114 A8
Ledbury Rd HU5 .... 139 D2
Lee Ave HU19 .... 75 A6
Lee Ct DN14 .... 77 A7
Lee Fair Gdns DN17 ..... 96 C1
Lee Smith St HU9 ...... 146 E7
Lee St HU8 .... 141 D3
Lee View DN14 .... 77 A7
Leeds Rd YO8 .... 148 A4
Leek Hill 9 DN15 .... 83 A5
Leeman Rd YO26 .... 156 A2
Leeming Garth 3 HU7 .... 57 B5
Lees Rest Houses
HU4 .... 144 D6
Lees Wlk HU3 .... 145 A7
Leeside YO24 .... 132 E8
Legard Ave DN16 .... 151 B2
Legard Dr HU10 .... 143 F6
Legarde Ave HU4 .... 144 C6
Leggott Way 1 DN41 .... 101 E6
Legion Cl 11 HU15 .... 68 C5
Legsby Ave DN32 .... 152 E2
Legsby Pl DN32 .... 102 F2
Leicester St HU3 .... 145 D8
Leicester Way YO1 ..... 156 C1
Leighton Croft 3 YO30 .. 126 F1
Leighton Gr 2 DN33 .... 102 E2
Leisure Pk YO32 .... 128 A2
Leitholm Cl 2 HU7 ...... 57 A6
Lelley Rd
Humbleton HU11 .... 58 F5
Preston HU12 .... 58 D2
Lendal YO1 .... 156 B2
Lenham La HU1 .... 155 A2
Leningrad Rd HU7 ...... 140 F6
Lennox Cl 2 YO14 .... 3 A8
Leonard Cl HU12 .... 72 A5
Leonard Cres DN15 ..... 150 F7
Leonard St
4 Kingston upon Hull
HU3 .... 145 D8
Kingston upon Hull HU2 .. 155 A4
Leopold Cl DN16 .... 151 A2
Lerecroft Rd YO24 ..... 132 D8
Lesley Ave YO10 .... 133 E8
Leslie Ct 6 DN15 ...... 151 B7
Lestrange St DN35 ..... 153 C3
Levels La DN9 .... 104 A4
Levels The HU18 .... 134 C4
Leven CE VC Prim Sch
HU17 .... 45 B7
Leven Gr HU9 .... 142 A2
Leven Rd
Scunthorpe DN16 .... 151 D2
York YO24 .... 132 D7
Leverstock Gn 36 DN7 ... 92 D4
Levington St DN32 ..... 153 A5
Levisham Cl HU6 ...... 139 F6
Levisham St YO10 ...... 130 D2
Levita Ave HU9 .... 142 C2
Levitt Lanes YO25 ...... 31 F2
Lewis Rd DN35 .... 153 D4
Lexington Dr HU4 ...... 144 C5
Leyburn Ave
Hornsea HU18 .... 134 C2
Kingston upon Hull HU6 .. 139 E4
Leyden Cl 18 DN40 ...... 87 B1
Leyes The YO10 .... 131 C4
Leyfield Cl 1 YO32 ...... 14 A7
Leyland Ave 6 DN7 ...... 92 E4
Leyland Rd YO31 .... 131 A5
Leys Ct YO16 .... 122 B4
Leys Farm Jun Sch
DN17 .... 96 C2
Leys La Darrington WF11 .. 76 A8
Little Smeaton WF8 ...... 76 B4
Skipsea YO25 .... 23 A1
Winterton DN15 .... 83 B6
Leys Rd
Bridlington YO16 .... 122 B4
Darrington WF11 .... 76 A7
Leys The HU18 .... 134 B4
Liberty La HU1 .... 155 C2
Library Sq YO1 .... 156 B3
Lichfield Ave DN17 ..... 150 C3
Lichfield Cl
Beverley HU17 .... 136 E1
Kingston upon Hull HU2 .. 155 A4
Lichfield Ct
Cleethorpes DN32 ...... 153 B2
6 York YO23 .... 130 B1
Lichfield Rd
Grimsby DN32 .... 153 B2
40 Hatfield DN7 .... 92 D4
Liddell St HU2 .... 155 A3
Lidgard Rd DN36 ...... 103 D1
Lidgett Cl DN20 .... 108 E8
Lidgett Gr YO26 .... 129 B6
Lidgett Gr Sch YO26 ... 129 B6
Lidgett The 7 DN9 ..... 105 D6
Lidice Rd DN14 .... 64 E2
Lighthouse Rd YO15 ...... 5 B2
Lilac Ave
Beverley HU17 .... 136 F7
Scunthorpe DN16 ...... 151 C5
Summergangs HU8 ...... 141 B2
Willerby HU10 .... 138 D1
York YO10 .... 131 B3
Lilac Cl YO25 .... 124 D3
Lilac Gr YO32 .... 127 D4
Lilac Rd 20 HU15 .... 68 C5
Lilacs The 10 YO42 ...... 29 A3
Lilbourne Dr YO30 ..... 130 A8
Lilling Ave 3 YO31 ..... 130 E8
Lily La YO15 .... 5 A2
Lilywood Rd DN20 .... 97 D3
Limber Ct DN34 .... 152 A2
Limber Hill LN8 .... 120 A4
Limber Rd
Humberside Airport
DN39 .... 100 A6
Swallow LN7 .... 112 A7
Limber Vale DN34 ...... 152 A2
Lime Ave Brough HU15 .... 68 C5
Kingston upon Hull
HU10 .... 138 E1
Scunthorpe DN16 .... 97 A3
York YO31 .... 130 F7
Lime Cl YO25 .... 124 F2
Lime Gr Goxhill DN19 .... 86 A8
Holton le Clay DN36 .... 114 A5
Humberston DN36 ...... 114 C7
Scunthorpe DN16 ...... 151 B3
Lime St Grimsby DN31 .. 152 C4
Kingston upon Hull HU8 .. 155 C4
Lime Tree 6 HU15 .... 66 D7
Lime Tree Ave
Beverley HU17 .... 137 A6
20 Gainsborough DN21 .. 117 B1
Goole DN14 .... 149 D5
Northfield HU13 .... 143 F2
Summergangs HU8 ...... 141 C2
York YO32 .... 127 D3
Lime Tree Gdns DN14 ... 149 D5
Lime Tree Gr
Selby YO8 .... 148 A6
4 Thorne/Moorends DN8 .. 93 A8
Lime Tree La HU11 .... 142 F6
Lime Tree Mews 15 YO19 .. 26 F7
Lime Tree Villas HU7 ... 141 D6
Limedale View 3 DN3 .... 92 A3
Limedane HU6 .... 139 F8
Limegarth 10 YO26 ...... 12 F1
Limekiln Hill YO25 .... 7 B3
Limekiln La YO16 ...... 123 A5
Limerick Cl HU8 .... 142 B6
Limes Ct YO31 .... 130 F6
Limes The
2 Beckingham DN10 .... 116 D1
3 South Cave HU15 ...... 53 F1
3 Stallingborough DN41 .. 101 D6
Stockton-on-the-Forest
YO32 .... 14 D2
Limes Wlk YO25 .... 124 F5
Limetree Ave
12 Grimsby DN33 .... 102 E2
Kingston upon Hull HU7 .. 141 D6
Limetree Cl 2 YO8 .... 48 B1
Lincoln Bvd DN31 ...... 152 B3
Lincoln Castle Way
DN19 .... 70 D2
Lincoln Cl 13 DN17 ...... 94 D7
Lincoln Cres 2 DN21 .... 119 C8
Lincoln Ct DN16 .... 151 B3
Lincoln Dr
24 Barton-upon-Humber
DN18 .... 84 F8
Caistor LN7 .... 111 B4
Winterton DN15 .... 83 A5
Lincoln Gate DN36 ..... 121 A5
Lincoln Gdns DN16 .... 151 A2
Lincoln Gdns Jun Sch
DN16 .... 151 A2
Lincoln Gdns Prim Sch
DN16 .... 151 B3
Lincoln Gn HU4 .... 144 C7
Lincoln Rd
Cleethorpes DN35 ..... 153 C1
Moorland Prison DN7 ... 104 A8
Lincoln St
22 Gainsborough DN21 .. 117 B1
Kingston upon Hull HU2 .. 155 B4
York YO26 .... 129 F5
Lincoln Way 9 HU17 ..... 55 E8
Lincolnshire Wolds Rly*
LN11 .... 121 C7
Lindale 2 YO24 .... 132 C7
Lindale Ave HU18 ...... 134 B2
Lindale Gdns DN16 .... 151 C3
Linden Ave HU16 ...... 139 C7
Linden Cl 6 Hatfield DN7 .. 92 D4
York YO32 .... 127 F5
Linden Gr 1 YO30 ..... 130 A8
Linden Way 9 YO8 .... 48 B2
Lindengate Ave HU7 ... 141 B4
Lindengate Way HU7 ... 141 B5
Lindholme DN21 .... 107 C3
Lindholme Bank Rd
DN7 .... 93 B1
Lindisfarne Ave 4
DN36 .... 113 F7
Lindley Rd YO30 ...... 126 F1
Lindley St
Scunthorpe DN16 ...... 151 A2
York YO24 .... 129 F3
Lindley Wood Gr
YO30 .... 126 E3
Lindrick Wlk 8 DN37 ... 113 D6
Lindsey DN36 .... 114 A6
Lindsey Ave YO26 ..... 129 D4
Lindsey Ct 21 DN9 ..... 105 E6
Lindsey Dr Crowle DN17 .. 94 D8
Healing DN41 .... 102 A5
Holton le Clay DN36 ... 114 A6
Lindsey Lower Sch The
DN35 .... 153 D2
Lindsey Pl HU4 .... 144 D6
Lindsey Rd DN35 ...... 153 F1
Lindsey Rise 30 DN33 .. 113 E8
Lindsey Sch & Com Arts Coll
The DN35 .... 103 C2
Lindsey St 2 DN16 ..... 151 C6
Lindum Ave 23 DN40 ..... 87 B1
Lindum Gr DN17 .... 94 C7
Lindum Rd DN35 .... 103 C2
Lindum St DN15 .... 151 B7
Lindum Wlk LN7 ...... 110 A4
Linecroft La DN10 .... 116 E4
Linegate 4 YO43 ...... 135 D4
Ling House La DN7 ..... 92 A5
Ling La YO41 .... 27 F6
Lingcourt HU6 .... 139 F7
Lingcroft Cl YO8 .... 63 D4
Lingcroft La YO19 ..... 133 E3
Lingdale Rd HU9 ...... 142 E3
Lingfield Cres YO24 ... 129 F1
Lings La DN7 .... 92 D3
Lings Rd HU17 .... 42 E3
Link Ave YO30 .... 130 C8
Link Rd
Huntington YO31 ...... 127 E2
Kingston upon Hull
HU16 .... 139 B5
Link Rd Ct YO19 ...... 131 D4
Link The
Copmanthorpe YO23 ... 132 A3
Kingston upon Hull HU4 .. 144 C5
Selby YO8 .... 148 A4
York YO10 .... 133 E8
Linkfield Rd HU5 ..... 139 E4
Links Rd DN35 .... 103 D2
Linkway Hatfield DN7 .... 92 F3
Norton DN6 .... 76 E2
Linley Cl HU17 .... 45 A8
Linleyhill Rd HU17 ..... 33 C1
Linnaeus St HU3 ...... 145 C6
Linnet Cl DN15 .... 96 B7
Linnet Dr HU7 .... 141 D7
Linnet Way YO24 ...... 132 C8
Linthorpe Gr HU10 .... 143 E8
Linton 23 HU15 .... 68 C6
Linton Cl HU17 .... 154 A1
Linton Garth HU17 ..... 43 A5
Linton on Ouse Prim Sch
YO30 .... 12 A7
Linton Rd YO26 .... 126 A1
Linton Rise DN15 .... 82 A4
Linton St 5 YO26 ...... 129 E5
Linton Woods YO30 ..... 12 A7
Linton Woods La YO30 ... 12 A8
Linwith La DN14 .... 63 C3
Linwood Ave 17 DN33 ... 113 E8
Lisburn Gr DN33 ...... 102 E1
Lisle Ct HU2 .... 155 B1
Lisle Marsden CE Aided Prim
Sch DN32 .... 102 F2
Lismore Ave HU9 ..... 142 A3
Lissett Cl HU17 .... 43 D6
Lissett Gr HU6 .... 140 C7
Lissett La YO25 .... 22 D4
Lister Rd DN15 .... 150 C7
Lister St Grimsby DN31 .. 152 B4
Kingston upon Hull HU1 .. 155 A1
Lister Way YO30 ...... 130 A7
Little Ave YO30 ...... 130 B8
Little Beck Rd YO16 ... 122 B4
Little Belt The DN21 ... 117 B2
Little Burton 3 YO25 ... 34 B2
Little Clover HU17 .... 136 F6
Little Coates Rd DN34 .. 102 C2
Little Comm La DN14 .... 77 C5
Little Dam La HU12 ..... 88 B8
Little Garth YO26 ..... 126 A2
Little George St HU8 .. 155 C4
Little Grimsby La
LN11 .... 121 D1
Little Hallfield Rd
YO31 .... 130 E5
Little Heck Comm La
DN14 .... 62 D1
Little John St DN34 ... 152 B3
Little La
Broomfleet HU15 .... 67 C6
Ellerton YO42 .... 38 C1
11 Haxby YO32 .... 13 E5
Little Smeaton DN6 ...... 76 D4
Mappleton HU11 .... 47 A5
Shipton Thorpe YO43 .... 40 E5
Watton YO25 .... 32 E5
Wrawby DN20 .... 98 D3
Little London La DN14 ... 78 D8
Little Mason St HU2 ... 155 C3
Little Mdws YO32 ..... 127 D8
Little Michael St
DN34 .... 152 B3
Little Moor La YO8 .... 148 A8
Little Queen St HU1 ... 155 A2
Little Reed St HU2 .... 155 A3
Little Shore HU11 ...... 45 E2
Little Stonegate YO1 .. 156 B3
Little Weighton Rd
Skidby HU16 .... 138 A8
Walkington HU17 .... 55 B7
Little Weighton Rowley CE
VC Prim Sch HU20 ...... 55 A4
Little Westfield YO25 .... 8 C3
Little Wlk DN21 .... 116 E5
Little Wold La HU15 ..... 54 A2
Littlebeck Cl HU3 ..... 145 A7
Littlebeck Rd 4 DN36 .. 114 C8
Littlecoates Prim Sch
DN31 .... 152 B5
Littlefair Rd HU9 ..... 147 A7
Littlefield Cl 5 YO26 .... 12 F1
Littlefield La
Grimsby DN34 .... 152 B2
Marsh Chapel DN36 .... 115 B1
Littleham Cl HU7 ..... 141 B8
Littlemoor Cl HU15 ..... 53 D3
Littlethorpe Cl 7 YO32 ... 14 B8
Littlewood Rd
Rowley HU17 .... 54 D7
11 Thorne/Moorends DN8 .. 93 B8
Littondale
Kingston upon Hull HU7 .. 140 F7
15 Welton HU15 .... 68 D6
Liverpool St HU3 ..... 145 A3
Livesey Rd DN36 ...... 121 B6
Livingstone Rd HU13 ... 69 F4
Livingstone St YO26 ... 129 F5
Lloyd Cl YO10 .... 131 B1
Lloyds Ave DN17 ...... 150 F4
Loatley Gn HU16 ...... 139 C5
Lob La YO41 .... 15 D2
Lobelia Dr DN16 .... 96 C1
Lochrin Pl 2 YO26 .... 129 B4
Lock Cl DN14 .... 77 F6
Lock Hill DN8 .... 93 A8
Lock Keepers Ct HU9 .. 146 B6
Lock La
Holme-on-Spalding-Moor
YO43 .... 52 B8
Thorne/Moorends DN8 .... 93 A8
Lock Rd DN36 .... 115 A4
Lockey Croft YO32 .... 127 C8
Lockgate Rd DN14 .... 77 C4
Lockham Rd HU12 .... 90 F4
Lockhill DN31 .... 152 E6
Locking Garth LN11 ... 121 F5
Lockington CE VC Sch
YO25 .... 32 B2
Lockington Rd YO25 ..... 31 F3
Lockside Rd DN40 .... 87 D3
Lockton Gr 1 HU5 ..... 144 D8
Lockwood Bank DN9 ... 105 E6
Lockwood Cl 6 DN8 ..... 93 B8
Lockwood Ct DN15 .... 150 E8
Lockwood Dr HU17 .... 136 E7
Lockwood Rd HU17 .... 136 D7
Lockwood St
Great Driffield YO25 .. 124 E3
Kingston upon Hull HU2 .. 155 B4
York YO31 .... 156 C3
Lockyer Cl 4 YO30 .... 130 A8
Lodge Ave DN18 .... 84 F8
Lodge Cl
Elloughton HU15 .... 68 C7
Kingston upon Hull
HU13 .... 143 F1
Lodge Ct 35 DN7 .... 92 D4
Lodge Farm Ct YO42 .... 39 B6
Lodge Gdns 5 DN14 ..... 63 C1
Lodge La
Flixborough DN15 .... 82 B2
Gowdall DN14 .... 62 F1
Kirk Bramwith DN7 ...... 92 A8
Snaith DN14 .... 78 D8
Lodge Rd DN15 .... 150 C6
Lodge St HU9 .... 141 E2
Lofthouse La YO41 ..... 27 D7
Loftsome Way 11 DN14 .. 65 B7
Loftus Gr HU9 .... 142 E3
Logan Cl HU7 .... 141 C7
Loganberry Dr HU4 ... 144 C4
Lombard St
Grimsby DN34 .... 152 A3
Kingston upon Hull HU2 .. 155 A3
Lombardy Cl 8 HU4 .... 144 C7
Lomond Gr 1 DN36 .... 114 C8
Lomond Rd HU5 .... 144 E8
Londesborough Ct
YO25 .... 124 C4
Londesborough Gr 5
YO8 .... 48 B2
Londesborough Hill
YO43 .... 41 A8
Londesborough Rd
Hutton Cranswick YO25 .. 32 E7
Market Weighton YO43 .. 135 D6
Londesborough St
Kingston upon Hull HU3 .. 145 C7
5 Selby YO8 .... 148 C5
London La DN6 .... 77 D1
London St 15 YO42 ...... 29 A4
Long Barrow*
Beelsby DN37 .... 112 D4
Thixendale YO17 .... 17 A7
Willerby YO12 .... 1 E7
Long Cl La YO10 ...... 156 C1
Long Field Dr DN3 ...... 92 A1
Long Field Rd DN3 ...... 92 A2
Long Furrow YO32 ..... 127 C8
Long Hill YO42 .... 29 D1
Long La Atwick YO25 ..... 35 D6
Beverley HU17 .... 154 B2
Bridlington YO16 ..... 122 C5
Catton YO41 .... 27 D6
Cawood YO8 .... 48 A6
Driffield YO25 .... 124 F7
Eastrington DN14 .... 65 D8
Ellerby HU11 .... 58 B8
Ellerton YO42 .... 38 F1
Foston YO25 .... 22 A3
Goole DN14 .... 149 E7
Great Driffield YO25 .. 124 F6
Heck DN14 .... 77 D8
Heslington YO10 .... 26 C3
Humbleton HU11 .... 58 F5
Kirk Smeaton WF8 .... 76 B1
Market Weighton YO43 ... 41 B2
Nafferton YO25 .... 20 E8
Pollington DN14 .... 78 A7
Skeffling HU12 .... 90 C5
Willoughton DN21 ..... 119 B3
Woodmansey HU17 ..... 154 B1
Long Mann Hills Rd
YO8 .... 148 B4
Long Marston CE VC Prim
Sch YO26 .... 24 A6
Long Rampart YO42 ..... 38 D3
Long Rd DN15 .... 150 E8
Long Ridge Dr YO26 ... 126 A1
Long Ridge La YO26 ... 126 A1
Long St YO25 .... 9 F6
Long Toft Prim Sch
DN7 .... 92 C6
Long Trods 5 YO8 ..... 148 C6
Long Wood Rd DN21 ... 117 D1
Longbrough La HU12 .... 59 E4
Longcroft 2 YO32 .... 13 E5
Longcroft Lower Sch
HU17 .... 136 B5
Longcroft Pk HU17 .... 136 C5
Longcroft Sch & Performing
Arts Coll HU17 .... 136 C5
Longdales La HU11 .... 142 F8
Longden St HU3 .... 145 A7
Longfield Rd 4 DN34 .. 102 C2
Longfield Terr YO30 .. 156 A3
Longford Gr HU9 ..... 142 E2
Longhill Prim Sch
HU8 .... 142 C6
Longhorn Cl 1 DN37 .. 113 C6
Longleat Ave YO16 ... 122 F7
Longmans Hill CP Sch
YO8 .... 148 C3
Longmans La HU16 .... 139 B6
Longmeadow Rise 7
DN41 .... 101 A4
Longmeadows Dr
DN37 .... 101 F1
Longton Rd 13 DN3 ..... 92 A3
Longwood Link 8 YO30 .. 126 E3
Longwood Rd YO30 ... 126 F3
Lonsdale Cl DN36 .... 114 D7
Lonsdale St 5 HU3 ... 145 A6
Lopham La DN37 ..... 112 F8
Lord Deramore's Prim Sch
YO10 .... 131 C1
Lord Dr 27 YO42 .... 29 A3
Lord Mayor's Wlk
YO31 .... 156 B3
Lord Roberts Rd HU17 .. 154 B2
Lord St Grimsby DN31 .. 152 B4
Stainforth DN7 .... 92 C6
Lords La
Barrow upon Humber
DN19 .... 85 D8
Upper Poppleton YO26 ... 12 E2
Lords Moor La YO32 ..... 14 C7
Lordship La 16 Barlby YO8 .. 49 A4
Wistow YO8 .... 148 D8
Lorenzo Way HU9 .... 141 F2
Loriners Dr 7 YO23 .. 132 B3
Lorne Cl HU2 .... 155 B4
Lorne St YO23 .... 130 B1
Lorraine Ave 3 YO41 ... 27 B2
Lorraine St HU8 ..... 141 A3
Loten Dr HU18 ...... 134 D6
Lothian Way HU7 ...... 57 A6
Lotting's La YO42 ..... 28 C4
Louis Dr HU5 .... 144 B8
Louis St HU3 .... 145 C8
Louth Rd
Fotherby LN11 .... 121 D3
Grimsby DN33 .... 102 E1
5 New Waltham DN36 .. 113 F7
Louville Ave HU19 ..... 75 A6
Lovat Cl HU3 .... 145 D5
Love La
Gainsborough DN21 .. 117 B1
Hedon HU12 .... 72 C7
Londesborough YO43 ... 41 A8
Nunthorpe YO10 ..... 133 C8
York YO24 .... 130 A2
Loveden Ct 7 DN35 .. 103 D2
Lovell Rd 8 DN17 ...... 96 C2
Loveridge Ave HU5 .. 140 A2
Lovett St DN35 ..... 153 B4
Low Balk Rd HU17 ..... 42 F2
Low Burgage DN15 ..... 68 B1
Low Catton Rd YO41 ... 27 C8
Low Comm La HU15 .... 68 D4
Low Croft 6 YO32 ..... 14 A7
Low Cross St 7 DN17 .. 94 D8
Low Deeps La DN10 .. 104 C1
Low Farm Rd HU11 .... 57 E5

Low Field La
Carnaby YO25 ....10 C3
Welton HU14 ....68 E5
Low Fields Dr YO24 ....129 C3
Low Garth DN17 ....96 C1
Low Gate DN36 ....115 C1
Low Gn
Copmanthorpe YO23 ....132 B2
13 Knottingley WF11 ....61 A2
Low La
Heslington YO10 ....131 D1
Kirk Bramwith DN7 ....92 A6
Low Levels Bank DN8 ....93 E3
Low Leys Rd DN17 ....96 C1
Low Mdw YO8 ....148 C6
Low Mill Cl YO10 ....131 D3
Low Mill La HU15 ....53 C2
Low Moor Ave 3 YO10 ....133 F8
Low Moor La
Askham Richard YO23 ....24 D3
Hessay YO26 ....24 C8
Low Ousegate YO1 ....156 B2
Low Peter La YO25 ....124 C8
Low Petergate YO1 ....156 B3
Low Poppleton La
YO26 ....129 B7
Low Rd
Blyborough DN21 ....119 B6
Gowdall DN14 ....63 A1
Healing DN41 ....101 F5
Kellington DN14 ....61 F4
Kirby Grindalythe YO17 ....6 F7
Marsh Chapel DN36 ....115 A1
North Cave HU15 ....53 E2
Worlaby DN20 ....98 C8
Low St
Beckingham DN10 ....116 E1
Carlton DN14 ....63 C2
Haxey DN9 ....105 D2
North Ferriby HU14 ....69 A5
Sancton YO43 ....41 D2
South Ferriby DN18 ....84 A7
Winterton DN15 ....83 A5
Low Well Pk YO19 ....37 F7
Low Westfield Rd
YO23 ....132 A1
Lowcroft Ave 3 DN9 ....105 D2
Lowcroft Cl 4 DN9 ....105 D2
Lowcroft Mdw 10 DN9 ....105 D2
Lowdale Cl HU5 ....139 E1
Lower Bridge St DN14 ....149 C3
Lower Darnborough St
YO23 ....156 B1
Lower Derwent Valley Nat
Nature Reserve*
YO42 ....50 C8
Lower Friargate YO1 ....156 B2
Lower Kenyon St 6 DN8 ....93 A8
Lower Mdws DN18 ....69 F1
Lower Priory St YO1 ....156 A1
Lower Spring St DN31 ....152 E5
Lowerdale 13 HU15 ....68 D6
Loweswater Rd 5 YO30 ....126 E1
Lowfield YO43 ....40 B1
Lowfield Cl
10 Barnby Dun DN3 ....92 A3
18 Kirton in Lindsey DN21 ....108 B1
Lowfield Dr YO32 ....13 E5
Lowfield House HU10 ....143 E6
Lowfield La
East Garton HU12 ....59 C5
Nunburnholme YO42 ....29 D3
Rufforth YO26 ....129 A4
Scrayingham YO41 ....16 A7
Lowfield Rd
Barlby with Osgodby YO8 ....49 B5
Beverley HU17 ....137 A7
Hillam LS25 ....61 C8
Kingston upon Hull
HU10 ....143 E5
Lowfield Sec Sch
YO24 ....129 D3
Lowgate Balne DN14 ....77 D5
Kingston upon Hull HU1 ....155 C2
Lowhill DN8 ....78 F1
Lowick YO24 ....132 C7
Lowland Cl 3 HU7 ....141 D8
Lowmoor Rd YO8 ....49 E6
Lown Hill YO24 ....129 C2
Lowndes Pk YO25 ....124 D5
Lowood Dr YO16 ....122 B4
Lowther Ct YO31 ....156 C4
Lowther Dr YO8 ....148 E3
Lowther St
Kingston upon Hull HU3 ....145 A7
York YO31 ....156 C4
Lowther Terr YO24 ....130 A3
Lowthorpe La YO25 ....125 F7
Loxley Cl YO30 ....126 F2
Loxley Gn HU4 ....144 B7
Loxley Way 7 HU15 ....68 D5
Loyd St HU10 ....143 F6
Loyds Cl 12 HU15 ....53 F1
Lucas Ave YO30 ....130 C8
Lucas Ct DN41 ....101 F5
Lucian Wlk HU4 ....144 A2
Luck La HU12 ....58 C1
Lucombe Way YO32 ....127 D4
Ludborough Pk DN36 ....121 B6
Ludborough Rd DN36 ....121 B8
Ludborough Way 21
DN35 ....103 C2
Luddington & Garthorpe
Prim Sch DN17 ....81 C4
Luddington Rd DN17 ....81 E5
Ludford St DN32 ....152 E2
Ludgate Cl 4 DN37 ....113 D6
Ludlow Ave DN34 ....152 A3
Ludlow Pl DN35 ....153 E1
Lulworth Ave HU4 ....144 A3
Lulworth Ct DN17 ....150 D4
Lumby Hill LS25 ....61 A8
Lumby La LS25 ....61 A8
Lumley Rd YO30 ....130 B7
Lumsden Cl YO25 ....124 B2
Lund Ave HU16 ....138 E6
Lund Cl YO32 ....127 C8
Lund La Bubwith YO8 ....50 C4
Cliffe YO8 ....49 D4
Lund Rd YO25 ....32 A2
Lunds The HU10 ....143 C6
Lundy Cl 10 YO30 ....127 A1
Lundy Ct DN40 ....101 C8
Luneburg Pl 14 DN15 ....96 B7
Luneburg Way DN15 ....96 B7
Lunedale Cl HU8 ....141 E7
Lunedale Rd DN16 ....151 D1
Lunn La DN14 ....61 D3
Lunn's Cres DN18 ....84 E8
Luton Rd HU5 ....144 F8
Luttons CP Sch YO17 ....7 B8
Lycett Rd YO24 ....132 F6
Lych Gate DN20 ....97 D3
Lydbrook Rd DN16 ....151 A5
Lydford Rd DN40 ....87 C1
Lydham Ct 2 YO24 ....132 C8
Lydia Ct 6 DN40 ....87 B1
Lygon St DN16 ....151 B5
Lymington Garth HU4 ....144 A3
Lyndale Ave
3 Kirk Sandall DN3 ....92 A1
York YO10 ....131 C3
Lynden Way YO24 ....129 D3
Lyndhurst Ave
17 Grimsby DN33 ....102 E2
Kingston upon Hull
HU16 ....139 D6
Lyndhurst Cl
Beverley HU17 ....137 B4
2 Norton DN6 ....76 F2
Thorne/Moorends DN8 ....92 F8
Lyndhurst Dr 1 DN6 ....76 F2
Lyndhurst Rise 3 DN6 ....76 F2
Lynesykes Rd YO25 ....21 F5
Lynhams Rd
Bempton YO15 ....4 E1
Bridlington YO15 ....123 B8
Lynmouth Cl 9 HU7 ....57 A5
Lynmouth Dr DN17 ....150 C4
Lynngarth Ave HU16 ....139 C6
Lynton Ave HU4 ....144 B3
Lynton Cl Brayton YO8 ....148 B1
Scunthorpe DN15 ....150 D8
Lynton Gdns YO8 ....148 B1
Lynton Par DN31 ....152 B3
Lynton Rise 10 DN35 ....103 C2
Lynwith Cl DN14 ....63 C3
Lynwith Ct DN14 ....63 C3
Lynwith Dr DN14 ....63 C3
Lynwood Ave
3 Copmanthorpe YO23 ....132 A3
Kingston upon Hull
HU10 ....143 E6
Lynwood Cl YO32 ....14 A4
Lynwood View 4 YO23 ....132 A3
Lyric Cl 1 HU3 ....145 C5
Lysaghts Way DN15 ....82 C1
Lysander Cl YO30 ....127 A3
Lysander Dr YO43 ....135 E4
Lyth Cl 5 YO16 ....123 A7
Lytham Dr
Barnoldby le Beck DN37 ....113 D6
Kingston upon Hull
HU16 ....139 D6
Lythe Ave HU5 ....139 E4

M

M62 Trad Est DN14 ....149 A3
Mablethorpe Rd DN36 ....115 A3
MacAulay Jun & Inf Sch
DN31 ....152 B4
MacAulay St DN31 ....152 B4
MacAulay Way DN31 ....152 C4
MacDonald Ct 12 YO42 ....29 A3
Mace View HU17 ....154 B1
Machray Pl DN35 ....153 D3
MacKender Ct 3 DN16 ....151 B2
MacKenzie Pl 24 DN40 ....87 B1
MacLagan Rd YO23 ....132 F4
Maclure St DN31 ....152 F6
Madeira Ct HU5 ....140 A1
Madeley St HU3 ....145 C4
Madison Gdns 4 HU5 ....140 A1
Madron Cl HU7 ....141 B8
Maegan Way DN35 ....153 E2
Magazine La YO8 ....49 B3
Magazine Rd YO8 ....49 B4
Magdalen Cl 3 DN16 ....96 D2
Magdalen Ct 8 HU12 ....72 D7
Magdalen Gate HU12 ....72 D7
Magdalen La HU12 ....72 D7
Magdalene Rd 8 DN34 ....102 C3
Magnolia Cl YO25 ....124 D3
Magnolia Dr DN36 ....114 A5
Magnolia Gr YO32 ....127 D2
Magnolia Rise 9 DN40 ....87 C1
Magnolia Way DN16 ....151 A3
Magrath Ct 3 DN20 ....98 C2
Maida Gr YO10 ....130 D2
Maiden Cl 1 DN40 ....87 B1
Maiden Ct 8 HU7 ....57 B5
Maidensgrave Henge*
YO25 ....2 F1
Maidenwell La LN7 ....110 A4
Maidwell Way 1 DN34 ....102 B2
Main App Rd DN16 ....151 C7
Main Ave
Scunthorpe DN17 ....150 C2
York YO31 ....130 F5
Main Rd
Ashby cum Fenby DN37 ....113 D3
Burton Agnes YO25 ....10 C3
Burton Pidsea HU12 ....59 C2
Drax YO8 ....63 F5
Gilberdyke DN14 ....66 B7
Holmpton HU19 ....75 C2
Kilpin DN14 ....65 D7
Kingston upon Hull
HU11 ....142 E6
Mappleton HU11 ....47 A4
Newport HU15 ....53 A1
Skeffling HU12 ....90 D6
Thorngumbald HU12 ....72 F5
Ulrome YO25 ....22 E6
Utterby LN11 ....121 C4
Main St
Askham Bryan YO23 ....24 F3
Asselby DN14 ....64 D7
Bainton YO25 ....31 E7
Barmby Moor YO42 ....28 D3
3 Beal DN14 ....61 D4
Beeford YO25 ....22 C1
Beswick YO25 ....32 C4
Bilbrough YO23 ....24 C1
Bishopthorpe YO23 ....133 A4
Bonby DN20 ....84 C2
Boynton YO16 ....10 D6
Brandesburton YO25 ....34 B2
Bridlington YO16 ....122 A1
Broomfleet HU15 ....67 C6
Brough HU15 ....68 C6
Bubwith YO8 ....50 C7
Buckton/Bempton YO15 ....4 C3
Bugthorpe YO41 ....16 D4
Burstwick HU12 ....73 A6
Burton Agnes YO25 ....10 A1
Cadney DN20 ....109 D6
Carnaby YO16 ....10 E4
Catwick HU17 ....45 C8
Cherry Burton HU17 ....43 A5
Cliffe YO8 ....49 E2
Coniston HU11 ....57 F6
Copmanthorpe YO23 ....132 A2
Cottingwith YO42 ....38 C5
Crowle DN17 ....94 E6
Dalton Holme HU17 ....42 E8
Deighton YO19 ....37 A7
East/West Stockwith
DN10 ....116 F6
Ellerker HU15 ....68 A8
Ellerton YO42 ....38 C1
Elvington YO41 ....27 C2
Escrick YO19 ....37 B5
Etton HU17 ....42 F6
Fishlake DN7 ....92 D8
Foston YO25 ....22 A4
Fulstow LN11 ....121 F8
Ganton YO12 ....1 A8
Garton YO25 ....19 F6
Goodmanham YO43 ....41 D6
Gowdall DN14 ....63 A1
Graiselound DN9 ....105 D1
Grasby DN38 ....110 E7
Harpham YO25 ....21 F8
Hatfield HU11 ....46 C5
Hatfield DN7 ....92 F3
Heck DN14 ....77 C8
Hemingbrough YO8 ....49 F1
Hensall DN14 ....62 D2
Heslington YO10 ....131 B1
Hessay YO26 ....24 B8
Horkstow DN18 ....84 A5
Hotham YO43 ....53 D5
Humberside Airport
DN39 ....100 A6
Hutton Cranswick YO25 ....32 E7
Keadby with Althorpe
DN17 ....95 D4
Kelfield YO19 ....36 D1
Kelk YO25 ....21 F6
Kellington DN14 ....61 F3
Keyingham HU12 ....73 C4
Kirk Smeaton WF8 ....76 B3
Kirkburn YO25 ....19 F1
Knapton YO26 ....129 A5
Leconfield HU17 ....43 D6
Long Riston/Arnold HU11 ....45 C5
Monk Fryston LS25 ....61 A8
1 Naburn YO19 ....36 D8
North Duffield YO8 ....50 A8
North Frodingham YO25 ....33 F8
Nunthorpe YO10 ....133 D8
Ottringham HU12 ....73 E3
Patrington HU12 ....89 C8
Paull HU12 ....72 A5
Pollington DN14 ....77 F6
Poppleton YO26 ....12 F1
Preston HU12 ....58 C1
Reighton YO14 ....3 E5
Riccall YO19 ....49 A8
Roos HU12 ....60 A1
Scawby DN20 ....108 E7
Sculcoates HU2 ....140 F1
Searby cum Owmby
DN38 ....110 D8
Seaton HU11 ....35 A1
Shipton YO30 ....12 F5
Sigglesthorne HU11 ....45 F8
Skerne & Wansford YO25 ....21 A2
Skidby HU16 ....138 B8
Skipsea YO25 ....23 A1
Stamford Bridge YO41 ....15 D2
Main St continued
Swanland HU14 ....69 B7
Swine HU11 ....57 D6
Thornton Curtis DN39 ....85 E5
Thwing YO25 ....2 B1
Tibthorpe YO25 ....19 D2
Tickton HU17 ....137 E8
Ulrome YO25 ....22 E5
Watton YO25 ....32 D5
Wawne HU7 ....56 F7
Welwick HU12 ....90 A7
Wheldrake YO19 ....37 F7
Whitton DN15 ....67 E3
Wilberfoss YO41 ....27 E5
Willerby HU10 ....138 C2
Withernwick HU11 ....46 D3
Womersley DN6 ....76 C6
Worlaby DN20 ....98 D8
Maine Ave DN15 ....96 A7
Mains La YO42 ....39 E3
Maister Rd 12 HU12 ....73 C4
Majestic Ct 7 HU9 ....142 A3
Malbys Gr YO23 ....132 B2
Malcolm Rd DN34 ....102 C2
Maldon Dr HU9 ....146 C6
Malet Lambert Sch Lang Coll
HU8 ....141 E4
Malham Ave HU4 ....144 C6
Malham Gr YO31 ....131 B5
Malkinson Cl 11 DN15 ....83 A5
Mallalieu Ct DN15 ....150 E8
Mallard Ave
Barnby Dun DN3 ....92 A4
2 Leven HU17 ....45 A8
Mallard Cl
Beverley HU17 ....136 F6
Driffield YO25 ....125 A4
2 Healing DN41 ....101 F5
Ulrome YO25 ....23 A3
Mallard Dr LN7 ....111 A4
Mallard Mews DN32 ....152 E2
Mallard Rd
Kingston upon Hull HU9 ....142 B4
Scunthorpe DN17 ....150 E2
Mallard Way 11 YO32 ....13 F5
Mallards Reach HU16 ....139 C8
Malling Wlk 13 DN16 ....96 D1
Mallory Cl YO32 ....127 D4
Mallory Rd DN16 ....151 D1
Mallyan Cl 15 HU8 ....141 E7
Malm St HU3 ....145 B6
Malmesbury Dr DN34 ....152 C2
Malmo Rd HU7 ....140 E5
Malpas Cl 8 HU7 ....56 F5
Malt Kilns The DN14 ....149 D4
Malt Shoval Ct YO1 ....156 C2
Maltby Ave DN37 ....102 B2
Maltby La 12 DN18 ....69 E1
Maltby Rd DN17 ....150 E1
Malthouse La 5 YO16 ....122 D5
Malthouse Row DN14 ....149 C3
Maltings Ct 6 YO8 ....148 C6
Maltings The
Beverley HU17 ....154 C3
Kingston upon Hull HU2 ....155 B3
Nafferton YO25 ....125 F6
Maltings Way DN32 ....152 E4
Maltkiln La 4 DN20 ....98 F7
Maltkiln Rd DN18 ....69 F1
Maltings The 5 YO43 ....135 D4
Malton Ave YO31 ....130 E6
Malton La YO17 ....7 A8
Malton Mews HU17 ....137 B3
Malton Rd
Hunmanby YO14 ....2 F8
Huntington YO32 ....128 A1
Molescroft HU17 ....136 B6
York YO31 ....130 F7
Malton St HU9 ....155 C3
Malton Way YO30 ....129 F8
Malvern Ave
Grimsby DN33 ....102 D2
York YO26 ....129 D5
Malvern Cl
Huntington YO32 ....128 A5
4 Thorne/Moorends DN8 ....93 A7
Malvern Cres 9 HU5 ....139 D2
Malvern Rd
Goole DN14 ....149 D5
Kingston upon Hull HU5 ....139 D2
Scunthorpe DN17 ....150 F3
Manby Rd
Immingham DN40 ....87 B3
Scunthorpe DN17 ....96 C2
Manchester Rd YO42 ....28 E3
Manchester St
Cleethorpes DN35 ....153 D4
Kingston upon Hull HU3 ....145 A4
Mancklin Ave HU8 ....141 D5
Mancroft YO32 ....127 C8
Mandela Link DN31 ....152 C3
Manderville Cl 18 HU12 ....72 D7
Manet Rd HU8 ....141 C1
Manifold Rd DN16 ....151 E1
Manilla La DN18 ....69 F2
Manlake Ave DN15 ....83 A5
Manley Cl YO32 ....127 D4
Manley Ct 1 DN9 ....105 D6
Manley Gdns
Brigg DN20 ....98 B2
Cleethorpes DN35 ....103 C2
Manley St 12 DN15 ....151 B7
Mann La DN9 ....94 D2
Mannaberg Way DN15 ....96 D7
Manningtree Cl DN32 ....152 E2
Manor Ave DN32 ....152 D2
Manor Barns HU20 ....55 A4
Manor Beeches The 3
YO19 ....26 E7
Manor CE Sec Sch
YO26 ....129 C7
Manor Cl
Beverley HU17 ....154 A4
Great Driffield YO25 ....124 F4
5 Hemingbrough YO8 ....49 F1
4 Keelby DN41 ....101 A5
Kirk Smeaton WF8 ....76 B3
Nafferton YO25 ....125 F6
6 North Duffield YO8 ....50 A7
12 Norton DN6 ....76 E2
Skipsea YO25 ....23 A2
Sproatley HU11 ....58 D5
Upper Poppleton YO26 ....24 F8
Manor Croft YO42 ....16 F1
Manor Ct 6 Bubwith YO8 ....50 D7
Kingston upon Hull HU10 ....69 C8
Stallingborough DN41 ....101 E7
2 York YO32 ....127 F6
Manor Ct Rd 7 DN9 ....105 E6
Manor Dr Beeford YO25 ....22 C1
Bonby DN20 ....84 C2
Brough HU15 ....68 C6
Camblesforth YO8 ....63 C4
4 Dunnington YO19 ....26 E7
10 Gilberdyke HU15 ....66 D8
5 North Duffield YO8 ....50 A7
Scawby DN20 ....108 E8
Waltham DN37 ....113 E7
Manor Dr N YO26 ....129 D4
Manor Dr S YO26 ....129 D4
Manor Farm Cl
1 Brayton YO8 ....148 A1
Carlton DN14 ....63 C2
Copmanthorpe YO23 ....132 A2
Kellington DN14 ....61 F3
Messingham DN17 ....107 D6
Manor Farm Ct YO8 ....62 C4
Manor Farm La DN14 ....78 A3
Manor Farm Rd DN17 ....150 E2
Manor Fields
Kingston upon Hull HU10 ....69 C8
Market Weighton YO43 ....135 D4
Rawcliffe DN14 ....64 B2
14 Welton HU15 ....68 D6
Manor Garth
Barmby Moor YO42 ....28 D3
Haxby YO32 ....127 B8
Kellington DN14 ....61 F3
Keyingham HU12 ....73 C4
7 Norton DN6 ....76 F2
1 Riccall YO19 ....49 A8
Skidby HU16 ....55 C4
Manor Gdns
8 Hatfield DN7 ....92 E4
6 Hunmanby YO14 ....3 A8
Manor Gn Bolton YO41 ....28 D7
Church End YO25 ....33 F8
Manor Heath YO23 ....132 A3
Manor House St HU1 ....155 A1
Manor La
Barrow upon Humber
DN19 ....85 D8
Goxhill DN19 ....85 F8
Hollym HU19 ....75 A4
Rawcliffe YO30 ....126 D2
Manor Mid Sch DN7 ....92 E4
Manor Pk
Beverley HU17 ....154 A4
Preston HU12 ....58 D1
Seaton HU11 ....35 A1
Manor Pk Cl YO30 ....126 E2
Manor Pk Gr 2 YO30 ....126 E2
Manor Pk Rd YO30 ....126 E2
Manor Rd Beal DN14 ....61 C4
Beverley HU17 ....154 A3
Crowle DN17 ....94 C7
Goole DN14 ....149 C1
Hatfield DN7 ....92 E4
Kingston upon Hull HU5 ....144 B8
9 North Cave HU15 ....53 D3
Northorpe DN21 ....118 D8
Preston HU12 ....58 C1
Reedness DN14 ....65 F1
Scunthorpe DN16 ....96 D2
South Cliffe YO43 ....53 B7
Stainforth DN7 ....92 C7
Swanland HU14 ....69 B6
Thorngumbald HU12 ....72 F5
Twin Rivers DN14 ....81 E7
Manor St
6 Bridlington YO15 ....122 E2
6 Keelby DN41 ....101 A5
Kingston upon Hull HU1 ....155 B2
Manor Way
Kingston upon Hull
HU10 ....143 F6
York YO30 ....126 E2
Manorfield Ave YO25 ....124 F5
Manorfield Rd YO25 ....124 F4
Manorhouse La HU17 ....55 B8
Mansel St DN32 ....153 B4
Mansfield Ct 6 DN32 ....153 A5
Mansfield Pk HU5 ....140 B3
Mansfield Rd DN15 ....150 B6
Mansfield St YO31 ....156 C3
Mansgate Hill LN7 ....111 B3
Mansion Ct Gdns DN8 ....93 A8
Manson Cl 13 DN34 ....102 B2
Manston Garth 4 HU7 ....57 B5
Manton Ct DN20 ....108 F6
Manton La DN20 ....108 E6
Manton Rd DN21 ....108 A4

Manuel St DN14 149 B4
Manvers St HU5 140 C3
Maple Ave
Bishopthorpe YO23 133 A3
Crowle DN17 94 D7
Flixborough DN15 96 B7
Grimsby DN34 102 C4
Keelby DN41 101 A4
Kingston upon Hull HU10 143 F8
Maple Cl
2 Bridlington YO16 123 A6
Brigg DN20 98 D2
Gainsborough DN21 117 A2
Hambleton YO8 48 B1
12 Keelby DN41 101 A4
5 Kingston upon Hull HU4 144 C7
Messingham DN17 107 D6
Maple Ct
Wheldrake YO19 37 D8
York YO10 133 E6
Maple Dr
Beverley HU17 136 F6
Goole DN14 149 F5
Maple Gr 12 Brayton YO8 48 D1
8 Healing DN41 101 F5
3 Immingham DN40 87 C2
6 New Waltham DN36 113 F7
Northfield HU13 143 B3
Summergangs HU8 141 C2
York YO10 130 D1
Maple Pk HU12 72 D8
Maple Rd
Bridlington YO16 123 A6
12 Thorne/Moorends DN8 79 B1
Maple St HU5 140 D2
Maple Tree Ave 10 YO8 49 B4
Maple Tree Cl E DN16 151 A5
Maple Tree Cl W DN16 151 A5
Maple Tree Way DN16 151 A5
Maple Wlk
8 Brandesburton YO25 34 B2
Goole DN14 149 F5
Maplehurst Ave YO31 130 D7
Mapleleaf Ct 9 HU16 138 F5
Maplewood Ave HU4 144 B7
Maplewood Paddock 2 YO24 129 C1
Mappleton Gr HU9 142 A2
Mappleton Rd HU11 46 D6
Marbury Pk
29 Dunswell HU7 56 F5
3 Kingston upon Hull HU6 140 A2
March St
6 Kirton in Lindsey DN21 108 B1
York YO31 156 C4
Marchant Cl HU17 136 D7
Marcus St Goole DN14 149 B4
Grimsby DN34 152 A2
Marfleet Ave HU9 147 B7
Marfleet Cnr DN36 114 B1
Marfleet La HU9 142 B3
Marfleet Prim Sch HU9 147 C8
Margaret Ave DN17 95 D5
Margaret Gr 1 HU13 143 F1
Margaret Philipson Ct YO31 156 C3
Margaret Pl 18 DN36 114 A7
Margaret St
Grimsby DN32 152 F3
Immingham DN40 101 C8
York YO10 156 C1
Margrave La
Garthorpe & Fockerby DN17 81 E5
Reedness DN14 80 E7
Marian Way DN37 113 C6
Marigold Cl YO8 148 C2
Marigold Wlk 22 DN35 103 C1
Marin Ct 7 HU17 137 B3
Marina Ave 3 DN14 63 B1
Marina Ct HU2 155 B1
Marina View 6 DN8 93 A7
Marine Ave HU14 69 A4
Marine Dr HU18 134 D5
Marine Valley 2 YO15 5 B3
Marine Wharf HU1 155 B1
Mariners Arms Flats DN17 95 D6
Mariners Cl HU9 146 C6
Mariners Ct HU17 154 C2
Mariners St 9 DN14 149 C4
Marjorie Waite Ct YO30 130 B7
Mark Rise DN21 117 F5
Market Cross Sh Ctr 13 YO8 148 C5
Market Ct 5 DN17 94 D7
Market Gn HU16 139 B6
Market Hall Sh Ctr DN31 152 D3
Market Hill DN15 151 B8
Market La
12 Barton-upon-Humber DN18 84 F8
5 Brigg DN20 98 B2
14 Selby YO8 148 C5
Market Pl
11 Barton-upon-Humber DN18 84 F8
Bridlington YO16 122 C5
Market Pl *continued*
8 Brigg DN20 98 B2
11 Caistor LN7 111 B4
2 Cawood YO8 48 B8
5 Epworth DN9 105 E6
Great Driffield YO25 124 E4
31 Hedon HU12 72 C7
Hornsea HU18 134 B4
Kingston upon Hull HU1 155 C1
22 Kirton in Lindsey DN21 108 B1
Market Weighton YO43 135 D4
Owston Ferry DN9 106 B2
Patrington HU12 74 D1
Pocklington YO42 29 A3
11 Selby YO8 148 C5
9 Snaith DN14 63 C1
South Cave HU15 54 A2
Market St
Cleethorpes DN35 153 F2
9 Pocklington YO42 29 A4
14 Winterton DN15 83 A5
York YO1 156 B2
Market Weighton Inf Sch YO43 135 D3
Market Weighton Rd
Barlby with Osgodby YO8 49 B6
Holme-on-Spalding-Moor YO43 40 B2
Market Weighton YO43 135 A2
Sancton YO43 41 D3
Market Weighton Sch YO43 135 F4
Market Wlk YO25 124 E4
Marketbridge La YO42 39 E7
Markham Cres YO31 156 B4
Markham Mews DN37 113 E6
Markham St YO31 156 B4
Markham Way DN20 98 E4
Markhams Orch DN33 113 E8
Marklew Ave DN34 152 B3
Markman La YO25 125 D5
Marlborough Ave
Goole DN14 149 C5
2 Haxey DN9 105 D2
Hornsea HU18 134 C1
Kingston upon Hull HU5 145 A8
Northfield HU13 143 D2
Marlborough Cl
15 Cleethorpes DN32 153 A5
Rawcliffe YO30 126 D3
Marlborough Dr DN16 151 B4
Marlborough Gr YO10 130 D2
Marlborough Rd 9 DN8 93 B7
Marlborough Terr
8 Bridlington YO15 122 F2
Kingston upon Hull HU2 155 A3
Marlborough Villas YO10 130 D2
Marlborough Way DN35 103 C1
Marlow Rd DN21 117 C1
Marlowe Rd DN17 150 D3
Marlowe St HU8 141 C2
Marmaduke St 3 HU3 145 C4
Marmiam Dr 2 YO32 14 D2
Marmion Dr DN15 83 A5
Marmion Rd DN16 151 C3
Marne St HU5 145 A8
Marples Mews DN35 153 F1
Marquis Ave DN36 114 A8
Marquis Ct YO26 129 D5
Marr La HU15 66 F7
Marris Dr DN15 83 B5
Marritt Way 9 HU12 73 C4
Marsdale HU7 140 F7
Marsden Dr DN15 150 D8
Marsden Gr 3 DN8 93 A8
Marsden Landing HU6 140 D8
Marsden Rd DN31 153 A5
Marsh Dr HU17 154 A1
Marsh End
17 Howden DN14 65 A7
Knottingley WF11 61 A3
Marsh Hill La DN14 78 C4
Marsh La Asselby DN14 64 D7
Barlow YO8 63 B8
Barnetby le Wold DN38 99 B4
Barrow upon Humber DN19 70 C2
Barton-upon-Humber DN18 69 F1
2 Beal DN14 61 D4
Cawood YO8 48 D8
Keyingham HU12 73 B3
Knottingley WF11 61 A2
Misterton DN10 116 D5
New Holland DN19 70 E2
Ryehill HU12 73 A4
South Killingholme DN40 87 B4
Thorne DN8 79 A2
Thorngumbald HU12 73 A4
West Haddlesey YO8 61 F5
Winteringham DN15 68 A1
Marsh La Gdns DN14 61 F4
Marsh Rd Crowle DN17 94 B7
Easington HU12 90 E5
Keyingham HU12 73 A2
Ottringham HU12 88 C8
Walkeringham DN10 116 E3
Marsh Way DN36 115 C5
Marshall Ave
Bridlington YO15 122 E2
Grimsby DN34 152 B3
Kingston upon Hull HU10 143 E8
Preston HU12 72 C8
Marshall Hill YO25 19 D2
Marshall St HU5 140 C2
Marshchapel Cl 20 DN35 103 C2
Marshchapel Prim Sch DN36 115 B2
Marshfield Ave DN14 149 E4
Marshfield Rd
Goole DN14 149 E4
Scunthorpe DN16 151 C1
Marshland Rd DN8 79 B2
Marshlands Prim Sch DN14 149 D1
Marske Wlk 1 HU5 139 E3
Marston Ave YO26 129 B3
Marston Cres YO26 129 B3
Marston La
Long Marston YO26 24 A8
Moor Monkton YO26 12 A1
Marten Cl 2 YO30 130 A8
Martin Cheeseman Ct 3 YO24 132 C8
Martin Cl HU9 142 B3
Martin La YO42 29 C6
Martin St HU17 137 B3
Martin Way 7 DN36 113 F8
Martin's Alley HU2 155 B1
Martin's Cl DN19 85 D8
Martins Ct YO26 130 A5
Martins Rd DN39 86 B1
Marton Ave YO16 122 E5
Marton Ct 6 YO16 123 A7
Marton Gr
8 Grimsby DN33 102 D2
43 Hatfield DN7 92 D4
Kingston upon Hull HU6 139 F5
Marton La YO25 9 F6
Marton Rd
Bridlington YO16 122 D5
Ellerby HU11 46 B1
Marton View YO15 123 B8
Martongate YO16 123 A7
Martongate Prim Sch YO16 122 F6
Martyn Rd DN32 153 D2
Marvel St HU9 146 B7
Marvelgarth La HU11 35 A2
Mary St DN15 151 A7
Mary Sumner Way DN15 150 E8
Marydene Dr HU6 140 C5
Marygate YO30 156 A3
Marygate La YO30 156 A3
Marylebone Wlk 3 DN33 102 D1
Mascotte Gdns HU18 134 D3
Mask La YO41 27 D4
Mason Dr DN17 96 C2
Mason St HU2 155 B3
Masons Ct 6 DN18 84 E8
Maspin Cl 19 HU7 56 F5
Maspin Moor Rd LS25 61 C7
Massey Cl
8 Epworth DN9 105 D6
Kingston upon Hull HU3 145 A5
Massey St
Kingston upon Hull HU3 145 A4
Selby YO8 148 C5
Mast Dr HU9 146 C6
Mathews St DN35 153 C3
Matlock Ct DN15 150 B6
Matlock Dr DN37 102 C4
Matson Cl YO16 122 C2
Matson Rd YO16 122 B1
Matthew Humberstone CE Sch DN35 103 B2
Mattison Way YO24 129 E2
Mattocks La HU12 72 D8
Matty La 10 YO43 53 F7
Maude Cl 10 HU12 73 C4
Maulson Dr HU11 58 A3
Maurice Ave HU8 141 A2
Mavis Rd DN17 150 E2
Mawson Gn La DN14 78 C3
Maxwell Ct 9 DN34 102 B3
Maxwell Rd YO42 29 A4
Maxwell St HU8 141 A2
May Ct 28 YO42 29 A3
May Gdns HU7 141 A4
May Gr HU13 143 D2
May St
Cleethorpes DN35 153 D4
Kingston upon Hull HU5 140 D3
May Tree Ave HU8 141 C2
Maybury Prim Sch HU9 142 B3
Maybury Rd HU9 141 F3
Maye Gr
Kingston upon Hull HU2 155 C4
Summergangs HU8 141 B1
Mayfair Cres 18 DN37 113 D6
Mayfair Ct
3 Humberston DN35 103 D1
Kingston upon Hull HU5 140 C2
Mayfair Dr W DN37 102 B4
Mayfield & Broompark Nature Reserve* DN14 149 E5
Mayfield DN14 149 E6
Mayfield Ave
2 Gainsborough DN21 117 B2
South Killingholme DN40 86 F2
Stainforth DN7 92 D7
Mayfield Cl DN33 113 D8
Mayfield Dr 5 YO8 148 A1
Mayfield Gr YO24 132 E8
Mayfield Rd
Brayton YO8 148 A1
Bridlington YO15 122 D1
Mayfield St HU3 145 C8
Mayflower Ave 6 DN40 87 C1
Mayflower Cl 2 DN40 86 E3
Mayland Ave HU5 144 A8
Mayland Dr HU16 138 E6
Maypole Gdns YO8 48 B8
Maypole Gr 3 YO19 36 D8
Maypole St DN21 119 A2
Maysfield Ct DN20 109 A5
Maythorn Rd YO31 127 E2
Maythorpe YO23 24 C6
Maythorpe Cl HU3 145 A7
Mayville Ave HU8 141 B3
Mcan Cl YO10 131 D4
McArthur Designer Outlet YO19 133 D4
McGrath Cl 25 YO42 29 A3
McKintosh Dr YO25 125 A3
McShane Ct 11 YO42 29 A3
McVeigh Ct 10 DN41 101 F5
Mead St HU8 141 D5
Mead The 1 DN37 101 F1
Mead Wlk HU4 144 C6
Meadlands YO31 131 B6
Meadley Ct HU17 137 C4
Meadow Ave DN39 86 A2
Meadow Bank 2 HU17 136 F7
Meadow Cl
5 Beeford YO25 22 D1
Thorpe Willoughby YO8 48 C2
Meadow Croft
Brayton YO8 148 A2
16 Kirk Sandall DN3 92 A2
Waltham DN37 113 D7
Meadow Ct
Grimsby DN37 102 C4
Hibaldstow DN20 108 F5
3 York YO24 132 E8
Meadow Ct Greyhound Stadium DN7 92 C5
Meadow Dr
Barton-upon-Humber DN18 84 F8
Burstwick HU12 73 B6
Grimsby DN33 113 D8
Healing DN41 102 A5
Market Weighton YO43 135 E4
Misterton DN10 116 C5
Thorpe Willoughby YO8 48 B2
Meadow Field YO43 40 A1
Meadow Garth
Kingston upon Hull HU6 56 D5
Thorpe Willoughby YO8 48 C2
Meadow La
Driffield YO25 125 B4
1 Haxby YO32 127 D8
9 Newport HU15 52 F1
Meadow Pl 5 YO8 148 B6
Meadow Rd
Bridlington YO16 122 B2
Great Driffield YO25 125 A4
Scunthorpe DN17 150 C2
Meadow Rise
Barnby Dun DN3 92 A3
Blyton DN21 117 F6
Meadow The LN7 111 B3
Meadow Vale DN20 108 F8
Meadow View
Bainton YO25 31 E7
Bridlington YO16 122 E7
28 Humberston DN35 103 C1
Meadow Way
Heworth YO31 130 F7
Huntington YO32 127 F4
Kingston upon Hull HU16 138 F5
3 Walkington HU17 55 C8
Meadow Wlk 6 HU14 69 B7
Meadowbank
4 Belton DN9 94 E1
Grimsby DN37 102 B4
Meadowbank Rd HU3 144 E7
Meadowbeck Cl YO10 131 B4
Meadowcroft Rd YO25 125 A6
Meadowfield
Barnby Dun DN3 92 A3
1 Bubwith YO8 50 D7
Meadowfield Cl 6 YO42 28 F4
Meadowfield Rd YO15 122 D1
Meadowfields Dr YO31 127 D2
Meadows The
Beverley HU17 137 B2
Brandesburton YO25 34 B2
Bransholme HU7 140 E7
4 Buckton/Bempton YO15 4 C3
Burringham DN17 95 D4
Carlton DN14 63 C3
Cherry Burton HU17 43 A4
Dunswell HU6 56 D5
Great Driffield YO25 125 A4
Howden DN14 65 A6
Leven HU17 45 A8
Messingham DN17 107 D7
7 Monk Fryston LS25 61 A8
Riccall YO19 48 F8
2 Skelton YO30 126 B5
13 South Cave HU15 53 F1
West Ella HU10 69 C8
5 Westwoodside DN9 105 A2
Meadway YO8 48 D2
Meadway Dr YO8 48 D2
Meam Cl YO10 131 D4
Measham Dr DN7 92 D7
Meaux Abbey (Site of)* HU17 44 F2
Meaux La HU17 44 F4
Meaux Rd HU7 56 F8
Mechanic La 9 HU3 145 D5
Meden Ave 8 HU15 68 D5
Medforth Rd YO16 122 C4
Medina Ave YO16 122 D3
Medina Rd HU8 142 C5
Medium Section Rd DN16 97 A4
Medlar Dr 2 HU15 68 D5
Medway Pl DN34 152 A1
Meggison's Turnpike YO25 32 F7
Meggitt La DN15 68 A1
Megson Way
Thorngumbald HU12 72 E5
Walkington HU17 55 D8
Melander Cl YO26 129 B4
Melander Gdns 5 YO32 127 D7
Melbourne Ave
Bridlington YO16 122 D3
18 Grimsby DN33 102 E2
Melbourne CP Sch YO42 39 A7
Melbourne Pk YO42 39 A6
Melbourne Sq HU17 43 D6
Melbourne St
4 Kingston upon Hull HU5 140 C3
York YO10 130 D2
Melbury Wlk DN17 150 C4
Melcombe Ave 11 YO32 14 A7
Melford Ct DN16 151 E1
Mellwood View DN9 106 A3
Melrose Cl 1 YO31 131 A5
Melrose Pk HU17 154 A2
Melrose Rd 5 DN21 117 B1
Melrose St HU3 144 F6
Melrosegate YO31 130 F5
Melton Ave YO30 129 F8
Melton Bottom HU14 68 E5
Melton Dr
Bishopthorpe YO23 133 A3
York YO30 129 F8
Melton Fields HU14 68 F5
Melton Gallows DN38 99 A5
Melton Old Rd HU14 68 E5
Melton Rd
North Ferriby HU14 69 A5
Wrawby DN20 98 F4
Meltonby Ave HU5 139 C2
Meltonby La YO42 28 E6
Melville Cl 19 HU12 73 C4
Melville St HU1 155 A1
Melwood Cl DN9 105 F6
Melwood Gr
Kingston upon Hull HU5 140 D2
York YO26 129 B5
Melwood Hill DN9 105 F6
Melwood View DN9 105 F6
Memorial Ave 14 HU19 75 A6
Menasha Way DN16 151 E3
Mendip Ave
Goole DN14 149 D5
Grimsby DN33 113 E8
Mendip Cl 2 YO32 127 F5
Mendip Rd DN17 150 D4
Menson Dr DN7 92 D4
Mercer Rd 1 DN21 117 A1
Merchant Adventurers Hall* YO1 156 C2
Merchant Way YO23 132 B3
Merchantgate YO1 156 C2
Merchants Ct YO31 130 E5
Mercia Way DN15 96 C8
Mere Cres DN16 151 D3
Mere Garth HU18 134 B4
Mere La
Dalton Holme HU17 42 F8
Edenthorpe DN3 92 A1
Winterton DN15 83 A7
Mere View Ave HU18 134 B2
Mere Way HU14 69 B7
Mere Wlk 6 HU18 134 C4
Meredith Ave DN17 150 C2
Meredyke Rd DN17 81 D3
Mereside 9 YO15 5 A2
Mereside Terr HU18 134 B4
Mereside View YO15 5 A2
Meridian Point Ret Pk DN35 103 D2
Merlin Cl HU7 141 D7
Merlin Covert 4 YO31 127 F3
Merlin Dr DN20 99 A8
Merlin Rd DN17 150 E2
Merrick St HU9 146 B7
Merryman Garth HU12 72 C7
Merryweather Ct 14 DN16 96 D1
Mersey Prim Sch HU8 141 C1
Mersey St HU8 141 C1
Merton Gr 5 HU9 141 F1
Merton Rd DN16 96 D2
Messingham La DN20 108 C7
Messingham Prim Sch DN17 107 D7
Messingham Rd
East Butterwick DN17 106 D8
Scotter DN21 107 C4
16 Scunthorpe DN17 96 C2
Scunthorpe DN16 151 A1
Metcalfe La YO19 131 C5
Metham La DN14 65 F4
Mews The HU3 145 C5
Meynell St DN21 117 A8
Micklegate 1 Selby YO8 148 D5
York YO1 156 A2
Micklegate Bar Mus* YO24 156 A1

Micklethwaite Gr 2 DN8 79 B2
Micklethwaite Rd 1 DN8 79 B2
Mickley Gr HU9 142 C2
Middle Banks 24 YO32 13 E5
Middle Barn Hill DN20 84 D1
Middle Ct DN31 152 E4
Middle Dike La HU16 139 D7
Middle Garth Dr HU15 54 A2
Middle La Amcotts DN17 95 E8
Brayton YO8 148 C1
14 Knottingley WF11 61 A2
Preston HU12 58 B1
5 Seaton HU11 35 A1
Middle St
Corringham DN21 118 B2
Foggathorpe YO42 39 A2
Kilham YO25 9 B3
Nafferton YO25 125 F7
North Kelsey LN7 110 A4
Rudston YO25 9 F6
Scotton DN21 107 C1
Wilberfoss YO41 27 F5
Willoughton DN21 119 B3
Middle St N YO25 124 E4
Middle St S YO25 124 F3
Middle Thorpe Rd
DN35 103 B2
Middlebrook Gdns
YO8 148 A2
Middlebrook La 23 DN8 93 A8
Middleburg St HU9 146 D8
Middlecroft Dr YO32 14 A7
Middlecroft Gr 2 YO32 14 B7
Middledyke La HU16 139 D6
Middlefield La WF8 76 A2
Middlegate Cl 9 DN19 85 C8
Middlegate La
Saxby All Saints DN20 84 B4
South Ferriby DN18 84 B7
Middleham Ave YO31 130 E8
Middleham Cl 3 HU9 146 E8
Middlehowe Gn 2 HU17 55 B8
Middlehowe Rd HU17 55 A8
Middlemarsh Cl 3 HU8 141 B4
Middleplatt Rd DN40 87 D2
Middlesex Rd HU8 141 F5
Middlethorpe Dr
YO24 132 E7
Middlethorpe Gr YO24 132 F7
Middlethorpe Prim Sch
DN35 103 B2
Middleton Cl
Beverley HU17 154 C4
Messingham DN17 107 D7
Middleton Ct
Bridlington YO16 122 D5
Kingston upon Hull HU5 145 B8
Middleton Hall* HU6 140 B4
Middleton Rd
Bainton YO25 31 D5
Scunthorpe DN16 96 D2
York YO24 129 C2
Middleton St HU3 145 C8
Middleton-on-the-Wolds CE
VC Sch YO25 31 C4
Middlewood Cl YO23 24 C6
Midfield Pl DN36 114 D8
Midfield Rd DN36 114 D8
Midfield Way 1 DN41 101 A4
Midgley Cl
Kingston upon Hull HU3 145 C5
21 Stamford Bridge YO41 15 D2
Midland Ind Est DN15 151 D5
Midland Rd DN16 151 D5
Midland St HU1 155 A2
Midmere Ave HU7 141 B7
Midmere Prim Sch
HU7 141 C6
Midway Ave
Bridlington YO16 122 D2
Poppleton YO26 126 A1
Midway Gr HU4 144 E4
Milcroft Cres 18 DN7 92 D4
Mildred Gr 5 YO24 129 F2
Mile End Ave DN7 92 D3
Mile End Pk YO42 29 A4
Mile The YO42 29 A4
Miles La HU17 43 C6
Milestone Ave YO23 24 C6
Milford Ave YO16 122 C5
Milford Cres 5 YO16 122 C5
Milford Ct 19 DN32 153 A5
Milford Gr HU9 142 E1
Milford Mews 7 YO32 127 D7
Milford Way 8 YO32 127 D7
Mill Ave DN31 152 C4
Mill Balk DN14 77 C8
Mill Balk Pl DN14 78 B8
Mill Baulk Rd DN10 116 C3
Mill Beck La HU16 139 B8
Mill Cl Bridlington YO16 122 C5
15 Broughton DN20 98 B2
Great Driffield YO25 124 D4
Marshchapel DN36 115 C2
Monk Fryston LS25 61 A8
7 Waltham DN37 113 E6
Mill Cres 11 DN21 107 C3
Mill Croft Scawby DN20 108 F8
11 Scunthorpe DN16 96 E2
Scunthorpe DN16 151 D3
Mill Ct 10 YO16 122 C5
Mill Dr HU17 45 A8
Mill Falls YO25 124 D4
Mill Field Ct 5 DN3 92 A3
Mill Field Rd
Chapel Haddlesey YO8 62 B5
Fishlake DN7 92 C8
Scunthorpe DN16 151 E7
Mill Garth
12 Cleethorpes DN35 103 B2
14 Hemingbrough YO8 49 F1
Mill Gate YO16 122 C5
Mill Hill Ellerker HU15 68 A8
Escrick YO19 37 B5
Mill Hill Cres DN35 153 E1
Mill Hill Dr
6 Scunthorpe DN16 96 E2
York YO32 127 F4
Mill Hill Rd DN7 92 E3
Mill House La DN15 83 B5
Mill House Way HU11 45 D2
Mill La
Acaster Malbis YO23 36 C8
Askham Richard YO23 24 D2
Barlow YO8 63 B7
Barrow upon Humber
DN19 85 C8
Beverley HU17 154 B4
Bielby YO42 39 E6
Bishop Burton HU17 43 B2
Brandesburton YO25 34 B2
Brayton YO8 62 C8
Bridlington YO16 122 C5
Brigg DN20 98 B1
Brough HU15 68 C6
Broughton DN20 97 E3
Caistor LN7 111 C4
Carlton DN14 63 D3
East Halton DN40 86 D6
Eastrington DN14 52 A1
Elstronwick HU12 58 F3
Foston YO25 21 F1
Gainsborough DN21 117 A2
Gilberdyke HU15 52 D1
Goxhill DN19 71 A1
Harpham YO25 21 E7
Haxby YO32 13 D5
Haxey DN9 105 B2
Hayton YO42 29 D1
2 Hemingbrough YO8 49 F1
Hessay YO23 24 B7
Holton le Clay DN36 114 B4
Hornsea HU18 134 B4
Huggate YO42 18 B1
Immingham DN40 87 A1
Inglemire HU16 138 E7
14 Keelby DN41 101 A4
Kilpin DN14 65 D5
Kirk Ella HU10 143 C6
Kirton in Lindsey DN21 108 C1
Langtoft YO25 8 C7
Laxton DN14 65 F3
Marshchapel DN36 115 C2
Newbald YO43 53 E6
Newland YO8 64 A3
Newport HU15 52 E1
3 North Cave HU15 53 D3
North Dalton YO25 31 C7
North Kelsey LN7 110 A4
Rawcliffe DN14 63 F1
1 Riccall YO19 37 A1
Rise HU11 45 E6
Scawby DN20 108 F8
Seaton HU11 35 A2
Seaton Ross YO42 39 D4
Skipsea YO25 23 B2
Sledmere YO25 6 F3
Snaith & Cowick DN14 78 C8
South Ferriby DN18 84 A7
Walkeringham DN10 116 C3
Warter YO42 30 A4
Watton YO25 32 D4
Welwick HU12 90 A7
Wilberfoss YO41 27 E6
Wrawby DN20 98 E3
York YO31 130 E6
Mill La Ct HU17 154 B3
Mill La W HU15 68 B6
Mill Mere Rd DN21 118 A2
Mill Mount YO24 130 A3
Mill Mount Ct YO24 130 A3
Mill Pl DN35 153 F2
Mill Race DN36 114 E4
Mill Rd Aldbrough HU11 47 C2
Burton Constable HU11 58 D7
Burton Fleming YO25 2 D4
Cleethorpes DN35 153 E1
Crowle DN17 94 D8
Hibaldstow DN20 108 E4
Keadby DN17 95 D5
Keyingham HU12 73 C4
Luddington & Haldenby
DN17 81 C4
Skidby HU16 138 C7
Sproatley HU11 58 D5
Swanland HU14 69 A6
Mill Rise
Great Driffield YO25 124 D4
Skidby HU16 138 B8
Swanland HU14 69 A6
Mill Side YO25 9 C3
Mill Side Cl 6 YO25 9 C3
Mill St
Great Driffield YO25 124 E4
Hutton Cranswick YO25 32 E8
Kingston upon Hull HU1 155 A2
York YO1 156 C1
Mill View DN37 113 D6
Mill View Ct DN14 149 E4
Mill View Pl 5 HU17 137 B3
Mill View Rd HU17 154 C2
Mill Wlk HU16 139 C5
Millard Ave DN7 92 D4
Millard Nook 18 DN7 92 D4
Millbank 11 YO16 122 C5
Millbank St DN14 149 F5
Millbeck Bank HU15 67 E8
Millbeck Cl YO43 135 D5
Millbrook Way 23 DN18 84 F8
Milldane HU16 139 E8
Millennium Way DN14 149 F5
Miller Ave DN32 153 C2
Miller Cl
Barmby Moor YO42 28 F4
10 Thorne/Moorends DN8 93 B7
Miller La
Thorne/Moorends DN8 93 B7
Yapham YO42 29 A6
Miller Rd DN21 117 D1
Miller's Wlk HU5 139 F2
Millers Brook DN9 94 E1
Millers Croft 6 YO23 132 B3
Millers Quay 14 DN20 98 B2
Millfield Ave
16 Grimsby DN33 102 E2
York YO10 130 F3
Millfield Cl YO41 27 E5
Millfield Ct YO19 37 F7
Millfield Dr YO8 63 D4
Millfield Garth YO25 31 C4
Millfield Gdns YO26 126 A2
Millfield La
Nether Poppleton YO26 129 B8
Poppleton YO26 126 A2
York YO10 131 A3
Millfield Rd
4 Bridlington YO16 122 C5
17 Hemingbrough YO8 49 F1
Hemingbrough YO8 63 F8
Thorne/Moorends DN8 93 A8
York YO23 130 B2
Millfield The DN20 109 A6
Millfields
Barton-upon-Humber
DN18 84 E8
23 Caistor LN7 111 B4
Millfields Way 7 DN19 85 C8
Millgate YO8 148 C6
Millgates YO26 129 C6
Millhill Rd DN14 149 E5
Millhouse La DN14 149 F5
Millhouse St Rise 3
DN40 87 B1
Millhouse Woods La
HU16 139 B8
Millington Woods Nature
Reserve* YO42 29 D8
Millom Way DN32 152 F4
Millport Dr HU4 144 B2
Mills Dr DN7 104 A8
Mills Service Rd DN16 97 A4
Millthorpe Sec Sch
YO23 130 B2
Millview Gdns DN20 98 E3
Milne Rd HU9 142 C4
Milner Pl YO16 122 D4
Milner Rd YO16 122 D4
Milner St YO24 129 D3
Milson Cl
4 Barton-upon-Humber
DN18 84 E8
Broughton DN20 97 D4
Milson Gr YO10 131 A3
Milson Rd 8 DN41 101 A4
Milton Carr 8 YO30 126 F1
Milton Cl
5 Gainsborough DN21 117 C1
12 Howden DN14 65 A7
Milton Rd
3 Gainsborough DN21 117 C1
Grimsby DN33 102 D2
Scunthorpe DN16 151 B1
Milton St Goole DN14 149 C4
York YO10 130 F3
Minchin Cl 3 YO30 127 B1
Minehead Rd HU7 57 A5
Mineral Quay Rd DN40 87 C3
Minerva Terr HU1 155 B1
Minnow Cl 14 DN37 102 B4
Minshull Rd 12 DN35 103 C2
Minster Ave
Beverley HU17 154 B2
York YO31 127 F2
Minster Cl
3 Haxby YO32 127 C8
Kingston upon Hull HU8 141 D5
York YO1 156 B3
Minster Ct
Beverley HU17 154 A2
11 Howden DN14 65 A7
York YO31 156 B3
Minster Moorgate
HU17 154 A2
Minster Moorgate W
HU17 154 A2
Minster Rd
Misterton DN10 116 C5
Scunthorpe DN15 150 B6
Minster Sch The YO1 156 B3
Minster View YO32 127 C8
Minster Yd YO1 156 B3
Minster Yd N HU17 154 B2
Minster Yd S HU17 154 B2
Mint Wlk HU17 154 B1
Minter Cl 2 YO24 129 B1
Mintfields Rd HU17 154 C3
Minton St HU5 140 D3
Mires La HU15 53 D2
Mires The YO43 53 F7
Mirfield Gr HU9 142 C1
Mirfield Rd
Grimsby DN32 102 F2
Scunthorpe DN15 150 C8
Mirkhill Rd YO8 148 B6
Misson Bank DN9 104 C3
Misterton Prim Sch
DN10 116 C4
Mistral Ct YO31 130 E8
Mitcham Rd HU8 142 A5
Mitchell Cl DN7 92 D5
Mitchell La YO41 27 D8
Mitchell Way YO30 126 E3
Mitchel's La YO10 133 F8
Miterdale 4 YO24 132 C7
Mitford Cl 3 YO14 2 F8
Mitford Rd 2 YO14 2 F8
Mitten Ave 10 DN14 78 C8
Mizzen Rd HU6 140 B8
MLS Bsns Centres
YO30 127 A2
Moat Field YO10 131 C4
Moat House Rd DN21 108 A1
Moat La 4 DN40 86 E3
Moat Rd DN15 82 C1
Moat Way YO8 48 D1
Moatside Ct YO31 156 B3
Modder St DN16 151 B2
Model Farm La DN39 86 B1
Moffat Cl HU8 141 C4
Moins Ct YO10 131 D4
Moira Cl DN7 92 D7
Moiser Cl YO32 127 D4
Molescroft Ave 3
HU17 136 D6
Molescroft Dr HU17 136 D6
Molescroft Mews
HU17 136 C6
Molescroft Pk 4 HU17 136 D6
Molescroft Prim Sch
HU17 136 D6
Molescroft Rd HU17 136 C6
Molescroft W Cl 2
HU17 136 D6
Mollison Ave DN35 153 F1
Mollison Rd HU4 144 A3
Monarch Way YO26 129 D6
Mond Ave DN14 149 D5
Money Hill (Tumulus)*
YO43 42 A8
Monic Ave HU13 143 F2
Monk Ave YO31 130 F7
Monk Bar & Richard III Mus*
YO31 156 C3
Monk Bar Ct YO31 156 B3
Monk Fryston CE VC Prim
Sch LS25 61 A8
Monk Fryston Prim Sch
LS25 61 A8
Monk La YO8 148 C7
Monkbridge Ct YO31 156 C4
Monkgate YO31 156 C3
Monkgate Cloisters
YO31 156 C3
Monks Cl DN7 92 D5
Monks Cross Dr YO32 128 A3
Monks Cross Link
YO32 128 B4
Monks Cross Sh Pk
YO32 128 B3
Monks Rd DN17 150 F2
Monks Wlk The HU17 154 B2
Monkton 11 HU15 68 D6
Monkton Cl 10 HU16 138 F5
Monkton Rd 5 YO31 127 F1
Monkton Wlk HU8 142 C6
Monmouth St HU4 144 E3
Mons St HU5 145 A8
Monson Rd DN21 118 D8
Montague Rd YO23 133 A3
Montague St
Cleethorpes DN35 153 B5
Goole DN14 149 C4
York YO23 130 C1
Montague Wlk 6 YO26 12 F1
Montbretia Dr 23 DN16 96 D1
Montcalm Wlk 8 HU16 138 F5
Montgomery Rd DN35 153 D1
Montgomery Sq YO25 124 C2
Montreal Cres 4 HU16 138 F5
Montrose Ave YO31 130 D8
Montrose Ct DN14 149 F5
Montrose Dr DN14 149 F5
Montrose St
Kingston upon Hull HU8 141 B1
Scunthorpe DN16 151 B6
Moody La DN31 152 A7
Mook St YO60 16 B8
Moor Carr La YO8 49 B5
Moor Cl YO19 37 F8
Moor Cottage Rd YO25 34 D5
Moor Dike Rd DN7 104 A8
Moor Edges Rd DN8 93 B8
Moor End YO43 52 B8
Moor Gn HU4 144 B7
Moor Gr YO24 132 E8
Moor La 6 Barlby YO8 49 B5
Bilbrough LS24 24 B1
Bishopthorpe YO23 132 E2
Burton Agnes YO25 10 C2
Caistor LN7 111 E4
Carnaby YO16 10 E4
Cliffe YO8 49 F4
Copmanthorpe YO23 132 A1
Earswick YO32 128 C8
Full Sutton YO41 15 F1
Harpham YO25 22 A8
Hatfield DN8 93 D3
Haxby YO32 13 D7
Humbleton HU11 58 E6
Kelfield YO19 36 E2
Murton YO19 131 F8
Naburn YO19 36 D8
Moor La *continued*
Newton-on-Ouse YO30 12 C7
Rufforth YO23 24 E6
Skelton YO30 126 D6
Strensall YO32 14 B7
Sykehouse DN14 78 A4
Thorne DN8 79 B1
Wroot DN9 104 C6
York YO24 132 C6
Moor Lee La
Eggborough DN14 77 B8
Heck DN14 62 B1
Moor Owners Rd DN8 93 D8
Moor Rd
Bottesford DN17 96 B1
Bridlington YO15 123 D7
Crowle DN17 94 C8
Hunmanby YO14 3 B7
Rawcliffe DN14 79 B7
Sancton YO43 53 C8
Stamford Bridge YO41 15 D2
Thorne DN8 93 C7
Moor Way YO32 128 A4
Moorbeck Cl HU6 139 F4
Moorcroft Rd YO24 132 D7
Moore Ave YO10 131 B4
Moorends Rd DN8 79 A4
Moorfield Dr YO41 27 E6
Moorfield Rd YO16 122 D3
Moorfield Way YO41 27 E6
Moorfields 3 YO8 48 D6
Moorfields La
Kilpin DN14 65 D3
Reedness DN14 80 F7
Moorfoot Cl 8 HU7 57 A6
Moorgarth Ave 10 YO24 129 F2
Moorgate YO24 129 D3
Moorhouse Rd 1 HU5 139 B1
Moorings Ct DN14 65 C4
Moorings The DN20 98 A2
Moorland Ave 3 DN10 116 C3
Moorland Cl 4 DN10 116 C3
Moorland Dr 16 DN36 114 A8
Moorland Garth 2 YO32 14 A7
Moorland Gdns YO23 132 A1
Moorland Rd
Goole DN14 149 D1
York YO10 133 D8
Moorland Way 12 DN9 105 E6
Moorlands Skelton YO32 13 B5
6 Westwoodside DN9 105 A2
Moorlands Cl YO10 131 C4
Moorlands Fields
YO10 133 E8
Moorlands La YO30 126 C6
Moorlands Nature Reserve*
YO32 13 B5
Moorlands The HU15 53 E1
Moors La HU15 53 E2
Moors Rd DN15 150 C7
Moortown Rd
Brandesburton YO25 34 B4
Nettleton LN7 111 A3
Moorwell Rd DN17 96 C1
Moot Hill* YO25 124 E5
Morcar Rd YO41 15 D1
Mordacks Dr YO16 123 B8
Mordacks Rd YO16 123 A7
Mordaunt Ave DN33 113 D8
More Hall Dr HU7 141 D7
Morecambe Ave DN16 151 A1
Morehall Cl YO30 126 F2
Moreton Bay HU11 142 E5
Morfield Gr 3 DN9 105 D6
Morgan Cl 32 YO42 29 A3
Morgan Way DN19 70 D2
Morley Rd DN17 150 F1
Morley St Goole DN14 149 D1
Kingston upon Hull HU8 141 A2
Morley's Yd HU17 154 A3
Morpeth St HU3 145 D7
Morpeth Wlk DN34 152 A3
Morrell Ct YO24 132 B8
Morrell Way YO10 131 A2
Morrets La YO8 48 A1
Morrill St HU9 141 D1
Morris Rd HU3 144 E7
Morritt Cl 3 YO31 130 F8
Morrow Ave HU18 134 D5
Mortal Ash Hill DN16 97 C2
Mortimer Dr HU10 143 F6
Mortimer Wlk YO25 125 A3
Mortlake Cl HU8 141 E5
Morton Cl
4 Gainsborough DN21 117 A2
Immingham DN40 87 B2
Morton La
Beverley HU17 154 B3
Hambleton YO8 62 A8
Morton Rd
Gainsborough DN21 117 B2
Grimsby DN34 152 B3
Laughton DN21 117 E8
Morton St HU3 145 C8
Morton Terr DN21 117 B1
Morton Trentside Prim Sch
DN21 117 A2
Moseley Hill HU11 142 E6
Moss Gn La
Brayton YO8 148 A2
Hirst Courtney YO8 62 F3
Moss Haven DN6 77 D1
Moss Rd Grimsby DN32 152 E3
Kirk Bramwith DN7 92 A8
Moss DN6 77 B1

Moss St YO24 156 A1
Mosscroft La DN7 92 E2
Motherwell Cl HU7 141 C4
Moulton Cl 6 DN34 102 B2
Mount Ave
13 Barton-upon-Humber DN18 84 E8
Bridlington YO16 122 E6
Kingston upon Hull HU13 143 D2
Selby YO8 148 B3
Winterton DN15 83 B5
Mount Cres YO16 122 E6
Mount Dr YO16 122 E6
Mount Ephraim 6 YO24 130 A3
Mount Gr YO8 148 B3
Mount Par YO24 130 A3
Mount Pk YO19 49 A8
Mount Pleasant
Aldbrough HU11 47 D2
Harpham YO25 9 D3
9 Holton le Clay DN36 114 A5
1 Hornsea HU18 134 B4
Kingston upon Hull HU8 141 A1
New Holland DN19 70 E2
Waltham DN37 113 D7
Mount Pleasant CE Jun Sch YO43 135 D3
Mount Pleasant Rd
Goole DN14 149 D5
North Frodingham YO25 34 A7
Thorne DN8 79 A2
Mount Pleasant Windmill* DN21 108 B2
Mount Royale Cl 4 DN39 86 A1
Mount Sch The YO24 130 A3
Mount Terr YO24 130 A3
Mount The
Great Driffield YO25 124 F5
7 Kirk Sandall DN3 92 A1
Selby YO8 148 B3
York YO24 156 A1
Mount Vale YO24 130 A2
Mount Vale Dr YO24 130 A2
Mount Vernon HU11 142 E6
Mount View HU14 69 A5
Mountbatten Cl 7 DN16 96 D2
Mountbatten Mews DN14 149 C5
Mountbatten Prim Sch HU9 142 E3
Mowbray Cl DN9 105 D3
Mowbray Ct 20 DN9 105 E6
Mowbray Dr YO26 129 C4
Mowbray Rd 18 DN8 93 B7
Mowbray St
Epworth DN9 105 E6
3 Gainsborough DN21 117 B1
Mowthorpe Medieval Village* YO17 6 C6
Moy Ct HU6 140 A6
Mucky La HU12 59 C6
Muirfield 16 DN37 113 D6
Muirfield Croft 4 DN40 87 C1
Muirfield Way 6 YO26 129 B5
Mulberry Ave 12 DN8 79 B2
Mulberry Cl
Great Driffield YO25 124 D3
North Thoresby DN36 114 B1
Mulberry Ct YO32 127 F6
Mulberry Dr
11 Crowle DN17 94 D7
7 Haxby YO32 13 E5
Mulberry La HU11 45 E2
Mulcourt HU6 139 F7
Mulgrave St HU8 155 C4
Mulgrave St S DN15 151 A8
Mull Way DN40 101 C8
Mullion Cl HU7 141 C7
Mulwith Cl YO31 131 A6
Mumby Cl 7 DN36 114 B1
Muncastergate YO31 130 E7
Munroe Cl HU8 141 C4
Munster Ct 5 DN32 153 A5
Murham Ave DN14 149 C6
Murray Cl 3 YO42 29 A4
Murray Cres HU16 138 F5
Murray St
Grimsby DN31 152 F6
York YO24 129 F3
Murrayfield Rd HU5 139 F1
Murrough Wilson Pl 3 YO31 130 C7
Murton Garth YO19 131 F6
Murton La YO19 26 D7
Murton Way YO19 131 E5
Museum St YO1 156 B2
Muston Ave HU16 139 A5
Muston Rd YO14 2 F8
Muswell Ct HU8 142 A5
Mutton La DN10 116 C1
Mylor Cl 10 HU7 57 A5
Myrtle Ave
Bishopthorpe YO23 133 B3
Selby YO8 148 B3
Myrtle Rd DN7 92 C4
Myrtle Way 14 HU15 68 D5
Myton St HU1 155 A2
Mytongate HU1 155 A1

N

Nab Dr DN14 149 C6
Nab La DN7 92 C8
Naburn CE Prim Sch YO19 36 D8
Naburn La
Deighton YO19 37 A7
Fulford YO19 133 D4
Naburn Pk Mews YO19 36 E8
Naburn St HU3 145 A4
Nacton St DN31 152 F5
Nafferton Prim Sch YO25 125 E6
Nafferton Sta YO25 125 F6
Nairn Cl YO24 132 C6
Nalton Cl YO23 132 A1
Nalton Ct HU16 139 A5
Nalton St YO8 148 C5
Nan Sampson Bank DN9 104 B4
Nandike Cl 4 HU10 143 F6
Napier Cl HU17 154 A4
Narrow Boats The 13 DN20 98 B2
Narrow La
Cottingwith YO42 38 D7
Eastrington DN14 52 A2
Kilpin DN14 65 D6
Twin Rivers DN14 81 C8
Narvick Rd HU7 140 E5
Naseby Cl 14 DN7 92 D3
Naseby Dr DN31 152 B3
Naseby Gr DN31 152 B4
Nashcourt HU6 139 F7
National Ave HU5 144 F8
National Ctr for Early Music* YO1 156 C2
National Fishing Heritage Ctr* DN31 152 D4
National Rly Mus* YO26 130 A4
Navensby Cl DN31 102 C5
Navigation La LN7 111 A4
Navigation Rd YO1 156 C2
Navigation Way HU9 146 C6
Nayfield Cl 7 YO25 124 F4
Naylor's Row 3 HU9 146 B7
Neap House Rd DN15 95 E6
Neasden Cl HU8 141 E5
Neasden Prim Sch HU8 141 E5
Neat Marsh Rd HU12 58 B1
Neatgangs La DN19 71 A3
Neath Rd DN16 151 A5
Neatshead Garth 9 HU7 57 B5
Needham Cl HU17 137 B4
Nelson Ct HU1 155 B1
Nelson Rd HU5 144 B7
Nelson St
Bridlington YO15 122 E2
Gainsborough DN21 117 B1
Grimsby DN32 152 F5
Kingston upon Hull HU1 155 C1
York YO31 156 C4
Nelson Way DN34 102 B3
Nelson's La YO24 129 F1
Nelthorpe Cl 6 DN39 86 A1
Neptune St
Bridlington YO15 122 E1
Cleethorpes DN35 153 E3
Kingston upon Hull HU1 145 D4
Ness La
Garthorpe & Fockerby DN17 81 E6
1 Preston HU12 58 C1
Ness Rd 5 YO8 148 D6
Nessgate YO1 156 B2
Nestlings The HU8 141 D4
Nestor Gr HU9 142 C5
Neswick La YO25 31 F7
Nether Way 20 YO26 12 F1
Nethergate
Nafferton YO25 125 F7
Westwoodside DN9 105 B2
Netherlands Way DN41 87 E1
Netherton Rd HU4 144 B4
Netherwindings 18 YO32 13 F5
Netherwoods 6 YO32 14 B8
Nettle Hill 12 HU15 52 F1
Nettleholme 2 DN7 92 D4
Nettleton Garth 3 HU12 73 A6
Nettleton Prim Sch LN7 111 A3
Nettleton Rd LN7 111 B3
Neville Ave HU17 154 C3
Neville Cl
2 Keadby with Althorpe DN17 95 D4
Kingston upon Hull HU3 145 D5
Neville Cres DN15 83 A5
Neville Dr YO23 133 A3
Neville Garth 27 HU12 72 D7
Neville La DN7 92 A8
Neville Pits La DN14 77 B4
Neville Rd DN16 151 C6
Neville St
Cleethorpes DN35 153 D4
York YO31 156 C4
Neville Terr YO31 156 C4
Neville Turner Way 9 DN37 113 D6
Nevinson Gr YO10 133 E8
Nevis Way YO24 132 B7
New Bridge La YO25 125 F5
New Bridge Rd HU9 146 C8
New Burlington Rd 2 YO15 122 D2
New Carr La DN14 52 A3
New Cartergate 5 DN31 152 D3
New Chapel La 6 DN37 101 F1
New Church Terr 12 YO8 148 C5
New Cl 1 DN33 102 E2
New Clee Sta DN31 153 B5
New Cleveland St HU8 155 C4
New Cross St HU2 155 B2
New Cut YO25 22 E5
New Delights DN36 114 F3
New Earswick Prim Sch YO32 127 D4
New Earswick Sports Club YO32 127 D3
New Fen La YO8 48 F6
New Finkle Ct HU16 139 A6
New Forge Ct 15 YO32 13 F5
New Gdn St HU1 155 B3
New George St HU2 155 B3
New Gn 2 DN7 92 C6
New Haven Terr DN31 152 B5
New Holland CE & Methodist Prim Sch DN19 70 E2
New Holland Rd DN19 85 D8
New Holland Sta DN19 70 E3
New Inn La DN7 92 C7
New La Beal DN14 61 D3
Bishopthorpe YO23 133 A4
Holgate YO24 129 E3
Holme-on-Spalding-Moor YO43 52 C4
Humbleton HU11 59 A5
Huntington YO32 127 F1
Huntington YO32 128 A1
Laxton DN14 65 E4
Long Marston YO23 24 B3
Newland YO8 64 A3
Rawcliffe DN14 79 A8
Reedness DN14 80 E8
Selby YO8 148 C5
Strensall YO32 14 B8
New Laids La HU12 73 B7
New Michael St HU1 155 A1
New Mill Field Rd DN7 92 E3
New Millgate YO8 148 C6
New Pasture Cl 6 YO16 122 C5
New Pasture La YO16 122 B5
New Pasture La Prim Sch YO16 122 B5
New Pasture Prim Sch YO16 122 B5
New Pasture Wlk YO16 122 B5
New Pk Est DN7 92 D7
New Potter Grange Rd DN14 64 E2
New Rd
Beningbrough YO30 12 C6
Brandesburton YO25 33 E3
Brantingham HU15 68 C8
Burton Pidsea HU12 59 C2
Cleethorpes DN35 153 F2
Etton HU17 43 A6
Foggathorpe YO42 39 A2
Great Driffield YO25 124 F4
Harpham YO25 21 C8
Heck DN14 62 D1
Hedon HU12 72 C7
Hessay YO26 24 C8
Holme-on-Spalding-Moor YO43 40 B1
Hornsea HU18 134 D4
Hunmanby YO14 2 F7
Keyingham HU12 73 D5
Kirby Grindalythe YO17 6 B6
Laceby DN37 113 A8
Long Drax YO8 63 E6
Nafferton YO25 125 D7
Norton DN6 76 F2
Ottringham HU12 73 E3
Reighton YO14 3 E5
Roos HU12 59 F3
Scunthorpe DN17 150 B2
Stapleton WF8 76 B5
Swinefleet DN14 80 C4
Waltham DN37 113 E6
Wheldrake YO19 37 C7
Worlaby DN20 98 D8
New Row DN17 107 D7
New St 18 Brigg DN20 98 C2
Gainsborough DN21 117 B1
Grimsby DN31 152 E3
Pocklington YO42 29 A3
York YO1 156 B2
New Trent St DN17 94 E6
New Village Rd
Kingston upon Hull HU16 139 C7
Little Weighton HU20 55 A4
New Walkergate HU17 154 A3
New Waltham Prim Sch DN36 114 A8
New Wlk
Beverley HU17 136 D5
Great Driffield YO25 124 F4
North Ferriby HU14 69 A4
New Wlk Cl YO25 124 F4
New Wlk Terr YO10 130 D2
Newbald Gr HU6 139 F6
Newbald Prim Sch YO43 53 F8
Newbald Rd HU17 136 A2
Newbald Way 1 HU16 138 E6
Newbegin
Beverley HU17 154 A3
Hornsea HU18 134 C4
Newbigg Crowle DN17 94 C8
Westwoodside DN9 105 B2
Newbolt Ave DN17 150 D3
Newbolt Cl LN7 111 A3
Newborn Ave DN15 150 E8
Newborough St YO30 156 A4
Newbridge La YO41 28 A7
Newbridge Rd HU12 73 B6
Newbury Ave
Grimsby DN37 102 C5
York YO24 129 D1
Newbury Gr 2 DN34 102 C2
Newby La DN14 77 F8
Newby Rd DN31 152 C3
Newby Terr YO31 130 C7
Newclose La DN14 149 D6
Newcomen St HU9 141 D1
Newcroft YO8 148 B4
Newdale 3 YO32 13 F5
Newdown Rd DN17 96 B2
Newfield Cl DN3 92 A3
Newfield La
Burstwick HU12 58 F2
South Cave HU15 53 E1
Newfields Ave DN8 79 B1
Newfields Cl DN8 79 B1
Newfields Dr DN8 79 B1
Newgate YO1 156 B2
Newgate Ct YO1 156 B2
Newgate St HU16 139 B6
Newhall Rd 8 DN3 92 A2
Newhay La YO8 49 E1
Newholme Cl HU6 139 F6
Newholme Dr 8 DN8 79 B2
Newington Ave HU4 144 E5
Newington Prim Sch HU3 145 A4
Newington St HU3 144 F4
Newland Ave
Great Driffield YO25 124 D4
Kingston upon Hull HU5 140 C2
Scunthorpe DN15 150 E6
Newland Ave Prim Sch HU5 140 C2
Newland Dr DN15 150 D7
Newland Gr 1 HU5 140 C3
Newland Pk HU5 140 A3
Newland Pk Ave HU6 140 B4
Newland Pk Cl YO10 131 A3
Newland Pk Dr YO10 130 F3
Newland Rd DN14 149 C5
Newland Sch for Girls HU6 140 A4
Newland St John CE VA Prim Sch HU6 140 D4
Newland View 11 DN9 105 E6
Newland Wlk DN15 150 D7
Newlands 17 DN21 117 C1
Newlands Dr YO26 129 B6
Newlands La Paull HU12 72 D3
Upper Poppleton YO26 24 E8
Newlands Pk 23 DN36 103 D1
Newlands Rd
Bishopthorpe YO23 132 F4
Sunk Island HU12 89 D6
Newlands The HU6 140 C4
Newlyn Cl
4 Kingston upon Hull HU13 144 A2
New Waltham DN36 114 A8
Sutton-on-Hull HU7 141 C7
Newmarket St DN32 152 F4
Newnham Cres 12 DN16 96 D2
Newport Ave YO8 148 B4
Newport Cl 4 HU3 145 D5
Newport Dr DN15 83 A6
Newport Prim Sch HU15 52 F1
Newport Rd HU15 53 C2
Newport St
Barton-upon-Humber DN18 69 E1
Goole DN14 149 B4
Newroad End WF8 76 A6
Newsam Cl 4 YO25 22 D1
Newsham Abbey (Site of)* DN39 100 C8
Newsham Dr DN34 152 A3
Newsham Garth HU4 144 C5
Newsham Gdns HU19 75 A5
Newsham Hill La YO16 4 C2
Newsham La DN39 100 D8
Newstead Ave DN36 114 B5
Newstead Cres YO16 122 D6
Newstead Rd DN35 103 C2
Newstead St HU5 145 A8
Newthorpe Rd 2 DN6 76 E2
Newton Dr HU17 154 A1
Newton La LN8 120 A5
Newton Marsh La DN36 114 F6
Newton Pk YO30 12 B7
Newton Rd DN16 151 E2
Newton St 3 HU3 145 B4
Newton Terr YO1 156 B1
Newtondale HU7 140 F7
Newtondale Garth YO16 122 F7
Newtown Ct HU9 146 E7
Newtown Sq HU9 146 E7
Nicholas Ct 7 DN18 84 E8
Nicholas Gdns YO10 130 F3
Nicholas St YO10 130 F3
Nicholson Cl HU17 137 B4
Nicholson Ct YO42 29 A3
Nicholson La 2 HU11 35 A1
Nicholson Rd
Healing DN41 102 A5
Immingham DN40 86 E4
Nicholson St
Cleethorpes DN35 153 F1
5 Kingston upon Hull HU5 140 E2
Nicholson Way 6 DN9 105 D7
Nicholson's La HU12 74 B3
Nicholsons Ct HU16 139 A6
Nickey Nackey La YO8 48 B8
Nicolgate La 27 DN20 98 C2
Nicolson Dr 16 DN18 84 F8
Nidd Cl YO26 129 B8
Nidd Gr YO24 132 E8
Nidd St DN14 149 D1
Nidderdale HU7 140 F6
Nidderdale Cl 1 YO16 123 A7
Nigel Gr 7 YO24 129 F2
Nightingale Cl
Scunthorpe DN15 96 B7
4 Walkington HU17 55 D8
York YO32 127 E1
Nightingale Dr YO16 122 F5
Nightingale Rd YO16 122 F5
Nine Dikes Rd YO25 9 D8
Ninescores La DN9 104 B4
Ninth Ave
Fixborough Stather DN15 82 A1
York YO31 130 F5
Nith Gr HU8 142 C6
Nithdale Gdns HU5 140 E2
Noddle Hill Way HU7 141 D8
Noel St 2 DN21 117 B1
Nolloth Cres HU17 154 B4
Noodle Hill Way HU7 57 B5
Nook The YO8 148 D6
Nooking La DN37 101 D2
Nooking The DN9 105 D3
Nookings Dr DN20 109 A5
Nordale Cl 9 HU8 141 E7
Nordham HU15 53 D3
Norfolk Ave DN15 82 B4
Norfolk Bank La HU15 67 E8
Norfolk Ct 11 DN32 153 A5
Norfolk La DN35 153 E3
Norfolk St
Beverley HU17 136 D5
Kingston upon Hull HU2 155 A3
York YO23 130 C2
Norland Ave HU4 144 C6
Norlands La YO16 4 A1
Norman Cl
Barton-upon-Humber DN18 84 F8
7 Thorpe Willoughby YO8 48 B1
Norman Cres DN17 150 F4
Norman Dr
3 Hatfield DN7 92 D3
York YO26 129 B6
Norman Rd
Grimsby DN34 152 B3
Hatfield DN7 92 D3
Norman St 5 YO10 131 A3
Normanby Ent Pk DN15 151 B8
Normanby Hall Ctry Pk* DN15 82 C3
Normanby Rd
Burton upon Stather DN15 82 B4
Nettleton LN7 111 B2
Scunthorpe DN15 151 A8
Normandy Ave HU17 55 E8
Normandy Cl 4 YO8 148 B6
Normandy Rd DN35 153 D1
Normandy Way DN14 149 A3
Normanton Rise HU4 144 C7
Nornabell Dr HU17 136 E7
Nornabell St 1 HU8 146 C8
Norrison Ave HU6 140 C8
Norsefield Ave 1 DN37 113 E7
Norseman Cl 7 YO19 48 F8
Norseway 2 YO41 15 D1
North Axholme Comp Sch DN17 94 D6
North Back La
2 Bridlington YO16 122 D4
Kilham YO25 9 B3
North Bar Within HU17 154 A3
North Bar Without HU17 136 D4
North Bridge St DN32 152 F5
North Burton La YO14 3 B4
North Carr Dales Rd HU19 74 F4
North Carr La
Saxby All Saints DN20 83 F3
Tickton HU17 44 D3
North Carr Rd
Scotter DN17 106 E5
West Stockwith DN10 116 E5
North Cave CE VC Prim Sch HU15 53 D3
North Cave Rd YO43 53 D4
North Cave Wetland Nature Reserve* HU15 53 C3
North Church Side
1 Easington HU12 90 F6
Kingston upon Hull HU1 155 B2
North Cliff Rd DN21 108 C2
North Cliffe Wood Nature Reserve* YO43 53 A8

North Coates Rd DN36 115 A4
North Comm Rd DN8 78 F2
North Cotes CE Sch DN36 115 B3
North Cotes Rd
Hunmanby YO25 2 C5
Wold Newton YO25 1 E5
North Ctry Ct 2 HU9 141 F1
North Cty Prim Sch The DN21 117 A1
North Dr
Kingston upon Hull HU10 143 E6
Swanland HU14 69 B7
North Duffield CP Sch YO8 50 A8
North Eastern Rd DN8 93 A8
North Eastern Terr YO24 132 E8
North Elkington La LN11 121 B1
North End
5 Flamborough YO15 5 A2
Goxhill DN19 86 A8
Seaton Ross YO42 39 D4
South Ferriby DN18 84 A8
North End Cres 13 DN36 114 D4
North End La LN7 110 A2
North End Rd
Halsham HU12 73 F5
Roos HU12 60 A2
1 Tetney DN36 114 D4
North Farm Rd DN17 96 B2
North Ferriby CE VC Prim Sch HU14 69 A5
North Field La
Askham Bryan YO23 24 F3
Upper Poppleton YO26 24 F7
North Frodingham Prim Sch YO25 33 F8
North Frodingham Rd YO25 34 B8
North Grange Ct YO30 156 A4
North Holme 8 DN36 114 D4
North Ings Rd DN7 92 E5
North Intake La DN9 116 F8
North Kelsey Prim Sch LN7 110 A4
North Kelsey Rd LN7 110 F4
North La
Dringhouses YO24 132 E8
Huntington YO32 127 F5
Marsh Chapel DN36 115 C2
Sykehouse DN14 78 B4
Wheldrake YO19 37 F7
North Leas Ave YO16 122 E7
North Leas Dr YO16 122 E7
North Leas Wlk YO16 122 E7
North Leys Rd HU19 75 B4
North Lincoln Rd DN16 151 D6
North Lindsey Coll DN17 150 E4
North Marine Dr YO15 123 A4
North Marine Rd 1 YO15 5 B3
North Marsh Rd HU12 91 B3
North Moor 7 YO32 127 F5
North Moor Dr 1 DN10 116 C3
North Moor Gdns YO32 127 F5
North Moor La
Bottesford DN17 96 B1
Cottingham HU16 139 D8
Messingham DN17 107 B8
North Moor Rd
3 Flamborough YO15 5 B3
Messingham DN17 107 C6
Walkeringham DN10 116 C3
York YO32 127 F5
North Moss La DN41 101 E8
North Newbald Becksies Nature Reserve* YO43 53 F8
North Ormsby Medieval Village* LN11 121 A3
North Parade
Scunthorpe DN16 151 D2
York YO30 156 A3
North Pinfold Way 2 YO16 122 D6
North Pk HU12 58 F2
North Promenade
Cleethorpes DN35 153 E3
Withernsea HU19 75 A7
North Quay DN31 153 A7
North Rd Atwick YO25 35 C6
Bewholme YO25 35 A5
Halsham HU12 73 F6
Hatfield HU11 46 C5
Keadby with Althorpe DN17 95 C6
Kingston upon Hull HU4 144 E4
Lund YO25 31 F3
Ulrome YO25 23 A4
Withernsea HU19 74 F7
North Rise 2 HU12 73 A6
North Sea La DN36 103 D1
North St Aldbrough HU11 47 C1
Barmby on the Marsh DN14 64 A7
Barrow upon Humber DN19 85 D8
Bridlington YO15 122 E2
Caistor LN7 111 B4
Cleethorpes DN35 153 F2
North St *continued*
Crowle DN17 94 D8
6 Gainsborough DN21 117 A2
Goole DN14 149 D4
Great Driffield YO25 124 E5
Kingston upon Hull HU2 155 A3
Kirk Ella HU10 143 E6
Leven HU17 45 A8
Nafferton YO25 125 E8
Owston Ferry DN9 106 B3
Roxby cum Risby DN15 83 A4
1 Scunthorpe DN15 151 B8
West Butterwick DN17 95 D1
West/East Butterwick DN17 106 D8
York YO1 156 B2
North Thoresby Prim Sch DN36 114 A1
North Townside Rd YO25 33 F8
North Turnpike YO25 23 A4
North View
Beverley HU17 137 C4
Skidby HU20 55 B4
North View Terr YO15 122 F3
North Walls HU1 155 C2
North Warren Rd DN21 117 A1
North Way DN36 115 B2
Northampton Rd DN16 151 C5
North's La DN37 112 D8
Northcote Ave YO24 129 E3
Northcott Specl Sch HU7 56 F5
Northcroft 5 YO32 13 F5
Northcroft Dr 13 HU8 141 E7
North-dale Ct 2 DN21 108 B2
Northdale Pk 3 HU14 69 B7
Northern Acad of Performing Arts HU1 155 A2
Northern Ave 3 DN20 98 C3
Northern Backlight Theatre YO31 156 C4
Northern Gateway HU9 147 A7
Northern Gateway Rd HU9 147 A7
Northferry La DN9 94 C1
Northfield 3 Barlby YO8 49 B5
Rimswell HU19 74 F7
Swanland HU14 69 B7
Northfield Ave
Great Driffield YO25 124 F6
Kingston upon Hull HU13 143 E3
Northfield Cl
Driffield YO25 124 F6
12 Pocklington YO42 28 F4
1 Scunthorpe DN16 151 C2
5 South Cave HU15 53 F1
2 Tetney DN36 114 D4
West Butterwick DN17 95 D1
Womersley DN6 76 C6
Northfield Cotts DN16 96 D1
Northfield Cres YO25 124 E5
Northfield Inf Sch YO25 124 F6
Northfield La
Amcotts DN17 81 F2
Kirton in Lindsey DN21 119 B8
3 Riccall YO19 36 F1
Thornton Curtis DN39 85 D5
Welwick HU12 90 A8
Willoughton DN21 119 A4
Womersley DN6 76 C7
Northfield Rd
Beverley HU17 136 C6
Bubwith YO8 50 E8
Coniston HU11 57 F7
Great Driffield YO25 124 E6
Kingston upon Hull HU3 144 F6
Market Weighton YO43 135 E4
Messingham DN17 107 D8
Pocklington YO42 28 F4
Wetwang YO25 19 A6
Northfield Rise 7 YO42 28 F4
Northfield Sch YO26 129 B5
Northfield Terr YO24 132 E8
Northfield Wlk YO25 124 F6
Northfields
Barmby Moor YO42 28 D4
5 Strensall YO32 14 B8
Northgate
Cottingham HU16 139 A7
Hornsea HU18 134 C5
Hunmanby YO14 2 F8
Northfield HU13 143 E2
Thorne/Moorends DN8 79 B2
Walkington HU17 55 B8
Northgate Gr YO43 135 C4
Northgate La YO41 15 A3
Northgate Vale YO43 135 C4
Northlands Ave
1 Earswick YO32 127 F7
2 Winterton DN15 83 A5
Northlands Rd DN15 83 A6
Northlands Rd S DN15 83 A5
Northminster Bsns Pk YO26 24 F7
Northmoor Rd DN17 80 C1
Northolmby St 20 DN14 65 A7
Northolme DN21 117 B1
Northolme Circ 2 HU13 143 E2
Northolme Cres
Kingston upon Hull HU13 143 E2
Northolme Cres *continued*
Scunthorpe DN15 150 F7
Northolme Dr YO30 126 E1
Northolme Rd HU13 143 E2
Northolt Cl HU8 141 E6
Northorpe Cl HU9 142 C1
Northorpe Rd DN21 107 D1
Northorpe Rise YO16 122 B5
Northorpe Wlk YO16 122 B5
Northside Haxey DN9 105 C2
Laxton DN14 65 F4
Patrington HU12 74 D1
Northside Ct 6 HU12 74 D1
Northside Rd HU19 75 A4
Northstead Cl HU10 138 E1
Northumberland Ave
Hornsea HU18 134 B5
Kingston upon Hull HU2 155 B4
Northumberland Cl DN34 152 B2
Northway Fulstow LN11 121 E8
Goole DN14 149 B6
Northwood Cl HU8 142 C6
Northwood Dr HU13 143 B3
Norton & Kirk Smeat WF8 76 C3
Norton Comm La DN6 76 F2
Norton Comm Rd DN6 77 A1
Norton Cty Jun & Inf Schs DN6 76 E2
Norton Gr HU4 144 D4
Norton La LN8 119 F2
Norton Mill La DN6 76 E2
Norton Priory DN6 76 E2
Norton Rd DN16 151 B1
Norton St HU17 154 A2
Norway Dr YO10 133 D8
Norwich Ave 3 DN34 102 D2
Norwich Ct HU17 136 E1
Norwood HU17 154 B4
Norwood Ave DN15 150 F6
Norwood Cl 3 HU10 143 E7
Norwood Ct HU17 154 B4
Norwood Dale HU17 154 A3
Norwood Far Gr HU17 154 B4
Norwood Gr HU17 154 B4
Norwood Rd DN7 92 C5
Norwood St HU3 145 C7
Noseley Way 31 HU7 56 F6
Nostell Gr YO16 122 D7
Nostell Rd DN16 151 D5
Nostell Way YO16 122 D7
Nottingham Rd 6 HU11 47 C1
Nouth-dale Cl 2 DN21 108 B2
Nova Scotia Way 4 YO19 49 A8
Novello Garth HU4 144 B4
Nuffield Cl 6 DN16 96 D2
Nun Monkton Foundation Prim Sch YO26 12 A5
Nunburnholme Ave HU14 69 A4
Nunburnholme Hill YO42 29 F3
Nunburnholme Pk HU4 144 B7
Nunmill St YO23 130 C2
Nunnerley Pl DN37 113 E7
Nunnery Hill* YO25 21 F6
Nunnery La YO23 156 B1
Nunnery Wlk 4 HU15 53 F1
Nunnington Cl HU5 140 B2
Nuns Rd DN17 150 F2
Nunsthorpe Com Sch DN33 102 D2
Nunsthorpe Jun Sch DN33 102 D2
Nunthorpe Ave YO23 130 B2
Nunthorpe Cl 17 DN7 92 D4
Nunthorpe Cres YO23 130 B1
Nunthorpe Gr YO23 130 B2
Nunthorpe Rd YO23 156 A1
Nurseries The HU17 136 D7
Nursery Cl
3 Barton-upon-Humber DN18 69 F1
19 Hemingbrough YO8 49 F1
Kingston upon Hull HU4 144 B5
Scunthorpe DN17 96 C2
Thorngumbald HU12 72 E5
Nursery Ct
14 Brough HU15 68 C5
Nether Poppleton YO26 126 A2
Nursery Dr YO24 129 E3
Nursery Gdns
Beverley HU17 154 A1
17 Holton le Clay DN36 114 A5
York YO10 131 C3
Nursery Gr YO16 122 B5
Nursery Rd YO26 126 A2
Nursery Vale DN21 117 A3
Nursery Wlk HU16 139 D6
Nutana Ave HU18 134 C7
Nutfields Gr 8 DN7 92 C6
Nuttles La HU12 58 E2
Nutwood View 22 DN16 96 E2

O

Oak Ave Brough HU15 68 C6
Goole DN14 149 D1
Grimsby DN32 102 F2
Kingston upon Hull HU10 138 D1
Scawby DN20 108 F8
Withernsea HU19 75 A5
Oak Cl Beverley HU17 137 A6
Oak Cl *continued*
Sproatley HU11 58 C5
Oak Cres 7 DN8 79 A1
Oak Dene DN14 149 E6
Oak Dr
Kingston upon Hull HU4 144 B7
Newport HU15 52 F1
5 Thorpe Willoughby YO8 48 B1
Oak Field YO8 148 A1
Oak Glade 6 YO31 127 F3
Oak Gr
9 Barnetby le Beck DN38 99 B4
Barrow upon Humber DN19 85 C7
9 Hedon HU12 72 C7
Oak Hill HU10 138 C2
Oak Rd Healing DN41 101 F5
Kingston upon Hull HU6 140 D5
2 North Duffield YO8 50 A7
Scunthorpe DN16 151 B3
Thorne/Moorends DN8 79 A1
Oak Rise 4 YO26 129 C3
Oak Sq 3 HU7 56 E7
Oak St 3 YO26 129 E5
Oak Tree Ave 14 DN21 117 C1
Oak Tree Cl
Beverley HU17 136 D6
Strensall YO32 14 B7
Oak Tree Ct
Bubwith YO8 50 D7
4 Wigginton YO32 127 D7
Oak Tree Dr HU17 136 D6
Oak Tree Est 10 HU12 58 C1
Oak Tree Gr YO32 127 D3
Oak Tree La YO32 127 C7
Oak Tree Way 10 YO32 14 B7
Oak Way DN35 103 B1
Oakdale Ave 3 HU10 143 E8
Oakdale Cl 6 DN14 78 C8
Oakdale Rd YO30 126 F2
Oakdene HU16 139 B6
Oakfield Cl DN20 98 D2
Oakfield Ct 1 HU6 139 F4
Oakfield Prim Sch DN16 151 A1
Oakford Cl DN17 150 D4
Oakhill Cres 3 YO32 14 A6
Oakington Garth HU7 141 C8
Oakland Ave
33 Hatfield DN7 92 D4
York YO31 131 A7
Oakland Dr YO31 131 A7
Oaklands
Beckingham DN10 116 D1
Camblesforth YO8 63 C5
Gilberdyke HU15 66 D8
Hornsea HU18 134 D2
Hutton Cranswick YO25 32 E6
6 Strensall YO32 14 B7
Oaklands Ave 3 DN14 65 B7
Oaklands Cres YO8 63 C5
Oaklands Dr
Northfield HU13 143 D3
Willberby HU10 138 C1
Oaklands Rd DN40 87 C2
Oaklands Sec Sch YO24 129 C2
Oaklands Small Sch DN14 64 E4
Oaklands Sports Ctr YO24 129 C2
Oakleigh 9 DN16 96 E2
Oakmoor Gr DN8 79 B2
Oakmoor Rd DN8 79 B2
Oakney Wood Dr YO8 148 D1
Oaks La DN10 116 C2
Oaktree Dr 4 HU7 141 D7
Oakville St YO31 130 D7
Oakwell Ave YO16 123 A6
Oakwell Gr 2 HU8 141 B1
Oakwood Cl HU4 144 A7
Oakwood Dr DN37 102 B3
Oakwood Pk DN14 77 F6
Oakwood Rise 1 DN16 96 D2
Oatlands Rd YO16 123 A6
Oban Ave HU9 142 A2
Oban Ct 32 DN40 87 B1
Occupation La
North Kelsey LN7 110 A4
Swanland HU14 69 B8
Ocean Bvd HU9 146 B6
Ocean Dr 7 HU15 52 F1
Ochrepit Hill YO42 17 A2
Octagon The HU10 138 D1
Octon Rd YO25 9 A8
Odin Ct DN31 102 D2
Ogilvy Dr DN17 96 C2
Ogle Rd 11 YO15 5 B2
Ogleforth YO31 156 B3
O'hanlon Ave DN20 98 C2
Old Annandale Rd HU10 143 C8
Old Boys Sch La 4 YO8 48 B8
Old Bridge Rd HU18 134 C2
Old Brumby St DN16 151 A4
Old Carpenter's Yd DN7 92 B6
Old Chapel Cl 2 HU11 45 C5
Old Chapel La DN37 101 F1
Old Clee Jun & Inf Sch DN32 153 B2
Old Coppice 14 YO32 13 F5
Old Courts Rd 6 DN20 98 C2
Old Crosby DN15 96 D7
Old Ct HU17 136 D5
Old Dairy DN19 85 D8
Old Dike Lands YO32 127 C8
Old Epworth Rd E DN7 92 F4
Old Farm Cl HU12 73 E3
Old Farm Ct 5 DN37 113 D6
Old Farm Way YO8 148 B2
Old Field La DN7 92 A5
Old Fleet 2 DN37 102 B3
Old Forge Rd 4 DN10 116 C5
Old Forge Way HU11 45 D2
Old Gn La YO41 28 A5
Old Hall La YO41 27 C5
Old Haxey Rd DN10 116 C6
Old House Gdns YO8 62 A5
Old Howe La YO25 22 A3
Old Ironside Rd DN16 151 D7
Old La Blacktoft DN14 66 C4
Hirst Courtney YO8 62 F3
Long Marston YO26 24 A6
Reedness DN14 80 E7
Sigglesthorne HU11 45 F8
Old Lea YO43 40 B1
Old Leys La DN21 119 C3
Old Main Rd
Barnetby le Beck DN37 113 B6
Irby DN37 112 D7
Old Manor Dr DN20 108 E8
Old Manor Lawns HU17 154 B2
Old Mill Cl YO43 135 F3
Old Mill La
7 Broughton DN20 97 E3
Whitton DN15 67 E3
Wrawby DN20 98 D4
Old Mkt Pl 6 DN31 152 D3
Old Moor La YO24 132 E7
Old Orchard YO32 127 D8
Old Orchard The
Fulford YO10 133 E7
Shipton YO30 12 F5
Old Penny Memories* YO15 122 F2
Old Plumtree La 2 DN36 114 B1
Old Pond Pl 16 HU14 69 A4
Old Post Office La
Barnetby le Wold DN38 99 B4
5 South Ferriby DN18 84 A7
Old Rd Healing DN37 102 B5
Holme-on-Spalding-Moor YO43 40 B1
Leconfield HU17 43 C6
Ottringham HU12 73 E3
Old Rectory Gdns DN16 151 A1
Old Row The DN15 82 A5
Old Rugby Pk DN14 149 C5
Old Sch Dr DN20 108 F5
Old Sch La
Allerthorpe DN17 95 D5
Barlby with Osgodby YO8 49 B5
Keadby DN17 95 D5
North Kelsey LN7 110 A4
20 Scunthorpe DN16 96 D2
Old Sch The
Kirk Bramwith DN7 92 A7
Roxby cum Risby DN15 82 F4
Old Sch Yd 8 DN21 108 B1
Old Showfields 8 DN21 117 B1
Old Smithy & Heritage Ctr The* DN9 106 B3
Old Stack Yd The DN20 98 D3
Old Sunderlandwick La YO25 20 D1
Old Tatham YO43 40 B1
Old Thorne Rd DN7 92 E4
Old Trent Rd DN10 116 F1
Old Trough La HU15 52 C2
Old Vicarage La 5 LS25 61 A8
Old Vicarage Pk DN20 108 E8
Old Village Rd HU20 55 A4
Old Village St DN15 95 E6
Old Village The YO32 127 F5
Old Warp La DN18 84 A7
Old Waste HU17 154 A3
Oldbeck Rd HU17 137 C4
Oldfield Ave HU6 140 C6
Oldfield Cl
Barnby Dun DN3 92 A4
Stainforth DN7 92 B6
Oldfield Cres DN7 92 C6
Oldfield La DN7 92 B6
Oldfield Rd 11 DN8 93 B7
Oldfleet Prim Sch HU9 142 E2
Oldlane Gate DN14 80 D4
Oldman Ct YO24 132 C8
Oldstead Ave HU6 139 F5
Olinda Rd 2 YO15 122 E2
Oliver Ct DN31 152 D4
Oliver St DN35 153 D4
Oliver's Cl 18 YO14 2 F8
Olivers La YO16 122 E3
Olivier Ct HU4 144 E3
Olympia Cres YO8 148 E6
Olympian Ct YO10 130 F4
Ombler Cl 11 HU12 73 C4
Omega Bvd DN8 92 F8
Omega Cl YO16 123 A5
Omega Rd YO16 122 F5
On Hill HU14 69 B6
Ontario Rd DN17 96 B2
Onyx Gr 2 HU3 145 A4
Oole Rd DN35 153 F2
Opsa Bsns Ctr YO1 156 B2
Orb La DN15 96 D8
Orby Gr 6 DN33 102 D2
Orchard Ave 8 DN21 107 C3

Orchard Cl
2 Barrow upon Humber DN19 .....85 C7
13 Barton-upon-Humber DN18 .....84 F8
Blyton DN21 .....117 F5
Bridlington YO16 .....122 E7
3 Burringham DN17 .....95 D4
Burton upon Stather DN15 .....82 B5
Driffield YO25 .....125 E7
Great Driffield YO25 .....124 D5
Hatfield DN7 .....92 C3
Kingston upon Hull HU10 .....143 F7
2 Kirton in Lindsey DN21 .....108 B1
Messingham DN17 .....107 D7
6 Monk Fryston LS25 .....61 A8
Morton DN21 .....117 A3
9 Norton DN6 .....76 E2
10 Pocklington YO42 .....28 F4
Roos HU12 .....74 A8
2 Scunthorpe DN16 .....151 B2
Selby YO8 .....148 A4
Wilberfoss YO41 .....27 E6
York YO24 .....129 E1
Orchard Cotts 4 YO19 .....26 F7
Orchard Croft
2 Epworth DN9 .....105 D7
10 Grimsby DN33 .....113 E8
Kingston upon Hull HU16 .....139 B8
Orchard Ct
3 Market Weighton YO43 .....135 E4
10 Waltham DN37 .....113 D6
Orchard Dr
Burton upon Stather DN15 .....82 B5
Goole DN14 .....65 C4
Gunness DN15 .....95 E6
Hatfield DN7 .....92 C3
Kingston upon Hull HU13 .....143 E1
Middleton-on-the-Wolds YO25 .....31 C4
1 Winteringham DN15 .....68 B1
Orchard End 20 YO8 .....49 F1
Orchard Garth
Beverley HU17 .....136 D6
Copmanthorpe YO23 .....132 B2
Orchard Gdns
4 Pocklington YO42 .....28 F4
York YO31 .....127 E2
Orchard Gr Hatfield DN7 .....92 D5
Misterton DN10 .....116 D4
Orchard La
Great Driffield YO25 .....124 E5
Hutton Cranswick YO25 .....32 E8
Thorne/Moorends DN8 .....79 B2
Orchard Paddock
34 Haxby YO32 .....13 E5
3 Haxby YO32 .....127 D8
Orchard Pk YO42 .....39 B6
Orchard Pk Rd HU6 .....139 F8
Orchard Rd
Kingston upon Hull HU4 .....144 B5
Selby YO8 .....148 A4
Skidby HU16 .....138 A8
Upper Poppleton YO26 .....126 A1
Orchard St DN8 .....93 A8
Orchard The
Beverley HU17 .....137 F8
Bishopthorpe YO25 .....133 A3
Fangfoss YO41 .....28 C8
Heslington YO10 .....131 A1
Kingston upon Hull HU9 .....142 B4
Leven HU17 .....45 A7
14 New Waltham DN36 .....114 A7
Orchard View 3 YO30 .....126 B5
Orchard Way
1 Gilberdyke HU15 .....66 D7
Hensall DN14 .....62 C2
Howden DN14 .....65 A6
9 Pocklington YO42 .....28 F4
Selby YO8 .....148 A4
Skirlaugh HU11 .....45 D2
1 Strensall YO32 .....14 B7
Thorpe Willoughby YO8 .....48 B2
York YO24 .....129 E1
Orchards The YO25 .....32 E8
Orchid Rise DN15 .....150 F6
Ordnance La YO10 .....130 D1
Ore Blending Rd DN16 .....97 A4
Oribi Cl HU4 .....144 C2
Oriel Cl 6 HU17 .....55 D8
Oriel Gr
Kingston upon Hull HU9 .....142 A1
York YO30 .....130 A8
Oriole Rd DN17 .....150 E2
Orion Cl 8 HU3 .....145 B5
Orion Way DN34 .....102 B2
Orkney Cl 7 HU8 .....141 E7
Orkney Pl 11 DN40 .....87 C1
Ormerod Cres 7 HU5 .....139 D2
Ormerod Rd HU5 .....139 D2
Ormesby Wlk 9 HU5 .....139 D3
Ormonde Ave HU6 .....140 D4
Ormsby Cl 9 DN35 .....103 B2
Ormsby Rd DN17 .....150 E1
Orniscourt HU6 .....139 F7
Orrin Cl YO24 .....132 C7
Orwell St DN31 .....152 F5
Osbaldwick La YO10 .....131 B4
Osbaldwick Link Rd YO19 .....131 D4
Osbaldwick Prim Sch YO10 .....131 C4
Osbaldwick Village YO10 .....131 C4
Osborne Dr DN36 .....114 A5
Osborne Rd DN41 .....101 E8
Osborne St
Cleethorpes DN35 .....153 F2
Grimsby DN31 .....152 D3
Kingston upon Hull HU1 .....155 A2
Osbourne Dr
Keyingham HU12 .....73 D4
4 York YO30 .....126 E3
Oshawa Dell YO42 .....29 A2
Oslear Cres DN35 .....153 E1
Oslo Rd HU7 .....140 F6
Osmington Gdns 10 YO32 .....14 A7
Osprey Cl
Kingston upon Hull HU6 .....140 B8
4 York YO24 .....132 B8
Ossett Cl HU8 .....141 C1
Ostler's Cl YO23 .....132 C3
Ostler's La DN18 .....84 A5
Ostman Rd YO26 .....129 C5
Oswald Rd DN15 .....151 A7
Otley Cl HU9 .....142 C2
Ottawa Cl 6 HU16 .....138 F5
Ottawa Rd 6 DN17 .....96 C2
Otterbirch Wharf HU17 .....137 B3
Otterburn St 6 HU3 .....145 A5
Otterwood Bank 6 YO24 .....129 B1
Otterwood La YO24 .....129 B1
Otterwood Paddock YO41 .....15 C2
Ottringham Rd HU12 .....73 D4
Oubrough La HU11 .....57 F8
Oundle Cl 5 DN16 .....96 E2
Our Ladys RC Prim Sch YO24 .....129 E1
Ouse Acres YO26 .....129 D6
Ouse Bank YO8 .....148 E5
Ouse Carr La DN14 .....65 A5
Ouse Lea YO30 .....130 A7
Ouseburn Ave YO26 .....129 C6
Ousecliffe Gdns YO30 .....130 A6
Ousegate YO8 .....148 D5
Out Gates Foston YO25 .....22 B3
Harpham YO25 .....21 E6
Out Holme La DN36 .....114 E3
Out Newton Rd
Holmpton HU19 .....75 C1
Skeffling HU12 .....90 D6
Outer Trinities HU17 .....154 B2
Outgaits Cl 4 YO14 .....2 F8
Outgaits La YO14 .....3 A8
Outgang La YO19 .....131 D6
Outgang The
Brantingham HU15 .....68 B7
South Cliffe YO43 .....53 B6
Outgate DN17 .....94 E6
Outlands Rd HU16 .....139 D5
Outram Cl HU2 .....155 A4
Outstray Rd HU12 .....89 C7
Oval The Brough HU15 .....68 C6
Grimsby DN33 .....102 E1
Hatfield DN7 .....92 C5
Kellingley DN14 .....61 C3
Kirk Ella HU10 .....143 E8
Pocklington YO42 .....29 A4
23 Scunthorpe DN17 .....96 C2
Summergangs HU8 .....141 C2
Overdale Cl YO24 .....132 D8
Overland Rd HU16 .....139 C5
Overstrand Dr HU7 .....141 D6
Overton Ave HU10 .....143 E8
Overton Ct 6 DN18 .....69 F1
Overton Rd YO30 .....12 F3
Ovington Terr YO23 .....130 B2
Owbridge Ct HU2 .....155 A2
Owen Ave HU13 .....144 A1
Owlwood Ct 7 YO19 .....26 E7
Owlwood La 6 YO19 .....26 E7
Owmby Hill DN38 .....110 D8
Owmby La LN7 .....110 C5
Owmby Mount DN38 .....110 D8
Owmby Rd DN38 .....110 D8
Owmby Wold La DN38 .....110 E8
Owst Rd HU12 .....73 C4
Owsthorpe La DN14 .....52 A1
Owston Ave 2 YO10 .....131 A3
Owston Ferry Rd DN9 .....116 E8
Owston Rd
1 Hunmanby YO14 .....2 F8
West Stockwith DN10 .....116 E6
Owthorne Cl YO16 .....122 B6
Owthorne Grange HU19 .....74 F6
Owthorne Wlk
Bridlington YO16 .....122 B5
Withernsea HU19 .....74 F7
Ox Calder Cl 16 YO19 .....26 F7
Ox Carr La YO32 .....14 B6
Ox Cl YO41 .....15 D2
Ox Pasture La DN17 .....81 C2
Oxcombe Cl DN37 .....113 D8
Oxen La YO8 .....49 E3
Oxenhope Rd HU6 .....140 D7
Oxford Cl 6 HU17 .....136 E1
Oxford Rd DN14 .....149 C5
Oxford St
Bridlington YO16 .....122 D3
Cleethorpes DN35 .....153 F1
Grimsby DN32 .....153 A4
Kingston upon Hull HU2 .....155 C4
Scunthorpe DN16 .....151 D2
5 York YO24 .....130 A3
Oxmardyke La HU15 .....66 E6
Oxmarsh La DN19 .....70 E2
Oyster Ct DN35 .....153 F1

P

Packman La HU10 .....143 B8
Paddock Cl
Askham Richard YO23 .....24 D3
Copmanthorpe YO23 .....132 A2
Paddock Ct
Bridlington YO16 .....122 E7
Great Driffield YO25 .....124 F5
33 Immingham DN40 .....87 B1
Paddock La
Blyton DN21 .....117 F5
West Butterwick DN17 .....95 C1
Paddock La E DN21 .....117 F5
Paddock Rise 8 DN19 .....85 C8
Paddock The
14 Airmyn DN14 .....64 E4
Beverley HU17 .....136 D6
1 Buckton/Bempton YO15 .....4 D3
3 Burton upon Stather DN15 .....82 B4
Cottingham HU16 .....139 C6
East Ella HU4 .....144 B5
18 Gilberdyke HU15 .....66 D8
1 North Ferriby HU14 .....69 A5
8 Selby YO8 .....148 C6
2 Swanland HU14 .....69 C7
Wilberfoss YO41 .....27 E5
York YO26 .....129 C6
Paddock Way YO26 .....129 C6
Paddocks The
Barnoldby le Beck DN37 .....113 B6
Beckingham DN10 .....116 D1
6 Crowle DN17 .....94 D7
Great Driffield YO25 .....124 D3
Hutton Cranswick YO25 .....32 E7
Kingston upon Hull HU10 .....143 B7
Middleton YO25 .....31 C4
Pademoor Terr DN17 .....81 A2
Padstow Cl 7 HU7 .....56 F5
Padstow Wlk DN17 .....150 C4
Pagehall Cl DN33 .....102 E1
Paghill Est HU12 .....72 A5
Pagnell Ave YO8 .....148 E4
Paignton Ct DN33 .....113 E7
Painsthorpe La YO41 .....17 B5
Paisley Prim Sch HU3 .....145 A6
Paisley St HU3 .....145 A7
Palace Ave YO15 .....122 E2
Palanza Terr 8 YO15 .....122 E2
Pale La YO8 .....61 F7
Palmcourt HU6 .....139 F7
Palmer Ave HU10 .....143 D8
Palmer Gr YO8 .....148 A3
Palmer La
Barrow upon Humber DN19 .....85 D8
York YO1 .....156 C2
Palmes Cl YO19 .....36 E8
Pam Cl 19 DN40 .....87 C1
Pamela Rd DN40 .....87 C1
Panama Dr HU11 .....45 D2
Panman La YO19 .....26 F8
Paper Mill Rd DN14 .....79 B8
Parade Ct YO31 .....130 F6
Parade The HU5 .....140 D1
Paradise Cotts YO17 .....17 F8
Paradise Pl 9 Brigg DN20 .....98 B2
3 Goole DN14 .....149 D4
Paradise Sq HU17 .....154 B2
Paragon Sq HU1 .....155 A2
Paragon St
Kingston upon Hull HU1 .....155 A2
York YO10 .....156 C1
Parcevall Dr 32 HU7 .....56 F5
Parish Church Prim Sch DN21 .....117 B1
Parishes Sh Ctr The DN15 .....151 B7
Park Ave Barlow YO8 .....63 C7
Barton-upon-Humber DN18 .....84 E8
Beverley HU17 .....154 A4
1 Brandesburton YO25 .....34 B2
Bridlington YO15 .....122 F3
Cottingham HU16 .....139 A7
Crowle DN17 .....94 D7
Goole DN14 .....149 B5
Great Driffield YO25 .....124 E6
Grimsby DN32 .....152 D1
Misterton DN10 .....116 C6
New Earswick YO32 .....127 D5
Northfield HU13 .....143 E3
Scunthorpe DN17 .....96 C2
Snaith DN14 .....78 D8
Withernsea HU19 .....75 A6
Park Ave W HU5 .....140 A1
Park Cl 6 Airmyn DN14 .....64 E4
Great Driffield YO25 .....124 E5
Immingham DN40 .....87 C1
Melbourne YO42 .....39 A7
Skelton YO30 .....126 B4
Westwoodside DN9 .....105 A2
Park Cres
11 Thorne/Moorends DN8 .....93 A7
York YO31 .....156 C4
Park Ct DN15 .....151 B8
Park Dr Campsall DN6 .....76 E1
Grimsby DN32 .....152 E1
4 Westwoodside DN9 .....105 A2
Park Est YO32 .....127 D8
Park Farm Rd DN15 .....96 C8
Park Gate YO32 .....14 B8
Park Gdns 5 DN14 .....78 C8
Park Gr
Kingston upon Hull HU5 .....140 C1
Selby YO8 .....148 B3
York YO31 .....156 C4
Park Gr Sch YO31 .....156 C4
Park Hill DN21 .....108 B1
Park La Balne DN14 .....77 C5
Barlow YO8 .....63 C7
Bishop Wilton YO42 .....16 F1
Burn YO8 .....62 D7
Humberston DN35 .....103 C1
Luttons YO17 .....7 C8
Redbourne DN21 .....108 F3
Rowley HU17 .....55 B6
Saxby All Saints DN20 .....84 A3
Scawby DN20 .....108 F8
Snaith & Cowick DN14 .....78 C6
Tickton HU17 .....44 D2
Westwoodside DN9 .....105 A2
Wilberfoss YO41 .....27 E5
Womersley DN6 .....76 D6
York YO24 .....129 F3
Park La Cl
Bishop Wilton YO42 .....16 F1
Hatfield DN7 .....92 C2
Park La E HU4 .....144 C6
Park La Rd DN7 .....92 C2
Park La W HU4 .....144 C5
Park Lodge YO32 .....127 D4
Park Pl YO31 .....156 C4
Park Rd Airmyn DN14 .....64 E4
Barlow YO8 .....63 C7
Brough HU15 .....68 E5
Dalton Holme HU17 .....42 C8
Kingston upon Hull HU3 .....140 D1
Sproatley HU11 .....58 C5
Thorne/Moorends DN8 .....79 B2
Park Rise 17 YO14 .....2 F8
Park Rose E Coast Leisure & Ret Park* YO15 .....10 F3
Park Row
Hornsea HU18 .....134 D4
Kingston upon Hull HU3 .....145 D7
Northfield HU13 .....143 E2
Selby YO8 .....148 D5
Sproatley HU11 .....58 C5
Park Sq DN15 .....151 A6
Park St
Cleethorpes DN35 .....153 B4
Hotham YO43 .....53 D5
Kingston upon Hull HU3 .....145 D6
Messingham DN17 .....107 D7
Selby YO8 .....148 D5
Swinefleet DN14 .....80 D8
Winterton DN15 .....83 B5
York YO24 .....156 A1
Park Terr YO32 .....127 D5
Park View
Barton-upon-Humber DN18 .....84 F8
2 Bridlington YO16 .....122 F4
Cleethorpes DN35 .....153 C3
Crowle DN17 .....94 D6
Kingston upon Hull HU4 .....144 E4
Messingham DN17 .....107 D7
10 Thorne/Moorends DN8 .....93 A7
Park View Cl DN19 .....85 C7
Park View Terr DN17 .....106 C8
Park Wlk HU4 .....144 B5
Parkdale 15 DN18 .....84 E8
Parker Ave YO26 .....129 B2
Parker Rd DN36 .....114 D8
Parker St DN35 .....153 F1
Parker's La DN16 .....151 C2
Parkfield Ave HU14 .....69 A4
Parkfield Dr
Bridlington YO16 .....122 B5
Kingston upon Hull HU3 .....144 F6
Parkhill Cres DN3 .....92 A4
Parkhill Rd DN3 .....92 A4
Parkhill Rise DN15 .....83 B5
Parkhurst Cl 4 HU8 .....142 C6
Parkin Ave YO8 .....148 E4
Parkin Rd DN17 .....96 C2
Parkinson Ave DN15 .....151 A7
Parkland Way YO32 .....127 D8
Parklands Beeford YO25 .....34 C8
Goole DN14 .....149 B5
3 West/East Butterwick DN17 .....106 D8
Parklands Cres 10 HU14 .....69 A5
Parklands Dr 9 HU14 .....69 A5
Parklands The 2 HU15 .....54 A2
Parks Cl 8 DN39 .....86 A1
Parks Prim Sch The HU6 .....139 E7
Parks Rd DN7 .....92 C4
Parkside YO43 .....135 D4
Parkside Cl
Cottingham HU16 .....138 F6
Newland HU5 .....140 B1
York YO24 .....129 E3
Parkside Commercial Ctr YO23 .....156 C1
Parkside Prim Sch DN14 .....149 B6
Parkstone Gr 8 DN7 .....92 D4
Parkstone Prim Sch HU6 .....140 D7
Parkstone Rd HU6 .....140 C7
Parkway The
Cottingham HU16 .....139 A5
Kirk Ella HU10 .....143 E8
9 Snaith DN14 .....78 C8
Parkways 12 Hatfield DN7 .....92 D4
Selby YO8 .....148 B3
Parkwood Jun & Inf Sch DN17 .....150 C4
Parkwood Rise DN3 .....92 A3
Parliament St
8 Brough HU15 .....68 D6
Goole DN14 .....149 C4
Kingston upon Hull HU1 .....155 B2
York YO1 .....156 B2
Parris Pl DN35 .....153 D3
Parsonage Cl YO25 .....125 E7
Parson's La DN14 .....65 A7
Parson's Wlk 11 DN14 .....64 E4
Parsons Cl 10 DN14 .....64 E4
Parsons La YO26 .....12 E1
Parthian Rd HU9 .....142 C3
Parthridge Cl YO15 .....11 B4
Partridge Cl
Caistor LN7 .....111 B4
Scunthorpe DN17 .....150 E2
Partridge Dr LN7 .....111 F2
Parva Rd HU18 .....134 D4
Pashley Rd 20 DN8 .....93 B7
Paston Wlk YO23 .....156 B1
Pasture Ave
5 Burringham DN17 .....95 D4
Goole DN14 .....149 D5
Pasture Cl Kilham YO25 .....9 B3
2 Leconfield HU17 .....43 D6
Market Weighton YO43 .....135 E4
Skelton YO30 .....126 B5
2 Strensall YO32 .....14 B6
Wistow YO8 .....48 D6
Pasture Farm Cl YO10 .....133 D6
Pasture Hill YO17 .....16 E8
Pasture House Mews HU17 .....136 D4
Pasture La
Amcotts DN17 .....81 D1
Beverley HU17 .....136 D4
23 Brough HU15 .....68 C5
Ellerton YO42 .....38 C1
Garthorpe & Fockerby DN17 .....81 D6
Heworth YO31 .....131 B8
Sproatley HU11 .....58 D6
Pasture Prim Sch DN14 .....149 C5
Pasture Rd
Barton-upon-Humber DN18 .....69 F1
Goole DN14 .....149 C4
Hornsea HU18 .....134 D4
Pasture Rd N DN18 .....69 F1
Pasture Rd S DN18 .....69 F1
Pasture Rise YO16 .....122 B5
Pasture St DN32 .....152 E3
Pasture Terr HU17 .....136 D4
Pasture Way YO8 .....48 D6
Pasture Wharf Nature Reserve* DN18 .....70 A1
Pastures Ct DN17 .....107 D7
Pastures La HU12 .....60 B4
Pastures The
Carlton DN14 .....63 C3
Hutton Cranswick YO25 .....32 F7
4 York YO24 .....132 E8
Pately Pl 1 YO26 .....129 D4
Patrick Pool YO1 .....156 B2
Patrick St DN32 .....152 E1
Patricks Cl LN7 .....110 A4
Patrington CE VC Prim Sch HU12 .....74 D1
Patrington Garth HU7 .....141 C8
Patrington Rd
Holmpton HU19 .....75 C2
Ottringham HU12 .....73 F3
Patterdale Dr YO30 .....126 E1
Patterdale Rd HU5 .....144 E8
Paul Cres 5 DN36 .....114 C8
Paul La DN15 .....83 D1
Paul's Wlk DN17 .....150 B3
Paull Lands Rd HU12 .....72 D5
Paull Prim Sch HU12 .....72 A5
Paull Rd HU12 .....72 B6
Pavement YO1 .....156 B2
Paver La YO1 .....156 C2
Pavilion Cl HU8 .....141 B2
Pavilion Gdns DN17 .....150 F6
Pavilion Leisure Ctr 20 HU19 .....75 A6
Pavilion Way 18 DN36 .....114 A5
Paxdale HU7 .....140 E8
Payton Cl 17 YO42 .....29 A4
Peace Haven 3 DN37 .....113 D7
Peace Wlk 6 HU12 .....58 D1
Peacehaven Cl 2 HU7 .....141 B7
Peach Tree Cl 3 DN16 .....96 E2
Peach Tree Ct 5 HU3 .....145 D5
Peacock St DN17 .....150 F1
Peaks Ave DN36 .....114 A8
Peaks La Grimsby DN32 .....152 F1
New Waltham DN36 .....114 A8
Peaks Parkway DN32 .....152 E2
Peaks Parkway Ret Park DN32 .....152 E3
Peaksfield Ave DN32 .....152 F1
Pear Tree Ave
Long Drax YO8 .....63 F7
8 Poppleton YO26 .....12 F1
Pear Tree Cl
Kingston upon Hull HU8 .....141 D4
11 Waltham DN37 .....113 D6
York YO32 .....127 F4
Pear Tree La
Covenham St Bartholomew LN11 .....121 E6
Kirk Bramwith DN7 .....92 A8
Utterby DN36 .....121 B5

Pearcy Lane (Smook Hills Rd) HU19 75 A4
Pearson Ave HU5 140 D1
Pearson Prim Sch HU3 145 D8
Pearson Rd DN35 103 C2
Pearson St HU2 155 A3
Peartree Ct YO1 156 C3
Peartree Pk 19 DN14 65 A7
Pease St HU3 155 A2
Peaseholme HU13 143 C1
Peasholme Gn YO1 156 C2
Peat Carr Bank DN9 104 C3
Peckham Cl HU8 141 E5
Peckitt St YO1 156 B1
Peel Castle Rd 8 DN8 93 B7
Peel Cl YO10 131 A1
Peel Hill Rd 5 DN8 93 B7
Peel Pl HU17 136 D4
Peel St
Kingston upon Hull HU3 145 D8
York YO1 156 C1
Pefham La YO17 17 F4
Pegasus Rd DN20 99 A8
Pegasus Way DN31 102 B6
Pelham Ave 8 DN33 102 E1
Pelham Cl
5 Barton-upon-Humber DN18 84 E8
5 Beverley HU17 55 F8
Pelham Cres 15 DN41 101 A4
Pelham Dr 1 HU9 146 C7
Pelham Ind Est DN40 87 C2
Pelham Pl
9 Grimsby DN33 102 E1
15 Strensall YO32 14 A7
Pelham Rd
Cleethorpes DN35 153 D3
Grimsby DN34 152 C2
1 Holton le Clay DN36 114 A5
Immingham DN40 87 C1
Pelham Sq DN35 153 E3
Pelham View DN20 108 F5
Pelham's Pillar* DN37 111 C6
Pem La 7 YO42 29 A4
Pemberton Dr 3 DN36 113 F7
Pemberton St 1 HU8 146 B7
Pembroke Ave
Grimsby DN34 152 A3
13 Scunthorpe DN16 96 D2
Pembroke Gr HU9 142 A1
Pembroke Rd DN34 152 A1
Pembroke St YO30 130 B7
Pembroke Terr YO15 122 E1
Pendeen Cl 7 DN21 117 C1
Pendeen Gr HU8 141 B3
Pendle Cl 18 HU7 57 A6
Pendreth Pl DN35 153 D3
Pendrill St HU3 140 E1
Penistone Ct 2 HU9 146 D7
Penley's Gr St YO31 156 C4
Pennine Cl
Immingham DN40 87 B2
York YO32 127 F4
Pennine Rd DN8 93 A7
Pennine Way HU7 57 A6
Pennington St HU8 146 B7
Penny La Ct YO1 156 C3
Pennyholme Cl 34 HU7 56 F6
Pennyman Rd HU17 154 C4
Penrose Cl 9 HU7 56 F5
Penshurst Ave HU13 143 F3
Penshurst Rd DN35 103 B2
Pentire Cl 11 YO30 127 A1
Pentland Ave DN14 149 D5
Pentland Cl HU8 141 F7
Pentland Dr YO32 127 E3
Penwith Dr HU10 143 F7
Penyghent Ave YO31 131 A5
Peploe Cres 6 DN19 70 E2
Peploe La DN19 70 E2
Peppercorn Cl 6 YO26 129 E4
Peppercorn Wlk
Grimsby DN32 152 E3
11 Holton le Clay DN36 114 A5
Peppercorns The 2 HU15 66 D8
Peppermint Way YO8 148 A5
Peppin La LN11 121 D2
Peppleton Cl HU8 141 C4
Percival St DN15 151 A8
Percy Cl HU17 43 C6
Percy Dr 4 DN14 64 E4
Percy Rd
14 Hunmanby YO14 3 A8
Pocklington YO42 29 A4
Percy St Goole DN14 149 C1
Kingston upon Hull HU2 155 A3
Scunthorpe DN16 151 B6
York YO31 156 B3
Percy's La YO1 156 C2
Peregrine Cl HU4 144 D2
Perivale Cl HU8 142 A5
Periwinkle Ct DN14 149 E6
Perkins Cl DN37 102 C4
Permain Cl DN33 102 F1
Perran Cl HU7 141 B7
Perry St HU3 145 A6
Pershore Ave DN34 102 B2
Perth St HU5 144 F8
Perth Way 3 DN40 101 B8
Petchell Way DN32 152 E4
Peter Hill Dr YO30 130 A8
Peter La YO1 156 B2
Peterborough Rd DN16 151 B3
Petercroft Cl 5 YO19 26 F7
Petercroft La YO19 26 F7
Peterhouse Rd DN34 152 A1
Petersfield Cl HU7 141 B6
Petersham Cl 1 HU8 142 A5
Petersway YO30 156 A4
Petre Ave YO8 148 E3
Petuaria Cl HU15 68 B6
Pevensey Cl 1 HU7 141 B7
Peveril Ave DN17 150 F4
Pew Tree Cl YO41 27 E6
Pexton Rd YO25 124 B3
Pheasant Cl DN17 150 E2
Pheasant Ct 1 LN7 111 B4
Pheasant Dr 5 YO24 132 B8
Phelps Pl DN32 153 C1
Phelps St DN35 153 B5
Philadelphia Terr 2 YO23 130 B2
Philip Ave
Cleethorpes DN35 103 B2
5 Waltham DN37 113 E7
Philip Gr DN35 103 B2
Philip Larkin Cl HU6 140 C4
Philips Cres DN15 150 F7
Phillips La 4 DN37 101 F1
Phoenix Bsns Ctr DN14 149 D2
Phoenix Bvd YO26 130 A4
Phoenix Cl HU8 141 F4
Phoenix House Sch DN32 153 B4
Phoenix Parkway DN15 96 B7
Phoenix St Goole DN14 149 D4
Grimsby DN32 152 E3
Phyllis Ave DN34 152 B3
Phyllis Taylor Gdns DN32 152 D3
Picadilly Ct YO1 156 C2
Piccadilly
8 New Waltham DN36 114 A7
York YO1 156 C2
Pick Haven Garth DN14 61 F3
Pickering Ave HU18 134 D2
Pickering Gr 9 DN8 93 A7
Pickering High Sch HU4 144 C4
Pickering Pk YO25 31 C4
Pickering Rd HU4 144 C3
Pickering View HU3 144 D3
Pickerings The 17 HU14 69 A4
Picksley Cres DN36 114 A5
Pidgeon Cote La 3 DN19 86 A8
Pier Rd HU19 75 A6
Pier St HU1 155 B1
Piggy La 4 HU19 75 A6
Pighill La HU17 136 D7
Pighill Nook Rd LS25 61 C7
Pike Hills Mount YO23 132 A3
Pilgrim Ave DN40 87 C1
Pilgrim St YO31 156 B4
Pilgrim's Cl 5 DN40 86 E3
Pilgrims Way DN40 87 B1
Pilham La DN21 117 E4
Pilmar La HU12 60 B1
Pilots Way HU9 155 C1
Pimpernel Way 15 DN16 96 E2
Pinchbeck Ave DN16 151 C6
Pincheon Gn La DN14 78 D4
Pindars Way YO8 49 B4
Pinderfield Cl 7 HU9 142 A5
Pine Cl DN37 102 B5
Pine Ct 8 DN35 103 B1
Pine Hall Rd DN3 92 A3
Pine Mdws HU10 143 B8
Pine Tree Cl YO8 48 B2
Pine Tree La 1 LS25 61 A7
Pine Wlk 4 Brough HU15 68 C6
Healing DN41 102 A5
Pinefield Ave 4 DN3 92 A3
Pinefield Pl 27 HU15 68 C6
Pinefield Rd DN3 92 A3
Pinelands 4 YO32 127 D7
Pinelands Way YO10 131 C3
Pinetree Ave 5 DN21 107 C3
Pinetree Cl 4 DN20 97 E4
Pinewood DN16 96 E2
Pinewood Cl 5 YO42 29 A3
Pinewood Cres DN33 102 C2
Pinewood Ct 4 YO42 29 A3
Pinewood Dr YO8 63 D4
Pinewood Gr
2 Kingston upon Hull HU4 144 C7
6 York YO31 127 E2
Pinewood Hill 4 YO10 131 C3
Pinewood Rd 3 YO42 29 A3
Pinfold 10 Epworth DN9 105 E6
South Cave HU15 53 F1
Pinfold Cl
4 Bridlington YO16 122 D6
Hutton YO25 32 E8
5 Riccall YO19 37 A1
Pinfold Ct
3 Bridlington YO16 122 D6
4 Preston HU12 58 C1
4 York YO30 130 A7
Pinfold Gdns
Bridlington YO16 122 D6
14 Holton le Clay DN36 114 B5
Pinfold Gr YO16 122 C6
Pinfold Hill YO8 48 D6
Pinfold Ind Est YO16 122 D6
Pinfold La Asselby DN14 64 F6
Bempton YO16 4 B1
Bridlington YO16 122 C7
Burstwick HU12 73 A6
Pinfold La *continued*
Fishlake DN7 92 D8
10 Grimsby DN33 102 E1
Holton le Clay DN36 114 A5
Kirk Smeaton WF8 76 B3
Misterton DN10 116 C5
Moss DN6 77 D1
Norton DN6 76 E2
Pollington DN14 77 F6
Roos HU12 60 A1
Stallingborough DN41 101 D6
25 Thorne/Moorends DN8 93 A8
Pinfold Mdws YO16 122 C6
Pinfold Mews HU17 154 B3
Pinfold St
Bridlington YO16 122 D5
Eastrington DN14 51 F1
Howden DN14 65 A6
Pinfold View DN14 77 F6
Pinfold Way N 2 YO16 122 D5
Pingley La DN20 98 C1
Pingley Mdw DN20 98 C1
Pinkney's La YO25 124 D4
Pinney's Ct 7 DN41 101 F5
Pinsent Ct YO31 130 E8
Piper Rd YO25 32 E8
Piper's La HU11 46 C2
Pippin Ct 11 DN15 96 B7
Pippin Dr 16 DN16 96 D1
Pit La HU12 73 A4
Pitbalk Hill YO43 53 E4
Pitman Ave DN18 84 E8
Pitmoor La 5 DN39 86 A1
Pitsfold Cl 11 HU7 57 A5
Pitt St HU3 144 F7
Plains La DN8 93 F3
Plane St HU3 145 A5
Plantain Cl 14 DN16 96 E2
Plantation Cl HU17 137 B4
Plantation Dr
Barlby with Osgodby YO8 49 B5
1 South Cave HU15 53 F1
Welton HU14 68 F5
York YO26 129 C6
Plantation Gr YO26 129 C6
Plantation Rd 22 DN8 93 A8
Plantation View YO16 123 A8
Plantation Way 23 YO32 13 E5
Plaxton Bridge Rd HU17 56 C7
Pleasure Island Theme Pk* DN35 103 E1
Plimsoll Way HU9 146 B6
Plough Garth The DN14 61 F3
Plough Hill 12 LN7 111 B4
Ploughlands 1 YO32 127 C7
Ploughman's Cl YO23 132 C3
Ploughmans' La YO32 127 C7
Plover Dr 9 HU15 68 C6
Plover Sq 2 LN7 111 B4
Plowden Rd HU3 144 F5
Plowright Theatre DN15 151 A6
Plum Tree Dr DN36 115 C2
Plum Tree Rd HU11 58 D5
Plum Tree Way DN16 151 A5
Plum Tree Wlk HU15 54 A2
Plume Cl YO43 135 D5
Plumer Ave YO31 131 A5
Plumtree Hill Rd DN7 92 C7
Plumtree La 1 DN36 114 B1
Plumtree Rd HU12 72 E4
Plym Gr HU8 142 C6
Plymouth Cl 8 DN15 83 A5
Plymouth Rd DN17 150 D4
Poacher's Croft 3 DN9 94 E1
Pochard Cl 3 HU15 52 F1
Pocklington CE VC Infants Sch YO42 29 A4
Pocklington Ind Est YO42 28 F3
Pocklington La
Bishop Wilton YO42 16 F2
Huggate YO42 18 A1
Pocklington Sch YO42 28 F3
Pockthorpe La YO25 8 F2
Poffinder Wood Rd DN7 92 E7
Poles Bank DN9 104 E6
Pollard Cl YO32 127 E3
Pollington Balne CE Prim Sch DN14 77 F6
Polton Cl DN7 92 D7
Polton Toft DN7 92 D7
Pomona Way YO25 124 D3
Pond Side DN39 85 E3
Pond St 3 YO8 148 D6
Ponds Way 6 DN18 69 E1
Pontefract Rd DN14 78 A8
Pool Ct 7 DN14 149 C4
Pool Dr DN17 96 C2
Poolbank La HU15 68 E5
Poorhouse La HU9 142 C1
Poplar Cl
Burstwick HU12 73 A6
Kingston upon Hull HU4 144 A5
Skirlaugh HU11 45 E2
Poplar Ct HU7 141 C6
Poplar Dr
Beverley HU17 136 F6
Bridlington YO16 123 A6
Brigg DN20 98 C3
3 Broughton DN20 97 D3
Goole DN14 65 C3
21 Humberston DN36 103 D1
Poplar Gdns Drax YO8 63 F5
Scunthorpe DN16 151 B3
Poplar Gr
Cleethorpes DN35 153 E3
10 Hedon HU12 72 C7
1 Scotter DN21 107 C3
York YO32 127 E3
Poplar La DN21 118 A2
Poplar Rd
Cleethorpes DN35 153 E3
Hatfield DN7 92 C4
Healing DN41 101 F5
Poplar St YO26 129 E5
Poplars The
15 Brandesburton YO25 34 B2
11 Brayton YO8 48 D1
Knottingley WF11 61 A1
5 Leconfield HU17 43 D6
Poplars Way HU17 136 D1
Popple St HU9 146 B6
Poppleton Hall Gdn YO26 126 A3
Poppleton Rd YO26 129 E4
Poppleton Rd Prim Sch YO26 129 E5
Poppleton Sta YO26 24 F8
Popplewell Cl DN9 94 E2
Popplewell Terr 14 DN9 105 E6
Poppy Cl
2 Scunthorpe DN15 96 B7
Selby YO8 148 C2
Poppyfield Way 23 DN20 98 B2
Porlock Dr HU7 57 A5
Port Ave HU6 140 C8
Portal Rd YO26 129 B6
Porter St
Kingston upon Hull HU3 155 A1
Scunthorpe DN15 151 A8
Portholme Cres 7 YO8 148 C5
Portholme Ct YO8 148 C4
Portholme Dr YO8 148 C4
Portholme Rd YO8 148 C5
Portington Rd DN14 51 F1
Portisham Pl 12 YO32 14 A7
Portland Ave DN32 152 E1
Portland Mews YO16 122 C3
Portland Pl
Bridlington YO16 122 C3
Grimsby DN32 102 F2
Kingston upon Hull HU2 155 A3
Portland St
Kingston upon Hull HU2 155 A3
Rawcliffe DN14 79 B8
York YO31 156 B4
Portmadoc Cl 5 HU7 56 F7
Portman Rd DN15 96 C7
Portobello St HU9 141 F3
Portsmouth Wlk HU4 144 B4
Post Office La
Ashby cum Fenby DN37 113 D3
Humberside Airport DN39 100 A6
Whitton DN15 67 E3
Post Office Row DN14 64 A1
Post Office St 12 YO15 5 A2
Postern Cl YO23 156 B1
Postern La YO42 38 D6
Posterngate HU1 155 B2
Postill Sq YO16 122 D4
Potter Cl YO43 135 D3
Potterdale Dr HU20 55 A4
Potterill La HU7 141 D6
Potters Dr 4 YO23 132 B3
Potters Way HU18 134 C1
Pottery La YO31 130 E7
Pottinger Gdns LN7 111 A2
Potts La DN17 94 D7
Poultney Garth 4 HU12 72 D7
Powell St YO8 148 B6
Powells Cres DN16 151 B2
Pratt's La HU11 46 D3
Prec The DN17 150 D3
Precentor's Ct YO31 156 B3
Prescott Ave 9 HU15 68 C5
Prescott Gr 23 DN7 92 D4
Preston Dr 1 DN20 98 C2
Preston La DN18 84 F8
Preston Prim Sch HU12 58 D1
Preston Rd Hedon HU12 72 C8
Kingston upon Hull HU9 141 F1
Prestongate HU13 143 E1
Prestwick Ct YO26 129 B5
Pretoria St HU3 144 F5
Pretymen Cres DN36 114 A7
Price's La YO23 156 B1
Prickett Rd YO16 122 C4
Priest Cl YO14 2 F8
Priest La YO19 26 F5
Priestgate
3 Barton-upon-Humber DN18 84 F8
Kingston upon Hull HU7 141 D6
Nafferton YO25 125 F6
Priestgate Cl YO25 125 F6
Primitive Chapel La DN40 86 F2
Primrose Cl 19 DN41 101 F5
Primrose Dr 1 HU5 144 C8
Primrose Gr YO8 148 A6
Primrose Hill 9 WF11 61 A3
Primrose Pk HU17 137 D1
Primrose Vale 1 WF11 61 A2
Primrose Way
Humberston DN35 103 C1
1 Scunthorpe DN15 96 B7
Prince Albert Gdns DN32 152 E5
Prince Charles Dr 20 DN18 84 F8
Prince Philip Dr 21 DN18 84 F8
Prince St
Bridlington YO15 122 F2
Kingston upon Hull HU1 155 B2
Prince's Ave HU19 75 A6
Prince's Dock St HU1 155 B2
Prince's Rd
Cleethorpes DN35 153 E2
Kingston upon Hull HU5 140 C2
Princes Ave
Grimsby DN31 152 C3
1 Hedon HU12 72 C7
Hessle HU13 143 E1
Kingston upon Hull HU5 145 C8
Princes Gdns HU17 154 A2
Princes St 17 DN20 98 C2
Princess Alexandra Co 14 DN17 96 C2
Princess Ave DN7 92 C6
Princess Cl YO43 135 D3
Princess Dr
22 Barton-upon-Humber DN18 84 F8
West Haddlesey YO8 62 A5
York YO26 129 D6
Princess Par YO43 135 D3
Princess Quay Sh Ctr HU1 155 B2
Princess Rd
Market Weighton YO43 135 D3
Strensall YO32 14 B7
Princess Royal Hospl The HU8 142 A6
Princess St
4 Bridlington YO15 122 F2
Goole DN14 149 C2
Immingham DN40 87 C1
Kingston upon Hull HU2 155 B3
Princess Terr 5 YO15 122 F2
Princess Way
8 Beverley HU17 55 E8
Woodmansey HU17 136 D1
Printing Office La 6 DN17 94 D8
Prior's Wlk YO26 129 D6
Priors Cl DN36 114 A7
Priory Ave 13 HU14 69 A4
Priory Cell (Rems of)* DN37 113 A2
Priory Cl
Bridlington YO16 122 E5
10 Swanland HU14 69 B7
Wilberfoss YO41 27 F6
Priory Cres
Bridlington YO16 122 E4
Kingston upon Hull HU16 139 B5
Scunthorpe DN17 151 A3
Ulceby DN39 86 A2
Priory Dr HU5 139 D2
Priory Farm Dr 4 HU4 144 D2
Priory Gr HU4 144 D3
Priory La
Barrow upon Humber DN19 85 D8
Scunthorpe DN17 150 E2
1 Snaith DN14 63 C1
Priory La Inf Sch DN17 151 A3
Priory La Jun Sch DN17 150 F2
Priory Pk HU13 144 A1
Priory Pk Cl 3 LS25 61 A8
Priory Pk Gr 2 LS25 61 B8
Priory Prim Sch HU5 139 D1
Priory Rd
Beverley HU17 154 C2
Cottingham HU5 139 C3
Grimsby DN37 102 B3
Kingston upon Hull HU16 139 B5
Scunthorpe DN17 151 A2
Priory Rd or H DN6 76 E2
Priory Rise DN17 150 F2
Priory St YO1 156 A1
Priory Way
Kingston upon Hull HU4 144 A1
1 Snaith DN14 63 B1
Priory Wlk YO16 122 D4
Priory Wood Way YO31 127 F2
Proctor's Way DN20 109 A5
Promenade YO15 122 F2
Promenade The 15 HU19 75 A6
Promenades Sh Ctr The YO15 122 F2
Prospect Cl
Camblesforth YO8 63 D5
Pollington DN14 77 F6
Prospect Pl
Kingston upon Hull HU9 146 B7
Wistow YO8 48 D6
Prospect Rd DN14 79 B8
Prospect Sh Ctr HU2 155 A3
Prospect St
Bridlington YO15 122 E2
Kingston upon Hull HU2 155 A3
Prospect Terr
Fulford YO10 133 D6
York YO1 156 B1
Prospect Way YO8 148 D4
Prospect Way Ind Est YO8 148 D4
Providence Cres DN18 84 E8

Providence Pl
10 Bridlington YO15 ...122 F3
1 Great Driffield YO25 ...124 F4
Providence Row HU2 ...155 A4
Prunus Ave HU10 ...143 F8
Pryme Rd DN16 ...151 C4
Pryme St Anlaby HU10 ...143 F6
Kingston upon Hull HU2 ...155 A3
Prystie Pl 1 DN35 ...103 B1
Puddiners La DN14 ...80 E7
Pudding Gate 8 HU17 ...43 A2
Pudding La 48 DN7 ...92 D4
Pulcroft Rd HU13 ...143 D2
Pulfin Bog Nature Reserve* HU17 ...44 A7
Pulham La YO25 ...19 B5
Pulleyn Cl 3 YO32 ...14 C8
Pulleyn Dr YO24 ...129 F1
Pulman St HU3 ...145 A7
Pump Hill DN20 ...109 D6
Pump La YO15 ...4 C3
Punton Wlk DN14 ...78 B8
Purbeck Rd
Grimsby DN33 ...113 E8
Scunthorpe DN17 ...150 C5
Purey Cust Nuffield Hospl The YO31 ...156 B3
Purton Gr HU7 ...141 A7
Putney Cl HU8 ...141 E5
Pyewipe Rd DN31 ...152 C5
Pykestone Cl 15 HU7 ...57 A6
Pyruss Dr HU4 ...144 B2
Pytchley Wlk 1 DN35 ...103 C1

Q

Quadrant The HU6 ...139 F4
Quaker Gn 1 YO24 ...132 C7
Quaker La HU17 ...136 D4
Quaker Rd HU12 ...59 F4
Quales Mews 2 HU18 ...134 C4
Quant Mews YO10 ...131 B3
Quantock Cl
7 Kingston upon Hull HU3 ...145 D5
Scunthorpe DN17 ...150 D4
5 Thorne/Moorends DN8 ...93 A7
Quantock Rd DN33 ...113 E8
Quarrington Gr 19 HU7 ...56 F6
Quarry Ave 20 WF11 ...61 A2
Quarry Rd DN6 ...76 F2
Quart La
Eastrington DN14 ...65 F7
Reedness DN14 ...80 D6
Quay La DN14 ...80 C7
Quay Rd
Bridlington YO16 ...122 D3
4 Thorne DN8 ...78 F1
Quay St HU1 ...155 B2
Quay The YO8 ...148 D6
Quayside 1 DN8 ...78 F1
Quebec Dr HU16 ...138 E5
Quebec Rd DN17 ...96 C2
Queen Annes Rd YO30 ...156 A3
Queen Dike* YO17 ...17 B8
Queen Elizabeth Ave 4 DN18 ...84 A7
Queen Elizabeth High Sch DN21 ...117 B2
Queen Elizabeth Rd 6 DN36 ...114 C8
Queen Elizabeth Way 19 DN18 ...84 F8
Queen Margaret's Sch YO19 ...37 A5
Queen Mary Ave DN35 ...153 C3
Queen Mary Ave Inf Sch DN35 ...153 C3
Queen St
Barton-upon-Humber DN18 ...69 F1
Bridlington YO15 ...122 E2
15 Brigg DN20 ...98 C2
13 Epworth DN9 ...105 E6
Great Driffield YO25 ...124 F4
Grimsby DN32 ...152 E3
Kingston upon Hull HU1 ...155 C1
Kirton in Lindsey DN21 ...108 B1
Scunthorpe DN16 ...151 C6
16 Thorne/Moorends DN8 ...93 A8
15 Winterton DN15 ...83 A5
Withernsea HU19 ...75 A6
York YO24 ...156 A2
Queen St N HU19 ...74 F7
Queen Victoria Sq HU1 ...155 B2
Queen Victoria St YO23 ...130 B1
Queen's Alley HU1 ...155 C1
Queen's Ave 5 DN18 ...69 F1
Queen's Cl Goole DN14 ...149 C4
2 Kingston upon Hull HU16 ...139 B7
Queen's Cres DN7 ...92 C6
Queen's Ct
17 Thorne/Moorends DN8 ...93 A8
York YO1 ...156 B2
Queen's Dr HU16 ...139 A7
Queen's Gate HU16 ...139 B7
Queen's Gate St HU3 ...145 B5
Queen's Par DN35 ...153 F1
Queen's Rd DN38 ...99 B4
Queen's Staith Rd YO1 ...156 B2
Queen's View Cres DN16 ...151 D3
Queen's Way HU16 ...139 B7
Queens Cres DN17 ...95 D6
Queens Dock Ave HU1 ...155 B2
Queens Dr
7 Crowle DN17 ...94 D7
Goole DN14 ...149 D6
Queens Gdns HU18 ...134 B3
Queens Par DN31 ...152 C3
Queens Rd
Beverley HU17 ...154 C4
Immingham DN40 ...87 D1
Kingston upon Hull HU5 ...140 C2
Queens Sq 13 YO16 ...122 E2
Queens Staith Mews YO1 ...156 B1
Queensbury Way 2 HU14 ...69 B6
Queensfield LN7 ...110 A1
Queensgate
Beverley HU17 ...154 A1
Bridlington YO16 ...122 E4
Queensgate Sq YO16 ...122 D3
Queensmead
Aldbrough HU11 ...47 C1
Beverley HU17 ...55 E8
Lund YO25 ...31 F2
Queensway
Goole DN14 ...149 D4
Grimsby DN37 ...102 C4
Scunthorpe DN16 ...151 A5
Woodmansey HU17 ...56 B8
Queensway Ind Est DN15 ...151 E2
Queensway The HU6 ...140 B8
Queenswood Gr YO24 ...129 D2
Queenswood Rd 7 DN16 ...96 E2
Quillcourt HU6 ...139 E7
Quilter Ave HU4 ...144 B5
Quilter Dr HU11 ...142 F7
Quinton Rd DN32 ...102 F2
Quorn Mews 26 DN35 ...103 C2
Quorum The HU4 ...144 D3

R

Racca Ave 11 WF11 ...61 A2
Racca Gn WF11 ...61 A2
Race La Carlton YO8 ...63 B4
Wootton DN39 ...85 C3
Racecourse Rd YO23 ...133 B8
Rachel Cl 3 DN21 ...117 B2
Radcliffe Ct DN16 ...151 D4
Radcliffe Rd DN41 ...101 F5
Radcroft La YO43 ...53 D5
Radstock Wlk HU8 ...142 C7
Raglan St HU5 ...140 C3
Raich Carter Way HU6 ...56 D5
Railway Cres 2 HU19 ...75 A6
Railway Pl DN31 ...152 F5
Railway St
Barnetby le Wold DN38 ...99 B4
Beverley HU17 ...154 B2
Grimsby DN32 ...152 F4
Hornsea HU18 ...134 D4
Kingston upon Hull HU1 ...155 B1
Railway Terr
Grimsby DN32 ...152 D3
York YO24 ...130 A4
Railway View YO24 ...132 E8
Raincliffe St 4 YO8 ...148 C5
Raines Cl 5 HU12 ...73 A6
Rainham Cl HU8 ...141 E7
Rainhill Rd 2 HU5 ...140 A2
Rainsborough Way 3 YO30 ...130 A8
Rainsburgh La YO25 ...2 A3
Rainsbutt Rd DN17 ...94 C8
Rainswood Cl 8 HU7 ...56 F6
Raithby Ave 3 DN41 ...101 A4
Raithby Gr 12 DN33 ...102 D2
Rake Bridge Bank DN7 ...92 D1
Raker Cl YO19 ...37 F7
Rakes Rd HU17 ...42 E2
Raleigh Dr
Kingston upon Hull HU9 ...146 D6
Sproatley HU11 ...58 D5
Ralph Butterfield Prim Sch YO32 ...13 F5
Ram Bvd DN15 ...96 C8
Ramsay Cl YO31 ...156 C4
Ramsden Ave DN18 ...84 E8
Ramsden Cl YO25 ...124 A1
Ramsden Ct HU17 ...154 C3
Ramsden Pl 11 HU16 ...138 F5
Ramsey Ave YO23 ...133 B3
Ramsey Cl YO16 ...122 C2
Ramsey Rd YO16 ...122 B2
Ramsgate Cl HU8 ...141 E7
Ramskir La DN7 ...92 C7
Ranby Cres HU18 ...134 C2
Ranby Dr HU18 ...134 C2
Ranby Rd DN17 ...150 E1
Randall Garth YO25 ...125 A3
Rands Est 7 HU12 ...58 D1
Randsfield Ave 17 HU15 ...68 C5
Rangely Cl 9 HU7 ...57 A6
Rannoch Cl 6 HU7 ...57 A6
Ransom Ct DN39 ...100 A6
Ransome Way 14 HU15 ...68 C6
Ratcliffe Ct YO30 ...126 C5
Ratcliffe St YO30 ...130 B7
Rattan Row YO25 ...8 C6
Ratten Row
4 Bishop Burton HU17 ...43 A2
11 North Newbald YO43 ...53 F7
Rauceby Cl 10 HU7 ...56 F6
Raven Cl DN20 ...97 D4
Raven Gr YO26 ...129 C4
Raven St HU9 ...146 D7
Ravencroft La 1 DN10 ...116 D1
Ravendale 18 DN18 ...84 F8
Ravendale Cl 1 DN36 ...114 B5
Ravendale Rd 10 DN35 ...103 D2
Ravendale St N DN15 ...151 B7
Ravendale St S DN15 ...151 B7
Ravenhill Cl 14 DN35 ...103 B2
Ravenscar Rd 9 DN37 ...102 C5
Ravensfleet Rd DN21 ...116 F6
Ravenspur Rd HU11 ...58 A4
Ravenspurn YO16 ...122 B6
Ravenspurn Gr 1 HU9 ...142 A2
Ravenspurn Rd HU12 ...89 C8
Ravenspurn St DN31 ...152 D4
Ravenspurn Way 1 DN31 ...152 D4
Raventhorpe Medieval Village* DN16 ...97 B2
Rawcliffe Ave YO30 ...129 F8
Rawcliffe Bridge Prim Sch DN14 ...79 B8
Rawcliffe Cl 5 YO30 ...126 E2
Rawcliffe Croft YO30 ...126 D2
Rawcliffe Dr YO30 ...129 F8
Rawcliffe Gr HU4 ...144 D5
Rawcliffe in Snaith Prim Sch DN14 ...64 A1
Rawcliffe Inf Sch YO30 ...126 E1
Rawcliffe La YO30 ...126 F1
Rawcliffe Landing YO30 ...126 C3
Rawcliffe Rd DN14 ...149 A4
Rawcliffe Sta DN14 ...79 A8
Rawcliffe Village YO30 ...126 E3
Rawcliffe Way YO30 ...126 E2
Rawdale Cl HU15 ...54 A2
Rawdon Ave YO10 ...130 F4
Rawling Way HU3 ...145 C5
Rawlinson Ave 22 LN7 ...111 B4
Raymond Rd DN16 ...151 C3
Raywell Cl HU10 ...143 F7
Raywell St HU2 ...155 A3
Read Cl YO8 ...63 F5
Read Sch YO8 ...63 F5
Reading Gate
Reedness DN17 ...80 C3
Swinefleet DN14 ...80 D7
Reading Rm Yd 4 HU14 ...69 A4
Real Aeroplane Mus The* YO8 ...50 D5
Reangamoor La YO42 ...39 D2
Reaper's Rise 15 DN9 ...105 E6
Reaper's Way 6 DN9 ...105 D2
Recreation Club La HU17 ...154 A4
Recreation Rd 2 YO8 ...148 D6
Recto Ave DN32 ...152 F1
Rectory Ave 33 DN21 ...117 B1
Rectory Cl YO25 ...125 F7
Rectory Gdns
3 Beckingham DN10 ...116 D1
York YO23 ...130 B1
Rectory La
Beeford YO25 ...22 C1
Preston HU12 ...58 C1
Roos HU12 ...60 C3
Rectory Rd HU12 ...74 A8
Rectory St DN9 ...105 E6
Rectory View YO25 ...32 C2
Rectory Way YO43 ...40 B1
Rectory Wlk YO16 ...122 B4
Red House La YO43 ...135 A4
Red La
Market Weighton YO43 ...135 E5
South Ferriby DN18 ...83 F7
Red Lion St 2 DN14 ...149 C4
Red Twr* YO1 ...130 E4
Redbarn Dr YO10 ...131 D4
Redbourn Cl DN16 ...151 B5
Redbourn E Rd DN16 ...97 A6
Redbourn Way DN16 ...151 B6
Redbourne Mere DN21 ...108 E2
Redbourne Rd
Grimsby DN33 ...102 D2
Hibaldstow DN20 ...108 F4
Waddingham DN21 ...119 F8
Redbourne St
Kingston upon Hull HU3 ...145 B5
3 Scunthorpe DN16 ...151 C6
Redcap La YO42 ...38 C5
Redcar Gr DN32 ...153 A1
Redcar St HU8 ...155 C4
Redcliff Dr 19 HU14 ...69 A4
Redcliff Rd HU13 ...69 E4
Redcoat Way 1 YO24 ...132 B8
Redcombe La DN20 ...98 B2
Redeness St YO31 ...130 E5
Redfern Cl HU3 ...145 D5
Redgates HU17 ...55 B7
Redgrave Cl 4 YO31 ...130 E8
Redhall Cl 7 DN3 ...92 A2
Redhill Field La YO23 ...24 D1
Redhouse La YO8 ...63 F6
Redland Cres 2 DN8 ...93 B8
Redland Dr HU10 ...143 C8
Redman Cl
15 Gainsborough DN21 ...117 C1
York YO10 ...133 C8
Redmayne Sq YO32 ...14 B8
Redmire Cl HU7 ...57 A6
Redmires Cl YO30 ...127 A2
Redruth Cl HU7 ...141 C6
Redthorn Dr YO31 ...127 F1
Redwing Dr YO25 ...125 A5
Redwood Cl YO16 ...122 E6
Redwood Ct DN16 ...96 E2
Redwood Dr
7 Cleethorpes DN35 ...103 B1
6 Haxby YO32 ...13 E5
Redwood Gdns YO25 ...124 F3
Redwood Way YO16 ...122 D6
Redwoods The HU10 ...138 C2
Reed St HU2 ...155 A3
Reedham Garth HU4 ...144 A3
Reedholme La DN8 ...78 F4
Reedness Prim Sch DN14 ...66 A1
Reedsway 12 YO25 ...34 B2
Rees Cl YO43 ...135 D5
Reeth Wlk HU5 ...139 D3
Reeves The YO24 ...129 C1
Refinery Rd DN16 ...151 F6
Reform St HU2 ...155 B3
Regency Ct 8 DN18 ...69 E1
Regency Mews 2 YO24 ...132 F8
Regent Arc DN32 ...152 D3
Regent Cl
Kingston upon Hull HU3 ...145 C6
Willerby HU10 ...138 E1
Regent Dr 15 DN17 ...94 D7
Regent Gdns DN34 ...152 C1
Regent St
Beverley HU17 ...154 B2
York YO10 ...130 E3
Regent St Pavement 8 YO42 ...29 A3
Regent Terr 7 YO15 ...122 F2
Regents Ct
Cottingham HU16 ...139 A6
14 York YO26 ...129 F5
Regimental Mus* YO1 ...156 B1
Regina Cres 2 HU5 ...140 A1
Reginald Gr YO23 ...130 C1
Reginald Rd DN15 ...96 C7
Reginald Terr YO8 ...148 D4
Regis Ct HU9 ...142 B3
Register Sq HU17 ...154 A2
Reigate Cl HU8 ...142 A4
Reighton Ave YO30 ...129 F8
Reighton Dr 10 YO30 ...126 F1
Reina Dr YO25 ...124 C4
Reldene Dr HU5 ...144 B7
Remembrance Ct YO16 ...122 A2
Remillo Ave DN32 ...152 F1
Remington Ave YO25 ...34 E3
Remple Ave DN7 ...93 A3
Remple Comm Rd DN7 ...92 F2
Remple La DN7 ...93 A3
Rendel St DN31 ...152 D5
Rensburg St HU9 ...141 D1
Renshaw Gdns 8 YO26 ...129 E4
Renton Ct HU13 ...143 F6
Reporto Ave DN32 ...152 F1
Repton Dr
Kingston upon Hull HU7 ...141 D5
21 Scunthorpe DN16 ...96 D2
Reservoir Rd HU6 ...140 F3
Responso Ave DN32 ...152 F1
Reston Ct 8 DN35 ...103 D2
Reston Gr 25 DN33 ...102 D2
Retford Gr HU9 ...142 E1
Retreat Hospl The YO10 ...130 F2
Revesby Ave
13 Grimsby DN34 ...102 C2
Scunthorpe DN16 ...151 A3
Revesby Ct DN16 ...151 A4
Revigo Ave DN32 ...152 F1
Revill Cl 17 DN21 ...107 C3
Reygate Gr YO23 ...132 B2
Reynolds Cl HU14 ...68 E5
Reynolds Inf Sch DN35 ...153 D3
Reynolds Jun Sch DN35 ...153 D3
Reynolds St DN35 ...153 D2
Reynoldson St HU5 ...140 C2
Rhodena Ave YO16 ...122 D2
Rhodes St HU3 ...144 F5
Rhyl Cl 4 HU7 ...56 F7
Rialto Ave DN32 ...152 F1
Ribble St 4 HU3 ...145 B4
Ribblesdale 3 HU7 ...141 A6
Ribblesdale Cl YO16 ...122 F7
Ribston Cl 9 DN16 ...96 D1
Ribstone Gr YO31 ...131 B6
Riby Ct DN36 ...114 B5
Riby Rd Cabourne LN7 ...111 D6
Keelby DN41 ...101 A4
Scunthorpe DN17 ...150 E1
Stallingborough DN41 ...101 C4
Swallow LN7 ...112 A7
Riby Sq DN32 ...152 F5
Riby St DN31 ...153 A5
Ribycourt HU6 ...139 E7
Riccall Cl HU6 ...140 A6
Riccall CP Sch YO19 ...36 F1
Riccall La YO19 ...36 D1
Richard Cooper St DN14 ...149 E4
Richard St
Grimsby DN31 ...152 C4
Selby YO8 ...148 B5
Richardson Cl DN36 ...114 D8
Richardson St YO23 ...130 C2
Richdale Ave DN21 ...108 B1
Richmond Cl YO43 ...135 F3
Richmond Dr
Goole DN14 ...149 F5
10 Scunthorpe DN16 ...96 E2
Richmond Gdns HU17 ...136 D1
Richmond Rd
Cleethorpes DN35 ...153 E1
Grimsby DN34 ...152 A2
Kingston upon Hull HU13 ...143 E2
Thorne/Moorends DN8 ...79 B2
Richmond St
Bridlington YO15 ...122 D1
2 Kingston upon Hull HU5 ...145 B8
York YO31 ...130 E5
Richmond Way 2 HU17 ...55 E8
Richmond Wlk HU17 ...136 D1
Rickaby Cl YO16 ...122 D4
Ridding Cres DN14 ...64 A1
Ridding La DN14 ...64 A1
Riddings Infants Sch DN17 ...96 C2
Riddings Jun Sch DN17 ...96 C2
Ridge View DN20 ...98 C2
Ridge Way DN17 ...150 E5
Ridgestone Ave HU11 ...142 E7
Ridgeway YO26 ...129 B3
Ridgeway Rd HU5 ...144 B7
Ridgeway The DN34 ...102 B2
Ridgewood Ave 6 DN3 ...92 A1
Ridgewood Dr DN15 ...82 A4
Riding Fields Sq HU17 ...154 C3
Riding Mews HU17 ...154 B3
Ridings The
Beverley HU17 ...136 C6
Cottingham HU16 ...138 E6
East Ella HU5 ...144 A8
Great Driffield YO25 ...125 A6
15 North Ferriby HU14 ...69 A4
Ridsdale HU7 ...140 F7
Rifle Butts Quarry Nature Reserve* YO43 ...41 D5
Rigby Cl HU17 ...136 D7
Rileston Pl 12 DN16 ...96 D1
Rillington Ave HU16 ...139 A5
Rimswell Gr HU9 ...142 A2
Ring Beck La HU15 ...68 A8
Ringley Mdws 5 YO15 ...4 C3
Ringrose St HU3 ...144 F5
Ringstead Garth 4 HU7 ...57 A5
Ringstone Rd
Bishopthorpe YO23 ...133 B5
York YO30 ...126 F3
Ringwood Cl DN16 ...151 B1
Ripley Cl
Bridlington YO16 ...122 D5
Kingston upon Hull HU6 ...140 B7
Ripley Ct DN15 ...150 B6
Ripley Gr 3 YO32 ...13 E5
Ripley Pl YO43 ...135 D4
Riplingham Rd
Kingston upon Hull HU10 ...143 A8
Skidby HU10 ...138 A1
Ripon Ave HU17 ...136 E1
Ripon Cl DN17 ...150 C3
Ripon St DN31 ...152 C3
Ripon Way HU9 ...146 C8
Risby Garth HU16 ...55 C4
Risby Gr HU6 ...139 F5
Risby Hill HU20 ...55 A4
Risby La HU17 ...55 B7
Risby Medieval Village* DN15 ...83 A2
Risby Pl HU17 ...154 A1
Risby Rd DN15 ...82 F1
Rise Cl HU11 ...45 C5
Rise La Catwick HU17 ...45 D8
Rise HU11 ...45 D5
Rise Rd HU11 ...45 F7
Rise The
7 North Ferriby HU14 ...69 A5
Scunthorpe DN17 ...96 C2
South Ferriby DN18 ...84 A8
Risedale 21 LN7 ...111 B4
Riseway HU11 ...45 C5
Risewood YO41 ...15 B2
Rishworth Cl 5 HU7 ...57 A6
Rishworth Gr YO30 ...126 F2
Riston CE VC Prim Sch HU11 ...45 C5
Riston Rd HU17 ...45 C7
Riston St HU3 ...145 C5
Rivan Ave 5 DN33 ...113 E8
Rivan Gr 6 DN33 ...113 E8
Rivelin Cres DN16 ...151 A4
Rivelin Pl DN16 ...151 A4
Rivelin Rd DN16 ...151 A3
Rivelin Way YO30 ...126 F2
River Cl 2 Barlby YO8 ...49 B5
Goole DN14 ...149 F5
River Gr HU4 ...144 E3
River Head YO25 ...124 F3
River Head Dr 3 YO25 ...124 F3
River La Fishlake DN7 ...92 D8
Market Weighton YO43 ...40 F2
West Haddlesey YO8 ...62 A5
River Mdw DN20 ...98 B1
River St 1 Selby YO8 ...148 D6
York YO23 ...156 B1
River View 1 Barlby YO8 ...49 B5
26 Barton-upon-Humber DN18 ...84 F8
Goole DN14 ...65 C3

River View *continued*
– Kingston upon Hull HU13 143 F1
River Wlk DN14 65 C4
Riverbank Cl DN17 95 D5
Riverbank Rise 24 DN18 84 E8
Riverdale 4 DN14 61 D4
Riverdale Rd
– Kilpin DN14 65 C1
– Scunthorpe DN16 151 A3
Riversdale 17 YO32 13 F5
Riversdale Dr DN14 149 F5
Riversdale Rd HU6 140 D6
Riverside
– 11 Broughton DN20 98 B2
– Great Driffield YO25 124 F3
– Rawcliffe DN14 64 A2
– Scotter DN21 107 C4
Riverside Cl
– 1 Elvington YO41 27 C2
– 6 Great Driffield YO25 124 F3
– West Haddlesey YO8 62 A5
Riverside Cres YO32 127 F6
Riverside Ct
– 5 Hessle HU13 69 E4
– Rawcliffe DN14 64 A2
Riverside Dr DN35 103 D1
Riverside Gdns
– 2 Elvington YO41 27 C2
– 2 Poppleton YO26 12 F1
Riverside Mews 5 YO25 124 F3
Riverside Specl Sch DN14 149 E5
Riverside Wlk
– 1 Poppleton YO26 12 F1
– 5 Strensall YO32 14 A7
Riversvale Dr 21 YO26 12 F1
Riverview Ave HU14 69 A4
Riverview Gdns HU7 140 E7
Riverview Rd HU17 137 C4
Rivesby Ave DN16 151 A3
Riviera Dr YO15 123 B6
Rix Rd HU7 141 A3
Roall La DN14 61 F4
Robert Cl
– Immingham DN40 87 B1
– 3 Withernsea HU19 75 A6
Robert St
– Scunthorpe DN15 151 B7
– Selby YO8 148 C5
Robert Wilkinson Prim Sch YO32 14 A7
Robert Wood Ave HU17 154 A2
Roberts St DN32 153 A3
Robertson Cl YO42 29 A3
Robin Gr 6 YO24 129 F3
Robin Hood Cres 5 DN3 92 A1
Robin Hood Rd 3 DN3 92 A1
Robinia Dr HU4 144 C2
Robinson Cl DN15 150 E8
Robinson Ct YO1 156 C2
Robinson Dr YO24 129 B2
Robinson La DN31 153 A6
Robinson Rd DN40 87 E2
Robinson Row HU1 155 B2
Robinson St E DN32 152 E3
Robinson's Gr DN20 109 A5
Robinson's La DN36 114 B1
Roborough Cl HU7 141 B8
Robson Ave HU6 140 B8
Robson Rd DN35 153 D3
Robson Way
– Kingston upon Hull HU7 141 D7
– 6 Preston HU12 72 C7
Rochdale Rd DN16 151 A1
Roche Ave YO31 130 E8
Roche Dr DN14 149 E6
Rochester Ave HU4 144 A3
Rochester Cl DN17 150 C3
Rochester Ct 2 DN35 103 D1
Rockford Ave HU8 141 B3
Rockford Gr HU8 141 B3
Rockingham Ave YO31 131 A5
Rockingham Ct 10 DN34 102 B2
Rockley Ct HU10 143 F6
Rod Mill Rd DN16 151 E5
Rodney Cl HU2 155 A4
Roe La LS25 61 C7
Rogers Ct YO24 132 C8
Rokeby Ave HU4 144 B5
Rokeby Cl
– Beverley HU17 154 A4
– Kingston upon Hull HU4 144 B5
Rokeby Pk HU4 144 B5
Rokeby Pk Prim Sch HU4 144 B4
Roland Ct YO32 127 E3
Roland Simpson Cl 1 DN14 78 C8
Rolston Ave 3 YO31 127 E2
Rolston Cl HU9 142 C1
Rolston Rd HU18 134 C2
Roman Ave N 17 YO41 15 D2
Roman Ave S YO41 15 D1
Roman Camps* YO30 127 B2
Roman Rd DN20 108 D8
Roman Rigg YO43 53 D8
Roman Way DN17 150 F2
Romans Cl YO19 48 F8
Rombalds Croft 26 HU15 68 C6
Romford Gr HU9 142 E1
Romney Gdns 4 HU5 140 E2
Romsey Ct 11 DN34 102 B3
Romwood Cl 17 HU15 68 D6
Romyn Cl YO16 122 B2
Ronaldsway Cl 6 HU9 142 A3
Ronson Cl HU9 142 D3
Rook's La DN10 116 C5
Rookery Ave 10 DN33 102 E2
Rookery Croft 9 DN9 105 E6
Rookery Rd 18 DN41 101 F5
Rookery The
– Scawby DN20 108 F8
– 22 Scotter DN21 107 C3
Rooklands 2 DN21 107 C3
Rookley Cl 3 HU8 142 C5
Roos CE VC Prim Sch HU12 60 B1
Roos Cl HU17 136 F7
Rootas La HU17 43 A6
Rope Wlk
– Bridlington YO15 122 E2
– Thorne/Moorends DN8 93 A8
Roper St HU1 155 A2
Ropers Ct YO23 132 C3
Ropery Cl
– Beverley HU17 137 B4
– Keyingham HU12 73 D3
– 3 Kilham YO25 9 C3
– Thorngumbald HU12 72 E5
Ropery La 1 DN18 69 E1
Ropery Rd DN21 117 A2
Ropery St
– Grimsby DN32 152 F3
– Kingston upon Hull HU3 145 D5
Ropewalk* DN18 69 F1
Ropewalk The
– 9 Caistor LN7 111 B4
– York YO31 130 E5
Rosaire Pl DN33 113 E8
Rosalind Ave DN34 152 B3
Rosamond St 7 HU3 145 B4
Rose Carr Wlk HU18 134 D6
Rose Gdns 4 DN40 87 C2
Rose La HU17 43 C5
Rose Lea Cl 2 LS25 61 A7
Rose St YO31 130 C7
Rose Tree Gr YO32 127 D4
Rose Wlk DN15 151 C7
Roseacres DN14 65 C4
Roseberry Ave
– Bridlington YO15 122 C1
– 15 Hatfield DN7 92 D4
Roseberry Gr YO30 126 F3
Rosebery St YO26 129 F6
Rosecomb Way 6 YO32 127 D7
Rosecroft Way YO30 129 E8
Rosedale Leven HU17 45 B8
– Scunthorpe DN17 96 C1
– Waltham DN37 113 D7
Rosedale Ave
– Kingston upon Hull HU9 141 E1
– York YO26 129 C4
Rosedale Gr HU5 144 D7
Rosedale St YO10 130 D2
Rosedale Wlk
– Beverley HU17 136 E1
– Bridlington YO16 122 B4
Rosefields DN21 117 C1
Rosemary Ave DN34 102 C3
Rosemary Ct YO1 156 C2
Rosemary Pl YO1 156 C2
Rosemary Way
– Beverley HU17 154 C1
– Humberston DN36 103 C1
Rosemoor Cl 19 YO14 2 F8
Rosemount Cl 3 HU6 140 B8
Rosemount Dr DN16 151 B2
Rosemount Grange HU13 143 C3
Roseveare Ave DN34 152 A3
Rosewood Cl
– 3 Bridlington YO16 123 A6
– 4 Kingston upon Hull HU4 144 B7
Rosewood Way 25 DN16 96 D2
Rosewood Wlk YO16 123 A6
Rosewoods DN14 65 C8
Rosey Row 4 HU9 146 C7
Rosina Gr N DN32 153 B2
Rosina Gr S DN32 153 B2
Roslyn Cres HU12 72 C7
Roslyn Rd HU3 144 E7
Rosmead St HU9 146 D8
Rosper Rd DN40 87 A4
Ross La Bainton YO25 31 D7
– Winterton DN15 83 B5
Ross Rd DN31 153 B5
Rossall Cl 4 DN16 96 E2
Rosslyn St 1 YO30 130 A6
Rostun Rd HU12 60 B2
Roth Hill La YO19 37 E3
Rothbury Rd DN17 150 F3
Rothesay Cl 1 HU9 141 E1
Rothwell Ave 15 DN33 102 D2
Rothwell Rd
– Cabourne LN7 111 C3
– Scunthorpe DN15 150 D8
Rotsea La YO25 33 B7
Rotterdam Rd HU7 141 A5
Rotton Sykes La DN15 67 F2
Rougier St YO1 156 A2
Round Hill Link YO30 126 F2
Roundhay Rd YO15 122 D1
Roundway
– Grimsby DN34 152 C1
– 7 Immingham DN40 87 C1
Roundway The HU4 144 C5
Routh Ave HU17 154 C3
Roval Dr DN40 87 B1
Row La HU12 90 A7
Rowan Ave
– Beverley HU17 136 F7
– York YO32 127 D4
Rowan Cl
– 3 Barrow upon Humber DN19 85 C8
– Gateforth YO8 48 B1
– 2 Keelby DN41 101 A4
– 10 Thorne/Moorends DN8 79 B2
Rowan Cres 2 DN16 96 E2
Rowan Ct 7 DN19 86 A8
Rowan Dr
– Healing DN41 101 F5
– 6 Humberston DN36 114 D8
Rowan Garth HU16 55 C4
Rowan Pl YO32 127 D4
Rowan Wlk HU18 134 D2
Rowans The
– 23 Gainsborough DN21 117 C1
– Holme-on-Spalding-Moor YO42 40 A1
– 1 Westwoodside DN9 105 A2
Rowedale Cl 15 YO14 2 F8
Rowland Rd DN16 151 A6
Rowlandhall La DN14 50 E1
Rowlandson St DN31 152 F6
Rowley CE Sch HU20 55 A4
Rowley Ct 2 YO32 127 F7
Rowley Gr HU6 139 F5
Rowley Rd HU20 54 F3
Rowlston Gr HU9 142 A2
Rowmans The YO30 126 C4
Rowmills Rd DN16 151 C4
Rowntree Ave YO30 130 C8
Rowpit La HU17 45 C8
Rowston Cl 7 DN21 117 B1
Rowston St DN35 103 D3
Rowton Dr HU11 45 D2
Roxburgh St 1 HU5 145 B8
Roxby Cswy DN15 83 C4
Roxby Rd DN15 82 F4
Roxton Ave DN41 101 A5
Roxton Hall Dr 13 HU14 69 A5
Roxton Medieval Village* DN40 101 A7
Royal Chase YO24 132 F8
Royal Cres YO15 122 F2
Royal Ct 25 DN35 103 D1
Royal Dr DN14 79 A8
Royal Garth HU17 154 A1
Royal Hull Hospitals NHS Trust HU3 145 C6
Royal St DN31 152 E6
Royal Wlk HU16 139 D5
Royd's Rd YO8 61 F6
Royston Gr HU8 141 B1
Ruard Rd DN19 86 B8
Ruards La DN19 71 A1
Ruby St 3 YO23 130 B1
Rudcarr La YO19 14 E1
Rudding Dr YO16 122 D7
Ruddings YO19 38 A8
Ruddings Cl 9 YO32 127 C8
Ruddings La YO42 38 E2
Ruddings The YO8 148 A4
Rudgate La DN14 78 E4
Rudham Ave DN32 102 F2
Rudston Beacon* YO25 9 F4
Rudston Gr HU9 142 A1
Rudston Monolith* YO25 9 F6
Rudston Rd YO25 9 F2
Rue De Nozay 2 DN20 97 E4
Ruffhams Cl YO19 37 F8
Rufford Rd 3 DN35 103 C2
Rufforth Dr HU17 43 D5
Rufforth Garth HU7 141 C8
Rufforth Prim Sch YO23 24 C6
Rugby Rd DN16 151 A4
Rugby St 5 HU3 145 B4
Ruislip Cl HU8 142 A5
Runcorn Garth HU4 144 B3
Rundle Ct 29 YO42 29 A3
Runner End YO43 40 A1
Runswick Ave YO26 129 B4
Runswick Ct DN32 153 A2
Runswick Rd DN32 153 B2
Rupert Rd 9 DN33 102 E2
Rushcarr La DN17 95 C1
Rusholme La YO8 64 A5
Rushtons Way DN20 108 F5
Rushwood Cl 6 YO32 13 F5
Ruskin St HU3 145 B6
Ruskington Cl DN31 102 C5
Russell Ct 13 DN35 103 D1
Russell Dr
– 20 Keyingham HU12 73 C4
– York YO30 129 E8
Russell Rd DN14 149 B4
Russell St
– Kingston upon Hull HU2 155 A3
– York YO23 130 B2
Russell Wlk DN17 107 D7
Russet Cl 12 DN15 96 B7
Russet Dr YO31 131 B5
Rustenburg St HU9 141 D1
Rustic La DN21 117 F6
Ruswarp Gr HU6 139 E6
Rutherglen Dr HU9 142 A3
Rutland Cl YO23 132 A3
Rutland Dr 16 DN36 114 A7
Rutland Rd
– Goole DN14 149 D6
– Kingston upon Hull HU5 144 E8
– Scunthorpe DN16 151 D3
Rutland St DN32 153 A4
Ryburn Cl YO30 126 F2
Rydal Ave
– 11 Grimsby DN33 113 D8
– York YO31 131 A6
Rydal Gr HU16 138 E6
Rydale Ct HU5 140 E3
Rydales The HU5 140 E3
Ryde Ave HU5 140 D3
Ryde St HU5 140 D2
Rye Cl YO32 127 C8
Ryecroft 7 YO32 14 A6
Ryecroft Ave
– 10 Norton DN6 76 E2
– York YO24 132 C7
Ryecroft Cl YO31 131 C8
Ryecroft Dr HU19 75 A6
Ryecroft Gdns DN14 62 A2
Ryecroft Rd DN6 76 E1
Ryedale 12 HU15 68 D6
Ryedale Ave DN15 83 A6
Ryedale Way YO8 148 C3
Ryehill Cl YO32 127 D5
Ryehill Gr HU9 141 F2
Ryehill La HU12 73 A4
Ryelands Ave YO16 123 A6
Ryemoor Rd YO32 127 C8
Rylatt Pl YO26 129 B3
Rymer Pl DN35 103 D2
Rysome La HU19 75 C1
Rysome Rd HU12 90 B7

S

Sabina Ct HU8 141 E7
Sable Cl HU4 144 C2
Sackville Cl
– 5 Beverley HU17 55 E8
– 14 Immingham DN40 87 C1
Sackville Rd 15 DN40 87 C1
Sackville St DN34 152 C3
Sacred Gate HU12 72 D6
Sadberge Ct YO10 131 C3
Saddler's Way DN9 105 D3
Saddlers Cl
– 1 Copmanthorpe YO23 132 B3
– Huntington YO32 127 F2
Saddlers Way YO26 24 A6
Saddleworth Cl 19 HU7 57 A6
Saffron Dr 6 DN14 63 C1
Saffron Garth 15 HU12 74 D1
Saffrondale HU10 143 E7
Sage Cl HU17 154 B1
Sagefield Cl 6 DN33 113 D8
Sailors Wharf HU9 146 C6
Sails Dr YO10 131 B3
Sainsbury Way HU4 144 A1
St Abbs Cl HU9 155 C1
St Aelreds Cl YO31 130 F4
St Aelreds RC Prim Sch YO31 131 B5
St Aidan Cres YO16 122 E4
St Aidan Ct YO16 122 E5
St Aidan Rd YO16 122 E4
St Aiden Cl YO43 135 E3
St Aiden Way HU9 141 F2
St Alban Cl YO16 122 E4
St Alban Rd YO16 122 E4
St Alban's Ct HU11 46 D3
St Albans Ave DN31 152 A4
St Albans Cl
– 7 Beverley HU17 136 E1
– Hibaldstow DN20 108 F5
– Scunthorpe DN17 150 C3
St Albans Mount HU6 140 C4
St Andrew Pl YO1 156 C2
St Andrew Rd YO16 122 E4
St Andrew St HU17 154 B2
St Andrew's CE VA Prim Sch HU7 140 E8
St Andrew's Cl
– Middleton-on-the-Wolds YO25 31 C4
– Paull HU12 72 A5
– Redbourne DN21 108 E3
St Andrew's Dr DN15 82 A4
St Andrew's Mount HU10 143 C8
St Andrew's St DN21 108 A1
St Andrew's Terr 6 DN14 149 C4
St Andrew's Way
– 2 Barnby Dun DN3 92 A3
– Epworth DN9 105 E7
St Andrewgate YO1 156 B2
St Andrews Ave DN17 96 C1
St Andrews Ct DN14 149 C4
St Andrews Gr 10 DN7 92 D4
St Andrews La 5 DN40 87 B2
St Andrews Prim Sch HU10 143 C7
St Andrews Way HU8 141 C3
St Ann Ct YO10 130 E2
St Ann's Ave DN34 152 B2
St Ann's Ct YO10 130 D2
St Anne's Cl HU17 137 B5
St Anne's Com Specl Sch HU15 68 E5
St Anne's Dr HU16 139 D6
St Anne's Rd 8 DN41 101 A5
St Anne's Wlk
– 9 Brough HU15 68 D6
– Driffield YO25 125 A3
St Annes Rd YO15 122 F3
St Anthony Rd YO16 122 E4
St Anthony's Dr 24 HU12 72 D7
St Anthony's Pk 25 HU12 72 D7
St Athony's Cl HU6 140 B4
St Aubyn's Pl YO24 130 A2
St Augustine Ave DN32 152 E1
St Augustine Cres DN16 151 B1
St Augustine Dr HU11 45 E2
St Augustine Webster RC Prim Sch DN15 150 D8
St Augustine's Ct 2 HU5 140 D3
St Augustine's Dr YO16 122 E5
St Augustine's Gate 30 HU12 72 C7
St Augustine's Gr YO16 122 E5
St Austells Cl HU9 141 F2
St Barbara's Cres 8 DN15 82 B4
St Barnabas' CE Prim Sch
– Barnetby le Wold DN38 99 B4
– Clifton Park YO26 129 F5
St Barnabas Ct
– 4 Kingston upon Hull HU3 145 C4
– 13 York YO26 129 F5
St Barnabas Dr HU14 69 C7
St Barnabas Rd DN38 99 B4
St Bartholemew's Way HU8 142 A5
St Bartholomew's Cl 17 DN41 101 A4
St Bede Ct HU4 144 E5
St Bede's RC Sch DN16 151 B2
St Benedict Cl HU7 57 B5
St Benedict Rd YO23 156 A1
St Bernadette's RC Prim Sch DN16 151 C2
St Bernard's Cl 9 DN20 97 E4
St Boltophs Cl 4 WF11 61 A2
St Botolph's Rd DN16 151 C3
St Bridget's Ct YO23 156 B1
St Catherine's Dr DN7 92 C2
St Catherines YO30 126 D6
St Catherines Cl YO30 126 C5
St Catherines Cres 8 DN16 96 D2
St Catherines Ct
– 6 Grimsby DN34 102 C3
– Kingston upon Hull HU5 140 E2
– Scunthorpe DN16 151 D2
St Catherines Dr HU17 43 C6
St Catherines Pl YO24 130 A3
St Chad DN19 85 D8
St Chad Cres YO16 122 E4
St Chad Gr YO16 122 E4
St Chad Rd YO16 122 E4
St Chad's Rd DN16 151 D3
St Chads Wharf YO23 133 C8
St Charles' RC Prim Sch HU2 155 A3
St Christopher Rd YO16 122 E4
St Christopher's Rd DN36 114 C8
St Clares Wlk 12 DN20 98 C2
St Clement's Gr YO23 130 C2
St Clements Pl HU2 155 A4
St Clements Way
– 17 Holton le Clay DN36 114 A5
– Kingston upon Hull HU9 141 F2
St Columba Rd YO16 122 F5
St Crispins Cl DN40 86 E4
St Cuthbert Rd YO16 122 E4
St David Cl HU17 154 B2
St David La YO15 5 B3
St David's Cl HU16 139 D6
St David's View 9 DN14 64 E4
St Davids Cres DN17 96 C2
St Deny's Cl 1 DN40 86 E3
St Denys' Rd YO1 156 C2
St Edmunds YO41 15 D2
St Edmunds's Ct 4 HU5 139 D2
St Edward's Cl YO24 132 F8
St Edwins Cl 27 DN7 92 D4
St Ellens Ct HU17 154 B2
St Francis Ave DN31 152 A4
St Francis Ct 1 HU5 139 D2
St Francis Gr DN37 101 E1
St Francis Prep Sch YO25 125 E7
St George's Ave
– Bridlington YO15 122 E3
– Hatfield DN7 92 C3
St George's Ct DN21 108 F3
St George's Pl YO24 129 F2
St George's Prim Sch HU3 145 A6
St George's RC Prim Sch YO10 130 D2
St George's Rd HU3 145 A5
St George's Wlk HU9 142 B2
St Georges Cl 19 DN8 93 B7
St Georges Gn DN14 149 D6
St Georges Rd 16 DN8 93 B7
St Giles' Ave DN33 102 E1
St Giles Ct
– Kingston upon Hull HU9 142 C1
– York YO31 156 B3
St Giles Rd YO30 126 B5
St Giles Way YO23 132 A2
St Giles's Croft HU17 154 A2
St Gregory's Mews YO1 156 A2

St Hedda's Ct 6 HU5 . . .139 D2
St Helena Gdns 3 HU5 . .140 E2
St Helen's Ave YO42 . . . . .29 B4
St Helen's Cl YO42 . . . . . . .29 B4
St Helen's Cres DN37 . . .113 D5
St Helen's Dr 10 HU15 . . . .68 D6
St Helen's La YO14 . . . . .3 C6
St Helen's Rd
Brigg DN20 . . . . .98 C2
Pocklington YO42 . . . . .29 B4
5 York YO24 . . . . .132 E8
St Helen's Rise YO19 . . . .38 A7
St Helen's Sq
Barmby Moor YO42 . . . . .28 D4
3 Market Weighton
YO43 . . . . .135 D4
York YO1 . . . . .156 B2
St Helen's Well* YO43 . . .41 D5
St Helens Ave 13 DN33 . . .102 E2
St Helens Way DN21 . . . .119 B2
St Helier's Rd DN35 . . . .153 E3
St Hilda St
3 Bridlington YO15 . . . . . .122 E2
Kingston upon Hull HU3 . . .140 E1
St Hilda's Ave DN34 . . . .152 B2
St Hildas Mews YO10 . . . .131 B4
St Hugh's Ave DN35 . . . .153 D2
St Hugh's Cres DN16 . . . .151 C4
St Hugh's Sec Specl Sch
DN16 . . . . .151 B5
St Hughs Hospl DN32 . . .102 F2
St Hybald's Gr DN20 . . . .108 F7
St Ives Cl HU7 . . . . .141 C7
St Ives Cres DN34 . . . . . .102 C3
St James Ave
Grimsby DN34 . . . . .152 A2
Hatfield DN7 . . . . .92 C3
St James' CE VC Prim Sch
HU7 . . . . .141 C6
St James Cl
12 Crowle DN17 . . . . .94 D7
Kingston upon Hull HU7 . . .141 D7
York YO30 . . . . .126 E3
St James' Ct DN34 . . . . .152 C2
St James Ct
Rawcliffe DN14 . . . . .64 A1
Scunthorpe DN15 . . . . .151 A6
St James Mount YO24 . . .130 A2
St James Pl 5 YO24 . . . .129 D1
St James' Rd YO15 . . . . .122 D1
St James Rd
22 Brigg DN20 . . . . .98 C2
Welton HU14 . . . . .68 F5
St James' Sch DN34 . . . .152 C2
St James St HU3 . . . . . . .145 D5
St James Terr YO8 . . . . . .148 C5
St James's Rd DN20 . . . .108 E8
St Joan's Dr DN20 . . . . . .108 E8
St John Mews YO8 . . . . . .148 B7
St John of Beverley RC VA
Prim Sch HU17 . . . . . . .154 C4
St John St
Beverley HU17 . . . . .154 B2
York YO31 . . . . .156 B3
St John's Ave YO16 . . . . .122 C3
St John's Ave W YO16 . . .122 C2
St John's Cl
Bridlington YO16 . . . . .122 C2
11 Pocklington YO42 . . . . . . .28 F4
St John's Cres YO31 . . . .156 C4
St John's Gdns YO25 . . . .124 E3
St John's Gr HU9 . . . . . . .141 F1
St John's Pl 2 YO25 . . . .124 F3
St John's Rd
Great Driffield YO25 . . . . .124 E3
8 Humberston DN36 . . . . .114 C8
Scunthorpe DN16 . . . . .151 C2
9 Stamford Bridge YO41 . . .15 D2
St John's St
Bridlington YO16 . . . . .122 D4
15 Howden DN14 . . . . .65 A7
St John's Well*
Harpham YO25 . . . . .21 F8
Scunthorpe DN16 . . . . . .96 D1
St John's Wlk
Bridlington YO16 . . . . .122 C3
1 Great Driffield YO25 . . .124 F3
Kingston upon Hull
HU13 . . . . .143 F2
St Johns Cl 1 HU17 . . . . . .55 F8
St Johns Ct
Goole DN14 . . . . .149 C4
Grimsby DN34 . . . . .152 A1
Kingston upon Hull HU6 . . .140 D4
St Joseph Dr HU4 . . . . . .144 C5
St Joseph's Cath Prim Sch
DN14 . . . . .149 D5
St Joseph's RC Prim Sch
Cleethorpes DN35 . . . . .103 B2
Goole DN14 . . . . .149 D5
St Jude Gr YO16 . . . . .122 D4
St Jude Rd YO16 . . . . .122 D4
St Jude's Ct 3 HU5 . . . . .139 D2
St Julian's Wells
HU10 . . . . .143 D7
St Katherine's Rd 2
HU15 . . . . .53 F1
St Lawrence Ave
Kingston upon Hull
HU16 . . . . .138 F5
Snaith DN14 . . . . .78 B8
St Lawrence Rd DN7 . . . .92 C4
St Lawrence Sq HU11 . . . .45 F8
St Lawrence's Pl
DN16 . . . . .151 D3
St Lawrence's Rd
DN16 . . . . .151 D2
St Lawrences CE Prim Sch
YO10 . . . . .130 E3
St Leonard's Ave
DN31 . . . . .152 A4
St Leonard's Cl 2 YO25 . .22 D1
St Leonard's Pl YO30 . . . .156 B3
St Leonard's Rd
Beverley HU17 . . . . .136 C6
Kingston upon Hull HU5 . . .140 D2
St Leonards Ave YO8 . . . .49 B4
St Luke's Cl DN7 . . . . .92 C2
St Luke's Cres 12 DN36 . .114 C8
St Luke's Ct DN32 . . . . . .152 F4
St Luke's Gr YO30 . . . . . .130 B7
St Luke's Sch DN16 . . . . .151 D3
St Luke's St HU3 . . . . . . .155 A2
St Lukes Ct HU10 . . . . . . .143 F8
St Margaret's Cl 9
DN37 . . . . .101 F1
St Margaret's Cres 4
DN40 . . . . .100 E8
St Margaret's Terr
YO1 . . . . .130 E4
St Margaret's Wlk
DN16 . . . . .151 C1
St Margarets Ave
HU16 . . . . .138 E6
St Margarets Cl
Driffield YO25 . . . . .124 E3
Kingston upon Hull
HU16 . . . . .138 E6
St Margarets Ct 3 HU8 .142 C6
St Margarets View 4
HU11 . . . . .45 C5
St Mark St HU8 . . . . .155 C4
St Mark's Gr YO30 . . . . . .126 E2
St Mark's Rd 18 DN36 . . .114 C8
St Mark's Sq HU3 . . . . . .145 D4
St Martin's Cl
Blyton DN21 . . . . .117 F5
2 Burton Agnes YO25 . . . . .10 A2
Fangfoss YO41 . . . . .28 C8
St Martin's Cres
6 Grimsby DN33 . . . . .102 E2
Scawby DN20 . . . . .108 E8
St Martin's Ct HU17 . . . .154 A2
St Martin's Dr 1 YO25 . . .10 A2
St Martin's Gr YO16 . . . .122 C2
St Martin's La YO1 . . . . .156 A2
St Martin's Pl 16 DN41 . . .101 A4
St Martin's Prep Sch
DN32 . . . . .152 D1
St Martin's Rd
Scawby DN20 . . . . .108 E8
Thorngumbald HU12 . . . . . . .72 E5
St Martins Ave 2 HU4 . . .144 E6
St Martins CE Prim Sch
DN9 . . . . .106 A3
St Martins CE VA Prim Sch
YO41 . . . . .28 C8
St Martins Dr YO16 . . . . .122 C3
St Mary Queen of Martyrs RC
Prim Sch HU7 . . . . .140 F7
St Mary's YO30 . . . . .156 A3
St Mary's Ave
1 Barnetby le Wold DN38 . . .99 B4
12 Hemingbrough YO8 . . . . .49 F1
Kingston upon Hull HU5 . . .139 D4
St Mary's CE Prim Sch
HU17 . . . . .136 D5
St Mary's CE VC Prim Sch
HU17 . . . . .136 D5
St Mary's Cl
Beverley HU17 . . . . .136 D5
Brough HU15 . . . . .68 C7
Grimsby DN32 . . . . .153 C2
15 Haxby YO32 . . . . .13 E5
Strensall YO32 . . . . .14 A7
7 Thorngumbald HU12 . . . .72 E5
St Mary's Coll HU6 . . . . .140 C5
St Mary's Cres YO16 . . . .122 D4
St Mary's Ct
9 Scunthorpe DN15 . . . . . . .96 B7
York YO24 . . . . .156 A1
St Mary's Dr
Hatfield DN7 . . . . .92 C2
38 Hedon HU12 . . . . .72 D7
St Mary's Gr YO10 . . . . . .131 C4
St Mary's La
5 Barton-upon-Humber
DN18 . . . . .84 F8
York YO30 . . . . .156 A3
St Mary's Mkt Weighton RC
Prim Sch YO43 . . . . .135 E3
St Mary's Mus* YO1 . . . .156 B2
St Mary's RC Prim Sch
Brigg DN20 . . . . .98 C3
Grimsby DN32 . . . . .152 F4
Selby YO8 . . . . .148 B2
St Mary's RC Sch
DN33 . . . . .102 D2
St Mary's Rd DN7 . . . . .92 C2
St Mary's Terr
Beverley HU17 . . . . .154 A3
York YO30 . . . . .156 A3
St Mary's Wlk
Beverley HU17 . . . . .154 A4
Bridlington YO16 . . . . .122 D4
St Marys CE Prim Sch
YO23 . . . . .24 D3
St Marys Cl
Cottingwith YO42 . . . . .38 C5
6 South Field HU13 . . . . . . .69 E5
St Marys La HU17 . . . . . .154 A3
St Marys Mount HU16 . .139 C6
St Marys RC VA Prim Sch
YO15 . . . . .122 C2
St Marys Terr YO30 . . . . .156 A3
St Matthew St HU3 . . . . .145 B5
St Matthew's Cl 4 YO19 . .36 D8
St Matthew's Ct HU17 . . .154 B2
St Matthew's Rd 11
DN36 . . . . .114 C8
St Matthews Ct HU17 . . .154 B2
St Maurice's Rd YO31 . . .156 C3
St Mawes Cres DN34 . . . .152 A3
St Mews 34 HU12 . . . . .72 C7
St Michael's Cl
Kingston upon Hull HU8 . . .142 B5
Skidby HU16 . . . . .138 A8
13 Thorne/Moorends DN8 . .93 B7
St Michael's Cres
DN16 . . . . .151 C4
St Michael's Ct DN19 . . . .86 A8
St Michael's Dr
39 Hedon HU12 . . . . .72 D7
Thorne DN8 . . . . .93 B7
St Michael's Mount
Kingston upon Hull HU6 . . .140 C5
14 Swanland HU14 . . . . .69 B7
St Michael's Rd DN34 . . .102 B2
St Michael's Wlk 3 YO15 . . .4 D3
St Monica's Ct 3 HU5 . . .140 C3
St Monicas Cl YO42 . . . . .39 B6
St Nectan Cl 9 HU3 . . . .145 A4
St Nicholas Ave
Kingston upon Hull HU4 . . .144 C2
York YO19 . . . . .133 D4
St Nicholas Cl
Copmanthorpe YO23 . . . . . .132 A3
8 Newbald YO43 . . . . .53 F7
St Nicholas Cres
YO23 . . . . .132 A3
St Nicholas Croft YO23 . .24 E3
St Nicholas Dr
Beverley HU17 . . . . .154 C2
Grimsby DN37 . . . . .102 B3
Hornsea HU18 . . . . .134 C6
St Nicholas Fields Nature
Reserve* YO10 . . . . .130 F4
St Nicholas Gate HU12 . .72 D7
St Nicholas Gdns HU4 . .144 C3
St Nicholas Pk 6 HU19 . . .75 A6
St Nicholas Pl 1 YO10 . .130 F3
St Nicholas Rd
Beverley HU17 . . . . .154 C2
Copmanthorpe YO23 . . . . . .132 A3
Thorne/Moorends DN8 . . . . .93 A8
St Nicholas' VA Prim Sch
HU6 . . . . .140 C4
St Nicholas Way 22 YO32 .13 E5
St Norbert's RC Prim Sch
DN17 . . . . .94 D7
St Olaf's Dr DN32 . . . . . .152 D2
St Olave's Rd YO30 . . . . .156 A4
St Olave's Sch YO30 . . . .156 A3
St Oswald Ct 5 HU5 . . . .139 D2
St Oswald Rd YO16 . . . . .122 E4
St Oswald's CE Prim Sch
YO10 . . . . .133 E7
St Oswald's Cl YO41 . . . . .27 F6
St Oswald's Rd YO10 . . . .133 D8
St Oswalds Ct YO10 . . . . .133 E7
St Patrick's Gn 14 HU12 . .74 D1
St Paul St HU2 . . . . .155 A4
St Paul's CE Prim Sch
YO24 . . . . .130 A3
St Paul's Rd
Gainsborough DN21 . . . . . .117 A2
Scunthorpe DN16 . . . . .151 B2
St Paul's Sq YO24 . . . . . .130 A3
St Paul's Terr YO24 . . . . .130 A4
St Paulinus Cres 20
HU15 . . . . .68 C6
St Pauls Dr HU17 . . . . . . .137 E8
St Pauls Mews YO24 . . . .130 A3
St Pauls Way HU17 . . . . .137 E8
St Peter St HU9 . . . . .155 C2
St Peter's Ave
Cleethorpes DN35 . . . . .153 E2
Kingston upon Hull
HU10 . . . . .143 E6
Scunthorpe DN16 . . . . .96 D2
St Peter's CE Prim Sch
DN35 . . . . .153 F2
St Peter's Cl
10 Holton le Clay DN36 . . .114 A5
16 Howden DN14 . . . . .65 A7
St Peter's Cres 7 DN36 .114 C8
St Peter's Gr
9 Scotter DN21 . . . . .107 C3
York YO30 . . . . .156 A4
St Peter's Rd Drax YO8 . . .63 F5
19 Scotter DN21 . . . . .107 C3
St Peter's Sch YO30 . . . .156 A4
St Peter's Sq 14 YO42 . . . .29 A4
St Peters Cl
East/West Stockwith
DN21 . . . . .116 E5
Hutton Cranswick YO25 . . . . .32 E8
Rufforth YO26 . . . . .129 A5
St Peters Ct YO30 . . . . . .156 A4
St Peters Gr DN37 . . . . . .101 E1
St Peters Orch DN18 . . . . .69 F1
St Peters View HU11 . . . .142 F6
St Peters Wlk HU12 . . . . . .59 D2
St Philip's Gr YO30 . . . . .130 A8
St Philips Rd HU12 . . . . . .73 C4
St Quintin Field YO25 . . .125 F7
St Quintin Pk 9 YO25 . . . .34 B2
St Quintins Cl 6 HU9 . . .146 C8
St Richard's RC Prim Sch
HU9 . . . . .142 C1
St Sampsons Sq YO1 . . .156 B2
St Saviour's Pl YO1 . . . . .156 C2
St Saviourgate YO1 . . . . .156 C2
St Silas St HU2 . . . . .155 B4
St Stephen Rd YO16 . . . .122 E4
St Stephen's Cl HU10 . . . .138 C2
St Stephen's Cres 4
HU15 . . . . .66 D8
St Stephen's Rd YO24 . . .129 C2
St Stephen's Sq YO24 . . .129 C1
St Stephens Cl YO25 . . . .124 E3
St Stephens Mews
YO30 . . . . .127 A2
St Stephens St HU2 . . . . .145 D6
St Swithin's Wlk YO26 . . .129 E4
St Thomas Moore Rd
HU4 . . . . .144 A4
St Thomas More RC Prim Sch
HU4 . . . . .144 B4
St Thomas' Pl YO31 . . . . .156 B4
St Thomas Rd YO16 . . . . .122 E4
St Thomas' Rd 14 DN36 . .114 C8
St Thomas's Cl 2 YO10 . .131 C4
St Thomas's Grange 2
HU5 . . . . .139 D2
St Vincent's Ave DN15 . . .96 D7
St Vincent's RC Prim Sch
HU5 . . . . .140 D2
St Wilfred Rd YO16 . . . . .122 E3
St Wilfred's RC Prim Sch
YO31 . . . . .156 C3
St Wilfrid's Cl 7 YO32 . . . .14 B6
St Wilfrid's Cres 9 YO8 . .48 D1
St Wilfrid's Ct YO31 . . . .156 C3
St Wilfrid's Rd 8 YO32 . . .14 B6
St Wilfrids Cl HU12 . . . . . .73 E3
St Williams Coll YO31 . . .156 B3
St Wulstan Cl YO31 . . . . .130 E7
Saints Cl HU9 . . . . .141 F2
Salacon Way 1 DN32 . . .153 A5
Saladine Ct 16 DN41 . . . .101 F5
Salamander Cl DN31 . . . .152 B4
Salcey Cl 23 HU7 . . . . .56 F6
Salents La YO17 . . . . .6 B6
Sales La DN14 . . . . .78 B3
Salisbury Ave
Beverley HU17 . . . . .136 E1
Goole DN14 . . . . .149 E4
Hornsea HU18 . . . . .134 C2
24 Waltham DN37 . . . . . . .113 D6
Salisbury Cl
Morton DN21 . . . . .117 A3
Scunthorpe DN17 . . . . .150 C3
Salisbury Rd YO26 . . . . .129 F5
Salisbury St
6 Gainsborough DN21 . . .117 B2
Northfield HU13 . . . . .143 D1
Sculcoates HU5 . . . . .140 B2
Salmon Gr HU6 . . . . .140 B4
Salmonby Rd
1 Scunthorpe DN17 . . . . . . .96 C2
Scunthorpe DN17 . . . . .150 E1
Salmond Rd 5 YO24 . . . .129 B1
Salsbury Ave DN34 . . . . .152 B2
Salt End La HU12 . . . . .72 A7
Saltash Rd HU4 . . . . .144 A2
Saltaugh Rd HU12 . . . . . . .88 B8
Saltburn Gr DN32 . . . . . .153 A1
Saltburn St HU3 . . . . . . .145 A4
Saltergate Rd DN17 . . . . .107 D7
Salters' La LN11 . . . . . . .120 E4
Saltford Ave HU9 . . . . . . .147 F8
Saltgrounds Rd HU15 . . . .68 B5
Salthouse La HU1 . . . . . .155 C2
Saltmarsh La HU12 . . . . . .89 D8
Saltmarshe Delph Nature
Reserve* DN14 . . . . .65 D1
Saltmarshe Sta DN14 . . . .65 E4
Salton Ave 4 HU5 . . . . . .139 E3
Saltshouse Rd HU8 . . . . .141 E6
Saltwell Pk 29 HU7 . . . . . . .56 F6
Salvesen Rd DN35 . . . . . .153 B5
Salvesen Way HU3 . . . . .145 A3
Samman Cl HU10 . . . . . .143 D6
Samman Rd HU17 . . . . . .154 C4
Samphire Cl DN36 . . . . . .115 C4
Sample Ave HU17 . . . . . .154 B4
Sampson St DN17 . . . . . . .81 A3
Samuel Ave DN32 . . . . . .153 B2
Sanbeds La DN9 . . . . . . .105 B2
Sancton Cl HU16 . . . . . . .138 E6
Sancton Rd YO43 . . . . . .135 E3
Sanctuary Way DN37 . . .102 B3
Sand Hutton CE VC Prim Sch
YO41 . . . . .15 B5
Sand Hutton Ct YO41 . . . .15 B5
Sand La
Barlby with Osgodby YO8 . . .49 B4
Broughton DN20 . . . . .97 D3
Bubwith YO8 . . . . .50 D5
Caistor LN7 . . . . .110 E4
Manton DN21 . . . . .108 A5
Messingham DN17 . . . . . . .107 A7
Newton on Derwent YO41 . . .28 B5
North Cave HU15 . . . . .53 D2
Sancton YO43 . . . . .53 D8
South Cliffe YO43 . . . . .52 E8
Thornton YO42 . . . . .39 D7
Wistow YO8 . . . . .48 E6
Wroot DN9 . . . . .104 C6
Sand Rd DN17 . . . . .106 B8
Sandacre Ct YO26 . . . . . .129 D5
Sandale Ct HU5 . . . . .139 E1
Sandbeck La DN21 . . . . .117 E6
Sandcroft Cl 4 YO24 . . . .132 D8
Sandcroft Rd YO24 . . . . .132 D8
Sanderson Cl
Driffield YO25 . . . . .124 D2
Sanderson Cl *continued*
Scunthorpe DN16 . . . . .151 A5
Sanderson's Bank
DN10 . . . . .104 C2
Sandfield Cl
Market Weighton YO43 . . . .135 B3
Scunthorpe DN17 . . . . .150 D1
Sandfield Dr 3 HU15 . . . . .68 C5
Sandfield Gn YO43 . . . . .135 B3
Sandford Cl HU7 . . . . .56 F5
Sandford St DN31 . . . . . .152 B4
Sandgate Rd YO16 . . . . .123 A6
Sandhall Dr DN14 . . . . . .149 F5
Sandhall Rd DN14 . . . . . . .65 C3
Sandhill La Brayton YO8 . .48 D2
Sutton upon Derwent
YO41 . . . . .27 E2
Sandhill Rd DN14 . . . . .81 B6
Sandholme
2 Haxby YO32 . . . . .13 F5
Market Weighton YO43 . . . .135 C3
Sandholme Cl 1 HU15 . . . .66 D8
Sandholme La HU17 . . . . .44 F8
Sandholme Pk HU15 . . . . .66 D8
Sandholme Rd HU15 . . . . .66 C8
Sandholme Way 4 DN14 .65 A7
Sandhouse Cres DN16 . .151 C5
Sandiacres 5 YO8 . . . . . . .48 D1
Sandlemere Cl 3 HU3 . . .145 A5
Sandmartin Ct YO24 . . . .132 D8
Sandmoor Cl HU8 . . . . . .142 B6
Sandown Cl YO24 . . . . . .129 E2
Sandpiper Ct HU18 . . . . .134 D6
Sandpiper Dr HU4 . . . . . .144 B1
Sandpits La HU11 . . . . . . .47 C1
Sandringham Cl
6 Bridlington YO16 . . . . . .122 D6
Haxby YO32 . . . . .127 C7
Kingston upon Hull
HU16 . . . . .139 A7
Sandringham Cres 15
DN17 . . . . .96 C2
Sandringham Dr
DN14 . . . . .149 B6
Sandringham Rd
DN35 . . . . .103 B2
Sandringham St
2 Kingston upon Hull
HU3 . . . . .145 A6
York YO10 . . . . .130 D2
Sands Cl Keadby DN17 . . . .95 D6
Reighton YO14 . . . . .3 D7
Sands Ct 3 HU14 . . . . .69 A4
Sands La Barmston YO25 . .22 F5
Bridlington YO15 . . . . .122 F3
Brough HU15 . . . . .68 C6
Ellerker HU15 . . . . .67 F6
Holme-on-Spalding-Moor
YO43 . . . . .39 F1
Hornsea HU18 . . . . .134 D4
Hunmanby YO14 . . . . .3 A8
Scotter DN21 . . . . .107 C3
South Ferriby DN18 . . . . . . .84 A7
Ulrome YO25 . . . . .23 B3
Sands Rd Barmston YO15 . .22 F7
Hunmanby YO14 . . . . .3 B7
Sands Top YO43 . . . . .53 E7
Sandsacre Ave YO16 . . .123 A6
Sandsacre Dr 1 YO16 . . .123 A6
Sandsacre Rd YO16 . . . .123 A6
Sandsacre Way YO16 . . .122 F6
Sandsfield Ave YO43 . . . . .40 E6
Sandstock Rd
Pocklington YO42 . . . . .29 A4
York YO31 . . . . .131 B7
Sandtoft Rd
Epworth DN9 . . . . .94 B3
Hatfield DN7 . . . . .93 A4
Sandwalk YO43 . . . . .135 C3
Sandway Ave 12 YO8 . . . . .48 B1
Sandway Cl 11 YO8 . . . . . .48 B1
Sandway Dr
Camblesforth YO8 . . . . .63 D4
1 Thorpe Willoughby YO8 . .48 B1
Sandwith Ct HU17 . . . . . .154 B4
Sandwith La YO8 . . . . .63 B4
Sandy Cl DN36 . . . . .115 C5
Sandy Gap YO32 . . . . . . .127 C7
Sandy La Harpham YO25 . . . .9 E2
Harton YO60 . . . . .15 B8
16 Haxby YO32 . . . . .13 E5
North Duffield YO8 . . . . .49 F8
Stockton on the Forest
YO32 . . . . .14 E4
Sandy Point HU9 . . . . . . .142 E5
Sandy Rise YO8 . . . . .148 C3
Sandycroft Cl HU10 . . . .139 A1
Sandyland 29 YO32 . . . . . .13 E5
Sandyridge YO26 . . . . . . .126 A1
Saner St HU3 . . . . .145 B6
Saner's Cl HU16 . . . . . . .139 B5
Santolina Way HU4 . . . . .144 C2
Sapperton Cl 16 HU7 . . . . .56 F6
Sapphire Gr 7 HU3 . . . . .145 A4
Sarah Rhodes La DN14 . . .65 C3
Sarge Cl 16 DN36 . . . . . . .114 A5
Sargent Ave YO23 . . . . . .132 F4
Sargent's Way 8 DN20 . .108 F5
Sargon Way DN31 . . . . . .102 C6
Sassaby Cl HU4 . . . . .144 C3
Saunby Gr DN35 . . . . . . .153 E3
Saunders Cres 21 YO42 . . .29 A3
Saunders Croft 4 HU17 . .55 B8
Saunders La HU17 . . . . . . .55 B7
Saunders St DN31 . . . . . .152 C4
Savage Rd YO15 . . . . .122 D2
Savery St HU9 . . . . .141 D1
Savile Cl HU17 . . . . .136 E6

Saville Gr YO30 ... 130 A8
Saville St HU1 ... 155 B2
Savoy Ct 12 DN36 ... 114 A7
Savoy Rd HU8 ... 141 F4
Sawcliffe Medieval Village* DN15 ... 82 F1
Sawley Cl HU18 ... 134 C5
Sawmill Yd 5 YO15 ... 122 E2
Sawston Ave HU5 ... 139 C2
Sawyer's Cres YO23 ... 132 C2
Sawyers Wlk 9 YO19 ... 26 F7
Saxby Gr 17 DN33 ... 102 D2
Saxby Hill DN20 ... 84 B3
Saxby Rd Bonby DN20 ... 84 B2
Kingston upon Hull HU8 ... 142 A5
Scunthorpe DN17 ... 150 E1
Saxcourt HU6 ... 139 E7
Saxford Way 8 YO32 ... 13 D5
Saxon Cl
Barton-upon-Humber DN18 ... 84 F8
Shipton YO30 ... 12 F5
6 Thorpe Willoughby YO8 ... 48 B1
Saxon Cres DN35 ... 153 D2
Saxon Ct Blyton DN21 ... 117 F5
Scunthorpe DN16 ... 96 D2
Saxon Pl YO31 ... 130 E7
Saxon Rd YO41 ... 15 D2
Saxon Rise HU17 ... 136 D7
Saxon Vale YO30 ... 12 F5
Saxon Villas 10 HU3 ... 145 A4
Saxon Way
4 Caistor LN7 ... 111 B4
Kingston upon Hull HU13 ... 143 F1
Saxondale HU4 ... 144 B7
Saxonfield LN7 ... 111 A4
Saxton Cl DN17 ... 150 E2
Scafell Cl 4 YO30 ... 126 E1
Scaife Cl HU17 ... 154 C2
Scaife Garth YO42 ... 28 F3
Scaife Gdns YO31 ... 130 C7
Scaife Mews HU17 ... 137 B3
Scaife St YO31 ... 130 C7
Scalby Gr HU5 ... 144 D8
Scalby La HU15 ... 66 D8
Scalby Pl HU18 ... 134 B4
Scale La HU1 ... 155 C2
Scale La Staith HU1 ... 155 C2
Scallow La DN17 ... 107 D6
Scalm La YO8 ... 48 A4
Scampton Cl DN34 ... 152 A1
Scampton Garth HU7 ... 141 C8
Scandinavian Way DN41 ... 87 E1
Scarborough Cres 8 YO16 ... 122 C5
Scarborough Rd
Bempton YO16 ... 4 A1
Blyton DN21 ... 117 E5
7 Bridlington YO16 ... 122 C5
Great Driffield YO25 ... 124 E6
Langtoft YO25 ... 8 C7
Scarborough St HU3 ... 145 A4
Scarborough Terr YO30 ... 156 B4
Scarcroft Hill YO24 ... 130 B2
Scarcroft La YO23 ... 156 A1
Scarcroft Prim Sch YO23 ... 156 A1
Scarcroft Rd YO24 ... 156 A1
Scarcroft View YO23 ... 156 A1
Scardale Ct YO8 ... 148 A2
Scargate Cl YO16 ... 123 A7
Scarrington Cres HU4 ... 144 B6
Scarrow Cl HU3 ... 145 A7
Scarsea Way YO15 ... 4 C3
Scartho Jun & Inf Sch DN33 ... 102 E1
Scartho Pk DN33 ... 102 D1
Scartho Rd DN33 ... 102 E2
Scaudercroft 13 YO19 ... 26 F7
Scawby Hall* DN20 ... 108 F8
Scawby Prim Sch DN20 ... 108 E8
Scawby Rd Brigg DN20 ... 98 A1
Broughton DN20 ... 97 E2
13 Grimsby DN33 ... 102 D2
Scunthorpe DN17 ... 150 E1
Scawton Ave 1 YO31 ... 127 E2
Schiphol Way DN38 ... 99 E5
Schofield Ave HU17 ... 154 C3
Schofield Cl 5 DN19 ... 85 C8
Scholefield Ave HU17 ... 56 B8
School Cl Selby YO8 ... 148 B3
16 Stamford Bridge YO41 ... 15 D2
School Dr DN17 ... 107 D7
School Hill YO16 ... 10 E4
School House La 2 DN10 ... 116 C3
School Houses 6 DN20 ... 97 E4
School La Appleby DN15 ... 83 D1
Askham Richard YO23 ... 24 D3
Beswick YO25 ... 32 B4
Beverley HU17 ... 154 B3
Bishopthorpe YO23 ... 133 A4
Bonby DN20 ... 84 C2
Buckton/Bempton YO15 ... 4 C3
Burton Fleming YO25 ... 2 E3
Cabourne LN7 ... 111 D5
Copmanthorpe YO23 ... 132 A2
10 Flamborough YO15 ... 5 A2
Goxhill DN19 ... 86 A8
Grayingham DN21 ... 119 B7
Heslington YO10 ... 131 B1
Holmton HU19 ... 75 D2
Irby DN37 ... 112 D7
15 Keyingham HU12 ... 73 C4
School La *continued*
Kingston upon Hull HU10 ... 143 C8
New Holland DN19 ... 70 E2
5 North Ferriby HU14 ... 69 A4
North Kelsey LN7 ... 110 A5
5 Pocklington YO42 ... 29 A4
23 Poppleton YO26 ... 12 F1
Redbourne DN21 ... 108 F2
Rothwell LN7 ... 111 E2
South Ferriby DN18 ... 84 A7
Tetney DN36 ... 114 C3
West/East Butterwick DN17 ... 106 D8
York YO10 ... 133 E7
School La Mews HU17 ... 154 B3
School Rd
Hemingbrough YO8 ... 49 F1
7 Preston HU12 ... 58 C1
Scunthorpe DN16 ... 151 B2
South Killingholme DN40 ... 86 E3
Winteringham DN15 ... 68 A1
School Rise YO43 ... 53 F7
School St
Kingston upon Hull HU1 ... 155 A2
York YO24 ... 129 D3
School Wlk DN35 ... 153 C1
Schooner Ct HU4 ... 144 B3
Schubert Cl HU9 ... 142 A3
Scorborough La YO25 ... 43 D8
Scoreby La YO41 ... 15 B1
Scotchman La YO60 ... 15 A8
Scotney Cl 5 HU3 ... 140 E1
Scott Ave DN17 ... 150 C2
Scott Cl 7 DN37 ... 102 C4
Scott Gdns 7 HU19 ... 75 A6
Scott Moncrieff Rd YO32 ... 14 B6
Scott Rd YO8 ... 148 C6
Scott St
27 Gainsborough DN21 ... 117 B1
Kingston upon Hull HU2 ... 155 B3
York YO23 ... 130 C2
Scotter Prim Sch DN21 ... 107 C3
Scotter Rd
Laughton DN21 ... 117 F8
Messingham DN17 ... 107 D5
Scotton DN21 ... 107 C2
Scunthorpe DN17 ... 150 C3
Scotter Rd S
Bottesford DN17 ... 96 B1
Scunthorpe DN17 ... 150 C1
Scotterthorpe Rd DN21 ... 107 B4
Scotton Rd DN21 ... 107 C3
Scotts Croft YO43 ... 135 D3
Scotts Garth Cl HU17 ... 137 F8
Scotts Garth Dr HU17 ... 44 C5
Scrap Bay Rd DN16 ... 97 A3
Scrivelsby Ct 9 DN35 ... 103 D2
Scriven Gr 8 YO32 ... 13 F5
Scrope Ave 4 YO31 ... 130 E5
Scrub La DN40 ... 86 E5
Scrubwood La HU17 ... 136 E6
Sculcoates La HU5 ... 140 E2
Scunthorpe CE Prim Sch DN15 ... 151 A8
Scunthorpe General Hospl DN15 ... 150 E6
Scunthorpe Leisure Ctr DN15 ... 151 B7
Scunthorpe Mus & Art Gall* DN15 ... 151 A6
Scunthorpe Sta DN16 ... 151 A6
Scunthorpe United Football Club DN15 ... 150 A6
Sea La DN36 ... 115 B3
Sea Rd
Cleethorpes DN35 ... 153 F2
Holmpton HU19 ... 75 D3
Sea View St DN35 ... 153 F1
Seabrook Dr DN16 ... 96 D1
Seacroft Rd
Cleethorpes DN35 ... 103 D3
Withernsea HU19 ... 75 A6
Seafield Ave HU9 ... 141 F3
Seafire Cl YO30 ... 127 A3
Seaford Rd DN35 ... 103 D1
Seagate YO15 ... 123 C6
Seagate View YO15 ... 123 E6
Seagull Cl HU4 ... 144 E2
Seakel La YO23 ... 24 C2
Seamer Gr DN32 ... 153 A1
Sean La DN14 ... 65 F4
Searby Hill DN38 ... 110 D8
Searby Rd DN17 ... 96 C2
Searby Wold La DN38 ... 99 E1
Seascale Wlk DN32 ... 152 F4
Seaside La HU12 ... 60 C2
Seaside Rd
Aldbrough HU11 ... 47 C2
Easington HU12 ... 91 A5
Holmpton HU19 ... 75 C2
Withernsea HU19 ... 75 A7
Seathorne HU19 ... 74 F7
Seathorne Rd 1 YO16 ... 122 C5
Seathorne Wlk YO16 ... 122 B5
Seaton Cl YO10 ... 131 C4
Seaton Gr
Grimsby DN32 ... 153 A1
Kingston upon Hull HU4 ... 144 E5
Seaton Rd
Bewholme YO25 ... 35 A4
Hornsea HU18 ... 134 A4
Kingston upon Hull HU13 ... 143 F2
Scunthorpe DN17 ... 150 D4
Seavy Carr La HU15 ... 52 F2
Seavy Rd DN14 ... 149 B3
Seawall La DN36 ... 115 C5
Second Ave
Bridlington YO15 ... 123 A4
Fixborough Stather DN15 ... 81 F1
4 Goole DN14 ... 149 C4
Grimsby DN33 ... 102 D2
Scunthorpe DN17 ... 150 C2
York YO31 ... 130 F6
Second Comm La YO8 ... 48 C4
Sedbergh Ave HU5 ... 139 D3
Sedbury Cl 5 HU7 ... 56 F6
Sedge Cl 4 DN18 ... 69 F1
Sedgebrook Gr 18 HU7 ... 56 F6
Sedgewood Way 13 DN15 ... 96 B7
Seed Cl La 3 DN37 ... 101 F1
Sefton Ave YO31 ... 130 F8
Sefton St 2 HU3 ... 145 B4
Seg La YO8 ... 63 F3
Segmere St DN35 ... 103 D3
Segrave Gr HU5 ... 144 D8
Segrave Wlk 10 YO26 ... 129 E4
Selbourne Rd 5 DN34 ... 102 C2
Selby Abbey YO8 ... 148 D5
Selby Abbey CE Prim Sch YO8 ... 148 C5
Selby Bsns Pk YO8 ... 148 D1
Selby Coll Selby YO8 ... 148 F3
Selby YO8 ... 148 C5
Selby CP Sch YO8 ... 148 B5
Selby Ct DN17 ... 150 D3
Selby High Sch YO8 ... 148 B4
Selby Ironworks Bsns Ctr YO8 ... 148 D5
Selby Rd
Eggborough DN14 ... 61 F1
Fulford YO19 ... 133 E6
Holme-on-Spalding-Moor YO43 ... 39 F1
Howden DN14 ... 65 A7
Riccall YO19 ... 49 A8
Snaith DN14 ... 63 C1
Thorne DN8 ... 92 F8
Wistow YO8 ... 48 D6
Womersley DN14 ... 77 A4
Selby Rly Sports Club YO8 ... 148 D5
Selby St HU3 ... 145 A5
Selby Sta YO8 ... 148 D5
Selby Town Football Club YO8 ... 148 B5
Seldon Rd YO26 ... 129 E5
Selge Way DN33 ... 102 C1
Selkirk St HU5 ... 145 A8
Sellers Dr HU17 ... 43 D6
Selmeston Ct DN34 ... 152 C2
Selsey Cl 2 HU5 ... 140 D2
Selvage La DN14 ... 78 A6
Selwick Dr YO15 ... 5 D2
Selworthy Cl 3 HU7 ... 57 A5
Selwyn Ave 14 HU14 ... 69 A4
Sennefleet Rd DN21 ... 107 B4
Sequana Ct HU9 ... 146 B6
Seraphim App Rd DN16 ... 151 E5
Seraphim Rd DN16 ... 151 F4
Service Rd 1 12 DN37 ... 102 C4
Service Rd 2 15 DN37 ... 102 C4
Service Rd 3 17 DN37 ... 102 C4
Service Rd 4 3 DN37 ... 102 C4
Service Rd 5 4 DN37 ... 102 C4
Service Rd 6 8 DN37 ... 102 C4
Service Rd 7 9 DN37 ... 102 C4
Service Rd 8 1 DN37 ... 102 C5
Service Rd 9 2 DN37 ... 102 C5
Service Rd 10 3 DN37 ... 102 C5
Service Rd 11 4 DN37 ... 102 C5
Service Rd 12 5 DN37 ... 102 C5
Service Rd 13 6 DN37 ... 102 C5
Service Rd 14 7 DN37 ... 102 C5
Service Rd 15 19 DN37 ... 102 C4
Service Rd 16 18 DN37 ... 102 C4
Service Rd 17 10 DN37 ... 102 C4
Service Rd 18 11 DN37 ... 102 C4
Service Rd 19 13 DN37 ... 102 C4
Service Rd 20 14 DN37 ... 102 C4
Service Rd 21 13 DN37 ... 102 B4
Service Rd 22 1 DN37 ... 102 C4
Service Rd 23 2 DN37 ... 102 C4
Service Rd 25 5 DN37 ... 102 C4
Service Rd 26 8 DN37 ... 102 C5
Service Rd No 1 DN32 ... 152 F5
Service Rd No 2 DN32 ... 152 F5
Services Rd DN16 ... 151 E6
Setterwood Garth 2 HU10 ... 143 E8
Setting Cres 8 HU5 ... 139 D2
Setting Rd HU5 ... 139 D2
Seven Corners La HU17 ... 136 D4
Seven Lakes L Pk* DN17 ... 94 D6
Seven Quay Rd DN40 ... 87 D3
Seventh Ave
3 Bridlington YO15 ... 122 F4
York YO31 ... 130 F5
Severn Gn YO26 ... 129 C8
Severn St HU8 ... 141 C1
Severus Ave YO26 ... 129 D4
Severus St YO24 ... 129 D3
Sewer La HU1 ... 155 B1
Sewerby Ave YO16 ... 122 E5
Sewerby Cres YO16 ... 122 D5
Sewerby Ct 6 YO16 ... 122 D5
Sewerby Hall & Gdns* YO15 ... 123 C7
Sewerby Headlands YO16 ... 122 F5
Sewerby Heads YO16 ... 122 F5
Sewerby Pk Cl YO15 ... 123 C7
Sewerby Rd YO16 ... 122 D5
Sewerby Rise YO16 ... 122 E5
Sextant Rd HU6 ... 140 C8
Seymour Gr YO31 ... 130 F6
Seymour Rd 6 HU12 ... 73 C4
Seymour St HU3 ... 144 F5
Shadwell Rise 5 DN18 ... 69 E1
Shady La 3 YO25 ... 10 A2
Shaftesbury Ave
Goole DN14 ... 149 A5
Grimsby DN34 ... 152 B3
Hornsea HU18 ... 134 C5
Kellingley DN14 ... 61 C3
Kingston upon Hull HU8 ... 141 F4
Shaftesbury Mews 1 DN36 ... 114 A7
Shaftesbury Rd YO15 ... 122 C1
Shakespeare Ave
2 Campsall DN6 ... 76 E1
Scunthorpe DN17 ... 150 C2
Shakespeare Cl 6 HU3 ... 145 D8
Shallowdale Gr 1 YO10 ... 131 C3
Shambles YO1 ... 156 B2
Shannon Rd HU8 ... 142 C6
Shardeloes HU9 ... 142 E5
Shardlow Rd HU18 ... 134 C5
Sharp Ave HU12 ... 73 A6
Sharp Hill La YO8 ... 63 F6
Sharp St HU5 ... 140 B2
Sharpe Cl 20 DN18 ... 84 E8
Sharpe Howe* YO11 ... 2 A8
Sharps La HU17 ... 55 B7
Shaw Dr 1 DN33 ... 113 F8
Shaw La DN6 ... 77 D2
Shaw Rd DN10 ... 116 A2
Shaw St HU9 ... 146 B7
Shaw's Terr YO24 ... 156 A1
Shawfield Cl 7 DN3 ... 92 A3
Shears Ct DN37 ... 113 E7
Sheep Cote La DN7 ... 92 D2
Sheep Dip La DN7 ... 92 C4
Sheep Marsh La DN36 ... 115 B3
Sheep Rake La YO25 ... 8 F4
Sheep Trod La HU12 ... 89 F6
Sheepdike La YO25 ... 21 F2
Sheepdyke La
Bonby DN20 ... 84 C2
Hunmanby YO14 ... 3 A8
Sheepfold St DN32 ... 152 E3
Sheepman La YO25 ... 32 F7
Sheeprake La YO15 ... 123 B8
Sheepswarth La HU20 ... 54 F3
Sheepwalk La YO17 ... 7 B7
Sheepwash La DN14 ... 77 A7
Sheffield Pk Ave DN15 ... 96 C7
Sheffield St DN15 ... 151 A8
Sheffield St E DN15 ... 151 A8
Sheffield St W DN15 ... 150 F8
Sheldon Cl HU7 ... 141 B8
Sheldrake Way HU17 ... 136 F6
Shelford Ave DN14 ... 65 A7
Shelford St DN15 ... 151 A7
Shelley Ave
Grimsby DN33 ... 102 D2
Kingston upon Hull HU9 ... 142 C2
Shelley Gr YO30 ... 126 F1
Shelroy Cl DN15 ... 96 B7
Shenley Cl 11 DN7 ... 92 D3
Shepherd La HU17 ... 55 F8
Shepherd's Croft DN9 ... 105 D7
Shepherds Lea 6 HU17 ... 55 E8
Shepherdton Mere YO25 ... 9 B1
Sheraton Dr 3 DN36 ... 114 D8
Sherbrooke Ave HU5 ... 139 E4
Sherburn Cres DN15 ... 150 D8
Sherburn Rd YO8 ... 148 A8
Sherburn St
1 Cawood YO8 ... 48 B8
Cleethorpes DN35 ... 153 F1
Kingston upon Hull HU9 ... 146 D8
Sherbuttgate Dr 13 YO42 ... 28 F4
Sherbuttgate Rd 14 YO42 ... 28 F4
Sheriff Highway HU12 ... 72 C6
Sherringham Dr YO24 ... 132 D8
Sherwood Ave HU9 ... 141 E1
Sherwood Cl
13 Norton DN6 ... 76 E1
4 Walkington HU17 ... 55 C8
Sherwood Ct HU9 ... 142 D5
Sherwood Dr HU4 ... 144 A7
Sherwood Gr
Huntington YO32 ... 127 F1
York YO26 ... 129 B6
Sherwood Rd DN34 ... 102 C2
Sherwood Vale DN15 ... 150 D7
Shetland Cl 6 HU7 ... 141 E7
Shetland Way 4 DN40 ... 101 C8
Shevington Wlk HU8 ... 142 C6
Shields Rd 2 HU12 ... 72 C7
Shildon Gr DN8 ... 79 C2
Shilling Cl 26 HU7 ... 56 F5
Shilton Garth Cl 3 YO32 ... 127 F7
Shipcote Rd DN14 ... 149 D1
Shipley Cl HU9 ... 142 C2
Shipman Rd YO43 ... 135 D3
Shipton Cl HU9 ... 142 C5
Shipton Cres 6 HU17 ... 43 D6
Shipton La YO43 ... 40 E3
Shipton Low Rd YO30 ... 12 E5
Shipton Rd
Clifton YO30 ... 129 F8
Rawcliffe YO30 ... 126 D2
Scunthorpe DN16 ... 151 C1
Shipton Rd *continued*
York YO30 ... 130 A7
Shipton St 3 YO30 ... 130 B7
Shipton St Inf Sch YO30 ... 130 B7
Shipyard Ind Est YO8 ... 148 E5
Shipyard Rd YO8 ... 148 E5
Shirbutt La YO26 ... 24 C8
Shirley Ave YO26 ... 129 C6
Shirley Cres DN16 ... 151 B4
Shoemaker's La DN21 ... 107 D5
Shopeth Way HU17 ... 56 B8
Shore Rd DN17 ... 81 F5
Shoreditch Cl 2 HU8 ... 141 F5
Short La Bempton YO16 ... 4 C1
12 Bridlington YO16 ... 122 C5
Fotherby LN11 ... 121 C2
Market Weighton YO43 ... 41 B2
West Haddlesey YO8 ... 61 F6
West Halton DN15 ... 82 E8
Short St
Cleethorpes DN35 ... 153 E2
Kingston upon Hull HU1 ... 155 A2
Shortacre La YO42 ... 38 E2
Shorthill Croft HU17 ... 154 A1
Shorwell Cl 2 HU8 ... 142 C5
Shotel Cl YO30 ... 129 F8
Shropshire Cl HU5 ... 139 D1
Shrubberies The YO8 ... 49 E2
Shuttleworth Ct HU18 ... 134 D4
Sibelius Rd HU4 ... 144 B4
Sicey La HU6 ... 56 D7
Side La DN33 ... 113 F8
Sidebottom St DN31 ... 152 F6
Siding La YO8 ... 49 B5
Sidings Ct HU15 ... 68 B5
Sidmouth Prim Sch HU5 ... 140 B3
Sidmouth St HU5 ... 140 C3
Sidney Ct DN35 ... 153 B4
Sidney Pl DN35 ... 153 B4
Sidney Rd
Grimsby DN34 ... 152 B3
Scunthorpe DN17 ... 150 D2
Sidney St DN35 ... 153 B4
Sidney Way DN35 ... 153 B4
Sidsaph Hill 2 DN10 ... 116 D3
Sigglesthorne CE VC Prim Sch HU11 ... 45 F8
Sigglesthorne Rd HU11 ... 46 B6
Sigglesthorne Sta Nature Reserve* HU11 ... 46 B6
Signhills Ave 1 DN35 ... 103 D2
Signhills Jun & Inf Sch DN35 ... 103 D2
Sigston Rd HU17 ... 154 C4
Silica Cres DN17 ... 150 D1
Silkstone Oval 15 DN8 ... 79 B2
Silkstone Wlk HU8 ... 141 C1
Sills La YO30 ... 12 B6
Silsden Ave 5 HU6 ... 140 C7
Silver Birch Rise 22 DN16 ... 96 D2
Silver St
Barnetby le Wold DN38 ... 99 B4
Barrow upon Humber DN19 ... 85 C7
Holton le Clay DN36 ... 114 A5
Huggate YO42 ... 18 C2
Kingston upon Hull HU1 ... 155 B2
Owston Ferry DN9 ... 106 B2
3 Riccall YO19 ... 49 A8
1 Stainforth DN7 ... 92 C6
24 Thorne/Moorends DN8 ... 93 A8
Whitley DN14 ... 77 A7
Winteringham DN15 ... 68 B1
York YO1 ... 156 B2
Silverdale Ct YO24 ... 132 D7
Silverdale Rd HU6 ... 140 C6
Silvergarth DN32 ... 153 A1
Silversides La DN20 ... 98 A1
Silvertree Wlk DN14 ... 149 F6
Sim Balk La YO24 ... 132 E5
Simon Howe YO12 ... 1 A5
Simons Pl DN35 ... 153 D3
Simpson Ave 6 YO14 ... 2 F8
Simpson Cl DN19 ... 85 D8
Simpson's Yd 3 YO8 ... 148 C6
Simson Ct HU17 ... 154 B4
Sinclair Cres HU8 ... 141 F6
Sinderby Wlk HU5 ... 139 D4
Sinderson Rd 18 DN36 ... 103 D1
Sir Henry Cooper Sch HU6 ... 56 D5
Sir James Reckitt Haven HU8 ... 141 C1
Sir John Nelthorpe Lower Sch DN20 ... 98 C2
Sir John Nelthorpe Sch DN20 ... 98 C2
Sirius Cl 3 HU3 ... 145 B5
Sirocco Ct YO31 ... 130 D8
Siskin Cres DN16 ... 96 D1
Sissons La HU15 ... 53 B1
Sissons Way HU5 ... 140 E3
Sittingbourne Cl HU8 ... 141 E8
Sitwell Gr YO26 ... 129 C5
Sitwell St HU8 ... 155 C4
Siward St YO10 ... 131 A3
Siwards How* YO10 ... 131 B1
Siward's Way YO10 ... 131 A2
Sixhills St DN32 ... 152 F3
Sixth Ave
Bridlington YO15 ... 122 F4
Fixborough Stather DN15 ... 82 A1

Sixth Ave *continued*
Scunthorpe DN17 ...150 B2
York YO31 ...130 E5
Skeckling Cl HU12 ...73 A6
Skeffling Rd HU12 ...90 B7
Skeldergate YO1 ...156 B2
Skelton Ave HU5 ...139 E2
Skelton Broad La DN14 ...65 C4
Skelton Cres YO43 ...135 C4
Skelton Ct 3 YO30 ...130 A6
Skelton La YO32 ...126 D8
Skelton Prim Sch YO30 ...126 C5
Skelton Rd DN17 ...150 C3
Skern Gr HU9 ...142 A2
Skerne Rd YO25 ...124 F2
Skewsby Gr YO31 ...127 F1
Skidby Carr La HU6 ...56 C6
Skidby CE VC Prim Sch HU16 ...138 A7
Skidby Gr HU6 ...139 F5
Skidby Rd HU20 ...55 A4
Skidby Windmill & Mus of E Riding Rural Life* HU16 ...138 C7
Skiddaw YO24 ...132 C7
Skiff La YO43 ...52 C7
Skiff La Ind Est YO43 ...52 D6
Skilgate Cl 7 HU7 ...57 A5
Skillings La HU15 ...68 C5
Skinners La
3 South Ferriby DN18 ...84 A7
Waltham DN37 ...113 E6
Skipper La YO25 ...1 E3
Skippingdale Rd DN15 ...96 C7
Skipsea Castle* YO25 ...23 A1
Skipsea La YO25 ...23 A3
Skipsea Prim Sch YO25 ...23 B1
Skipsea Rd Atwick YO25 ...35 C7
Beeford YO25 ...22 D1
Bewholme YO25 ...35 A5
Skipwith Cl HU6 ...140 B6
Skipwith Comm Nature Reserve* YO8 ...49 E8
Skipwith Rd YO19 ...37 B6
Skirbeck Rd HU8 ...141 D5
Skirlaugh CE VC Prim Sch HU11 ...45 E2
Skirlaugh Rd
Ellerby HU11 ...45 F1
Swine HU11 ...57 E8
Skirlaw Cl 18 DN14 ...65 A7
Skitter Rd DN40 ...86 D8
Skylark Cl YO25 ...125 A5
Skylark Dr DN16 ...96 D1
Slack The DN17 ...94 D8
Slay Pit Cl DN7 ...92 F4
Slay Pit La DN7 ...92 F3
Sleaford Ave 3 HU9 ...142 E2
Sledmere CE VC Prim Sch YO25 ...7 B3
Sledmere Gr HU4 ...144 E5
Sledmere House* YO25 ...7 B3
Sledmere Rd YO25 ...8 B6
Sleightholme Cl 21 HU7 ...56 F6
Sleights Cl HU3 ...145 A7
Sleights La Acklam YO17 ...16 E7
Broomfleet HU15 ...67 B6
Eastrington DN14 ...51 E3
Slessor Rd YO24 ...129 B1
Slingsby Cl HU5 ...139 D2
Slingsby Gr YO24 ...132 E8
Sloe La HU17 ...136 D2
Sluice La DN18 ...83 D8
Sluice Rd DN18 ...83 F8
Smales' St YO1 ...156 B1
Smary La YO19 ...26 D7
Smeatley's La DN6 ...76 C4
Smeaton Gr YO26 ...129 C5
Smeaton Rd YO41 ...27 D7
Smedley Cl HU17 ...154 C2
Smith Cl YO10 ...133 F8
Smith Field 4 DN36 ...114 B1
Smith St Grimsby DN31 ...152 F6
Scunthorpe DN15 ...150 F8
Smithall Rd HU17 ...136 E7
Smithfield Rd DN16 ...151 D2
Smithie Cl YO32 ...127 D5
Smithy La 7 DN38 ...99 B4
Smitton St DN31 ...153 A6
Smook Hills Rd (Pearcy Lane) HU19 ...75 A4
Smythy La YO25 ...1 D4
Snainton Gr 4 HU5 ...144 D8
Snaith Rd
Pollington DN14 ...77 F7
Rawcliffe DN14 ...64 A1
Snaith DN14 ...78 D8
Snaith Sch The DN14 ...78 C8
Snaith Sec Sch DN14 ...78 B8
Snaith Sta DN14 ...63 C1
Snatchells La DN14 ...78 C2
Snowdon Cl YO23 ...24 D3
Snowdon Way HU7 ...57 A7
Snowdonia Ave DN15 ...96 B8
Snowdrop Garth YO42 ...40 A1
Snowhill Cl 4 HU7 ...57 A6
Snuff Mill La HU16 ...139 B6
Sober Hill Dr YO43 ...40 A1
Soft La DN19 ...86 A6
Solomon Ct DN35 ...153 D1
Somerby Rd DN17 ...150 D1
Somerby Wold La DN38 ...99 C1
Somerden Rd HU9 ...147 E7
Somersby St DN31 ...152 D4
Somerscales St HU2 ...155 A4
Somerset Cl 6 YO30 ...126 E3
Somerset Dr 6 DN15 ...82 B4
Somerset Rd YO31 ...130 D8
Somerset St HU3 ...145 A5
Somerton Dr DN7 ...92 F4
Somerton Rd DN40 ...87 C1
Somervell Rd DN16 ...151 C1
Sonia Crest DN40 ...87 B1
Sophia Ave 7 DN33 ...102 E1
Sophia Cl HU2 ...155 A4
Sorbus Ct 5 HU3 ...145 D6
Sorbus View 4 HU4 ...144 C7
Sorrel Cl HU17 ...136 E1
Sorrel Dr 5 HU5 ...144 D8
Sorrel Way DN15 ...96 B7
Sorrell La DN14 ...78 D1
Soss La DN10 ...116 D5
Sotheron St DN14 ...149 D4
Sour La DN8 ...92 E8
Soutergate 12 DN18 ...69 F1
South Ave YO25 ...31 F2
South Axholme Com Sch DN9 ...105 D6
South Back La YO16 ...122 B4
South Bank DN17 ...95 D6
South Bank Ave YO23 ...130 B1
South Bridge Rd HU9 ...155 C1
South Carr Dales Rd HU19 ...74 F3
South Carr La DN20 ...109 B4
South Carr Rd DN20 ...109 A4
South Carrs HU17 ...45 A8
South Cave CE VC Prim Sch HU15 ...53 F1
South Church Side
2 Easington HU12 ...90 F6
Kingston upon Hull HU1 ...155 B2
South Cl 7 Kilham YO25 ...9 C3
Kingston upon Hull HU6 ...140 C6
South Cliff Rd
4 Bridlington YO15 ...122 E2
Kirton in Lindsey DN21 ...108 B1
South Dale LN7 ...111 B4
South Down Rd 3 YO32 ...127 F5
South Dr YO25 ...31 C4
South Duffield Rd YO8 ...49 C4
South Ella Dr HU10 ...143 D7
South Ella Way HU10 ...143 D7
South End
Seaton Ross YO42 ...39 E3
Thorne/Moorends DN8 ...93 A7
South End La DN14 ...77 B4
South End Rd
Ottringham HU12 ...73 E3
Roos HU12 ...60 B1
South Espl YO1 ...156 B1
South Ferriby Prim Sch DN18 ...84 A7
South Field Ct 5 HU16 ...138 F5
South Furlong Croft 17 DN9 ...105 E6
South Gate YO25 ...32 E6
South Glebe YO25 ...32 B1
South Gr 8 YO25 ...9 C3
South Holderness Tech Coll HU12 ...72 D8
South Hunsley Sch HU14 ...68 E5
South Ings La HU15 ...53 C2
South Intake La DN9 ...116 F7
South La
Bishop Wilton YO42 ...16 F1
Cawood YO8 ...48 B7
Kingston upon Hull HU13 ...143 E1
South Landing Nature Reserve* YO15 ...5 A1
South Leys Comp Sch DN17 ...96 C2
South Leys Rd HU19 ...75 A4
South Marine Dr YO15 ...122 D1
South Marsh Rd DN41 ...101 F7
South Moor Rd DN10 ...116 C3
South Newbald Rd YO43 ...53 F7
South Parade
Grimsby DN31 ...152 D4
Leven HU17 ...45 A7
8 Selby YO8 ...148 C5
Thorne DN8 ...93 A7
York YO24 ...156 A1
South Par Jun Sch DN31 ...152 D4
South Parkway 4 DN14 ...78 C8
South Pk HU12 ...60 B1
South Pk Rd DN17 ...96 B2
South Prom HU18 ...134 D4
South Rd
Keadby with Althorpe DN17 ...95 C6
Thorne/Moorends DN8 ...79 B2
South Rise HU16 ...138 B8
South Rise Cres 20 DN17 ...96 C2
South Ruddings La YO19 ...37 F7
South Sea Ave 26 YO15 ...5 A2
South Sea La DN36 ...114 D7
South Sea Rd YO15 ...5 A2
South Side Kilham YO25 ...9 B3
Winteringham DN15 ...68 A1
South Side La YO25 ...9 F6
South St
Barmby on the Marsh DN14 ...64 A7
Barnetby le Wold DN38 ...99 B4
South St *continued*
Bridlington YO15 ...122 E1
Burton Fleming YO25 ...2 E2
Cottingham HU16 ...139 A6
8 Gainsborough DN21 ...117 A2
Goole DN14 ...149 C2
Keelby DN41 ...101 A5
Kingston upon Hull HU1 ...155 A2
Leven HU17 ...45 A7
Middleton-on-the-Wolds YO25 ...31 C4
North Kelsey LN7 ...110 A4
Owston Ferry DN9 ...106 B2
Roxby cum Risby DN15 ...82 F3
West Butterwick DN17 ...106 D8
Winterton DN15 ...83 A5
South St Mary's Gate 4 DN31 ...152 D3
South Townside Rd YO25 ...34 A8
South View
Broughton DN20 ...97 D4
Grimsby DN34 ...152 A2
Healaugh LS24 ...24 A2
Holton le Clay DN36 ...114 B5
6 Humberston DN36 ...103 D1
Kingston upon Hull HU4 ...144 B6
South View Ave
Brigg DN20 ...98 C2
Burringham DN17 ...95 D4
South Wold HU20 ...55 A4
South Wolds Sch HU17 ...43 A7
South Wood Dr 12 DN8 ...93 A7
Southburn Ave HU4 ...144 E7
Southburn Rd YO25 ...20 A1
Southcliff Rd HU19 ...75 A6
Southcliffe Rd 12 DN21 ...107 C3
Southcoates Ave HU9 ...141 E2
Southcoates La HU9 ...146 E8
Southcoates Prim Sch HU9 ...141 F1
Southcote Cl 4 HU15 ...54 A2
Southcroft Dr 8 HU8 ...141 E7
South-Dale Cl 1 DN21 ...108 B2
Southern Dr HU4 ...144 C5
Southern Way DN40 ...87 C3
Southern Wlk DN33 ...113 E8
Southfield 1 Belton DN9 ...94 E1
Kingston upon Hull HU13 ...69 E4
Southfield Cl
Great Driffield YO25 ...124 F6
Rufforth YO23 ...24 D6
14 Thorne/Moorends DN8 ...93 B7
Ulceby DN39 ...86 B1
Wetwang YO25 ...19 B5
Southfield Cres 2 YO24 ...132 E8
Southfield Dr
1 Beverley HU17 ...137 A6
4 Epworth DN9 ...105 D6
North Ferriby HU14 ...69 A4
Southfield La
Barmston YO25 ...23 A6
Elstronwick HU12 ...59 C3
Everingham YO42 ...40 B4
Kellington DN14 ...61 E2
Roos HU12 ...60 C1
Seaton Ross YO42 ...39 D1
Skipsea YO25 ...23 B2
Willoughton DN21 ...119 A3
Southfield Pk YO43 ...135 D3
Southfield Rd
1 Broughton DN20 ...97 D3
8 Crowle DN17 ...94 D7
Elstronwick HU12 ...59 A2
Great Driffield YO25 ...124 F6
Grimsby DN33 ...113 E8
15 Holton le Clay DN36 ...114 A5
Kingston upon Hull HU5 ...140 A2
North Kelsey LN7 ...109 E2
Pocklington YO42 ...28 F4
Scunthorpe DN16 ...151 C1
Thorne/Moorends DN8 ...93 B7
Wetwang YO25 ...19 A5
Winterton DN15 ...82 F5
Southfield Well Balk YO25 ...19 B5
Southfields HU15 ...52 E1
Southfields Rd YO32 ...14 B7
Southgate
Hornsea HU18 ...134 C3
Kingston upon Hull HU13 ...143 E1
Market Weighton YO43 ...135 E3
4 Scunthorpe DN15 ...151 B7
Southgate Cl HU10 ...138 E2
Southgate Gdns 2 HU18 ...134 C3
Southlands
4 Haxby YO32 ...13 E5
16 Hemingbrough YO8 ...49 F1
Southlands Ave 1 DN21 ...117 A2
Southlands Cl YO19 ...37 B6
Southlands Dr 3 DN21 ...117 A2
Southlands Gdns 2 DN21 ...117 A2
Southlands Rd YO23 ...130 B2
Southmoor La WF11 ...61 B1
Southmoor Rd
Crowle DN17 ...94 C8
Thorganby YO19 ...37 F5
Southolme Dr 7 YO30 ...126 F1
Southorpe Cl YO16 ...122 B5
Southorpe La DN21 ...118 D7
Southorpe Nature Reserve* HU11 ...46 D8
Southorpe Rd HU11 ...134 A1
Southside HU12 ...74 D1
Southside Rd HU12 ...73 F5
Southwell Ave HU9 ...147 E8
Southwell Cl HU17 ...136 E1
Southwold Cres 25 DN33 ...113 E8
Southwood Ave HU16 ...138 F6
Southwood Dr HU16 ...139 A6
Southwood Gdns HU16 ...138 F5
Southwood Rd
Kingston upon Hull HU16 ...138 F5
Sutton upon Derwent YO41 ...38 C8
Soutter Gate HU12 ...72 C7
Sovereign Cl 14 DN34 ...102 B2
Sovereign Way 7 HU7 ...56 E5
Sow Hill Rd HU17 ...154 A3
Sowerby Rd YO26 ...129 D4
Sowers La DN15 ...83 A5
Spa Hill DN21 ...108 B1
Spa Well La DN14 ...78 C8
Spalding Ave YO30 ...130 B7
Spalding Rd DN16 ...151 B4
Spark Mill La HU17 ...154 C1
Spark St DN34 ...152 A3
Sparkmill Terr HU17 ...154 C2
Sparrowcroft La DN14 ...66 E3
Speculation St YO1 ...130 E4
Speedwell Cres DN15 ...96 B7
Speedwell La 1 HU17 ...55 D8
Speeton Gate YO15 ...4 B4
Spellowgate YO25 ...20 C7
Spellowgate Cl YO25 ...124 D5
Spen La
Holme-on-Spalding-Moor YO43 ...39 F2
York YO1 ...156 C3
Spencer Ave DN15 ...150 F8
Spencer Cl
22 Hedon HU12 ...72 C7
Kingston upon Hull HU16 ...138 F6
Spencer St
Beverley HU17 ...154 A3
Grimsby DN31 ...153 B5
Kingston upon Hull HU2 ...155 A3
3 York YO23 ...156 B1
Spencer Way 1 HU16 ...139 B7
Spencers Mead YO25 ...124 E3
Spencers Way YO25 ...124 E4
Speng La YO26 ...24 B4
Spenser St DN14 ...149 C5
Sperrin Cl 2 HU9 ...142 A3
Spey Bank YO24 ...132 C6
Spicer's Rd HU12 ...72 C6
Spilsby Rd DN17 ...150 E1
Spindle Cl YO24 ...132 C8
Spindlewood 1 HU15 ...68 C7
Spinnaker Cl HU3 ...145 D5
Spinney Cl 2 DN40 ...87 C1
Spinney Croft Cl 12 HU14 ...69 A5
Spinney The
1 Barnby Dun DN3 ...92 A3
8 Barrow upon Humber DN19 ...85 D8
Grimsby DN34 ...152 C3
Kingston upon Hull HU16 ...139 A5
6 Newport HU15 ...52 F1
7 Swanland HU14 ...69 B7
York YO24 ...132 F7
Spinney Wlk HU4 ...144 C6
Spire View 1 HU13 ...143 E1
Spital Hill DN21 ...117 B1
Spital Terr DN21 ...117 B1
Spittlerush La DN6 ...76 D2
Spout H YO42 ...28 D3
Spout Hill HU15 ...68 C8
Spratton Ct 2 DN37 ...102 B2
Spring Bank
Grimsby DN34 ...152 A3
Kingston upon Hull HU2 ...155 A3
4 North Newbald YO43 ...53 F7
Spring Bank W HU4 ...144 D7
Spring Cl YO25 ...124 D5
Spring Cottage Prim Sch HU8 ...141 F6
Spring Field Cl HU11 ...45 F8
Spring Gdns
Goole DN14 ...149 E4
Kingston upon Hull HU8 ...141 D5
Spring Gdns E HU4 ...144 B6
Spring Gdns S HU4 ...144 B5
Spring Gdns W HU4 ...144 B6
Spring Gr HU3 ...145 A7
Spring La
2 Buckton/Bempton YO15 ...4 D3
11 Laceby DN37 ...101 F1
Long Marston YO26 ...24 A5
York YO10 ...131 A1
Spring Rd 1 YO43 ...135 E4
Spring St
Immingham DN40 ...87 C1
Kingston upon Hull HU2 ...155 A3
Spring Vale HU9 ...142 D5
Spring Wlk YO8 ...148 A1
Springbank DN20 ...98 C2
Springbank Ave
Dunnington YO19 ...26 E7
Hornsea HU18 ...134 B4
Springbok Cl HU4 ...144 D2
Springburn St HU3 ...145 A5
Springdale Cl HU10 ...143 F8
Springdale Rd YO43 ...135 E5
Springdale Way HU17 ...154 A1
Springfield
Holme-on-Spalding-Moor YO43 ...40 A1
6 Howden DN14 ...65 B7
Springfield Ave
Bridlington YO15 ...122 E2
18 Brough HU15 ...68 C6
5 Hatfield DN7 ...92 E4
Springfield Cl
Barlby with Osgodby YO8 ...49 B5
Heworth YO31 ...131 C7
2 Scunthorpe DN16 ...151 C2
Springfield Cres 3 WF8 ...76 C3
Springfield Dr
9 Barlby YO8 ...49 B5
Beverley HU17 ...137 A6
Springfield Gdns YO43 ...40 A1
Springfield Prim Sch DN33 ...113 D8
Springfield Rd
26 Brigg DN20 ...98 C2
Grimsby DN33 ...113 D8
Kingston upon Hull HU3 ...144 F6
Pocklington YO42 ...29 B3
4 Poppleton YO26 ...12 F1
Springfield Rise DN20 ...98 D2
Springfield Way
Hook DN14 ...149 F6
Kingston upon Hull HU10 ...143 E7
York YO31 ...131 B7
Springfields 18 WF11 ...61 A2
Springfields Ave 17 WF11 ...61 A2
Springhead Ave HU5 ...144 A7
Springhead Cl 6 DN14 ...65 A7
Springhead Ct HU10 ...144 A6
Springhead Gdns HU10 ...144 A7
Springhead La HU4 ...144 A7
Springhead Prim Sch HU10 ...143 F7
Springs Rd DN10 ...104 C1
Springs Way DN20 ...98 B2
Springthorpe Rd DN21 ...118 B1
Springville Ave HU13 ...143 F2
Springway Cres DN34 ...152 A3
Springwood YO32 ...127 D7
Springwood Cres 7 DN33 ...113 D8
Springwood Gr 16 HU15 ...68 D6
Sproatley Endowed CE VC Prim Sch HU11 ...58 D5
Sproatley Rd HU12 ...58 D3
Spruce Cl YO32 ...127 D2
Spruce La DN39 ...86 A1
Spruce Rd
Kingston upon Hull HU1 ...155 A1
Leven HU17 ...45 B8
Spurn Ave 16 DN33 ...113 E8
Spurn Lightship* YO23 ...155 B1
Spurn Rd HU12 ...91 B2
Spurr Ct YO24 ...132 C8
Spurriergate YO1 ...156 B2
Spyvee St HU8 ...155 C3
Square The
4 Easington HU12 ...90 F6
Goxhill DN19 ...86 A8
Kingston upon Hull HU10 ...138 D1
Kingston upon Hull HU13 ...143 E1
Skerne & Wansford YO25 ...21 C3
Yapham YO42 ...28 E7
Squire La YO16 ...122 C4
Stable La 4 DN18 ...69 E1
Stable Rd YO8 ...63 D7
Stabler Cl 15 YO32 ...13 D5
Stablers Wlk YO32 ...127 F7
Staddlethorpe Broad La HU15 ...66 D7
Stafford St
6 Kingston upon Hull HU2 ...140 E1
Kingston upon Hull HU2 ...155 A4
Staindale Cl YO30 ...126 E2
Staindale Rd DN16 ...151 E1
Staines Cl HU8 ...142 A4
Stainforth Moor Rd DN7 ...93 C3
Stainforth Rd DN7 ...92 A5
Stainton Dr
Grimsby DN33 ...102 D2
15 Immingham DN40 ...87 B1
9 Scunthorpe DN17 ...96 C2
Staithe St 3 YO8 ...50 D7
Staithes Cl 4 YO26 ...129 B4
Staithes Rd HU12 ...72 B8
Stallingborough CE Prim Sch DN41 ...101 E6
Stallingborough Rd
Healing DN41 ...101 E5
Immingham DN40 ...87 B1
Keelby DN41 ...101 A5
Stallingborough Sta DN41 ...101 E6
Stalybridge Ave HU9 ...142 E1
Stamford Bridge Inf Sch YO41 ...15 D2
Stamford Bridge Rd YO19 ...26 E7
Stamford Bridge W YO41 ...15 C2
Stamford Gr HU9 ...142 E1
Stamford St E 10 YO26 ...129 F5
Stamford St W 8 YO26 ...129 F5

Stamford Wlk YO16 ....122 C2
Stan Valley 2 WF8 ....76 C3
Stanage Wlk DN32 .....152 F4
Stanbury Rd HU6 ......140 C7
Standage Rd 12 HU12 ......72 E5
Standidge Dr HU8 ......142 A5
Standish La 1 DN40 .....87 B2
Stanfield Rd 2 DN9 ....105 D6
Stanford Cl DN37 ....101 F1
Stanford Jun & Inf Sch
DN37 ....101 F1
Stanholme La DN36 ....114 A1
Stanhope Ave HU9 .....141 E2
Stanhope Pl DN35 .....153 C3
Stanhope St DN14 ......149 C4
Stanhurst La DN7 ....93 A5
Staniland Dr YO8 ......148 A5
Staniland Way 1 DN36 .114 D8
Staniwell Rise DN17 ...150 D3
Staniwells Dr 9 DN20 ....97 D3
Stanley Ave
Haxby YO32 ....127 D7
Hornsea HU18 ....134 C2
Stanley Gdns 15 DN7 .....92 C6
Stanley Rd
Scunthorpe DN15 ....150 C7
16 Stainforth DN7 ....92 C6
Stanley St Goole DN14 ..149 D4
Grimsby DN32 ....153 A4
Kingston upon Hull HU3 ...145 C7
York YO31 ....156 C4
Stannington Dr HU8 ...142 D6
Stansfield Cl HU9 ......142 D1
Stansted St DN31 ......152 B5
Staple Rd DN40 ....86 F3
Stapleford Cl 4 HU9 ....142 E2
Star Carr La DN20 ....98 C4
Star Hill Rd YO25 ....124 F5
Starboard Ave HU6 .....140 C8
Starcarr La YO25 ....34 A1
Starella Gr HU3 ....145 A4
Starham Rd LN7 ....109 C4
Starkbridge La DN14 ....78 A3
Starkey Cres YO31 .....131 A5
Startforth Wlk HU5 .....139 E3
Stather Rd
Burton upon Stather
DN15 ....82 A5
Flixborough DN15 ....82 A1
Stathers Wlk 3 HU10 ....143 F6
Station App
Bridlington YO15 ....122 E2
Cleethorpes DN35 ....153 F3
Station Ave
Bridlington YO16 ....122 D2
New Earswick YO32 ......127 D3
New Waltham DN36 ......114 A7
York YO1 ....156 A2
Station Ct 47 Hatfield DN7 .92 D4
Hornsea HU18 ....134 D4
Station Dr HU3 ....140 D1
Station Hill YO25 ....19 B6
Station La
Barmby on the Marsh
DN14 ....64 B7
Cliffe YO8 ....49 E3
Hedon HU12 ....72 C8
Holme-on-Spalding-Moor
YO43 ....39 F1
Searby cum Owmby
DN38 ....110 D7
Shipton YO30 ....12 E5
Station Mews HU18 ....134 D4
Station Rd Bainton YO25 ..31 E6
Blyton DN21 ....117 F6
Bridlington YO15 ....122 D2
Brough HU15 ....68 B5
Burringham DN17 ....95 D4
7 Burstwick HU12 ....73 A6
Burton Agnes YO25 ....10 A1
Carlton DN14 ....63 C3
Cleethorpes DN35 ....153 E3
Copmanthorpe YO23 .....132 B2
Cottingham HU13 ....143 E1
East Halton DN40 ....86 D7
Eastrington DN14 ....65 F8
Epworth DN9 ....105 D7
Fulstow LN11 ....121 D7
Garthorpe & Fockerby
DN17 ....81 E6
Garton YO25 ....20 A5
Gilberdyke HU15 ....66 D8
Grasby DN38 ....110 E6
Grimsby DN37 ....102 B5
Gunness DN15 ....95 E5
Habrough DN40 ....100 E8
Harpham YO25 ....21 E8
Hatfield DN7 ....92 D4
Haxby YO32 ....13 F5
Haxey DN9 ....116 C7
Healing DN41 ....101 F5
Hensall DN14 ....62 C1
Holton le Clay DN36 ......114 A4
Howden DN14 ....65 B8
Hutton Cranswick YO25 .....32 E7
Keadby with Althorpe
DN17 ....95 D6
Keyingham HU12 ....73 C4
Killingholme High DN40 ....87 B5
Kingston upon Hull
HU16 ....139 C7
Kirton in Lindsey DN21 ....108 B2
Lockington YO25 ....32 D1
Ludborough DN36 ....121 B6
Market Weighton YO43 ....135 D4
Middleton YO25 ....31 C5
Misterton DN10 ....116 D5
Nafferton YO25 ....125 F6
Station Rd continued
New Waltham DN36 ......114 A7
North Cave HU15 ....53 D3
North End DN19 ....71 A1
North Ferriby HU14 ....69 A4
North Kelsey LN7 ....110 A4
North Thoresby DN36 .....114 B1
Norton DN6 ....76 F2
Ottringham HU12 ....73 F4
Owston Ferry DN9 ....106 A2
Patrington HU12 ....74 C2
Pocklington YO42 ....29 A3
24 Poppleton YO26 ....12 F1
Preston HU12 ....72 C8
Rawcliffe DN14 ....64 A1
Riccall YO19 ....49 A8
Scawby DN20 ....108 F7
Scunthorpe DN15 ....151 B6
Selby YO8 ....148 D5
South Cave HU15 ....54 A2
South Kelsey LN7 ....110 D2
South Killingholme DN40 ....87 A5
Stainforth DN7 ....92 C5
Stallingborough DN41 ....101 D6
Thorngumbald HU12 ....73 A5
Thornton Curtis DN39 ......85 F5
Ulceby DN39 ....86 B1
Walkeringham DN10 ......116 D3
Waltham DN37 ....113 E7
Wharram YO17 ....6 A4
Whitton DN15 ....67 D3
Wistow YO8 ....48 C6
5 Withernsea HU19 ....75 A6
Womersley DN6 ....76 D5
York YO1 ....156 A2
Station Rise YO1 ......156 A2
Station Sq 4 YO32 ....14 B7
Station St DN10 ....116 C5
Station View Cliffe YO8 ...49 D3
Little Weighton HU20 ......55 A4
Staveley Rd HU9 ....142 C3
Staves Ct 10 DN36 .....114 D4
Staxton Ct HU9 ....146 D8
Staxton Hill YO12 ....1 C8
Staynor Ave YO8 ....148 E3
Steadings The DN15 .....82 B1
Steele Cl YO43 ....135 D3
Steep Hill HU15 ....54 B2
Steeping Dr 11 DN40 .....87 B1
Steeple Cl 4 YO32 ....13 D5
Steeton Ave 4 HU6 .....140 C7
Stembridge Cl 1 HU9 ....142 E1
Stephen Cl 2 DN39 ......86 A1
Stephen Cres
14 Barton-upon-Humber
DN18 ....84 F8
Grimsby DN34 ....102 C2
10 Humberston DN36 .....114 C8
Stephen's Wlk YO8 .....148 B1
Stephenson Cl
37 Hedon HU12 ....72 D7
Market Weighton YO43 ....135 C3
York YO31 ....127 E1
Stephenson St HU9 .....141 E1
Stephenson Way
YO26 ....129 F5
Stephenson's Wlk
HU16 ....139 D6
Stephenwath La YO41 ...16 C5
Stepney Ave 13 YO16 ....122 C5
Stepney Gr YO16 ....122 C4
Stepney La HU5 ....140 E1
Stepney Prim Sch
HU5 ....140 E1
Sterling Cres DN37 .....113 D6
Sterling Pk YO30 ....127 A3
Sterne Ave
7 Broughton DN20 ....97 D3
York YO31 ....131 A5
Stevenson Pl DN35 .....153 D1
Stevenson's Way 18
DN18 ....84 E8
Steward Cl YO8 ....48 D1
Stewart Garth HU16 ....138 E6
Stewart La YO19 ....36 C4
Steynburg St HU9 ......141 D1
Stirling Cl 2 DN21 ......117 C1
Stirling Gr YO10 ....133 F8
Stirling Rd
Barmby Moor YO42 ....28 E3
York YO30 ....126 F3
Stirling St
Grimsby DN31 ....153 B5
Kingston upon Hull HU3 ...144 F6
Stirrup Cl YO24 ....132 B8
Stockbridge Ave HU9 ...142 E1
Stockbridge La YO25 ....32 F6
Stockbridge Pk 2 HU15 ..68 C7
Stockbridge Rd HU15 ....68 B7
Stockhill Cl 1 YO19 ......26 E7
Stockholm Cl 1 YO10 ...133 D8
Stockholm Pk 23 HU12 ...72 D7
Stockholm Rd
Kingston upon Hull HU7 ...140 E5
16 Thorngumbald HU12 ....72 E5
Stocking La Hillam LS25 ..61 B7
Knottingley WF11 ....61 B2
Stockleigh Cl HU7 ......140 F8
Stocks Dr DN14 ....79 B8
Stocks Hill Belton DN9 ....94 E1
Huggate YO42 ....18 C1
Stockshill Rd DN16 .....151 C2
Stockton Hall YO32 ......14 D3
Stockton La
Heworth YO32 ....128 D1
York YO31 ....131 A7
Stockton on the Forest Prim
Sch YO32 ....14 D3
Stockwell Gr HU9 ......147 E8
Stockwell La 13 YO25 .....34 B2
Stockwell Prim Sch
HU9 ....147 E8
Stockwith La YO8 ....63 A4
Stockwith Rd
Haxey DN9 ....105 E1
Owston Ferry DN9 ....116 E8
Walkeringham DN10 .....116 D3
Walkerith DN21 ....116 E4
Stoke St HU2 ....155 A4
Stone Bridge Dr YO41 ...27 F5
Stone Dale YO42 ....17 D3
Stone Hill DN7 ....93 A4
Stone Hill Rd DN7 ....93 A4
Stone La DN17 ....95 D4
Stone Riggs YO32 ....14 D2
Stonebow The YO1 .....156 C2
Stonebridge Ave HU9 ..142 D1
Stonecarr Ct 2 HU7 .....56 F7
Stoneferry Prim Sch
HU8 ....141 A3
Stoneferry Rd HU8 .....141 A2
Stonegate
Hunmanby YO14 ....2 F8
Thorne/Moorends DN8 .....93 A8
York YO1 ....156 B3
Stonegate Cl 3 HU7 ....141 D7
Stoneknowle Hill YO43 ..54 A8
Stonelands Ct 2 YO30 ..127 A1
Stonepit Balk YO17 ....6 C5
Stonepit Hill YO17 ....6 C4
Stonepit La YO15 ....4 E3
Stonepit Rd
Ellerker HU15 ....54 A1
Welton HU15 ....68 E6
Stones Cl YO24 ....129 E2
Stones Mount HU16 ....139 A7
Stonesdale HU7 ....141 A6
Stonethwaite 5 YO24 ...132 C7
Stoney La HU15 ....53 A3
Stoney Way DN36 ....114 D4
Stony La HU15 ....53 A2
Stool Cl Rd DN9 ....94 E1
Stoop Cl YO32 ....127 C8
Storkhill Rd HU17 ......154 C4
Storking La YO41 ....27 F6
Stornaway Sq HU8 .....141 F7
Stortford St DN31 ......152 B5
Story St HU1 ....155 A3
Stothards La 1 DN19 ....86 A8
Stottlebink 17 YO15 ....5 A2
Stovin Cres DN15 ....83 A5
Stow Cl 11 DN37 ....102 B4
Stow Ct YO32 ....127 E3
Stow Rd Atwick YO25 .....35 D5
Scunthorpe DN16 ....151 B3
Stowe Garth YO16 ......122 F7
Straight La YO19 ....26 F8
Straits Rd HU11 ....46 D2
Strand Cl HU2 ....155 A4
Strand Inf Sch DN32 ...153 A5
Strand Jun Sch DN32 ...152 F5
Strand St DN32 ....152 F5
Stratford Ave 4 DN33 ...102 D2
Stratford Dr DN16 ......151 C5
Stratford Way YO32 .....127 E3
Stratford Wlk HU9 ......142 E1
Strathcona Ave HU5 ....139 E4
Strathearn St 1 HU5 ...140 D3
Strathmore Ave
Burstwick HU12 ....73 A7
Kingston upon Hull HU6 ...140 C6
Stratton Cl HU8 ....142 B7
Stratton Pk 3 HU14 ......69 B6
Strawberry Gdns
Hornsea HU18 ....134 C1
Kingston upon Hull HU9 ...145 B7
Strawberry Hill 2
DN37 ....113 C6
Strawberry St HU9 .....146 B7
Stray Garth YO31 ....130 F7
Stray Rd
Sunk Island HU12 ....89 B6
York YO31 ....131 B6
Stray The HU15 ....54 A2
Straylands Gr YO31 ....130 F8
Street YO25 ....9 E1
Street La Bubwith YO8 ....50 F5
North Kelsey LN7 ....110 B4
Street Life Mus of
Transport* HU1 ....155 C2
Street The YO42 ....28 A2
Strensall Comm Nature
Reserve* YO60 ....14 D8
Strensall Pk YO32 ....14 A5
Strensall Rd
Earswick YO32 ....128 A7
Kingston upon Hull HU5 ...139 C1
York YO32 ....127 F6
Strickland Rd
Eastoft DN17 ....81 A2
13 Hunmanby YO14 ....3 A8
Strickland St HU3 ......145 C4
Strines Gr 9 HU7 ....141 D7
Stripe La YO30 ....126 B5
Stromness Way HU8 ....141 F7
Stroud Cres E HU7 .....141 A7
Stroud Cres W HU7 .....141 A8
Strouther Cl YO42 ....29 A3
Stroykins Cl DN34 .....102 C3
Strubby Cl 6 DN35 .....103 D2
Stuart Cl
Bridlington YO15 ....122 C1
Scunthorpe DN17 ....96 C1
4 Strensall YO32 ....14 C8
Stuart Gr
Eggborough DN14 ....62 A2
Stuart Gr continued
9 Thorpe Willoughby YO8 ..48 B1
Stuart Rd YO24 ....129 D1
Stuart Wortley St
DN31 ....152 F6
Stubbs La
Cridling Stubbs WF11 ......76 A8
Norton DN6 ....76 E2
Stubbs Rd DN6 ....76 D3
Stubden Gr YO30 ......126 F2
Studcross DN9 ....105 D6
Studley Mdws YO16 ....122 D7
Studley St HU8 ....146 B8
Stump Cross* HU17 ......43 C2
Sturdee Gr YO31 ....130 D7
Sturmer Ct 15 DN16 ......96 D1
Sturton Gr 23 DN33 ....102 D2
Sturton La DN20 ....108 E7
Stygate La DN6 ....76 E1
Stylefield Rd 15 YO15 .....5 A2
Styles Croft HU14 ....69 C7
Subway St HU3 ....145 B3
Subway The DN16 ....97 A4
Suddaby Cl HU9 ....141 F2
Suddle Way 4 DN41 .....101 A4
Sudforth La DN14 ....61 C3
Suffolk Ct 13 DN32 .....153 A5
Suffolk St HU5 ....140 D3
Sugar Mill Ponds Nature
Reserve* DN14 ....79 B8
Suggitt's Ct DN35 ......153 D4
Suggitt's La DN35 ......153 D4
Suggitt's Orch DN35 ....153 D4
Sullivan Rd HU4 ....144 B4
Summer Hill DN21 ......117 C1
Summerdale DN18 ....84 E8
Summerfield Ave 3
DN37 ....113 E7
Summerfield Cl
Great Driffield YO25 ......124 D5
4 Waltham DN37 ....113 E7
Summerfield Rd
Bridlington YO15 ....122 D1
York YO24 ....132 C7
Summergangs Dr 17
HU12 ....72 E5
Summergangs Rd
HU8 ....141 C3
Summergroves Way
HU4 ....144 B2
Summermeadows
HU11 ....142 D6
Sunbeam Rd HU4 ....144 D5
Sundrew Ave DN14 .....149 D6
Sunk Island Rd HU12 ....88 E8
Sunningdale 12 DN37 ...113 D6
Sunningdale Ave 1
DN20 ....98 C3
Sunningdale Cl 1 YO26 .129 B5
Sunningdale Dr 7 DN40 .87 C2
Sunningdale Rd
Gipseyville HU4 ....144 E4
Northfield HU13 ....143 F2
Scunthorpe DN17 ....96 B2
Sunny Bank
Kingston upon Hull HU3 ...145 B7
3 Knottingley WF11 ....61 A2
Sunny Cnr 13 DN33 .....102 E1
Sunny Hill 9 DN21 ......108 B1
Sunnybank 1 DN18 ......84 E8
Sunnydale 3 YO32 ......127 D7
Sunway Gr DN16 ....151 A1
Surbiton Cl HU8 ....141 F5
Surrey Ct 12 DN32 .....153 A5
Surrey Garth HU4 ......144 B4
Surrey Way YO30 ......129 F8
Surtees St
Grimsby DN31 ....152 F6
York YO30 ....130 B7
Sussex Cl
5 Kingston upon Hull
HU5 ....139 D1
York YO10 ....131 C2
Sussex Ct 14 DN32 .....153 A5
Sussex Rd YO10 ....131 C2
Sussex St DN35 ....153 B4
Sussex Way 14 YO32 .....14 A7
Susworth Rd DN17 .....106 D4
Sutcliffe Ave 18 DN33 ...102 D2
Sutherland Ave HU6 ....140 B6
Sutherland St YO23 ....130 B1
Sutor Cl YO23 ....132 B3
Sutton Bridge* YO41 .....27 C2
Sutton CE Sch HU7 .....141 D7
Sutton Cl HU7 ....141 B8
Sutton Ct HU8 ....141 E6
Sutton Fields Ind Est
HU2 ....155 C4
Sutton Gdns HU7 ....141 B7
Sutton Ho Rd HU8 ......141 D5
Sutton La
Barmby Moor YO42 ....28 B3
Byram cum Sutton WF11 ....61 A4
Sutton Pk Prim Sch
HU7 ....140 F7
Sutton Pl DN20 ....108 F7
Sutton Rd Howden DN14 ..65 A6
Kingston upon Hull HU6 ...140 D6
12 Kirk Sandall DN3 ....92 A3
Wawne HU7 ....56 F7
Sutton St DN14 ....149 D4
Sutton Upon Derwent CE VC
Prim Sch YO41 ....27 C2
Sutton Way
Kingston upon Hull HU9 ...142 B2
York YO30 ....130 B8
Swaby Dr DN35 ....103 B2
Swaby's Yd HU17 ......154 A3
Swaddale Ave HU10 ....138 F2
Swainby Cl HU7 ....141 D7
Swale Ave YO24 ....132 E8
Swaledale Ave HU9 ....141 E1
Swaledale Mews
YO16 ....122 F6
Swaledale Pl DN16 .....151 D2
Swales Dr YO43 ....135 D3
Swales Rd DN36 ....114 D8
Swallow Ct 4 DN9 .....105 D7
Swallow Dr 3 DN41 .....101 F5
Swallow Grange 6
HU8 ....141 D7
Swallow La DN39 ....85 E2
Swallow Rd YO25 ....125 B5
Swallowfield Dr HU4 ...144 B2
Swallows The 3 YO32 ....14 B8
Swan Cl YO19 ....37 A7
Swan Farm Ct YO19 .....37 A7
Swan Hill* HU11 ....142 F6
Swan La DN14 ....149 D6
Swan Syke Dr 8 DN6 .....76 F2
Swanage Wlk HU4 ......144 B4
Swanella Gr HU3 ....145 A4
Swanfield Rd HU9 ......142 C2
Swanland Ave 3 YO15 ..122 F3
Swanland Butts Cl
HU10 ....143 C6
Swanland Cl 17 DN8 ......93 B7
Swanland Ct 23 DN8 .....93 B7
Swanland Dale HU14 ....69 B8
Swanland Garth 4 HU14 .69 A5
Swanland Hill HU14 .....69 B5
Swanland Prim Sch
HU14 ....69 B6
Swanland Rd HU13 .....143 C2
Swanland Way 3 HU16 .138 E6
Swann St
Kingston upon Hull HU2 ...155 C4
York YO23 ....156 A1
Swannacks View
DN20 ....108 F7
Sweep Cl YO43 ....135 D3
Sweet Briar Cl 7 DN37 .113 D7
Sweet Dews Gr HU9 ....146 D8
Sweyne Garth DN14 .....65 D1
Swift Ave YO25 ....125 B5
Swift Dr DN20 ....98 B2
Swift Rd DN17 ....150 D2
Swiftsure Cres 16 DN34 .102 B2
Swinburne La DN17 ....150 D3
Swinburne Rd DN17 ....150 D3
Swinburne St HU8 ......141 D2
Swinderby Garth 19 HU7 .57 A5
Swinderby Gdns DN34 ..152 A1
Swindon St YO16 ......122 D3
Swine Bank HU5 ....139 B2
Swine La HU11 ....57 E5
Swine Rd HU11 ....45 C1
Swinefleet Prim Sch
DN14 ....65 C1
Swinefleet Rd
Goole DN14 ....149 D2
Goole Fields DN14 ....80 C8
Swinegate
Kingston upon Hull
HU13 ....143 E1
York YO1 ....156 B2
Swinegate Ct E YO1 ....156 B3
Swinemoor Ind Est
HU17 ....137 B5
Swinemoor Inf Sch
HU17 ....154 C4
Swinemoor Jun Sch
HU17 ....154 C4
Swinemoor La HU17 ....137 B5
Swineridge Hill YO42 ....29 B6
Swineridge La YO42 .....29 C6
Swinescaif Hill Swine
HU15 ....54 A3
Swinescaif Rd HU15 .....54 A3
Swinster La DN40 ....86 E6
Swinsty Ct YO30 ....126 F1
Switchback LN8 ....120 A1
Swithin Cl HU13 ....144 A2
Sycamore Ave
15 Grimsby DN33 ....102 E2
York YO32 ....127 D4
Sycamore Cl
3 Barnetby le Wold DN38 ...99 B4
2 Broughton DN20 ....97 D3
Driffield YO25 ....124 D2
East Ella HU4 ....144 C7
14 Gilberdyke HU15 ....66 D8
Goole DN14 ....149 E6
1 Haxby YO32 ....127 D7
Hessle HU13 ....143 C3
Nafferton YO25 ....125 F7
8 Preston HU12 ....58 C1
Selby YO8 ....148 A4
Skelton YO30 ....126 C5
12 Snaith & Cowick DN14 ...78 C8
Sycamore Cres YO25 ....32 E7
Sycamore Ct HU5 ......140 C1
Sycamore Dr
9 Gainsborough DN21 ...117 C1
3 Thorngumbald HU12 .....72 E5
Sycamore Pl
New Earswick YO32 ......127 D4
York YO30 ....156 A3
Sycamore Rd YO8 ....49 B5
Sycamore Terr YO30 ...156 A3
Sycamore View 17 YO26 ..12 F1
Sycamores The HU17 ...137 B3

Sydney Smith Sch HU10 144 A5
Sykehouse Rd DN14 78 C4
Sykes Balk YO25 21 E8
Sykes Cl
6 Kingston upon Hull HU10 143 F6
Swanland HU14 69 B7
Sykes La Garton YO25 124 A5
Goxhill DN19 71 A2
Sykes St HU2 155 B3
Sylvan Falls YO25 124 C4
Sylvan Lea YO25 124 C4
Sylvan Mead YO25 124 C4
Sylvester La HU17 154 A3
Sylvester Sq HU1 155 B3
Sylvester St 13 DN21 108 B1
Sylvia Cl HU6 139 F5
Symmons Cl 4 HU17 137 A6
Symons Cl HU2 155 A4
Symons Way 13 YO42 29 A3

T

Tabard Hamlet 5 DN14 61 F2
Tabard Rd 6 DN14 61 F2
Tabards The 7 DN14 61 F2
Tadcaster Rd YO24 129 F1
Tadcaster Rd Dringhouses YO23 132 E5
Tadman Cl HU17 136 E7
Tadman St HU3 145 D4
Talbot Circ DN3 92 A4
Talbot Rd DN40 87 C1
Talbot Wlk DN16 151 B6
Talisman Dr 6 DN16 96 D1
Tall Trees HU13 143 C3
Tallert Way 28 DN33 102 C2
Tamar Dr 14 DN36 114 A8
Tamar Gr HU8 142 C7
Tamar Wlk DN17 150 C4
Tamarisk Way 18 DN16 96 E2
Tamworth Rd 9 YO30 127 A1
Tan Dyke Way HU17 154 C2
Tanfield Gr HU9 142 C2
Tang Hall La YO31 131 A5
Tang Hall Prim Sch YO31 130 F5
Tanner Row YO1 156 A2
Tanner's Moat YO1 156 A2
Tanpit La DN6 76 E3
Tansley Ct DN15 150 B7
Tansley La HU18 134 D1
Tansterne La HU11 59 A7
Tarbert Cres 2 YO24 132 B7
Tardrew Cl HU17 136 E6
Target La 16 YO42 29 A4
Tarleton Cl 3 DN3 92 A2
Tarran Ave HU6 140 B8
Tasburgh St DN32 152 F2
Tate Cl YO8 48 D6
Tattersall Cl DN17 150 D1
Tattersall Dr 1 HU17 137 B3
Tattershall Ave 14 DN34 102 C2
Tattershall Cl HU2 140 E1
Tatton Cl YO30 127 A1
Taunton Rd HU4 144 A3
Taunton Way 19 DN33 113 E8
Taurus Ct YO23 156 A1
Tavella Ct 1 DN9 105 B2
Tavistock St HU5 140 C3
Taylor Ave HU9 142 C3
Taylor Cl DN9 94 E2
Taylor St DN35 153 B5
Taylor's Ave DN35 103 C2
Taylor's La HU19 75 C2
Taylors Cl 5 HU17 55 B7
Taylors Field YO25 124 E4
Teal Cl 12 Broughton DN20 98 B2
Walkington HU17 55 B7
Teal Dr
23 Barton-upon-Humber DN18 84 E8
York YO24 132 C8
Teal Garth YO15 11 B4
Teal Pl LN7 111 A4
Teal Rd 1 HU15 52 F1
Tealby Gr 19 DN33 102 D2
Tealby Rd DN17 150 D1
Teale St DN15 151 A8
Team Gate 1 DN37 102 B3
Teanby Dr DN15 83 A5
Tedder Rd YO24 129 B1
Teddington Cl HU8 141 E6
Tedworth Rd HU9 142 C5
Tee La DN15 82 B5
Tees Gr HU8 142 C7
Teesdale Ave HU9 146 E8
Teesdale Mews YO16 122 F7
Telford Pl DN34 152 A3
Telford St HU9 141 E2
Telford Terr 1 YO24 130 B2
Temper Rd DN16 151 F4
Temperance Ave DN17 107 D7
Temperton's La DN9 106 A2
Templar Cl DN14 61 F1
Templar Ct 17 DN16 96 D2
Templar Way YO8 148 C2
Templar's Bath* DN16 96 D1
Temple Ave YO10 131 B4
Temple Cl Belton DN9 94 E2
Welton HU15 68 E6
Temple Garth YO23 132 C1
Temple La
Aylesby DN37 101 E1
Carnaby YO16 10 E5
Copmanthorpe YO23 132 C1
Temple Manor* YO8 62 D4
Temple Rd YO23 132 F4
Temple St HU5 140 E1
Temple Wlk 2 HU15 68 E6
Templefield Rd DN21 119 A3
Templemans La DN36 114 A1
Templemead YO31 130 E8
Templewaters 31 HU7 56 F5
Temsdale 2 HU7 141 A6
Ten Thorn La YO26 129 A4
Tennant St YO8 148 B6
Tennent Rd YO24 129 B2
Tennison Ct HU16 139 A7
Tennyson Ave
Bridlington YO15 122 E3
1 Campsall DN6 76 E1
Kingston upon Hull HU5 140 A1
7 Thorne/Moorends DN8 93 B8
York YO30 130 C7
Tennyson Cl Brigg DN20 98 C1
Caistor LN7 111 A3
Tennyson Ct HU12 72 D7
Tennyson Mews 4 DN31 152 D4
Tennyson Rd
Cleethorpes DN35 153 E3
Scunthorpe DN16 151 D3
Tennyson St
32 Gainsborough DN21 117 B1
Goole DN14 149 C5
Grimsby DN31 152 D4
Tensing Rd DN16 151 C1
Tenterden Cl HU7 141 A6
Tern Gr HU8 142 C5
Terrington Cl YO32 14 B8
Terrington Pl 4 DN35 103 B2
Terry Ave YO1 156 B1
Terry St
Kingston upon Hull HU3 140 D1
York YO23 130 C1
Teskey King Specl Sch HU6 140 A5
Tetley Rd DN16 151 C3
Tetley View 2 DN17 94 E6
Tetney CP Sch DN36 114 D4
Tetney La DN36 114 B5
Tetney Lock Rd DN36 114 D4
Tetney Rd DN36 114 C8
Tewkesbury Dr DN34 152 C2
Thanet Prim Sch HU9 142 D6
Thanet Rd
Kingston upon Hull HU9 142 D5
York YO24 129 D1
Thatch Cl YO8 148 C4
Thatchers Croft YO23 132 C3
Thaxted Cl HU8 142 B6
Theaker Ave DN21 117 C1
Theakston Mews HU17 136 D1
Thealby La DN15 82 D5
Thearne Cl 7 HU5 140 C3
Thearne La HU17 56 D7
Theatre Mews HU2 155 B3
Theodore Rd DN15 150 E8
Theresa Cl 6 YO31 127 F1
Therm Rd HU8 155 C4
Thesiger St DN32 152 F5
Thesiger Wlk 2 DN32 152 F5
Thief La Barlow YO8 148 F1
York YO10 130 F3
Thimblehall La HU15 52 E2
Thinholme La DN9 105 A1
Third Ave
Bridlington YO15 123 A4
Fixborough Stather DN15 82 A1
Goole DN14 149 C4
Scunthorpe DN17 150 C2
York YO31 130 F5
Third La DN37 113 D3
Thirkleby Cres DN32 103 A2
Thirkleby Way YO10 131 C4
Thirlby Wlk HU5 139 D3
Thirlmere Ave DN33 113 E8
Thirlmere Dr YO31 131 A6
Thirlmere Wlk DN14 149 E6
Thirsk Mews HU5 139 D4
Thirtle Bridge La HU19 74 C8
Thirtleby La HU11 57 F6
Thirty Acre La 13 HU12 72 D7
Thiseldine Cl 6 YO43 53 F7
Thistle Cl YO8 148 C2
Thistleton Gdns 6 HU5 140 E2
Thixendale Rd
Bridlington YO16 122 F7
Fridaythorpe YO25 18 A7
Thomas Clarkson Way HU7 140 E8
Thomas Rd
Scunthorpe DN17 150 F4
17 Stainforth DN7 92 C5
Thomas St
Grimsby DN32 152 F3
Kingston upon Hull HU9 146 B7
6 Selby YO8 148 D6
2 York YO10 130 E3
Thomas Sumpter Comp Sch DN17 150 E3
Thompson Ave HU17 154 C3
Thompson Cl 9 YO8 49 B4
Thompson Dr
16 Hatfield DN7 92 D4
2 Strensall YO32 14 B8
Thompson Nook 14 DN7 92 D4
Thompson Pl 6 YO26 129 E5
Thompson Rd HU12 72 B7
Thompson St
Bridlington YO16 122 D3
Scunthorpe DN15 151 B7
Thonock Rd DN21 117 D4
Thoresby Ave YO16 122 D6
Thoresby Cl YO16 122 D6
Thoresby Mews 7 YO16 122 D6
Thoresby Pl 2 DN35 103 C2
Thoresby Prim Sch HU5 145 B8
Thoresby Rd
Fulstow LN11 121 D8
North Coates DN36 115 A2
Scunthorpe DN17 150 D1
Tetney DN36 114 D3
York YO24 129 B1
Thoresby St HU5 145 B8
Thoresway Gr 9 DN33 102 D2
Thorgam Ct DN31 152 C3
Thorganby Rd DN35 103 D2
Thorgill Gr HU5 139 E3
Thorn Bank DN9 104 E4
Thorn Barn Cl HU12 72 F5
Thorn Fields HU12 72 D5
Thorn La DN19 86 A8
Thorn Leigh 3 HU3 145 C6
Thorn Marsh Rd HU12 72 E2
Thorn Nook YO31 130 F8
Thorn Rd HU12 72 D7
Thornbridge Cl HU9 142 B3
Thornbury Rd DN40 87 C1
Thorncroft 8 YO19 26 F7
Thorndale HU7 140 E8
Thorndale Croft YO25 19 B5
Thorndale La YO25 19 A5
Thornden Bldgs YO8 148 D5
Thorndike Way DN21 117 D1
Thorne & Dikesmarsh DN8 79 A2
Thorne Brooke Prim Sch DN8 93 B7
Thorne Gram Sch DN8 93 B8
Thorne N Sta DN8 93 A8
Thorne Rd Hatfield DN7 92 F5
Kirk Sandall DN3 92 A1
3 Stainforth DN7 92 C6
Thorne S Sta DN8 93 B7
Thorne Swimming Baths DN8 93 B8
Thorne Waste Drain Rd DN8 79 D1
Thorneycroft Rd 14 HU12 72 E5
Thornfield Ave 5 YO31 130 F8
Thornfield Dr 7 YO31 127 E2
Thorngarth La DN19 85 C8
Thorngumbald Inf Sch HU12 72 D5
Thorngumbald Jun Sch HU12 72 F5
Thorngumbald Rd HU12 72 B4
Thornham Cl HU15 53 F1
Thornham's Way 6 HU15 68 C7
Thornhill Ave HU8 141 C4
Thornhill Cres 19 DN17 96 C2
Thornhill Gdns DN34 152 A3
Thornhills 19 YO32 13 F5
Thornholme Dr 14 DN16 96 D2
Thornleys HU17 43 A4
Thornton 10 HU15 68 C6
Thornton Abbey (Rems of)* DN39 86 B5
Thornton Abbey Sta DN39 86 A5
Thornton Ave DN16 151 A3
Thornton Cl HU13 143 D1
Thornton Cres DN35 103 C2
Thornton Ct 22 DN36 114 A8
Thornton Dam La HU15 66 D8
Thornton Gdns 5 DN41 101 A4
Thornton Gr
7 Grimsby DN34 102 C2
3 Preston HU12 58 C1
Thornton La YO25 20 A1
Thornton Moor Cl YO30 126 F2
Thornton Pl DN40 87 B1
Thornton Rd
Barrow upon Humber DN19 85 D6
Bridlington YO16 122 B2
Goxhill DN19 85 F6
South Kelsey LN7 110 A1
Thornton St DN19 85 C7
Thorntondale Dr YO16 122 F7
Thorntree Cl DN14 149 E6
Thorntree Gr YO30 127 B2
Thorntree La
Balne DN14 77 C6
Goole DN14 149 E6
Thornwick Ave HU10 143 E8
Thornwick Cl 2 HU3 145 C5
Thornwick Rd YO15 5 B3
Thornwood Covert 1 YO24 129 C1
Thorny La YO42 16 F2
Thorold Pl 11 DN3 92 A3
Thorold St DN31 153 A5
Thorpe YO25 32 B1
Thorpe La YO8 48 B8
Thorpe Leys YO25 32 B2
Thorpe Rd
6 Brough HU15 68 C5
Howden DN14 65 C8
Thorpe Rd Ave 2 DN14 65 B7
Thorpe St
9 Bridlington YO15 122 E2
York YO23 130 B2
Thorpe Willoughby CP Sch YO8 48 B2
Thorpehall Rd DN3 92 A2
Thorpepark Prim Sch HU6 140 A8
Thorpepark Rd HU6 139 F8
Three Lakes Ind Est YO8 148 D2
Three Lakes Ret Pk YO8 148 D3
Thrislington Sq 19 DN8 79 B2
Thronton Ct YO43 135 D5
Throughleys La YO42 39 A5
Thrunscoe Inf Sch DN35 153 F1
Thrunscoe Rd DN35 153 F1
Thrussendale Rd YO17 16 E8
Thurlow Ave
Beverley HU17 136 E6
22 Pocklington YO42 29 A3
Thurlow Garth YO25 125 F7
Thurlstone Cl 18 HU7 56 F6
Thurstan Cl
Beverley HU17 136 D2
Kingston upon Hull HU9 142 D2
Thurstan Rd HU17 154 A2
Thwaite St HU16 139 C6
Thwing Rd
Burton Fleming YO25 2 E2
Kilham YO25 9 B5
Thyme Way HU17 55 F8
Tibby La YO25 32 C4
Tichbourne Cl 6 HU3 145 C5
Tickton CE VC Prim Sch HU17 137 F8
Tickton Gr HU6 139 F4
Tickton Mdws HU17 137 F8
Tideswell Ct DN15 150 B6
Tideworth Hague La DN14 78 C3
Tiger La HU17 154 A3
Tilbury Prim Sch HU4 144 B3
Tilbury Rd HU4 144 B3
Tilia Cl
Kingston upon Hull HU4 144 B2
Scunthorpe DN16 96 E2
Tilmire Cl 2 YO10 133 F8
Tilworth Rd HU8 141 F4
Timberland DN16 96 E2
Timberley Dr 7 DN37 102 B4
Tindale Bank Rd DN10 116 C7
Tinker La YO23 24 D6
Tinkler's La WF11 61 D6
Tinley Cl HU16 139 B7
Tintagel Way DN36 114 A8
Tintern Ave YO16 122 E6
Tippaty La WF11 61 A4
Tippet La HU17 44 F2
Tison Garth HU10 143 F6
Tithe Barn Cl 9 HU12 74 D1
Tithe Barn La
8 Patrington HU12 74 D1
13 Thorne/Moorends DN8 93 B8
Tithe Barn Rd 2 WF11 61 A2
Tithe Barn Way DN14 61 F3
Tithe Cl YO24 129 B1
Tithe La YO25 22 E5
Tithe Rd HU12 58 A1
Tiverton Rd HU7 141 A8
Tiverton St DN35 153 C4
Tivoli Gdns DN32 152 F4
Toadham La DN14 77 C5
Toby Ct YO32 14 A7
Todd La DN21 117 F4
Todd's La HU15 68 A8
Todds Cl HU14 69 C6
Todds Ct DN17 107 D7
Todds La DN15 82 A4
Toft Gn YO1 156 A2
Tofts Rd 2 DN18 84 E8
Tokenspire Bsns Pk & Ret Outlet HU17 137 C2
Toll Bar Ave DN36 113 F7
Toll Gavel HU17 154 A3
Tollerton Rd YO30 12 B7
Tollesby La 9 DN7 92 D4
Tollymore Pk 28 HU7 56 F5
Tom Hammond Way DN32 153 A4
Tomline Rd 2 DN41 101 A5
Tomline St DN31 152 F5
Tomlinson Ave DN15 150 E7
Tonbridge 21 DN33 113 E8
Tonbridge Gr 2 HU9 142 E2
Tongue La HU15 66 E6
Tonnant Way 6 DN34 102 B3
Toogood St HU2 155 B4
Toothill Gdns 2 DN34 102 C3
Toothill Rd 1 DN34 102 C3
Top La
Copmanthorpe YO23 132 B3
Kirk Bramwith DN7 92 A7
Top Rd
South Killingholme DN40 86 E3
Winterton DN15 82 F6
Worlaby DN20 98 D8
Topaz Gr 3 HU3 145 A4
Topcliff Ct YO8 148 B7
Topcliffe Garth HU7 141 C8
Tophill Low Nature Reserve* YO25 33 D4
Torbay Dr DN33 113 E7
Torchil Cl HU10 143 C6
Toremill Cl YO32 127 D4
Torksey Dr DN33 102 D2
Torksey Pl 28 DN33 102 D2
Torksey St DN21 108 B2
Tornville Cres DN14 79 B8
Torridge Gr HU8 142 C6
Torridge Rd HU8 142 C6
Torridon Pl YO24 132 B7
Torrington Rd DN17 150 C4
Torrington St
Grimsby DN32 152 F1
5 Kingston upon Hull HU5 140 C3
Tostig Ave YO26 129 C5
Tostig Cl 14 YO41 15 D2
Totnes Rd DN33 113 E7
Tottenham Cl 3 HU8 141 F5
Tottering La DN14 51 B5
Tottermire La DN9 105 D7
Towan Cl 11 HU7 56 F5
Tower Hill
Kingston upon Hull HU13 143 E1
Westwoodside DN9 105 B2
Tower Hill Dr HU13 143 E1
Tower Hill Mews 2 HU13 143 E1
Tower House La HU12 147 F7
Tower Pl YO1 156 B1
Tower Rd
Rimswell HU12 74 C6
Roos HU11 60 A4
Tower St
Flamborough YO15 5 A2
31 Gainsborough DN21 117 B1
Kingston upon Hull HU9 155 C1
York YO1 156 B1
Tower View
Carlton DN14 63 C2
Kingston upon Hull HU10 143 C5
Town End Ave DN14 63 C3
Town End Gdns 3 YO32 13 D5
Town End La YO42 18 C2
Town End Rd HU12 72 A5
Town Farm Cl YO25 23 A2
Town Hall Sq DN31 152 E3
Town Hall St 1 DN31 152 E3
Town Hill DN20 97 E4
Town Hill Dr DN20 97 E4
Town Rd DN36 114 D4
Town St Hayton YO42 40 C8
Immingham DN40 86 E4
Nunburnholme YO42 29 F3
Shiptonthorpe YO43 40 F6
Townend Cswy DN14 66 D2
Townend La HU15 53 C3
Townend Rd
Ellerton YO42 38 D1
12 Newbald YO43 53 F7
Walkington HU17 55 B8
Townend St YO31 156 B4
Townsend Cl DN36 103 E1
Townshend Dr 1 HU16 138 F5
Townside DN40 86 D6
Townside Cl 1 YO43 53 F7
Townside Rd YO43 53 F7
Towthorpe YO43 135 D8
Towthorpe La YO43 135 B7
Towthorpe Medieval Village* YO43 135 B8
Towthorpe Moor La YO32 14 C5
Towthorpe Rd YO32 13 F5
Towton Ave 9 YO24 129 F2
Toynton Rd 27 DN33 102 D2
Trafalgar Ave 10 DN34 102 B3
Trafalgar Cres YO15 11 B4
Trafalgar Pk DN36 114 A8
Trafalgar St
5 Kingston upon Hull HU3 145 D7
Kingston upon Hull HU2 155 A4
York YO23 130 B1
Trafford Rd
Kingston upon Hull HU10 143 E8
4 Norton DN6 76 E2
Trafford St DN15 151 B8
Traffords Way DN20 108 F6
Train Ave HU6 140 C7
Train Gate DN21 108 B1
Tranby Ave
Kingston upon Hull HU13 143 D2
York YO10 131 D4
Tranby Croft HU10 143 C5
Tranby Dr DN32 103 A2
Tranby La Hessle HU10 143 B5
Swanland HU14 69 B6
Tranby Lodge Gdns HU13 143 C1
Tranby Mdws Pk HU13 143 C3
Tranby Ride HU10 143 C5
Trandy La DN14 65 D5
Tranmere Cl HU3 145 B5
Tranmere Pk HU18 134 D3
Tranmore La DN14 62 B3
Travis Ave 18 DN8 93 B8
Travis Cl 16 DN8 93 B8
Travis Cty Prim Sch DN7 92 E4
Travis Gr 17 DN8 93 B8
Travis Rd HU16 138 F5
Travis St YO15 122 E3
Traviss Cl DN16 151 B4
Trawden Cl HU7 56 F6

Treasurer's House* YO31 ....156 B3
Tree Cl 9 DN9 ....105 D6
Treece Gdns 10 DN18 ....69 F1
Trees The HU6 ....140 C4
Treeton Rd DN14 ....65 A6
Tremayne Ave 2 HU15 ....68 C5
Trenchard Cl 3 DN40 ....87 D2
Trenchard Rd YO26 ....129 B6
Trenfield Ct YO24 ....129 F3
Trent Ave 4 YO32 ....127 F6
Trent Pk 6 HU7 ....56 F6
Trent Rd DN17 ....95 D6
Trent Side
4 Amcotts DN17 ....81 F1
Keadby with Althorpe DN17 ....95 D6
Trent St DN16 ....151 B6
Trent View DN17 ....95 D5
Trent Way YO24 ....132 D7
Trentham Cl YO16 ....122 D6
Trentham Dr YO16 ....122 D6
Trentham Mews 1 YO16 ....122 D6
Trentholme Dr
Messingham DN17 ....107 D7
2 York YO24 ....130 A2
Trenton Ave HU4 ....144 B6
Trentside
Keadby with Althorpe DN17 ....95 D3
Morton DN21 ....117 A2
Trentvale Prep Sch DN17 ....95 D6
Trevor Cl 15 DN37 ....101 F1
Trevor Gr 8 YO24 ....129 F2
Trevor St HU2 ....155 B4
Triangle Dr HU14 ....69 A4
Triangle The 11 HU14 ....69 A4
Tribune Way YO30 ....127 B2
Trinity Ave YO15 ....122 F3
Trinity Cl
Burstwick HU12 ....73 A6
Goxhill DN19 ....86 A8
Leven HU17 ....45 B8
Trinity Ct
5 Broughton DN20 ....97 D4
Kingston upon Hull HU2 ....155 B1
Trinity Garth HU16 ....138 A8
Trinity Gr
Beverley HU17 ....154 B3
1 Bridlington YO15 ....122 F3
3 Kingston upon Hull HU9 ....141 F1
Kingston upon Hull HU13 ....143 E2
Trinity House La HU1 ....155 B2
Trinity La
Beverley HU17 ....154 B2
York YO1 ....156 A2
Trinity Mews 2 YO15 ....122 F3
Trinity Rd
Bridlington YO15 ....122 F3
Cleethorpes DN35 ....153 E1
Hornsea HU18 ....134 C2
10 Scunthorpe DN16 ....96 D2
Trinity St
Grimsby DN31 ....153 A5
Kingston upon Hull HU3 ....145 C7
Trinity Wlk 2 DN18 ....69 E1
Trippett St HU2 ....155 C3
Triton Rd HU9 ....142 D3
Trolleybus Mus at Sandtoft The* DN8 ....94 A3
Trondheim Way DN41 ....101 E8
Troon Cl 2 YO26 ....129 B5
Troon Ct HU8 ....142 B6
Troon Rd DN7 ....92 D4
Troutbeck 7 YO24 ....132 C7
Troutsdale Ave YO30 ....126 E2
Troutsdale Cl YO16 ....122 F7
Troutsdale Gr HU9 ....146 F8
Trumfleet La DN6 ....77 D1
Trundle Gate YO43 ....53 F6
Trundle La DN7 ....92 C8
Trundles La 7 WF11 ....61 A2
Trunkass La DN37 ....112 D6
Trunscoe Jun Sch DN35 ....153 E1
Truro Cl HU7 ....141 C6
Tudor Cl
Bridlington YO15 ....122 C1
10 Thorpe Willoughby YO8 ....48 B1
Tudor Ct HU10 ....138 C1
Tudor Dr HU6 ....140 B8
Tudor Rd YO24 ....129 C2
Tudor Way YO32 ....14 C8
Tudworth Field Rd DN7 ....93 B5
Tudworth Rd DN7 ....93 A5
Tuke Ave YO10 ....131 B4
Tulip Rd DN15 ....151 C7
Tummel Ct 4 DN40 ....101 B8
Tune St YO8 ....49 B4
Tunis St HU5 ....140 E2
Tunnard St DN32 ....153 A4
Tunnel Rd DN20 ....98 D4
Turbary La YO32 ....128 E6
Turbary Rd
Epworth DN9 ....105 B6
Haxey DN9 ....105 C3
Turf Moor Rd DN7 ....93 A3
Turkey La YO16 ....10 E4
Turks Head Ct YO1 ....156 C3
Turks Head Gdns 10 HU15 ....52 F1
Turmar View HU11 ....58 A4
Turmarr Rd HU12 ....89 C8
Turmarr Villas 6 HU12 ....90 F6
Turmer Ave YO15 ....122 F3
Turnberry App DN37 ....113 D6
Turnberry Dr YO26 ....129 B4
Turnbull Dr 18 YO42 ....29 A3
Turner Ave HU19 ....75 A5
Turner Cl YO43 ....135 D3
Turner Ct HU3 ....155 A2
Turner Rd HU17 ....154 B4
Turner St 5 DN21 ....108 B1
Turner's Croft YO10 ....131 A1
Turner's La 15 HU14 ....69 A5
Turners Sq 9 YO8 ....148 C5
Turnham La YO8 ....49 C2
Turnhead Cres YO8 ....49 B5
Turnhead Ct YO8 ....49 B6
Turnmire Rd 1 YO24 ....132 E8
Turpin Cl DN21 ....117 C1
Turpin Ct YO1 ....156 C1
Turpit La HU12 ....72 A5
Turrets The 15 HU12 ....72 E5
Turver's La WF11 ....61 C2
Tuxford Gr HU9 ....142 E2
Tweed Gr HU8 ....142 B5
Tween Dykes Rd HU7 ....141 D6
Tweendykes Specl Sch HU7 ....141 C6
Twickenham Cl 2 HU8 ....142 A5
Twin Pike Way 14 YO32 ....13 D5
Two Riggs HU17 ....43 A4
Twyford Cl 5 HU9 ....142 E2
Twyning Pl DN35 ....153 D3
Tydeman Cl 1 DN16 ....96 D1
Tyler Ave DN34 ....152 A3
Tyn Garth YO19 ....36 D8
Tyne St HU3 ....145 B4
Tynedale 1 HU7 ....141 A6
Tynedale Ct 1 DN3 ....92 A2
Tysons Cl 7 DN18 ....69 F1
Tythe Garth 8 HU15 ....53 D3

U

Ulceby Rd
Scunthorpe DN17 ....96 B2
South Killingholme DN39 ....86 C2
Wootton DN39 ....85 F3
Ulceby St Nicholas' CE Prim Sch DN39 ....86 A1
Ulceby Sta DN39 ....86 C2
Ullswater YO24 ....132 D7
Ullswater Cl HU8 ....141 D4
Ullswater Gr DN14 ....149 E5
Ulrome Ct 1 HU9 ....142 B1
Ulster Ave 5 DN33 ....102 E1
Ulster Rd DN21 ....117 B1
Ulverston Rd HU4 ....144 A3
Ulyett La DN17 ....106 C8
Undercroft 7 YO19 ....26 F7
Underground Bunker* HU19 ....75 C1
Underwit Rd YO8 ....63 C4
Unicorn Row 10 DN21 ....108 B1
Union La YO8 ....148 C4
Union Pl DN14 ....149 D6
Union Rd DN8 ....93 A8
Union St
Great Driffield YO25 ....124 E4
Kingston upon Hull HU2 ....155 B3
20 Pocklington YO42 ....29 A4
Union Terr YO31 ....156 B4
Unity Ave HU13 ....143 F1
Unity Rd DN32 ....153 C2
University of Hull
Cottingham HU16 ....138 F8
Kingston upon Hull HU16 ....139 C5
Kingston upon Hull HU6 ....140 B4
University of Humberside
Kingston upon Hull HU6 ....140 C4
Kingston upon Hull HU6 ....140 A4
University of Lincoln HU1 ....155 B3
University of York
Heslington YO10 ....130 F1
York YO10 ....130 E3
York YO30 ....156 A3
University Rd YO10 ....130 F2
Upavon Garth HU7 ....141 C7
Upper Burgess St DN31 ....152 D4
Upper Hanover St 6 YO26 ....129 F5
Upper Kenyon St 5 DN8 ....93 A8
Upper Newborough St 1 YO30 ....130 C7
Upper Poppleton Jun Sch YO26 ....12 F1
Upper Price St YO23 ....156 A1
Upper St Paul's Terr YO24 ....130 A4
Upper Union St HU1 ....155 A2
Uppercommon La DN14 ....61 F3
Uppercroft 4 YO32 ....127 C8
Upperthorpe Hill DN9 ....105 A2
Upton St HU8 ....141 B1
Uredale Pl DN16 ....151 E1
Usher La YO32 ....13 F6
Utgard Way 4 DN33 ....102 D1
Utterby Dr DN34 ....152 C1
Utterby Prim Sch DN36 ....121 B5
Uxbridge Gr HU9 ....142 E1

V

Valda Vale 34 DN40 ....87 B1
Vale Cres YO42 ....16 F2
Vale of Ancholme Tech Coll DN20 ....98 B2
Vale The
Beverley HU17 ....137 B2
Kingston upon Hull HU10 ....143 B7
Skelton YO30 ....126 B5
Valentine Cl
1 Kingston upon Hull HU4 ....144 A2
6 Pocklington YO42 ....29 A3
Valiant Dr HU9 ....142 D4
Valletta St HU9 ....147 D7
Valley Dr HU10 ....143 B7
Valley View YO19 ....37 F7
Valley View Dr DN16 ....96 D1
Vanbrugh Dr YO10 ....131 C3
Vanbrugh Way YO10 ....131 A2
Vancouver Cres 5 DN17 ....96 C2
Vane St HU3 ....145 D7
Vanessa Dr DN21 ....117 B2
Varah Cl DN18 ....84 E8
Varlow Rd LN7 ....111 B4
Varsity Cl 6 DN7 ....104 A8
Vaughan Ave DN36 ....103 A2
Vaughan Rd
10 Campsall DN6 ....76 E1
1 Kingston upon Hull HU13 ....69 F4
Vavasour Ct YO23 ....132 B2
Veal St DN31 ....152 C3
Ventnor St HU5 ....140 C3
Venture Bsns Pk DN31 ....152 B6
Vere Terr DN31 ....152 C4
Verity Way YO25 ....125 A3
Vermont St HU5 ....140 D3
Vermuyden Rd DN8 ....79 C2
Vermuyden Sch DN14 ....149 B5
Vermuyden Terr DN14 ....149 D2
Vermuyden Villas DN8 ....94 A3
Vernon Cl YO23 ....133 A3
Vernon Rd
Bridlington YO15 ....122 F3
York YO30 ....126 E2
Vernon St HU1 ....155 B2
Vesper Dr YO24 ....129 B3
Vesper Wlk YO32 ....127 F6
Veterinary Cl YO25 ....9 A2
Vicar La Beverley HU17 ....154 A3
Eastrington DN14 ....51 F1
Hollym HU19 ....75 A4
Kingston upon Hull HU1 ....155 B1
Vicarage Ave DN20 ....98 D3
Vicarage Cl
Beswick YO25 ....32 D4
2 Bubwith YO8 ....50 D7
12 Hunmanby YO14 ....2 F8
Vicarage Cres DN15 ....82 B5
Vicarage Gdns
2 Brough HU15 ....68 C6
Grimsby DN34 ....152 C2
Scunthorpe DN15 ....150 F6
Wrawby DN20 ....98 E4
1 York YO10 ....131 C4
Vicarage La
Beckingham DN10 ....116 D1
Bishop Wilton YO42 ....16 F2
8 Buckton/Bempton YO15 ....4 D3
Cadney DN20 ....109 D6
Elsham DN20 ....98 F7
Grasby DN38 ....110 E7
Immingham DN40 ....86 E4
3 Kingston upon Hull HU13 ....143 E1
Naburn YO19 ....36 E8
Redbourne DN21 ....108 F2
Scawby DN20 ....108 E8
Skirlaugh HU11 ....45 D2
Wootton DN39 ....85 E3
Vicarage Lawn DN34 ....152 C2
Vicarage Pk DN15 ....83 D1
Vicarage Rd
Willoughton DN21 ....119 B4
Wrawby DN20 ....98 D3
Vicar's La HU12 ....91 A6
Vicar's Wlk 1 DN17 ....94 D7
Vicars Cl YO23 ....132 B2
Viceroy Cl HU2 ....155 B4
Vickerman's La HU12 ....59 A3
Victor Charles Terr YO43 ....135 D4
Victor St Grimsby DN32 ....153 A4
2 Kingston upon Hull HU9 ....146 C8
York YO1 ....156 B1
Victoria Ave
Hatfield DN7 ....92 D4
Hornsea HU18 ....134 D5
Sculcoates HU5 ....140 A1
Willerby HU10 ....138 C2
12 Withernsea HU19 ....75 A6
Victoria Cl
Marshchapel DN36 ....115 C2
Stainforth DN7 ....92 C5
Wike Well End DN8 ....93 A7
Victoria Ct
Burton upon Stather DN15 ....82 B5
15 York YO26 ....129 F5
Victoria Dock Prim Sch HU9 ....146 B6
Victoria Dr
3 Barton-upon-Humber DN18 ....69 E1
3 Gilberdyke HU15 ....66 D8
Victoria Farm Cl YO23 ....24 C6
Victoria Gdns
Hornsea HU18 ....134 C6
1 Kingston upon Hull HU5 ....140 A1
Victoria Rd
Barnetby le Wold DN38 ....99 B4
Beverley HU17 ....154 A1
Bridlington YO15 ....122 E3
Great Driffield YO25 ....124 D5
5 Keelby DN41 ....101 A5
2 Pocklington YO42 ....29 A4
Scunthorpe DN16 ....151 A1
Woodmansey HU17 ....55 E8
Victoria Ret Pk DN31 ....152 E5
Victoria St Goole DN14 ....149 D4
Kingston upon Hull HU13 ....144 A1
1 York YO23 ....156 B1
Victoria St N DN31 ....152 E4
Victoria St S 3 DN31 ....152 E3
Victoria St W 2 DN31 ....152 E3
Victoria Way 2 YO32 ....130 F8
Victoria's Way HU16 ....139 B6
Victory Way
1 Barton-upon-Humber DN18 ....69 F1
9 Grimsby DN37 ....102 B2
Viking Cl
2 Immingham DN40 ....87 B1
Kingston upon Hull HU10 ....138 C2
20 Stamford Bridge YO41 ....15 D2
Viking Dr 5 YO19 ....48 F8
Viking Rd
Bridlington YO16 ....123 B6
Stamford Bridge YO41 ....15 D2
York YO26 ....129 C5
Villa Cl YO8 ....49 F1
Villa Ct YO26 ....129 B7
Villa Fields 4 DN14 ....63 C1
Villa Gr 2 YO31 ....130 E6
Village Farm Cl 11 HU15 ....52 F1
Village Farm Ct 7 DN14 ....61 D4
Village Farm Rd 5 HU12 ....58 C1
Village Garth 1 YO32 ....13 E5
Village Rd
Kingston upon Hull HU8 ....141 C1
Sunk Island HU12 ....88 E5
Village St YO30 ....126 E3
Village The Haxby YO32 ....13 E5
Skelton YO30 ....126 B5
Stockton on the Forest YO32 ....14 D3
Strensall YO32 ....14 B7
York YO10 ....131 C4
Ville Rd DN16 ....151 D2
Villiers Ct 7 HU12 ....72 D7
Vincent Cl 3 HU4 ....144 A2
Vincent Way YO24 ....132 C8
Vine Cl HU16 ....139 A7
Vine Gdns YO8 ....50 D7
Vine St YO23 ....130 C2
Vinegarth 2 DN9 ....105 E6
Vinehall Rd DN9 ....105 C2
Vinery The 18 DN14 ....65 A7
Vineyards The 3 HU17 ....45 A8
Violet Cl 16 DN35 ....103 C1
Viscount Way 12 DN36 ....114 D8
Vivars Way YO8 ....148 D5
Vivian Ave DN32 ....153 B1
Voases Cl HU10 ....143 E6
Voases La HU10 ....143 E6
Volage Ct 18 YO42 ....29 A4
Volta St YO8 ....148 E4
Vulcan St HU6 ....140 F4
Vulcan Way DN7 ....93 A1
Vyner St YO31 ....130 C7

W

Waby Cl DN37 ....102 B4
Waddingham Pl
3 Habrough DN40 ....100 E8
19 New Waltham DN36 ....114 A7
Waddingham Rd LN7 ....109 F1
Waddington Ct HU5 ....140 B3
Waddington Dr 24 DN17 ....96 C2
Waddington Pl DN34 ....152 A1
Wade Ave HU18 ....134 C6
Wade House La YO8 ....63 F4
Wadebridge Gr 4 HU9 ....142 E1
Wadham Gr 4 HU9 ....141 F1
Wadhurst Cl HU7 ....141 A6
Wadsworth Ave HU6 ....140 C8
Wadsworth Rd YO25 ....124 B3
Waggoners Dr 3 YO23 ....132 B3
Wain's Gr YO24 ....132 D7
Wain's Rd YO24 ....132 D8
Waincroft 8 YO32 ....14 A6
Wainers Cl 5 YO23 ....132 B3
Wainfleet Ave HU16 ....139 A6
Wainfleet Rd 33 DN33 ....102 D2
Waite Cl 17 YO42 ....29 A3
Waithe La DN37 ....113 E4
Wake Ave HU16 ....139 A5
Wakefield Ave
Kingston upon Hull HU9 ....142 C2
Scotter DN21 ....107 D4
Wakefield La HU19 ....75 A2
Wakerley Rd 13 DN21 ....107 C3
Walcot Rd DN15 ....82 B8
Walcott St HU3 ....145 C4
Waldby Garth Rd HU12 ....73 C4
Waldegrave Ave HU8 ....142 A4
Walden Stubbs Rd DN6 ....76 E2
Waldo Way DN15 ....82 C1
Waldorf Rd DN35 ....103 C1
Walesby Cl 8 DN33 ....113 D8
Walesby Rd DN17 ....150 E1
Walgrave St HU5 ....140 C3
Walk La
Humberston DN36 ....114 C7
Irby DN37 ....112 D7
Walker Ave DN33 ....113 E8
Walker Cl DN15 ....82 E7
Walker Dr
Winterton DN15 ....83 A5
York YO24 ....132 C8
Walker La YO19 ....37 F7
Walker St HU3 ....145 C5
Walker's Cl 2 DN38 ....99 B4
Walkergate HU17 ....154 A3
Walkergate Prim Sch HU17 ....154 A3
Walkeringham Cty Prim Sch DN10 ....116 C3
Walkeringham Nature Reserve* DN10 ....116 B3
Walkeringham Rd
Beckingham DN10 ....116 D2
Gringley on the Hill DN10 ....116 A2
Walkerith Rd 11 DN21 ....117 A2
Walkers Cl 10 DN15 ....151 B7
Walkers Ct DN17 ....107 D7
Walkers Way DN39 ....86 B2
Walkington Dr YO43 ....135 C5
Walkington Heads HU17 ....54 D8
Walkington La YO30 ....12 B8
Walkington Prim Sch HU17 ....55 C7
Walkington Rd
Beverley HU17 ....136 B1
Rowley HU20 ....55 A5
Wall St DN34 ....152 A3
Waller St
3 Hornsea HU18 ....134 C3
Kingston upon Hull HU9 ....146 C8
Walliker St HU3 ....145 A6
Wallingfen La HU15 ....53 A1
Wallis Ct 9 DN33 ....102 D1
Walmgate YO1 ....156 C2
Walmsgate DN33 ....102 D2
Walmsgate Pl 24 DN33 ....102 D2
Walmsley Cl 1 YO15 ....4 C3
Walmsley St HU3 ....145 D7
Walney Rd YO31 ....131 A5
Walnut Cl
Kingston upon Hull HU16 ....139 D5
York YO10 ....131 A1
Walnut Cres
9 Cleethorpes DN35 ....103 B1
11 Snaith & Cowick DN14 ....78 C8
Walnut Dr DN20 ....108 F7
Walnut Gr YO25 ....125 F8
Walnut Rd 1 DN8 ....79 A1
Walnut Way DN17 ....107 C7
Walpole St YO31 ....130 D7
Walsall Garth HU4 ....144 A4
Walter St 5 HU19 ....74 F7
Walter's Terr 6 HU5 ....140 C3
Waltham Ct HU17 ....154 B4
Waltham Grange 24 DN35 ....103 C2
Waltham La HU17 ....154 A3
Waltham Rd
Barnoldby le Beck DN37 ....113 C6
Brigsley DN37 ....113 D5
Grimsby DN33 ....113 E8
Waltham St HU1 ....155 B2
Waltham Tollbar Bsns & Ent Coll DN36 ....113 F7
Waltham Windmill* DN37 ....113 D6
Walton Gr 3 DN33 ....102 E2
Walton La YO43 ....53 E6
Walton Pl YO26 ....129 B3
Walton St HU3 ....145 A7
Walton St L Ctr HU3 ....145 A6
Walworth Cl HU8 ....141 E5
Walworth St N 4 YO26 ....129 F5
Walworth St S 9 YO26 ....129 F5
Wand La DN14 ....62 C3
Wandell's View HU15 ....68 C8
Wandhill 31 YO32 ....13 E5
Wandle The YO26 ....129 A2
Wanlass Dr HU16 ....139 C7
Wansbeck 3 YO24 ....132 B7
Wansbeck Prim Sch HU8 ....142 D7
Wansbeck Rd HU8 ....142 C7
Wansford Gr HU9 ....142 A1
Wansford Rd
Driffield YO25 ....125 B3
Nafferton YO25 ....125 F5
Ward Ave HU11 ....142 F7
Ward Ct YO23 ....156 B1
Ward Lea YO25 ....125 F7
Ward St DN35 ....153 C4
Wardall St DN35 ....153 F1
Waredale Cl YO16 ....122 F7
Wareham Cl HU7 ....141 B6
Wares Way DN15 ....150 B7
Warfield Rd YO25 ....124 B2
Warley Ave DN16 ....151 C4

Warley Dr DN16 151 C4
Warley Rd DN16 151 C3
Warmer La HU12 90 E7
Warn Ave 18 HU12 72 C7
Warneford Gdns HU5 145 A8
Warneford Rd DN35 153 D4
Warping Way DN15 150 B7
Warren Cl DN21 117 A1
Warren Farm Cotts YO42 28 C1
Warren Rd DN15 96 D7
Warrendale DN18 84 E8
Warrenne Cl 31 DN7 92 D4
Warrenne Rd DN7 92 D4
Warter CE VC Prim Sch YO42 30 A5
Warter Rd Etton HU17 42 F6
Middleton YO25 31 A4
Warthill CE VC Prim Sch YO19 14 F2
Warton Ave HU17 137 B4
Warton Dr HU17 56 B8
Warwick Ave 5 DN33 102 D2
Warwick Cl DN7 92 F4
Warwick Dr
Barton-upon-Humber DN18 84 E8
Molescroft HU17 136 E6
Warwick Rd
Cleethorpes DN35 153 D1
Scunthorpe DN16 151 C5
Warwick St
Kingston upon Hull HU9 146 B7
York YO31 130 D7
Warwickshire Cl 6 HU5 139 D1
Wascana Cl HU4 144 B3
Wasdale Ave HU9 142 D4
Wasdale Cl 2 YO30 126 E1
Wasdale Gn 4 HU16 139 B7
Waseley Hill Way HU7 57 B5
Washdyke La
Elsham DN20 98 E6
Immingham DN40 87 B2
Washinghall La DN17 81 A2
Washington St
Great Driffield YO25 124 E4
Kingston upon Hull HU5 140 D3
Wassand Balk HU11 46 A8
Wassand Hall & Gdns* HU11 35 B1
Wassand Rd HU11 35 B1
Wassand St HU3 145 C4
Water Bank DN9 104 E5
Water End YO26 129 E5
Water Garth DN14 61 F4
Water Hill La YO8 148 D6
Water La
Bewholme YO25 35 A5
Camblesforth YO8 63 D5
8 Clifton YO30 127 A1
Dunnington YO19 26 F7
Eggborough DN14 62 A2
20 Flamborough YO15 5 A2
Goole DN14 65 C4
Harpham YO25 21 E7
Hemingbrough YO8 49 F1
Kirby Grindalythe YO17 6 B6
Kirby Underdale YO41 17 A5
Kirk Bramwith DN7 92 C7
Kirk Smeaton WF8 76 C3
Selby YO8 148 C6
South Cave HU15 53 F1
West Halton DN15 82 E8
York YO30 130 A7
Water Side DN15 68 A2
Water Way Garth DN14 77 F6
Waterdale HU7 140 E8
Waterdale Pk YO31 127 E1
Waterhouse La HU1 155 A1
Wateringdike La YO43 135 F7
Waterings 19 YO32 13 D5
Waterland Cl 15 HU12 72 D7
Waterloo Dr 14 DN33 102 D1
Waterloo St HU2 155 A4
Waterlow Dr 7 DN15 83 A5
Waterman Ct 3 YO24 129 B1
Waters Edge DN20 98 B2
Waters Edge Ctry Pk* DN18 69 F2
Watersedge YO25 124 F3
Waterside Goole DN14 65 C4
3 Thorne DN8 78 F1
Waterside Dr DN31 152 C4
Waterside Rd
Barton-upon-Humber DN18 69 E2
Beverley HU17 137 B3
2 Thorne DN8 78 F1
Waterton La DN7 92 D2
Waterways Mus & Adventure Ctr The* DN14 149 B2
Waterworks La HU11 142 E6
Waterworks St DN40 87 C2
Watford Ave DN34 102 C2
Watford Wlk HU9 142 E1
Wath Gr HU8 141 C1
Wath La YO41 27 C8
Watkin St N DN31 152 C5
Watkin St S DN31 152 D5
Watkinson Cl 8 HU12 58 D1
Watson Ave HU9 142 C2
Watson Cl 9 YO14 3 A8
Watson Dr 30 HU12 72 D7
Watson St
Kingston upon Hull HU7 141 D6
York YO24 130 A3
Watson Terr 2 YO24 130 A3
Watson's La YO14 3 D6
Watsons Ave YO16 122 D5
Watsons Croft DN7 92 D6
Watt St HU9 141 E1
Wattlers Cl YO23 132 C3
Watton Abbey* YO25 32 E4
Watton Gr HU6 140 B7
Watton Carr Nature Reserve* YO25 33 C2
Watts Rd HU17 154 B4
Waudby Cl 2 HU17 55 C8
Wauldby Cl 4 HU10 143 E7
Wauldby View 2 HU14 69 B7
Wavell St YO8 148 A6
Waveney Cl DN15 82 B5
Waveney Gr YO30 130 B8
Waveney Rd HU8 142 B6
Waverley Cl DN14 63 C2
Waverley St
Kingston upon Hull HU1 155 A1
York YO31 156 C3
Wawne Lodge HU7 56 F6
Wawne Prim Sch HU7 56 E7
Wawne Rd HU7 141 C8
Waxholme Rd HU19 74 E8
Wayfbain La 20 HU12 72 C7
Waynefleet Gr 3 YO10 131 A3
Wayside Cl
Holton le Clay DN36 114 A5
15 Scunthorpe DN16 96 D2
Wayside Cres YO16 122 B4
Wayside Dr DN36 114 A8
Wayside Rd YO16 122 B4
Weald Pk HU7 56 E6
Weardale HU7 140 F8
Weatherill St DN14 149 C4
Weaver Gr HU8 142 C7
Weavers Cl YO23 132 B3
Weavers Croft 8 DN9 105 A2
Weavers Pk YO23 132 B3
Webb Cl DN18 84 E8
Webster Ave DN15 150 E7
Weddall Cl YO24 129 F1
Weekes Rd 13 DN35 103 C2
Weel Rd HU17 137 D8
Weeland Ct 16 WF11 61 A2
Weeland Rd Beal DN14 61 E3
Hensall DN14 62 E2
Weelsby Ave DN32 152 E1
Weelsby Gr DN32 102 F2
Weelsby Prim Sch DN32 153 A4
Weelsby Rd DN32 152 E1
Weelsby St DN32 152 A4
Weelsby St S DN32 153 A3
Weelsby View DN36 114 A8
Weelsby Way HU13 143 C2
Weeping Elm Way DN16 96 E2
Weeton Cl HU11 58 A4
Weeton Dr YO25 19 B5
Weeton N La HU12 90 B8
Weeton Rd HU12 90 C7
Weeton Way 5 HU10 143 E7
Weghill Rd HU12 58 D1
Weighton Ct 9 DN14 65 A7
Weighton Gr HU6 139 F5
Weighton Hill YO43 135 F4
Weir Cl DN9 105 A2
Weir Rd DN9 105 A2
Weir The HU13 143 E1
Welbeck Pl 9 DN34 102 C2
Welbeck Rd DN35 153 C1
Welbeck St HU5 145 B8
Welborn Cl YO10 131 A4
Welbourn Wlk HU4 144 B6
Welburn Ct 8 YO25 22 D1
Welburn Gr HU5 139 E2
Welbury Gr HU9 142 C2
Weldon Rd DN21 119 B1
Welgarth YO25 31 B7
Welham Cl 10 DN14 65 B7
Welholme Ave DN32 152 D1
Welholme Inf Sch DN32 152 F2
Welholme Jun Sch DN32 152 F2
Welholme Mus & Gall* DN32 152 F2
Welholme Rd DN32 152 E2
Well La Beverley HU17 154 B2
Bridlington YO16 122 B4
Kingston upon Hull HU10 138 E2
Tibthorpe YO25 19 D2
Well St
Messingham DN17 107 C7
Tibthorpe YO25 19 D2
Well Vale 3 DN33 113 D8
Welland Ave DN34 102 C2
Welland Dr DN15 82 B5
Welland Rd HU8 142 C7
Welland Rise YO26 129 D5
Wellbeck Cl 20 DN20 98 C2
Wellbeck Rd 8 DN34 102 C2
Wellesley Ave HU6 140 D4
Wellesley Cl YO30 127 A2
Wellgarth DN32 153 B1
Wellington Ave HU18 134 C2
Wellington Cl 5 YO42 28 F4
Wellington Ct DN32 153 A4
Wellington La HU3 145 D8
Wellington Rd
Beverley HU17 154 B4
Wellington Rd *continued*
Bridlington YO15 122 E2
Pocklington YO42 28 E3
Wellington Row YO1 156 A2
Wellington St
Grimsby DN32 152 F4
Kingston upon Hull HU1 155 B1
York YO10 130 E3
Wellington St W HU1 155 B1
Wellington Way DN20 99 A8
Wellingtonia Dr 5 DN6 76 E1
Wellowgate DN32 152 D3
Wellowgate Mews DN32 152 D2
Wells Cl YO8 148 A5
Wells Cres 3 DN35 103 C1
Wells Gr DN14 149 B6
Wells La DN14 61 E3
Wells Rd DN37 101 D4
Wells St Grimsby DN34 152 B3
Kingston upon Hull HU3 145 A5
Scunthorpe DN15 151 B8
Wellsted St HU3 145 C5
Welshpool Cl 3 HU7 56 F7
Welton Ave
2 Kingston upon Hull HU16 138 E6
York YO26 129 D5
Welton Cl
17 Barton-upon-Humber DN18 84 E8
9 Beverley HU17 136 E1
Welton Gr HU6 139 F4
Welton Low Rd HU15 68 C6
Welton Old Rd HU15 68 E6
Welton Prim Sch HU15 68 D5
Welton Rd HU15 68 C5
Welton Wold View HU14 69 B7
Welwick Rd HU12 74 D1
Welwick Saltmarsh Nature Reserve* HU12 89 F6
Welwyn Dr YO10 133 E8
Welwyn Pk Ave HU6 140 C7
Welwyn Pk Dr HU6 140 D7
Welwyn Pk Rd HU6 140 C7
Wembley Pk Ave HU8 141 E5
Wembley Rd DN8 79 B2
Wenchirst La DN14 78 D2
Wendan Rd 7 DN8 93 A7
Wendover Cl
Humberston DN36 114 D8
Messingham DN17 107 D7
Wendover Rd DN17 107 D7
Wendover Rise DN35 153 E1
Wendron Cl HU7 141 C6
Wenham Rd YO24 132 C8
Wenlock Dr YO19 37 B6
Wenlock St HU3 145 C7
Wenlock Terr
Kingston upon Hull HU9 141 E1
York YO10 130 D1
Wenning Gr HU8 142 D7
Wensley Ave HU6 139 E4
Wensleydale HU7 140 F8
Wensleydale Cl YO16 122 F6
Wensleydale Dr YO10 131 D4
Wensleydale Rd DN16 151 E2
Wentdale 1 WF8 76 C3
Wentworth Cl
3 Beverley HU17 55 E8
Camblesforth YO8 63 D4
Kellington DN14 62 A2
Kingston upon Hull HU10 143 F8
Wentworth Cres 1 DN19 70 E2
Wentworth Dr
Goole DN14 149 E5
Messingham DN17 107 D7
Wentworth Gr 5 HU11 47 C1
Wentworth Rd
Bottesford DN17 96 B1
Bridlington YO16 122 C4
Grimsby DN34 152 B3
York YO24 130 B2
Wentworth Way
5 Hunmanby YO14 2 F8
Kingston upon Hull HU9 146 C7
York YO10 130 F2
Werkdyke The YO1 156 C3
Werneth Rd DN32 152 F4
Wesley Cl
3 Epworth DN9 105 E6
South Cave HU15 54 A2
Winterton DN15 83 A5
Wesley Cres 15 DN35 103 C2
Wesley Ct
10 Cleethorpes DN32 153 A5
7 Kingston upon Hull HU3 145 C5
Wesley Pl YO1 156 C2
Wesley Rd 5 Brigg DN20 98 C2
Scunthorpe DN16 151 E3
Wesley Sq 5 DN14 149 D4
Wesley St DN21 108 B1
West Acridge DN18 69 E1
West Ave
Burton Fleming YO25 2 E3
Stainforth DN7 92 C6
West Back Side YO25 10 C4
West Bank
Stainforth DN7 92 B7
York YO24 129 E3
West Butterwick CE Prim Sch DN17 106 D8
West Carr La HU7 140 F6
West Cl Fangfoss YO41 28 C8
Nafferton YO25 125 E6
West Cl *continued*
Newport HU15 52 E1
West Coates Rd DN31 152 B6
West Comm Cres DN17 150 F4
West Comm Gdns DN17 150 F2
West Comm La DN17 150 F3
West Comm N Rd DN17 107 A8
West Comm Rd DN17 150 F3
West Crayke YO16 122 F6
West Cross St 16 DN21 108 B1
West Ct 8 Riccall YO19 48 F8
8 Thorne/Moorends DN8 93 A7
West Dale Cres DN21 108 B2
West Dock Ave HU3 145 B4
West Dock St HU3 145 B3
West Dr YO25 125 F6
West Edge Rd WF8 76 A3
West Ella Rd
Kingston upon Hull HU10 143 A7
Swanland HU14 69 C7
West Ella Way HU10 143 C7
West End Bainton YO25 31 E7
Dalton Holme HU17 42 E8
Garthorpe & Fockerby DN17 81 E6
Kilham YO25 9 B3
Lund YO25 31 E2
Pollington DN14 77 F6
Rawcliffe DN14 64 A2
Seaton Ross YO42 39 D4
South Cave HU15 53 F1
Strensall YO32 14 A7
Swanland HU14 69 B6
Walkington HU17 55 B7
Winteringham DN15 68 A1
West End Cl
North Duffield YO8 50 A8
9 Strensall YO32 14 B7
West End Farm Cl 6 HU15 53 F1
West End Gdns
Driffield YO25 125 F6
Pollington DN14 77 F6
West End La DN36 115 B1
West End Rd
Epworth DN9 105 C7
2 Habrough DN40 100 E8
Kingston upon Hull HU16 138 F7
Norton DN6 76 E2
Ulceby DN39 85 F1
West Field La
1 Swanland HU14 69 B6
Upper Poppleton YO26 12 E1
West Garth Kilham YO25 9 B3
Rowley HU20 55 A4
West Gn
Kingston upon Hull HU10 69 C8
Messingham DN17 107 D7
Pocklington YO42 28 F3
West Gn Dr YO42 29 A3
West Gr
Barton-upon-Humber DN18 69 E1
Kingston upon Hull HU4 144 D4
West Hall Garth 10 HU15 53 F1
West Halton La DN15 82 C8
West Hann La DN19 70 C1
West Haven Way DN40 87 B3
West Hill 1 HU13 69 E4
West Ings Cl 4 WF11 61 A3
West Ings Cres 5 WF11 61 A3
West Ings Ct 1 WF11 61 A3
West Ings La 2 WF11 61 A3
West Ings Mews 6 WF11 61 A3
West Ings Way 3 WF11 61 A3
West La Burn YO8 62 C6
Burton Fleming YO25 2 E3
Keelby DN41 101 A4
Laxton DN14 65 D2
Sykehouse DN14 77 F2
Winterton DN15 83 B5
West Lambwath Rd HU11 46 D3
West Lea DN33 113 E8
West Leys Pk HU14 69 B6
West Leys Rd HU14 69 B6
West Marsh Ind Est DN31 152 D5
West Marsh La
Barrow upon Humber DN19 70 B1
Goxhill DN19 71 A3
West Mid Mere Rd DN40 86 D3
West Mill Rise 4 HU17 55 B7
West Moor Rd DN10 116 C3
West Newton Rd HU11 58 D8
West Par Rd HU3 145 D6
West Parade
Grimsby DN31 152 C3
Kingston upon Hull HU3 145 C7
West Parklands Dr 8 HU14 69 A5
West Pk YO8 148 A4
West Point Trading Pk HU3 145 A3
West Promenade YO25 124 D4
West Rd
Keadby with Althorpe DN17 95 C6
Sigglesthorne HU11 34 E1
West Rd *continued*
Thorne/Moorends DN8 79 B2
West Rd Fst Sch DN8 79 B2
West Riverside DN40 87 C3
West St
Barnetby le Wold DN38 99 B4
Beverley HU17 137 C4
Bridlington YO15 122 E1
Cleethorpes DN35 153 F2
21 Flamborough YO15 5 A2
9 Gainsborough DN21 117 A2
Goole DN14 149 C5
Hibaldstow DN20 108 F5
Kingston upon Hull HU1 155 A2
Leven HU17 44 F8
North Kelsey LN7 110 A4
Roxby cum Risby DN15 82 F3
Scawby DN20 108 E8
Scunthorpe DN15 151 A7
Thorne/Moorends DN8 93 A7
West Butterwick DN17 106 C8
West Halton DN15 82 E7
Winterton DN15 83 A5
West St Mary's Gate DN31 152 D3
West Terr
Beverley HU17 154 C2
18 Brigg DN20 98 B2
West Terr St 3 DN17 94 D7
West Thorpe YO24 132 D8
West View
Messingham DN17 107 C7
12 North Ferriby HU14 69 A4
Scunthorpe DN17 96 C2
West View Cl 9 DN41 101 A4
West Wood La YO23 24 E4
Westbeck Hill YO42 30 A5
Westbeck La DN21 118 F5
Westborough Way HU4 144 B6
Westbourne Ave
Bridlington YO16 122 D3
3 Hessle HU13 143 E2
Kingston upon Hull HU5 140 A1
Westbourne Ave W HU5 140 A1
Westbourne Dr DN17 94 D7
Westbourne Gdns YO8 148 C4
Westbourne Gr
Goole DN14 149 D6
15 Grimsby DN33 113 E8
Kingston upon Hull HU13 143 D2
Selby YO8 148 C4
Westbourne Rd
Hornsea HU18 134 D4
Selby YO8 148 C4
Westbourne St 5 HU3 145 A4
Westbourne Terr YO8 148 C4
Westbrook Cres 3 HU15 66 D7
Westbrook Rd 12 HU15 66 D8
Westbrooke Gr 18 LN7 111 B4
Westburn Ave 2 DN19 70 E2
Westbury Pk 10 DN35 103 D1
Westbury Rd DN35 103 C1
Westcliff Gdns DN17 150 F3
Westcliffe Prim Sch DN17 150 D2
Westcliffe Rd 16 DN21 107 C3
Westcott Prim Sch HU8 141 C3
Westcott St HU8 141 D2
Westcroft 11 YO43 53 F7
Westend Falls YO25 125 E6
Westend La DN14 77 B6
Westenders Way HU1 155 A1
Westerdale 4 HU14 69 B7
Westerdale Cl 8 HU12 73 C4
Westerdale Ct 2 YO30 130 A6
Westerdale Gr HU9 146 E8
Westerdale Rd DN16 151 D1
Western Access Rd DN40 87 C3
Western Ave DN20 98 C3
Western Dr 7 DN18 69 E1
Western Gailes Way HU8 142 B5
Western Gn DN15 68 A1
Western Outway DN34 102 D2
Western Prim Sch DN34 102 B3
Western Rd DN14 149 C6
Western Tech Sch The DN34 102 C3
Western Terr YO32 127 D3
Westfield
Patrington HU12 74 C1
Selby YO8 148 B4
Westfield Ave
Beverley HU17 136 D6
3 Eggborough DN14 61 F2
Goole DN14 149 D5
11 Grimsby DN33 102 E2
Rawcliffe DN14 64 A1
Selby YO8 148 B4
Westfield Cl
Easington HU12 90 F6
2 Eggborough DN14 61 F2
21 Haxby YO32 13 E5
Kingston upon Hull HU16 138 F6
Nafferton YO25 125 E6
3 Pocklington YO42 28 F4
Westfield Cres YO43 135 C4
Westfield Ct YO23 132 A2

Westfield Dr
Messingham DN17 107 D7
York YO10 133 D8
Westfield Garth
1 Crowle DN17 94 E6
1 Walkington HU17 55 B8
Westfield Gr
4 Eggborough DN14 61 F2
Grimsby DN35 153 D2
12 Haxby YO32 13 D5
Westfield La
East Garton HU12 59 D5
Fishlake DN7 92 B8
Hook DN14 149 D8
Kirk Bramwith DN7 78 B1
Norton WF8 76 C2
Preston HU12 58 B1
Thorganby YO19 38 A5
Wigginton YO32 13 D5
Westfield Pk HU15 68 C6
Westfield Pl
19 Haxby YO32 13 E5
York YO24 129 A1
Westfield Prim Com Sch
YO24 129 B2
Westfield Prim Sch
HU16 138 F6
Westfield Rd
Barton-upon-Humber
DN18 69 C1
Cottingham HU16 138 F6
Easington HU12 90 F5
East Ella HU4 144 D5
1 Eggborough DN14 61 F2
4 Goxhill DN19 86 A8
4 Hatfield DN7 92 E4
20 Haxby YO32 13 E5
Kirk Bramwith DN7 92 A8
Market Weighton YO43 135 C4
3 North Duffield YO8 50 A7
Pocklington YO42 28 F4
Rawcliffe DN14 64 A1
Scunthorpe DN17 150 B2
Selby YO8 148 B4
Skidby HU16 138 A5
Waltham DN37 113 D6
Westfield Rise
Beeford YO25 34 B8
Kingston upon Hull
HU13 143 D2
13 Withernsea HU19 75 A6
Westfield Sq DN14 149 D6
Westfield Terr YO43 135 C4
Westfield Villas 3 DN7 92 E4
Westgarth Ave HU6 139 F5
West-Gate YO25 124 E5
Westgate
Bridlington YO16 122 B4
Grimsby DN31 152 D5
Hornsea HU18 134 B4
Nafferton YO25 125 E6
North Cave HU15 53 D3
North Newbald YO43 53 E7
Patrington HU12 74 D1
Scotton DN21 107 C1
Westgate Manor 4
HU12 74 D1
Westgate Mdws YO25 125 E6
Westgate Rd DN9 94 D2
Westhill Rd DN34 152 A1
Westholme Ave HU18 134 C7
Westholme Cl 10 DN15 82 B4
Westholme Dr YO30 126 E1
Westholme La DN38 99 C5
Westkirke Ave 2 DN33 113 F8
Westland Rd
Kingston upon Hull
HU10 143 B7
3 Westwoodside DN9 105 B2
Westlands Ave
Grimsby DN34 152 C1
Tetney DN36 114 D4
Westlands Cl 13 HU12 72 C7
Westlands Dr HU12 72 C7
Westlands Gr YO31 130 F7
Westlands Mews
YO25 124 D5
Westlands Rd
Hedon HU12 72 C7
Kingston upon Hull HU5 144 B8
Sproatley HU11 58 C5
Westlands Way HU17 45 A8
Westminster Ave HU8 141 E3
Westminster Bsns Ctr
YO26 129 C8
Westminster Cl DN21 117 A3
Westminster Ct DN14 149 E6
Westminster Dr
Grimsby DN34 152 C2
Hatfield DN7 92 C2
Westminster Pl YO26 126 B1
Westminster Rd
2 Broughton DN20 97 D4
York YO30 130 A6
Westmoreland Ave 3
YO15 122 F2
Westmoreland Cl DN9 105 A2
Westmoreland Gr 2
YO15 122 F2
Westmoreland St HU2 155 B4
Westoby La
Barrow upon Humber
DN19 85 C7
Rowley HU15 54 E3
Weston Gr 3 DN40 87 B2
Westover Dr DN15 82 A4
Westparkside DN14 149 A6
Westpit La YO32 14 A7
Westport Rd 27 DN35 103 C1
Westridge Rd YO15 122 C1
Westrum La DN20 98 C1
Westside Rd DN31 152 C6
Westview Cl YO26 129 B7
Westward Cl DN34 152 C1
Westward Ho DN34 152 B1
Westway Ave HU6 139 F6
Westwick 25 HU12 72 C7
Westwinds Gdns DN15 83 A5
Westwinds Rd 10 DN15 83 A5
Westwold Rd 20 LN7 111 B4
Westwood
Beverley HU17 136 D2
4 Broughton DN20 97 D4
Westwood Ave HU18 134 B4
Westwood Cl HU7 141 C6
Westwood Dr 3 HU4 144 B6
Westwood Gate HU17 154 A1
Westwood Hospl
HU17 136 D3
Westwood Mews 12
YO19 26 F7
Westwood Rd
Beverley HU17 154 A3
12 Healing DN41 101 F5
Westwood Terr YO23 130 B1
Westwood Way HU17 136 D4
Westwoodside CE Prim Sch
DN9 105 B2
Wetherby Cl HU6 139 F7
Wetherby Rd YO26 129 B3
Wetwang CE VC Prim Sch
YO25 19 B5
Wexford Ave HU9 142 E1
Weyford Rd 9 DN35 103 D1
Weymouth Cl HU7 141 B6
Weymouth Cres DN17 150 C5
Whales La DN14 61 E3
Wharf Rd Crowle DN17 94 D7
Misterton DN10 116 C5
Wharf The DN36 115 A5
Wharfdale Cl DN15 95 E5
Wharfe Dr YO24 132 D8
Wharfedale Ave HU9 141 E1
Wharfedale Dr YO16 122 F7
Wharfedale Pl DN16 151 D2
Wharfedale Way 3
DN31 152 D4
Wharncliffe Rd N
DN31 153 A7
Wharncliffe St HU5 145 A8
Wharnscliffe Dr YO30 126 F2
Wharram Field 3 YO25 22 D1
Wharram St HU2 140 F1
Wharton Ave YO30 130 B7
Wharton Rd
Blyton DN21 117 D5
8 Stamford Bridge YO41 15 D2
Wharton St DN31 152 B3
Wheatcroft 6 YO32 14 A6
Wheatcroft Ave HU10 138 E2
Wheatfield Cl
9 Barnby Dun DN3 92 A3
Epworth DN9 105 F6
2 Kingston upon Hull
HU4 144 D2
Wheatfield Dr 2 DN37 113 D6
Wheatfield La YO32 127 C8
Wheatland Cl YO42 29 B3
Wheatlands Dr HU17 136 C6
Wheatlands Gr YO26 129 C6
Wheatley Dr
Bridlington YO16 123 A6
Haxby YO32 127 C8
Wheatley Gdns HU8 141 D3
Wheeldale Cl 2 HU7 141 D7
Wheeler Prim Sch
HU3 144 F5
Wheeler St HU3 144 F6
Wheelhouse The 4
YO30 126 B5
Wheels La YO8 63 F3
Wheelwright Cl
Copmanthorpe YO23 132 B2
Sutton upon Derwent
YO41 27 C1
Wheldrake CE Prim Sch
YO19 38 A8
Wheldrake Ings Nature
Reserve* YO19 38 C7
Wheldrake La
Deighton YO19 26 B1
Escrick YO19 37 B5
Whenby Gr YO31 127 F1
Whernside Ave YO31 131 A5
Whernside Cl 12 HU7 57 A6
Whimbrel Ave HU18 134 C2
Whimbrel Way 12 DN36 114 A8
Whin Cl 3 Strensall YO32 14 B6
York YO24 132 F7
Whin Garth YO24 132 F6
Whin La Burstwick HU12 73 C7
South Cave YO43 54 B6
Whin Moor La HU15 68 A7
Whin Rd YO24 132 F6
Whincroft Ave DN14 149 C6
Whinhill La HU12 73 F4
Whinns The HU17 154 C1
Whinny Hagg La YO8 48 A2
Whinny La YO60 15 A7
Whins Gate DN17 81 A4
Whins La HU11 45 D6
Whip-ma-whop-ma-gate
YO1 156 C2
Whisby Ct DN36 114 B5
Whistler Cl YO23 132 C3
Whiston Way 9 DN18 69 F1
Whitby Ave YO31 131 A7
Whitby Dr
Grimsby DN32 153 A1
York YO31 131 A7
Whitby St HU8 146 B8
White Cross* HU11 45 A6
White Cross Rd YO31 130 D7
White Cross Way YO41 16 A2
White Gap La HU20 54 E5
White Gap Rd HU20 54 F4
White Horse Cl 6 YO32 127 F5
White Horse La HU12 73 E3
White House Cl
19 Hatfield DN7 92 D4
Kingston upon Hull
HU10 138 C2
Kirk Bramwith DN7 92 C7
White House Dale
YO24 129 F1
White House Dr YO24 129 F1
White House Garth 15
HU14 69 A5
White House Gdns 4
YO24 130 A2
White House Gr 1 YO41 27 B2
White House La DN15 82 E8
White House Mews 16
HU14 69 A5
White House Rise
YO24 129 F1
White La DN8 92 F8
White Ley Rd DN6 76 C1
White Lodge YO8 148 B4
White Rose Ave 3
YO32 127 D3
White Rose Cl YO26 126 C1
White Rose Gr 5 YO32 127 D3
White Rose Way YO26 129 C8
White Sprunt Hill YO17 1 A1
White St
Kingston upon Hull HU3 144 F5
Selby YO8 148 B6
White Wlk HU10 143 C6
White's Cl La HU12 59 A2
White's Rd DN35 153 F1
Whitebeam Cl HU3 145 D5
Whitecarr La YO42 39 E8
Whitecross Gdns
YO31 130 D7
Whitecross Rd HU11 45 B6
Whitecross St DN18 84 F8
Whitefield Bglws DN14 76 F8
Whitefield La DN14 61 E1
Whitefields Cl HU17 136 E7
Whitefriargate HU1 155 B2
Whitegate Hill LN7 111 C3
Whitehall Gdns 3 HU5 140 A1
Whitehall Rd 5 DN35 103 D1
Whitehead Cl HU17 154 B2
Whitehope Cl 13 HU7 57 A6
Whitehouse Wlk HU6 56 D5
Whitelands YO25 124 D5
Whitemoor La YO8 49 C6
Whiterose Dr YO41 15 D2
Whitestone Dr YO31 127 E2
Whitestone Rd DN17 150 C2
Whitethorn Ave 11 HU19 75 A6
Whitethorn Cl YO31 127 E2
Whitethorn Way HU8 141 D4
Whitewell Cl 3 DN21 108 B1
Whitfield Rd DN17 150 D2
Whitgift Cl 13 DN37 101 F1
Whitgift Sch DN37 102 B4
Whiting Cl HU16 139 A6
Whitley & Eggborough CP
Sch DN14 61 F1
Whitley Bridge Sta
DN14 61 F1
Whitley Cl YO30 127 A1
Whitley Rd YO41 27 A3
Whitley Thorpe La
DN14 76 F7
Whitman Rd DN17 150 C2
Whitstable Cl 3 HU8 141 E7
Whitstone Cl HU7 140 F8
Whitton Pl YO10 131 C4
Whitton Rd DN15 82 C8
Whitworth St HU9 141 E2
Whoofer La DN21 117 B7
Wickenby Cl 18 DN34 102 C2
Wickenby Garth HU7 141 C8
Wickham Rd DN31 153 A6
Wickham Way YO25 124 D3
Wicklow Ave 22 DN33 113 E8
Wickware Rd HU17 137 A6
Wicstun Way YO43 135 C3
Wide La YO14 3 E5
Widford Gn 7 DN7 92 D3
Widop St DN14 149 C5
Wigginton Prim Sch
YO32 13 D5
Wigginton Rd YO31 156 B4
Wigginton Terr YO31 130 C8
Wike Gate Cl 7 DN8 93 B7
Wike Gate Gr 6 DN8 93 B7
Wike Gate Rd DN8 93 B8
Wilbar Gr HU5 140 B2
Wilberforce Ave YO30 130 B7
Wilberforce Cres
HU17 154 C4
Wilberforce Dr HU1 155 C3
Wilberforce House Mus*
HU1 155 C2
Wilberforce Mon*
HU1 155 C3
Wilberforce St HU3 145 D6
Wilberforce VI Form Coll
HU8 142 A5
Wilberfoss CE VC Prim Sch
YO41 27 E6
Wilbert Ct HU17 154 B3
Wilbert Gr HU17 154 B3
Wiles Ct HU17 154 C2
Wilfholme Rd YO25 32 F3
Wilflete Ct HU9 142 B3
Wilfreds Gr 8 YO8 49 B4
Wilfreds Rd 5 YO8 49 B4
Wilkie Cl DN15 150 C7
Wilkinson Ave DN8 79 B1
Wilkinson Way
20 Bottesford DN16 96 E2
3 Strensall YO32 14 A7
Willans Gr YO26 129 E4
Willerby Carr Cl 2 HU5 139 B1
Willerby Carr La Infants Sch
HU10 138 E1
Willerby Carr La Jun Sch
HU10 138 E1
Willerby Dr 2 DN14 65 A7
Willerby Low Rd
HU10 138 D3
Willerby Rd HU5 144 C8
Willesden Cl 4 HU8 141 F5
William Barcroft Jun Sch
DN32 153 C3
William Jacques Dr
YO8 49 E2
William Plows Ave
YO10 130 E2
William Rd YO8 49 B4
William St
Cleethorpes DN35 153 E1
Kingston upon Hull HU1 155 A1
Scunthorpe DN16 151 B6
William Wright Dock
HU1 145 B3
Williams Dr DN39 86 B1
Williamson St HU9 146 C7
Willing Way DN32 152 F4
Willingham Garth 4
HU12 72 E5
Willingham St DN32 152 E2
Willingham Way HU10 138 B1
Willis St YO10 130 E3
Willitoft Rd YO8 50 F6
Willoughby Gr 12 DN34 102 C2
Willoughby Rd
Hibaldstow DN20 109 A5
Scunthorpe DN17 150 E1
Willoughby Way YO24 132 B8
Willoughton CP Sch
DN21 119 A4
Willow Ave
2 Misterton DN10 116 C5
Thorne/Moorends DN8 79 A1
Willow Bank
14 Brayton YO8 48 D1
York YO32 127 E4
Willow Cl
Barnetby le Beck DN38 99 B4
13 Gainsborough DN21 117 A2
Laceby DN37 101 E1
Pollington DN14 78 A6
Snaith DN14 78 B8
Ulceby DN39 86 B1
Willow Cres DN8 79 A1
Willow Ct
Beverley HU17 136 C6
Hutton Cranswick YO25 32 E6
Kexby YO41 15 C2
Kingston upon Hull
HU10 138 E1
9 Pocklington YO42 29 A3
Willow Dr
11 Barton-upon-Humber
DN18 69 F1
Bridlington YO16 123 A6
12 Brough HU15 68 D5
Goole DN14 65 C3
Kingston upon Hull
HU10 143 D8
Messingham DN17 107 D7
1 North Duffield YO8 50 A7
1 Thorngumbald HU12 72 E5
Willow Garth
Eastrington DN14 51 F1
Pollington DN14 78 A6
Willow Garth La DN6 77 A1
Willow Gdns 2 DN19 85 D8
Willow Glade YO32 127 F3
Willow Gn 7 HU15 66 D8
Willow Gr
3 Aldbrough HU11 47 C1
Beverley HU17 136 D4
Earswick YO32 128 A7
Keadby DN17 95 D6
Kingston upon Hull HU5 140 C2
Pollington DN14 78 A6
Scawby DN20 108 F8
Scunthorpe DN16 151 B3
3 Thorne/Moorends DN8 79 B1
York YO31 130 F7
Willow La Goxhill DN19 86 A8
Pollington DN14 78 A6
Woodmansey HU17 154 B1
Willow Pk DN37 113 C6
Willow Pk Rd YO41 27 F5
Willow Rd
Burstwick HU12 73 B6
9 Campsall DN6 76 E1
10 Knottingley WF11 61 A3
6 Thorne/Moorends DN8 79 A1
Willow Rise YO8 48 B1
Willow Tree Cl 9 DN40 87 C2
Willow Tree Garth 5
HU17 136 F7
Willow View YO8 49 E3
Willowbridge Rd WF8 76 C2
Willowbrook Dr DN20 98 D2
Willowdale HU7 140 F8
Willowdale Cl YO16 123 A7
Willowfield HU6 140 A6
Willows Ave HU9 141 F3
Willows Dr HU18 134 C4
Willows Prim Sch
DN37 102 C4
Willows The
Hornsea HU18 134 C3
Howden DN14 65 A6
Kingston upon Hull
HU13 143 E4
8 Strensall YO32 14 B7
Willy Howe* YO25 2 C3
Wilmore La DN38 110 E7
Wilson Cl
Market Weighton YO43 135 D3
7 North Ferriby HU14 69 A4
Wilson St
Cleethorpes DN35 153 D4
Gainsborough DN21 117 A1
5 Goole DN14 149 C4
4 Kingston upon Hull
HU9 146 B7
Kirk Ella HU10 143 E6
Wilsons Cl 9 DN15 151 B7
Wilsthorpe Gr 1 YO10 133 F8
Wilstrop Farm Rd
YO23 132 A2
Wilton Rd
Hornsea HU18 134 D3
Humberston DN36 114 B8
Wilton Rd Ind Est
DN36 114 B8
Wilton Rise YO24 129 F3
Wilton St HU8 146 B8
Wilton Terr HU18 134 D4
Wiltshire Ave DN15 82 B4
Wiltshire Rd HU4 144 E2
Wimbledon Cl 4 HU8 142 A5
Wimborn Ave DN34 152 B2
Wimbourne Cl HU7 141 C6
Wimpole Cl 6 YO30 127 A1
Winceby Ave DN31 152 A4
Winchcombe Ave 3
DN34 102 C2
Winchester Ave
5 Beverley HU17 136 E1
Grimsby DN33 102 D2
Kingston upon Hull HU9 142 B4
3 York YO26 129 E4
Winchester Cl HU9 142 B4
Winchester Dr DN16 96 E2
Winchester Gr 1 YO26 129 E4
Winchester Rd 29 DN7 92 D4
Wincolmlee HU2 155 C3
Windass Ct HU13 143 E1
Windermere YO24 132 D7
Windermere Ave
DN33 113 D8
Windermere Cres
9 Humberston DN36 103 C1
10 Kirk Sandall DN3 92 A2
Windermere Ct HU7 140 F7
Windermere Dr
Bridlington YO16 122 E7
Goole DN14 149 E5
Windgate Hill La YO8 48 B6
Windham Cres 1 HU7 56 F7
Windlass Cl 29 DN8 93 A8
Windle Ave HU6 140 C7
Windlesham Ave 10
DN33 113 D8
Windlestone Sq 17 DN8 79 B2
Windmill Gdns YO8 148 B7
Windmill Hill YO25 124 E5
Windmill La Norton DN6 76 D1
York YO10 131 B2
Windmill Mdw 13 DN6 76 E2
Windmill Mdws YO41 27 E6
Windmill Rise YO26 129 E3
Windmill Way HU13 143 F1
Windsor Ave HU10 143 E7
Windsor Cl
Beverley HU17 137 B5
3 Keelby DN41 101 A5
Kingston upon Hull
HU16 139 B5
Windsor Cres
Bridlington YO15 122 E2
Crowle DN17 94 C7
Scunthorpe DN17 96 C1
Windsor Ct
Cleethorpes DN32 153 A5
22 Grimsby DN35 152 A5
Hatfield DN7 92 C2
Windsor Dr
Caistor LN7 111 B4
Goole DN14 149 B5
2 Haxby YO32 13 D5
Windsor Garth YO24 129 D1
Windsor Gr DN19 71 A1
Windsor La DN17 94 C7
Windsor Rd
Cleethorpes DN35 153 C1
Crowle DN17 94 C7
Kingston upon Hull HU5 139 F1
Windsor St 1 YO23 130 B1
Windsor Way
Barnetby le Wold DN38 99 B5
Broughton DN20 97 E4
Winestead Gr 3 HU9 142 A2

Winestead Ings La
HU12 74 A1
Winestead La HU12 74 B3
Wingate Rd DN37 102 B4
Wingfield Rd HU9 142 C2
Wingfield Way HU17 55 E8
Winifred Holtby Tech Coll
HU7 141 B7
Winn Ct DN35 153 E1
Winn St 1 DN16 151 B6
Winscar Croft 8 HU7 141 D7
Winscar Gr 9 YO30 126 E3
Winsetts Rd HU12 90 D5
Winship Cl 4 HU3 145 C5
Winslow Dr DN40 87 B1
Winslow Gr 15 DN34 102 C2
Winston Ave DN34 152 B2
Winston Cl HU12 73 A7
Winston Dr HU16 138 F5
Winston Way DN20 98 D2
Winterdale YO25 124 D5
Winteringham La DN15 82 E8
Winteringham Prim Sch
DN15 68 A1
Winteringham Rd DN15 83 B6
Winteringham Wlk
HU16 139 A5
Winterscale Ct TO1 130 D2
Winterscale St YO10 130 D2
Winterton CE Inf Sch
DN15 83 B5
Winterton Comp Sch
DN15 83 A6
Winterton Jun Sch DN15 83 B5
Winterton Rd
Roxby cum Risby DN15 82 F2
Scunthorpe DN15 151 B8
Winteringham DN15 83 B8
Winthorpe Rd
Grimsby DN33 102 D1
4 Kingston upon Hull
HU13 144 A3
Wintringham 25 HU15 68 C6
Wintringham Rd DN32 152 E2
Wintringham Sch DN32 102 F2
Wirral Ave 19 DN34 102 C2
Wise Cl HU17 136 E7
Wises Farm Rd 2 HU5 139 F1
Wiske Ave 6 HU15 68 D5
Wisker La YO32 128 C7
Wisteria Dr DN41 101 E5
Wisteria Way DN16 151 E1
Wistow Gr HU4 144 D5
Wistow Parochial CE VC Prim
Sch YO8 48 D6
Wistow Rd YO8 148 A8
Wistowgate YO8 48 B8
Witch La YO25 3 B2
Witham HU9 155 C3
Witham Dr
Burton upon Stather
DN15 82 B5
York YO32 128 A6
Withern Rd DN33 102 D2
Withernsea High Sch & Tech
Coll HU19 74 F7
Withernsea Hospl HU19 75 A6
Withernsea Inf Sch
HU19 74 F7
Withernsea Jun Sch
HU19 74 F7
Withernsea Lighthouse
Mus* HU19 74 F6
Withernsea Rd
Hollym HU19 75 A4
Holmpton HU19 75 C3
Rimswell HU19 74 D8
Roos HU19 60 C1
Withernsea St HU8 141 A1
Withernwick La HU11 47 A4
Withernwick Prim Sch
HU11 46 D3
Withernwick Rd
Aldbrough HU11 47 A2
Hatfield HU11 46 C5
Witty St HU3 145 A3
Witty's Pass 7 HU18 134 C4
Wittys Paddock 4 HU11 35 A1
Wivell Dr DN41 101 A5
Wivern Rd HU9 142 D3
Woad La DN37 102 C5
Woburn Cl
Bridlington YO16 122 F6
Strensall YO33 14 B8
Woburn Dr DN14 149 E5
Woburn St HU3 144 F4
Wold Ave YO43 135 E3
Wold Garth YO42 29 A3
Wold Hill HU15 53 E4
Wold La YO12 1 E8
Wold Newton Foundation
Sch YO25 2 A4
Wold Newton Rd YO25 2 E3
Wold Prim Sch HU5 139 B1
Wold Rd
Barrow upon Humber
DN19 85 D7
Kingston upon Hull HU5 139 B1
Kirby Grindalythe YO17 6 E8
Market Weighton YO43 135 F2
Nafferton YO25 125 E8
Pocklington YO42 29 A4
Walkington HU17 54 E7
Worlaby DN20 84 E1
Wold Rise YO43 41 E2
Wold View Brigg DN20 98 C2
Caistor LN7 111 B4
Elloughton-cum-Brough
HU15 68 C6
Fotherby LN11 121 D2
Fridaythorpe YO25 18 B5
6 Holton le Clay DN36 114 A5
Rothwell LN7 111 F2
3 South Cave HU15 54 A2
Wold View Rd N YO25 124 E3
Wold View Rd S YO25 124 E3
Wold Wlk YO16 122 B4
Woldcarr Rd HU3 144 F6
Woldcroft YO41 27 C2
Woldgate
Bridlington YO16 122 A3
Carnaby YO16 10 E6
Harpham YO25 9 D3
5 North Newbald YO43 53 F7
Woldgate Coll YO42 29 B4
Woldgate View 1 YO42 29 A3
Woldholme Ave YO25 124 D3
Wolds Cl 14 DN17 94 D7
Wolds The Goole DN14 149 D5
Kingston upon Hull
HU16 138 E6
Wolds Village* YO25 31 E8
Woldview Rd YO41 27 F5
Wolfe Ave YO31 130 F5
Wolfe Cl 7 HU16 138 F5
Wolfreton Ct HU10 143 E6
Wolfreton Dr HU10 143 F6
Wolfreton Garth HU10 143 D8
Wolfreton La HU10 143 F8
Wolfreton Mews HU10 143 F7
Wolfreton Rd HU10 143 F7
Wolfreton Sch HU10 138 D1
Wolfreton Villas HU10 143 F7
Wollaston Rd DN35 153 E2
Wolsey Ave YO8 48 B8
Wolsey Dr
3 Barrow upon Humber
DN19 85 C7
Bishopthorpe YO23 133 A3
Wolsley St YO10 130 E3
Wolviston Ave YO10 131 C3
Wombwell Gr 3 HU8 141 B1
Womersley CE VC Jun & Inf
Sch DN6 76 C6
Womersley Pk Gdns
DN6 76 D5
Womersley Rd
Grimsby DN31 153 A6
Knottingley WF11 61 A2
Wood Carr La DN9 94 C2
Wood Cl
8 Grimsby DN33 113 E8
7 Strensall YO32 14 A7
14 Thorpe Willoughby YO8 48 B1
Wood Dr 1 HU14 69 A4
Wood Gate YO42 29 D7
Wood Hill Way HU16 138 C8
Wood La
Acaster Selby YO23 36 B2
Beverley HU17 154 A3
Birkin WF11 61 D6
Bubwith DN14 51 A5
Cottingham HU16 139 B4
Fishlake DN7 92 D8
13 Thorpe Willoughby YO8 48 B1
Wressle DN14 51 B2
Wood St Grimsby DN32 152 F4
York YO31 130 E6
Wood Vale DN16 96 E2
Wood View Airmyn DN14 64 E3
Messingham DN17 107 D8
Swanland HU14 69 B7
Wood Way YO32 128 A4
Woodale Cl 3 DN15 96 B7
Woodall Ct 9 YO8 48 D6
Woodapple Ct 2 DN41 101 E6
Wood's La HU1 155 A1
Woodbine Ave DN20 98 C2
Woodbine Cl HU2 155 A4
Woodclose Rd DN17 150 D2
Woodcoates Cl 1 HU17 136 F7
Woodcock Cl 9 YO32 13 F5
Woodcock Rd 1 YO15 5 A2
Woodcock St HU3 145 A4
Woodcroft Ave HU6 139 F5
Wooden Beck Hill
DN10 116 B2
Woodfield Cl 4 DN36 114 D8
Woodfield La HU13 143 C1
Woodfield Rd
Gainsborough DN21 117 C1
Goole DN14 149 B6
Woodford Cl HU8 141 E2
Woodford Pl 1 YO24 129 D1
Woodgarr Ave 1 DN17 95 D6
Woodgate La HU5 144 F8
Woodgate Rd
Kingston upon Hull HU5 144 F7
Newbald YO43 54 A8
Woodgates Cl 6 HU14 69 A5
Woodgates La HU14 69 A5
Woodgates Mount 3
HU14 69 A5
Woodhall Dr
1 Beverley HU17 136 D6
Waltham DN37 113 D6
Woodhall La
Hemingbrough YO8 50 B3
Womersley DN6 76 D6
Woodhall Pk HU17 136 D7
Woodhall St HU8 141 A2
Woodhall Way HU17 154 A4
Woodhill Ave DN21 117 C1
Woodhill Cl 2 HU10 143 E7
Woodhill Rd DN21 107 A3
Woodhill Rise HU13 143 C2
Woodhouse Gn Rd DN7 92 B8
Woodhouse Gr 4 YO31 131 A5
Woodhouse La
Beeford YO25 22 C1
Belton DN9 94 E2
Hatfield DN7 92 D2
Pocklington YO42 29 A5
Riston HU11 45 B3
Woodhouse Rd
Scunthorpe DN16 151 E4
Thorganby YO19 38 A3
Woodhouse St HU9 146 D7
Woodings Ct 5 DN14 65 A7
Woodland Ave
17 Brough HU15 68 C6
14 Gainsborough DN21 117 A2
Goole DN14 149 C6
Woodland Chase YO30 127 B1
Woodland Dr
Broughton DN20 97 D4
1 Elsham DN20 98 F7
Kingston upon Hull
HU10 143 C6
Woodland End HU4 144 C5
Woodland Pl YO32 127 E4
Woodland Rise YO25 125 A6
Woodland View
Barnetby le Wold DN38 99 B4
Scunthorpe DN15 150 C7
Woodland Way
8 Airmyn DN14 64 E4
19 Epworth DN9 105 E6
York YO32 127 F4
Woodland Wlk 6 DN35 103 C1
Woodlands
Beverley HU17 136 D4
8 Driffield YO25 124 F3
Escrick YO19 37 B5
Woodlands Ave
Haxby YO32 127 C8
Immingham DN40 87 C2
Keelby DN41 101 A4
Woodlands Cl
15 Barlby with Osgodby
YO8 49 B4
4 Barrow upon Humber
DN19 85 C7
Bridlington YO15 123 B7
Woodlands Ct 13 YO8 49 B4
Woodlands Dr
14 Barlby with Osgodby
YO8 49 B4
Beverley HU17 136 D4
Woodlands Gr YO31 131 A7
Woodlands La
8 Brough HU15 68 C6
Hillam LS25 61 B7
Woodlands Prim Sch
DN33 102 D1
Woodlands Rd HU5 144 B7
Woodlands Rise
5 North Ferriby HU14 69 A5
Norton DN6 76 E1
Woodlands Sports Ctr
DN40 87 C2
Woodlands The
Kingston upon Hull HU5 140 B2
Preston HU12 72 B7
2 Stallingborough DN41 101 D6
The Lawns HU16 138 F7
Woodlands View 11 YO8 49 B4
Woodlea Ave YO26 129 C4
Woodlea Bank YO26 129 D4
Woodlea Cres YO26 129 D4
Woodlea Gr YO26 129 D5
Woodleigh Cl 2 YO32 14 A6
Woodleigh Dr HU7 141 C5
Woodman's Way HU17 154 C1
Woodmansey CE VC Prim
Sch HU17 56 C8
Woodmansey Mile
HU17 154 A1
Woodmarketgate 26
HU12 72 C7
Woodrow Pk DN33 102 E1
Woods La DN40 86 F2
Woods Mdw DN20 108 F6
Woods Terr 7 DN21 117 B2
Woodside
10 Gilberdyke HU15 66 D7
Kingston upon Hull
HU13 143 D1
Woodside Ave YO31 131 A6
Woodside La DN9 104 D6
Woodside Rd YO12 1 A8
Woodsley Ave DN35 153 E1
Woodsmill Quay YO1 156 B2
Woodstock Cl HU16 138 F6
Woodstock Rd DN16 151 D4
Woodthorpe Prim Sch
YO24 132 C7
Woodview Cl DN14 77 A7
Woodville Terr YO8 148 E3
Woolam Hill HU12 73 A6
Woollin Ave DN17 151 A2
Woolnough Ave YO10 131 B3
Woolsheds Cl 1 HU5 139 F1
Woolsthorpe Gr 20 HU7 56 F6
Woolwich Dr 2 HU4 144 B2
Wootton Cl DN17 150 C4
Wootton Rd
Grimsby DN33 102 D2
Wootton DN39 85 F2
Wootton St Andrew's CE Prim
Sch DN39 85 E3
Worcester Ave DN34 152 A1
Worcester Cl 11 DN16 96 D1
Worcester Dr YO31 131 B5
Worcester Rd HU5 139 C1
Worcestershire Cl 1
HU5 139 D1
Wordsworth Ave 4 DN6 76 E1
Wordsworth Cres
YO24 132 D7
Wordsworth Ct
Cleethorpes DN35 153 A5
21 Grimsby DN35 152 A5
Wordsworth Rd DN17 150 D2
Wordsworth St HU8 141 D2
Workington Ave 8 HU4 144 B6
Worlaby Prim Sch
DN20 98 D8
Worlaby Rd 1 DN33 113 D8
Worldwide Way
Immingham DN41 101 F8
Stallingborough DN41 87 F1
Wormley Hill La DN14 78 E2
Worsborough Cl 10
HU7 141 D7
Worsendale Rd YO42 16 F2
Worship St HU2 155 B3
Worsley Cl
7 Holton le Clay DN36 114 A5
Immingham DN40 87 D1
Worsley Rd DN40 87 C1
Worthing St HU5 140 D3
Wortley St DN16 151 A6
Wragby Rd DN17 150 D1
Wragby St DN32 152 F3
Wrangbrook Cl 3 DN14 65 A7
Wrangham Dr 1 YO14 3 A8
Wrangman Dale Rd
YO43 54 A8
Wrawby La HU12 58 D2
Wrawby Postmill*
DN20 98 E3
Wrawby Rd Brigg DN20 98 C2
Scunthorpe DN17 150 E1
Wrawby St 8 DN20 98 C2
Wrawby St Mary's CE Prim
Sch DN20 98 E3
Wray Cl Beverley HU17 154 B4
9 Waltham DN37 113 D7
Wray St 14 DN21 108 B1
Wray's Ave YO31 127 E1
Wren Cl 4 Healing DN41 101 F5
17 Scunthorpe DN16 96 D1
Wren Cres DN33 102 D1
Wren Hall La YO8 63 E6
Wren La 2 YO8 148 D5
Wressle Rd DN20 97 E4
Wressle Sta YO8 50 D2
Wright Cl YO16 122 B2
Wright Cres YO16 122 B2
Wright St HU2 155 A3
Wrights Gdns 1 DN10 116 D3
Wrights La WF11 76 B8
Wroot Rd DN9 104 A2
Wroot Travis Charity Prim
Sch DN9 104 D5
Wroots Ave DN14 149 D1
Wroxham Ave DN34 102 C3
Wrygarth Ave 7 HU15 68 C5
Wyatt Ave DN20 97 D3
Wybeck Rd DN15 96 D7
Wybers Way DN37 102 B4
Wybers Wood Jun & Inf Sch
DN37 102 B4
Wycliffe Ave YO10 131 B3
Wycliffe La YO15 122 E2
Wydale Rd YO10 131 D4
Wyham Medieval Village*
DN36 120 F5
Wyke St HU9 146 D7
Wyke VI Prim Coll HU5 139 E2
Wykeham Cl
2 Bridlington YO16 122 C5
1 Kingston upon Hull
HU7 141 D7
Wykehan Cl YO25 124 D3
Wylies Rd HU17 154 A3
Wymark View 26 DN33 102 C2
Wymersley Rd HU5 144 A8
Wynam La YO41 27 C1
Wynburg St HU9 141 D1
Wyndham Cl 4 HU17 43 D6
Wyndham Rd 10 DN36 114 A7
Wyndham St HU3 145 C7
Wynmoor Rd DN17 150 F3
Wyntryngham Cl 14
HU12 72 D7
Wyredale Rd DN16 151 D1
Wysteria Way HU8 141 E7
Wytherstone Cl 3 HU7 56 F6
Wyton Gr HU9 142 A2
Wyton Rd HU12 58 B2
Wyvern Cl DN17 94 D8

Y

Yapham Rd YO42 28 F5
Yarborough Camp*
DN39 99 E7
Yarborough Cl 2 DN36 114 A5
Yarborough Cres 6
DN20 97 D4
Yarborough Ct 4 DN15 150 B6
Yarborough Dr DN31 152 C4
Yarborough Jun Sch
DN34 152 A3
Yarborough Prim Sch
DN34 102 C4
Yarborough Rd
25 Brigg DN20 98 C2
Grimsby DN34 152 A3
Keelby DN41 101 A5
Scunthorpe DN16 97 A4
Yarburgh Cl 4 DN14 63 B1
Yarburgh Gr 2 YO26 129 E5
Yarburgh Way YO10 131 C3
Yardley Way 3 DN34 102 B2
Yarmouth Ave 3 HU4 144 A3
Yarra Rd DN35 153 F2
Yarrow Rd DN34 102 C4
Yatesbury Garth 18 HU7 57 A5
Yeadon Garth HU7 141 C8
Yearsley Cres YO31 130 D7
Yearsley Gr YO31 127 E1
Yearsley Gr Prim Sch
YO32 127 F1
Yearsley Swimming Pool
YO31 130 D8
Yedingham Wlk HU16 139 A5
Yeoman Dr 1 HU17 136 D1
Yew Dr DN16 96 D1
Yew Tree Cl
Acaster Malbis YO23 36 C8
Rufforth YO23 24 C6
Selby YO8 148 C6
Yew Tree Mews YO19 131 C5
Yew Tree Pk DN14 77 A7
Yews La DN37 101 E1
Yewtree Dr HU4 144 B7
Yiewsley Cl HU8 141 E6
Yokegate DN14 51 E3
Yordas Ct 3 YO16 123 A7
York Abbey* YO30 156 A3
York Art Gall* YO30 156 B3
York Ave DN16 96 D2
York Barbican Leisure Ctr
YO10 156 C1
York Castle Mus*
YO1 156 C1
York City Football Club
YO30 156 A4
York Cl YO43 135 D4
York Coll YO24 132 E6
York District Hospl
YO30 156 B4
York Dungeon* YO1 156 B2
York La Flaxton YO60 14 E8
Huggate YO42 18 A2
York Minst* YO1 156 B3
York Model Rly*
YO24 156 A2
York Pl DN35 103 B2
York Racecourse (The
Knavesmire)* YO24 130 A1
York Rd Barlby YO8 49 B5
Beverley HU17 136 D4
Bilbrough YO23 24 B2
Bishop Burton HU17 42 F3
Bridlington YO15 122 F3
Brigg DN20 98 C2
Cliffe YO8 49 E3
Cottam YO25 8 B2
Driffield YO25 124 B5
Dunnington YO19 26 D6
Fridaythorpe YO25 18 B5
Garton YO25 19 D8
Great Driffield YO25 124 D5
28 Hatfield DN7 92 D4
Haxby YO32 127 D7
Kilham YO25 8 F3
Kingston upon Hull HU6 139 F7
1 Kirton in Lindsey DN21 119 C8
Long Marston YO26 24 A6
Market Weighton YO43 135 A5
Naburn YO19 36 D8
North Duffield YO8 50 A8
Riccall YO19 37 A1
Shipton Thorpe YO43 40 E6
Sledmere YO25 7 E1
Stillingfleet YO19 36 D4
Strensall YO32 14 A6
Sutton-on-the-Forest
YO61 13 C8
York YO26 129 C3
York Rd Gallows Hill
YO43 135 A6
York St
5 Dunnington YO19 26 E7
Grimsby DN31 152 C4
Kingston upon Hull HU2 155 C4
1 Selby YO8 148 C5
York St John Coll
YO31 156 B3
York St John Coll of the Univ
of Leeds YO10 131 B3
York Sta YO24 156 A2
York Steiner Sch
YO10 130 D1
York Terr DN10 116 D5
Yorklands YO25 124 D5
Yorkshire Air Mus*
YO41 26 F3
Yorkshire Cl 3 HU5 139 D1
Yorkshire Mus* YO30 156 A3
Yorkshire Mus of Farming*
YO19 26 D7
Yorkshireside DN17 81 A3
Young Pl DN35 153 B3
Young St HU19 75 A7
Youth Ctr YO25 125 A5

Z

Zeigfield Ct 11 HU9 142 A3
Zetland St HU3 145 A5

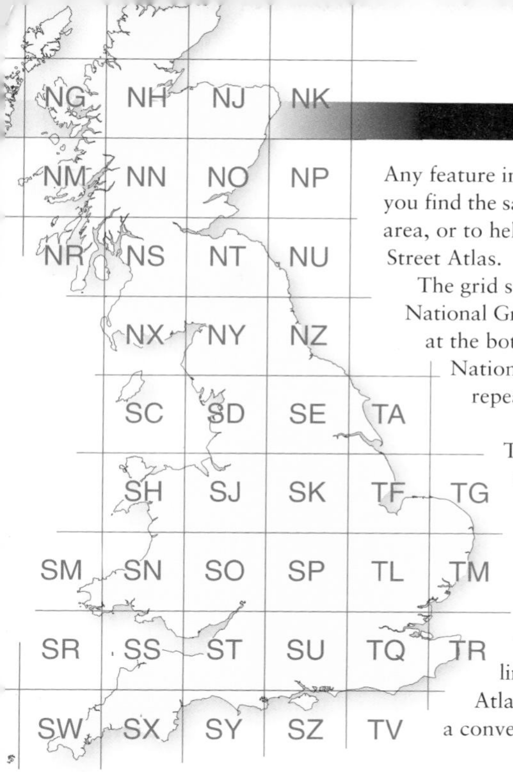
NG
NH
NJ
NK
NM
NN
NO
NP
NR
NS
NT
NU
NX
NY
NZ
SC
SD
SE
TA
SH
SJ
SK
TF
TG
SM
SN
SO
SP
TL
TM
SR
SS
ST
SU
TQ
TR
SW
SX
SY
SZ
TV

Using the Ordnance Survey National Grid

Any feature in this atlas can be given a unique reference to help you find the same feature on other Ordnance Survey maps of the area, or to help someone else locate you if they do not have a Street Atlas.

The grid squares in this atlas match the Ordnance Survey National Grid and are at 500 metre intervals. The small figures at the bottom and sides of every other grid line are the National Grid kilometre values (**00** to **99** km) and are repeated across the country every 100 km (see left).

To give a unique National Grid reference you need to locate where in the country you are. The country is divided into 100 km squares with each square given a unique two-letter reference. Use the administrative map to determine in which 100 km square a particular page of this atlas falls.

The bold letters and numbers between each grid line (**A** to **F**, **1** to **8**) are for use within a specific Street Atlas only, and when used with the page number, are a convenient way of referencing these grid squares.

Example *The railway bridge over DARLEY GREEN RD in grid square B1*

Step 1: Identify the two-letter reference, in this example the page is in **SP**

Step 2: Identify the 1 km square in which the railway bridge falls. Use the figures in the southwest corner of this square: Eastings **17**, Northings **74**. This gives a unique reference: **SP 17 74**, accurate to 1 km.

Step 3: To give a more precise reference accurate to 100 m you need to estimate how many tenths along and how many tenths up this 1 km square the feature is (to help with this the 1 km square is divided into four 500 m squares). This makes the bridge about **8** tenths along and about **1** tenth up from the southwest corner.

This gives a unique reference: **SP 178 741**, accurate to 100 m.

Eastings (read from left to right along the bottom) come before Northings (read from bottom to top). If you have trouble remembering say to yourself "Along the hall, THEN up the stairs"!

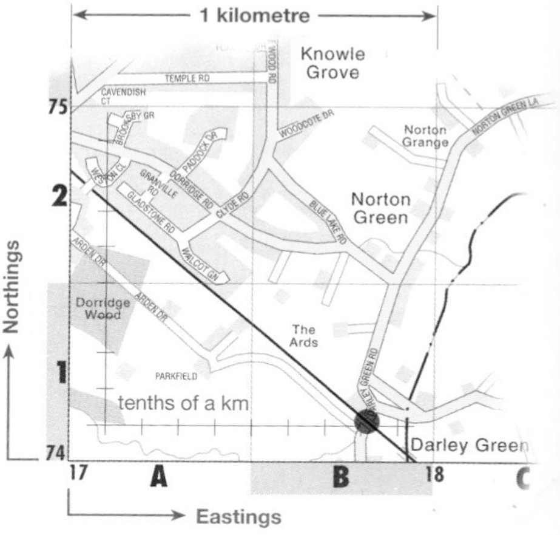
1 kilometre
Knowle Grove
TEMPLE RD
CAVENDISH CT
WOODCOTE DR
Norton Grange
NORTON GREEN LA
Norton Green
PADDOCK DR
GRANVILLE RD
DORRIDGE RD
GLADSTONE RD
CLYDE RD
BLUE LAKE RD
WALCOT GN
ARDEN DR
Dorridge Wood
The Ards
PARKFIELD
tenths of a km
Darley Green
75
2
1
74
17
A
B
18
C
Northings
Eastings